DEFINING DOCUMENTS
IN WORLD HISTORY

Nationalism & Populism

(320 BCE–2017 CE)

DEFINING DOCUMENTS
IN WORLD HISTORY

Nationalism & Populism (320 BCE–2017 CE)

Editor

David Simonelli

Volume 1

SALEM PRESS
A Division of EBSCO Information Services
Ipswich, Massachusetts

GREY HOUSE PUBLISHING

#982386612

Cover Image: Parchment Replica of the Magna Carta of King John (istockphoto.com/DavidSmart)

Publisher's Cataloging-In-Publication Data
(Prepared by The Donohue Group, Inc.)

Names: Simonelli, David, editor.
Title: Nationalism & populism (320 BCE-2017 CE) / editor, David Simonelli.
Other Titles: Nationalism and populism (320 BCE-2017 CE) | Defining documents in world history.
Description: [First edition]. | Ipswich, Massachusetts : Salem Press, a division of EBSCO Information Services ; [Amenia, New York] : Grey House Publishing, [2017] | Includes bibliographical references and index.
Identifiers: ISBN 978-1-68217-293-3 (set) | ISBN 978-1-68217-295-7 (v. 1) | ISBN 978-1-68217-296-4 (v. 2)
Subjects: LCSH: Nationalism--History--Sources. | Populism--History--Sources.
Classification: LCC JC311 .N38 2017 | DDC 320.54--dc23
V. 1

FIRST PRINTING
PRINTED IN THE UNITED STATES OF AMERICA

Table of Contents

Volume 1

NATIONALISM IN THE ANCIENT AND MEDIEVAL ERAS   1

THE AMERICAN AND FRENCH REVOLUTIONS   87

THE NINETEENTH CENTURY   167

THE FIRST WORLD WAR

235

Volume 2

SECOND WORLD WAR

309

THE COLD WAR

367

The Twentieth and Twenty-First Centuries

Appendixes

Publisher's Note

Defining Documents in World History series, produced by Salem Press, consists of a collection of essays on important historical documents by a diverse range of writers on a broad range of subjects in world history. This established series include *Ancient World (2700 BCE–c. 500 CE)*, *Middle Ages (476–1500)*, and *Renaissance & Early Modern Era (1308–1600)* in addition to the latest title: *Nationalism & Populism (320 BCE–2017 CE)*.

Nationalism & Populism offers in-depth analysis of a broad range of historical documents and historic events that illustrate the origin and evolution of the political ideas of nationalism and populism. The volume begins with a set of constitutions written by Aristotle and moves forward in time to the present day, with the forty-fifth president of the United States and his speeches that emphasis "America First." The constitutions, declarations, speeches, articles, essays, laws and court orders cover a broad span of world history to demonstrate the ways in which the idea of a nation as more than a geographic location has come into being. The fifty-nine articles in this volume are organized into seven sections:

- **Nationalism in the Ancient and Medieval Eras**, with three constitutions written by Aristotle, as well as an excerpt from the Magna Carta and Japan's Closed Country Edict, intended to maintain control of trade by Japanese merchants;
- **The American and French Revolutions** examines the Declaration of Independence and the Constitution of the United States, along with other writings from the same era, including the Declaration of the Rights of Man and of the Citizen, a document that ended the ancien régime in France and the Cartagena Manifesto was a key document in the Spanish American wars of independence that took place in Mexico and South America from 1808 to 1829;
- **The Nineteenth Century** includes the National Petition from the People's Charter, a product of the dissatisfaction within the working classes with the conditions in the United Kingdom during the early period of the Industrial Revolution and Rudyard Kipling's poem, "The White Man's Burden," which presents a rationale for empire as a necessary and noble intervention by the more

"civilized" European white nations in other parts of the world;

- **The First World War** takes a look at the Austro-Hungarian ultimatum to Serbia and the Serbian reply, the Balfour Declaration, one of a number of contradictory British pledges regarding the future disposition of Ottoman territories, and the Treaty of Lausanne, the final treaty that brought World War I (1914–1918) to a close;
- **Second World War** includes Benito Mussolini's declarations concerning fascism, Adolf Hitler's address to the German people, the United Nations' Charter, and a Vietnam's declaration of independence from French colonial domination;
- **The Cold War** marked a time when nations sought to secure their identities and borders and writings in this section examine Japan's constitution of 1947, India's constitution of 1949, and the Arusha declaration, the policies that constituted "Ujamaa";
- **The Twentieth and Twenty-First Centuries** includes the Constitution of the People's Republic of China, which was adopted by the Fifth National People's Congress in 1982, Treaty on European Union that provided the framework for the European Union, and the speeches of Donald Trump and his promise to put America first.

Historical documents provide a compelling view of dissent and protest, an important aspect of world history. Designed for high school and college students, the aim of the series is to advance historical document studies as an important activity in learning about history.

Essay Format

Nationalism & Populism contains thirty primary source documents—many in their entirety. Each document is supported by a critical essay, written by historians and teachers, that includes a Summary Overview, Defining Moment, Author Biography, Document Analysis, and Essential Themes. Readers will appreciate the diversity of the collected texts, including treaties, letters, speeches, political and religious sermons, laws, memoirs, and diplomatic communications among other genres. An important feature of each essay is a close reading of the primary source that develops evidence of broader themes, such as the author's rhetorical purpose, social or class position, point of view, and other relevant issues. In addition, essays are organized by section themes, listed above, highlighting major issues of the period, many of which extend across eras and continue to shape life as we know it around the world. Each section begins with a brief introduction that defines questions and problems underlying the subjects in the historical documents. Each essay also includes a Bibliography and Additional Reading section for further research.

Appendixes

- **Chronological List** arranges all documents by year.

- **Web Resources** is an annotated list of websites that offer valuable supplemental resources.
- **Bibliography** lists helpful articles and books for further study.

Contributors

Salem Press would like to extend its appreciation to all involved in the development and production of this work. The essays have been written and signed by scholars of history, humanities, and other disciplines related to the essays' topics. Without these expert contributions, a project of this nature would not be possible. A full list of contributor's names and affiliations appears in the front matter of this volume.

Editor's Introduction

The "nation" is a peculiar and recent concept in world history. Terms like "nation" are thrown around liberally in the media without any concept of what the proper definition of the term means. For the purposes of this document collection:

- a "country" is the topography of a territory and the people, plants and animals which live there;
- a "nation" is the people themselves and the institutions that they share and which define them: ethnicity, language, economy, religion, history, culture, geography, education, values;
- a "state" is the permanent institutions that organize and manage the country and nation;
- a "government" is the ideological regime in charge of the state at that time.

In the larger span of world history, most states have been empires, and most governments have been some form of monarchy, hereditary one-person rule. Empires and their emperors dominated numerous ethnicities, established their own histories, advanced their geographical borders and celebrated the diversity of cultures and people within those borders. Empires were made up of all the institutions of multiple "nations" at the same time. Most of all, empires were created through simple military power, more powerful peoples beating up less powerful peoples and later controlling their populations, resources and economies to maintain that power.

The idea of a nation, then, is a highly unusual one. In particular, a nation-state – a set of permanent institutions whose reason for existence, whose basis for organizing and managing an ethnicity, language, economy, religion, and history comes from those institutions' distinctions from those of other nations – is positively bizarre and unnatural in world history. Empires were based on power, and their greatness was measured in the wide variety of nations they dominated. "Nationalism" and nationalists asserted that just because one people was different from another, they should have the right to run their own state. A people might have to fight and die to achieve that goal, purely because they spoke a different language, had different values, or worshipped a different god in a different way. In its assertion of the distinctions between peoples as beautiful, nationalism was inspiring and uplifting; in its insistence that people be willing to die for the concept, nationalism was dangerous. Over the span of 5500 years of civilized history, the nation-state has only existed as a concept in the past three hundred years or so; furthermore, as documents like the Treaty on European Union and the Constitutive Act of African Union demonstrate, nation-states are trying to reunite themselves across borders and bring the concept of nationalism to a peaceful end.

The essential element in a nation is people and their distinctions – their distinctions from other peoples, and the distinctions that bring them together as one. "Populism" is a good word to define this concept. The history of civilization has seen the revelation of the growing power of common people as individuals and communities, asserting their interests over those of emperors, kings, gods, warriors, economic and social elites, anyone who had been able to define themselves as the few in charge of the lives of the many. European civilization, with its basis in Greco-Roman and Judeo-Christian traditions, has always emphasized the power of the individual and the rationality the individual uses to make choices. So it is no mistake that as Europeans have come to spread their power around the world through colonization and emigration, so have the ideas of nationalism and populism that one finds in these documents spread around the world too.

An original conception of the relationship between nationalism and populism can best be found, then, in the original Greco-Roman tradition. Aristotle lectured on his ideas of the best forms of government, as collected in *Politics*, three excerpts from which appear here. Aristotle basically believed that the best states balanced the relationship between the people, monarchy and aristocracy. Variations on this theme abounded in European history for the next two thousand years, from the aristocracy trying to tame the power of monarchy in England's Magna Carta to Dutch merchants and aristocrats begging for a new monarch to take them on as subjects in 1581. The exception to the European emphasis in this period comes from Japan, perhaps the most "western-like" of all non-western countries. That exception proves the rule. In its Seventeen Article Constitution, the Yamato clan tried to prove their legitimacy to the Japanese people; in the Closed Country Edict of 1635, the Tokugawa Shogunate tried to shut their country off from foreign influences specifically to keep their national character intact.

With the American and French Revolutions, the ideas of nationalism and populism began to found nation-states, for better and for worse. The historian and political scientist Benedict Anderson defined a nation as an "imagined community", meaning that people pick and choose their own traditions to uphold in definition as a nation, and likewise ignore others that are just as valid because they are perceived as negative. In fact, following up on Anderson's ideas, other historians even asserted that some nations simply invented traditions in order to establish a positive ideal to uphold. The documents from the American and French Revolutions are excellent examples of these concepts. Jefferson's Declaration of Independence asserted that "all men are created equal", despite the paradox of slavery that he practiced on his own plantation. Frenchmen used the Declaration of the Rights of Man and Citizen to define the freedoms they believed they deserved as individuals, then promptly surrendered those rights during Napoleon's rule in favor of power and empire. As this era proved, nationalism and populism allowed men to aspire to their highest levels of individuality, freedom and progress – at the same time they were pitted against one another, often to the death, as in the Napoleonic Wars and the American Civil War.

Nevertheless, the concept of nationalism grew along with the ideals of democracy and the institution of capitalism. It also spread through European imperialism in the nineteenth century. The Treaty of Guadalupe Hidalgo cemented the United States' status as the most powerful nation-state in the western hemisphere; Frederick Jackson Turner's lecture on the American frontier led many Americans to carry their vision of national expansion abroad. The Meiji constitution in Japan was a marvel of the absorption of western values; it also laid the foundation for the emperor's status as a god – literally, an invented tradition – and prepared the Japanese people for expansion and empire in the twentieth century. Theodor Herzl aspired to reinvent the Jewish people as rooted in a homeland, to imagine themselves as a community in the same way that other European peoples did in the late nineteenth century. The result in the twentieth century would be the righteous creation of the state of Israel after the Holocaust, and the Palestinian problem which lasts to this day.

Imperialism – the expansion and maintenance of empire – led Europeans to spread their values on nationalism and populism all over the world. It also led in part to the First World War, kicked off by Austria-Hungary's ultimatum to Serbia in 1914. The war's savagery and the involvement of colonies in its carnage led to the first widespread efforts to establish independence both during (the Irish Easter Rebellion) and after the war. The Covenant of the League of Nations spelled out the desire to bring all the nations of the world together in peace; now that colonized peoples like the Syrians and Koreans had experienced nationalism and populism, they wanted to be independent parts of that future world. Other populations at the end of empires – the Chinese and the Turks – wanted redefinition as nations in a world where their imperial domains had been dismantled.

The hope occasioned by the founding of the League of Nations fell apart quickly. Nationalism and populism had ugly sides that revealed themselves often in the 1920s and 1930s. Benito Mussolini's conception of fascism and Hitler's proclamation to the German people upon attaining the chancellery in 1933 defined nationalism in prejudicial terms, glorifying in people's distinctions as making them racially superior and, in the Nazis' case, identifying a scapegoat in opposition to the nation and people: the Jewish population of Europe. Come the war, nationalism fanned the flames of populist hatreds in the British Indian colony between Muslims and Hindus. Even the hopefulness of the United Nations Charter and Ho Chi Minh's declaration of Vietnam's independence would not last once the war was over.

By 1945 it was clear that nationalism and populism were responsible for the deaths of millions, and the coming Cold War between the United States and the Soviet Union promised even worse. The two sides split into military alliances, and conflicts in Cuba, the Suez Canal and the Congo were attached overtly or obliquely to the populist facedown between capitalist democracy and communism. At the same time, however, the wave of colonial independence movements had grown into an irreversible tide. New states like Israel, India, Algeria and Tanzania struck for their freedom and defined themselves as nations, triumphantly. The documents attached to these states in this collection are sacred to their peoples, imagined communities and invented traditions that came true and gave their peoples pride and meaning and purpose. Even older states like Japan and South Africa remade themselves as nation-states: Japan with the help of the United States after the destruction of the war, South Africa in preparation for a hoped-for future of freedom and equality that the Freedom Charter plotted out as a beacon to follow out of apartheid.

In the late twentieth and twenty-first centuries, our world has come full circle in some respects, and searches for a way past nationalism in other respects. The births of the EU and the African Union have been projects of peace, efforts to break down national distinctions to keep violence from breaking out within states and between states. They are also projects of prosperity and diversity, trying to break down national borders and barriers to employment based on ethnicity or skin color or religion or gender. The concept of populism in some respects opposes nationalism – many of the world's citizens want to be one people, freely moving, exchanging goods and services and accepting the differences that once divided us into nations. Yet Donald Trump's speech announcing his candidacy for the presidency of the US and the failure of reconciliation between North and South Korea say that we still have a long way to go.

David Simonelli
Department of History
Youngstown State University
Youngstown Ohio

March 12, 2017

Contributors

Paul M. Edwards
Center for the Study of the Korean War

James Ellison
Dickinson College

Sadan Jha
Centre for Social Studies, Surat, India

Marisa Lerer
The Graduate Center, CUNY

Tereasa Maillie
University of Alberta, Canada

Michael J. O'Neal, PhD
Independent Scholar, Moscow, ID

Dianne White Oyler
Fayetteville State University

Tobias Rettig
Singapore Management University

Carl Rollyson, PhD
Baruch College

Christopher Saunders
University of Cape Town, South Africa

Carole Schroeder
Boise State University

David Simonelli
Youngstown University

Robert N. Stacy
Independent Scholar

Dan Tamir
University of Zürich, Switzerland

DEFINING DOCUMENTS
IN WORLD HISTORY

Nationalism & Populism
(320 BCE–2017 CE)

Nationalism in the Ancient and Medieval Eras

The ancient and medieval eras in world history had no concepts s nationalism, at least any that could be defined. Political organizations amounted to empires, city-states, some combination of the two or the meritocracy and egalitarianism of the nomadic society. Yet from the time of the Babylonian empire and Hammurabi's law code around 1750 BCE, rulers believed that they had a responsibility to establish a relationship with their peoples in order to exercise authority. Most of these relationships had some sort of religious or military basis; the ruler flaunted a connection to unknown forces that governed the world, or simply beat up all comers to place themselves in power—usually both.

The first inklings of the sort of populism that might lead to the development of distinct nations arose in ancient Greece. The Greeks had a different relationship with their gods because they had a different relationship to the environment and geography that the gods represented. Greece (or Hellas, as they called it) was barren, mountainous, with little fresh water to use for agriculture. It was a tough place to live, and individuals who lived there considered themselves hardy and independent despite their many flaws. Not surprisingly, they saw their gods in the same way; more importantly, they saw themselves as being like the gods in their ability to manage the living space they inhabited. That meant they managed their own fates in government and the state, just as they did on their own land. The Greek city-states had positive connections to their many gods, but free men did not have to get the gods' input in order to make decisions. The Greek term for this concept was *Politics*, the term Aristotle used to describe his many different forms of government in the Mediterranean world in the fourth century BCE, three of which are included here.

Past the era of the ancient empires, men began to question their relationships with the states that dominated them, to question their legitimacy and the social contract that was implicit in the relationship. It's important to note that at the time when Magna Carta was drawn up (1215), the Plantagenet family that served as monarchs of England were rebellious vassals of the French king, the Dukes of Normandy. The reason English barons tired of King John I was because he demanded that they fight and die in his wars to try to secure the French throne for himself too. Therefore, limiting John's powers in the Magna Carta was simultaneously defining a distinction between being English and being French (whether John liked it or not).

By the early modern era, empires and city-states still dominated forms of state organization, but differences between peoples began to be recognized, fought over, massaged and defined. The Spanish Netherlands lost interest in being Spanish-owned. Its peoples' predominantly Protestant religious proclivities were in danger of repression as a part of the staunchly Catholic Spanish Empire, and the Dutch economy flourished in international trade, commerce and finance at the same time that Spain's economy remained mired in the colonial exploitation of precious metal reserves. The Japanese people had accepted their Yamato emperors as their link to the Shinto gods in the Seventeen Article Constitution. The introduction of Christianity in the late sixteenth century threatened to disrupt not just the Japanese state, but the Japanese way of life, and the Tokugawa shoguns who manipulated the emperors decided that Christianity and the Europeans who brought it to Japan needed to be excised from the islands altogether. Even the Great Muscovite Law Code, promulgated largely to make the terms of the manorial relationship between aristocrats and serfs more concrete, became a method of defining the Russian state as feudal in an early modern era. There may not have been nations, nor much people-oriented power in the early modern era, but world history was ready to see them arise.

■ *Athenian Constitution*

Date: ca 328 BCE
Author: Aristotle
Genre: Expository essay

Summary Overview

The *Athenian Constitution*, attributed to Aristotle, is a commentary on the development of constitutional democracy in ancient Greece. The text of *Athenian Constitution*, portions of which have not survived, is essentially a history of ancient Greece from a political, constitutional perspective. Thus it traces the progression of Greek rulers and the constitutional reforms they initiated—or in some cases their suppression of constitutional rights and privileges—up to the year 403 BCE. Portions of the *Athenian Constitution* contain information about ancient Greece that is found in no other surviving text.

Defining Moment

The *Athenian Constitution* was probably not written for publication; most likely, like much of Aristotle's writing, it was intended as a text for his students. The Lyceum that Aristotle directed was a school, but it was organized far more informally than a modern school is. There was no fixed curriculum, nor were there any specific course requirements. Students were not required to pay fees. Rather, the Lyceum was an informal gathering of young men who were interested in attending philosophical and scientific lectures and in conducting research on topics of interest. Very often the "classes" consisted of discussion and debate. Their efforts were often self-directed, with one student elected every ten days on a revolving basis to handle the school's administrative chores. The students were divided into two groups, junior members and senior members. The younger junior members attended lectures and often served as assistants to the senior members. The latter spent most of their time conducting research in philosophy and sci-

ence and in many cases writing documents to which Aristotle's name was attached.

Author Biography

Aristotle (along with his mentor, Plato, and Plato's mentor, Socrates) holds a firm place as one of the foundational figures in Western civilization. Virtually no discipline escaped his scholarship: aesthetics, music, morality, ethics, metaphysics, logic, rhetoric, politics, physics, anatomy, biology, zoology, optics, astronomy, geography, medicine—the list could go on and on. He virtually created the study of logic. His work laid the foundation for the modern scientific method.

Aristotle was born in Stagira, Chalcidice, near modern-day Thessaloníki, in 384 BCE. As a young adult, he attended the academy run by Plato in Athens, where he remained for two decades as a student and then as a teacher. After Plato's death, Aristotle traveled throughout Asia Minor (modern-day Turkey), married, and became the father of a daughter. In 343 BCE Philip II of Macedon, a kingdom in northeastern Greece, invited him to become director of an academy, where Aristotle's students included Philip's son, Alexander the Great, as well as the scientist Ptolemy. Aristotle returned to Athens in 335 BCE, where he established his own academy, the Lyceum. Although only about a third of Aristotle's written work survives, it is believed that the bulk of his works were written during this period, from 335 to 323 BCE. Late in his life, he was charged with impiety—with not holding the gods in sufficient reverence—probably because of his association with Macedon at a time when anti-Macedonian sentiment in Athens ran high. He fled to his mother's country estate, where he died in 322 BCE.

HISTORICAL DOCUMENT

Part 5

Since such, then, was the organization of the constitution, and the many were in slavery to the few, the people rose against the upper class. The strife was keen, and for a long time the two parties were ranged in hostile camps against one another, till at

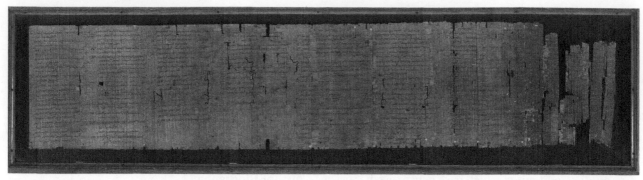

The Aristotelian Constitution of the Athenians, now in the British Library (commons.wikimedia.org/Papyrus 131) [Public Domain]

last, by common consent, they appointed Solon to be mediator and Archon, and committed the whole constitution to his hands. The immediate occasion of his appointment was his poem, which begins with the words:

I behold, and within my heart deep sadness has claimed its place,

As I mark the oldest home of the ancient Ionian race

Slain by the sword.

In this poem he fights and disputes on behalf of each party in turn against the other, and finally he advises them to come to terms and put an end to the quarrel existing between them. By birth and reputation Solon was one of the foremost men of the day, but in wealth and position he was of the middle class, as is generally agreed, and is, indeed, established by his own evidence in these poems, where he exhorts the wealthy not to be grasping.

But ye who have store of good, who are sated and overflow,

Restrain your swelling soul, and still it and keep it low:

Let the heart that is great within you be trained a lowlier way;

Ye shall not have all at your will, and we will not for ever obey.

Indeed, he constantly fastens the blame of the conflict on the rich; and accordingly at the beginning of the poem he says that he fears "the love of wealth and an overweening mind," evidently meaning that it was through these that the quarrel arose.

Part 6

As soon as he was at the head of affairs, Solon liberated the people once and for all, by prohibiting all loans on the security of the debtor's person: and in addition he made laws by which he cancelled all debts, public and private. This measure is commonly called the Seisachtheia [removal of burdens], since thereby the people had their loads removed from them. In connexion with it some persons try to traduce the character of Solon. It so happened that, when he was about to enact the Seisachtheia, he communicated his intention to some members of the upper class, whereupon, as the partisans of the popular party say, his friends stole a march on him; while those who wish to attack his character maintain that he too had a share in the fraud himself. For these persons borrowed money and bought up a large amount of land, and so when, a short time afterwards, all debts were cancelled, they became wealthy; and this, they say, was the origin of the families which were afterwards looked on as having been wealthy from primeval times. However, the story of the popular party is by far the most probable. A man who was so moderate and public-spirited in all his other actions, that when it was within his power to put his fellow-citizens beneath his feet and establish himself as tyrant, he preferred instead to incur the hostility of both parties by placing his honour and the general welfare above his personal aggrandisement, is not likely to have consented to defile his hands by such a petty and palpable fraud. That he had this absolute power is, in the first place, indicated by the desperate condition the country; moreover, he mentions it himself repeatedly in his poems, and it is universally admitted. We are therefore bound to consider this accusation to be false.

Part 7

Next Solon drew up a constitution and enacted new laws; and the ordinances of Draco ceased to be used, with the exception of those relating to murder. The laws were inscribed on the wooden stands, and set up in the King's Porch, and all swore to obey them; and the nine Archons made oath upon the stone, declaring that they would dedicate a golden statue if they should transgress any of them. This is the origin of the oath to that effect which they take to the present day. Solon ratified his laws for a hundred years; and the following was the fashion in which he organized the constitution. He divided the population according to property into four classes, just as it had been divided before, namely, Pentacosiomedimni, Knights, Zeugitae, and Thetes. The various magistracies, namely, the nine Archons, the Treasurers, the Commissioners for Public Contracts (Poletae), the Eleven, and Clerks (Colacretae), he assigned to the Pentacosiomedimni, the Knights, and the Zeugitae, giving offices to each class in proportion to the value of their rateable property. To who ranked among the Thetes he gave nothing but a place in the Assembly and in the juries. A man had to rank as a Pentacosiomedimnus if he made, from his own land, five hundred measures, whether liquid or solid. Those ranked as Knights who made three hundred measures, or, as some say, those who were able to maintain a horse. In support of the latter definition they adduce the name of the class, which may be supposed to be derived from this fact, and also some votive offerings of early times; for in the Acropolis there is a votive offering, a statue of Diphilus, bearing this inscription:

> The son of Diphilus, Athenion hight,
> Raised from the Thetes and become a knight,
> Did to the gods this sculptured charger bring,
> For his promotion a thank-offering.

And a horse stands in evidence beside the man, implying that this was what was meant by belonging to the rank of Knight. At the same time it seems reasonable to suppose that this class, like the Pentacosiomedimni, was defined by the possession of an income of a certain number of measures. Those ranked as Zeugitae who made two hundred measures, liquid or solid; and the rest ranked as Thetes, and were not eligible for any office. Hence it is that even at the present day, when a candidate for any office is asked to what class he belongs, no one would think of saying that he belonged to the Thetes.

Part 8

The elections to the various offices Solon enacted should be by lot, out of candidates selected by each of the tribes. Each tribe selected ten candidates for the nine archonships, and among these the lot was cast. Hence it is still the custom for each tribe to choose ten candidates by lot, and then the lot is again cast among these. A proof that Solon regulated the elections to office according to the property classes may be found in the law still in force with regard to the Treasurers, which enacts that they shall be chosen from the Pentacosiomedimni. Such was Solon's legislation with respect to the nine Archons; whereas in early times the Council of Areopagus summoned suitable persons according to its own judgement and appointed them for the year to the several offices. There were four tribes, as before, and four tribe-kings. Each tribe was divided into three Trittyes [Thirds], with twelve Naucraries in each; and the Naucraries had officers of their own, called Naucrari, whose duty it was to superintend the current receipts and expenditure. Hence, among the laws of Solon now obsolete, it is repeatedly written that the Naucrari are to receive and to spend out of the Naucraric fund. Solon also appointed a Council of four hundred, a hundred from each tribe; but he assigned to the Council of the Areopagus the duty of superintending the laws, acting as before as the guardian of the constitution in general. It kept watch over the affairs of the state in most of the more important matters, and corrected offenders, with full powers to inflict either fines or personal punishment. The money received in fines it brought up into the Acropolis, without assigning the reason for the mulct. It also tried those who conspired for the overthrow of the state, Solon having enacted a process of impeachment to deal with such offenders. Further, since he saw the state often engaged in internal disputes, while many of the citizens from sheer indifference accepted whatever might turn up, he made a law with express reference to such persons, enacting that any one who, in a time civil factions, did not take up arms with either party, should lose his rights as a citizen and cease to have any part in the state.

Part 9

Such, then, was his legislation concerning the magistracies. There are three points in the constitution of Solon which appear to be its most democratic features: first and most important, the prohibition of loans on the security of the debtor's person; secondly, the right of every person who so willed to claim redress on behalf of any one to whom wrong was being done; thirdly, the institution of the appeal to the jurycourts; and it is to this last, they say, that the masses have owed their strength most of all, since, when the democracy is master of the voting-power, it is master of the constitution. Moreover, since the laws were not drawn up in simple and explicit terms (but like the one concerning inheritances and wards of state), disputes inevitably occurred, and the courts had to decide in every matter, whether public or private. Some persons in fact believe that Solon deliberately made the laws indefinite, in order that the final decision might be in the hands of the people. This, however, is not probable, and the reason no doubt was that it is impossible to attain ideal perfection when framing a law in general terms; for we must judge of his intentions, not from the actual results in the present day, but from the general tenor of the rest of his legislation.

Part 10

These seem to be the democratic features of his laws; but in addition, before the period of his legislation, he carried through his abolition of debts, and after it his increase in the standards of weights and measures, and of the currency. During his administration the measures were made larger than those of Pheidon, and the mina, which previously had a standard of seventy drachmas, was raised to the full hundred. The standard coin in earlier times was the two-drachma piece. He also made weights corresponding with the coinage, sixty-three minas going to the talent; and the odd three minas were distributed among the staters and the other values.

Part 11

When he had completed his organization of the constitution in the manner that has been described, he found himself beset by people coming to him and harassing him concerning his laws, criticizing here and questioning there, till, as he wished neither to alter what he had decided on nor yet to be an object of ill will to every one by remaining in Athens, he set off on a journey to Egypt, with the combined objects of trade and travel, giving out that he should not return for ten years. He considered that there was no call for him to expound the laws personally, but that every one should obey them just as they were written. Moreover, his position at this time was unpleasant. Many members of the upper class had been estranged from him on account of his abolition of debts, and both parties were alienated through their disappointment at the condition of things which he had created. The mass of the people had expected him to make a complete redistribution of all property, and the upper class hoped he would restore everything to its former position, or, at any rate, make but a small change. Solon, however, had resisted both classes. He might have made himself a despot by attaching himself to whichever party he chose, but he preferred, though at the cost of incurring the enmity of both, to be the saviour of his country and the ideal lawgiver.

Part 12

The truth of this view of Solon's policy is established alike by common consent, and by the mention he has himself made of the matter in his poems. Thus:

I gave to the mass of the people such rank as befitted their need,
I took not away their honour, and I granted naught to their greed;
While those who were rich in power, who in wealth were glorious and great,
I bethought me that naught should befall them unworthy their splendour and state;
So I stood with my shield outstretched, and both were sale in its sight,
And I would not that either should triumph, when the triumph was not with right.

Again he declares how the mass of the people ought to be treated:

But thus will the people best the voice of their leaders obey,
When neither too slack is the rein, nor violence holdeth the sway;
For indulgence breedeth a child, the presumption that spurns control,
When riches too great are poured upon men of unbalanced soul.

And again elsewhere he speaks about the persons who wished to redistribute the land: So they came in search of plunder, and their cravings knew no bound, Every one among them deeming endless wealth would here be found. And that I with glozing smoothness hid a cruel mind within. Fondly then and vainly dreamt they; now they raise an angry din, And they glare askance in anger, and the light within their eyes Burns with hostile flames upon me. Yet therein no justice lies. All I promised, fully wrought I with the gods at hand to cheer, Naught beyond in folly ventured. Never to my soul was dear With a tyrant's force to govern, nor to see the good and base Side by side in equal portion share the rich home of our race.

Once more he speaks of the abolition of debts and of those who before were in servitude, but were released owing to the Seisachtheia:

Of all the aims for which I summoned forth
The people, was there one I compassed not?
Thou, when slow time brings justice in its train,
O mighty mother of the Olympian gods,

Dark Earth, thou best canst witness, from whose breast
I swept the pillars broadcast planted there,
And made thee free, who hadst been slave of yore.
And many a man whom fraud or law had sold
For from his god-built land, an outcast slave,
I brought again to Athens; yea, and some,
Exiles from home through debt's oppressive load,
Speaking no more the dear Athenian tongue,
But wandering far and wide, I brought again;
And those that here in vilest slavery
Crouched 'neath a master's frown, I set them free.
Thus might and right were yoked in harmony,
Since by the force of law I won my ends
And kept my promise. Equal laws I gave
To evil and to good, with even hand
Drawing straight justice for the lot of each.
But had another held the goad as
One in whose heart was guile and greediness,
He had not kept the people back from strife.
For had I granted, now what pleased the one,
Then what their foes devised in counterpoise,
Of many a man this state had been bereft.
Therefore I showed my might on every side,
Turning at bay like wolf among the hounds.

And again he reviles both parties for their grumblings in the times that followed:

Nay, if one must lay blame where blame is due,
Wer't not for me, the people ne'er had set
Their eyes upon these blessings e'en in dreams:
While greater men, the men of wealthier life,
Should praise me and should court me as their friend.

For had any other man, he says, received this exalted post,
He had not kept the people back, nor ceased
Til he had robbed the richness of the milk.
But I stood forth a landmark in the midst,
And barred the foes from battle.

Part 13

Such then, were Solon's reasons for his departure from the country. After his retirement the city was still torn by divisions. For four years, indeed, they lived in peace; but in the fifth year after Solon's government they were unable to elect an Archon on account of their dissensions, and again four years later they elected no Archon for the same reason. Subsequently, after a similar period had elapsed, Damasias was elected Archon; and he governed for two years and two months, until he was forcibly expelled from his office. After this, it was agreed, as a compromise, to elect ten Archons, five from the Eupatridae, three from the Agroeci, and two from the Demiurgi, and they ruled for the year following Damasias. It is clear from this that the Archon was at the time the magistrate who possessed the greatest power, since it is always in connexion with this office that conflicts are seen to arise. But altogether they were in a continual state of internal disorder. Some found the cause and justification of their discontent in the abolition of debts, because thereby they had been reduced to poverty; others were dissatisfied with the political constitution, because it had undergone a revolutionary change; while with others the motive was found in personal rivalries among themselves. The parties at this time were three in number. First there was the party of the Shore, led by Megacles the son of Alcmeon, which was considered to aim at a moderate form of government; then there were the men of the Plain, who desired an oligarchy and were led by Lycurgus; and thirdly there were the men of the Highlands, at the head of whom was Pisistratus, who was looked on as an extreme democrat. This latter party was reinforced by those who had been deprived of the debts due to them, from motives of poverty, and by those who were not of pure descent, from motives of personal apprehension. A proof of this is seen in the fact that after the tyranny was overthrown a revision was made of the citizen-roll, on the ground that many persons were partaking in the franchise without having a right to it. The names given to the respective parties were derived from the districts in which they held their lands.

Part 14

Pisistratus had the reputation of being an extreme democrat, and he also had distinguished himself greatly in the war with Megara. Taking advantage of this, he wounded himself, and by representing that his injuries had been inflicted on him by his political rivals, he persuaded the people, through a motion proposed by Aristion, to grant him a bodyguard. After he had got these "club-bearers," as they were called, he made an attack with them on the people and seized the Acropolis. This happened in the archonship of Comeas, thirty-one years after the legislation of Solon. It is related that, when Pisistratus asked for his bodyguard, Solon opposed the request, and declared that in so doing he proved himself wiser than half the people and braver than the rest, wiser than those who did not see that Pisistratus designed to make himself tyrant, and braver than those who saw it and kept silence. But when all his words availed nothing he carried forth his armour and set it up in front of his house, saying that he had helped his country so far as lay in his power (he was already a very old man), and that he called on all others to do the same. Solon's exhortations, however, proved fruitless, and Pisistratus assumed the sovereignty. His administration was more like a constitutional government than the rule of a tyrant; but before his power was firmly established, the adherents of Megacles and Lycurgus made a coalition and drove him out. This took place in the archonship of Hegesias, five years after the first establishment of his rule. Eleven years later Megacles, being in difficulties in a party struggle, again opened negotiations with Pisistratus, proposing that the latter should marry his daughter; and on these terms he brought him back to Athens, by a very primitive and simple-minded device. He first spread abroad a rumour that Athena was bringing back Pisistratus, and then, having found a woman of great stature and beauty, named Phye (according to Herodotus, of the deme of Paeania, but as others say a Thracian flower-seller of the deme of Collytus), he dressed her in a garb resembling that of the goddess and brought her into the city with Pisistratus. The latter drove in on a chariot with the woman beside him, and the inhabitants of the city, struck with awe, received him with adoration.

Part 15

In this manner did his first return take place. He did not, however, hold his power long, for about six years after his return he was again expelled. He refused to treat the daughter of Megacles as his wife, and being afraid, in consequence, of a combination of the two opposing parties, he retired from the country. First he led a colony to a place called Rhaicelus, in the region of the Thermaic gulf; and thence he passed to the country in the neighbourhood of Mt. Pangaeus. Here he acquired wealth and hired mercenaries; and not till ten years had elapsed did he return to Eretria and make an attempt to recover the government by force. In this he had the assistance of many allies, notably the Thebans and Lygdamis of Naxos, and also the Knights who held the supreme power in the constitution of Eretria. After his victory in the battle at Pallene he captured Athens, and when he had disarmed the people he at last had his tyranny securely established, and was able to take Naxos and set up Lygdamis as ruler there. He effected the disarmament of the people in the following manner. He ordered a parade in full armour in the Theseum, and began to make a speech to the people. He spoke for a short time, until the people called out that they could not hear him, whereupon he bade them come up to the entrance of the Acropolis, in order that his voice might be better heard. Then, while he continued to speak to them at great length, men whom he had appointed for the purpose collected the arms and locked them up in the chambers of the Theseum hard by, and came and made a signal to him that it was done. Pisistratus accordingly, when he had finished the rest of what he had to say, told the people also what had happened to their arms; adding that they were not to be surprised or alarmed, but go home and attend to their private affairs, while he would himself for the future manage all the business of the state.

Part 16

Such was the origin and such the vicissitudes of the tyranny of Pisistratus. His administration was temperate, as has been said before, and more like constitutional government than a tyranny. Not only was he in every respect humane and mild and ready to forgive those who offended, but, in addition, he advanced money to the poorer people to help them in their labours, so that they might make their living by agriculture. In this he had two objects, first that they might not spend their time in the city but

might be scattered over all the face of the country, and secondly that, being moderately well off and occupied with their own business, they might have neither the wish nor the time to attend to public affairs. At the same time his revenues were increased by the thorough cultivation of the country, since he imposed a tax of one tenth on all the produce. For the same reasons he instituted the local justices, and often made expeditions in person into the country to inspect it and to settle disputes between individuals, that they might not come into the city and neglect their farms. It was in one of these progresses that, as the story goes, Pisistratus had his adventure with the man of Hymettus, who was cultivating the spot afterwards known as "Tax-free Farm." He saw a man digging and working at a very stony piece of ground, and being surprised he sent his attendant to ask what he got out of this plot of land. "Aches and pains," said the man; "and that's what Pisistratus ought to have his tenth of." The man spoke without knowing who his questioner was; but Pisistratus was so pleased with his frank speech and his industry that he granted him exemption from all taxes. And so in matters in general he burdened the people as little as possible with his government, but always cultivated peace and kept them in all quietness. Hence the tyranny of Pisistratus was often spoken of proverbially as "the age of gold"; for when his sons succeeded him the government became much harsher. But most important of all in this respect was his popular and kindly disposition. In all things he was accustomed to observe the laws, without giving himself any exceptional privileges. Once he was summoned on a charge of homicide before the Areopagus, and he appeared in person to make his defence; but the prosecutor was afraid to present himself and abandoned the case. For these reasons he held power long, and whenever he was expelled he regained his position easily. The majority alike of the upper class and of the people were in his favour; the former he won by his social intercourse with them, the latter by the assistance which he gave to their private purses, and his nature fitted him to win the hearts of both. Moreover, the laws in reference to tyrants at that time in force at Athens were very mild, especially the one which applies more particularly to the establishment of a tyranny. The law ran as follows: "These are the ancestral statutes of the Athenians; if any persons shall make an attempt to establish a tyranny, or if any person shall join in setting up a tyranny, he shall lose his civic rights, both himself and his whole house."

GLOSSARY

Agroeci, Demiurgi, and Eupatridae: a reference to classes of people: the peasants, the artisans and tradespeople, and the nobility, respectively

ancient Ionian race: broadly speaking, the Greeks who were Aristotle's ancestors

deme: a country district or village, part of a city-state (polis)

glozing: flattering

King's Porch: the seat of the archon (king)

Ion, Medon, Acastus, and Codrus: a reference to various reputed leaders of Athens: Ion was commander in chief of the Athenian army under the archaic mythological king Erechtheus. Medon was the son of Codrus (the last of Athens's legendary kings) and the first archon of Athens. Acastus was the successor to Medon.

Lycurgus: Spartan lawgiver of the eighth century BCE

Naucrari: subdivisions of the population of the Athenian state

Pheidon: king of Argos in the eighth century BCE who instituted a system of standard measurements

the Eleven: the panel in charge of prisoners and executions—a group with immense discretion in determining who was arrested and in ordering summary executions

Thermaic gulf: gulf in the Aegean Sea now called the Gulf of Salonika

Document Analysis

In the section of Athenian Constitution preceding this excerpt, Aristotle documents the political situation in Athens prior to and during the time of Draco, who instituted a law code in 621 BCE. Athens was ruled by an oligarchy, so few people participated in the political process. For farmers, the economic situation was hard. The geography of Greece made trade difficult, so even though farmers tended to be self-sufficient, their farms were usually small, and one poor harvest could cast a farmer into debt. To satisfy this debt, the farmer and his family were often reduced to the condition of slaves; they paid their debt through service to their creditor.

Membership in the oligarchy was based on birth and wealth; the king ruled with the advisement of an aristocratic council with life tenure, so it was clearly an undemocratic institution. Facing the political pressure of a farmer's revolt, an archon (or oligarchical official) named Draco instituted a law code that was intended to reduce some of the conflict between the aristocracy and the lower classes. He extended voting rights to anyone who could furnish himself with military equipment. A person could become an archon if he owned property free of debt equal to ten minas. A mina was a unit of currency equal to a hundred drachmas; one drachma was roughly the amount that a skilled worker could earn in a day, so ten minas equaled something in the range of three years' wages for a skilled worker—a significant amount of property, but not the wealth that had formerly defined the aristocracy. The property qualifications for generals and cavalry commanders were higher, reflecting the greater skills these men would need. An important point about Draco's administration is that the archons were selected by lot from among those of voting age, and those who failed to attend meetings were fined according to their class: The highest class, based on wealth (the *pentacosiomedimnus*), paid more than knights or members of the *zeugite* class. Although historians debate who the *zeugites* were, it is clear they occupied a lower rung, perhaps as farmers or foot soldiers in the army. The Council of Areopagus remained "guardian of the laws," and citizens had redress for wrongs before the council.

With Part 5, Aristotle takes up the administration of Solon, who was not only a lawgiver and reformer but also a poet, though most of his poetry—only fragments of which survive—consists of commentary on his administration. Aristotle notes that when Solon assumed office, "many were in slavery to the few" and "the people rose against the upper class." After the people put the constitution into Solon's hands, he directed his efforts to making the contending classes "come to terms and put an end to the quarrel existing between them." Solon was particularly distressed by what he saw as a moral decay, much of it because the rich and their "love of wealth and an overweening mind." The chief step that Solon took was to cancel debts: He "liberated the people once and for all, by prohibiting all loans on the security of the debtor's person," meaning that people could no longer be reduced to a condition of servitude because of debt.

Additionally, "he made laws by which he cancelled all debts, public and private." Solon met with resistance from members of the upper class, some of whom accused Solon of perpetrating a fraud for his own benefit. Aristotle, though, rejects these stories as false, for Solon was "moderate and public-spirited in all his other actions," and the "desperate condition" of the country required him to take bold action without regard to what anyone thought.

Part 7 details changes Solon made to the constitution. Draco's laws, with the exception of those pertaining to murder, were rendered null. Solon retained the class structure from Draco: At the top were the *pentacosiomedimni*, who owned the most productive tracts of land. Beneath them were knights, or *hippeis*, followed by the *zeugitae* and a fourth class, the *thetes*, who were hired farmworkers and often served as foot soldiers in the military. A noteworthy reform was that Solon distributed archonships and other public offices according to a person's "rateable property," meaning that each class would have at least some representation and even

the *thetes* would have some public role as members of the assembly or juries.

In Part 8, Aristotle details the structure of the government under Solon. He notes that candidates for high office, including archonships, were to be selected by lot (rather than by birth). He notes that Athens comprised four tribes, the broadest classification of Athenian society; each tribe, which was headed by a king, was made up of three villages. Each of these villages comprised thirty clans. The clans consisted of a group of households, generally subsistence farmers, their dependents, and any slaves they might have owned. To ensure that the Athenian population was broadly represented, Solon instituted the Council of the Four Hundred, with a hundred representatives from each tribe. Solon, however, retained Draco's Council of the Areopagus, which had the "duty of superintending the laws, acting as before as the guardian of the constitution in general." In Part 9, Aristotle sums up the chief democratic features of Solon's administration: "the prohibition of loans on the security of the debtor's person"; "the right of every person who so willed to claim redress on behalf of any one to whom wrong was being done"; and "the institution of the appeal to the jurycourts." Aristotle goes on to note that "it is to this last … that the masses have owed their strength most of all, since, when the democracy is master of the voting-power, it is master of the constitution." Part 10 deals with Solon's reforms in coinage and weights and measurements.

Parts 11–16 of the *Athenian Constitution* examines the aftermath of Solon's constitutional reforms. Solon "found himself beset by people coming to him and harassing him concerning his laws." The upper classes were critical of his abolition of debts, and the lower classes expected that he would redistribute property more extensively. Accordingly, he left Athens. In Part 12, Aristotle reproduces passages of Solon's poetry in which he responded to the "grumblings" of Athens's citizens about his reforms. Thus, Solon wrote that "I gave to the mass of the people such rank as befitted their need, / I took not away their honour, and I granted naught to their greed." He defended his abolition of debt in terms such as these:

> Thus might and right were yoked in harmony,
> Since by the force of law I won my ends
> And kept my promise. Equal laws I gave
> To evil and to good, with even hand
> Drawing straight justice for the lot of each.

Solon was also highly critical in his poetry of the rich, referring to a situation "when riches too great are poured upon men of unbalanced soul."

After Solon's departure, his constitutional reforms began to collapse. The city was "torn by divisions" and had trouble electing archons. Party factionalism caused dissension in Athenian society. Aristotle goes on to detail how Pisistratus, under these circumstances, assumed power and declared himself tyrant. Pisistratus's administration, though, was marked by "vicissitudes" and he was expelled and then returned to power. Despite being a tyrant, "the majority alike of the upper class and of the people were in his favour; the former he won by his social intercourse with them, the latter by the assistance which he gave to their private purses, and his nature fitted him to win the hearts of both." According to Aristotle, then, his administration was "more like constitutional government than a tyranny."

Essential Themes

Aristotle's *Athenian Constitution* is a survey of the development of democratic institutions in ancient Greece. In the excerpt reproduced here, he identifies Solon as the progenitor of Greek democracy.

In the years before Solon promulgated his law code, Athens was in a state of crisis. The rich and poor were pitted against each other. The poor were enslaved to the rich, often because of debt. Food was in short supply. The oligarchs who had ruled Athens were arrogant and indifferent to the plight of the lower social orders. Further, they were often incompetent and corrupt, for the aristocracy that ruled Athens was based on heredity, not competence. Solon believed that Athens was falling into moral decay. He replaced this emphasis on hereditary rule by dividing Athenian society into classes based on wealth and income. In the twenty-first century, such a legal and social system does not seem very democratic. Yet in Solon's time it was a step forward in an ongoing process of placing political power in the hands of broader classes of people.

Solon was essential to Greek thinking about democracy and constitutional reform, for he was the first to encourage direct citizen participation in democratic institutions. Ultimately, these institutions would take hold in the Western world after knowledge of the institutions of Greece (and Rome) became widespread in the West during the Renaissance. European Enlightenment thinkers of the eighteenth century would use these models in overthrowing monarchies and creating the democracies that have dominated Europe, North America, and a large and growing number of other countries since then.

———*Michael J. O'Neal, PhD*

Bibliography and Further Reading

Day, James, and Mortimer Chambers. *Aristotle's History of Athenian Democracy*. Berkeley: University of California Press, 1962.

Irwin, Elizabeth. *Solon and Early Greek Poetry: The Politics of Exhortation*. New York: Cambridge University Press, 2005.

Keaney, John J. *The Composition of Aristotle's* Athenaion Politeia: *Observation and Explanation*. New York: Oxford University Press, 1992.

Moore, J. M. *Aristotle and Xenophon on Democracy and Oligarchy*. Berkeley: University of California Press, 1975.

Raaflaub, Kurt A., et al. *Origins of Democracy in Ancient Greece*. Berkeley: University of California Press, 2007.

Rhodes, Peter John. *Commentary on the Aristotelian Athenaion Politeia*. Oxford, U.K. Clarendon Press, 1981.

Robinson, Eric W., ed. *Ancient Greek Democracy: Readings and Sources*. Oxford, U.K: Blackwell, 2003.

Web Sites

"A History of Ancient Greece: Solon's Early Greek Legislation." International World History Project Web site. http://history-world.org/solon.htm.

■ Constitution of Carthage

Date: ca 328 BCE
Author: Aristotle
Genre: Book chapter

Summary Overview

The eleventh chapter of the second book of Aristotle's *Politics* (ca. 335–323 BCE) is on the constitution of the Phoenician Mediterranean city of Carthage, located near modern-day Tunis in Tunisia. This work is a response to the political philosophy of Aristotle's teacher, Plato, expanding on an attempt to describe an ideal organization for a national government. In *Politics* Aristotle develops his idea of how cities should function from his discussion of how people ought to live, giving real-world examples of well-governed cities whose constitutions are balanced between various forms of government. Aristotle settles on Carthage as the closest approximation to his ideal. Partly this was because of the relatively imperfect information about Carthage available to the Greek world, allowing Aristotle to interpret the history of the city in the best light for his purposes.

Defining Moment

Carthage, a Phoenician colony whose true name was Qart Hadasht, or "New Town," ruled over modern-day Tunisia and northeastern Algeria, a land far more fertile in antiquity than now. The Carthaginians also controlled Sardinia and Corsica and eventually Spain. The Carthaginian Empire, and the pre-Roman city at its center, were powers in the western Mediterranean from about 600 to 200 BCE.

Carthage produced no literary tradition of its own; about the historical development of the Carthaginian constitution we are completely in the dark. What we do know is that the city was dominated by great families. The Carthaginian Empire was ruled from the late sixth to the fourth centuries by Mago and his descendants, most prominently the fifth-century navigator Hanno, who led the drive both to conquer the North African hinterland and to explore the Atlantic. Early in the fourth century, the aristocratic form of government at Carthage described by Aristotle became established with the creation of the Council of the One Hundred and Four. In 308 BCE, the attempt of Bomilcar to make himself tyrant of the city steered Carthage in a new political direction, toward increasing democracy.

Meanwhile, Aristotle's treatise *Politics*, which contains his remarks on the constitution of Carthage, was com-posed in response to the *Republic* and *Laws* of his teacher, Plato. All three works aimed toward a philosophical description of the ideal form of government. The Greeks conceived that there were three possible forms. The first was monarchy, in which a single man held all the political power. A second was aristocracy, in which power was exercised by a council of leading citizens. The third was democracy, in which all power was exercised by the citizen body as a whole. Aristotle envisioned that a mixed constitution, which had a role for all three types of governance, was best. Aristotle felt that the constitution of Carthage most nearly approached his ideal.

Author Biography

The Greek philosopher Aristotle was the chief student of Plato and the tutor of Alexander the Great. His own school was located in the Athens neighborhood called the Lyceum, and his philosophy is often called peripatetic (meaning "to walk up and down"), after the enclosed walkway at the front of his school. He is one of the most influential founding figures of the Western intellectual tradition. His achievements range from creating the forerunner of the modern university curriculum to devising formal logic. Aristotle was born in 384 BCE in the village of Stagira in Macedonia. His father, Nicomachus, was the court physician to Amyntas II of Macedonia. Aristotle studied with Plato; when he did not become his successor as head of the academy, he moved on to teach philosophy in various Greek cities. One of his most important positions at this time was tutoring the future Alexander the Great. He also lectured for a time in Lesbos, where he performed most of the biological experiments (including dissections of animals) that he later incorporated into his books on biology. He returned to Athens but was forced to flee due to anti-Macedonian agitation in 323 BCE and died a year later in Euripus (modern-day Khalkís). Aristotle's surviving works can best be described as the first attempt at an encyclopedia, since they cover every field of knowledge known in antiquity. He organized human knowledge into a systematic arrangement where all of the physical and social sciences were subordinated to philosophy.

HISTORICAL DOCUMENT

The Carthaginians are also considered to have an excellent form of government, which differs from that of any other state in several respects, though it is in some very like the Lacedaemonian. Indeed, all three states—the Lacedaemonian, the Cretan, and the Carthaginian—nearly resemble one another, and are very different from any others. Many of the Carthaginian institutions are excellent. The superiority of their constitution is proved by the fact that, although containing an element of democracy, it has been lasting; the Carthaginians have never had any rebellion worth speaking of, and have never been under the rule of a tyrant.

Among the points in which the Carthaginian constitution resembles the Lacedaemonian are the following:—The common tables of the clubs answer to the Spartan phiditia, and their magistracy of the 104 to the Ephors; but, whereas the Ephors are any chance persons, the magistrates of the Carthaginians are elected according to merit—this is an improvement. They have also their kings and their gerusia, or council of elders, who correspond to the kings and elders of Sparta. Their kings, unlike the Spartan, are not always of the same family, and this an ordinary one, but if there is some distinguished family they are selected out of it and not appointed by seniority—this is far better. Such officers have great power, and therefore, if they are persons of little worth, do a great deal of harm, and they have already done harm at Lacedaemon.

Most of the defects or deviations from the perfect state, for which the Carthaginian constitution would be censured, apply equally to all the forms of government which we have mentioned. But of the deflections from aristocracy and constitutional government, some incline more to democracy and some to oligarchy. The kings and elders, if unanimous, may determine whether they will or will not bring a matter before the people, but when they are not unanimous, the people may decide whether or not the matter shall be brought forward. And whatever the kings and elders bring before the people is not only heard but also determined by them, and anyone who likes may oppose it; now this is not permitted in Sparta and Crete. That the magistracies of

five who have under them many important matters should be co-opted, that they should choose the supreme council of 100, and should hold office longer than other magistrates (for they are virtually rulers both before and after they hold office)—these are oligarchical features; their being without salary and not elected by lot, and any similar points, such as the practice of having all suits tried by the magistrates, and not some by one class of judges or jurors and some by another, as at Lacedaemon, are characteristic of aristocracy. The Carthaginian constitution deviates from aristocracy and inclines to oligarchy, chiefly on a point where popular opinion is on their side. For men in general think that magistrates should be chosen not only for their merit, but for their wealth: a man, they say, who is poor cannot rule well—he has not the leisure. If, then, election of magistrates for their wealth be characteristic of oligarchy, and election for merit of aristocracy, there will be a third form under which the constitution of Carthage is comprehended; for the Carthaginians choose their magistrates, and particularly the highest of them—their kings and generals—with an eye both to merit and to wealth.

But we must acknowledge that, in thus deviating from aristocracy, the legislator has committed an error. Nothing is more absolutely necessary than to provide that the highest class, not only when in office, but when out of office, should have leisure and not demean themselves in any way; and to this his attention should be first directed. Even if you must have regard to wealth, in order to secure leisure, yet it is surely a bad thing that the greatest offices, such as those of kings and generals, should be bought. The law which allows this abuse makes wealth of more account than virtue, and the whole state becomes avaricious. For, whenever the chiefs of the state deem anything honourable, the other citizens are sure to follow their example; and, where virtue has not the first place, there aristocracy cannot be firmly established. Those who have been at the expense of purchasing their places will be in the habit of repaying themselves; and it is absurd to suppose that a poor and honest man will be wanting to make gains, and that a lower stamp of man who has incurred a great expense will not. Wherefore they should rule who are able to rule best. And even if the legislator does not care to protect the good from poverty, he should at any rate secure leisure for those in office.

It would seem also to be a bad principle that the same person should hold many offices, which is a favourite practice among the Carthaginians, for one business is better done by one man. The legislator should see to this and should not appoint the same person to be a flute-player and a shoemaker. Hence, where the state is large, it is more in accordance both with constitutional and with democratic principles that the offices of state should be distributed among many persons. For, as I was saying, this arrangement is more popular, and any action famil-iarized by repetition is better and sooner performed. We have a proof in military and naval matters; the duties of command and of obedience in both these services extend to all.

The government of the Carthaginians is oligarchical, but they successfully escape the evils of oligarchy by their wealth, which enables them from time to time to send out some portion of the people to their colonies. This is their panacea and the means by which they give stability to the state. Accident favours them, but the legislator should be able to provide against revolution without trusting to accidents. As things are, if any misfortune occurred, and the people revolted from their rulers, there would be no way of restoring peace by legal methods.

GLOSSARY

aristocracy: government by those believed to be best qualified, in the ancient world almost always those who had inherited wealth and privilege

chance persons: in this context, persons from the entire adult population of Sparta, compared with the circumstances among the Carthaginians, who imposed qualifications on candidates for the magistracy

Ephors: the five annually elected Spartan magistrates who had power over the king

Lacedaemonian: from the Spartan city-state of Lacedaemonia

phiditia: a communal arrangement comprising the mess hall and barracks for twenty to thirty Spartan infantrymen

tyranny: in the Greek concept of the word, a temporary dictatorship led by a persuasive citizen who convinced others to allow him to seize power and abandon the rule of law in order to handle some sort of local crisis. A tyrant in ancient Greece was not necessarily cruel or power-mad, but his status as a political leader above the constitution meant that a city-state's political organization was weakened.

Document Analysis

Aristotle begins by stating that the constitution of Carthage is of the same general type as Sparta's (Lacedaemonia) and Crete's but is superior because it has endured through time and its democratic element has never produced a demagogic tyrant. Aristotle lists several similarities with Sparta's constitution. All Spartan citizens dined together in the same mess hall (which Aristotle considered a good means of encouraging civic equality), since they formed a permanent standing army. He attributes the same practice to Carthage. But this is a point on which Aristotle is confused. Citizenship in Carthage was conferred by belonging to one of several religious brotherhoods traditional in the city. These brotherhoods celebrated an annual religious feast similar to Easter or Passover, which is hardly comparable to the daily Spartan custom.

Aristotle next compares the kings of Carthage to those of Sparta. Many historians have made the mistake of taking Aristotle too literally here and transferring all the associations of Greek kings to the officials he talks about in Carthage. This parallel is extremely unlikely, given what else is known about Carthaginian history. The point of the comparison is more probably that just as Sparta had two kings ruling at the same time, Carthage had two chief magistrates who shared power in a joint term of office. Aristotle describes the Carthaginian kings as being "not always of the same family" and as being "selected" and "not appointed by seniority." It is clear, therefore, that he is not talking about a royal dynasty at all, but about elected officials. Indeed, Carthage was ruled by two chief executive officers who were elected annually. They were not called kings, but *suffetes*. This is the same Semitic word translated as "judge" in the Hebrew Bible, meaning an official who is not a king but who is chosen to lead a state for a specific period of time. In practice, the office of *suffete* was limited to the most powerful families in Carthage, and it often happened that a *suffete* would be elected to the same office that had been held by his father, uncle, or grandfather (not continuously but only for a few years each, with other families intervening). The same phenomenon has occurred among American presidents, but that hardly means that a royal dynasty has been established.

Aristotle also talks about the "gerusia, or council of elders." In fact, Carthage seems to have had two such councils. The Council of Thirty was composed of the leading aristocrats in the city and ruled almost in conjunction with the *suffetes*, who would have been first among equals in this council. The second council, which Aristotle appears to have in mind, was the Council of the One Hundred and Four, whose members were selected by holding certain magistracies other than the *suffetes*. This council's members exercised the judicial functions Aristotle talks about. In particular, they judged each *suffete* at the end of his administration; if they found any financial irregularities, they could, and often did, condemn him to be crucified. Aristotle's "magistracies of five" are harder to understand in the light of other sources about Carthage. They may have been special committees of the Council of Thirty given tasks such as negotiating treaties or settling land disputes.

Aristotle gives more information about the popular assembly of all Carthaginian citizens than does any other historical source. Modern-day historians generally accept that if either of the *suffetes* wished to pursue a policy that the Council of Thirty did not approve, he could bring it before the assembly as an alternative source of validation. Note that while this assembly might have included all citizens, it was far from democratic in any modern sense, since it would have ex-

cluded women and slaves (much more than half of the population) and might have required a minimal property qualification for voting rights.

Aristotle finally turns to the defects that prevent the constitution of Carthage from creating a perfect state. Carthage, through chance, has avoided the tendency of monarchy to become tyranny and of democratic government to give rise to a demagogue and so again producing tyranny. But Aristotle thinks that the aristocracy in Carthage was devolving into oligarchy. For Aristotle, aristocracy was the ideal principle of government, the rule of the best men—that is, the wisest and most just. There is a tendency for such a government to change into an oligarchy, in which power is put into the hands of a few men chosen for their wealth and status within society rather than for their virtue. Carthage avoids this tendency entirely, in Aristotle's view, since its people voted for those who were best and wealthiest.

Aristotle's discussion of the corrupting influence of money in oligarchic politics is not hypothetical. We know from the ancient Greek historian Polybius that it was a general practice, and a perfectly legal one, for candidates for office in Carthage simply to buy the votes of citizens for cash payments from their own private wealth. Similarly, the main reason the One Hundred and Four existed was to curb officials' enriching themselves from their offices. Such a measure would hardly have been necessary had it not been all too common a practice.

Aristotle settled on Carthage as having an ideal constitution in part because it was one of his own making. His relative ignorance of conditions in Carthage allowed him to interpret the little information he had in light of current ideas of good government. As a result, what Aristotle says must always be checked against the little other information we have about Carthage. Despite its importance in the history of the ancient world, Carthage is virtually in a black hole as far as literary sources go. Thus, Aristotle's disquisition on the city constitution is all the more important. As political philosophy, Aristotle's work looks backward to the organization of the city-state, even though he was writing at a time when the Mediterranean world was on the verge of organizing itself into governments on a national level.

Essential Themes

Throughout the period of Aristotle's writing, Carthage's main overseas enterprise was the effort to conquer the Greek cities on the island of Sicily, chief among them being the great city of Syracuse. By the beginning of the third century, Carthage had gained the upper hand in Sicily and seemed to be in permanent control of about two-thirds of the island. However, in 264 BCE a trivial diplomatic incident sparked war with Rome, which had just solidified its control of the entire Italian peninsula. From 264 to 241 BCE, Rome and Carthage fought the First Punic War (from the Latin Poeni, their name for the Phoenicians), mostly on Sicily but including an invasion of North Africa by a Roman army in 255 BCE. Rome was ultimately successful and forced Carthage to abandon Sicily. The defeated officer Hamilcar Barca became the leading figure in Carthaginian politics and directed the conquest of a new Carthaginian empire in Spain, where rich silver deposits were available. His son-in-law Hasdrubal and then his son Hannibal also became the leading figures in Carthage. In 218 BCE, Hannibal began a new war with Rome (known as the Second Punic War), lasting until 201 BCE. Hannibal led an army from Spain to Italy over the Alps, winning devastating victories over the Romans at present-day Lake Trasimeno in 217 BCE and Cannae in 216 BCE that are still studied as among the most perfect examples of the art of war in all history. The scope of the war was so great that for the first time Carthaginians themselves were compelled to serve in the army instead of hiring mercenaries. Nevertheless, the Romans were ultimately victorious after another successful invasion of Africa. Victory in the war established Rome as the dominant military power in the Western world, laying the foundations of the Roman Empire.

The ancient Greek historian Polybius, who was well aware of Aristotle's work, judged that Rome finally defeated Carthage because of the superiority of its constitution, a better mixture of the very characteristics Aristotle praised in his discussion of the constitution of Carthage. Although Carthage continued to exist as an independent state, it was completely subject to Rome, to the degree that it could not even defend itself against military attack by North African Numidian tribesmen without Rome's express approval. In 149 BCE, Rome launched the Third Punic War, which resulted in the destruction of the city. In 146 BCE the city was captured after a siege, its population enslaved, and every building leveled. Salt was sown into the earth to symbolically make it sterile. No ancient civilization was ever so thoroughly obliterated.

The impact of the city of Carthage is often underestimated because Carthaginian civilization was destroyed by defeat in the Punic Wars. Because Carthage produced no literary tradition of its own (at least none that survives) modern histories of Carthage concentrate to a great extent on the archaeological remains of physical culture.

Aristotle gives a snapshot of the Carthaginian constitution in the mid-fourth century. We do not have such a detailed treatment for any earlier or later period. The only impetus to change the constitution seems to have come from military disasters. In 360 and 308 BCE the *suffetes* Hanno and Bomilcar both tried to become tyrant (dictator) of Carthage during military crises, but both attempts failed because they lacked popular support. After the Second Punic War, Hannibal tried to move in this direction, too, and passed a great deal of democratic reform legislation by taking it to the people rather than the Council of Thirty. One of his changes was to have the assembly directly elect the Council of the One Hundred and Four and change the term of membership from life to one year. If his popularity gave him control of the assembly, as seems to have been the case, this would effectively have given Hannibal complete power in the state at the expense of the wealthy oligarchic faction. This led to Hannibal's exile, and his constitutional reforms probably were quickly overturned.

Polybius is the only other author who treats the Carthaginian constitution with anything approaching the detailed discussion Aristotle gives it. Polybius wished to contrast it to the Roman constitution, as part of his explanation to his Greek readers of Rome's rise to imperial power over the Greek world. He believed, as many ancient theorists did, that a constitution had a natural life span, like a human being—with a prime of life, a decline into old age, and an eventual death. He felt that Carthage's constitution had been at its prime when Aristotle described it, two hundred years before his own writing, but had since gone through a natural decline. It was Carthage's misfortune to find itself opposed to Rome, whose constitution Polybius judged the most perfect in the world and just at its prime during the Punic Wars. Ultimately, Polybius attributed Carthage's defeat to the differences between the two constitutions.

——*Bradley A. Skeen, PhD*

Bibliography and Further Reading

Articles

Sanders, Lionel J. "Punic Politics in the Fifth Century b.c." *Historia* 37 (1988): 72–89.

Scullard, H. H. "Carthage." *Greece & Rome* 2 (1955): 98–107.

Walbank, F. W. "Polybius on the Roman Constitution." *Classical Quarterly* 37 (1943): 73–89.

Books

Lancel, Serge. *Carthage: A History*, trans. Antonia Nevill. Oxford: Blackwell, 1995.

Polybius. *The Histories*, vol. 3, trans. W. R. Paton. Cambridge, Mass. Harvard University Press, 1923.

Simpson, Peter L. *A Philosophical Commentary on the Politics of Aristotle*. Chapel Hill: University of North Carolina Press, 1998.

Warmington, B. H. *Carthage*. 2nd ed. New York: Praeger, 1969.

Web Sites

"Aristotle's Political Theory." Stanford Encyclopedia of Philosophy Web site. http://plato.stanford.edu/entries/aristotle-politics.

"Carthage." Livius.org Web site. http://www.livius.org/cao-caz/carthage/carthage.html.

■ Constitution of Sparta

Date: ca 328 BCE
Author: Aristotle
Genre: Book chapter

Summary Overview

The Constitution of Sparta was a written document, composed in the middle to late seventh century BCE. No known copy of it remains, and there is debate about whether Lycurgus, its supposed creator, actually existed. What is known about the constitution comes from Aristotle's *Politics*, written probably in the 320s BCE. Many of the laws in the Constitution of Sparta deal with strengthening the military, so the document is critical to the formation of the elite fighting force that put Sparta on the map in the ancient world.

The Constitution of Sparta is one of the earliest documents of its kind. If the dates of the ancient historians are trustworthy, the Spartan constitution predates that of Athens by 150 years. While the constitution established a mixed government that was occasionally monarchical, oligarchic, and even at times tyrannical, it did stress democracy. All male citizens were allowed to participate in the Domos, the Spartan assembly, which gave them immense power. Sparta was the earliest known democracy, and its constitution was both imitated and improved upon by many societies, ranging from those in the ancient world to various others throughout Western civilization.

Defining Moment

Aristotle's survey of the various types of government in *Politics* is one of the earliest, most thorough, and balanced accounts of politics in the entire history of political thought. He discusses a range of the functions of politics, from the origin and purpose of the state to why regimes are classified in a certain way and why they ultimately fail. In doing so, Aristotle provides a model for other civilizations to live by. Aristotle's list of the three best governments in the ancient Mediterranean included Sparta, Crete and Carthage; yet he spent most of his time in critique of the Spartan constitution (a constitution that was revered by others too as one of the best) to show others what *not* to do.

Book 2 of Aristotle's work focuses on the various constitutions of the ancient world, citing which ones are the best and the worst. Part 9 of book 2 is about the Spartan constitution and is mostly a critique that lays out why this constitution is not ideal. Each paragraph deals with a specific problem in the Spartan form of government. The Spartan constitution was clearly regarded in its time as one of the first forms of democracy, but Aristotle focuses mostly on its failings. Throughout, Aristotle refers to "the legislator." His reference is to Lycurgus.

Author Biography

Aristotle was born in 384 BCE in Stagira, Macedonia, the son of the physician to the royal court. He was bright, as evidenced by the fact that he went to study at Plato's Academy early in life. Plato was the Mediterranean world's greatest philosopher, and Aristotle was clearly influenced very strongly by the ideas of his teacher; many of Aristotle's own works were modifications of the arguments of Plato. Plato died in 348 or 347 BCE, and Aristotle left the Academy shortly after and went to Asia Minor, where he became the tutor to Hermias, the king of Assos. It is also around this time that he is thought to have become the tutor of the young Alexander of Macedon, later Alexander the Great. It is believed that Aristotle taught Alexander not only the basics of ethics and politics but also philosophy. When Alexander became king, Aristotle left his court and moved back to Athens, where he founded his own school, the Lyceum. Aristotle taught in this school until 323 BCE, the year before he died. It was during his time teaching at the Lyceum that Aristotle wrote the lectures that became his *Politics*. Aristotle had experience with many different types and forms of government, and he used this experience in writing about the advantages and disadvantages of all forms of government.

HISTORICAL DOCUMENT

Part IX.

In the governments of Lacedaemon and Crete, and indeed in all governments, two points have to be considered: first, whether any particular law is good or bad, when compared with the perfect state; secondly, whether it is or is not consistent with the idea and character which the lawgiver has set before his citizens. That in a well-ordered state the citizens should have leisure and not have to provide for their daily wants is generally acknowledged, but there is a difficulty in seeing how this leisure is to be attained. ...

... [T]he license of the Lacedaemonian women defeats the intention of the Spartan constitution, and is adverse to the happiness of the state. For, a husband and wife being each a part of every family, the state may be considered as about equally divided into men and women; and, therefore, in those states in which the condition of the women is bad, half the city may be regarded as having no laws. And this is what has actually happened at Sparta; the legislator [Lycurgus] wanted to make the whole state hardy and temperate, and he has carried out his intention in the case of the men, but he has neglected the women, who live in every sort of intemperance and luxury. The consequence is that in such a state wealth is too highly valued, especially if the citizens fall under the dominion of their wives, after the manner of most warlike races, except the Celts and a few others who openly approve of male loves. The old mythologer would seem to have been right in uniting Ares and Aphrodite, for all warlike races are prone to the love either of men or of women. This was exemplified among the Spartans in the days of their greatness; many things were managed by their women. But what difference does it make whether women rule, or the rulers are ruled by women? The result is the same. Even in regard to courage, which is of no use in daily life, and is needed only in war, the influence of the Lacedaemonian women has been most mischievous. The evil showed itself in the Theban invasion, when, unlike the women other cities, they were utterly useless and caused more confusion than the enemy. This license of the Lacedaemonian women existed from the earliest times, and was only what might be expected. For, during the wars of the Lacedaemonians, first against the Argives, and afterwards against the Arcadians and Messenians, the men were long away from home, and, on the return of peace, they gave themselves into the legislator's hand, already prepared by the discipline of a soldier's life (in which there are many elements of virtue), to receive his enactments. But, when Lycurgus, as tradition says, wanted to bring the women under his laws, they resisted, and he gave up the attempt. These then are the causes of what then happened, and this defect in the constitution is clearly to be attributed to them. We are not, however, considering what is or is not to be excused, but what is right or wrong, and the disorder of the women, as I have already said, not only gives an air of indecorum to the constitution considered in itself, but tends in a measure to foster avarice.

The mention of avarice naturally suggests a criticism on the inequality of property. While some of the Spartan citizens have quite small properties, others have very large ones; hence the land has passed into the hands of a few. And this is due also to faulty laws; for, although the legislator rightly holds up to shame the sale or purchase of an inheritance, he allows anybody who likes to give or bequeath it. Yet both practices lead to the same result. And nearly two-fifths of the whole country are held by women; this is owing to the number of heiresses and to the large dowries which are customary. It would surely have been better to have given no dowries at all, or, if any, but small or moderate ones. As the law now stands, a man may bestow his heiress on any one whom he pleases, and, if he die intestate, the privilege of giving her away descends to his heir. Hence, although the country is able to maintain 1500 cavalry and 30,000 hoplites, the whole number of Spartan citizens fell below 1000. The result proves the faulty nature of their laws respecting property; for the city sank under a single defeat; the want of men was their ruin. There is a tradition that, in the days of their ancient kings, they were in the habit of giving the rights of citizenship to strangers, and therefore, in spite of their long wars, no lack of population was experienced by them; indeed, at one time Sparta is said to have numbered not less than 10,000 citizens. Whether this statement is true or not, it would certainly have been better to have maintained their numbers by the equalization of property. Again, the law which relates to the procreation of children is adverse to the correction of this inequality. For the legislator, wanting to have as many Spartans as he could, encouraged the citizens to have large families; and there is a law at Sparta that the father of three sons shall be exempt from military service, and he who has four from all the burdens of the state. Yet it is obvious that, if there were many children, the land being distributed as it is, many of them must necessarily fall into poverty.

The Lacedaemonian constitution is defective in another point; I mean the Ephoralty. This magistracy has authority in the highest matters, but the Ephors are chosen from the whole people, and so the office is apt to fall into the hands of very poor men, who, being badly off, are open to bribes. There have been many examples at Sparta of this evil in former times; and quite recently, in the matter of the Andrians, certain of the Ephors who were bribed did their best to ruin the state. And so great and tyrannical is their power, that even the kings have been compelled to court them, so that, in this way as well together with the royal office, the whole constitution has deteriorated, and from being an aristocracy has turned into a democracy. The Ephoralty certainly does keep the state together; for the people are contented when they have a share in the highest office, and the result, whether due to the legislator or to chance, has been advantageous. For if a constitution is to be permanent, all the parts of the state must wish that it should exist and the same arrangements be maintained. This is the case at Sparta, where the kings desire its permanence because they have due honor in their own persons; the nobles because they are represented in the council of elders (for the office of elder is a reward of virtue); and the people, because all are eligible to the Ephoralty. The election of Ephors out of the whole people is perfectly right, but ought not to be carried on in the present fashion, which is too childish. Again, they have the decision of great causes, although they are quite

ordinary men, and therefore they should not determine them merely on their own judgment, but according to written rules, and to the laws. Their way of life, too, is not in accordance with the spirit of the constitution—they have a deal too much license; whereas, in the case of the other citizens, the excess of strictness is so intolerable that they run away from the law into the secret indulgence of sensual pleasures.

Again, the council of elders is not free from defects. It may be said that the elders are good men and well trained in manly virtue; and that, therefore, there is an advantage to the state in having them. But that judges of important causes should hold office for life is a disputable thing, for the mind grows old as well as the body. And when men have been educated in such a manner that even the legislator himself cannot trust them, there is real danger. Many of the elders are well known to have taken bribes and to have been guilty of partiality in public affairs. And therefore they ought not to be irresponsible; yet at Sparta they are so. But (it may be replied), 'All magistracies are accountable to the Ephors.' Yes, but this prerogative is too great for them, and we maintain that the control should be exercised in some other manner. Further, the mode in which the Spartans elect their elders is childish; and it is improper that the person to be elected should canvass for the office; the worthiest should be appointed, whether he chooses or not. And here the legislator clearly indicates the same intention which appears in other parts of his constitution; he would have his citizens ambitious, and he has reckoned upon this quality in the election of the elders; for no one would ask to be elected if he were not. Yet ambition and avarice, almost more than any other passions, are the motives of crime.

Whether kings are or are not an advantage to states, I will consider at another time; they should at any rate be chosen, not as they are now, but with regard to their personal life and conduct. The legislator himself obviously did not suppose that he could make them really good men; at least he shows a great distrust of their virtue. For this reason the Spartans used to join enemies with them in the same embassy, and the quarrels between the kings were held to be conservative of the state.

Neither did the first introducer of the common meals, called 'phiditia,' regulate them well. The entertainment ought to have been provided at the public cost, as in Crete; but among the Lacedaemonians every one is expected to contribute, and some of them are too poor to afford the expense; thus the intention of the legislator is frustrated. The common meals were meant to be a popular institution, but the existing manner of regulating them is the reverse of popular. For the very poor can scarcely take part in them; and, according to ancient custom, those who cannot contribute are not allowed to retain their rights of citizenship. ...

The charge which Plato brings, in the *Laws*, against the intention of the legislator, is likewise justified; the whole constitution has regard to one part of virtue only—the virtue of the soldier, which gives victory in war. So long as they were at war,

therefore, their power was preserved, but when they had attained empire they fell, for of the arts of peace they knew nothing, and had never engaged in any employment higher than war. There is another error, equally great, into which they have fallen. Although they truly think that the goods for which men contend are to be acquired by virtue rather than by vice, they err in supposing that these goods are to be preferred to the virtue which gains them.

Once more: the revenues of the state are ill-managed; there is no money in the treasury, although they are obliged to carry on great wars, and they are unwilling to pay taxes. The greater part of the land being in the hands of the Spartans, they do not look closely into one another's contributions. The result which the legislator has produced is the reverse of beneficial; for he has made his city poor, and his citizens greedy.

Enough respecting the Spartan constitution, of which these are the principal defects.

GLOSSARY

Lacedaemon: the central city-state in Sparta.

Intestate: without property of any kind.

license of the Lacedaemonian women: participation in government and other civic activities by Spartan women, contrary to Old World norms

old mythologer: unknown, but perhaps Homer

Ephoralty/ephors: magistrates in the Spartan government, dedicated to making decisions in the best interests of the city

Phiditia: a common every-day meal, or mess, shared by soldiers in Spartan society.

Document Analysis

Aristotle opens this passage in discussion of the role of Spartan women, which Aristotle cites as a second flaw in Spartan governance. Women were revered in Sparta for their role in creating a military society. It was their job and duty to produce sons who could participate in the *agoge* and become strong soldiers for Sparta. Spartan women were thought to be tougher than other women and were heavily influenced by the militaristic atmosphere of their society. When Sparta went to war, the women famously told their sons and husbands to come home either *with* their shields or *on* them—that is, they were to return victorious or die on the field of battle.

Aristotle, however, singles out the behavior of Spartan women as undermining the Spartan constitution and therefore the state's well-being. Women made up 50 percent of the population of Sparta; thus, when they behaved badly, the whole state was weakened. Spartan women lived licentiously, says Aristotle, which went against the steadfast endurance of the regime. Women, he thinks, had too much power. They were given the right to rule in many situations, and their men were inclined to care more about wealth than the good of the regime. Women had achieved this status in Sparta because the men were frequently off fighting wars against the Argives, the Arcadians, and the Messenians; thus, women had gained more power than they had in other ancient Greek city-states. Aristotle appears to make a glancing reference to homosexuality among Greek warriors, who spend more time with men than with women. He also alludes to the Greek god Ares, the god of war and violence, and to Aphrodite, the goddess of love and beauty. Sparta was a warlike society, and the women were "utterly useless," especially during Sparta's invasion by Thebes, and caused even more confusion for the Spartan soldiers than the Theban invaders did. Aristotle notes that Lycurgus tried to bring the women under the law, but they resisted, and he gave up trying. He cites this as a problem for Sparta, because the disorder of the women weakened the constitution and fostered avarice.

According to Aristotle, it was because of the inability to rein in the women that greed was prevalent and land was concentrated in the hands of a few people in Sparta. Some citizens in the city-state had small property holdings, while others had rather large estates, raising the question of inequality. The inequality was made worse by laws concerning inheritance and dowries. Nearly 40 percent of the land in Sparta, Aristotle says, was owned by women as a result of the laws governing dowries and heiresses' ownership of land. Aristotle believes that it would have been better for Sparta to give no dowries at all or at the least make permissible dowries much smaller. As larger dowries became more common, the land was concentrated in the hands of fewer people. To be considered a "citizen" at the time, a person had to own land. If fewer people owned land, then fewer people could be considered citizens. The population of citizens, says Aristotle, had dwindled to a mere one thousand.

The lack of citizens led to the city's ruin as it was beaten in a single battle by its enemies. The fault was with the property laws. Property ownership equalization would have been the solution. The Spartans, in earlier times ("the days of the ancient kings"), had alleviated the problem by bringing in people from the outside, granting the rights of citizenship to "strangers," or foreigners. Such was no longer the case. Exacerbating the problem were the laws governing procreation. In an effort to swell population numbers, fathers of three

sons were exempted from military service and fathers with four or more sons from all "burdens of the state." This did not help matters, because the land laws, coupled with the fact that people were encouraged to have large families, led many in Sparta to fall into poverty. Issues involving land ownership, dowries, and family size provide Aristotle with a clear example of how poorly conceived laws can lead to the weakening of a state, for the laws had unintended consequences.

In Sparta, five ephors were elected annually by the people, and every month they swore to uphold the rule of the two kings of Sparta. This was in direct contrast to how many of them actually operated. While the ephors held an immense amount of power, they were each elected for only one year. At the end of their one-year term, they could never run for reelection.

Aristotle, though, finds the institution defective. The ephors were chosen from the entire population, so poor men were eligible, and poor men were open to bribes. Such was the case when the ephors were bribed by the Andrians. According to Aristotle, the Andrians—the people of the island of Andros, one of many in the Greek archipelago—were almost able to bring about the complete ruin of Sparta by bribing the ephors, but historians remain uncertain about the specific events Aristotle is referencing. Many of the ephors tended to be tyrannical, even to the point of forcing the kings to do their bidding. Their usurpation of power had undermined the constitution and turned the regime away from the aristocracy, making it resemble a democracy—a form of government that Aristotle found inferior to oligarchy and monarchy, for it was government for and by the needy. Still, the ephors managed to hold together the state, in that all segments of society had a stake in the status quo. Aristotle supports the democratic eligibility of all people for the post of ephor but calls the manner in which they were elected "childish." Then, too, as ordinary men, he says, they should judge according to the law, but many tried to make judgments on their own, without reference to laws. These men did not live up to the spirit of the constitution because they cared too much for license and avarice. This type of lifestyle was in contrast to the strict military nature of the regime.

The council of elders, or *gerousia*, consisted of twenty-eight men over the age of sixty. They were elected for life and were also usually members of one of the two royal houses of Sparta. The two kings of Sparta were part of this council, making a total of thirty members.

Their main job was to discuss matters of state policy and then present alternative solutions to the Demos, or general assembly, for consideration and implementation.

Aristotle starts his critique on a positive note. He sees the senators as good men who were well trained in manly virtue, an obvious advantage to the state. Their election to a life term, however, was not beneficial to the state. These men were judges of important state matters, and as they grew older, they did not always act for the good of the regime. Certain members of the council were even accused of taking bribes and showing partiality in judgments. Moreover, they were irresponsible in many affairs of state and often controlled by the ephors. Aristotle contends that those vying to be elected should not canvass for the position; instead, the most worthy person should be appointed, whether or not he wanted the position. To campaign for office, citizens must be ambitious. But ambition, combined with avarice, could be the motives for crime and thus detrimental to Spartan society. Aristotle's comments on the inherent weaknesses of Sparta's council of elders illustrates well his belief that pure democracy is problematic and that governance was best placed in the hands of the most worthy citizens, as well as in those who have the means and leisure to cultivate virtue.

Aristotle then deals with the Spartan monarchy. There were two monarchs, with one king from each royal house in the city-state: the Agiad and Eurypontids families. According to tradition, these families were the descendants, respectively, of Eurysthenes and Procles, who in turn were the descendants of Heracles, the supposed conqueror of Sparta after the Trojan War. Again according to tradition, the Agiad family arrived in Sparta first and claimed the best land, making it the more important of the two dynastic lines. While Aristotle usually debates whether kings are beneficial or not and says here that he will take up the matter elsewhere, he states unequivocally that the kingship is not good in Sparta because the hereditary kings are usually unworthy of the position. They should be chosen with regard to their personal life and conduct, but they are not. Lycurgus did not think he could make them into good men, and he distrusted their supposed virtues. The dual kingship was ineffective, because the two kings could never agree, and the resulting tension was harmful to the overall government.

The common mess, or *phiditia*, was an important aspect of Spartan society. It was through these common meals that solidarity was created, especially among the soldiers. Only those who had completed training in the *agoge* could participate in the common mess. The institution was not very well regulated in Sparta. If a person was not able to contribute to the expenses of the common mess or was caught stealing to gather funds for his contribution, he would be expelled from the mess and shamed for the rest of his life. Those expelled also lost their citizenship and often the property associated with that right. Aristotle says that the entertainment should have been paid at public expense, as in Crete. In Sparta the problem was that some were too poor to contribute. Those who could not contribute could not take part in the *phiditia*, and those who could not take part lost their citizenship. The *phiditia* was supposed to be a popular institution, but again Aristotle cites the laws governing the institution as poorly crafted, creating consequences that undermined the intention of the laws. The laws pertaining to the *phiditia* were examples of laws that had the effect of reducing the number of citizens, weakening the state.

Aristotle is slightly vague about the office of admirals in Sparta. He appears to be referring to the tradition in Sparta that military commanders, whether generals or naval admirals, held the position for life. Aristotle notes that this law had often been rightly condemned, for the kings were seen as perpetual generals and the office of admiral was nothing more than a third king. Again, for Aristotle, this institution was flawed, for it left men in power who might no longer have deserved it. Further, it diffused the power of the monarchy, for it placed too much power in the hands of a military class that might often have operated independently of the government. Accordingly, laws pertaining to admirals (and generals) were examples of laws that failed to define precisely the role in government of a class and to vest power in a stable, recognized government institution.

The only virtue in Sparta was that exhibited by the soldiers, and this was a problem for society as a whole. When the Spartans were at war, all was well; when they were not at war, however, they tended to become idle and fall prey to too much leisure time. The state had nearly been ruined during times of peace because the Spartans did not know anything but war. Aristotle also faults them for believing that the goods acquired by virtue rather than vice were more important than the actual virtue through which the goods were obtained. Aristotle was a firm believer in virtue for its own sake. The purpose of virtue was not to gain worldly advantage but to a lead a good life. It was an end in itself, not a means to an end. Thus, Aristotle finds purely military virtues such as courage in battle inadequate for a well-ordered state, for the state that is not at war becomes unable to exercise virtue.

The revenues of Sparta were poorly managed; there was no money in the treasury. The people of Sparta wanted to continue to wage war, but they did not want to pay the taxes required to win wars. One of the problems had to do with land ownership. Typically, in a monarchy land was held either by the king or in the name of the king. The land, then, became a source of income for the king, and that income, in the case of Sparta, could be used to finance wars. In Sparta, however, large landowners held land in their own names. Their financial affairs were independent of the king, and each landowner had little interest in the financial affairs of the others. Thus, no one in Sparta was keeping an eye on the public treasury. This state of affairs fostered greed, and by leaving the public treasury bare, it also fostered poverty. Again, these weaknesses in the law and social structure undermined the state. Aristotle ends his discussion of the Spartans with one line, constituting an eleventh paragraph, saying that all he has discussed were the major defects of the Spartan constitution.

Essential Themes

While it was relatively conservative even by ancient standards, the Spartan constitution provided a model of democracy for others. It was considered one of the greatest forms of government of its day. The Spartan constitution was a model for Athens some 150 years later, when Cleisthenes took it upon himself to reform Athens, much as Lycurgus had done in Sparta. Athens had a council like that of Sparta's, called the boule. Cleisthenes introduced the reform of allowing the people to vote on certain issues and even vote for legislators. In other words, Sparta provided the model, which was then perfected by Athens, and it was from the Athenian constitution that modern democracies evolved.

Sparta was not always the fearsome military power that it was known to be in its later history. The Spartans suffered numerous defeats at the hands of their enemies. Nevertheless, the Spartans were intent on expanding their influence in the surrounding area. They invaded and subdued neighboring Messenia. Once the Messenians were defeated, they were incorporated into Sparta as slaves known as Helots. These slaves revolted around 670 BCE, which led to the Second Messenian War and the further subjugation of the citizens of Messenia to Sparta. Sparta's biggest enemy, however, was the neighboring city-state of Argos. It was the Spartan defeat at the hands of Argos at Hysiae in 669 BCE that started the Spartans down the path of reform. Shortly after, Lycurgus was said to have made the reforms that make up the bulk of the new constitution of Sparta, or Great Rhetra, as it is often called. After the reforms of the new constitution, Sparta was strengthened militarily enough to challenge the power of Argos.

Spartan society was radically changed after the reforms of Lycurgus. One of the most sweeping changes was the land-redistribution program. This plan called for all citizens of Sparta to have an equal amount of property. While this system did not last long, Sparta was the only city-state in ancient Greece at the time to have such a program. Another major reform helped Sparta become a great military power. This was the creation of the *agoge*, an institution by which boys were taken from their homes when they were seven years old and not returned to society until they were thirty and had undergone intensive military training. This military training turned them into the most elite fighting force in the ancient world at that time, the hoplites. The hoplites, named for the shields they carried, were feared by everyone and helped Sparta maintain control over the area for years. It was necessary to have completed training at the *agoge* to become a citizen. Once a Spartan male was a citizen, he took part in the *phiditia*, or common mess, where citizens would gather to take part in a communal meal. This system helped strengthen the Spartan army and society as a whole by creating a sense of unity and brotherhood. All these reforms occurred after the Messenian Helots revolted in 670 BCE and after Sparta lost to Argos at Hysiae in 669 BCE. Had these two events not occurred, Lycurgus might not have been as inclined to reform Spartan society so radically.

The impact of the constitution of Sparta was felt almost immediately in the city-state. The military was significantly strengthened through the creation of the *agoge* and the common mess. The Spartan hoplites became the most elite fighting force in the ancient world. Sparta had already become the dominant power in the Peloponnesus as a result of the Second Messenian War. What followed were numerous military triumphs, the most famous of which was in the Battle of Thermopylae in 480 BCE, when a small force of Spartans made a heroic stand against a much larger Persian force. A year later Spartan military prowess was on display against the Persians in the Battle of Plataea. During the Peloponnesian Wars (431–404 BCE), Sparta developed a navy that rivaled that of its adversary, Athens. By the end of the fifth century BCE, Sparta was becoming the dominant power throughout the region, though its power began to wane later with the rise of Athens and the increasing number of Helot revolts. Under the constitution, commoners were given a large role in Sparta with the creation of the Damos (an assembly composed of free adult males, who in turn elected the council of elders) and the possibility of being elected to the ephorate. Land was redistributed so that all people, at least in theory, would have equal property rights and thus become equal citizens. This did not last long, but the idea was a radical one nevertheless. All in all, the Spartan constitution helped Sparta become the power that dominated the ancient world and the power that people still remember today.

————*Scott Cashion*

Bibliography and Further Reading

Articles

Dickens, Guy. "The Growth of Spartan Policy." *Journal of Hellenic Studies* 32 (1912): 1–42.

Hammond, N. G. L. "The Lycurgean Reform at Sparta." *Journal of Hellenic Studies* 70 (1950): 42–64.

Salmon, John. "Political Hoplites?" *Journal of Hellenic Studies* 97 (1977): 84–101.

Sihler, E. G. "Aristotle's Criticisms of the Spartan Government." *Classical Review* 7, no. 10 (December 1893): 439–443.

Books

Cartledge, Paul. *The Spartans: The World of the Warrior-Heroes of Ancient Greece, from Utopia to Crisis and Collapse.* Woodstock, N.Y. Overlook Press, 2003.

Forrest, W. G. *The Emergence of Greek Democracy: The Character of Greek Politics, 800–400 B.C.* London: Weidenfield & Nicolson, 1966.

Huxley, George Leonard. *Early Sparta.* New York: Barnes & Noble, 1970.

Powell, Anton, and Stephen Hodkinson. *The Shadow of Sparta.* London: Routledge for the Classical Press of Wales, 1994.

Web Sites

"Sparta Reconsidered—Sparta the First Democracy." Elysium Gates Web site.
http://elysiumgates.com/~helena/Revolution.html.

"Sparta." Plato and His Dialogues Web site. http://plato-dialogues.org/tools/loc/sparta.htm.

■ Japanese Seventeen-Article Constitution

Date: 604
Author: Prince Shotoku
Genre: Constitution

Summary Overview

Composed in the year 604, Japan's Seventeen-Article Constitution contains a series of moral admonitions drawn from Buddhist and Confucian ideals of sage government. The Seventeen-Article Constitution is considered the earliest Japanese articulation of the ethical foundations of government and an indigenous political vision for a centralized, bureaucratic Japanese state. Authorship of the constitution has been generally attributed to Crown Prince Shotoku, though there is some evidence that the text had been written by others and posthumously credited to him. Prince Shotoku oversaw the affairs of the early Japanese state for twenty-nine years in the capacity of acting regent for his childless aunt, Empress Suiko. He has since been hailed widely as Japan's earliest native example of a wise ruler. Questions of authorship notwithstanding, the Seventeen-Article Constitution is considered an accurate reflection of Shotoku's personal erudition in the Chinese classics and dedication to the recently imported doctrine of Buddhism. While the original manuscript is no longer extant, the text of the Seventeen-Article Constitution was preserved in *Nihon shoki* (*Chronicles of Japan*), an imperial history compiled in the year 720.

Defining Moment

According to Chinese historical records, by the fourth century, the islands the Chinese called "Wa"—Japan—were ruled by the Yamato clan. Yamato rule had taken the form of federations called *kuni*, which were made up of smaller clan units called *uji*. Most historians agree that between the third and fifth centuries the location of the rulers moved from Kyushu to the Yamato Plain, the place from which the early state would have taken its name. During the fifth century, Chinese accounts like the *Sung shu* (Book of the Sung) continued to describe how the kings of Wa had achieved political dominance through warfare and the subjugation of rival groups. Leaders were recognized with various titles under a detailed system of social ranks that established a clear political hierarchy among multiple rulers.

Throughout the sixth century, powerful *uji* clans continued to struggle with one another for regional domination and for influence over the Yamato kings. The rise of the influential Soga clan signified an important shift in the political structure during the late sixth century. The Yamato gradually relinquished their reliance on military clans and began to favor clans like the Soga, who were capable of assisting with administrative tasks such as levying taxes and economic oversight of state-owned rice fields. Additionally, Soga backing for the newly imported doctrine of Buddhism eventually led to increased power in government positions. In 593 it resulted in the placement of a Soga woman of royal birth on the throne, Empress Suiko. This was the historical context in which Prince Shotoku, a nephew of the new empress, was named her regent and thus stepped onto the national stage.

The reign of Empress Suiko was a watershed moment in the transition to centralized rule. During this time, there emerged the first concentrated attempts to redefine Japanese kingship and establish a ruler who could exercise supreme authority over a unified state. Chinese state structures heavily influenced the model for the new sense of Japanese kingship in the figure of the *tenno*, or emperor. Official state doctrine held that the hereditary position of emperor was derived from his or her innate divinity and was thus unassailable. It was in this national context—the need to establish the legitimacy of the Yamatos as an imperial family and of the Soga as their dominant advisors—that Prince Shotoku's constitution was written.

Author Biography

Shotoku appears to have been a posthumous appellation for the prince who had previously been known as Umayakado or Kamitsumiya. The second son of Emperor Yomei, the prince was born in 574 and raised in an atmosphere rife with political intrigue. At the age of nineteen, Prince Shotoku was named crown prince and regent for Empress Suiko shortly after her enthronement. He would remain in that position until his death in 622. During an administration that native histories have hailed as exemplary, Prince Shotoku maintained key links with continental Asia. He sent an envoy to

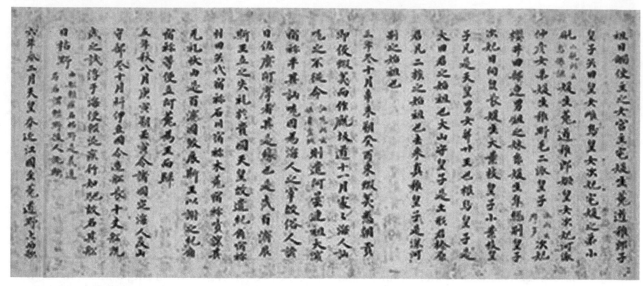

Page from a copy of the Nihon Shoki, early Heian period (commons.wikimedia.org) [Public Domain]

the Korean kingdom of Silla and established a variety of cultural and religious exchanges with China's Sui Dynasty. He is also credited with the creation of the twelve-rank system for court bureaucracy and the compilation of two now-lost historical chronicles, *Tennoki* (Record of the Emperors) and *Kokki* (Record of the Nation).

Key components of Prince Shotoku's cultural legacy include his sponsorship of state-sanctioned Buddhism through authorship of an undated commentary on three Buddhist scriptures known as the *Sangyo gisho* (Annotated Commentaries on the Three Sutras) and the creation of the Seventeen-Article Constitution in 604. While historians have raised questions concerning Shotoku's authorship of these documents, both

can be reliably dated to the era of Suiko's reign, and it seems clear that Shotoku provided key direction, if not direct authorship, for both texts. Together, they have earned Shotoku an historical reputation as the penultimate model of sage rule for the Japanese nation. While the prince never took Buddhist orders himself, there is evidence that he spent his entire life as a devout lay Buddhist and scholar of Chinese culture. Shotoku's writings offered Japanized interpretations of Buddhist doctrine and Chinese models of statecraft, and his ideas helped establish universal rule within the Yamato state. In this respect, Shotoku's career and literary productions provide key evidence of the importance and impacts of continental Asian culture, particularly that of China, upon the early Japanese state.

HISTORICAL DOCUMENT

Summer, 4th month, 3rd day [12th year of Empress Suiko, 604 AD].

The Crown Prince personally drafted and promulgated a constitution consisting of seventeen articles, which are as follows:

I. Harmony is to be cherished, and opposition for opposition's sake must be avoided as a matter of principle. Men are often influenced by partisan feelings, except a few sagacious ones. Hence there

are some who disobey their lords and fathers, or who dispute with their neighboring villages. If those above are harmonious and those below are cordial, their discussion will be guided by a spirit of conciliation, and reason shall naturally prevail. There will be nothing that cannot be accomplished.

II. With all our heart, revere the three treasures. The three treasures, consisting of Buddha, the Doctrine, and the Monastic Order, are the final refuge of the four generated beings, and are the supreme objects of worship in all countries. Can any man in any age ever fail to respect these teachings? Few men are utterly devoid of goodness, and men can be taught to follow the teachings. Unless they take refuge in the three treasures, there is no way of rectifying their misdeeds.

III. When an imperial command is given, obey it with reverence. The sovereign is likened to heaven and his subjects are likened to earth. With heaven providing the cover and earth supporting it, the four seasons proceed in orderly fashion, giving sustenance to all that which is in nature. If earth attempts to overtake the functions of heaven, it destroys everything. Therefore when the sovereign speaks, his subjects must listen: when the superior acts, the inferior must follow his examples. When an imperial command is given, carry it out with diligence. If there is no reverence shown to the imperial command, ruin will automatically result.

IV. The ministers and functionaries must act on the basis of decorum for the basis of governing the people consists of decorum. If the superiors do not behave with decorum, offenses will ensue. If the ministers behave with decorum, there will be no confusion about ranks. If the people behave with decorum, the nation will be governed well of its own.

V. Cast away your ravenous desire for food and abandon your covetousness for material possessions. If a suit is brought before you, render a clear-cut judgment. … Nowadays, those who are in the position of pronouncing judgment are motivated by making private gains and, as a rule, receive bribes. Thus the plaints of the rich are like a stone flung into water, while those of the poor are like water poured over a stone. Under these circumstances, the poor will be denied recourses to justice, which constitutes a dereliction of duty of the ministers.

VI. Punish that which is evil and encourage that which is good. This is an excellent rule from antiquity. Do not conceal the good qualities of others, and always correct that which is evil which comes to your attention. Consider those flatterers and tricksters as constituting a superb weapon for the overthrow of the state, and a sharp sword for the destruction of people. Smooth-tongued adula-

tors love to report to their superiors the errors of their inferiors; and to their inferiors, castigate the errors of their superiors. Men of this type lack loyalty to the sovereign and have no compassion for the people. They are the ones who can cause great civil disorders.

VII. Every man must be given his clearly delineated responsibility. If a wise man is entrusted with office, the sound of praise arises. If a wicked man holds office, disturbances become frequent. … In all things, great or small, find the right man, and the country will be well governed. On all occasions, in an emergency or otherwise, seek out a wise man, which in itself is an enriching experience. In this manner, the state will be lasting and its sacerdotal functions will be free from danger. Therefore did the sage kings of old seek the man to fill the office, not the office for the sake of the man.

VIII. The ministers and functionaries must attend the court early in the morning and retire late. The business of the state must not be taken lightly. A full day is hardly enough to complete work, and if the attendance is late, emergencies cannot be met. If the officials retire early, the work cannot be completed.

IX. Good faith is the foundation of righteousness, and everything must be guided by good faith. The key to the success of the good and the failure of the bad can also be found in good faith. If the officials observe good faith with one another, everything can be accomplished. If they do not observe good faith, everything is bound to fail.

X. Discard wrath and anger from your heart and from your looks. Do not be offended when others differ with you. Everyone has his own mind, and each mind has its own leanings. Thus what is right with him is wrong with us, and what is right with us is wrong with him. We are not necessarily sages, and he is not necessarily a fool. We are all simply ordinary men, and none of us can set up a rule to determine the right from wrong. … Therefore, instead of giving way to anger as others do, let us fear our own mistakes. Even though we may have a point, let us follow the multitude and act like them.

XI. Observe clearly merit and demerit and assign reward and punishment accordingly. Nowadays, rewards are given in the absence of meritorious work, punishments without corresponding crimes. The ministers, who are in charge of public affairs, must therefore take upon themselves the task of administering a clear-cut system of rewards and punishments.

XII. Provincial authorities or local nobles are not permitted to levy exactions on the people. A country cannot have two sovereigns nor the people two masters. The people of the whole country must have the sovereign as their only master. The officials who are given certain functions are all his subjects. Being the subjects of the sovereign, these officials have no more right than others to levy exactions on the people.

XIII. All persons entrusted with office must attend equally to their functions. If absent from work due to illness or being sent on missions, and work for that period is neglected, on their return, they must perform their duties conscientiously by taking into account that which transpired before and during their absence. Do not permit lack of knowledge of the intervening period as an excuse to hinder effective performance of public affairs.

XIV. Ministers and functionaries are asked not to be envious of others. If we envy others, they in turn will envy us, and there is no limit to the evil that envy can cause us. We resent others when their intelligence is superior to ours, and we envy those who surpass us in talent. This is the reason why it takes five hundred years before we can meet a wise man, and in a thousand years it is still difficult to find one sage. If we cannot find wise men and sages, how can the country be governed?

XV. The way of a minister is to turn away from private motives and to uphold public good. Private motives breed resentment and resentful feelings cause a man to act discordantly. If he fails to act in accord with others, he sacrifices public interests for the sake of his private feelings. When resentment arises, it goes counter to the existing order and breaks the law. Therefore it is said in the first article that superiors and inferiors must act in harmony. The purport is the same.

XVI. The people may be employed in forced labor only at seasonable times. This is an excellent rule from antiquity. Employ the people in the winter months when they are at leisure. However, from spring to autumn, when they are engaged in agriculture or sericulture, do not employ them. Without their agricultural endeavor, there is no food, and without their sericulture, there is no clothing.

XVII. Major decisions must not be made by one person alone, but must be deliberated with many. On the other hand, it is not necessary to consult many people on minor questions. If important matters are not discussed fully there may always be fear of committing mistakes. A thorough discussion with many can prevent it and bring about a reasonable solution.

GLOSSARY

attendance: in this context, ministers and functionaries who are obliged to be present in the court to perform their duties

four generated beings: a collective designation for the four classes of life-forms recognized in Buddhism, distinguished by mode of birth—live-born, born from eggs, moisture-bred, and formed by metamorphosis

levy exactions on the people: extract additional taxes from citizens, without sanction

Document Analysis

Prince Shotoku's Seventeen-Article Constitution contains Confucian, Buddhist, and Taoist elements, reflecting the syncretic nature of Japanese philosophical systems during the Yamato period (ca. 300–710) and providing compelling evidence of the importance of Chinese cultural influence in Yamato state structures. The constitution outlines a three-tiered social hierarchy consisting of a morally upright ruler, ethical officials, and an obedient populace. The document primarily describes the roles of the sovereign and the officials who carry out his or her will, utilizing both Confucian and Buddhist concepts to define the proper roles and behavior of government officials. Building on diverse Chinese models, the constitution strove to place the emerging Japanese state on an equal cultural footing with Sui and Tang Dynasty China by articulating a notion of kingship that legitimated the rule of Prince Shotoku and his successors.

In Article I, Shotoku clearly and strongly advocates the importance of "harmony" in human relations. The placement of this statement at the beginning of the document is deliberate and sets the tone for the remainder of the text. In Japanese, "harmony," or "concord," is expressed with the character *wa*, and this same concept frequently appears in the *Analects* of Confucius to denote propriety or decorum. It should be noted that this word for harmony is not the same "Wa" used as an early Chinese appellation for the emergent Japanese state. Those were written with a different Chinese character, meaning "dwarf." Later, the Japanese would replace that offensive character with the more flattering character employed in Article I to mean "harmony." The date of the transition in nomenclature is uncertain. In this original context, "harmony" is also tied directly to social status. The constitution suggests that harmony is achieved when men pursue "cordial" discussions that are free of "partisan feelings" and "guided by a spirit of conciliation." Only thus may reason prevail. This argument presupposes that human nature is innately contrary, even bigoted. Human beings must learn to supersede their latently contentious nature in the name of creating a harmonious society. Harmony depends, Shotoku suggests, not purely on a blind obedience to a rule of law but rather upon the moral nature of the person or persons directing or governing society. If rulers and officials ("those above") earnestly seek concord, then "those below" (the polity) will follow suit.

The *Analects* make repeated reference to morally upright and benevolent rulership as the basis for an ordered society, stating, for example: "Ruling is straightening. If you lead along a straight way, who will dare go by a crooked one?" (Book 12, Verse 17). In Confucian thought the ideal society is one in which the rule of law is no longer necessary because the people have fully internalized the notion of right action, or *li*.

Notably, Article II is the only section in the constitution that makes direct reference to Buddhism. This is remarkable when considered from the perspective of Prince Shotoku's purported role as a key sponsor of Buddhism in the early Japanese state. Here, Shotoku perceives the usefulness of the imported doctrine in government; the "three treasures consisting of Buddha, the Doctrine and the Monastic Order" provide a framework for spiritual growth and self-reflection that is also conducive to ethical governance. The admonition in Article II to "revere" these treasures with all one's heart would be one echoed by later emperors such as Shomu, in the early eighth century—a ruler who would adopt the appellation of "servant of the three treasures."

Article II rejects any sense of human nature as essentially corrupt or sinful and instead argues that "few men are utterly devoid of goodness." Shotoku suggests that all sentient beings are capable of recognizing and respecting the Buddhist "three treasures" as "supreme objects of worship" and a "final refuge" from the consequences of their misdeeds. In seeking to found a centralized, universal state, Shotoku looked toward the equally universal law of Buddhist doctrine. Empress Suiko's issuance in 594 of an imperial edict that granted official support to the promulgation of Buddhism offered additional evidence of the court's dedication to promoting the dissemination of Buddhist thought and practice. Shotoku himself undertook many years of study of Buddhist doctrine under the tutelage of the Korean monk Eji from the kingdom of Koguryo. Numerous Buddhist temples were built in quick succession during the sixth and seventh centuries.

In Article III, Shotoku comments upon the ideal relationship between ruler and subject, relating it to the cosmic relationship of heaven (the "sovereign") and earth ("subjects"). In this thoroughly naturalized hierarchy, an "imperial command" is to be obeyed with "reverence" and "diligence." Comparing the relationship between the ruler and the ruled to other natural phenomena (for example, the progression of the "four seasons" and "all that which is in nature"), Shotoku posits that any resistance to the will of the ruler constitutes an unnatural response—one that "destroys everything" and results in "ruin." Modeled on Han Chinese notions of government, this formulation states that the relationship between the emperor (and by extension, his or her official functionaries) and state subjects (the "people") is naturally sanctioned and therefore unassailable. This new model of government was undoubtedly connected to the challenges to and decline in clan status and power during the sixth and seventh centuries.

The fourth article expands upon Article III's definition of the ideal ruler-subject relationship to specifically include government officials charged with the intermediate roles of carrying out the will of the imperial house. Article IV directs these "ministers" and "functionaries" to observe strict "decorum" as the "basis of governing the people." If officials are not themselves observing ethical and decorous behavior, "offenses" and insurrection will surely result. It is interesting to note that the term used in the original for "offenses" is *tsumi*, a word most often translated in Buddhist contexts as "sin." Conversely, correct behavior on the part of officials will ensure smooth administration, and the "nation will be governed well of its own." This philosophy concerning the moral righteousness of government officials can be related to the Confucian notion of the "exemplary person" (Chinese, *junzi*; Japanese, *kunshi*) whose self-cultivation naturally inspires reverence, peace, and stability in others. In its original content, *jun* had been a general term for a ruler. The term *junzi* (literally, "the ruler's child") came to be broadly applied to the upper classes of Chinese society, the "gentlemen." While the term had originally denoted high social status, Confucian thinkers came to define it as describing superior character and comportment based upon personal merit, rather than social class.

Article V cautions officials to guard against materialism, greed, and corruption. Specific injunctions are made against accepting bribes and lending a biased ear to rich or influential constituencies. This last warning against corruption is delivered in simile form: "Thus the plaints of the rich are like a stone flung into water," causing ripples to spread far and wide, while the voices of the poor are inefficacious, "like water poured over a stone." The result of corrupt, greedy self-interest will be the denial of justice to the poor, which is clearly denounced as a "dereliction of duty." Thus, this article expresses the author's paramount concern with ethical self-improvement and rectitude for members of the ruling class. Similar injunctions against corruption are found in Chinese models, including the *Analects* of Confucius and writings by the Chinese Legalist scholar Han Feizi (ca. 280–233 BCE; also known as Han Fei-tzu).

In Article VI, officials are sternly enjoined to "punish" evil and "encourage that which is good." Shotoku's comment that "this is an excellent rule from antiquity" alludes to his formal training in the Chinese Confucian classics. He warns government officials, the intended audience of the constitution, to view "flatterers and tricksters" as direct threats to the sovereignty of the unified state as well as to its people. "Men of this type"—that is, men who do not observe *li*, or *rei* as it was termed in Japanese—lack "loyalty to the sovereign" and "compassion for the people" and are capable of fomenting "civil disorders."

Clear delineation and separation of assigned duties are the central concerns of Article VII, which admonishes rulers to find and correctly place the "right man" in each government position. This is essentially an espousal of Chinese meritocracy, the origins of which may be traced back to Qin Dynasty reforms. Shotoku seems to allude to that history by referring to the manner in which "sage kings of old" sought the proper "man to fill the office, not the office for the sake of the man." Article VIII simply expounds the importance of promptitude and diligence in the fulfillment of official government duties. Article IX defines "good faith" as "the foundation of righteousness," which is crucial to the success of the state. Shotoku thus distinguishes truth as the hallmark of good government. This should be read as a reiteration of Article IV's encouragement of decorum and Article V's counsel concerning the dangers of official corruption.

Article X suggests that state problems can be effectively addressed only when discussed in a harmonious environment free of acrimony and petty concerns. Shotoku concedes that while not all persons in positions of political power are "sages," even "ordinary men" are capable of reaching a consensus in determining right from wrong. In this respect, Article X hearkens directly back to Shotoku's unequivocal advocacy of harmony (*wa*) in Article I. Article XI expands on the discussion of what constitutes ethical government. Here, Shotoku instructs government functionaries to create and govern according to a "clear-cut system of rewards and punishments." Some commentators have tied this description of a minutely articulated legal code to the influence of Han Feizi, who lived during China's late Warring States period.

Article XII is important insofar as it is perhaps the most direct statement of Shotoku's principle of centralized rule under a hierarchy of government officials overseen by the imperial court. Article XII expressly forbids the levying of taxes by "provincial authorities" and "local nobles." Therefore, it reflects the contemporary decline of regional and local rule during Shotoku's lifetime and foreshadows the full flowering of the imperial institution by the Nara period (710–784). Article XIII is comparable to Article VIII; it specifically cites neglect of work because of absenteeism (even when due to illness) as among the behaviors unacceptable in government officials. Shotoku is here advocating the professionalism he envisions as important to the success of his merit-based bureaucracy.

Like Articles IX through XI, Article XIV continues the repeated appeals for personal virtue among government officials. The plea takes the form of a request to avoid envy, particularly of the kind engendered by encounters with intellectual superiors. Shotoku argues that envy directed toward "those who surpass us in talent" will impede the creation of a sense of community and thus a cohesive society: "If we cannot find wise men and sages, how can the country be governed?" Article XV defines the "way of a minister" as the path that upholds the "public good" over "private motives" and thus avoids the resentment that self-serving action arouses. Citing social discord and lawbreaking as the natural result of official egoism, Shotoku again makes reference to Article I's valorization of harmony to bolster his point.

Another important peacekeeping directive, Article XVI prohibits the arbitrary use of corvée (forced labor exacted by the government, typically for public construction projects and the like), especially at times when it would interfere with the "agricultural endeavor" of those conscripted into labor. This directive could reduce the possibility of unrest and uprisings among the governed. Like Articles V, VI, and XII, Article XVI expresses concern for the common people and an awareness of their needs. The Seventeen-Article Constitution is perhaps the earliest example of a document that clearly addresses the needs of commoners in such benevolent terms.

The author's denunciation of one-person rule and despotism in Article XVII appears to be directly drawn from Chinese Legalist thought. Consider this excerpt from the section entitled "The Way of the Ruler" in the *Han Feizi*: "This is the way of the enlightened ruler: he causes the wise to bring forward all their schemes" (Watson, p. 17). Some commentators have hailed Article XVII's emphasis on collaborative decision making in government as the "embryonic beginning" of democratic thought in the early Japanese state.

Essential Themes

The Seventeen-Article Constitution was the first Japanese articulation of a vision for a centralized state. This was to be a state that could fully utilize the new imperial bureaucracy, which Prince Shotoku had put into effect in 603. His reliance on Chinese models encouraged Japan's continued cultural borrowing from Sui and Tang Dynasty China.

However, the Seventeen-Article Constitution was more than a mere imitation of Chinese models. It also outlined a newly appropriated sense of Japanese sovereignty and provided a naturalized vision of the ruler-subject relationship that was not subject to the whims of the Chinese Mandate of Heaven. In this new model, the emperor was understood to be a supreme ruler imbued with authority as the earthly symbol of heaven. The far-reaching implications of this view of the imperial person for later Japanese history cannot be overstated. The location of ultimate governmental authority in the person of the emperor persisted for more than a millennium, even during long periods when de facto political power rested in the hands of aristocratic regents or military leaders outside the imperial family. As government doctrine, the text presaged the later Taika Reforms (645) and Taiho Code (702), which were similarly modeled after Chinese precedents.

The prestige of Prince Shotoku increased exponentially after his death in 622. Various legends arose about him. Some held that the prince had been a reincarnation of Eshi, an early Zen master and patriarch of Chinese Buddhism. Other persistent mythologies claimed that he had been a manifestation of the popular Buddhist figure Kannon (Avalokitesvara). During Japan's medieval period from the twelfth through fifteenth centuries, worship of Shotoku as an incarnation of Kannon enjoyed tremendous popularity.

Prince Shotoku is still held up as an icon of Japanese Buddhism. Scholarly discussion about Shotoku—both the man and the legend—has continued into contemporary times. Recently, Shotoku and his attendant mythology have been connected to Japanese nationalist discourse and narratives of state formation by scholars such as Ienaga Saburo and Michael Como. Perhaps Shotoku's most lasting and readily recognized legacy is his status as an emblem of the monumental shifts in Japanese statecraft that took place during his lifetime—changes that shaped the very essence of Japan's then-emerging national identity.

——*Melinda S. Varner*

Bibliography and Further Reading

Como, Michael. *Shotoku: Ethnicity, Ritual, and Violence in the Japanese Buddhist Tradition*. New York: Oxford University Press, 2008.

Deal, William. "Hagiography and History: The Image of Prince Shotoku." In *Religions of Japan in Practice*, ed. George J. Tanabe Jr. Princeton: Princeton University Press, 1999.

Hall, David L., and Roger T. Ames. *Thinking through Confucius*. Albany: State University of New York Press, 1987.

Lee, Kenneth Doo Young. *The Prince and the Monk: Shotoku Worship in Shinran's Buddhism*. Albany: State University of New York Press, 2007.

Nakamura, Hajime. *History of Japanese Thought*. London: Kegan Paul, 2002.

Tamura, Yoshiro. *Japanese Buddhism: A Cultural History*, trans. Jeffrey Hunter. Tokyo: Kosei Publishing Company, 2000.

Watson, Burton, trans. *Basic Writings of Mo Tzu, Hsuün Tzu, and Han Fei Tzu*. New York: Columbia University Press, 1967.

Waley, Arthur, trans. *The Analects of Confucius*. New York: Macmillan, 1939.

Williams, Yoko. *Tsumi—Offence and Retribution in Early Japan*. London: RoutledgeCurzon, 2003.

■ Magna Carta

Date: 1215
Authors: Stephen Langton, William Marshal. Robert Fitzwalter
Genre: Legal document

Summary Overview

In June 1215 a group of English barons forced King John of England to accept the sixty-three provisions of the Magna Carta ("Great Charter") at Runnymede, England. The Magna Carta was not originally intended to secure rights for all English citizens. Rather, it was meant to assert the feudal rights of England's barons, who had become disenchanted with King John's rule, and soon after it was signed, John ignored the charter and began warring with his barons again. Yet despite the motivations of the authors and signers, the document contains political principles that remain important today. After its original issuance in 1215, the Magna Carta was revised and reissued. The 1297 version of the charter, which is the version used here, was renewed under King Edward I and remains on the statute books to this day, although numerous provisions have been repealed by specific legislation.

The Magna Carta has gained significance as the centuries have passed and has come to symbolize the very foundation of the concept of civil liberties. By using the word *freemen* in its introduction and first clause and "all Men of this our Realm" in Clause 37, the charter potentially had an audience that was much larger than the assemblage of men at Runnymede. There has been much dispute about what this language implied and to whom the rights granted by the Magna Carta applied. The jurist and legal scholar Sir Edward Coke used the term to include almost all men and, in 1628, promulgated the Magna Carta as a constitution by which the rights of Englishmen were guaranteed. Its simple issuance and acceptance by the crown limited royal power and asserted that monarchs also were subject to the rule of law implied by the idea of a constitution. Regardless of what the writers of Magna Carta may have originally intended, its scope came to include all men and eventually all people.

In different royal dynasties and different centuries, the Magna Carta took on different levels of meaning and was transformed into a symbol of personal freedom. The Magna Carta would have its heyday not in the thirteenth century but rather hundreds of years later during the Enlightenment, when political thinkers drew on the Magna Carta to resist absolute monarchy and advocate more representative constitutional government. This new significance was not lost on British colonists in North America, who drew upon the Magna Carta as they came into conflict with King George III over rights and taxation.

Defining Moment

On October 14, 1066, William, Duke of Normandy, also known as William the Conqueror, defeated the recently crowned King Harold II of England at the Battle of Hastings. On Christmas Day, 1066, he was crowned King William I of England. The Norman Conquest ushered in many changes in England, particularly with respect to government. The Normans brought a more centralized style of rule than had previously existed in England. William set up the Great Council, which would eventually become Parliament. The Anglo-Saxon nobles were dispossessed of their lands, which were then given to a much smaller group of Norman barons. This concentrated a degree of power and wealth among these barons, and they were thus often emboldened to resist royal authority.

In the century that followed the Norman Conquest, power had become more centralized in the hands of the monarch, oftentimes at the expense of baronial authority. Taxes continually increased to finance numerous endeavors. The issues that led to the signing of the Magna Carta at Runnymede in 1215 grew in importance during the rule of King John's predecessor, King Richard I, who was his brother. Richard ruled England from 1189 to 1199, but he spent much of his reign in Aquitaine, a region in western France where he had grown up with his mother, Eleanor of Aquitaine. He also spent time outside his realm as a crusader. For fourteen months beginning in December 1192, he was the prisoner of Duke Leopold V of Austria, who held him for ransom after his capture by pirates while returning home from the Third Crusade. Since Richard was mostly an absentee monarch, he put ministers in charge of the day-to-day administration of his kingdom. These ministers had to raise taxes continually to sup-

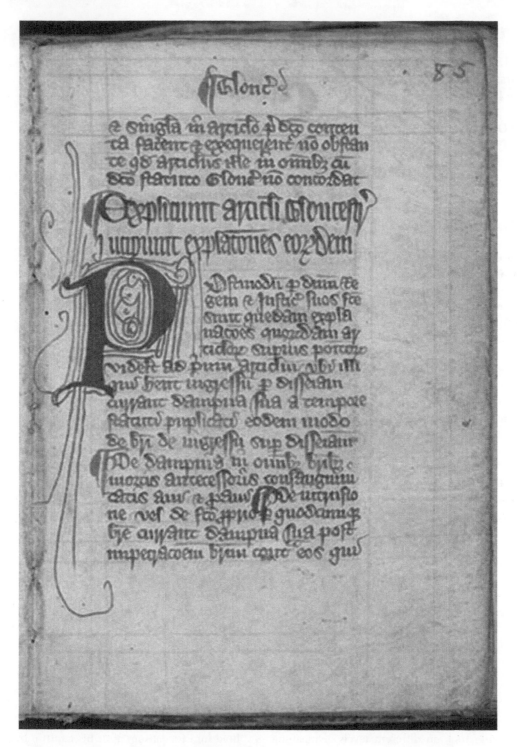

Magna carta cum statutis angliae (Great Charter with English Statutes), early 14th-century (commons.wikimedia.org) [Public Domain]

port Richard's endeavors overseas, including money for the ransom, which nearly bankrupted England. After his return from captivity, Richard spent most of the remainder of his life in combat in France. The barons and ministers who ran the country in his stead became very comfortable with this arrangement, but it would cause considerable trouble for the next king, John, who ascended the throne after Richard died on April 6, 1199. John's rule was often heavy-handed and despotic, and the barons were naturally resentful. In many regards, John was set up to fail, since he was always compared with his iconic brother, who was nicknamed "Richard the Lion-Hearted."

Trouble began in 1190, when Richard I had named as his successor Duke Arthur of Brittany, a nephew. Upon Richard's death, John acted quickly and declared himself king. After years of fighting to resolve the succession issue, he captured his teenage nephew and imprisoned him. The story goes that in 1203 John murdered his captive nephew in cold blood. This act of cowardice was not lost on his barons and cost John a great deal of political capital. John also was not as effective a military tactician as his brother and father, King Henry II, had been. King Philip II of France, also known as Philip Augustus, managed to take most of England's territorial possessions in France, including Normandy itself, the land of John's ancestors.

The next major controversy of John's rule was his conflict with Pope Innocent III over the election of the archbishop of Canterbury, Cardinal Stephen Langton. Innocent III refused to accept John's candidate, the bishop of Norwich John de Grey, and a confrontation ensued. John saw this as a direct assault on his power, and after he refused to back down, the pope put England under a papal interdict, which meant that no sacraments could be performed in England except baptism and the last rites. John essentially ignored the interdict, prompting the pope to depose him—in effect, to strip him of his crown. After a protracted struggle that saw John excommunicated and church lands seized by the Crown, John capitulated in 1212 and allowed Langton to assume his duties as archbishop of Canterbury. The damage to John's reputation, however, was already done.

During this same period, John had come into increasing conflict with his nobles and had begun to resort to ever more cruel and unusual tactics to control his barons, such as holding hostage the wives and children of those with whom he was quarrelling. John thus cultivated considerable antagonism among the barons on whom he greatly depended for financial and military support. John also continued the burdensome tax-collection policies of Richard I.

In 1214 John suffered a major military defeat at the hands of the French and returned to England in disgrace. Once again, his standing in the eyes of his people had suffered, and the stage was set for his acceptance of the Magna Carta the following year. As part of the uprising against him, the barons seized control of the Tower of London in May 1215. One month later at Runnymede, a meadow along the Thames west of London, the barons persuaded John to affix his seal to a charter of liberties intended to rein in the king's power.

Author Biographies

The authorship of the Magna Carta is not entirely known. Some historians believe that a document called the "Articles of Barons" formed the basis of the Magna Carta. The consensus is that these articles were worked into a final document by a group of learned men, most likely headed by Stephen Langton, William Marshal, and Robert Fitzwalter.

Langton was born around 1150. After the death of the archbishop of Canterbury, Hubert Walter, in 1205, Langton became embroiled in a power struggle between King John and Pope Innocent III. Langton was the pope's choice to succeed Walter, but John had another candidate in mind. Eventually, John capitulated, and Langton became the archbishop of Canterbury. During the baronial conflict with John, Langton supported and advised the barons. However, he extricated himself from the conflict when the opposition turned to violence, and he was one of the king's emissaries at Runnymede. He died in 1228.

William Marshal, the First Earl of Pembroke, was born in about 1146 and died in 1219. He was considered one of the greatest warriors of his day, and his bravery in battle became the stuff of legend. Marshal aided in the succession of John to the throne after the death of Richard I. By 1213 he had become one of John's most important counselors, and he remained loyal to the king during the baronial conflict. He represented the king at Runnymede and was probably among the authors of the final document. After John's death, Marshal acted as the regent for the underage Henry III and thus became the de facto ruler of England.

The birth date of Robert Fitzwalter is unknown. It is known, however, that he died on November 9, 1235.

He came to prominence as the leader of the opposition to John. In 1212 he was accused of actions against the king and fled to France. His lands were seized and his castles destroyed. The following year, his lands were restored by John, but he remained a staunch opponent of the king. He was one of the chief negotiators of the Magna Carta, though it is not known exactly how much input he had.

HISTORICAL DOCUMENT

[Preamble]
Edward by the grace of God, King of England, Lord of Ireland, and Duke of Guyan, to all Archbishops, Bishops, etc. We have seen the Great Charter of the Lord Henry, sometimes King of England, our father, of the Liberties of England, in these words: Henry by the grace of God, King of England, Lord of Ireland, Duke of Normandy and Guyan, and Earl of Anjou, to all Archbishops, Bishops, Abbots, Priors, Earls, Barons, Sheriffs, Provosts, Officers, and to all Bailiffs and other our faithful Subjects, which shall see this present Charter, Greeting. Know ye that we, unto the honour of Almighty God, and for the salvation of the souls of our progenitors and successors, Kings of England, to the advancement of holy Church, and amendment of our Realm, of our meer and free will, have given and granted to all Archbishops, Bishops, Abbots, Priors, Earls, Barons, and to all freemen of this our realm, these liberties following, to be kept in our kingdom of England for ever.

[1] First, We have granted to God, and by this our present Charter have confirmed, for us and our Heirs for ever, That the Church of England shall be free, and shall have her whole rights and liberties inviolable. We have granted also, and given to all the freemen of our realm, for us and our Heirs for ever, these liberties underwritten, to have and to hold to them and their Heirs, of us and our Heirs for ever.

[2] If any of our Earls or Barons, or any other, which holdeth of Us in chief by Knights service, shall die and at the time of his death his heir be of full age, and oweth us Relief, he shall have his inheritance by the old Relief; that is to say, the heir or heirs of an Earl, for a whole Earldom, by one hundred pound; the heir or heirs of a Baron, for a whole Barony, by one hundred marks; the heir or heirs of a Knight, for one whole Knights fee, one hundred shillings at the most; and he that hath less, shall give less, according to the custom of the fees.

[3] But if the Heir of any such be within age, his Lord shall not have the ward of him, nor of his land, before that he hath taken him homage. And after that such an heir hath been in ward (when he is come of full age) that is to say, to the age of one and twenty years, he shall have his inheritance without Relief, and without Fine; so that if such an heir, being within age, be made Knight, yet nevertheless his land shall remain in the keeping of his Lord unto the term aforesaid.

[4] The keeper of the land of such an heir, being within age, shall not take of the lands of the heir, but reasonable issues, reasonable customs, and reasonable services, and that without destruction and waste of his men and goods. And if we commit the custody of any such land to the Sheriff, or to any other, which is answerable unto us for the issues of the same land, and he make destruction or waste of those things that he hath in custody, we will take of him amends and recompence therefore, and the land shall be committed to two lawful and discreet men of that fee, which shall answer unto us for the issues of the same land, or unto him whom we will assign. And if we give or sell to any man the custody of any such land, and he therein do make destruction or waste, he shall lose the same custody; and it shall be assigned to two lawful and discreet men of that fee, which also in like manner shall be answerable to us, as afore is said.

[5] The keeper, so long as he hath the custody of the land of such an heir, shall keep up the houses, parks, warrens, ponds, mills, and other things pertaining to the same land, with the issues of the said land; and he shall deliver to the Heir, when he cometh to his full age, all his land stored with ploughs, and all other things, at the least as he received it. All these things shall be observed in the custodies of the Archbishopricks, Bishopricks, Abbeys, Priories, Churchs, and Dignities vacant, which appertain to us; except this, that such custody shall not be sold.

[6] Heirs shall be married without Disparagement.

[7] A Widow, after the death of her husband, incontinent, and without any Difficulty, shall have her marriage and her inheritance, and shall give nothing for her dower, her marriage, or her inheritance, which her husband and she held the day of the death of her husband, and she shall tarry in the chief house of her husband by forty days after the death of her husband, within which days her dower shall be assigned her (if it were not assigned her before) or that the house be a castle; and if she depart from the castle, then a competent house shall be forthwith provided for her, in the which she may honestly dwell, until her dower be to her assigned, as it is aforesaid; and she shall have in the meantime her reasonable estovers of the common; and for her dower shall be assigned unto her the third part of all the lands of her husband, which were his during coverture, except she were endowed of less at the Church-door. No widow shall be distrained to marry herself: nevertheless she shall find surety, that she shall not marry without our licence and assent (if she hold of us) nor without the assent of the Lord, if she hold of another.

[8] We or our Bailiffs shall not seize any land or rent for any debt, as long as the present Goods and Chattels of the debtor do suffice to pay the debt, and the debtor himself be ready to satisfy therefore. Neither shall the pledges of the debtor be distrained, as long as the principal debtor is sufficient for the payment of the debt. And if the principal debtor fail in the payment of the debt, having nothing wherewith to pay, or will not pay where he is able, the pledges shall answer for the debt. And if they will, they shall have the lands and rents of the debtor, until they be satished of that which they before paid for him, except that the debtor can show himself to be acquitted against the said sureties.

[9] The city of London shall have all the old liberties and customs, which it hath been used to have. Moreover we will and grant, that all other Cities, Boroughs, Towns, and the Barons of the Five Ports, and all other Ports, shall have all their liberties and free customs.

[10] No man shall be distrained to do more service for a Knights fee, nor any freehold, than therefore is due.

[11] Common Pleas shall not follow our Court, but shall be holden in some place certain.

[12] Assises of novel disseisin, and of Mortdancestor, shall not be taken but in the shires, and after this manner: If we be out of this Realm, our chief Justicer shall send our Justicers through every County once in the Year, which, with the Knights of the shires, shall take the said Assises in those counties; and those things that at the coming of our foresaid Justicers, being sent to take those Assises in the counties, cannot be determined, shall be ended by them in some other place in their circuit; and those things, which for difficulty of some articles cannot be determined by them, shall be referred to our Justicers of the Bench, and there shall be ended.

[13] Assises of Darrein Presentment shall be alway taken before our Justices of the Bench, and there shall be determined.

[14] A Freeman shall not be amerced for a small fault, but after the manner of the fault; and for a great fault after the greatness thereof, saving to him his contenement; and a Merchant likewise, saving to him his Merchandise; and any other's villain than ours shall be likewise amerced, saving his wainage, if he falls into our mercy. And none of the said amerciaments shall be assessed, but by the oath of honest and lawful men of the vicinage. Earls and Barons shall not be amerced but by their Peers, and after the manner of their offence. No man of the Church shall be amerced after the quantity of his spiritual Benefice, but after his Lay-tenement, and after the quantity of his offence.

[15] No Town or Freeman shall be distrained to make Bridges nor Banks, but such as of old time and of right have been accustomed to make them in the time of King Henry our Grandfather.

[16] No Banks shall be defended from henceforth, but such as were in defence in the time of King Henry our Grandfather, by the same places, and the same bounds, as they were wont to be in his time.

[17] No Sheriff, Constable, Escheator, Coroner, nor any other our Bailiffs, shall hold Pleas of our Crown.

[18] If any that holdeth of us Lay-fee do die, and our Sheriff or Bailiff do show our Letters Patents of our summon for Debt, which the dead man did owe to us; it shall be lawful to our Sheriff or Bailiff

to attach or inroll all the goods and chattels of the dead, being found in the said fee, to the Value of the same Debt, by the sight and testimony of lawful men, so that nothing thereof shall be taken away, until we be clearly paid off the debt; and the residue shall remain to the Executors to perform the testament of the dead; and if nothing be owing unto us, all the chattels shall go to the use of the dead (saving to his wife and children their reasonable parts).

[19] No Constable, nor his Bailiff, shall take corn or other chattels of any man, if the man be not of the Town where the Castle is, but he shall forthwith pay for the same, unless that the will of the seller was to respite the payment; and if he be of the same Town, the price shall be paid unto him within forty days.

[20] No Constable shall distrain any Knight to give money for keeping of his Castle, if he himself will do it in his proper person, or cause it to be done by another sufficient man, if he may not do it himself for a reasonable cause. And if we lead or send him to an army, he shall be free from Castle-ward for the time that he shall be with us in fee in our host, for the which he hath done service in our wars.

[21] No Sheriff nor Bailiff of ours, or any other, shall take the Horses or Carts of any man to make carriage, except he pay the old price limited, that is to say, for carriage with two horse, x.d. a day; for three horse, xiv.d. a day. No demesne Cart of any Spiritual person or Knight, or any Lord, shall be taken by our Bailiffs; nor we, nor our Bailiffs, nor any other, shall take any man's wood for our Castles, or other our necessaries to be done, but by the licence of him whose wood it shall be.

[22] We will not hold the Lands of them that be convict of Felony but one year and one day, and then those Lands shall be delivered to the Lords of the fee.

[23] All Wears from henceforth shall be utterly put down by Thames and Medway, and through all England, but only by the Sea-coasts.

[24] The Writ that is called Praecipe in capite shall be from henceforth granted to no person of any freehold, whereby any freeman may lose his Court.

[25] One measure of Wine shall be through our Realm, and one measure of Ale, and one measure of Corn, that is to say, the Quarter of London; and one breadth of dyed Cloth, Russets, and Haberjects,

that is to say, two Yards within the lists. And it shall be of Weights as it is of Measures.

[26] Nothing from henceforth shall be given for a Writ of Inquisition, nor taken of him that prayeth Inquisition of Life, or of Member, but it shall be granted freely, and not denied.

[27] If any do hold of us by Fee-ferm, or by Socage, or Burgage, and he holdeth Lands of another by Knights Service, we will not have the Custody of his Heir, nor of his Land, which is holden of the Fee of another, by reason of that Fee-ferm, Socage, or Burgage. Neither will we have the custody of such Fee-ferm, or Socage, or Burgage, except Knights Service be due unto us out of the same Fee-ferm. We will not have the custody of the Heir, or of any Land, by occasion of any Petit Serjeanty, that any man holdeth of us by Service to pay a Knife, an Arrow, or the like.

[28] No Bailiff from henceforth shall put any man to his open Law, nor to an Oath, upon his own bare saying, without faithful Witnesses brought in for the same.

[29] No Freeman shall be taken, or imprisoned, or be disseised of his Freehold, or Liberties, or free Customs, or be outlawed, or exiled, or any otherwise destroyed; nor will we pass upon him, nor condemn him, but by lawful Judgment of his Peers, or by the Law of the Land. We will sell to no man, we will not deny or defer to any man either Justice or Right.

[30] All Merchants (if they were not openly prohibited before) shall have their safe and sure Conduct to depart out of England, to come into England, to tarry in, and go through England, as well by Land as by Water, to buy and sell without any manner of evil Tolts, by the old and rightful Customs, except in Time of War. And if they be of a land making War against us, and such be found in our Realm at the beginning of the Wars, they shall be attached without harm of body or goods, until it be known unto us, or our Chief Justice, how our Merchants be intreated there in the land making War against us; and if our Merchants be well intreated there, theirs shall be likewise with us.

[31] If any man hold of any Eschete, as of the honour of Wallingford, Nottingham, Boloin, or of any other Eschetes which be in our hands, and are Baronies, and die, his Heir shall give none other

Relief, nor do none other Service to us, than he should to the Baron, if it were in the Baron's hand. And we in the same wise shall hold it as the Baron held it; neither shall we have, by occasion of any such Barony or Eschete, any Eschete or keeping of any of our men, unless he that held the Barony or Eschete hold of us in chief.

[32] No Freeman from henceforth shall give or sell any more of his Land, but so that of the residue of the Lands the Lord of the Fee may have the Service due to him, which belongeth to the Fee.

[33] All Patrons of Abbies, which have the King's Charters of England of Advowson, or have old Tenure or Possession in the same, shall have the Custody of them when they fall void, as it hath been accustomed, and as it is afore declared.

[34] No Man shall be taken or imprisoned upon the Appeal of a Woman for the Death of any other, than of her husband.

[35] No County Court from henceforth shall be holden, but from Month to Month; and where greater time hath been used, there shall be greater: Nor any Sheriff, or his Bailiff, shall keep his Turn in the Hundred but twice in the Year; and nowhere but in due place, and accustomed; that is to say, once after Easter, and again after the Feast of St. Michael. And the View of Frankpledge shall be likewise at the Feast of St. Michael without occasion; so that every man may have his Liberties which he had, or used to have, in the time of King Henry our Grandfather, or which he hath purchased since: but the View of Frankpledge shall be so done, that our Peace may be kept; and that the Tything be wholly kept as it hath been accustomed; and that the Sheriff seek no Occasions, and that he be content with so much as the Sheriff was wont to have for his Viewmaking in the time of King Henry our Grandfather.

[36] It shall not be lawful from henceforth to any to give his Lands to any Religious House, and to take the same Land again to hold of the same House. Nor shall it be lawful to any House of Religion to take the Lands of any, and to lease the same to him of whom he received it. If any from henceforth give his Lands to any Religious House, and thereupon be convict, the Gift shall be utterly void, and the Land shall accrue to the Lord of the Fee.

[37] Escuage from henceforth shall be taken like as it was wont to be in the time of King Henry our Grandfather; reserving to all Archbishops, Bishops, Abbots, Priors, Templers, Hospitallers, Earls, Barons, and all persons, as well Spiritual as Temporal, all their free liberties and free Customs, which they have had in time passed. And all these Customs and Liberties aforesaid, which we have granted to be holden within this our Realm, as much as appertaineth to us and our Heirs, we shall observe; and all Men of this our Realm, as well Spiritual as Temporal (as much as in them is) shall observe the same against all persons in like wise. And for this our Gift and Grant of these Liberties, and of other contained in our Charter of Liberties of our Forest, the Archbishops, Bishops, Abbots, Priors, Earls, Barons, Knights, Freeholders, and other our Subjects, have given unto us the Fifteenth Part of all their Moveables. And we have granted unto them for us and our Heirs, that neither we, nor our Heirs shall procure or do anything whereby the Liberties in this Charter contained shall be infringed or broken; and if anything be procured by any person contrary to the premisses, it shall be had of no force nor effect.

These being Witnesses; Lord B. Archbishop of Canterbury, E. Bishop of London, J. Bishop of Bathe, P. of Winchester, H. of Lincoln, R. of Salisbury, W. of Rochester, W. of Worester, J. of Ely, H. of Hereford, R. of Chichester, W. of Exeter, Bishops; the Abbot of St. Edmunds, the Abbot of St. Albans, the Abbot of Bello, the Abbot of St. Augustines in Canterbury, the Abbot of Evesham, the Abbot of Westminster, the Abbot of Bourgh St. Peter, the Abbot of Reading, the Abbot of Abindon, the Abbot of Malmsbury, the Abbot of Winchcomb, the Abbot of Hyde, the Abbot of Certefey, the Abbot of Sherburn, the Abbot of Cerne, the Abbot of Abbotebir, the Abbot of Middleton, the Abbot of Seleby, the Abbot of Cirencester; H. de Burgh Justice, H. Earl of Chester and Lincoln, W. Earl of Salisbury, W. Earl of Warren, G. de Clare Earl of Gloucester and Hereford, W. de Ferrars Earl of Derby, W. de Mandeville Earl of Essex, H. de Bygod Earl of Norfolk, W. Earl of Albermarle, H. Earl of Hereford, J. Constable of Chester, R. de Ros, R. Fitzwalter, R. de Vyponte, W. de Bruer, R. de Muntefichet, P. Fitzherbert, W. de Aubenie, F. Grefly, F. de Breus, J. de Monemue, J. Fit-

zallen, H. de Mortimer, W. de Beauchamp, W. de St. John, P. de Mauly, Brian de Lisle, Thomas de Multon, R. de Argenteyn, G. de Nevil, W. de Mauduit, J. de Balun, and others.

We, ratifying and approving these Gifts and Grants aforesaid, confirm and make strong all the same for us and our Heirs perpetually, and, by the Tenour of these Presents, do renew the same; willing and granting for us and our Heirs, that this Charter, and all and

singular his Articles, for ever shall be stedfastly, firmly, and inviolably observed; although some Articles in the same Charter contained, yet hitherto peradventure have not been kept, we will, and by Authority Royal command, from henceforth firmly they be observed. In witness whereof we have caused these our Letters Patents to be made. T. Edward our Son at Westminster, the Twenty-eighth Day of March, in the Twenty-eighth Year of our Reign.

GLOSSARY

Advowson: the right, in English ecclesiastical law, to nominate a person to fill a vacant Church office

contenement: property other than real estate necessary to maintaining one's present way of life

evil Tolts: excessive royal taxes

Five Ports: the confederation, established in 1155, of five towns in southeastern England located where the channel was narrowest, hence crossing to the Continent quickest

Guyan: old spelling of Guyenne, or Aquitaine

Haberjects: the materials from which chain mail was made

incontinent: person not under control; in this context, describing a woman not under the authority of a male relative or guardian

Justicer: person appointed to administer justice

King Henry our Grandfather: King Henry II of England

Lay-fee: debt owed to the Crown by a Crown tenant

Lord Henry … King Henry our father: King Henry III of England

meer: pure

keep his Turn in the Hundred: hold court in the county

Viewmaking: the process of gathering and inspecting the men in the Frankpledge

villain: villein; a free common villager of the peasant class

wainage: vehicles a freeman needed to make a living

wears … utterly put down: dams or breakwaters in a river, taken down or removed

Document Analysis

The Magna Carta originally contained sixty-three "chapters," or clauses, that asserted what the barons considered to be their ancient rights in an effort to protect themselves and their property. By the time Edward I agreed to reissue the Magna Carta in 1297, there were thirty-seven clauses. The clauses that pertained solely to the conflict leading up to the signing of the document in 1215 had been eliminated, and all clauses concerned with the administration of forests had been transferred to a separate Forest Charter in 1217.

The document commences with a preamble, which states that it is a declaration of liberties granted to "Archbishops, Bishops, Abbots, Priors, Earls, Barons, and … all freemen of this our realm." The clauses that follow enumerate various types of liberties, including freedom of the church, feudal law regarding the holding of land, the rights of widows, the reformation of the justice system, property rights, the rights of people accused of crimes, and the rights of merchants. They appear in no particular order, and the language of the clauses often reflects the influence of Norman French legal and feudal practices.

Clause 1 contains at least two important provisions. The first is its assertion that "the Church of England shall be free." Stephen Langton was in all likelihood the architect of this clause. After the bitter confrontation between Pope Innocent III and King John over Langton's appointment as archbishop of Canterbury, Langton wanted to prevent any such confrontations in the future. This provision would become an antecedent to later concepts of the division of church and state. The phrase "Church of England" assigned an idiosyncratic nature to the Church of England, distinguishing it from the Roman Catholic Church. This concept of a distinct Church of England would be played out in the sixteenth century during the reign of Henry VIII.

A second important aspect of Clause 1 is the use of the word *freemen*. Although it is not entirely clear what the authors meant by this term at the time, what is important is what it later came to mean. Over time, the category of freemen came to apply to an increasingly broad range of people, and this usage is one of the features that has allowed the Magna Carta to be interpreted flexibly over the centuries.

Clauses 2 through 7 address feudal relationships and rights. In the early thirteenth century English society was defined by feudal relationships and agreements. The nobility held their lands as direct grants from the king in exchange for military service and payment of taxes. These taxes came in many forms, many of which involved the transference of estates from one generation to the next. Many of the barons' complaints against John pertained to the king's having overstepped his authority. These clauses define the boundaries of feudal relationships with the king and protect the rights of the nobles from abuses by royal authority.

Clauses 2 and 3, for example, deal with issues of inheritance and who may profit from the transference of property. Both address the amount of "relief" that could be assessed to someone receiving an inheritance. Relief was a fee paid in order to collect one's inheritance, but there was no limit on the amount of relief to be paid, which Clause 2 tried to correct. Clause 3 prevented the king from receiving relief when he had already profited from having been the guardian of an inheritance. Clauses 4 and 5 protected the rights of heirs who were too young to collect their inheritance from king's representatives, who might otherwise have tried to profit dishonestly from the property of their charges.

In Clause 6 the marriage of heirs is addressed. The king had made a practice of selling female heirs to men wishing to gain the women's title and fortune. In many cases these marriages were seen as inequitable because the man was from a lower social station than the woman. The barons wanted to curtail this practice. Clause 7 stipulates the rights of widows and states that a widow could not have her inheritance denied to her. The implication of the second portion of the clause is perhaps more significant. The clause states, "No widow shall be distrained to marry herself." In other words, no widow had to marry if she chose not to do so. Allowing widows autonomy in deciding whether to remarry represented a small step toward granting rights not just to men but also to women.

Clause 8 spells out the relationship between debtors and sureties. A surety was someone who was responsible for a debt if the debtor could not pay. This clause says that a debt collector could not go to the surety without first endeavoring to collect the debt from the debtor. It further states that if a surety satisfied the debt, he was entitled to compensation from the debtor equal to the amount settled.

The city of London played a major role in the conflict between King John and the barons. By siding with the barons in the conflict, the people of London earned a special position with the barons, and that position earned them Clause 9 of the Magna Carta. Clause 9 stipulates that London was granted all of the traditional rights and privileges that the city had previously enjoyed. These rights and privileges were protected now by law.

Clause 10 reflected an effort to define the terms of military service under the feudal code. The exact amount of service was not well defined, and the Magna Carta did not do much to rectify this murkiness. However, this clause put in writing the principle that the amount of service required was to be based on the amount of land a noble had been granted.

Clauses 11 through 14 deal with issues of justice. Clause 11, for example, was intended to limit the expenses individuals incurred while seeking justice. Prior to 1215, individuals who had to go to court literally had to go to court—that is, to the location of the king. If the king was moving from place to place, those seeking justice had to follow him at their own expense. This clause fixed where court would be held and limited expenses. Clause 12 was aimed at making justice more convenient by stating that certain trials would be held in the county. It names two types of legal proceedings, using language that had been imported from Norman French. "Assises of novel disseisin" were court proceedings for the recovery of land of which a person had recently lost ownership; an "assise," spelled "assize" now, was simply a sitting of the court. Assises of "Mortdancestor," usually spelled *mort d'ancestor*, were actions to recover land of which a person had been deprived by the death of an ancestor. Clause 13 introduces another legal term: "Assises of Darrein Presentment." "Darrein Presentment" translates to "last presentation" and had to do with legal complications that could ensue over conflicting claims to a benefice, or an ecclesiastical office.

Clause 14 expresses the view that there should not be excessive punishment for those convicted of a crime. The clause addresses the assessment of fines, and its thrust is that the fine should be commensurate with the severity of the crime. The principle that the punishment should fit the crime has become important in the judicial systems of democratic nations and was later set forth in the Eighth Amendment to the U.S. Constitution.

It was the practice of the day in England for the king's subjects to build and maintain bridges. Villages and individuals had no option to refuse when the king ordered them to build a bridge. Clause 15 sought to end this practice. Clause 16 deals with riverbanks and fishing rights, stating that fishing rights were not to be curtailed, save on those rivers that were designated in the time of King Henry II. Later, Clause 23 deals with fish weirs, or traps that were used to catch fish by placing wooden posts in the riverbed. Since these wooden posts often were impediments to commerce, the barons wanted them removed.

Clause 17 returns to the administration of justice by stating that trials must be conducted by the proper authorities. This instruction was to ensure that proper jus-

tice would be dispensed and people would be protected from the brand of justice doled out by local officials, whose sentences were often much harsher than those passed by the king's officials. Clause 18 deals with estates of Crown tenants who owed debts to the Crown. It specifies how a Crown tenant would be protected from abuses by royal authorities who tried to collect debts. The clause states that documentation was required from royal officials in order to settle debts. An escheator was a royal official responsible for holding an inquest on the death of a tenant in chief and determining who should inherit the property.

Clauses 19 through 21 share the common theme of property rights. In general, they established the principle that property could not be taken from a person arbitrarily without proper remuneration. This concept later became the linchpin in English philosopher John Locke's understanding of property and enumeration of "natural rights" in the seventeenth century.

Clause 22 represented another attempt to define the scope of the king's power and make that power less arbitrary. The clauses pertaining to feudal relationships do not say that the king did not have certain powers; rather, they defined and limited those powers. Clause 22 limited the king's power to take away the land of a noble convicted of a felony. By attaching a specific timetable to when a baron's land could be taken from him after conviction of a felony, another safeguard was put in place against the abuse of royal power. Clause 24 deals with Writs Praecipe, also called writs of covenant. These writs, issued by the king, gave local sheriffs the authority to take away a noble's land and remit it to another party who claimed the land. Practices such as these had been at the heart of the conflict between the barons and King John.

The purpose of Clause 25, one of the more straightforward of the Magna Carta's clauses, was to establish standard measurements for the sale of certain items in order to protect buyers. A "haberject" was a type of dyed cloth. Clause 26 pertains to the subject of trial by combat. A "Writ of Inquisition" was the right to trial by combat for an accuser, an important function of justice at that time. Governments had not yet fully developed their judicial function, and trial by combat was one of the main forms of redress for someone wronged by another. This clause simply provided that this right could not be taken away and would be granted without charging a fee. The Magna Carta takes up this issue again later, in Clause 34. Clause 27 reined in the king's ability to collect a tax from guardianship when it was not within the scope of the law to do so. The term *fee-ferm* means "fee-farm," or a farm on which a farmer paid rent. Under the practice of socage, a farmer held land in exchange for service; the term *burgage* referred to property in towns on which the holder paid rent.

Clauses 28 and 29 would later become quite influential in the practice of criminal law. The most accepted interpretation of Clause 28 is that a bailiff (meaning any number of different officials) may not charge a person with a crime without first producing a credible witness. Clause 29 is perhaps the most well-known clause and the one that was seized on by later legal scholars, for from it the concept of trial by jury evolved:

No Freeman shall be taken, or imprisoned, or be disseised of his Freehold [have his property taken away], or Liberties, or free Customs, or be outlawed, or exiled, or any otherwise destroyed; nor will we pass upon him, nor condemn him, but by lawful Judgment of his Peers, or by the Law of the Land.

In other words, a person could not be convicted by the arbitrary whim of another person but must be found guilty of a legitimate crime by a group of his peers. Trial by jury has since become the foundation of democratic judicial systems. The clause concludes with a strong statement that justice may not be bought.

Clause 30 provided for free trade with merchants of all nations not at war with the king. It states that trade was to be unencumbered by excessive royal taxation. Another clause designed to rein in the power of the king, Clause 31, enabled barons to regain rights that they had held under previous kings but that had not been recognized by King John. Before John's reign, the rights to property ownership and inheritance of subtenants, another layer of the feudal order, had been recognized. John ignored these rights when land was escheated (left without an heir). Instead of allowing the land to pass to the proper tenant, John claimed the land for himself. An addition to the original 1215 version, Clause 32, deals with the practice of subdividing fiefs (feudal estates) in order to break down the feudal order. Extreme fragmentation of estates could have broken down the feudal order and made tenants independent of their feudal lords. Clause 32 sought to end this practice.

Clause 33 specifies who would have guardianship over churches and thus have had the right to an appointment at a church. Churches were founded by either the king or a lesser feudal lord. The founder of a particular church had the right to appoint its head. In certain cases,

John ignored this and appointed heads of the churches. This clause was meant to define legally another feudal relationship and protect the feudal rights of the barons. Taking up again the issue of trial by combat, Clause 34 eliminated the advantage women were seen to have, for female accusers had been able to hire a champion to fight in their stead, but an accused man had to fight for himself. Clause 34 sought to end this practice.

Clause 35 returns to the issue of judicial procedure. It makes reference to two institutions: "Frankpledge" and "Tything." The latter was a group of ten men; the former referred to the obligation of the ten to stand as sureties for the members of the group and to produce any one of the members if he was summoned to a legal proceeding. The purpose of this clause was to specify when and under what circumstances these institutions could be invoked while preventing their misuse to harass people. Clause 36 attempted to prevent another abuse: in this case, abuse over the ownership of church lands, particularly the practices of granting land to a church and taking it back and of the church's taking land and leasing it back to the donor. Finally, Clause 37 regulated the practice of escuage, also called scutage. This term referred to the obligation of a tenant to follow his lord in military service at his own expense.

Essential Themes

Upon its inception, the Magna Carta did not make much of an impact, as King John largely ignored it. It faded in importance during the Tudor period of English history, but the document was revived in the seventeenth century during the Stuart period, when Parliament was at odds with the king. Sir Edward Coke was the seventeenth-century champion of the Magna Carta. He asserted that it was proof of an ancient set of liberties that English people possessed. Coke invoked an ideal of the Magna Carta, rather than the probable intention of its authors. Although Coke died in 1634, his view of the Magna Carta was used as a spark to ignite the English Civil War of the 1640s and later the Glorious Revolution of 1688, which brought King William III and Queen Mary II to the English throne and produced the English Bill of Rights. It was also the inspiration behind the Habeas Corpus Act of 1679. As time went on, power shifted increasingly from the king to Parliament, and many historians argue that the Magna Carta was at the center of this evolution. Coke's idealized interpretation of the Magna Carta would eventually become reality.

In the American colonies, the Magna Carta became a symbol. Many colonies were being founded and settled concurrently with the strife between Parliament and the Stuart kings James I and Charles I in the seventeenth century. As a result, colonists were often mindful of the Magna Carta when colonial charters were being drawn up. Colonists saw themselves as entitled to the ancient rights granted to them by the Magna Carta, and they invoked the Magna Carta in their arguments against British taxation and infringements upon their rights. The ideal of the Magna Carta remained powerful in the writing of the U.S. Constitution, and many interpretations of the Magna Carta live on in the American Constitution and Bill of Rights.

———*Matthew Fiorillo*

Bibliography and Further Reading

Daniell, Christopher. *From Norman Conquest to Magna Carta: England, 1066–1215*. New York: Routledge, 2003.

Danziger, Danny, and John Gillingham. *1215: The Year of Magna Carta*. New York: Simon & Schuster, 2004.

Erickson, Carolly. *Royal Panoply: Brief Lives of the English Monarchs*. New York: St. Martin's Press, 2006.

Howard, A. E. Dick. *Magna Carta: Text and Commentary*. Rev. ed. Charlottesville: University Press of Virginia, 1998.

Turner, Ralph V. *Magna Carta: Through the Ages*. New York: Pearson/Longman, 2003.

Web Sites

McKechnie, William Sharp. "Magna Carta: A Commentary on the Great Charter of King John." Online Library of Liberty. http://oll.libertyfund.org/titles/mckechnie-magna-carta-a-commentary [accessed March 4, 2017].

Sommerville, J. P. "The Crisis of John's Reign." University of Wisconsin https://faculty.history.wisc.edu/sommerville/123/123%20114%20John%20in%20crisis.htm [accessed March 4, 2017].

"Magna Carta." British Library http://www.bl.uk/magna-carta [accessed March 4, 2017].

■ Dutch Declaration of Independence

Date: 1581
Authors: Jacques Tayaert, Jacob Valcke, Pieter van Dieven, Andries Hessels
Genre: Declaration of independence

Summary Overview

The Dutch Declaration of Independence, signed on July 26, 1581, was formally called the Act of Abjuration or, in Dutch, the Plakkaat van Verlatinghe. A coalition of Dutch provinces in the northern portion of the federation called the United Provinces issued the declaration to announce their independence from Spanish rule under King Philip II. A literal English translation of Plakkaat van Verlatinghe would be "Placard of Desertion"; this title was given to the document because Dutch rebels believed that Philip had essentially deserted the Low Countries, like a shepherd who had deserted his flock, and the document outlines his abuses against the provinces.

The declaration represented the northern provinces' formal renunciation of the authority of Philip II to rule in the Netherlands. To accomplish this in the sixteenth century, the Dutch rebels needed aid, in the forms of manpower, finances, and supplies for the ongoing Dutch Revolt as well as political or royal leadership. The need for the latter would become even more pressing upon the assassination of the most powerful prince and champion, William of Orange, three years later. Although they eventually became a republic, the rebels' initial instinct was to have the country ruled by a monarch. For these reasons, France's duke of Anjou, England's Queen Elizabeth I, the Turkish Ottoman Empire, and other international figures and states were a significant part of the audience.

The Dutch Declaration of Independence, regarded as the first modern declaration of independence, was forged during the Eighty Years' War, often called the Dutch War of Independence. The first phase of this war was the Dutch Revolt of 1568–1609, during which the Netherlands' northern provinces achieved independence from Spain. After Spain and the northern provinces signed the Twelve Years' Truce in 1609 at Antwerp, ending hostilities, the southern provinces continued to live under Spanish domination until the Treaty of Münster was signed in 1648. This treaty, part of the realignment brought about that year by the Treaty of Westphalia—which ended the Eighty Years' War as well as the Thirty Years' War, fought in central Europe—confirmed the existence of the Dutch provinces as an independent nation variously called the Dutch Republic, the Republic of the Seven United Netherlands, or the Republic of the Seven United Provinces.

In the twenty-first century, the names of Holland and the Netherlands tend to be used interchangeably. The terminology, though, is complex and oftentimes confusing. Netherlands literally means "Low Countries" or "Lowlands" and historically dates to the period when the Dutch Republic consisted of a loose confederation of seven provinces; the declaration refers to this confederation in the opening line as the United Provinces of the Low Countries. In 1830 two of those provinces broke off from the recently established United Kingdom of the Netherlands to form Belgium. Today, the phrase "Low Countries" is often used to refer collectively to the countries of the Netherlands, Belgium, and Luxembourg. The phrase actually has little to do with the countries' "lowness" relative to sea level; rather, it refers to the provinces' originally being the more southerly portions of earlier empires. Holland is a name commonly used to refer to the country of the Netherlands, but more accurately it reflects the names of two provinces, North Holland and South Holland, that historically were the most prominent members of the Dutch Republic. Finally, "Dutch" refers to the language spoken in the Netherlands, though the word is also used to refer to the people and the nation's institutions; it is etymologically related to "Deutsche," or German.

Defining Moment

The Dutch Declaration of Independence was signed in the midst of a complex set of events that would radically alter the balance of power in Western Europe. In the fifteenth century, the successive dukes of Burgundy held control of what were called the Seventeen Provinces, a collection of counties and fiefdoms roughly corresponding to the Dutch Republic and also including small portions of modern-day France and Germany. Accordingly, the region was often called the Burgundian Netherlands. The Burgundian Netherlands were inherited by Charles, the duke of Burgundy, in 1506.

Charles was a descendant of the House of Habsburg, a branch of the Austrian royal succession that ruled a large portion of central Europe, and as such he became King Charles I of Spain in 1516; he was also the grandson of King Ferdinand II of Aragon and Isabella I of Castile, famous for backing Christopher Columbus's voyage to the New World in 1492. Charles was Spanish, but he was born in Ghent (in Flanders, now part of Belgium), so he spoke Dutch and was sympathetic to Dutch concerns. In 1519, upon the death of his grandfather, he became the head of the House of Habsburg and was elected the monarch of the Holy Roman Empire as Charles V (though the pope did not officially crown him until 1530). He thus presided over a large swath of western, central, and southern Europe, including the Netherlands. He asserted his control over the Netherlands in 1549 when he issued the Pragmatic Sanction, which recognized the Seventeen Provinces as a unified political entity to which the Habsburgs were heirs.

During the sixteenth century, three major issues caused friction in Charles V's Dutch domains. One issue was taxation. Flanders had become a particularly wealthy province, but the other Dutch provinces were affluent as well, largely through trade and industry as spurred by an entrepreneurial ethic. Charles became embroiled in a series of wars, particularly against France as a part of the Italian Wars, and against the Ottoman Turks in the Mediterranean. He needed funds to finance these wars, and the affluent Dutch bore more than their fair share of the tax burden. Dutch merchants and exporters opposed the wars because France and the Ottoman Empire were important trading partners. The second issue that caused friction was the rise of Protestantism, which Catholic Spain regarded as heresy. Protestantism had been tolerated locally throughout the Dutch provinces, but Charles believed that it had to be suppressed and sent troops into the provinces to that end. He enacted harsh measures against Dutch Protestants, creating numerous grievances. His attempts to suppress Dutch Protestantism took place against the backdrop of the notorious Spanish Inquisition, the oftentimes cruel effort to root out heresy, blasphemy, witchcraft, sodomy, and other departures from Catholic orthodoxy.

The third source of friction was efforts to centralize the government. The Netherlands had historically consisted of numerous principalities operating more or less autonomously under the control of local nobles.

Charles wanted to increase efficiency in his empire, so he attempted to impose more centralized rule over these principalities. Charles replaced local Dutch stadtholders (heads of state) and members of the States-General, the governing body of the Seventeen Provinces, with his own appointments. He also replaced bishops and other religious authorities. Both the nobles and the increasingly influential merchants of the Netherlands resented these encroachments on their traditional prerogatives.

Charles relinquished the throne of Spain to his son, Philip II, in 1556. While the Dutch had grown annoyed with Charles, they grudgingly tolerated his rule, for he spoke Dutch and appeared to be at least somewhat interested in Dutch welfare. Philip II, though, was more Spanish than Dutch and showed little interest in the Netherlands. The issues that had arisen during the first half of the sixteenth century became more pronounced under Philip, who governed the Dutch provinces harshly; he was at loggerheads with the Dutch nobles throughout his first decade of rule. They resisted his efforts to increase taxes. They demanded the withdrawal of Spanish troops. They resented Antoine Perrenot de Granvelle, Philip's appointed head of the States-General, and several prominent nobles resigned from the States-General in protest. Religious protests increased, as Dutch Protestants—and even Dutch Catholics—called for an end to persecution of Protestantism. In 1566 a petition to that end was submitted by some four hundred nobles to Philip's governor of the Netherlands, Margaret of Parma, who passed it along to Philip—who promptly ignored it.

As if matters were not troubled enough, they turned worse in 1566 when rioting broke out in Flanders and other provinces. These riots were led by Dutch Calvinists and were part of a so-called iconoclastic ("image breaking") movement. Calvinists in numerous cities looted churches and destroyed religious images of Catholic saints, which Calvinists thought of as idols. In response to the vandalism, in 1567 Philip sent troops to Brussels under the command of Fernando Álvarez de Toledo, the third duke of Alba. Given broad license by Philip, the duke of Alba created the Council of Troubles (in Dutch, Raad van Beroerten) to enforce harsh measures against anyone he thought to be disloyal to the king. Numerous nobles were executed, including most prominently Lamoraal, the count of Egmond, and Filips van Montmorency, the count of Hoorn, who were decapitated in Brussels in 1568. Over the next year, a thousand people were executed, prompting

Netherlanders to refer to the Council of Troubles as the "Council of Blood."

Amid this turmoil, William I, an influential stadtholder, assumed leadership of the opposition to Philip, though William was politically savvy and did not renounce his allegiance to the king. Initially, he fled to his domains in Germany to avoid the wrath of the duke of Alba. In 1568 he returned in an effort to drive Alba out, invading the Netherlands in concert with armies led by his two brothers and a fourth army led by French Huguenots. On May 23, 1568, his forces defeated a Spanish force at the Battle of Heiligerlee, marking the first Dutch victory of the Dutch Revolt and the Eighty Years' War. Although William was victorious, the other invading armies were not. William ran out of money, his army fell apart, and the rebellion was effectively quelled until 1572.

The duke of Alba meanwhile retained his position of authority. He provoked the ire of Netherlanders anew when he instituted a tax to fund the Spanish king's war against the Ottoman Empire. The Ottoman Turks, for their part, offered direct aid to the Dutch rebels, hoping thereby to counter Habsburg hegemony over Europe. Discontent continued to grow until Dutch rebels seized the town of Brielle on April 1, 1572. This victory, entirely unexpected, emboldened the rebels, who reappointed William of Orange as their leader. William faced a difficult challenge, for he needed to find a way to unite three different factions: Calvinists who wanted to impose Dutch Protestantism, Catholics who yet remained loyal to Philip, and a large group of Catholics and Protestants who were primarily interested in ending Spanish rule over their country and restoring their privileges.

Throughout the 1570s, Philip had problems of his own. His wars were bankrupting Spain; his unpaid soldiers mutinied, and in 1576 they sacked and looted Antwerp in an event called the Spanish Fury. Again the rebels were emboldened. That same year the Seventeen Provinces signed an internal treaty called the Pacification of Ghent, an agreement to join forces against the Spanish and to enforce religious tolerance. The union, however, was still in disarray. In early 1579 the southern provinces, through the Union of Arras, withdrew from the greater union and confirmed their loyalty to the Spanish king, largely because they were uncomfortable with the fundamentalist religious fervor of the Calvinists. In response, the northern provinces of Holland, Zeeland, Utrecht, and Groningen formed the Union of Utrecht on January 23, 1579, leaving the Seventeen Provinces divided between north and south. By 1581, Gelder, Overijssel, and Friesland had also joined with the northern provinces, which then declared their independence from Spain as the Republic of the Seven United Provinces.

Author Biographies

The Dutch Declaration of Independence was drafted by a committee of four men; details of their lives are sketchy. Andries Hessels held the position of *greffier*, or secretary, of Brabant. Jacques Tayaert was a pensionary, or chief functionary and legal adviser, in the city of Ghent. Jacob Valcke held the same position in the city of Ter Goes, now called Goes. Finally, Pieter van Dieven was pensionary of the city of Mechelen. A fifth name is often mentioned, that of Jan de Asseliers, the *audiencer* of the States-General (the official charged with drafting its declarations), who may have physically written out the declaration and may have composed the preamble. His name appears at the very end of the document as a signer.

Although he was not strictly speaking an author of the declaration, William I of Orange, often called William the Silent for his circumspection in negotiations with the king of France, was the leader of the Dutch Revolt and thus can be considered the inspiration behind the document. (This William of Orange is not to be confused with the William of Orange who assumed the throne of England in 1689 through the Glorious Revolution; the latter was William III of Orange.) William I of Orange was born on April 24, 1533, in Nassau, a province in what is now Germany. Upon the death of his cousin in 1544, as the family's only recognized heir, he assumed the title of prince of Auranja, or Orange, a province in southern France. Both Nassau and Orange were parts of the Holy Roman Empire at the time, so that made William a vassal of the emperor Charles V. Through marriage, William gained additional royal titles and rose in the emperor's hierarchy of aristocratic advisors. In 1555 Charles V appointed him to the Council of State; later, Philip II appointed him stadtholder of Holland, Zeeland, Utrecht, and Burgundy.

During the religious disturbances that followed the accession of Philip, William refused to appear before the Council of Troubles and was declared an outlaw. He then became leader of the armed resistance to Spain and won several important battles. His leadership of the Dutch was validated by the signing of the

Act of Abjuration in 1581, uniting the Republic of the Seven United Provinces and rejecting Philip II as their king. Philip, though, had placed a bounty on William's head, which proved too hard to resist on the part of one Balthasar Gérard, a Catholic Frenchman who believed that William had betrayed his king. On July 10, 1584, Gérard presented himself at William's home and shot him with a handgun—one of the earliest political assassinations by handgun in history. Nevertheless, William became a legendary champion of Dutch independence, and even though neither of the provinces in his inheritance was located in the Netherlands, the House of Orange-Nassau became the most recognizable aristocratic political family in the United Provinces.

HISTORICAL DOCUMENT

The States General of the United Provinces of the Low Countries, to all whom it may concern, do by these Presents send greeting:

As it is apparent to all that a prince is constituted by God to be ruler of a people, to defend them from oppression and violence as the shepherd his sheep; and whereas God did not create the people slaves to their prince, to obey his commands, whether right or wrong, but rather the prince for the sake of the subjects (without which he could be no prince), to govern them according to equity, to love and support them as a father his children or a shepherd his flock, and even at the hazard of life to defend and preserve them. And when he does not behave thus, but, on the contrary, oppresses them, seeking opportunities to infringe their ancient customs and privileges, exacting from them slavish compliance, then he is no longer a prince, but a tyrant, and the subjects are to consider him in no other view. And particularly when this is done deliberately, unauthorized by the states, they may not only disallow his authority, but legally proceed to the choice of another prince for their defense. This is the only method left for subjects whose humble petitions and remonstrances could never soften their prince or dissuade him from his tyrannical proceedings; and this is what the law of nature dictates for the defense of liberty, which we ought to transmit to posterity, even at the hazard of our lives. And this we have seen done frequently in several countries upon the like occasion, whereof there are notorious instances, and more justifiable in our land, which has been always governed according to their ancient privileges, which are expressed in the oath taken by the prince at his admission to the government; for most of the Provinces receive their prince upon certain conditions, which he swears to maintain, which, if the prince violates, he is no longer sovereign.

Now thus it was that the king of Spain after the demise of the emperor, his father, Charles the Fifth, of the glorious memory (of whom he received all these provinces), forgetting the services done by the subjects of these countries, both to his father and himself, by whose valor he got so glorious and memorable victories over his enemies that his name and power became famous and dreaded over all the world, forgetting also the advice of his said imperial majesty, made to him before to the contrary, did rather hearken to the counsel of those Spaniards about him, who had conceived a secret hatred to this land and to its liberty, because they could not enjoy posts of honor and high employments here under the states as in Naples, Sicily, Milan and the Indies, and other countries under the king's dominion. Thus allured by the riches of the said provinces, wherewith many of them were well acquainted, the said counselors, we say, or the principal of them, frequently remonstrated to the king that it was more for his Majesty's reputation and grandeur to subdue the Low Countries a second time, and to make himself absolute (by which they mean to tyrannize at pleasure), than to govern according to the restrictions he had accepted, and at his admission sworn to observe. From that time forward the king of Spain, following these evil counselors, sought by all means possible to reduce this country (stripping them of their ancient privileges) to slavery, under the government of Spaniards having first, under the mask of religion, endeavored to settle new bishops in the largest and principal cities, endowing and incorporating them with the richest abbeys, assigning to each bishop nine canons to assist him as counselors, three whereof should superintend the inquisition.

By this incorporation the said bishops (who might be strangers as well as natives) would have had the first place and vote in the assembly of the states, and always the prince's creatures at devotion; and by the addition of the said canons he would have introduced the Spanish inquisition, which has been always as dreadful and detested in these provinces as the worst of slavery, as is well known, in so much that his imperial majesty, having once before proposed it to these states, and upon whose remonstrances did desist, and entirely gave it up, hereby giving proof of the great affection he had for his subjects. But, notwithstanding the many remonstrances made to the king both by the provinces and particular towns, in writing as well as by some principal lords by word of mouth; and, namely, by the Baron of Montigny and Earl of Egmont, who with the approbation of the Duchess of Parma, then governess of the Low Countries, by the advice of the council of state were sent several times to Spain upon this affair. And, although the king had by fair words given them grounds to hope that their request should be complied with, yet by his letters he ordered the contrary, soon after expressly commanding, upon pain of his displeasure, to admit the new bishops immediately, and put them in possession of their bishoprics and incorporated abbeys, to hold the court of the inquisition in the places where it had been before, to obey and follow the decrees and ordinances of the Council of Trent, which in many articles are destructive of the privileges of the country.

This being come to the knowledge of the people gave just occasion to great uneasiness and clamor among them, and lessened that good affection they had always borne toward the king and his predecessors. And, especially, seeing that he did not only seek to tyrannize over their persons and estates, but also over their consciences, for which they believed themselves accountable to God only. Upon this occasion the chief of the nobility in compassion to the poor people, in the year 1566, exhibited a certain remonstrance in form of a petition, humbly praying, in order to appease them and prevent public disturbances, that it would please his majesty (by showing that clemency due from a good prince to his people) to soften the said points, and especially with regard to the rigorous inquisition, and capital punishments for matters of religion. And to inform the king of this affair in a more solemn manner, and to represent to him how necessary it was for the peace and prosperity of the public to remove the aforesaid innovations, and moderate the severity of his declarations published concerning divine worship, the Marquis de Berghen, and the aforesaid Baron of Montigny had been sent, at the request of the said lady regent, council of state, and of the states-general as ambassadors to Spain, where the king, instead of giving them audience, and redress the grievances they had complained of (which for want of a timely remedy did always appear in their evil consequences among the common people), did, by the advice of Spanish council, declare all those who were concerned in preparing the said remonstrance to be rebels, and guilty of high treason, and to be punished with death, and confiscation of their estates; and, what is more (thinking himself well assured of reducing these countries under absolute tyranny by the army of the Duke of Alva), did soon after imprison and put to death the said lords the ambassadors, and confiscated their estates, contrary to the law of nations, which has been always religiously observed even among the most tyrannic and barbarous princes.

And, although the said disturbances, which in the year 1566 happened on the aforementioned occasion, were now appeased by the governess and her ministers, and many friends to liberty were either banished or subdued, in so much that the king had not any show of reason to use arms and violence, and further oppress this country, yet for these causes and reasons, long time before sought by the council of Spain (as appears by intercepted letters from the Spanish ambassador, Alana, then in France, writ to the Duchess of Parma), to annul all the privileges of this country, and govern it tyrannically at pleasure as in the Indies; and in their new conquests he has, at the instigation of the council of Spain, showing the little regard he had for his people, so contrary to the duty which a good prince owes to his subjects), sent the Duke of Alva with a powerful army to oppress this land, who for his inhuman cruelties is looked upon as one of its greatest enemies, accompanied with counselors too like himself. And, although he came in without the least opposition, and was received by the poor subjects with all marks of honor and clemency, which the king had often hypocritically promised in his letters, and that himself intended to come in person to give orders to their general satisfaction, having since the departure of the Duke of Alva equipped a fleet to carry him from Spain, and another in Zealand to come to meet him at the great expense of the country, the better to deceive his subjects, and allure them into the toils, nevertheless the said duke, immediately after his arrival (though a stranger, and no way related to the royal family), declared that he had a captain-general's commission, and soon after that of governor of these provinces, contrary to all its ancient customs and privileges; and, the more to manifest his designs, he immediately garrisoned the principal towns and castles, and caused fortresses and citadels to be built in the great cities to awe them into subjection, and very courteously sent for the chief nobility in the king's name, under pretense of taking their advice, and to employ them in the service of their country. And those who believed his letters were seized and carried out of Brabant, contrary to law, where they were imprisoned and prosecuted as criminals before him who had no right, nor could be a competent judge; and at last he, without hearing their defense at large, sentenced them to death, which was publicly and ignominiously executed.

The others, better acquainted with Spanish hypocrisy, residing in foreign countries, were declared outlawed, and had their estates confiscated, so that the poor subjects could make no use of their fortresses nor be assisted by their princes in defense of their liberty against the violence of the pope; besides a great number of other gentlemen and substantial citizens, some of whom were executed, and others banished that their estates might be confiscated, plaguing the other honest inhabitants, not only by the injuries done to their wives, children and estates by the Spanish soldiers lodged in their houses, as likewise by diverse contributions, which they were forced to pay toward building citadels and new fortifications of towns even to their own ruin, besides the taxes of the hundredth, twentieth, and tenth penny, to pay both the foreign and those raised in the country, to be employed against their fellow-citizens and against those who at the hazard of their lives defended their liberties. In order to impoverish the subjects, and to incapacitate them to hinder his design, and that he might with more ease execute the instructions received in Spain, to treat these countries as new conquests, he began to alter the course of justice after the Spanish mode, directly contrary to our privileges; and, imagining at last he had nothing more to fear, he endeavored by main force to settle a tax called the tenth penny on merchandise and manufacture, to the total ruin of these countries, the prosperity of which depends upon a flourishing trade, notwithstanding frequent remonstrances, not by a single province only, but by all of them united, which he had effected, had it not been for the Prince of Orange with diverse gentlemen and other inhabitants, who had followed this prince in his exile, most of whom were in his pay, and banished by the Duke of Alva with others who between him and the states of all the provinces, on the contrary sought, by all possible promises made to the colonels already at his devotion, to gain the German troops, who were then garrisoned in the principal fortresses and the cities, that by their assistance he might master them, as he had gained many of them already, and held them attached to his interest in order, by their assistance, to force those who would not join with him in making war against the Prince of Orange, and the provinces of Holland and Zealand, more cruel and bloody than any war before. But, as no disguises can long conceal our intentions, this project was discovered before it could be executed; and he, unable to perform his promises, and instead of that peace so much boasted of at his arrival a new war kindled, not yet extinguished.

All these considerations give us more than sufficient reason to renounce the King of Spain, and seek some other powerful and more gracious prince to take us under his protection; and, more especially, as these countries have been for these twenty years abandoned to disturbance and oppression by their king, during which time the inhabitants were not treated as subjects, but enemies, enslaved forcibly by their own governors.

Having also, after the decease of Don Juan, sufficiently declared by the Baron de Selles that he would not allow the pacification of Ghent, the which Don Juan had in his majesty's name sworn to maintain, but daily proposing new terms of agreement less advantageous. Notwithstanding these discouragements we used all possible means, by petitions in writing, and the good offices of the greatest princes in Christendom, to be reconciled to our king, having lastly maintained for a long time our deputies at the Congress of Cologne, hoping that the intercession of his imperial majesty and of the electors would procure an honorable and lasting peace, and some degree of liberty, particularly relating to religion (which chiefly concerns God and our own consciences), at last we found by experience that nothing would be obtained of the king by prayers and treaties, which latter he made use of to divide and weaken the provinces, that he might the easier execute his plan rigorously, by subduing them one by one, which afterwards plainly appeared by certain proclamations and proscriptions published by the king's orders, by virtue of which we and all officers of the United Provinces with all our friends are declared rebels and as such to have forfeited our lives and estates. Thus, by rendering us odious to all, he might interrupt our commerce, likewise reducing us to despair, offering a great sum to any that would assassinate the Prince of Orange.

So, having no hope of reconciliation, and finding no other remedy, we have, agreeable to the law of nature in our own defense, and for maintaining the rights, privileges, and liberties of our countrymen, wives, and children, and latest posterity from being enslaved by the Spaniards, been constrained to renounce allegiance to the King of Spain, and pursue such methods as appear to us most likely to secure our ancient liberties and privileges. Know all men by these presents that being reduced to the last extremity, as above mentioned, we have unanimously and deliberately declared, and do by these presents declare, that the King of Spain has forfeited, ipso jure, all hereditary right to the sovereignty of those countries, and are determined from henceforward not to acknowledge his sovereignty or jurisdiction, nor any act of his relating to the domains of the Low Countries, nor make use of his name as prince, nor suffer others to do it.

In consequence whereof we also declare all officers, judges, lords, gentlemen, vassals, and all other the inhabitants of this country of what condition or quality soever, to be henceforth discharged from all oaths and obligations whatsoever made to the King of Spain as sovereign of those countries. And whereas, upon the motives already mentioned, the greater part of the United Provinces have, by common consent of their members, submitted to the government and sovereignty of the illustrious Prince and Duke of Anjou, upon certain conditions stipulated with his highness, and whereas the most serene Archduke Matthias has resigned the government of these countries with our approbation, we command and order all justiciaries, officers, and all whom it may concern, not to make use of the name, titles, great or privy seal of the King of Spain from henceforward; but in lieu of them, as long as his highness the Duke of Anjou is absent upon urgent affairs relating to the welfare of these countries, having so agreed with his highness or otherwise, they shall provisionally use the name and title of the President and Council of the Province.

And, until such a president and counselors shall be nominated, assembled, and act in that capacity, they shall act in our name, except that in Holland and Zealand where they shall use the name of the Prince of Orange, and of the states of the said provinces until the aforesaid council shall legally sit, and then shall conform to the directions of that council agreeable to the contract made with his highness. And, instead of the king's seal aforesaid, they shall make use of our great seal, center-seal, and signet, in affairs relating to the public, according as the said council shall from time to time be authorized. And in affairs concerning the administration of justice, and transactions peculiar to each province, the provincial council and other councils of that country shall use respectively the name, title, and seal of the said province, where the case is to be tried, and no other, on pain of having all letters, documents, and despatches annulled. And, for the better and effectual performance hereof, we have ordered and commanded, and do hereby order and command, that all the seals of the King of Spain which are in these United Provinces shall immediately, upon the publication of these presents, be delivered to the estate of each province respectively, or to such persons as by the said estates shall be authorized and appointed, upon peril of discretionary punishment.

Moreover, we order and command that from henceforth no money coined shall be stamped with the name, title, or arms of the King of Spain in any of these United Provinces, but that all new gold and silver pieces, with their halfs and quarters, shall only bear such impressions as the states shall direct. We order likewise and command the president and other lords of the privy council, and all other chancellors, presidents, accountants-general, and to others in all the chambers of accounts respectively in these said countries, and likewise to all other judges and officers, as we hold them discharged from henceforth of their oath made to the King of Spain, pursuant to the tenor of their commission, that they shall take a new oath to the states of that country on whose jurisdiction they depend, or to commissaries appointed by them, to be true to us against the King of Spain and all his adherents, according to the formula of words prepared by the states-general for that purpose. And we shall give to the said counselors, justiciaries, and officers employed in these provinces, who have contracted in our name with his highness the Duke of Anjou, an act to continue them in their respective offices, instead of new commissions, a clause annulling the former provisionally until the arrival of his highness. Moreover, to all such counselors, accomptants, justiciaries, and officers in these Provinces, who have

not contracted with his highness, aforesaid, we shall grant new commissions under our hands and seals, unless any of the said officers are accused and convicted of having acted under their former commissions against the liberties and privileges of this country or of other the like maladministration.

We farther command of the president and members of the privy council, chancellor of the Duchy of Brabant, also the chancellor of the Duchy of Guelders, and county of Zutphen, to the president and members of the council of Holland, to the receivers of great officers of Beoostersheldt and Bewestersheldt in Zealand, to the president and council of Friese, and to the Escoulet of Mechelen, to the president and members of the council of Utrecht, and to all other justiciaries and officers whom it may concern, to the lieutenants all and every of them, to cause this our ordinance to be published and proclaimed throughout their respective jurisdictions, in the usual places appointed for that purpose, that none may plead ignorance. And to cause our said ordinance to be observed inviolably, punishing the offenders impartially and without delay; for so it is found expedient for the public good. And, for better maintaining all and every article hereof, we give to all and every one of you, by express command, full power and authority. In witness whereof we have hereunto set our hands and seals, dated in our assembly at the Hague, the six and twentieth day of July, 1581, indorsed by the orders of the states-general, and signed J. De Asseliers.

GLOSSARY

accomptants: an archaic term for accountants

Escoulet of Mechelen: governing body of this small region of southern Holland

ipso jure: automatically (literally: by the law itself)

justiciaries: officials who administer justice

king of Spain: Philip II

remonstrances: forceful, vehement protests

Zealand: misspelling of Zeeland, the Dutch province comprising a strip of coastline that borders on Belgium

Document Analysis

The Dutch Declaration of Independence begins with a lengthy exposition detailing the abuses of the Spanish king, Philip II, and the historical circumstances that led to the signing of the document. This is followed by the "declaration of independence" per se, indicating that the duke of Anjou agreed to function as the Netherlands' monarch, listing specific ways in which Spanish influence was to be eliminated, and outlining provisions for the governance of the provinces.

The first seven paragraphs of the declaration effectively constitute a preamble, although the section is not specifically identified as such. In the preamble, the Dutch rebels outline in detail the historical circumstances that led to their renunciation of Spanish rule. After a very brief introduction, the document opens with harsh criticism of Spain's King Philip. Using traditional Christian imagery, the document compares the king to a shepherd and the Netherlands to his flock. Paragraph 2 argues that a king is supposed to look to the welfare of his flock. In contrast, Philip has subjected the Dutch to oppression, slavery, and tyranny and has infringed upon "their ancient customs and privileges." Accordingly, the Dutch have decided to "disallow his authority" and choose another prince to rule over them. They have been forced to take this step because their "humble petitions and remonstrances" to the king have been ignored. The paragraph asserts that the provinces accept a ruler only "upon certain conditions, which he swears to maintain"; if the prince violates these conditions, "he is no longer sovereign."

In a small gesture of political goodwill, the third paragraph casts the blame for the current circumstances less on the king and more on his "evil counselors," who, according to the document, wanted to exploit the Netherlands for their own gain, as they had in other realms. Nevertheless, the king is culpable because he listened to those counselors and took steps to subdue the Netherlands. The paragraph makes reference to the Spanish Inquisition, which locally was part of a broad effort to subjugate the Dutch by imposing church authorities on them. The fourth paragraph continues this theme, referring to the Inquisition as being "as dreadful and detested in these provinces as the worst of slavery." The document then makes reference to various petitions for religious toleration submitted by the nobles to Margaret of Parma, Philip's appointed governor of the Netherlands. Margaret, born in 1522, was Charles V's illegitimate daughter and became the duchess of Parma, in Italy, when she married Ottavio Farnese, the duke of Parma, who happened to be Pope Paul III's grandson. (The duke was just thirteen at the time, while Margaret was just sixteen—and this was her second marriage.) Philip responded to the nobles' petitions with more oppression through the Inquisition, which was charged with enforcing the doctrines enunciated at the Council of Trent—a Catholic ecumenical council that ran from 1545 to 1563 and whose primary purpose was to answer and resist Protestant heresy.

The fifth paragraph makes reference to the events that took place in 1566 and the immediate aftermath. Yet another petition for religious toleration was submitted to Margaret and, through her, to the Spanish king. Envoys were dispatched to seek relief from the king, but the king, rather than receiving them to discuss the matter and find common ground, declared that anyone who had taken part in the effort to remonstrate with him was a rebel and an outlaw, subject to punishment by death and the confiscation of his estates. It was at this point that the king empowered the duke of Alba (spelled Alva in the document), who cruelly enforced the Inquisition and later boasted that he had put to death over eighteen thousand men. Alba's rule became prominent in the so-called Black Legend, a term coined in 1914 by the Spanish writer Julián Juderías to refer to the reputation of the Spanish during the sixteenth century as cruel, oppressive, tyrannical, and intolerant. Paragraph 6 continues to outline Alba's abuses. Because so many people had been executed, there would have been little reason to send an invading army into the Netherlands, yet such an army did invade under Alba's generalship with the purpose of ruling the country as tyrannically as Spain ruled the "Indies," or its colonies in the New World. The document states that throughout all this turmoil, the people of the Netherlands yet tried to find ways to submit themselves to the king and treat his representative with courtesy. In response, they were subjected to conquest, violence, and executions.

The seventh and final paragraph of the preamble lists numerous other abuses. Dutch nobles, including William of Orange and "diverse gentlemen," were forced to flee into exile, and their lands were then confiscated by the Spanish. Spanish soldiers were quartered in people's houses. Dutch citizens were forced to pay taxes for the construction of military posts; the "tenth penny" was a 10 percent tax levied on merchandise. German mercenaries were brought into the Netherlands, again with the purpose of waging war and denying the Dutch their traditional liberties.

Having catalogued the abuses of the Spanish king, the document states in paragraph 8 that the provinces have "more than sufficient reason to renounce the King of Spain, and seek some other powerful and more gracious prince to take us under his protection." In paragraph 9, still more abuses are listed. Reference is made to Don Juan of Austria, yet another illegitimate child of Charles V. Don Juan was a military commander who was sent to the Netherlands to fulfill the role of governor-general. Like Alba, he directed a number of campaigns that led to the sacking of various Dutch cities and the execution of large numbers of rebels, until his death in 1578. His mandate in the Netherlands was to disrupt and destroy the alliance created by the Pacification of Ghent of 1576. Again, the document emphasizes that efforts were made to secure peace, particularly through the Congress of Cologne, convened in 1579. Although it was mediated by Pope Gregory XIII, the congress was unsuccessful; again, Spain refused to back down, to the extent that a price was put on William of Orange's head.

Paragraph 10 constitutes the actual declaration of independence from Spanish rule. The authors, representing "the greater part of the United Provinces," proclaim that the Dutch are renouncing their allegiance to the Spanish king, who "has forfeited, ipso jure, all hereditary right to the sovereignty of those countries." None of the members of the States-General aligned with the document would thenceforth recognize the authority of the Spanish king. All inhabitants of the Low Countries, including civil servants, the nobility, and the common people, were relieved from their oaths of allegiance to Spain. The document then indicates that the duke of Anjou—François, the youngest son of King Henry II of France—agreed to accept sovereignty over the Netherlands, replacing the authority of Archduke Matthias, a member of the House of Habsburg who had succeeded the duke of Alba but had since resigned his position as governor of the Netherlands (to later become Holy Roman Emperor). The duke of Anjou never proved popular in the Netherlands, holding but limited power; he died in 1584.

The remaining paragraphs outline the specific political steps that the rebellious provinces were taking. Paragraph 11 establishes a council that was to govern the affairs of the Netherlands until the duke of Anjou could assume his responsibilities. Paragraph 12 outlines specific issues of governance, such as the coining of money, justice, and financial affairs. Paragraph 13 gives specifics relating to the establishment, membership, and powers of the president and governing council.

Essential Themes

The Dutch Declaration of Independence by no means brought peace to the United Provinces. Through the 1580s, Spain continued to send troops to the Netherlands. Yet Spanish forces were stretched thin; they continued to fight the Turks in the Mediterranean, and the Spanish Armada was defeated by the English navy in 1588—just as the northern provinces of the Netherlands were building up their own navy. Spain was virtually bankrupt, and the Spanish people, burdened with high taxes and war casualties, grew increasingly unwilling to back the war in the Netherlands. Finally, Spain capitulated and agreed to a suspension of hostilities at Antwerp in 1609, a treaty known as the Twelve Years' Truce. War erupted again, however, in 1621 over issues of religious toleration—of Protestants in the Catholic south and Catholics in the Protestant north—and sea trade routes. In 1639 the Dutch dealt the Spanish a decisive defeat in the last major campaign of the Eighty Years' War. The war officially ceased with the 1648 Treaty of Münster, which ended Spanish control over the Netherlands. This treaty was part of the larger realignment in Europe brought about by the Treaty of Westphalia, which also ended the Thirty Years' War, a complex war between Catholics and Protestants in the Holy Roman Empire that engulfed most of Europe.

Ultimately, the Dutch Revolt and the Dutch Declaration of Independence would have a far-reaching impact on Europe. The Dutch Revolt essentially challenged the divine right of kings to rule. As of 1648 the Netherlands was no longer a monarchy, a circumstance that sowed seeds of discontent with monarchical rule throughout the continent. The ultimate results of antiroyalist sentiment were the decline of the Spanish Empire, the English Civil Wars of the mid-seventeenth century, and the French Revolution of the late eighteenth century. It has also been argued that the Dutch Declaration of Independence, read by Thomas Jefferson, had a significant effect on the crafting of the American Declaration of Independence of 1776.

———Michael J. O'Neal, PhD

Bibliography and Further Reading

Arnade, Peter. *Beggars, Iconoclasts, and Civic Patriots: The Political Culture of the Dutch Revolt*. Ithaca, NY: Cornell University Press, 2008.

Darby, Graham, ed. *The Origins and Development of the Dutch Revolt*. London: Routledge, 2001.

Geyl, Pieter. *History of the Dutch-Speaking Peoples, 1555–1648*. London: Phoenix Press, 2001.

Israel, Jonathan I. *The Dutch Republic: Its Rise, Greatness and Fall, 1477–1806*. Oxford: Clarendon Press, 1998.

Koenigsberger, H. G. *Monarchies, States Generals and Parliaments: The Netherlands in the Fifteenth and Sixteenth Centuries*. Cambridge: Cambridge University Press, 2001.

Limm, Peter. *The Dutch Revolt, 1559–1648*. London: Longman, 1999.

Tracy, James D. *The Founding of the Dutch Republic: War, Finance, and Politics in Holland, 1572–1588*. Oxford, U.K. Oxford University Press, 2008.

Van Gelderen, Martin. *The Political Thought of the Dutch Revolt, 1555–1590*. Cambridge, U.K. Cambridge University Press, 2002.

Web Sites

Wolff, Barbara. "Was Declaration of Independence Inspired by Dutch?" *University of Wisconsin–Madison News* (June 29, 1998). http://www.news.wisc.edu/3049 [accessed February 26, 2017].

■ Japan's Closed Country Edict

Date: 1635
Author: Tokugawa Iemitsu
Genre: State directive

Summary Overview

In 1635 the Tokugawa Shogunate, Japan's military government at that time, issued a regulatory code known as the Closed Country Edict. This was one of several sets of laws issued during the 1630s that caused Japan to become largely closed off from the rest of the world for over two centuries. During the sixteenth and seventeenth centuries, European exploration had begun to radically alter both the shape of the world and relations between peoples from different parts of the globe. Accordingly, the fact that Japan's rulers took steps to halt those developments as they affected Japan was significant.

The Closed Country Edict of 1635 was one of several codes that led to Japan's status as a "closed country." Although historians have long debated the impetus behind the Closed Country Edict and its effectiveness and results, they are nonetheless in agreement that its impact was immense. Without it, Japan's early modern history might have developed in a dramatically different manner. Among the edict's effects were the following: (1) It limited Japan's relations with other nations and peoples from 1635 until the 1850s; (2) it forced the country as a whole to focus on internal developments during these centuries; (3) it added to the country's stability, since it was one of a number of measures that gave the Tokugawa increased control over the Japanese people; (4) it gave the government power to regulate all aspects of foreign relations, which it did to its advantage (and to the detriment of the great lords).

Defining Moment

In the autumn of 1543 a Portuguese ship arrived in southern Japan; it was the first Western vessel to reach that land. Lacking a central government at the time, Japan conducted no formal foreign relations. However, there was much international activity in the area, and the Japanese were part of it. A number of the *daimyo*, particularly those in southwestern Japan, were active in overseas trade. Many Japanese pirates (and pirates of other nationalities) plied the waters of Southeast Asia and East Asia, and there were a number of small Japanese colonies established by traders at ports throughout

the region. The arrival of the westerners saw the emergence of a robust intra-Asian trade network, in which goods and precious metals moved between China, Japan, South Asia, and Southeast Asia on boats of many nationalities. This trade would thrive for another century, with the Portuguese and later the Dutch acquiring most of their wealth in Asia by becoming major trade participants in the region, rather than by sending spices and other luxury items back to Europe.

Christian missionaries—members of the Society of Jesus, or Jesuits—first came to Japan in 1549, only six years after the first Portuguese ship arrived. The Jesuits were part of the Counter-Reformation, the Catholic Church's effort to regain Europe from the Protestants and spread the Gospel to the far reaches of the earth. They were learned and devout, dedicated to the cause they had joined. And they were supported in their efforts by the Portuguese traders, who gave them passage and donated funds to their work. Thus, as the Portuguese traders worked to enlarge their portion of trade with Japan, their Jesuit associates worked to convert the Japanese to Christianity.

Because the Portuguese brought wealth to the regions in which they stopped, the *daimyo* of southwestern Japan were anxious that the traders make use of their harbors. Some, like Omura Sumitada, who controlled Nagasaki, even donated lands and harbors, which, in effect, allowed the Portuguese to establish foreign enclaves within the country. Some *daimyo* also converted to Christianity and encouraged (occasionally with a heavy hand) their subjects to do likewise. The result was that by 1580 there may have been as many as one hundred thousand Japanese Christians and by 1600 as many as three hundred thousand, though what percentage of those were committed to the faith is difficult to say. Nonetheless, Christianity and the foreigners who brought it began to have an impact upon Japan.

Politically, Japan began to change during this time as well. In 1600, Tokugawa Ieyasu was the last of three great generals to unite Japan's warring factions around his leadership. Ieyasu's heirs followed in his footsteps for the next 250 years as the Tokugawa Shogunate. To bring lasting stability to Japan, the shogunate needed steady sources of revenue, the *daimyo* needed to be controlled, lawlessness needed to be brought to an end, and foreign affairs and foreign trade needed to be regulated. A major concern was the foreign trade activity of the southwestern *daimyo*, men with large domains and large armies; their ability to dominate foreign trade added to the threat they posed to the central regime. The fact that so many of the *daimyo* had converted to Christianity also warranted careful consideration.

Around the turn of the century other westerners arrived in Japanese ports: Spanish (both traders and Franciscan missionaries), Dutch, and English. The Franciscans and Jesuits were soon at odds, and there was evidence to suggest that many of the foreigners presented a threat to the peace—a threat that needed to be addressed. In 1614 Ieyasu finally issued an edict banning Christianity and expelling all missionaries. With the death of Ieyasu in 1616, persecution of Christians began in earnest, carried out under the direction of Tokugawa Hidetada and Tokugawa Iemitsu, the second and third Tokugawa shoguns. Particularly noteworthy was the "Great Martyrdom" of 1622, in which 132 Christians, both Jesuits and Japanese converts, were executed in Nagasaki.

One reason the Tokugawa shoguns were willing to undertake such harsh measures is that foreign trade was unlikely to be hurt, since the Dutch had begun to supplant the Iberian powers on the seas. And whereas the Portuguese and Spanish were zealous in their religion, the Dutch were not. Moreover, in order to solidify their position, the Dutch took steps to undermine their European rivals, playing off Tokugawa fears of Christianity.

From an economic standpoint, a key aspect of Tokugawa policy in these early decades was the regulation of the silk trade under *ito wappu*, or the "raw silk apportionment" system. Because the Portuguese had been able to gain restricted access to trade with China in the late sixteenth century, they were the sole purveyors of raw silk to Japan, the most highly prized and profitable of goods in this market. Stiff competition for silk among Japanese merchants led to steep prices and enormous profits for the Portuguese. In order to change this situation and regulate the import silk market, in 1604 the Tokugawa established the *ito wappu* system, which took control away from the Portuguese and gave it to powerful Japanese merchants from several of the large cities (at first Kyoto, Nagasaki, and Sakai, to which

were shortly added Osaka and Edo: thus the "five trading cities" referred to in article 12 of the edict). These merchants negotiated terms, set prices, and allocated goods both to their benefit and the benefit of the government. The Portuguese continued to make a profit from the silk trade, but it was much reduced.

This was the general context in which the Closed Country Edict was issued in 1635. Its issuance (as well as those edicts that preceded and followed it in the same decade) was not immediately precipitated by a particular incident or crisis, involving, for example, foreign affairs, Christianity, or international commerce—suggesting that these laws reflected a set of policies that had been many years in the making, here at last put into final form.

Author Biography

Just who the author or authors of this document were is hard to know. The edict was issued under the rule of the third shogun, Tokugawa Iemitsu (1604–1651). Although it is highly unlikely that he wrote it (common practice was to have learned advisers or high officials draft edicts), he no doubt had a large say in what was in it. Like the other early Tokugawa shoguns, Iemitsu was a personal ruler who took an active role in establishing policy and laying down laws. Iemitsu differed from his two predecessors, however, in that he was the first shogun to have no experience in battle. Probably for this reason he did much to establish the bureaucratic structure of the shogunate, shifting it away from the military organization that had characterized it under his father and grandfather. In this sense, the Closed Country Edict was appropriate to him. Accordingly, it is fair to say that the content reflected Iemitsu's concerns and ideas and that it had been worked out in conjunction with his advisers.

As for the five individuals who signed the edict of 1635—Hotta Masamori, Abe Tadaaki, Matsudaira Nobutsuna, Sakai Tadakatsu (1587–1662), and Doi Toshikatsu (1573–1644)—we must be careful not to ascribe authorship to them without appropriate caveats. In the first place, since most of the 1635 edict had already appeared in a decree of 1633, the authorship of the earlier document must also be considered. At that time, only two of these men (Sakai and Doi) were serving as senior councillors (the council being the governmental body that issued these edicts). Sakai and Doi may, in fact, have been the principal authors, as they were influential *daimyo* (wealthy landowners or businessmen) with close ties to the Tokugawa. Moreover, both were longtime appointees, having served as senior councillors for more than a decade. Sakai Tadakatsu had established his worth to the Tokugawa in 1600 when he fought with Tokugawa Ieyasu in the battle that brought Ieyasu to power. Doi Toshikatsu had even longer and closer connections to the Tokugawa, having become a powerful retainer to Tokugawa Hidetada in 1579. Both men were rewarded with large fiefs and eventually important positions in the shogunate.

HISTORICAL DOCUMENT

Items: for Nagasaki

1. Japanese ships are strictly forbidden to leave for foreign countries.

2. No Japanese is permitted to go abroad. If there is anyone who attempts to do so secretly, he must be executed. The ship so involved must be impounded and its owner arrested, and the matter must be reported to the higher authority.

3. If any Japanese returns from overseas after residing there, he must be put to death.

4. If there is any place where the teachings of padres (Christianity) is practiced, the two of you must order a thorough investigation.

5. Any informer revealing the whereabouts of the followers of padres (Christians) must be rewarded accordingly. If anyone reveals the whereabouts of a high ranking padre, he must be given one hundred pieces of silver. For those of lower ranks, depending on the deed, the reward must be set accordingly.

6. If a foreign ship has an objection [to the measures adopted] and it becomes necessary to report the matter to Edo, you may ask the Omura domain to provide ships to guard the foreign ship, as was done previously.

7. If there are any Southern Barbarians (Westerners) who propagate the teachings of padres, or otherwise commit crimes, they may be incarcerated in the prison maintained by the Omura domain, as was done previously.

8. All incoming ships must be carefully searched for the followers of padres.

9. No single trading city shall be permitted to purchase all the merchandise brought by foreign ships.

10. Samurai are not permitted to purchase any goods originating from foreign ships directly from Chinese merchants in Nagasaki.

11. After a list of merchandise brought by foreign ships is sent to Edo, as before you may order that commercial dealings may take place without waiting for a reply from Edo.

12. After settling the price, all white yarns (raw silk) brought by foreign ships shall be allocated to the five trading cities and other quarters as stipulated.

13. After settling the price of white yarns (raw silk), other merchandise [brought by foreign ships] may be traded freely between the [licensed] dealers. However, in view of the fact that Chinese ships are small and cannot bring large consignments, you may issue orders of sale at your discretion. Additionally, payment for goods purchased must be made within twenty days after the price is set.

14. The date of departure homeward of foreign ships shall not be later than the twentieth day of the ninth month. Any ships arriving in Japan later than usual shall depart within fifty days of their arrival. As to the departure of Chinese ships, you may use your discretion to order their departure after the departure of the Portuguese *galeota*.

15. The goods brought by foreign ships which remained unsold may not be deposited or accepted for deposit.

16. The arrival in Nagasaki of representatives of the five trading cities shall not be later than the fifth day of the seventh month. Anyone arriving later than that date shall lose the quota assigned to his city.

17. Ships arriving in Hirado must sell their raw silk at the price set in Nagasaki, and are not permitted to engage in business transactions until after the price is established in Nagasaki.

You are hereby required to act in accordance with the provisions set above. It is so ordered.

From:

Lord of Kaga, seal [Hotta Masamori]

Lord of Bungo, seal [Abe Tadaaki]

Lord of Izu, seal [Matsudaira Nobutsuna]
Lord of Sanuki, seal [Sakai Tadakatsu]
Lord of Oi, seal [Doi Toshikatsu]

To:
Sakakibara, Lord of Hida [Motonao]
Sengoku, Lord of Yamato [Hisataka]

GLOSSARY

fifth day of the seventh month: The Japanese dating system is not equivalent to Western dating. This date can be construed as sometime in the summer.

galeota: galleon

twentieth day of the ninth month: The Japanese dating system is not equivalent to Western dating. This date can be pinpointed to the autumn.

Document Analysis

The Closed Country Edict of 1635 consists of seventeen articles and can be roughly divided into three sections. Understanding these divisions provides a key to understanding the concerns and intent of the Tokugawa leadership that produced the document. Three articles address the question of Japanese travel and trade abroad, both of which are prohibited, five articles deal with Christian missionaries and their teachings, and the remaining nine articles are directed at foreign trade and the protocols and requirements associated with it.

It is important to note that the title given the document, Closed Country Edict, was a later addition ascribed by historians as they attempted to classify it. To call this document the Closed Country Edict suggests an interpretation that the authors may not have expected or desired, and this is something that must be kept in mind. The edict, in fact, had no title beyond the simple "Items: for Nagasaki," meaning a list of articles or instructions. Considered in that light, we might also ask which of the seventeen articles actually established policy that led to Japan's becoming a closed country.

The first three articles, those that address Japanese travel and trade abroad, clearly do establish policy leading to a closed country. By restricting both Japanese ships and individuals of Japanese birth from traveling to foreign countries, or returning from foreign countries after having resided there, the Tokugawa government made it clear that if foreign relations and trade were maintained, they would be conducted by foreigners *in their ships*, not by Japanese in Japanese vessels. In this

sense, the edict did indeed define one type of closed country, a country in which resident nationals must remain. Leaving for any purpose, long-term or short-term, was unacceptable. It also put an end to (or at least cut off irrevocably) the several small Japanese colonies in the Southeast Asian coastal region, which meant that Japan would remain limited in size and space to more traditional borders.

Beyond the first three articles, there is very little in this edict that specifies or decrees, implicitly or explicitly, that Japan is to be a closed country. Only article 14 hints at this; it stipulates that foreign vessels must depart for home by the autumn, unless they reached Japan late, in which case they must leave within fifty days of arrival. From this alone, it is difficult to know just when in a given year foreign vessels arrived in Japan, but it must have been during the first week or so of the seventh month (as the Japanese dated it), since article 16 states that Japanese merchants are to arrive in Nagasaki by the summer. Taken together, these two articles suggest that foreign trading vessels were probably allowed in Japan for approximately two months each summer, but the edict says nothing further about foreign relations or foreign residents except where Christianity is at issue.

The five articles that deal with Christianity are not the harsh, strongly prohibitive declarations about the religion or threats against missionaries and believers that one might expect. Article 4, for example, requires the two Nagasaki commissioners (to whom the Closed Country Edict is addressed) to carry out investigations into suspected gatherings of believers, while article 5 notes that those who inform on Christians should be given rewards, and article 6 suggests that precedence be followed in having the Omura domain guard any foreign ship that has an objection to Tokugawa policy (usually related to Christianity, the reason the article is placed here). Finally, article 7 concerns the protocol surrounding the incarceration of Christians and instructs the commissioners to have suspects placed in the prison of the Omura domain. In short, these articles deal with secondary or administrative matters. Prohibitions against Christianity, missionaries, and Japanese Christian believers had all been explicitly stated in earlier edicts, beginning with that of Ieyasu in 1613. The authors of the 1635 edict saw no need to reiterate those prohibitions.

The remaining nine articles deal with foreign trade. The detailed stipulations suggest that much here is new or at least had not already been made explicit in edict form, and that was in fact the case. Officials could turn back to earlier laws and edicts to chart policies that regulated and prohibited Christianity, but that was not true of the *ito wappu* system, which had been laid out in rudimentary form in 1604 but lacked specific prohibitions and regulations until the five edicts of the 1630s.

Closer examination of these nine articles reveals that three are directed at Japanese merchants, three at foreign merchants (those who brought the goods in their ships), and three at both groups. Articles 9 and 16 define acceptable behavior for Japanese merchants, ensuring that no merchants from one city monopolize trade, and require Japanese merchants to arrive in Nagasaki by a certain day (in the summer) in order to be able to purchase goods. As the Tokugawa stipulate here and elsewhere, things are to be done with order. Those who failed to do so would inevitably lose their privileges. Article 10 is likewise directed at Japanese merchants, though it is more difficult to understand. It prohibits samurai from purchasing goods from Chinese vessels, suggesting that at least some warriors in the new and peaceful world of Tokugawa Japan were engaged in commerce, an activity the Tokugawa shoguns did not look highly upon. The reason was that trade and commercial activities were regarded as unbefitting the warrior (that is, gentlemanly) class, whose work was to be noble and uplifting.

The three articles directed at foreign merchants are article 14, which sets the date of departure for foreign ships; article 15, which prohibits the deposit of unsold goods in Nagasaki; and article 17, which requires traders on foreign ships arriving in Hirado (another port in southwestern Japan) to sell their silk at the price established in Nagasaki. At this point in time, given the extent of state control over the sale of raw silk, none of these articles was particularly onerous; they merely ensured that no irregularities would occur in the system as already established. Also, as suggested in article 17, foreign trade in Japan was becoming limited in location; no longer could traders on a foreign vessel arrive at any harbor that they wished and there carry out trade with local inhabitants.

The articles that are relevant to both foreign and Japanese merchants are articles 11–13; they all deal with the protocols of foreign trade regarding silk and other commodities. Article 11 confirms an earlier practice regarding permission to engage in buying and selling, while article 12 reiterates the privileged position of the "five trading cities" in the silk market. Article 13 states that non-silk merchandise may be traded after the price on raw silk is set. It also provides two caveats: It gives the local commissioners discretion to regulate the quantity of goods brought for sale in Chinese ships, since the vessels are small and can carry only limited loads, and it requires purchasers to pay for their goods within twenty days of the date when the price for the item is set.

Essential Themes

Without the Closed Country Edict (and accompanying policies such as the ban on Christianity), early modern Japan might have developed in radically different ways than it did. For example, Christianity might have become an influential religious and social force, altering Japan's culture in fundamental ways. Likewise, relations with foreign peoples might have increased in extent and depth, with Japanese travelers journeying frequently to other parts of Asia, the Near East, and even Europe. Another possibility is that an open Japan would have been less internally stable than it was. Those were all possibilities, but they did not occur. Instead, Japan was closed (if imperfectly), and it followed a distinct path largely unshaped by foreign intercourse for well over two hundred years.

Although the Tokugawa leadership may have considered its policy of prohibiting foreign travel by Japanese vessels and individuals merely a matter of security, there is no question that the impact of these articles was considerable. The measures forced the Japanese to turn inward, to consider first themselves and their world rather than the broader world beyond their borders. As a result, the rich and unique early-modern culture of Tokugawa Japan—with its kabuki theater, ukiyo-e woodblock prints, and distinctive crafts—developed within a closed country, a land in which foreign ideas and habits had limited influence.

Although the Closed Country Edict was effective at "keeping Japanese in," it was less effective at "keeping foreigners out," primarily because that was not its intent. Nonetheless, there was constriction over time, some of it brought about by decree and some the result of external factors. Important factors included the state's decision to ban entry to all Europeans of the Catholic faith; the English decision early in the seventeenth century to abandon Japan as unprofitable, which left only the Dutch on the European side and the Chinese among the Asians; and a Tokugawa decree of 1639, which restricted the Dutch and Chinese to the harbor of Nagasaki, where small numbers of them resided in foreign enclaves and carried out trade annually when their ships arrived from abroad. The only other foreign intercourse the shogunate allowed was trade between the *daimyo* of Tsushima and Korea (which faced each other across the straits of Japan) and trade between the *daimyo* of Satsuma and the Kingdom of the Ryukyus (islands to the south of Japan, the most prominent being Okinawa). Despite these annual contacts, Japan was indeed a land that saw and housed very few foreigners during the Tokugawa era. Native Japanese could not help but feel that the rest of the world was far away and its peoples very different.

Because Japan became largely closed off to outsiders, by the late eighteenth century the idea of *sakoku*, or "Japan as a closed country," had become accepted policy, despite the fact that no formal declaration of closure had ever been made. This was a case in which a practice had become doctrine over time, a tradition shaped by years of acceptance.

For the Tokugawa, the Closed Country Edict was one of a handful of critical policies that gave the shoguns firm control over the country. Peace reigned for 250 years, during which time Japan experienced unprece-

dented population growth and commercial activity. The Tokugawa Period was not without problems, some of them severe, but it was also a remarkable period, a time when Japan moved from having been a medieval society to being an early-modern one, and at least some of the credit for that must go to the influence of the Closed Country Edict.

Finally, it is important to note that Japan's closed country policy led to confrontations with the West in the early and middle nineteenth century. These confrontations nearly resulted in Japan's subjugation, as it stubbornly held to a practice that was shortsighted and impractical, at least by the 1850s. Nonetheless, Japan emerged independent and largely unscathed, though the Tokugawa government and the old military order collapsed in the process.

———*Lee Butler, PhD*

Bibliography and Further Reading

Articles

Tashiro, Kazui. "Foreign Relations during the Edo Period: Sakoku Reexamined." *Journal of Japanese Studies* 8, no. 2 (1982): 283–306.

Toby, Ronald. "Reopening the Question of Sakoku: Diplomacy in the Legitimation of the Tokugawa Bakufu." *Journal of Japanese Studies* 3, no. 2 (1977): 323–364.

Books

Boxer, Charles. *The Christian Century in Japan, 1549–1650*. Berkeley: University of California Press, 1951.

Elison, George. *Deus Destroyed: The Image of Christianity in Early Modern Japan*. Cambridge: Harvard University Asia Center, 1988.

Hall, John Whitney. *The Cambridge History of Japan*. Volume 4: *Early Modern Japan*. New York: Cambridge University Press, 1991.

Sansom, George. *A History of Japan, 1615–1867*. Stanford, Calif. Stanford University Press, 1963.

Toby, Ronald. *State and Diplomacy in Early Modern Japan: Asia in the Development of the Tokugawa Bakufu*. Princeton, N.J. Princeton University Press, 1984.

■ Treaty of Westphalia

Date: 1648
Author: Various
Genre: International peace agreement

Summary Overview

The Treaty of Westphalia was actually a pair of treaties negotiated in the Westphalian towns of Münster and Osnabrück and concluded on October 24, 1648, ending the Thirty Years' War (1618–1648). The Thirty Years' War, a period of violence and destruction unmatched in Europe until the twentieth century, had brought about a perspectival change in the way states dealt with one another. The medieval notion of universality, whereby rulers acted in the best interests of the church, had given way to the brutal emergence of raison d'état, or the view that state interests trump all other concerns. The treaty was the European community's first attempt to reign in national aggression through fostering a balance of power and collective peace.

The Treaty of Westphalia set the year 1648 as the ultimate diplomatic and religious break between the medieval and early modern periods. The rupture, however, was neither simple nor accomplished by mutual consent, as demonstrated by the attitudes of two leaders of the time. The Habsburg Archduke Ferdinand, who in 1619 became Holy Roman Emperor, had declared in 1596 that he would sooner die than make any concessions to the sectarians on the topic of religion. His contemporary, Cardinal Richelieu of France, wrote: "The state has no immortality; its salvation is now or never." In twenty-first century terms, the former would be derided as a fanatic, while the latter would be considered a political realist.

Defining Moment

In the sixteenth century the Protestant Reformation had split much of Europe into opposing camps defined by religion. The rulers of Spain, France, and the Holy Roman Empire had initially pledged their support to the papacy against the then-heretical position of Martin Luther and his followers. Within a short time, however, many rulers—particularly German electors and princes from the northern states and principalities of the Holy Roman Empire as well as the kings of Sweden and Denmark—had decided to embrace Lutheranism, whether they were motivated by religious conviction, humanist inclinations, antipapal sentiment, or territorial greed.

The situation was most problematic for the Holy Roman Empire, since its Habsburg emperor, Charles V, was also King Charles I of staunchly Catholic Spain. In the early seventeenth century, the Holy Roman Empire encompassed modern-day Germany, Austria, the Czech Republic, Slovenia, Luxembourg and parts of Poland, Slovakia, eastern France, and northern Italy. It also included the United Provinces, or the modern-day Netherlands; the Spanish Netherlands, or present-day Belgium; and the Swiss Confederation, or what was to become Switzerland. Charles V undertook a series of wars to root out Protestantism. Since the empire never enjoyed the political unity of other European states, the outcome of these conflicts was compromise. The most significant treaty resulting from Charles V's wars was the Peace of Augsburg (1555), in which the empire was effectively divided between Lutheran and Catholic principalities. The Peace of Augsburg established the principle of *cuius regio, eius religio*, which meant that the prince or elector of a certain territory would determine the religion for all of its inhabitants. This peace agreement, however, was more of a truce and demonstrated the weakness of the empire. Additionally, by 1555, the range of Protestant confessions had come to include not only Lutherans but also groups not permitted under the Peace of Augsburg: Calvinists, Anabaptists, and Unitarians.

Charles V's abdication shortly after the Peace of Augsburg temporarily settled religious controversy in the Holy Roman Empire. Other Habsburgs, though, saw themselves as defenders of Catholicism against the growing threats of both the Protestants and the Ottoman Turks. The tension between Protestants and Catholics in Europe, therefore, ought to be seen from the perspective of a wider threat to the Catholic faith, which was under attack on many fronts. In 1564 the imperial crown fell to Charles V's nephew, Maximilian II, who only added to the cauldron by preferring Lutheran to Catholic preachers and protecting Protestants from persecution. His son and successor, Rudolf II, believed that moderation and toleration served to undermine the unity of the empire.

In addition, by the early seventeenth century, the economic prosperity once enjoyed by many German states had been undermined. The bulk of economic trade no longer flowed from the Mediterranean across the Alps and up through the German principalities but instead was being routed directly to northern Europe by sea. This was largely because England and the Netherlands, rather than Spain and Portugal, had come to dominate the Atlantic and many trade routes. Major German banking families were in steady decline. By 1600, the various currencies used within the empire were becoming unstable. As the economic situation worsened, the population continued to increase, which amplified the potential for unrest among the peasantry.

As is often typical during periods of economic instability, many tenaciously clung to religious beliefs. This served to rekindle strife over religious divisions. What formerly had been more of an academic debate between Catholics and Protestants was quickly becoming more heated. Protestant princes in the Holy Roman Empire formed the Protestant Union in 1608. In response, Catholic leaders formed the Catholic League the following year. Both had outside support; the French king, Henry IV, offered support to the Protestant Union, while the Spanish Habsburgs stood ready to help fellow Catholics.

In 1617 the Habsburg Archduke Ferdinand, a fervent Catholic, was made king of Bohemia, a mostly Protestant principality. On May 23, 1618, in Prague, the capital of Bohemia, a group of Protestant nobles, angry at the growing influence of Catholicism—and particularly the appointment of Archduke Ferdinand to the Bohemian throne—tossed two representatives of Holy Roman Emperor Matthias and their secretary out of a window. The three survived, but the action was an affront not only to the empire but also Ferdinand and the Catholic League. Ferdinand immediately sent two armies into Bohemia. In response, the Calvinist elector of the Palatinate, Frederick V, organized a counterforce. By the end of November 1618, Protestant forces had captured Pilsen, the Catholic stronghold in Bohemia. The following spring, Matthias was dead and Ferdinand had become his presumptive heir as Holy Roman Emperor. The Bohemian Diet declared that Ferdinand was deposed as king and offered the Bohemian crown to Frederick V, who accepted. There followed two years of war in central Europe, in which Ferdinand defended his claims to the thrones of the Empire and Bohemia, defeating Frederick at the Battle of White Mountain in

November 1620. The Bohemian Protestants were defeated, and their land was confiscated. Ferdinand, who had become Holy Roman Emperor Ferdinand II by this time, was restored as Bohemian king, and he proceeded to sell former Protestant estates to Catholics, thereby creating a new Catholic nobility in Bohemia. The initial salvos of the Thirty Years' War in Bohemia were over, but many yearned for vengeance.

In the second phase of the conflict, the mantle of Protestant resistance was taken up by King Christian IV of Denmark. He intervened not so much to assist his fellow Protestants but primarily to acquire territory in northern Germany. Christian received nominal support from England, France, and the Netherlands, then known as the United Provinces, although none of these lands provided significant financial or military support. Unfortunately for Christian, the Holy Roman Empire found a brilliant general in Albrecht von Wallenstein, a Bohemian nobleman who sought to increase his own power by supporting Ferdinand II. In 1625 Wallenstein was commissioned to supply twenty thousand troops for the emperor's cause. By mid-1629, imperial forces had gained the upper hand, forcing Christian to renounce any claims to northern Germany. Ferdinand then confiscated the lands of those who had supported the Danish king and gave land to Wallenstein, including the North German duchy of Mecklenburg. Ferdinand also issued the Edict of Restitution in 1629, which prohibited Calvinist worship but, more important, restored all Catholic property that had been secularized since 1552, much of which had been bought and paid for. This edict convinced even Catholic princes that Ferdinand had overstretched his authority. Many had benefited economically from the decentralized structure of the empire, but Ferdinand's centralization of power, enforced by Wallenstein, was perceived as a threat.

Like Christian IV of Denmark, the Swedish king, Gustavus II Adolph, was primarily concerned about his state's political independence and economic development. For these reasons, in 1630 he positioned Sweden as the rescuer of Protestantism in the northern German states and a check against the power of the Habsburgs under Ferdinand II. While Gustavus, a Lutheran, prohibited forced conversions and tolerated Catholicism, the forces of the empire were brutal. For example, in 1631 an imperial army under Johann Tserclaes (also known as Count Tilly) massacred twenty thousand in the Protestant archbishop city of Magdeburg and even destroyed its cathedral. After the first major Protestant victory in this phase of the war at Breitenfeld in Saxony in September 1631, many of Ferdinand's allies began entering the Swedish alliance. Gustavus moved into central and southern Germany, devastating the countryside as he marched, but he was mortally wounded in battle in 1632. Wallenstein was assassinated two years later, but thanks to the imperial army's reinforcement with Spanish troops, Sweden's military advance was halted at the South German town of Nördlingen in September 1634. In May 1635, Ferdinand II signed the Peace of Prague with the Saxons; this treaty also suspended the Edict of Restitution and prohibited German princes from forming military alliances with foreign powers.

The final phase of the Thirty Years' War came as a result of France's fear of being surrounded by powerful Habsburgs in both the Holy Roman Empire and Spain. The first minister of France, the Catholic Cardinal Richelieu, supported Lutheran Sweden and garnered the support of Pope Urban VIII, who feared that Habsburg power might threaten his holdings in Italy. Thus, leadership of the Protestant forces passed from Sweden to France, and the war became a wider European conflict. Since the entry of France meant the infusion of forces superior to those of the emperor, many Protestant leaders began to defect from their alliance with Ferdinand III, Ferdinand II's son who had become Holy Roman Emperor upon his father's death in 1637. At the Battle of Breitenfeld outside Vienna in 1642, the imperial army suffered a loss of ten thousand troops at the hands of the Swedes. In 1643 the French won a decisive victory at the Battle of Rocroi over the Spanish on the border of the Spanish Netherlands (modern-day Belgium). By 1646, Ferdinand III had sent representatives to Westphalia to seek peace negotiations.

The war had devastated most of central Europe. The six armies—of the Holy Roman Empire, Denmark, Sweden, Bohemia, Spain, and France—were made up primarily of mercenaries who had no attachment to the places where the fighting occurred; they would fight for any faith for a fee. These armies did not respect the right of surrender; they treated civilians as legitimate targets and made rape and torture general instruments of war. As armies traveled, so did disease. Typhus, dysentery, bubonic plague, and syphilis added to the demographic catastrophe. The war, the flight of refugees, and the ravages of disease brought about a drastic population decline. By the war's end in Germany and Austria, the population had fallen by nearly one-third,

from an estimated 21 million to 13.5 million. Starvation was also a consequence of the long war. Farmers saw no reason to plant crops, since there was no assurance they would still be alive to harvest them. As at Versailles at the end of the First World War, diplomats gathered in Westphalia at the end of 1644 in the hope of creating a lasting peace.

Author Biography

There is no solitary author of the treaty. However, since the treaty's original language was French and considering France's advantageous position at the war's end, the French delegation perhaps had the most influence. It was headed by Henri II d'Orléans, the duke of Longueville, who, as a French prince, had previously served in the French military in both Italy and the Holy Roman Empire. Usually cast as a rebel of sorts, he used his role at Westphalia not only for the benefit of France but also to secure the independence of the Swiss Confederation. He was joined by the French diplomat Abel Servien, marquis de Sablé, and Claude de Mesmes, the count d'Avaux, a diplomat and public administrator.

While Sweden was in a rather advantageous position at war's end, the Swedish attempt to secure one of the electoral college votes within the empire was thwarted by the stronger influence of France at the conference. The Swedish representatives were Johann Adler Salvius and Count Bengt Gabrielsson Oxenstierna. The Holy Roman Empire's chief delegate was Count Maximilian von Trauttmansdorff. Trauttmansdorff had a long tenure in the service of the Habsburgs, securing both the Bohemian and the Hungarian crowns for the future Ferdinand II and, later, serving as the most influential minister to Ferdinand III.

The Spanish delegation was headed by Gaspar de Bracamonte y Guzmán. Many delegations were sent from the German principalities of the Holy Roman Empire. The representative of the Catholic Church, Fabio Chigi (later Pope Alexander VII), and the Venetian envoy, Alvise Contarini (who became the doge, or duke, of Venice) served as mediators. Many of the imperial states of the Holy Roman Empire also sent delegations. The most important was Brandenburg, which was represented by Count Johann von Sayn-Wittgenstein, the most prominent of the empire's Protestant representatives. He was able to increase the holdings of Brandenburg by obtaining eastern Pomerania as well as other smaller territories.

HISTORICAL DOCUMENT

In the name of the most holy and individual Trinity: Be it known to all, and every one whom it may concern, or to whom in any manner it may belong, That for many Years past, Discords and Civil Divisions being stir'd up in the Roman Empire, which increas'd to such a degree, that not only all Germany, but also the neighbouring Kingdoms, and France particularly, have been involv'd in the Disorders of a long and cruel War: ... It has at last happen'd, by the effect of Divine Goodness, seconded by the Endeavours of the most Serene Republick of Venice, who in this sad time, when all Christendom is imbroil'd, has not ceas'd to contribute its Counsels for the publick Welfare and Tranquillity; so that on the side, and the other, they have form'd Thoughts of an universal Peace.

...

I. That there shall be a Christian and Universal Peace, and a perpetual, true, and sincere Amity, between his Sacred Imperial Majesty, and his most Christian Majesty; as also, between all and each of the Allies. ... That this Peace and Amity be observ'd and cultivated with such a Sincerity and Zeal, that each Party shall endeavour to procure the Benefit, Honour and Advantage of the other; that thus on all sides they may see this Peace and Friendship in the Roman Empire, and the Kingdom of France flourish, by entertaining a good and faithful Neighbourhood.

II. That there shall be on the one side and the other a perpetual Oblivion, Amnesty, or Pardon of all that has been committed since the beginning of these Troubles ...

VI. According to this foundation of reciprocal Amity, and a general Amnesty, all and every one of the Electors of the sacred Roman Empire, the Princes and States (therein comprehending the Nobility, which depend immediately on the Empire) their Vassals, Subjects, Citizens, Inhabitants (to whom on the account of the Bohemian or German Troubles or Alliances, contracted here and there, might have been done by the one Party or the other, any Prejudice or Damage in any manner, or under what pretence soever, as well in their Lord-ships, their fiefs, Underfiefs, Allodations, as in their Dignitys, Immunitys, Rights and Privileges) shall be fully re-establish'd on the one side and the other, in the Ecclesiastick or Laick State, which they enjoy'd, or could lawfully enjoy, notwithstanding any Alterations, which have been made in the mean time to the contrary. ...

VII. It shall also be free for the Elector of Treves, as well in the Quality of Bishop of Spires as Bishop of Worms, to sue before competent Judges for the Rights he pretends to certain Ecclesiastical Lands, situated in the Territorys of the Lower Palatinate, if so be those Princes make not a friendly Agreement among themselves. ...

XXVIII. That those of the Confession of Augsburg, and particularly the Inhabitants of Oppenheim, shall be put in possession again of their Churches, and Ecclesiastical Estates, as they were in the Year 1624. as also that all others of the said Confession of Augsburg, who shall demand it, shall have the free Exercise of their Religion, as well in publick Churches at the appointed Hours, as in private in their own Houses, or in others chosen for this purpose by their Ministers, or by those of their Neighbours, preaching the Word of God. ...

XXXIX. That the Debts either by Purchase, Sale, Revenues, or by what other name they may be call'd, if they have been violently extorted by one of the Partys in War, and if the Debtors alledge and offer to prove there has been a real Payment, they shall be no more prosecuted, before these Exceptions be first adjusted. That the Debtors shall be oblig'd to produce their Exceptions within the term of two years after the Publication of the Peace, upon pain of being afterwards condemn'd to perpetual Silence.

XL. That Processes which have been hitherto enter'd on this Account, together with the Transactions and Promises made for the Restitution of Debts, shall be look'd upon as void; and yet the Sums of Money, which during the War have been exacted bona fide, and with a good intent, by way of Contributions, to prevent greater Evils by the Contributors, are not comprehended herein.

XLI. That Sentences pronounc'd during the War about Matters purely Secular, if the Defect in the

Proceedings be not fully manifest, or cannot be immediately demonstrated, shall not be esteem'd wholly void; but that the Effect shall be suspended until the Acts of Justice (if one of the Partys demand the space of six months after the Publication of the Peace, for the reviewing of his Process) be review'd and weigh'd in a proper Court, and according to the ordinary or extraordinary Forms us'd in the Empire: to the end that the former Judgments may be confirm'd, amended, or quite eras'd, in case of Nullity.

XLII. In the like manner, if any Royal, or particular Fiefs, have not been renew'd since the Year 1618. nor Homage paid to whom it belongs; the same shall bring no prejudice, and the Investiture shall be renew'd the day the Peace shall be concluded.

XLIII. Finally, That all and each of the Officers, as well Military Men as Counsellors and Gownmen, and Ecclesiasticks of what degree they may be, who have serv'd the one or other Party among the Allies, or among their Adherents, let it be in the Gown, or with the Sword, from the highest to the lowest, without any distinction or exception ... shall be restor'd by all Partys in the State of Life, Honour, Renown, Liberty of Conscience, Rights and Privileges, which they enjoy'd before the abovesaid Disorders; that no prejudice shall be done to their Effects and Persons, that no Action or accusation shall be enter'd against them; and that further, no Punishment be inflicted on them, or they to bear any damage under what pretence soever: And all this shall have its full effect in respect to those who are not Subjects or Vassals of his Imperial Majesty, or of the House of Austria.

XLIV. But for those who are Subjects and Hereditary Vassals of the Emperor, and of the House of Austria, they shall really have the benefit of the Amnesty, as for their Persons, Life, Reputation, Honours: and they may return with Safety to their former Country; but they shall be oblig'd to conform, and submit themselves to the Laws of the Realms, or particular Provinces they shall belong to.

XLV. As to their Estates that have been lost by Confiscation or otherways, before they took the part of the Crown of France, or of Swedeland, notwithstanding the Plenipotentiarys of Swedeland have made long instances they may be also restor'd. Nevertheless his Imperial Majesty being to receive Law

from none, and the Imperialists sticking close thereto, it has not been thought convenient by the States of the Empire, that for such a Subject the War should be continu'd: And that thus those who have lost their Effects as aforesaid, cannot recover them to the prejudice of their last Masters and Possessors. But the Estates, which have been taken away by reason of Arms taken for France or Swedeland, against the Emperor and the House of Austria, they shall be restor'd in the State they are found, and that without any Compensation for Profit or Damage.

XLIX. And since for the greater Tranquillity of the Empire, in its general Assemblys of Peace, a certain Agreement has been made between the Emperor, Princes and States of the Empire, which has been inserted in the Instrument and Treaty of Peace, ... touching the Differences about Ecclesiastical Lands, and the Liberty of the Exercise of Religion; it has been found expedient to confirm, and ratify it by this present Treaty, in the same manner as the abovesaid Agreement has been made with the said Crown of Swedeland; also with those call'd the Reformed, in the same manner, as if the words of the abovesaid Instrument were reported here verbatim. ...

LVI. ... That if within the term of nine Months, the whole Sum be not paid to Madam the Landgravine, not only Cuesfeldt and Newhaus shall remain in her Hands till the full Payment, but also for the remainder, she shall be paid Interest at Five per Cent. and the Treasurers and Collectors of the Bayliwicks appertaining to the abovesaid Archbishopricks, Bishopricks and Abby, bordering on the Principality of Hesse, ... they shall yearly pay the Interest of the remaining Sum notwithstanding the Prohibitions of their Masters. If the Treasurers and Collectors delay the Payment, or alienate the Revenues, Madam the Landgravine shall have liberty to constrain them to pay, by all sorts of means, always saving the Right of the Lord Proprietor of the Territory. ...

LVIII. ... The Fortifications and Ramparts, rais'd during the Possession of the Places, shall be destroy'd and demolish'd as much as possible, without exposing the Towns, Borroughs, Castles and Fortresses, to Invasions and Robberys. ...

LXIII. And as His Imperial Majesty, upon Complaints made in the name of the City of Basle, and of all Switzerland, in the presence of their Plenipotentiarys deputed to the present Assembly, touching some Procedures and Executions proceeding from the Imperial Chamber against the said City, and the other united Cantons of the Swiss Country, and their Citizens and Subjects having demanded the Advice of the States of the Empire and their Council; these have, by a Decree of the 14th of May of the last Year, declared the said City of Basle, and the other Swiss-Cantons, to be as it were in possession of their full Liberty and Exemption of the Empire; so that they are no ways subject to the Judicatures, or Judgments of the Empire, and it was thought convenient to insert the same in this Treaty of Peace, and confirm it, and thereby to make void and annul all such Procedures and Arrests given on this Account in what form soever.

LXIV. And to prevent for the future any Differences arising in the Politick State, all and every one of the Electors, Princes and States of the Roman Empire, are so establish'd and confirm'd in their antient Rights, Prerogatives, Libertys, Privileges, free exercise of Territorial Right, as well Ecclesiastick, as Politick Lordships, Regales, by virtue of this present Transaction, that they never can or ought to be molested therein by any whomsoever upon any manner of pretence.

LXV. They shall enjoy without contradiction, the Right of Suffrage in all Deliberations touching the Affairs of the Empire; but above all, when the Business in hand shall be the making or interpreting of Laws, the declaring of Wars, imposing of Taxes, levying or quartering of Soldiers, erecting new Fortifications in the Territorys of the States, or reinforcing the old Garisons; as also when a Peace of Alliance is to be concluded, and treated about, or the like, none of these, or the like things shall be acted for the future, without the Suffrage and Consent of the Free Assembly of all the States of the Empire: Above all, it shall be free perpetually to each of the States of the Empire, to make Alliances with Strangers for their Preservation and Safety; provided, nevertheless, such Alliances be not against the Emperor, and the Empire, nor against the Publick Peace, and this Treaty, and without prejudice to the Oath by which every one is bound to the Emperor and the Empire.

LXVI. That the Diets of the Empire shall be held within six Months after the Ratification of the Peace; and after that time as often as the Publick Utility, or Necessity requires. That in the first Diet the Defects of precedent Assemblys be chiefly remedy'd; and that then also be treated and settled by common Consent of the States, the Form and Election of the Kings of the Romans, by a Form, and certain Imperial Resolution; the Manner and Order which is to be observ'd for declaring one or more States, to be within the Territorys of the Empire, besides the Manner otherways describ'd in the Constitutions of the Empire; that they consider also of re-establishing the Circles, the renewing the Matricular-Book, the re-establishing suppress'd States, the moderating and lessening the Collects of the Empire, Reformation of Justice and Policy, the taxing of Fees in the Chamber of Justice, the Due and requisite instructing of ordinary Deputys for the Advantage of the Publick, the true Office of Directors in the Colleges of the Empire, and such other Business as could not be here expedited.

LXVII. That as well as general as particular Diets, the free Towns, and other States of the Empire, shall have decisive Votes; they shall, without molestation, keep their Regales, Customs, annual Revenues, Libertys, Privileges to confiscate, to raise Taxes, and other Rights, lawfully obtain'd from the Emperor and Empire, or enjoy'd long before these Commotions, with a full Jurisdiction within the inclosure of their Walls, and their Territorys: making void at the same time, annulling and for the future prohibiting all Things, which by Reprisals, Arrests, stopping of Passages, and other prejudicial Acts, either during the War, under what pretext soever they have been done and attempted hitherto by private Authority, or may hereafter without any preceding formality of Right be enterpris'd. As for the rest, all laudable Customs of the sacred Roman Empire, the fundamental Constitutions and Laws, shall for the future be strictly observ'd, all the Confusions which time of War have, or could introduce, being remov'd and laid aside. ...

LXX. The Rights and Privileges of Territorys, water'd by Rivers or otherways, as Customs granted by the Emperor, with the Consent of the Electors, and among others, to the Count of Oldenburg on the Viserg, and introduc'd by a long Usage, shall remain in their Vigour and Execution. There shall be a full Liberty of Commerce, a secure Passage by Sea and Land: and after this manner all and every one of the Vassals, Subjects, Inhabitants and Servants of the Allys, on the one side and the other, shall have full power to go and come, to trade and return back, by Virtue of this present Article, after the same manner as was allowed before the Troubles of Germany; the Magistrates, on the one side and on the other, shall be oblig'd to protect and defend them against all sorts of Oppressions, equally with their own Subjects, without prejudice to the other Articles of this Convention, and the particular laws and Rights of each place. And that the said Peace and Amity between the Emperor and the Most Christian King, may be the more corroborated, and the publick Safety provided for, it has been agreed with the Consent, Advice and Will of the Electors, Princes and States of the Empire, for the Benefit of Peace. ...

LXXII. That Monsieur Francis, Duke of Lorain, shall be restor'd to the possession of the Bishoprick of Verdun, as being the lawful Bishop thereof; and shall be left in the peaceable Administration of this Bishoprick and its Abbys (saving the Right of the King and of particular Persons) and shall enjoy his Patrimonial Estates, and his other Rights, wherever they may be situated (and as far as they do not contradict the present Resignation) his Privileges, Revenues and Incomes; having previously taken the Oath of Fidelity to the King, and provided he undertakes nothing against the Good of the State and the Service of his Majesty.

LXXIII. In the second place, the Emperor and Empire resign and transfer to the most Christian King, and his Successors, the Right of direct Lordship and Sovereignty, and all that has belong'd, or might hitherto belong to him, or the sacred Roman Empire, upon Pignerol. ...

LXXVI. Item, All the Vassals, Subjects, People, Towns, Boroughs, Castles, Houses, Fortresses, Woods, Coppices, Gold or Silver Mines, Minerals, Rivers, Brooks, Pastures; and in a word, all the Rights, Regales and Appurtenances, without any reserve, shall belong to the most Christian King, and shall be for ever incorporated with the Kingdom France, with all manner of Jurisdiction and Sovereignty, without any contradiction from the Emperor, the Empire, House of Austria, or any other: so that no Emperor, or any Prince of the House of Austria, shall, or ever ought to usurp, nor so much as pretend any Right and Power over the said Countrys, as well on this, as the other side the Rhine.

LXXVII. The most Christian King shall, nevertheless, be oblig'd to preserve in all and every one of these Countrys the Catholick Religion, as maintain'd under the Princes of Austria, and to abolish all Innovations crept in during the War. ...

LXXXI. For the greater Validity of the said Cessions and Alienations, the Emperor and Empire, by virtue of this present Treaty, abolish all and every one of the Decrees, Constitutions, Statutes and Customs of their Predecessors, Emperors of the sacred Roman Empire, tho they have been confirm'd by Oath, or shall be confirm'd for the future; particularly this Article of the Imperial Capitulation, by which all or any Alienation of the Appurtenances and Rights of the Empire is prohibited: and by the same means they exclude for ever all Exceptions hereunto, on what Right and Titles soever they may be grounded.

LXXXII. Further it has been agreed, That besides the Ratification promis'd hereafter in the next Diet by the Emperor and the States of the Empire, they shall ratify anew the Alienations of the said Lordships and Rights: insomuch, that if it shou'd be agreed in the Imperial Capitulation, or if there shou'd be a Proposal made for the future, in the Diet, to recover the Lands and Rights of the Empire, the abovenam'd things shall not be comprehended therein, as having been legally transfer'd to another's Dominion, with the common Consent of the States, for the benefit of the publick Tranquillity; for which reason it has been found expedient the said Seigniorys shou'd be ras'd out of the Matricular-Book of the Empire. ...

LXXXIX. ... No King of France can or ought ever to pretend to or usurp any Right or Power over the said Countrys situated on this and the other side the Rhine: ...

XCII. That the most Christian King shall be bound to leave not only the Bishops of Strasburg and Basle, with the City of Strasburg, but also the other States or Orders, ... so that he cannot pretend any Royal Superiority over them, but shall rest contented with the Rights which appertain'd to the House of Austria, and which by this present Treaty of Pacification, are yielded to the Crown of France. In such a manner, nevertheless, that by the present Declaration, nothing is intended that shall derogate from the Sovereign Dominion already hereabove agreed to. ...

XCIX. Who hereafter, with the Authority and Consent of their Imperial and most Christian Majestys, by virtue of this solemn Treaty of Peace, shall have no Action for this account against the Duke of Savoy, or his Heirs and Successors. ...

CIV. As soon as the Treaty of Peace shall be sign'd and seal'd by the Plenipotentiarys and Ambassadors, all Hostilitys shall cease, and all Partys shall study immediately to put in execution what has been agreed to; ... That when it shall be known that the signing has been made in these two Places, divers Couriers shall presently be sent to the Generals of the Armys, to acquaint them that the Peace is concluded, and take care that the Generals chuse a Day, on which shall be made on all sides a Cessation of Arms and Hostilitys for the publishing of the Peace in the Army; and that command be given to all and each of the chief Officers Military and Civil, and to the Governors of Fortresses, to abstain for the future from all Acts of Hostility: and if it happen that any thing be attempted, or actually innovated after the said Publication, the same shall be forthwith repair'd and restor'd to its former State.

CV. The Plenipotentiarys on all sides shall agree among themselves, between the Conclusion and the Ratification of the Peace, upon the Ways, Time, and Securitys which are to be taken for the Restitution of Places, and for the Disbanding of Troops; of that both Partys may be assur'd, that all things agreed to shall be sincerely accomplish'd.

CVI. The Emperor above all things shall publish an Edict thro'out the Empire, and strictly enjoin all, who by these Articles of Pacification are oblig'd to restore or do any thing else, to obey it promptly and without tergi-versation, between the signing and the ratifying of this present Treaty; commanding as well the Directors as Governors of the Militia of the Circles, to hasten and finish the Restitution to be made to every one, in conformity to those Conventions, when the same are demanded. ...

CVII. If any of those who are to have something restor'd to them, suppose that the Emperor's Commissarys are necessary to be present at the Execution of some Restitution (which is left to their Choice) they shall have them. In which case, that the effect of the things agreed on may be the less hinder'd, it shall be permitted as well to those who restore, as to those to whom Restitution is to be made, to nominate two or three Commissarys immediately after the signing of the Peace, of whom his Imperial Majesty shall chuse two, one of each Religion, and one of each Party, whom he shall injoin to accomplish without delay all that which ought to be done by virtue of this present Treaty. ...

CVIII. Finally, That all and every one either States, Commonaltys, or private Men, either Ecclesiastical or Secular, who by virtue of this Transaction and its general Articles, or by the express and special Disposition of any of them, are oblig'd to restore, transfer, give, do, or execute any thing, shall be bound forthwith after the Publication of the Emperor's Edicts, and after Notification given, to restore, transfer, give, do, or execute the same, without any Delay or Exception, or evading Clause either general or particular, contain'd in the precedent Amnesty, and without any Exception and Fraud as to what they are oblig'd unto. ...

CXII. That the very Places, Citys, Towns, Boroughs, Villages, Castles, Fortresses and Forts ... shall be restor'd without delay to their former and lawful Possessors and Lords, whether they be mediately or immediately States of the Empire, Ecclesiastical or Secular, comprehending therein also the free Nobility of the Empire: and they shall be left at their own free disposal, either according to Right and Custom, or according to the Force this present Treaty. ...

CXIII. And that this Restitution of possess'd Places, as well by his Imperial Majesty as the most Christian King, and the Allys and Adherents of the one and the other Party, shall be reciprocally and bona fide executed.

CXIV. That the Records, Writings and Documents, and other Moveables, be also restor'd. ...

CXV. That the Inhabitants of each Place shall be oblig'd, when the Soldiers and Garisons draw out, to furnish them without Money the necessary Waggons, Horses, Boats and Provisions, to carry off all things to the appointed Places in the Empire. ...

CXVII. That it shall not for the future, or at present, prove to the damage and prejudice of any Town, that has been taken and kept by the one or other Party; but that all and every one of them, with their Citizens and Inhabitants, shall enjoy as well the general Benefit of the Amnesty, as the rest of this Pacification. And for the Remainder of their Rights and Privileges, Ecclesiastical and Secular, which they enjoy'd before these Troubles, they shall be maintain'd therein; save, nevertheless the Rights of Sovereignty, and what depends thereon, for the Lords to whom they belong.

CXVIII. Finally, that the Troops and Armys of all those who are making War in the Empire, shall be disbanded and discharg'd; only each Party shall send to and keep up as many Men in his own Dominion, as he shall judge necessary for his Security.

CXIX. The Ambassadors and Plenipotentiarys of the Emperor, of the King, and the States of the Empire, promise respectively and the one to the other, to cause the Emperor, the most Christian King, the Electors of the Sacred Roman Empire, the Princes and States, to agree and ratify the Peace which has been concluded in this manner, and by general Consent; and so infallibly to order it, that the solemn Acts of Ratification be presented at Munster, and mutually and in good form exchang'd in the term of eight weeks, to reckon from the day of signing. ...

CXXI. That it never shall be alledg'd, allow'd, or admitted, that any Canonical or Civil Law, any general or particular Decrees of Councils, any Privileges, any Indulgences, any Edicts, any Commissions, Inhibitions, Mandates, Decrees, Rescripts, Suspensions of Law, Judgments pronounc'd at any time, Adjudications, Capitulations of the Emperor, and other Rules and Exceptions of Religious Orders, past or future Protestations, Contradictions, Appeals, Investitures, Transactions, Oaths, Renunciations, Contracts, and much less the Edict of 1629 or the Transaction of Prague, with its Appendixes, or the Concordates with the Popes, or the Interims of the Year 1548. or any other politick Statutes, or Ecclesiastical Decrees, Dispensations, Absolutions, or any other Exceptions, under what pretence or colour they can be invented; shall take place against this Convention, or any of its Clauses and Articles neither shall any inhibitory or other Processes or Commissions be ever allow'd to the Plaintiff or Defendant.

CXXXII. That he who by his Assistance or Counsel shall contravene this Transaction or Publick Peace, or shall oppose its Execution and the abovesaid Restitution, or who shall have endeavour'd, after the Restitution has been lawfully made, and without exceeding the manner agreed on before, without a lawful Cognizance of the Cause, and without the ordinary Course of Justice, to molest those that have been restor'd, whether Ecclesiasticks or Laymen; he shall incur the Punishment of being an Infringer of the publick Peace, and Sentence given against him according to the Constitutions of the Empire, so that the Restitution and Reparation may have its full effect.

CXXIII. That nevertheless the concluded Peace shall remain in force, and all Partys in this Transaction shall be oblig'd to defend and protect all and every Article of this Peace against any one, without distinction of Religion; and if it happens any point shall be violated, the Offended shall before all things exhort the Offender not to come to any Hostility, submitting the Cause to a friendly Composition, or the ordinary Proceedings of Justice. ...

CXXVI. And as often as any would march Troops thro' the other Territorys, this Passage shall be done at the charge of him whom the Troops belong to, and that without burdening or doing any harm or damage to those whole Countrys they march thro'. In a word, all that the Imperial Constitutions determine and ordain touching the Preservation of the publick Peace, shall be strictly observ'd. ...

CXXVIII. In Testimony of all and each of these things, and for their greater Validity, the Ambassadors of their Imperial and most Christian Majestys, and the Deputys, in the name of all the Electors, Princes, and States of the Empire, sent particularly for this end (by virtue of what has been concluded the 13th of October, in the Year hereafter mention'd, and has been deliver'd. …

And that on condition that by the Subscription of the abovesaid Ambassadors and Deputys, all and every one of the other States who shall abstain from signing and ratifying the present Treaty, shall be no less oblig'd to maintain and observe what is contain'd in this present Treaty of Pacification, than if they had subscrib'd and ratify'd it; and no Protestation or Contradiction of the Council of Direction in the Roman Empire shall be valid, or receiv'd in respect to the Subscription and said Deputys have made.

Done, pass'd and concluded at Munster in Westphalia, the 24th Day of October, 1648.

GLOSSARY

Allodations: lands or estates held outright, with no ties of feudal obligation

Cessions and Alienations: territories ceded or otherwise conveyed to other parties

Diets of the Empire: qualified legislative bodies of the participating states

his most Christian Majesty: Louis XIV, king of France

his Sacred Imperial Majesty: Ferdinand III, ruler of the Holy Roman Empire, and eldest son of Emperor Ferdinand II

Imperial Capitulation: approval of the treaty, a statement saying that the emperor will have to capitulate to the dictates of Westphalia

Laick: secular

renewing the Matricular-Book: renewal of imperial allegiance within the Holy Roman Empire

Moveables: personal property

regales: royal prerogatives

Document Analysis

The Treaty of Westphalia is named for the northern German region where the negotiations were conducted. Representatives did not gather at one location, however. At the town of Münster, the delegates from France and the Holy Roman Empire met under the mediation of the papacy and the republic of Venice. A mere fifty kilometers away in Osnabrück, the delegates of France, the Holy Roman Empire, and Sweden gathered with Christian IV of Denmark as mediator. This segregation of powers was necessary, since Sweden refused to be mediated by a representative of the papacy and the papal representative refused to sit in the same room with a "heretic."

The Congress of Westphalia opened in December 1644 and was concluded with much fanfare on October 24, 1648. The comprehensive treaty's introduction declares a "universal Peace," which, according to article I, is to be founded not on a common religion or dictated by religious authority but is to occur "between all and each of the Allies … that each Party shall endeavour to procure the Benefit, Honour and Advantage of the other." In other words, abiding by the principles of the treaty was intended to benefit all parties. In order to halt the cycle of violence, articles II and VI provided for amnesty and pardon for all offenses committed since the beginning of the war while avoiding the rhetoric typical of an imposed peace.

The language of the treaty was new to diplomatic discourse in that it is conciliatory toward different religious sects. This was clearly an effort to remove religious difference as a cause of conflict. To this end, article XLV proclaims "the Liberty of the Exercise of Religion" throughout the Holy Roman Empire, thus strengthening the position of the Protestants. Article

XXVIII specifically granted religious freedom to Lutherans (called "those of the Confession of Augsburg" in the document) and restored ecclesiastical property to them based on their holdings as of 1624. Articles XXII, XXV, and XXVI offered an olive branch to Charles I Louis of the Lower Palatinate, who was the son of Frederick V, the Calvinist elector whom the Protestants had selected as Bohemian king in 1619 in their attempted rebellion against Ferdinand II.

The monetary cost of the war had been significant, and the treaty attempted to anticipate and address economic concerns. Article XXXIX gave all parties a period of two years to show claim, after which debts were to be considered settled. Since economic conditions had worsened throughout the Holy Roman Empire during the war, the signatories wanted to ensure that indemnities either would be paid quickly or would be forgiven to avoid future strife and acts of vengeance. For similar reasons, article XLI upheld secular judicial pronouncements issued during the war.

The latter half of the treaty dealt, in particular, with the Holy Roman Emperor and his subjects. Article XLIV repeated the earlier proclamation of general amnesty, and article XLV provided for the return of some royal land but without compensation for damages. Herein the overriding influence of France and Sweden in drafting the document is evident; while the emperor and Austria, whom the delegates wanted to conciliate, could regain lost property, these provisions implied that others within the empire who lost property might not have it returned. Article XLIX restated the principle regarding religious liberty and the return of church land. It refers to an agreement among those powers that were meeting at Münster and extended it to apply to the Swedish delegation at Osnabrück.

Specific regions and allies are mentioned in the treaty. For example, article LVI stipulated the repayment of a sum to "Madam the Landgravine," whose family had been a long-term supporter of the Protestant cause in the state of Hesse. Article XCIX absolved the House of Savoy, which assisted in the French cause, of any retribution on the part of the empire. Article LVIII stipulated that fortresses of war throughout the empire were to be dismantled as long as they did not leave an area lacking in security. Article LXXXII called upon each prince of the empire to respect the traditions and rights of other states, participate in the empire's assemblies, and regard the authority of the Holy Roman Emperor.

Territorial realignments were recognized in the treaty. For example, the United Provinces of the Nether-lands were pronounced independent of Spain. Article LXXVI recognized France's right to the towns of Metz, Toul, and Verdun on the western border of the empire, as well as most of Alsace, although article LXXXIX required France to renounce further claims to territory in the vicinity of the Rhine. Article LXXVII stipulates that the French king is obligated to "preserve" Catholicism in areas where it is dominant. Contrary to the Edict of Restitution, only territory that the empire had conquered by 1624 was to be returned to the Catholic Church. French territorial gains were small, but the treaty assured that France, while being obliged to respect religious traditions, could achieve its security goals by maintaining a buffer between itself and the Holy Roman Empire.

Articles CIV through CXIX provided for the implementation of peace. Specifically, articles CIV and CV spelled out the time and method for cessation of hostilities, CVI the publication of the peace, CVII through CXIV the restoration or transfer of property, CXV the responsibilities of local inhabitants toward departing soldiers, and CXVIII the demobilization of troops and the maintenance of those necessary for security.

With respect to the treaties and covenants established during the course of the war, such as the Edict of Restitution and Peace of Prague, article CXXI made clear that the Treaty of Westphalia superseded all other provisions, treaties, and agreements. Article CXXXII warned anyone who might infringe on what the treaty termed "Publick Peace." While no specific punishment was given, Article CXXIII enjoined all signatories to "defend and protect all and every Article of this Peace." This provision gave France and Sweden the ability to frustrate the Habsburgs. France and Sweden thus became the guarantors of the new imperial constitution with the obligation to protect the rights of princes against the Holy Roman Emperor. They became the counterbalance to ensure that future conflict over or within the empire would be quelled.

Essential Themes

The significance of the Treaty of Westphalia is often underestimated. It would serve as a model for resolving future European conflicts. Six armies had participated in the conflict. Those six states as well as many princes of the empire participated in a gathering that brought together more than one hundred delegations. For the first time, a congress with representatives from all parties involved in a multinational conflict not only addressed international disputes but also agreed to abide by the resulting settlement.

France and Sweden gained the most from the treaty. Ultimately, France would replace Spain as the dominant power on the continent (and the two countries would not officially cease hostilities until 1659). Sweden emerged as the major power in the Baltic, a position it would enjoy for a half-century until military defeat by Czar Peter I of Russia. The Habsburgs lost the most. The Austrian branch, the traditional rulers of the Holy Roman Empire, agreed to the independence of the Swiss Confederation. In addition, German princes were not only recognized as independent but also were given the right to establish Lutheranism, Catholicism, or Calvinism within their territories. The treaty also required the Spanish Habsburgs to recognize the independence of a Dutch Republic, which included two provinces taken from the Spanish Netherlands (present-day Belgium).

These territorial and political realignments were significant, and many would last well into the nineteenth century. The treaty also determined religious distribution within the empire by confirming the Peace of Augsburg, which had first established the principle that the prince's religion would determine the religion of his people and expanded it to include Calvinism. As a result, the northern parts of the empire remained largely Lutheran and the area along the Rhine Calvinist, and Catholicism prevailed in the south.

With the catastrophic decline in agriculture, many farmers lacked the capital to remain independent and were forced to become day laborers. In parts of central Europe, especially areas east of the Elbe River, the loss of peasant holdings resulted in the consolidation of large estates and the expansion of serfdom.

The treaty also brought about a formal break between German principalities and territories controlled by the Austrian Habsburgs. Princely power demonstrated during the war and guaranteed by the treaty revealed how little most German states and principalities had to offer the Habsburgs. After 1648, the Austrian Habsburgs increasingly focused attention on their own territories, both inside and outside the empire, and expanded farther into southeastern Europe. This absence of Habsburg influence coupled with the religious and territorial provisions of the treaty enabled a formerly weak principality, such as Brandenburg-Prussia, to begin the process of state building, especially under the Calvinist Frederick William who was both the elector of Brandenburg and the duke of Prussia.

Finally, the Treaty of Westphalia signaled the loss of power of the papacy. Since late antiquity, the church had battled for supremacy over European princes and kings, in particular, the Holy Roman Emperor. Even though the Holy Roman Empire had fought on behalf of the Catholic religion in the Thirty Years' War, its loss and the emergence of Richelieu's version of statecraft left little room for the Catholic Church as a power player after 1648.

In the broadest sense, the Treaty of Westphalia may be considered the culmination of the European medieval experience. The significance of this ambitious document is often neglected, since it cannot be read simply as the treaty that ended the Thirty Years' War. It addressed social, political, economic, and religious trends, as well as other issues arising from domestic and international perspectives, in order to create a collective and enduring peace.

———*Christopher Ohan*

Bibliography and Further Reading

Asch, Robert G. *The Thirty Years War: The Holy Roman Empire and Europe, 1618-1648*. New York: St. Martin's Press, 1997.

Bireley, Robert. *Ferdinand II, Counter-Reformation Emperor, 1578-1637*. New York: Cambridge University Press, 2014.

Ingrao, Charles W. *The Habsburg Monarchy, 1618–1815*. New York: Cambridge University Press, 1994.

Wedgwood, C.V. *The Thirty Years War*. New York: New York Review Books, 2005.

Wilson, Peter H. *The Thirty Years War: Europe's Tragedy*. Cambridge, MA: Belknap Press, 2011.

Web Sites

"The Thirty Years' War." *New Advent: Catholic Encyclopedia* http://www.newadvent.org/ cathen/14648b.htm [accessed February 21, 2017].

Cavendish, Richard. "The Treaty of Westphalia." *History Today* 48 Issue 10 (November 1998) http://www.historytoday.com/richard-cavendish/treaty-westphalia [accessed February 21, 2017].

P.C. "The Economist Explains—What Happened in the Thirty Years War?" *The Economist* (17 January 2016) http://www.economist.com/blogs/economist-explains/2016/01/economist-explains-5 [accessed February 21, 2017].

Great Muscovite Law Code

Date: 1649
Author: Czar Alexis I
Genre: Law code

Summary Overview

The Ulozhenie, or Great Muscovite Law Code, was Muscovite Russia's main legal code, issued by Alexis I Mikhaylovich ("Alexei Mikhailovich" in the document) in 1649. Its full title, Sobornoe Ulozhenie, literally means "Collected Code of Laws." It replaced the Sudebniki (law codes) of Ivan III Vasilyevich (1497) and Ivan IV Vasilyevich (1550). These codes had promoted state centralization and the rise of state and legal bureaucracies. The Ulozhenie—a complex document running well over two hundred pages in modern printings—continued this process. It is primarily known, however, for its passages on serfdom, which take up only a few pages. In this, the code represented the legal climax of a long historical process whereby Russia's once-free peasants (about 90 percent of the total population) had been reduced to a form of serfdom often compared to slavery. The new code terminated the few remaining rights of movement left to serfs from earlier legislation; ended time limitations on the return of runaways; eroded the differences between serf and slave classes (the two categories remained legally distinct until 1723, however); and pronounced the resulting system hereditary, permanent, and irrevocable. More generally, the Ulozhenie was a striking statement of political authority and social hierarchy, covering topics that included the relation of various social classes to the state and questions of authority within families.

Defining Moment

The Ulozhenie was an effort to bring order to a corpus of law that, owing to the issuance of numerous edicts over the previous two centuries, had become confusing, contradictory, and ineffective. A specific trigger was a major riot that shook Moscow in 1648. The riot was in response to an unpopular salt tax and perceived corruption and abuses among state officials. More generally, the Ulozhenie was intended as a means of enforcing authority, order, and social hierarchy in a state that had suffered numerous major upheavals in the preceding decades, including foreign invasions, civil war, peasant uprisings, "false" czars, and mass migrations, many of them connected with the difficult interregnum of 1598

to 1613 known as the Time of Troubles. This traumatic period followed the death in 1598 of Fyodor I Ivanovich, son of Ivan IV (known as Ivan the Terrible). Fyodor was the last member of the seven-century-old Rurik Dynasty of Russian rulers. The Time of Troubles almost led to the complete collapse of Russia and the establishment of Polish Catholic rule in Moscow. Ultimately, however, it instead spawned a broad-based national movement for the regeneration of Muscovite and Orthodox Christian Russia as well as a deeply ingrained sense of the need for strong, central rule and clear lines of authority. The Ulozhenie addressed all these concerns.

In the early summer of 1648, Alexis consulted with Patriarch Joseph of Moscow, church officials, boyars (nobles), and other prominent advisers. Then, on July 16, he appointed a five-person commission headed by the talented and prominent state servant Nikita Odoevsky and ordered them to compile a draft law. This was done by October 3. Odoevsky, a favorite also of the previous czar, was a minor noble who had already carved out successful careers for himself as a diplomat and military commander. Before being recruited for work on the Ulozhenie, he had proved himself in legal affairs, running the chancelleries of Kazan and Siberia. His commission drew on a wide body of existing legislation, including past legal cases, earlier Russian secular law codes, Orthodox ecclesiastical law, and Byzantine and Lithuanian codes. The draft was then amended and expanded by an "Assembly of the Land," comprising men from every rank of society (except the peasant masses) and two noblemen from each town. All these men were required to read and sign the finished product. The Ulozhenie was essentially a compilation and codification of existing laws, rather than an original composition. Nonetheless it is considered one of the great achievements of Russian literature prior to the nineteenth century.

Author Biography

The Ulozhenie was established at the order of Czar Alexis I. Alexis was born in March 1629 and took the throne at the age of sixteen. His father and royal predecessor, Mikhail, was the founder of the Romanov

Dynasty. Most historians consider Alexis to have been a pious and fairly effective ruler. Conservative rather than reactionary, he was cautiously favorable to reforms that appeared likely to strengthen or preserve tradition and authority, such as a new and more comprehensive law code. He was also distinguished by an ability to choose wise and talented advisers and to give them sufficient freedom of action. This latter trait is also clearly exemplified by the Ulozhenie, which Alexis authorized but did not compose. He died in 1676.

HISTORICAL DOCUMENT

Chapter 10.—The Judicial Process. In It Are 287 Articles.

1. The judicial process of the Sovereign, Tsar, and Grand Prince of all Russia Aleksei Mikhailovich shall be directed by boyars, and *okol'nichie*, and counselors, and state secretaries, and various chancellery officials, and judges. All justice shall be meted out to all people of the Muscovite state, from the highest to the lowest rank, according to the law. Moreover, arriving foreigners and various people from elsewhere who are in the Muscovite state shall be tried by that same judicial process and rendered justice by the sovereign's decree according to the law. No one on his own initiative shall out of friendship or out of enmity add anything to or remove anything from judicial records. No one shall favor a friend nor wreak vengeance on an enemy in any matter. No one shall favor anyone in any matter for any reason. All of the sovereign's cases shall be processed without diffidence to the powerful. Deliver the wronged from the hand of the unjust.

2. Disputed cases which for any reason cannot be resolved in the chancelleries shall be transferred from the chancelleries in a report to the Sovereign, Tsar, and Grand Prince of all Russia Aleksei Mikhailovich and to his royal boyars, and *okol'nichie*, and counselors. The boyars, and *okol'nichie*, and counselors shall sit in the Palace [of Facets], and by the sovereign's decree shall handle the sovereign's various cases all together.

3. If a judge is an enemy of the plaintiff and a friend, or relative, of the defendant, and the plaintiff proceeds to petition the sovereign about that prior to the trial, [saying] that he is unable to bring a suit before that judge; or if a defendant proceeds to petition prior to a trial that the judge is a friend, or relative, or his plaintiff, and that he is unable to defend himself before that judge: that judge against whom there is such a petition shall not try that plaintiff and defendant. Another judge, whom the sovereign will appoint, shall try them.

4. But if a plaintiff or defendant proceeds to petition against a judge after a trial on grounds that the latter is a relative [of the opposing litigant], or was hostile: do not believe that petition, and do not transfer the case from chancellery to chancellery so that there will be no excessive delay for the plaintiff and defendant in this matter.

5. If a boyar, or *okol'nichii*, or counselor, or state secretary, or any other judge, in response to bribes of the plaintiff or defendant, or out of friendship or enmity convicts an innocent party and exculpates the guilty party, and that is established conclusively: collect from such judges the plaintiff's claim threefold, and give it to the plaintiff. Collect the legal fees, and the judicial transaction fee, and the legal tenth for the sovereign from them as well. For that offense a boyar, and *okol'nichii*, and counselor shall be deprived of his rank. If a judge not of counselor rank commits such an injustice: inflict on those people a beating with the knout in the market place, and henceforth they shall not try judicial cases [i.e., they shall be deprived of their offices].

6. In the provincial towns, apply that same decree to governors, and state secretaries, and various chancellery officials for such injustices. ...

Chapter 11.—The Judicial Process for Peasants. In It Are 34 Articles.

1. Concerning the sovereign's peasants and landless peasants of court villages and rural taxpaying districts who, having fled from the sovereign's court villages and from the rural taxpaying districts, are now living under the patriarch, or under the metropolitans, and under the archbishops, and the bishop [sic]; or under monasteries; or under boyars, or under *okol'nichie*, and under counselors, and under chamberlains, and under *stol'niki*, and under

striapchie, and under Moscow *dvoriane*, and under state secretaries, and under *zhil'tsy*, and under provincial *dvoriane* and *deti boiarskie*, and under foreigners, and under all hereditary estate owners and service landholders; and in the cadastral books, which books the census takers submitted to the Service Land Chancellery and to other chancelleries after the Moscow fire of the past year 1626, those fugitive peasants or their fathers were registered [as living] under the sovereign: having hunted down those fugitive peasants and landless peasants of the sovereign, cart them [back] to the sovereign's court villages and to the rural taxpaying districts, to their old allotments as [registered in] the cadastral books, with their wives, and with their children, and with all their movable peasant property, without any statute of limitations.

2. Similarly, if hereditary estate owners and service landholders proceed to petition the sovereign about their fugitive peasants and about landless peasants; and they testify that their peasants and landless peasants, having fled from them, are living in the sovereign's court villages, and in rural taxpaying districts, or as townsmen in the urban taxpaying districts, or as musketeers, or as cossacks, or as gunners, or as any other type of servicemen in the trans-Moscow or in the frontier towns; or under the patriarch, or under the metropolitans, or under the archbishops and bishops; or under monasteries; or under boyars, and under *okol'nichie*, and under counselors, and under chamberlains, and under *stol'niki*, and under *striapchie*, and under Moscow *dvoriane*, and under state secretaries, and under *zhil'tsy*, and under provincial *dvoriane* and *deti boiarskie*, and under foreigners, and under any hereditary estate owners and service landholders: return such peasants and landless peasants after trial and investigation on the basis of the cadastral books, which books the census takers submitted to the Service Land Chancellery after the Moscow fire of the past year 1626, if those fugitive peasants of theirs, or the fathers of those peasants of theirs, were recorded [as living] under them in those cadastral books, or [if] after those cadastral books [were compiled] those peasants, or their children, were recorded in new grants [as living] under someone in books allotting lands or in books registering land transfers.

Return fugitive peasants and landless peasants from flight on the basis of the cadastral books to people of all ranks, without any statute of limitations.

3. If it becomes necessary to return fugitive peasants and landless peasants to someone after trial and investigation: return those peasants with their wives, and with their children, and with all their movable property, with their standing grain and with their threshed grain. Do not impose a fine for those peasants [on their current lords] for the years prior to this present Law Code.

Concerning peasants who, while fugitives, married off their unmarried daughters, or sisters, or kinswomen to peasants of those estate owners and service landholders under whom they were living, or elsewhere in another village or hamlet: do not fault that person and, on the basis of the status of those unmarried women, do not hand over the husbands to their former estate owners and service landholders because until the present sovereign's decree there was no rule by the sovereign that no one could receive peasants [to live] under him. [Only] statutes of limitations [on the recovery of] fugitive peasants were decreed and, moreover, in many years after the census takers [did their work], the hereditary estates and service landholdings of many hereditary estate owners and service landholders changed hands.

4. If fugitive peasants and landless peasants are returned to someone: chancellery officials of the sovereign's court villages and the rural taxpaying districts, and estate owners, and service landholders shall get from those people [to whom the fugitives are returned] inventory receipts, signed by them, for those peasants and landless peasants of theirs and their movable property in case of dispute in the future.

Order the town public square scribes to write the inventory receipts in Moscow and in the provincial towns; in villages and hamlets where there are no public square scribes, order the civil administration or church scribes of other villages to write such inventories. They shall issue such inventory receipts signed by their own hand.

Concerning people who are illiterate: those people shall order their own spiritual fathers, or people of the vicinity whom they trust, to sign those inventory receipts in their stead. No one shall order his own priests, and scribes, and slaves to write such inventories so that henceforth there will be no dispute by anybody or with anybody over such inventories.

5. Concerning the vacant houses of peasants and landless peasants, or [their] house lots, registered in the cadastral books with certain estate owners and service landholders; and in the cadastral books it is written about the peasants and landless peasants of those houses that those peasants and landless peasants fled from them in the years prior to [the compilation of] those cadastral books, but there was no petition from them against anyone about those peasants throughout this time: do not grant a trial for those peasants and landless peasants on the basis of those vacant houses and vacant lots because for many years they did not petition the sovereign against anyone about those peasants of theirs.

6. If fugitive peasants and landless peasants are returned from someone to plaintiffs after trial and investigation, and according to the cadastral books; or if someone returns [fugitives] without trial according to [this] Law Code: on the petition of those people under whom they had lived while fugitives, register those peasants in the Service Land Chancellery [as living] under those people to whom they are returned.

Concerning those people from whom they are taken: do not collect any of the sovereign's levies [due from the peasants] from such service landholders and hereditary estate owners on the basis of the census books. Collect all of the sovereign's levies from those estate owners and service landholders under whom they proceed to live as peasants upon their return.

7. If, after trial and investigation, and according to the cadastral books, peasants are taken away from any hereditary estate owners and returned to plaintiffs from their purchased estates; and they purchased those estates from estate owners with those peasants [living on them] after [the compilation of] the cadastres; and those peasants are registered on their lands in the purchase documents: those estate owners, in the stead of those returned peasants, shall take from the sellers similar peasants with all [their] movable property, and with [their] standing grain and with [their] threshed grain, from their other estates.

8. Concerning those estate owners and service landholders who in the past years had a trial about fugitive peasants and landless peasants; and at trial someone's [claims] to such fugitive peasants were rejected, prior to this decree of the sovereign, on the basis of the statute of limitations on the recovery of fugitive peasants in the prior decree of the great Sovereign, Tsar, and Grand Prince of all Russia Mikhail Fedorovich of blessed memory; and those fugitive peasants and landless peasants were ordered to live under those people under whom they lived out the years [of the] statute of limitations; or certain service landholders and hereditary estate owners arranged an amicable agreement in past years, prior to this decree of the sovereign, about fugitive peasants and landless peasants, and according to the amicable agreement someone ceded his peasants to someone else, and they confirmed it with registered documents, or they submitted reconciliation petitions [to settle court suits]: all those cases shall remain as those cases were resolved prior to this decree of the sovereign. Do not consider those cases anew and do not renegotiate [them].

9. Concerning peasants and landless peasants registered under someone in the census books of the past years 1645/46 and 1646/47; and after [the compilation of] those census books they fled from those people under whom they were registered in the census books, or they proceed to flee in the future: return those fugitive peasants and landless peasants, and their brothers, and children, and kinsmen, and grandchildren with [their] wives and with [their] children and with all [their] movable property, and with [their] standing grain and with threshed grain, from flight to those people from whom they fled, on the basis of the census books, without any statute of limitations. Henceforth no one ever shall receive others' peasants and shall not retain them under himself.

10. If someone after this royal Law Code proceeds to receive and retain under himself fugitive peasants, and landless peasants, and their children, and brothers, and kinsmen; and hereditary estate owners and service landholders demand those fugitive peasants of theirs from them [in a trial]: after trial and investigation, and according to the census books, return those fugitive peasants and landless

peasants of theirs to them with [their] wives and with [their] children, and with all their movable property, and with [their] standing grain, and with [their] threshed grain, and with [their] grain still in the ground, without any statute of limitations. .

Concerning the length of the time they live under someone as fugitives after this royal Law Code: collect from those under whom they proceed to live 10 rubles each for any peasant per year for the sovereign's taxes and the service landholder's incomes. Give [the money] to the plaintiffs whose peasants and landless peasants they are.

11. If someone proceeds to petition the sovereign against someone about such fugitive peasants and landless peasants; and those peasants and their fathers are not registered in the cadastral books under either the plaintiff or the defendant, but those peasants are registered under the plaintiff or the defendant in the census books of the past years 1645/46 and 1646/47: on the basis of the census books, return those peasants and landless peasants to that person under whom they are registered in the census books. ...

20. If any people come to someone on [his] hereditary estate and service landholding and say about themselves that they are free; and those people desire to live under them as peasants or landless peasants: those people whom they approach shall interrogate them—what kind of free people are they? And where is their birth place? And under whom did they live? And whence did they come? And are they not someone's fugitive slaves, and peasants, and landless peasants? And do they have manumission documents?

If they say that they do not have manumission documents on their person: service landholders and hereditary estate owners shall find out about such people accurately, whether they really are free people. Having investigated accurately, bring them in the same year for registration to the Service Land Chancellery in Moscow; Kazan'-area residents and residents of Kazan' by-towns shall bring them to Kazan'; Novgorodians and residents of the Novgorodian by-towns shall bring them to Novgorod; Pskovians and residents of the Pskov by-towns shall bring them to Pskov. [Chancellery officials] in the Service Land Chancellery and governors in the provincial towns shall interrogate such free people on that subject and shall record their testimonies accurately.

If it becomes necessary to give those people who are brought in for registration, on the basis of their testimony under interrogation, as peasants to those people who brought them in for registration: order those people to whom they will be given as peasants to affix their signatures to the testimonies of those people after they have been taken.

21. If an estate owner or a service landholder brings in for registration the person who approached him without having checked accurately, and they proceed to take such people in as peasants: return such people as peasants to plaintiffs after trial and investigation, and according to the census book, along with [their] wives, and with [their] children, and with [their] movable property.

Concerning [what shall be exacted] from those people who take in someone else's peasant or landless peasant without checking accurately: collect for those years, however many [the peasant] lived under someone, 10 rubles per year for the sovereign's taxes and for the incomes of the hereditary estate owner and service landholder because [of this rule]: without checking accurately, do not receive someone else's [peasant]. ...

Chapter 19.—Townsmen. In It Are 40 Articles.

1. Concerning the [tax-exempt] settlements in Moscow belonging to the patriarch, and metropolitans, and other high church officials, and monasteries, and boyars, and *okol'nichie*, and counselors, and [tsar's] intimates, and people of all ranks; and in those settlements are living merchants and artisans who pursue various trading enterprises and own shops, but are not paying the sovereign's taxes and are not rendering service: confiscate all of those settlements, with all the people who are living in those settlements, for the sovereign [and place them] all on the tax rolls [and force them to render] service without any statute of limitations and irrevocably, except for limited service contract slaves.

If it is said in an inquiry that the limited service contract slaves are their perpetual slaves, return them to those people to whom they belong. Order them moved back to their houses. Concerning those limited service contract slaves whose fathers and whose clan ancestors were townsmen, or from the sovereign's rural districts: take those [people] to live in the urban taxpaying districts.

Henceforth, except for the sovereign's settlements, no one shall have [tax-exempt] settlements in Moscow or in the provincial towns.

Confiscate the patriarch's settlements completely, excepting those palace court officials who for a long time lived under former patriarchs in their patriarchal ranks as *deti boiarskie*, singers, secretaries, scribes, furnace tenders, guards, cooks and bakers, grooms, and as his palace court officials of other ranks who are given an annual salary and grain. ...

Chapter 22.—Decree: For Which Offenses the Death Penalty Should Be Inflicted on Someone, and for Which Offenses the Penalty Should Not Be Death, But [Another] Punishment Should Be Imposed. In It Are 26 Articles.

1. If any son or daughter kills his father or mother: for patricide or matricide, punish them also with death, without the slightest mercy.

2. If any son or daughter kills his or her father or mother with some other people, and that is established conclusively after investigation, also punish with death, without the slightest mercy, those who committed such a deed with them.

3. If a father or mother kills a son or daughter: imprison them for a year after that. After having sat in prison for a year, they shall go to God's church, and in God's church they shall declare aloud that sin of theirs to all the people. Do not punish a father or mother with death for [killing] a son or daughter.

4. If someone, a son or a daughter, forgetting Christian law, proceeds to utter coarse speeches to a father or mother, or out of impudence strikes a father or mother, and the father or mother proceeds to petition against them for that: beat such forgetters of Christian law with the knout for the father and mother.

5. If any son or daughter plunder[s] a father's or mother's movable property by force; or not honoring the father and mother and [attempting] to drive them out, proceed[s] to denounce them for some evil deeds; or a son or daughter does not proceed to respect and feed a father and mother in their old age, does not proceed to support them materially in any way, and the father or mother proceed[s] to petition the sovereign against him or her about that: inflict a severe punishment on such children for such deeds of theirs, beat them mercilessly with the knout, and command them to attend to their father and mother in all obedience without any back-talk. Do not believe their denunciation.

6. If any son or daughter proceed[s] to petition for a trial against a father or mother: do not grant them a trial in any matter against a father or mother. Beat them with the knout for such a petition and return them to the father and mother. ...

14. If a wife kills her husband, or feeds him poison, and that is established conclusively: punish her for that, bury her alive in the ground and punish her with that punishment without any mercy, even if the children of the killed [husband], or any other close relatives of his, do not desire that she be executed. Do not show her the slightest mercy, and keep her in the ground until that time when she dies.

15. If a woman is sentenced to the death penalty and she is pregnant at that time: do not punish that woman with death until she gives birth, and execute her at the time when she has given birth. Until that time, keep her in prison, or in the custody of reliable bailiffs, so that she will not depart.

16. If someone with felonious intent comes into someone's house, and desires to do something shameful to the mistress of that house, or desires to carry her away somewhere out of that house; and her slaves do not defend her against that felon, and proceed to assist those people who have come for her in the commission [of the crime]; and subsequently such a deed of theirs is discovered: punish with death all those felons who with such intent come into another's house and those slaves who assist them in the commission of such a felony. ...

20. If someone shoot[s] from a handgun or from a bow at a wild animal, or at a bird, or at a target; and the arrow or bullet goes astray and kills someone over a hill or beyond a fence; or if someone by any chance kills someone with a piece of wood, or a rock, or anything else in a non-deliberate act; and previously there was no enmity or other animosity between that person who killed and that [person] he

killed; and it is established about that conclusively that such a homicide occurred without deliberation and without intent: do not punish anyone with death for such a homicide and do not incarcerate anyone in prison because that event occurred accidently, without intent. …

24. If a Muslim by any means whatsoever, by force or by deceit, compels a Russian [to convert] to his Islamic faith; and he circumcises that Russian according to his Islamic faith; and that is established conclusively: punish that Muslim after investigation, burn him with fire without any mercy.

Concerning the Russian whom he converted to Islam: send that Russian to the patriarch, or to another high ecclesiastical figure, and order him to compile a decree according to the canons of the Holy Apostles and the Holy Fathers.

25. If someone of the male gender, or the female gender, having forgotten the wrath of God and Christian law, proceeds to procure adult women and mature girls for fornication, and that is established conclusively: inflict a severe punishment on them for such a lawless and vile business, beat them with the knout.

26. If a woman proceeds to live in fornication and vileness, and in fornication begets children with someone; and she herself, or someone else at her command, destroys those children; and that is established conclusively: punish with death without any mercy such lawless women and that person who destroyed her children at her order so that others looking on will not commit such a lawless and vile deed and will refrain from fornication.

GLOSSARY

knout: a barbed whip used for state-ordered physical punishments in czarist Russia

manumission documents: official papers stating that the bearer, a former slave, has been freed

Mikhail Fedorovich: Mikhail Fedorovich Romanov (1596–1645)

service landholding: rented land whose tenant was required to serve the state lifelong or until too infirm to continue his duties (that is, until superannuated)

spiritual fathers: Orthodox clergy and other personnel

stol'niki, …, striapchie, …, dvoriane, … zhil'tsy: specific ranks or titles within the service gentry, with *dvoriane* referring to nobles and gentry in state service

Document Analysis

The complete Ulozhenie is divided into twenty-five chapters, each dealing with a different general topic or legislative area. They are presented in a specific order, corresponding to the importance or status accorded to each at the time, from the highest to the lowest. Thus, chapter 1 considers the honor and authority of God and his church, the second chapter treats the personal honor of the czar, the third looks at matters of conduct in the czar's court, and so on. The final chapter (the "lowest") treats unlawful taverns. The chapters between consider a wealth of issues, including the mint and currency, travel and foreigners, various ranks of service personnel, tolls and fees, the judicial process at various social levels, monasteries, different categories of landholding, social and political estates, slaves and serfs, robbery and theft, the death penalty, and palace musketeers. Some chapters are short—the one on palace musketeers has only three articles. Others are much longer. There are, for instance, 104 articles on robbery and theft and 119 on the judicial process regarding slaves. The longest of all, at 287 articles, considers the judicial process in general.

Chapter 10, The Judicial Process, speaks to a basic goal of the Ulozhenie: the creation of a state of law, with all the apparatuses, offices, and procedures that might require. Alexis's concept of a state of law should not be misunderstood, however. In the Ulozhenie there is no concept of people as individuals, imbued with natural rights or equal before the law. Instead, the assumptions are that the law exists to serve the interests of the state (largely synonymous with the person and authority of the czar) and that persons will be treated collectively according to social order, religion, nationality, and other factors. As evidence of the high level of concern for creating a state of law, the chapter contains 287 articles, the most by far of any in the code. Only the first six are reproduced here; but they suggest the basic parameters of the overall system.

The czar emphasizes his own authority. The Ulozhenie and the legal system more generally are *his* possessions and expressions of *his* will—even if specific and important tasks must be delegated to boyars, *okol'nichie*, and others. Boyars were hereditary nobles in state service and held the highest rank in the Muscovite social hierarchy; *okol'nichie* were second in rank. There were at least eighteen different service ranks at the time. Beyond this initial statement, however, the czar calls for impartiality, honesty, and adherence to the principles and rulings of his code, both by the Muscovite court and in the provinces.

Chapter 11 includes thirty-four articles; about two-thirds of them are reproduced here. It is in this chapter that we find the legal basis for the full-fledged system of serfdom with which the social history of Russia from the seventeenth to nineteenth centuries is nearly synonymous.

Article 1 establishes the tone of the chapter. It takes as a reference point the cadastral books of 1626, which showed the place of registration of peasant families at that time. In some cases, a later census of 1646–1647 provided the reference point. The article calls for all runaway peasants and their descendants—along with their wives, children, and "movable property"—to be returned to their original estates "without any statute of limitations" regardless of where they currently reside. Article 1 deals specifically with peasants originally registered on crown lands (the "sovereign's peasants"); article 2 extends the ruling to all categories of landowners. According to the law, a peasant originally registered with a member of the service gentry (such as a *stol'nik* or *striapchii*) but now living elsewhere must also be returned to his place of registration as of 1626. Note that this rule applied even to peasants who had moved onto lands belonging directly to the czar. Thus, the first two

articles establish a basic and draconian principle: Peasants have only one rightful and lawful place to live, the place at which they were properly and originally registered. They and their descendants were to be returned there no matter how long they had lived at some other place.

Article 3 establishes that the law would not be used to punish landlords who have previously held runaway peasants, only those landlords who would do so henceforth. This surely suggests the scale of the issue. No doubt "runaways" were extremely common. More generally, this article and numerous others throughout the code deal with the many problems, disputes, and uncertainties bound to arise as soon as efforts began to establish the "rightful" place of residence of any given peasant or peasant family. What should one do, for example, when marriages have been made among peasants not registered on the same estate in 1626? To which estate should the resulting family and any descendants properly belong? Should the larger family be broken up? And what about the "vacant houses" of runaway peasants (article 5)? On these and other similar issues, the Ulozhenie generally calls for proper investigations and trials, and it establishes that complications based on actions taken before passage of the law should be treated with some sympathy. Future actions, by contrast, are to be dealt with more legalistically. Article 10, for example, specifically calls for a fine of ten rubles per peasant per year to be levied against any landlord under whom fugitive peasants are living.

The law greatly affected not only peasants but also landowners. For the most part, the idea was to help them secure and retain labor for their landholdings. But the code could also cause them problems. Article 7, for example, treats the case of a landowner whose peasants are found after investigation to be the lawful property of another and therefore subject to removal. Articles 20 and 21 place upon landowners the responsibility of properly ascertaining the current legal status of persons wishing to settle on their estates. No doubt this would have presented a burden to landowners, and there was always the chance that a landlord, even one who intended to follow the law properly, might make a mistake or be deceived by his peasants. That landlord would still risk being levied a hefty fine.

Chapter 19 establishes yet another social category: the "townsmen." Only the first article of a total of forty is reproduced here. It shows the czar's intent to exert his will, centralize control, and improve the collection of taxes from people and places either previously exempt under the authority of other high-ranking persons, such as the Russian Orthodox patriarch, or from whom it had otherwise been hard to collect taxes. By the seventeenth century, towns had become the loci of significant commercial activity and thus also of potential taxable wealth. When townsmen moved, those taxes, which generally were levied collectively rather than individually, often went uncollected. Beginning with the official approval of the Ulozhenie in 1649, townsmen were required to remain where they were, and they could, like serfs, be forcibly returned if they moved elsewhere without authorization. In return, they obtained certain monopolies on trade and commercial activities. In this article, a "limited service contract slave" is distinguished by possession of a contract stipulating the duration and nature of servitude. "*Deti boiarskie*" refers to a middle rank within the provincial, as opposed to the Muscovite, service class.

Chapter 22 contains twenty-six articles, half of which are reproduced here. Many of these articles exemplify the Ulozhenie's emphasis on clear hierarchy, unquestionable authority, and strict punishment. They are largely untempered by concerns for mitigating circumstances and possible exceptions. When reading the first articles, dealing with murders within families, it should be kept in mind that the law's authors imagined the nuclear family as a microcosm of the larger "state family." The authority given to parents, especially fathers, as heads of families mirrors that assumed by the czar over his larger "family"—the population of the Muscovite state. Similarly, the lack of power given to children represents in microcosm the subordination of all subjects to their social superiors and ultimately to the czar. Thus, crimes committed by children against their parents are considered extremely serious, while crimes committed by parents against their children are reckoned to be minor. Following articles 5 and 6, any complaints made by children against their parents are to be ignored and even punished, but their responsibility to care for and feed their parents in old age is sacrosanct. Of course, one can also see in these articles the influence of some of the Ten Commandments, rather strictly and literally applied.

Returning to family themes, articles 14 to 16 reflect the harsh patriarchal culture of the time. A man's authority over his wife is considered absolute and sacred. A woman who violates this order by murdering her husband has committed a terrible crime. Whereas clauses

treating the murder of a master by his slave (not reproduced here) simply call for the slave's death, article 14 goes so far as to prescribe the manner of the offending wife's execution. The seriousness of her action, as viewed by Muscovite culture, is further emphasized in the same article by the refusal to contemplate any mitigating circumstances or calls for leniency made by the children or other relatives. This stands in stark contrast to some other parts of the code, where a clear concern is indeed shown for mitigating circumstances and intent (see, for example, article 20 in this chapter).

Note, however, that article 15 stipulates that the wife's crime, though unpardonable, is not to be paid for by the death of any innocent unborn child. The concern shown in article 16 for a woman's honor echoes the patriarchal tone of article 14 in that it seeks primarily to protect the exclusive ownership of the wife by her husband. The use of the term "mistress of that house" speaks to the fact that the law had in mind primarily elite women and not the ordinary peasant, whose affairs were largely regulated by this time by their landlords. Articles 24 to 26 return to religious themes and freely mix elements of harsh legalism with Christian compassion.

Essential Themes

As a general statement of state authority and social hierarchy, the Ulozhenie was intended ultimately for the entire Russian populace. It would, however, have been directly read or encountered only by a small literate minority, especially members of the service gentry, court officials, and the church hierarchy. Twelve hundred copies were made in the spring of 1649, and a further twelve hundred in the winter. Both quickly sold out, with the majority of copies probably going to courts and other government offices in Moscow and throughout provincial towns, where it henceforth provided the framework for legal cases and procedures (the main exception being cases coming under church jurisdiction).

Some of the Ulozhenie's most important articles involve serfdom, specifically its transformation into virtual slavery. Muscovite Russia's aristocrats received land grants from the czarist state as a function of inheritance or as a reward for service to the czar. The value of a land grant was determined almost entirely by the presence of peasants, who provided income in the form of labor and crops—the primary and often the only sources of revenue for the landlord. Until the late fifteenth century, it had remained common for landlords to negotiate terms of labor with peasants residing upon their lands. The two groups often had opposite interests, however. The landlords wanted permanent and reliable workers and ever-higher incomes. The peasants valued their freedom and independence, and they resented encroaching authority and rising taxation. Often, they simply moved on, leaving their landlords to face untended fields and economic hardship. The absence of natural boundaries and the lure of seemingly endless horizons to the east and south compounded the problem. Flight was especially common during the dislocations of the Time of Troubles.

Among landlords, however, the service gentry were especially vulnerable, since they faced the additional threat of having their peasants seized and transferred wholesale to the estates of higher-ranking and more powerful nobles. Thus, it was the service gentry who most actively pressured the state for help. Since Muscovy relied heavily on them for services and loyalty, as well as on military recruits from their lands, their pleas were taken to heart. Continued peasant flight spurred ever-more repressive countermeasures. In 1570 in parts of the province of Novgorod, Ivan IV declared a one-off "prohibited year," during which peasants would not be able to move for any reason, regardless of their ability to pay all debts and release fees. Thereafter, the concept was applied more widely. By the 1580s prohibited years had become the norm throughout Muscovite Russia. Instead, the state designated occasional "free years." The last one was in 1602. Around the same time, the statute of limitations on recovery of a runaway peasant was increased, reaching fifteen years in the first part of the sixteenth century. The Ulozhenie abolished the limitation altogether, and subsequent legislation criminalized peasant flight.

All classes of persons were affected by the Ulozhenie. The law's most enduring and significant consequences centered on its codification of serfdom, however. This system became the backbone of the economy and a fundamental determinant of the historical trajectory of the Russian state. Although serfdom had long provided both elites and the state with more or less stable sources of income, labor, and conscripts, it also fostered diverse and huge challenges that ultimately hampered the country's development. Under conditions of serf labor, for example, there was little incentive for investment in more productive or efficient farming methods and technologies, with the result that agriculture in Russia remained less efficient and productive than in many Western European regions. Russia's industrial and military development also lagged for similar reasons. Not surprisingly, the peasants themselves chafed under the burden of serfdom. After 1649, rebellions grew in frequency and scale. Peasant unrest, along with Russia's humiliating defeat in the Crimean War (1853–1856), which also could be traced to serfdom, eventually persuaded Alexander II to abolish the system "from above" in 1861, before the peasants abolished it themselves "from below." By 1861 serfdom was widely blamed for a stifling backwardness in many aspects of Russian society, whether in agriculture, industry, military effectiveness, or public morality.

— —*Brian Bonhomme*

Bibliography and Further Reading

Hellie, Richard, ed. and trans. *The Muscovite Law Code (Ulozhenie) of 1649*. Irvine, CA: Charles Schlacks, Jr., 1988.

———. "Russian Law from Oleg to Peter the Great." Foreword to *The Laws of Rus': Tenth to Fifteenth Centuries*, ed. and trans. Daniel H. Kaiser. Salt Lake City, UT: Charles Schlacks, Jr., 1992.

Longworth, Philip. *Alexis, Tsar of All the Russias*. London: Franklin Watts, 1984.

Pipes, Richard. *Russia under the Old Regime*. 2nd ed. London: Penguin, 1995.

Poe, Marshall T. *The Russian Elite in the Seventeenth Century*. Vol. 2: *A Quantitative Analysis of the "Duma Ranks," 1613–1713*. Helsinki: Finnish Academy of Science and Letters, 2004.

Wirtschafter, Elise Kimerling. *Russia's Age of Serfdom 1649–1861*. Malden, MA. Blackwell Publishers, 2008.

THE AMERICAN AND FRENCH REVOLUTIONS

The American and French Revolutions created the concept of the nation and nationalism, because they brought about the concept of people power. Their impacts can be read from the Declaration of Independence and the Declaration of the Rights of Man and Citizen, and the US Constitution. The reach of those documents has been extensive, as the Constitution of Haiti and the Cartagena Manifesto demonstrate. Yet it is important to define what was "revolutionary" about the two revolutions to determine their impacts, which were actually quite different despite the similarity in values.

A revolution is a fast change in history—as opposed to evolution, the way things usually change. When a "revolution" takes place, it brings about a dramatic transformation, and in a short period of time. But a transformation of what? The Industrial Revolution took place in two stages over the course of some 250 years, hardly a short period. The Information Revolution we are living through today has seen cellphones add computers to their series of functions to create smartphones, a transformation but not a particularly dramatic one. Yet these are both revolutionary events, not so much for the actual material transformation inasmuch as for the way they change our actions, our attitudes, our futures and our fortunes. In short, a revolution takes place in one's mind: life changes so dramatically that it seems impossible to ever again live in the same way before the revolution took place. The first time someone saw a railroad engine or entered a factory to make money as opposed to growing food to survive, that was revolutionary. Similarly, once people had computers literally at their fingertips as opposed to having to use them on their laps or at a desk, that was revolutionary too. So it was with the American and French Revolutions and the developments of nationalism and populism that they brought about.

When Americans talk about "the American Revolution," they tend to be thinking of the Revolutionary War, as it is misleadingly termed; better to refer to the event as the American War (or wars, since the British ended up engaged with half of Europe by the end of it) of Independence. In point of fact, the colonists fought a war not to bring about fast changes, but to be left alone as they were: not to have to pay taxes or quarter troops or see their colonial governments subordinated to that of the British Empire in London. The real revolution was in the documents—the Declaration of Independence, the Articles of Confederation, the Constitution and the Bill of Rights attached to it. These documents put rules and privileges in writing that Americans had to respect; the revolutionary concept was to follow them to maintain a state, as opposed to being forced to abide by the rules of an empire through the implied threat of violence if one did not. Of course, this has proved difficult over two and a half centuries. It has required a civil war, a civil rights movement, immigration and immigration quotas, the suppression of freedoms and tests of those freedoms for Americans to learn to follow the rules of the Constitution. In other words, the American Revolution was a revolution of ideas, and Americans have had to live up to those ideas in their actions.

The French Revolution, in following, then, was not particularly revolutionary in the ideas presented in the Declaration of the Rights of Man and Citizen, since they already existed in the United States. Several efforts at constitutions over the next decade after 1789 came up with similar institutions and ideas to that of the US government, albeit with the added proviso of the end of slavery in France and its imperial territories. No war was necessary to bring them about, though the French ended up at war with all of Europe by the 1790s. But there was no event in American history equivalent to that of the fall of the Bastille in July 1789. Average people in Paris decided to defend the National Assembly in France by picking up whatever weapons they could make available and create their own political event to assert their wishes to their state, in this case Louis XVI, their monarch. At pain of his own potential death, Louis was forced to listen. In world history, nothing similar had ever happened before—previous peasant revolts had never required a monarch to fear for his own life (and Louis would lose his life to his people in 1793). In fact, the Chinese premier Zhou Enlai famously said, when asked his opinion about the impact of the French Revolution, "it's too soon to tell"—since there are still elite powers in the world and people still need to periodically assert their interests to those elites with the threat of removal if they are not addressed. The French people themselves had to challenge and sometimes remove their states from power and write new constitutions five times from 1789 forward in their history. In other words, the French Revolution was a revolution of actions, and the French people have had to use ideas to keep them under control.

The French Revolution has proved far more impactful in world history, as revolutions go, than the American Revolution—the reason Edmund Burke and Madame de Stael castigated the French Revolution and Napoleon was because of their potentially dangerous and destabilizing impacts on Europe and the world. The stability represented by the American example has been more aspired to; whether the US is the greatest nation on earth is questionable depending on the measurement, but there is no doubt that it is the essential nation because all other states have intended to develop a peaceable and solid constitution in a similar fashion. Both revolutions are the models for the development of the concepts of nationalism and populism, in concert: they were brought about by average people who wrote down their ideas on what would make their future states, governments and other institutions unique in the world.

■ Declaration of Independence

Date: 1776
Author: Thomas Jefferson, et al
Genre: Declarative speech

Summary Overview

On July 4, 1776, the Continental Congress adopted Thomas Jefferson's amended draft of the Declaration of Independence from Britain. The initial effort by the framers of the American system of government was not to separate from Britain but to be accepted by Britain as an equal partner—to be given the rights and responsibilities of full British citizenship. Early efforts to secure such acceptance met with contempt and refusal. By 1776 the Founding Fathers were forced to make a choice: subservience or revolution.

Concluding that independence was their only option, they felt, as men of the Enlightenment, in the Age of Reason, that they were bound by honor to declare to the world the reasons for their radical act. The Continental Congress thus selected a committee of five men to draft a statement calling for independence. That committee—consisting of Thomas Jefferson, John Adams, Benjamin Franklin, Robert R. Livingston, and Roger Sherman—surprisingly chose the thirty-four-year-old Virginian Jefferson to write the first draft of what would become the Declaration of Independence. These men could hardly have imagined the full impact their handiwork would have, for in modern times the Declaration of Independence is one of the most read and honored documents produced by the revolutionaries of that age. It is a document that has had a profound impact not only on that revolutionary generation but also on future generations.

Defining Moment

When the Seven Years' War between Britain and France ended in 1763, Britain was in deep debt. To alleviate this debt, Parliament passed legislation designed to increase tax revenues from Britain's American colonies. Among these measures were the Sugar Act of 1764, the Stamp Act of 1765 and the Townshend Revenue Act of 1767. Many colonists objected to these measures, arguing that because the colonies were not represented in Parliament, that body had no authority to tax them. They expressed their dissatisfaction through the well-known phrase "no taxation without representation." By the early 1770s numerous colonists, Thomas Jefferson among them, were beginning to believe that Parliament had no authority of any type over the colonies, each of which had its own legislature that was more representative of their interests.

Matters came to a head in December 1773. The British government reduced the cost of transporting tea from India to the American colonies, making the cost of the tea—with its accompanying legal tariff—cheaper than smuggled tea. The colonists in Boston responded with the Boston Tea Party, dumping Indian tea into Boston Harbor. To restore order in the unruly colony of Massachusetts, Parliament imposed what came to be called the Intolerable Acts, shutting down the port of Boston until the cost of the tea had been recouped.

In response to these laws, the colonists held the First Continental Congress in Philadelphia between September 5 and October 26, 1774. The delegates' chief goal was to settle the dispute with Britain, which resulted in two measures. One was to petition the king of England, George III, asking him to repeal the acts. The other was to organize a boycott of British goods. Hope remained high among many Americans who were still loyal to the British Crown that some accommodation could be reached.

King George III, however, refused to grant the requests made by the colonies. The colonies thus agreed to form another congress to discuss the refusal. On April 19, 1775, however, even before the Second Continental Congress could meet, fighting broke out at Lexington and Concord, Massachusetts, between colonial militia and British troops. Several colonists were killed, and the losses inflamed passions and put additional pressure on the Congress to become bolder. The Second Continental Congress convened on May 10, 1775, with the delegates more radicalized and inclined toward revolution. Even then, though, most of the delegates to the Congress were unwilling to declare independence from Britain and continued to hope that the king would intervene. When the king refused and issued the Proclamation for Suppressing Rebellion and Sedition, George Washington was named commander of the fledgling colonial militia, and both sides committed to engage in war. The movement for American independence gained ground.

The case for revolution was best articulated by the pamphleteer Thomas Paine, who in January 1776 published his famous broadside *Common Sense*. In that brief but powerfully argued pamphlet, Paine boldly outlined the intellectual underpinnings for what would become the American Revolution. Such ideas had been percolating in the colonies for several decades, and Paine demonstrated a talent for defining revolutionary sentiment in a manner that proved both compelling and convincing. *Common Sense* created a firestorm. Over 120,000 copies of the pamphlet were sold in the first three months of publication alone—roughly one in every thirteen adult colonists owned a copy, with most citizens who lacked a copy reading someone else's. To Paine, the king of England was "the Royal Brute of Britain." In America, Paine asserted, "the law is king." Paine called for the colonies to declare their independence and establish a republic.

On June 7, 1776, Richard Henry Lee, representing Virginia, submitted a resolution of independence to the Second Continental Congress. Some delegations opposed the resolution. Others had not yet been authorized by their colonies to support independence. Lee's resolution was tabled while the Congress formed a committee to draft a document that would be published to explain why the resolution of independence was approved, if in fact it later was. Accordingly, on June 11, Thomas Jefferson joined John Adams, Robert Livingston, Benjamin Franklin, and Roger Sherman on the "Committee of Five," assigned the task of drafting a declaration of independence. The committee in turn relied on Jefferson to write a draft of the declaration. Jefferson based the document on three primary sources: the preamble to the Virginia constitution, the Virginia Declaration of Rights, written by George Mason in May 1776, and the English Declaration of Rights, written in 1689 to end the reign of King James II. Ironically, the task was regarded as a routine assignment; the goal was to produce a statement of political position to be read out loud to gathered audiences in the major cities in British North America so they would know why the rebellion was taking place. The goal was not to produce a foundational document that would inspire Americans for generations—though that is what the declaration became.

After some discussion and revision the committee submitted the declaration to Congress on June 28.

Debate continued until July 2, when Congress, with twelve affirmative votes and one abstention, voted to approve Lee's resolution. After two additional days of discussion and debate over the wording of Jefferson's declaration, Congress approved it for publication on July 4. The document then published in newspapers all over the colonies and read out loud publically, and it was eventually signed by the members of the Second Continental Congress on August 2, 1776.

Author Biography

Thomas Jefferson, the principal author of the Declaration of Independence, is considered by many to be the greatest person the United States has ever produced. A true Renaissance man, Jefferson was a statesman, author, politician, philosopher, diplomat, inventor, scientist, and much more. He was also a prominent slaveowner, and the hypocrisy of writing a Declaration of Independence for the colonies that echoed some of the same tyrannies Jefferson himself exercised over his own slaves has not been lost on historians. Regardless of opinion, Jefferson was obviously a fascinating man, full of contradictions and genius, one of the pivotal and defining figures in world history at the turn of the nineteenth century.

In declaring the states' independence, Jefferson sought to persuade as many colonists as possible to take part in the Revolution. Taking on the most powerful nation in the world was an enormous risk, and the chances for success seemed quite slim. This aspect of the document reveals an obvious narrow self-interest on the part of Jefferson and his colleagues, but the Revolution was also to be fought for timeless and universal principles. No revolution can be successful without a significant portion of the population backing the rebels, and uncertainty remained regarding just how much support could be mustered for the revolt against Britain. In that sense, Jefferson's work was one grand piece of recruiting propaganda aimed at inspiring the people to take up arms against the British. As such, it indeed proved quite effective.

The Declaration of Independence was, of course, also aimed at the British government—but it was likewise aimed at the British people. Some sympathy for the American cause could be found both in the Parliament and among the British people, and the colonists were waging a battle for British public opinion as much as they were informing the government of Britain that they were declaring independence.

Finally, Jefferson aimed at a worldwide audience. He and his fellow drafters were men of the Enlightenment, and felt compelled to make the case for revolution to an audience of like-minded persons who might be persuaded that, indeed, their cause was just and their goals admirable. Believing that honorable men would rally to the cause of freedom, Jefferson sought to make their case against the British government and for the rights for which they were fighting. It is testament to the power of the ideas in the declaration that the news of its proclamation to the people of British North America was censored in places like the Austrian and Russian Empires, for fear that people in eastern Europe might be inspired to rise up against their emperors themselves and strike for freedom.

After the Declaration of Independence, Jefferson served as governor of Virginia and, upon the United States' independence, as ambassador to France. He served in Washington's cabinet as secretary of state and as Adams' vice president before assuming the presidency himself in 1801. As president, he used a variety of means to press his agenda in Congress while respecting the legislature's constitutional prerogatives. Jefferson's use of his political party allowed him to build a strong presidency, responsive to the majority will of the people, as expressed through the party. He doubled the United States' size for a relatively low cost, as France sold the territory of Louisiana to the United States. All the while, he conducted scientific experiments at his Virginia plantation, Monticello, read voraciously, wrote regular works on the politics of the time, and conducted a long-term relationship with one of his slaves, Sally Hemings. He died in 1826.

HISTORICAL DOCUMENT

IN CONGRESS, July 4, 1776.

The unanimous Declaration of the thirteen united States of America,

When in the Course of human events, it becomes necessary for one people to dissolve the political bands which have connected them with another, and to assume among the powers of the earth, the separate and equal station to which the Laws of Nature and of Nature's God entitle them, a decent respect to the opinions of mankind requires that they should declare the causes which impel them to the separation.

We hold these truths to be self-evident, that all men are created equal, that they are endowed by their Creator with certain unalienable Rights, that among these are Life, Liberty and the pursuit of Happiness.—That to secure these rights, Governments are instituted among Men, deriving their just powers from the consent of the governed,—That whenever any Form of Government becomes destructive of these ends, it is the Right of the People to alter or to abolish it, and to institute new Government, laying its foundation on such principles and organizing its powers in such form, as to them shall seem most likely to effect their Safety and Happiness. Prudence, indeed, will dictate that Governments long established should not be changed for light and transient causes; and accordingly all experience hath shewn, that mankind are more disposed to suffer, while evils are sufferable, than to right themselves by abolishing the forms to which they are accustomed. But when a long train of abuses and usurpations, pursuing invariably the same Object evinces a design to reduce them under absolute Despotism, it is their right, it is their duty, to throw off such Government, and to provide new Guards for their future security.—Such has been the patient sufferance of these Colonies; and such is now the necessity which constrains them to alter their former Systems of Government. The history of the present King of Britain is a history of repeated injuries and usurpations, all having in direct object the establishment of an absolute Tyranny over these States. To prove this, let Facts be submitted to a candid world.

- He has refused his Assent to Laws, the most wholesome and necessary for the public good.

- He has forbidden his Governors to pass Laws of immediate and pressing importance, unless suspended in their operation till his Assent should be obtained; and when so suspended, he has utterly neglected to attend to them.

- He has refused to pass other Laws for the accommodation of large districts of people, unless those people would relinquish the right of Representation in the Legislature, a right inestimable to them and formidable to tyrants only.

- He has called together legislative bodies at places unusual, uncomfortable, and distant from the depository of their public Records, for the sole purpose of fatiguing them into compliance with his measures.

- He has dissolved Representative Houses repeatedly, for opposing with manly firmness his invasions on the rights of the people.

- He has refused for a long time, after such dissolutions, to cause others to be elected; whereby the Legislative powers, incapable of Annihilation, have returned to the People at large for their exercise; the State remaining in the mean time exposed to all the dangers of invasion from without, and convulsions within.

- He has endeavoured to prevent the population of these States; for that purpose obstructing the Laws for Naturalization of Foreigners; refusing to pass others to encourage their migrations hither, and raising the conditions of new Appropriations of Lands.

- He has obstructed the Administration of Justice, by refusing his Assent to Laws for establishing Judiciary powers.

- He has made Judges dependent on his Will alone, for the tenure of their offices, and the amount and payment of their salaries.

- He has erected a multitude of New Offices, and sent hither swarms of Officers to harass our people, and eat out their substance.

- He has kept among us, in times of peace, Standing Armies without the Consent of our legislatures.

- He has affected to render the Military independent of and superior to the Civil power.

- He has combined with others to subject us to a jurisdiction foreign to our constitution, and unacknowledged by our laws; giving his Assent to their Acts of pretended Legislation: For Quartering large bodies of armed troops among us: For protecting them, by a mock Trial, from punishment for any Murders which they should commit on the Inhabitants of these States: For cutting off our Trade with all parts of the world: For imposing Taxes on us without our Consent: For depriving us in many cases, of the benefits of Trial by Jury: For transporting us beyond Seas to be tried for pretended offences For abolishing the free System of English Laws in a neighbouring Province, establishing therein an Arbitrary government, and enlarging its Boundaries so as to render it at once an example and fit instrument for introducing the same absolute rule into these Colonies: For taking away our Charters, abolishing our most valuable Laws, and altering fundamentally the Forms of our Governments: For suspending our own Legislatures, and declaring themselves invested with power to legislate for us in all cases whatsoever.

- He has abdicated Government here, by declaring us out of his Protection and waging War against us.

- He has plundered our seas, ravaged our Coasts, burnt our towns, and destroyed the lives of our people.

- He is at this time transporting large Armies of foreign Mercenaries to compleat the works of death, desolation and tyranny, already begun with circumstances of Cruelty & perfidy scarcely paralleled in the most barbarous ages, and totally unworthy the Head of a civilized nation.

- He has constrained our fellow Citizens taken Captive on the high Seas to bear Arms against their Country, to become the executioners of their friends and Brethren, or to fall themselves by their Hands.

- He has excited domestic insurrections amongst us, and has endeavoured to bring on the inhabitants of our frontiers, the merciless Indian Savages, whose known rule of warfare, is an undistinguished destruction of all ages, sexes and conditions.

In every stage of these Oppressions We have Petitioned for Redress in the most humble terms: Our repeated Petitions have been answered only by repeated injury. A Prince whose character is thus marked by every act which may define a Tyrant, is unfit to be the ruler of a free people.

Nor have We been wanting in attentions to our Brittish brethren. We have warned them from time to time of attempts by their legislature to extend an unwarrantable jurisdiction over us. We have reminded them of the circumstances of our emigration and settlement here. We have appealed to their native justice and magnanimity, and we have conjured them by the ties of our common kindred to disavow these usurpations, which, would inevitably interrupt our connections and correspondence. They too have been deaf to the voice of justice and of consanguinity. We must, therefore, acquiesce in the necessity, which denounces our Separation, and hold them, as we hold the rest of mankind, Enemies in War, in Peace Friends.

We, therefore, the Representatives of the united States of America, in General Congress, Assembled, appealing to the Supreme Judge of the world for the rectitude of our intentions, do, in the Name, and by Authority of the good People of these Colonies, solemnly publish and declare, That these United Colonies are, and of Right ought to be Free and Independent States; that they are Absolved from all Allegiance to the British Crown, and that all political connection between them and the State of Britain, is and ought to be totally dissolved; and that as Free and Independent States, they have full Power to levy War, conclude Peace, contract Alliances, establish Commerce, and to do all other Acts and Things which Independent States may of right do. And for the support of this Declaration, with a firm reliance on the protection of divine Providence, we mutually pledge to each other our Lives, our Fortunes and our sacred Honor.

GLOSSARY

consanguinity: the state of being related by blood or common ancestors or of being closely related or linked

divine Providence: the foreseeing care and guidance of God or nature over the creatures of the earth

perfidy: deliberate breach of faith or trust; treachery

Document Analysis

On July 2, 1776, Jefferson's amended draft of a document declaring independence from Britain was presented to the Continental Congress for a vote. This Declaration of Independence was a powerful statement of principle and high purpose. It was also a call to revolution. While the majority of the document consists of an exhaustive list of grievances against the British king, the driving creed can be found in the powerful opening sentence. In it, Jefferson acknowledges that if the American colonies were going to break with Britain, the grounds for doing so must be reasonable and the colonists should explain them to the world. In this sentence Jefferson invokes the "Laws of Nature." In doing so he was bringing into the discussion the concept of natural rights, particularly as articulated by the English political philosopher John Locke in his *Second Treatise on Government*. The next paragraph begins with a paraphrase from Locke that became the most widely known words from the Declaration: "We hold these truths to be self-evident, that all men are created equal, that they are endowed by their Creator with certain unalienable Rights, that among these are Life, Liberty and the pursuit of Happiness." The word *unalienable* meant that these rights could not be taken away. They were not granted by the state or a king, nor could the state or a king deny to citizens the full enjoyment of these rights. People possessed rights by virtue of being human.

Given these natural rights, Jefferson goes on to say that a government, because it is "instituted among Men," could have legitimacy only from the "consent of the governed." Accordingly, if a government deprived its citizens of "Life, Liberty and the pursuit of Happiness," citizens were justified in abolishing their government and forming a new one. This idea would have particular resonance in England, since the English people had deposed their own king, James II, from the throne in 1688 for essentially similar reasons. Jefferson acknowledges that governments should not be abolished for "light and transient causes" and then goes on to say that the "abuses and usurpations" of the British government showed a clear desire to reduce the colonies under "absolute Despotism." Thus, colonists had not only the right but also the duty to "provide new Guards for their future security."

The bulk of the Declaration of Independence consists of a lengthy list of ways in which King George had violated the rights of the colonists. The first three grievances state that the king had "refused his Assent to Laws," that he had "forbidden his governors to pass Laws of immediate and pressing importance," that he opposed laws "for the accommodation of large districts of people." In 1767, under George III, eighteen Massachusetts laws for the establishment of new townships went ignored by the British Crown. Given the means of the era, expanding the colonies without developing new towns would have been difficult. Modes of transportation were limited, such that political representatives could not feasibly maintain contact with constituents in farther locations. Thus, new towns were needed in order to provide all citizens with access to political representation.

Many of the grievances pertain to administrative and legislative matters. Jefferson accuses George III of imposing taxes without the colonies' consent, that he "dissolved Representative Houses," that he obstructed trade, and that in general he had harassed the colonies with burdensome and "fatiguing" requirements.

Additionally, says Jefferson, the king had prevented efforts to populate the colonies by passing obstructive laws for migration and naturalization. By this Jefferson is referring to two British laws. One is a proclamation issued by King George III following Britain's acquisition of French territory in North America. The proclamation forbade colonists of the thirteen colonies from settling or buying land west of the Appalachians and gave the Crown a monopoly on land bought from Native Americans. The proclamation angered the colonists, since these were lands that they had helped fight for in the French and Indian War. Another grievance admonishes the king "for abolishing the free System of English Laws in a neighbouring Province, establishing therein an Arbitrary government, and enlarging its Boundaries so as to render it at once an example and fit instrument for introducing the same absolute rule into these Colonies." This grievance is a reference to the Quebec Act of 1774, which expanded British territory to include modern-day Illinois, Indiana, Michigan, Ohio, Wisconsin, and parts of Minnesota. The colonists denounced the act for establishing procedures of governance in this territory. The act also guarantees the free practice of the Roman Catholic faith in these lands, such that it was also denounced for giving preference to Catholicism.

The king had created "swarms" of administrators whose only purpose seemed to be to "harass our people, and eat out their substance." He had kept standing armies in the colonies without the consent of the legislatures, elevated the military over the civil authorities, required the colonies to "quarter" armed troops (that is, to provide food and housing for them), seized colonists on the seas and forced them to serve in the British military, and transported mercenary soldiers into the colonies for the purpose of fighting the war. Although "cutting off our Trade with all parts of the world" appears as a general complaint, it specifically refers to the Boston Port Act of 1774. The Boston Port Act was a response to the Boston Tea Party; it outlawed the use of the port of Boston for "landing and discharging, loading or shipping, of goods, wares, and merchandise" until such time as restitution was made to the king's treasury and to the East India Company for damages suffered.

It is noteworthy that the document never refers directly to Parliament. The colonists regarded the British Empire as a compact of territories under the authority of the king; because colonies were not represented in Parliament, the delegates to the Continental Congress believed that body had no authority over them. Thus Jefferson refers to Parliament as a "jurisdiction foreign to our constitution." This would have been news to fully ninety percent of the British people, who did not meet the property requirement to vote and therefore did not elect their representatives in the House of Commons themselves. They still saw Parliament as having jurisdiction over them—of all Jefferson's statements in the declaration, this one was the most objectionably close to treason under the British state's standards.

Jefferson also said the king had submitted the courts and judges to his will alone in matters of administration of justice, abolished colonial charters, transported criminals for trial, and deprived citizens of trial by jury. Here Jefferson refers to the brand of "mock Trial" received by British officials stationed in the colonies in accord with the Administration of Justice Act of 1774. The Administration of Justice Act granted a change of venue to another British colony or to Britain in trials of officials charged with crimes stemming from their enforcement of the law or suppression of riots. The purpose of this act was to ensure that the trials in question would be more conducive to the Crown than they would have been if held in the colonies, owing to the prejudices of local juries.

One further grievance charges the King with the grave crimes of "taking away our Charters, abolishing our most valuable Laws, and altering fundamentally the Forms of our Governments." This complaint refers to the Massachusetts Government Act of 1774. In the wake of the Boston Tea Party, Parliament launched a legislative offensive against Massachusetts to punish its errant behavior. British officials realized that part of their inability to control the colony was rooted in the highly independent nature of local government there. The Massachusetts Government Act effectively abrogated the colony's charter and provided for an unprecedented amount of royal control. Severe limits were placed on the powers of town meetings, the essential ingredient of American self-government. Under the Massachusetts Government Act, most elective offices in the colony were to be filled with royal appointees, not with popularly elected officials.

After listing these "usurpations," Jefferson notes that the colonists had repeatedly petitioned the king for "Redress" and had met with "repeated injury." This observation was included because even after the outbreak of hostilities, many Americans still remained loyal to the British Crown. Jefferson adds that the colonists had tried to appeal to "our Brittish [sic] brethren" and their "native justice and magnanimity" but that the British people had been "deaf to the voice of justice and of consanguinity"—that is, of ties of blood. Accordingly, while the British would be friends in peace, they were "Enemies in War."

In the final paragraph, Jefferson incorporates the language of the resolution of independence adopted on July 2, 1776, in proclaiming that the colonies were now free and independent of Britain.

Essential Themes

The Declaration of Independence had a profound impact in its age and far beyond its time. Along with Thomas Paine's *Common Sense*, the Declaration of Independence was a rousing call to arms at a time when armed insurrection against British rule was not yet a certainty—indeed, when no colony in the history of the world had ever rejected its metropole for independence. Jefferson's document launched a revolution, one where people could subscribe to a national identity based not on blood ties or birth or geography or language, but on political ideals that were defined in his preamble. In essence, the Declaration of Independence was the first statement in the American Revolution that anyone on earth willing to believe that all men were created equal with the right to life, liberty and the pursuit of happiness could be an American.

Widely read and oft cited, the Declaration remains one of the world's most influential political documents. While the immediate impact of the Declaration of Independence was felt primarily in colonial America, the long-term impact has been much broader, if harder to measure. The document's creed has been invoked to justify revolutions in Africa, Asia, Latin America, and elsewhere. The American Revolution was contained in ideas; the United States' history and that of the states that followed its lead has been about trying to live up to those ideas in their actions. Thirteen years later, when Parisians stormed the Bastille in 1789, the French Revolution would introduce the idea that men could take their political lives into their own hands, whatever their economic status, and forcefully demand the same natural rights that Jefferson elucidated in the Declaration of Independence. The French Revolution, then, was a revolution of actions, and French history and the history of other states that followed the French example has been about trying to rein in those actions with ideas. Combined, the American Revolution as defined in the Declaration of Independence and the French Revolution as defined by the storming of the Bastille transformed the world's conception of government, nation, and state as rightfully being defined by a people's majority wishes instead of by whatever monarch had the power to assert his will over them.

——*Michael A. Genovese and Kristina L. Rioux, additional commentary by Michael J. O'Neal, PhD*

Bibliography and Further Reading

Armitage, David. *The Declaration of Independence: A Global History*. Cambridge, MA: Harvard University Press, 2008.

Curry, Robert. *Common Sense Nation: Unlocking the Forgotten Power of the American Idea*. New York: Encounter Books, 2015.

Dyer, Justin Buckley, editor. *The Contested Legacy of the Declaration of Independence*. Lanham, MD: Rowman & Littlefield Publishers, 2012.

Hogeland, William. *Declaration: The Nine Tumultuous Weeks when America Became Independent, May 1-July 4, 1776*. New York: Simon & Schuster, 2010.

Pincus, Steven. *The Heart of the Declaration: The Founders' Case for an Activist Government*. New Haven, CT: Yale University Press, 2016.

Shain, Barry Alan, editor and compiler. *The Declaration of Independence in Historical Context: American State Papers, Petitions, Proclamations, & Letters of the Delegates to the First National Congresses*. Indianapolis, IN: Liberty Fund, 2014

Web Sites

"Declaration of Independence." *America's Founding Documents*. National Archives (October 12, 2016) https://www.archives.gov/founding-docs/declaration [accessed February 25, 2017].

Jefferson, Thomas. "Letter to Henry Lee." *TeachingAmericanHistory.org*. Ashland University http://www.ashbrook.org/constitution/henry_lee.html [accessed February 25, 2017].

"Jefferson's Draft of the Declaration of Independence, 28 June, 1776." *American History: From Revolution to Reconstruction and Beyond* http://www.let.rug.nl/usa/D/1776-1800/ independence/doitj.htm **[accessed February 25, 2017].**

■ Constitution of the United States

Date: 1787
Author: Gouverneur Morris, James Madison et al.
Genre: Constitution

Summary Overview

In May 1787 representatives of twelve of the thirteen states (all but Rhode Island) convened the Constitutional Convention in Philadelphia to draft a constitution for the union that bound them together. Since the end of the Revolutionary War, the United States had been operating under the Articles of Confederation, but sentiment was growing that the articles were too weak and that the infant nation was in danger of collapsing because it lacked a strong federal government. After weeks of discussion and negotiation, the framers adopted a new constitution on September 17 that opens with the stirring words "We the people of the United States, in order to form a more perfect union." The Constitution of the United States remains a master work in balancing the powers of the executive branch led by the president, the legislative branch, and the judiciary and in balancing the power of the federal government with that of the states. Like any constitution, the U.S. Constitution specifies the rules under which the new nation's government would operate. Two years later, ten amendments constituting a Bill of Rights were added. A testament to the enduring power of the Constitution is that, after the Bill of Rights, it has been amended only seventeen times in more than two centuries. After oftentimes contentious debates in the states, the new Constitution became the law of the land on June 21, 1788, when New Hampshire became the ninth state to ratify the document.

Defining Moment

The presence of a common enemy had inspired the thirteen colonies to cooperate during the American War of Independence. After declaring independence from Great Britain, the thirteen American colonies adopted new constitutions for themselves and for the union that bound them together. The U.S. Constitution, which in 1787 proposed the federal government in the form known in the modern era, was in fact the second national constitution. The Articles of Confederation, ratified in 1781 as the first national constitution, provided for a weak central government that was little more than a league of friendship.

At the state level, despite universal support for the concept of separation of powers, assemblies were dominant. State constitutions placed few or no controls upon the actions of state assemblies, which were elected annually. Few problems surfaced until the inevitable postwar depression developed beginning in mid-1784. Farmers were overproducing, but their markets, particularly in the West Indies, were restricted. Consequently, prices for American agricultural produce plunged. At the same time, taxes were raised, as Congress and the state legislatures had heavy war debts to pay, to both foreign and domestic creditors. Individuals and organizations that could not pay their taxes or their debts had their property confiscated by local authorities and sold at public auction. Debtors petitioned their assemblies for relief, and half of the states succumbed; in the other states, violence occurred. In western Virginia, courthouses were burned, destroying tax records. In Massachusetts, farmers in the western counties forcibly closed the civil courts in order to forestall future foreclosures on farms. Creditors, in the minority, worried that state assemblies would yield to vocal majorities—the debtors—and enact measures that would endanger their property rights. Anti-creditor legislation, some modest, some radical, coupled with violence throughout the country frightened men like George Washington who believed that there were "combustibles" in every state ready to be ignited by a single spark. Worst of all, a former Revolutionary War officer named Daniel Shays led a rebellion in Massachusetts against the state government, in demand of lower taxes and debt cancellation; when the state militia looked for help from the central government to put down the revolt, there was no army to be had.

Shays' rebellion was crushed by the Massachusetts militia, but it prompted a small group of nationalists to call for a more powerful central government. Their efforts in drafting the Articles of Confederation had clearly failed, as did their efforts to amend them and to give the Congress of the Confederation additional powers. The states were clearly less willing than they had been to abide by the dictates of Congress. Finally, those who wished to preserve the Union decided to move outside of Congress and call a convention of the states to propose amendments to the articles.

The Constitutional Convention convened in May 1787. With George Washington and Benjamin Franklin present at the convention, a predilection swept over the country to accept whatever the convention proposed. Over the next year, Americans participated in a profound public debate over government and how best to preserve liberty. Many Americans viewed the Constitutional Convention as a last opportunity to peacefully adopt a viable federal constitution that would preserve the Union, promote justice and prosperity, and provide defense from both external aggression and domestic insurrection, and the entire country waited anxiously while delegates deliberated in secret for four months.

Controversy raged between delegates from the large and small states, between delegates from the northern and southern states, and between those who were nationalists and those who supported merely strengthening the existing confederation. Several compromises were eventually made, and a unique new form of government was presented to the states for ratification. After almost a year of public debate, the new U.S. Constitution was adopted, and Congress called for the first federal elections. Two years later the Bill of Rights was added to the Constitution, taking away one of the primary fears of the document's opponents—that it would reduce individual freedoms.

Author Biography

Fifty-five delegates attended the Constitutional Convention between May 25 and September 17, 1787. Averaging forty-four years old, the delegates were primarily lawyers, farmers, and merchants. The fifty-five-year-old George Washington was elected president of the convention. When the convention operated as a committee of the whole—that is, for the purpose of discussion under less official terms—Nathaniel Gorham, of Massachusetts, presided. Thirty-nine delegates signed the final document. Three delegates—Elbridge Gerry, from

Massachusetts, and Edmund Randolph and George Mason, both from Virginia—were in attendance on the last day but refused to sign the Constitution.

All of the delegates were political leaders in their home states. Many had served in Congress and in their state governments. Only two—Randolph, of Virginia, and William Livingston, of New Jersey—were incumbent governors. All of the delegates and subsequent scholars acknowledged the leadership of the thirty-six-year-old James Madison, of Virginia. He was soon dubbed and is still often referred to as the "father of the Constitution"—an appellation he steadfastly rejected, as he believed that the Constitution was the product of many hands and many hearts. In essence, no one person was the "father of the Constitution"; instead, perhaps, a half dozen or so might be called "uncles."

James Madison was the primary author of the Virginia Resolutions, presented on the first day of debates, which became the outline that the convention debated. Several key provisions of the Virginia proposal were rejected by the convention, leaving Madison despondent. Other proposals were presented by William Paterson (N.J.), Alexander Hamilton (N.Y.), and Charles Pinckney (S.C.). Other key delegates performed significant roles. The eighty-one-year-old Benjamin Franklin, though too frail to stand and speak himself, gave his Pennsylvania colleague James Wilson written speeches that Wilson then read. Franklin's speeches were often delivered when tempers flared, and his humor helped to reduce the tension. John Rutledge (S.C.) chaired the Committee of Detail; Elbridge Gerry (Mass.) chaired the committee that proposed the Great Compromise, aimed at balancing representation from small and large states; and William Samuel Johnson (Conn.) chaired the Committee of Style. Gouverneur Morris (N.J.) wrote the preamble and the final version of the text of the entire Constitution. Jacob Shallus, the assistant clerk of the Pennsylvania Assembly, was the scribe who actually wrote the four-page engrossed copy of the Constitution.

HISTORICAL DOCUMENT

We the People of the United States, in Order to form a more perfect Union, establish Justice, insure domestic Tranquility, provide for the common defense, promote the general Welfare, and secure the Blessings of Liberty to ourselves and our Posterity, do ordain and establish this Constitution for the United States of America.

Article I
Section 1
All legislative Powers herein granted shall be vested in a Congress of the United States, which shall consist of a Senate and House of Representatives.

Section 2
The House of Representatives shall be composed of Members chosen every second Year by the People of the several States, and the Electors in each State shall have the Qualifications requisite for Electors of the most numerous Branch of the State Legislature.

No Person shall be a Representative who shall not have attained to the Age of twenty five Years, and been seven Years a Citizen of the United States, and who shall not, when elected, be an Inhabitant of that State in which he shall be chosen.

Representatives and direct Taxes shall be apportioned among the several States which may be included within this Union, according to their respective Numbers, which shall be determined by adding to the whole Number of free Persons, including those bound to Service for a Term of Years, and excluding Indians not taxed, three fifths of all other Persons. The actual Enumeration shall be made within three Years after the first Meeting of the Congress of the United States, and within every subsequent Term of ten Years, in such Manner as they shall by Law direct. The Number of Representatives shall not exceed one for every thirty Thousand, but each State shall have at Least one Representative; and until such enumeration shall be made, the State of New Hampshire shall be entitled to chuse three, Massachusetts eight, Rhode-Island and Providence Plantations one, Connecticut five, New-York six, New Jersey four, Pennsylvania eight, Delaware one, Maryland six, Virginia ten, North Carolina five, South Carolina five, and Georgia three.

When vacancies happen in the Representation from any State, the Executive Authority thereof shall issue Writs of Election to fill such Vacancies.

The House of Representatives shall chuse their Speaker and other Officers; and shall have the sole Power of Impeachment.

Section 3
The Senate of the United States shall be composed of two Senators from each State, chosen by the Legislature thereof for six Years; and each Senator shall have one Vote.

Immediately after they shall be assembled in Consequence of the first Election, they shall be divided as equally as may be into three Classes. The Seats of the Senators of the first Class shall be vacated at the Expiration of the second Year, of the second Class at the Expiration of the fourth Year, and of the third Class at the Expiration of the sixth Year, so that one third may be chosen every second Year; and if Vacancies happen by Resignation, or otherwise, during the Recess of the Legislature of any State, the Executive thereof may make temporary Appointments until the next Meeting of the Legislature, which shall then fill such Vacancies.

No Person shall be a Senator who shall not have attained to the Age of thirty Years, and been nine Years a Citizen of the United States, and who shall not, when elected, be an Inhabitant of that State for which he shall be chosen.

The Vice President of the United States shall be President of the Senate, but shall have no Vote, unless they be equally divided.

The Senate shall chuse their other Officers, and also a President pro tempore, in the Absence of the Vice President, or when he shall exercise the Office of President of the United States.

The Senate shall have the sole Power to try all Impeachments. When sitting for that Purpose, they shall be on Oath or Affirmation. When the President of the United States is tried, the Chief Justice shall preside: And no Person shall be convicted without the Concurrence of two thirds of the Members present.

Judgment in Cases of Impeachment shall not extend further than to removal from Office, and disqualification to hold and enjoy any Office of honor, Trust or Profit under the United States: but the Party convicted shall nevertheless be liable and subject to Indictment, Trial, Judgment and Punishment, according to Law.

Section 4

The Times, Places and Manner of holding Elections for Senators and Representatives, shall be prescribed in each State by the Legislature thereof; but the Congress may at any time by Law make or alter such Regulations, except as to the Places of chusing Senators.

The Congress shall assemble at least once in every Year, and such Meeting shall be on the first Monday in December, unless they shall by Law appoint a different Day.

Section 5

Each House shall be the Judge of the Elections, Returns and Qualifications of its own Members, and a Majority of each shall constitute a Quorum to do Business; but a smaller Number may adjourn from day to day, and may be authorized to compel the Attendance of absent Members, in such Manner, and under such Penalties as each House may provide.

Each House may determine the Rules of its Proceedings, punish its Members for disorderly Behaviour, and, with the Concurrence of two thirds, expel a Member.

Each House shall keep a Journal of its Proceedings, and from time to time publish the same, excepting such Parts as may in their Judgment require Secrecy; and the Yeas and Nays of the Members of either House on any question shall, at the Desire of one fifth of those Present, be entered on the Journal.

Neither House, during the Session of Congress, shall, without the Consent of the other, adjourn for more than three days, nor to any other Place than that in which the two Houses shall be sitting.

Section 6

The Senators and Representatives shall receive a Compensation for their Services, to be ascertained by Law, and paid out of the Treasury of the United States. They shall in all Cases, except Treason, Felony and Breach of the Peace, be privileged from Arrest during their Attendance at the Session of their respective Houses, and in going to and returning from the same; and for any Speech or Debate in either House, they shall not be questioned in any other Place.

No Senator or Representative shall, during the Time for which he was elected, be appointed to any civil Office under the Authority of the United States, which shall have been created, or the Emoluments whereof shall have been encreased during such time; and no Person holding any Office under the United States, shall be a Member of either House during his Continuance in Office.

Section 7

All Bills for raising Revenue shall originate in the House of Representatives; but the Senate may propose or concur with Amendments as on other Bills.

Every Bill which shall have passed the House of Representatives and the Senate, shall, before it become a Law, be presented to the President of the United States: If he approve he shall sign it, but if not he shall return it, with his Objections to that House in which it shall have originated, who shall enter the Objections at large on their Journal, and proceed to reconsider it. If after such Reconsideration two thirds of that House shall agree to pass the Bill, it shall be sent, together with the Objections, to the other House, by which it shall likewise be reconsidered, and if approved by two thirds of that House, it shall become a Law. But in all such Cases the Votes of both Houses shall be determined by yeas and Nays, and the Names of the Persons voting for and against the Bill shall be entered on the Journal of each House respectively. If any Bill shall not be returned by the President within ten Days (Sundays excepted) after it shall have been presented to him, the Same shall be a Law, in like Manner as if he had signed it, unless the Congress by their Adjournment prevent its Return, in which Case it shall not be a Law.

Every Order, Resolution, or Vote to which the Concurrence of the Senate and House of Representatives may be necessary (except on a question of Adjournment) shall be presented to the President of the United States; and before the Same shall take Effect, shall be approved by him, or being disapproved by him, shall be repassed by two thirds of the Senate and House of Representatives, according to the Rules and Limitations prescribed in the Case of a Bill.

Section 8

The Congress shall have Power To lay and collect Taxes, Duties, Imposts and Excises, to pay the Debts and provide for the common Defence and general Welfare of the United States; but all Duties, Imposts and Excises shall be uniform throughout the United States;

To borrow Money on the credit of the United States;

To regulate Commerce with foreign Nations, and among the several States, and with the Indian Tribes;

To establish an uniform Rule of Naturalization, and uniform Laws on the subject of Bankruptcies throughout the United States;

To coin Money, regulate the Value thereof, and of foreign Coin, and fix the Standard of Weights and Measures;

To provide for the Punishment of counterfeiting the Securities and current Coin of the United States;

To establish Post Offices and post Roads;

To promote the Progress of Science and useful Arts, by securing for limited Times to Authors and Inventors the exclusive Right to their respective Writings and Discoveries;

To constitute Tribunals inferior to the supreme Court;

To define and punish Piracies and Felonies committed on the high Seas, and Offences against the Law of Nations;

To declare War, grant Letters of Marque and Reprisal, and make Rules concerning Captures on Land and Water;

To raise and support Armies, but no Appropriation of Money to that Use shall be for a longer Term than two Years;

To provide and maintain a Navy;

To make Rules for the Government and Regulation of the land and naval Forces;

To provide for calling forth the Militia to execute the Laws of the Union, suppress Insurrections and repel Invasions;

To provide for organizing, arming, and disciplining, the Militia, and for governing such Part of them as may be employed in the Service of the United States, reserving to the States respectively, the Appointment of the Officers, and the Authority of training the Militia according to the discipline prescribed by Congress;

To exercise exclusive Legislation in all Cases whatsoever, over such District (not exceeding ten Miles square) as may, by Cession of particular States, and the Acceptance of Congress, become the Seat of the Government of the United States, and to exercise like Authority over all Places purchased by the Consent of the Legislature of the State in which the Same shall be, for the Erection of Forts, Magazines, Arsenals, dock-Yards, and other needful Buildings;—And

To make all Laws which shall be necessary and proper for carrying into Execution the foregoing Powers, and all other Powers vested by this Constitution in the Government of the United States, or in any Department or Officer thereof.

Section 9

The Migration or Importation of such Persons as any of the States now existing shall think proper to admit, shall not be prohibited by the Congress prior to the Year one thousand eight hundred and eight, but a Tax or duty may be imposed on such Importation, not exceeding ten dollars for each Person.

The Privilege of the Writ of Habeas Corpus shall not be suspended, unless when in Cases of Rebellion or Invasion the public Safety may require it.

No Bill of Attainder or ex post facto Law shall be passed.

No Capitation, or other direct, Tax shall be laid, unless in Proportion to the Census or enumeration herein before directed to be taken.

No Tax or Duty shall be laid on Articles exported from any State.

No Preference shall be given by any Regulation of Commerce or Revenue to the Ports of one State over those of another; nor shall Vessels bound to, or from, one State, be obliged to enter, clear, or pay Duties in another.

No Money shall be drawn from the Treasury, but in Consequence of Appropriations made by Law; and a regular Statement and Account of the Receipts and Expenditures of all public Money shall be published from time to time.

No Title of Nobility shall be granted by the United States: And no Person holding any Office of Profit or Trust under them, shall, without the Consent of the Congress, accept of any present, Emolument, Office, or Title, of any kind whatever, from any King, Prince, or foreign State.

Section 10

No State shall enter into any Treaty, Alliance, or Confederation; grant Letters of Marque and Reprisal; coin Money; emit Bills of Credit; make any Thing but gold and silver Coin a Tender in Payment of Debts; pass any Bill of Attainder, ex post facto Law, or Law impairing the Obligation of Contracts, or grant any Title of Nobility.

No State shall, without the Consent of the Congress, lay any Imposts or Duties on Imports or Exports, except what may be absolutely necessary for executing its inspection Laws: and the net Produce of all Duties and Imposts, laid by any State on Imports or Exports, shall be for the Use of the Treasury of the United States; and all such Laws shall be subject to the Revision and Controul of the Congress.

No State shall, without the Consent of Congress, lay any Duty of Tonnage, keep Troops, or Ships of War in time of Peace, enter into any Agreement or Compact with another State, or with a foreign Power, or engage in War, unless actually invaded, or in such imminent Danger as will not admit of delay.

Article II
Section 1

The executive Power shall be vested in a President of the United States of America. He shall hold his Office during the Term of four Years, and, together with the Vice President, chosen for the same Term, be elected, as follows:

Each State shall appoint, in such Manner as the Legislature thereof may direct, a Number of Electors, equal to the whole Number of Senators and Representatives to which the State may be entitled in the Congress: but no Senator or Representative, or Person holding an Office of Trust or Profit under the United States, shall be appointed an Elector.

The Electors shall meet in their respective States, and vote by Ballot for two Persons, of whom one at least shall not be an Inhabitant of the same State with themselves. And they shall make a List of all the Persons voted for, and of the Number of Votes for each; which List they shall sign and certify, and transmit sealed to the Seat of the Government of the United States, directed to the President of the Senate. The President of the Senate shall, in the Presence of the Senate and House of Representatives, open all the Certificates, and the Votes shall then be counted. The Person having the greatest Number of Votes shall be the President, if such Number be a Majority of the whole Number of Electors appointed; and if there be more than one who have such Majority, and have an equal Number of Votes, then the House of Representatives shall immediately chuse by Ballot one of them for President; and if no Person have a Majority, then from the five highest on the List the said House shall in like Manner chuse the President. But in chusing the President, the Votes shall be taken by States, the Representation from each State having one Vote; A quorum for this purpose shall consist of a Member or Members from two thirds of the States, and a Majority of all the States shall be necessary to a Choice. In every Case, after the Choice of the President, the Person having the greatest Number of Votes of the Electors shall be the Vice President. But if there should remain two or more who have equal Votes, the Senate shall chuse from them by Ballot the Vice President.

The Congress may determine the Time of chusing the Electors, and the Day on which they shall give their Votes; which Day shall be the same throughout the United States.

No Person except a natural born Citizen, or a Citizen of the United States, at the time of the Adoption of this Constitution, shall be eligible to the Office of President; neither shall any Person be eligible to that Office who shall not have attained to the Age of thirty five Years, and been fourteen Years a Resident within the United States.

In Case of the Removal of the President from Office, or of his Death, Resignation, or Inability to discharge the Powers and Duties of the said Office, the Same shall devolve on the Vice President, and the Congress may by Law provide for the Case of Removal, Death, Resignation or Inability, both of the President and Vice President, declaring what Officer shall then act as President, and such Officer shall act accordingly, until the Disability be removed, or a President shall be elected.

The President shall, at stated Times, receive for his Services, a Compensation, which shall neither be increased nor diminished during the Period for which he shall have been elected, and he shall not receive within that Period any other Emolument from the United States, or any of them.

Before he enter on the Execution of his Office, he shall take the following Oath or Affirmation:— "I do solemnly swear (or affirm) that I will faithfully execute the Office of President of the United States, and will to the best of my Ability, preserve, protect and defend the Constitution of the United States."

Section 2
The President shall be Commander in Chief of the Army and Navy of the United States, and of the Militia of the several States, when called into the actual Service of the United States; he may require the Opinion, in writing, of the principal Officer in each of the executive Departments, upon any Subject relating to the Duties of their respective Offices, and he shall have Power to grant Reprieves and Pardons for Offences against the United States, except in Cases of Impeachment.

He shall have Power, by and with the Advice and Consent of the Senate, to make Treaties, provided two thirds of the Senators present concur; and he shall nominate, and by and with the Advice and Consent of the Senate, shall appoint Ambassadors, other public Ministers and Consuls, Judges of the supreme Court, and all other Officers of the United States, whose Appointments are not herein otherwise provided for, and which shall be established by Law: but the Congress may by Law vest the Appointment of such inferior Officers, as they think proper, in the President alone, in the Courts of Law, or in the Heads of Departments.

The President shall have Power to fill up all Vacancies that may happen during the Recess of the Senate, by granting Commissions which shall expire at the End of their next Session.

Section 3
He shall from time to time give to the Congress Information of the State of the Union, and recommend to their Consideration such Measures as he shall judge necessary and expedient; he may, on extraordinary Occasions, convene both Houses, or either of them, and in Case of Disagreement between them, with Respect to the Time of Adjournment, he may adjourn them to such Time as he shall think proper; he shall receive Ambassadors and other public Ministers; he shall take Care that the Laws be faithfully executed, and shall Commission all the Officers of the United States.

Section 4
The President, Vice President and all civil Officers of the United States, shall be removed from Office on Impeachment for, and Conviction of, Treason, Bribery, or other high Crimes and Misdemeanors.

Article III
Section 1
The judicial Power of the United States shall be vested in one supreme Court, and in such inferior Courts as the Congress may from time to time ordain and establish. The Judges, both of the supreme and inferior Courts, shall hold their Offices during good Behaviour, and shall, at stated Times, receive for their Services a Compensation, which shall not be diminished during their Continuance in Office.

Section 2
The judicial Power shall extend to all Cases, in Law and Equity, arising under this Constitution, the Laws of the United States, and Treaties made, or which shall be made, under their Authority;—to all Cases affecting Ambassadors, other public Ministers and Consuls;—to all Cases of admiralty and maritime Jurisdiction;—to Controversies to which the United States shall be a Party;—to Controversies between two or more States;— between a State and Citizens of another State;—between Citizens of different States;—between Citizens of the same State claiming Lands under Grants of different States, and between a State, or the Citizens thereof, and foreign States, Citizens or Subjects.

In all Cases affecting Ambassadors, other public Ministers and Consuls, and those in which a State shall be Party, the supreme Court shall have original Jurisdiction. In all the other Cases before mentioned, the supreme Court shall have appellate Jurisdiction, both as to Law and Fact, with such Exceptions, and under such Regulations as the Congress shall make.

The Trial of all Crimes, except in Cases of Impeachment, shall be by Jury; and such Trial shall be held in the State where the said Crimes shall have been committed; but when not committed within any State, the Trial shall be at such Place or Places as the Congress may by Law have directed.

Section 3
Treason against the United States, shall consist only in levying War against them, or in adhering to their Enemies, giving them Aid and Comfort. No Person shall be convicted of Treason unless on the Testimony of two Witnesses to the same overt Act, or on Confession in open Court.

The Congress shall have Power to declare the Punishment of Treason, but no Attainder of Treason shall work Corruption of Blood, or Forfeiture except during the Life of the Person attainted.

Article IV
Section 1
Full Faith and Credit shall be given in each State to the public Acts, Records, and judicial Proceedings of every other State. And the Congress may by general Laws prescribe the Manner in which such Acts, Records and Proceedings shall be proved, and the Effect thereof.

Section 2
The Citizens of each State shall be entitled to all Privileges and Immunities of Citizens in the several States.

A Person charged in any State with Treason, Felony, or other Crime, who shall flee from Justice, and be found in another State, shall on Demand of the executive Authority of the State from which he fled, be delivered up, to be removed to the State having Jurisdiction of the Crime.

No Person held to Service or Labour in one State, under the Laws thereof, escaping into another, shall, in Consequence of any Law or Regulation therein, be discharged from such Service or Labour, but shall be delivered up on Claim of the Party to whom such Service or Labour may be due.

Section 3
New States may be admitted by the Congress into this Union; but no new State shall be formed or erected within the Jurisdiction of any other State; nor any State be formed by the Junction of two or more States, or Parts of States, without the Consent of the Legislatures of the States concerned as well as of the Congress.

The Congress shall have Power to dispose of and make all needful Rules and Regulations respecting the Territory or other Property belonging to the United States; and nothing in this Constitution shall be so construed as to Prejudice any Claims of the United States, or of any particular State.

Section 4
The United States shall guarantee to every State in this Union a Republican Form of Government, and shall protect each of them against Invasion; and on Application of the Legislature, or of the Executive (when the Legislature cannot be convened), against domestic Violence.

Article V
The Congress, whenever two thirds of both Houses shall deem it necessary, shall propose Amendments to this Constitution, or, on the Application of the Legislatures of two thirds of the several States, shall call a Convention for proposing Amendments, which, in either Case, shall be valid to all Intents and Purposes, as Part of this Constitution, when ratified by the Legislatures of three fourths of the several States, or by Conventions in three fourths thereof, as the one or the other Mode of Ratification may be proposed by the Congress; Provided that no Amendment which may be made prior to the Year One thousand eight hundred and eight shall in any Manner affect the first and fourth Clauses in the Ninth Section of the first Article; and that no State, without its Consent, shall be deprived of its equal Suffrage in the Senate.

Article VI

All Debts contracted and Engagements entered into, before the Adoption of this Constitution, shall be as valid against the United States under this Constitution, as under the Confederation.

This Constitution, and the Laws of the United States which shall be made in Pursuance thereof; and all Treaties made, or which shall be made, under the Authority of the United States, shall be the supreme Law of the Land; and the Judges in every State shall be bound thereby, any Thing in the Constitution or Laws of any State to the Contrary notwithstanding.

The Senators and Representatives before mentioned, and the Members of the several State Legislatures, and all executive and judicial Officers, both of the United States and of the several States,

shall be bound by Oath or Affirmation, to support this Constitution; but no religious Test shall ever be required as a Qualification to any Office or public Trust under the United States.

Article VII

The Ratification of the Conventions of nine States, shall be sufficient for the Establishment of this Constitution between the States so ratifying the Same. ...

Done in Convention by the Unanimous Consent of the States present the Seventeenth Day of September in the Year of our Lord one thousand seven hundred and Eighty seven and of the Independence of the United States of America the Twelfth In witness whereof We have hereunto subscribed our Names[.]
...

GLOSSARY

Bill of Attainder: a legislative statement of guilt or conviction without a trial

Duties: governmental taxes placed on goods, typically exports or imports

Emoluments: compensations arising from office or employment

enumeration: a listing

Excises: taxes on the manufacture, sale, or use of goods within a country

ex post facto: retroactively; applying to previous events

quorum: the minimum number of members needed to be present for a group to conduct valid business

Republican: based upon representation

Securities: evidences of debt or of ownership

Writ of Habeas Corpus: an order to bring a person before a court or judge, usually as a protection against illegal imprisonment

Document Analysis

In terms of governmental concepts, nothing in the Constitution is new; every part came from the Articles of Confederation, the state constitutions and bills of rights, or the Northwest Ordinance. The genius of the Founding Fathers lay in how they mixed together these disparate "old" provisions to create a federal republic different from any other previously formed state. The

genesis of the Constitution came about through a series of compromises struck among delegates representing states with different interests. Delegates from large and small states first vied with each other over representation. Southern delegates differed with northern delegates on representation and a host of other issues. The southern delegates sought an agricultural society in which slavery would be protected from those who wished to abolish the South's peculiar institution, while northerners wanted to encourage commerce, fishing, and manufacturing. The country as a whole was divided between those who wanted a strong central government and those who merely wanted to give the Confederation Congress a few more necessary powers while keeping the primary political authority with the states. These competing forces were in fact essential to the shaping of the Constitution. By dividing power between the federal and state governments and by separating the different branches of the federal government through an intricate system of checks and balances, the convention created a uniquely strong and efficient federal government that could better protect the rights of its citizens.

The Constitution is introduced by a fifty-two-word preamble, written by Gouverneur Morris, that announces a major change in national philosophy. Opening with the famous words "We the People of the United States," the Constitution replaced the loose confederation of states with a contract forged among all of the nation's people. The new federal government would "form a more perfect Union, establish Justice, insure domestic Tranquility, provide for the common defence, promote the general Welfare, and secure the Blessings of Liberty to ourselves and our Posterity."

Seven articles follow the preamble. Article I—in length, half of the entire Constitution—gave all legislative power to a bicameral Congress. To be elected biennially by the people, the larger House of Representatives was apportioned among the states based upon population, including three-fifths of the slaves. Reapportionment in the House would occur every ten years after a federal census. For the smaller Senate, each state legislature would elect two federal senators to serve six-year terms. One-third of the Senate was to be elected every two years. Senators and representatives would vote individually, not as a state delegation. The vice president of the United States would serve as president of the Senate, casting votes only to break ties.

The states would set their own rules for electing members of Congress, but Congress could regulate elections that were not held. Congress would be required to sit at least once annually. Each house would elect its own officers, create its own rules, keep its own records, set qualifications for its own members, and determine the results of disputed elections. By law, Congress would set all governmental salaries, which would be paid out of the federal treasury. Mandatory rotation

in office and the power of recall were eliminated. No member of Congress would be allowed to coincidentally hold another federal office.

Congress would be entitled to levy and collect taxes; regulate foreign and interstate commerce; declare war; raise and maintain an army and navy; provide rules for training state militias; establish post offices and post roads; borrow and coin money; punish counterfeiters; set uniform bankruptcy laws; pass laws for naturalization; fix standards for weights and measures; grant copyrights and patents; define and punish piracy and crimes at sea; create inferior federal courts; exercise exclusive jurisdiction over a federal capital and over federal forts, arsenals, and magazines; and "make all Laws which shall be necessary and proper, for carrying into Execution the foregoing Powers." Only the House could initiate money bills, but, unlike Great Britain's House of Lords, the Senate could amend money bills. The president could veto bills, but Congress could override the veto by a two-thirds vote in each house.

The last two sections of Article I placed limits on the actions of Congress and the states. Both were prohibited from passing bills of attainder, enacting ex post facto laws, and granting titles of nobility. Congress specifically could not levy export duties, close the foreign slave trade before 1808, or suspend the writ of habeas corpus except during rebellions and foreign invasion. The states were also prohibited from passing laws that would impair the obligation of contracts, coining money, issuing paper money, declaring anything but gold and silver legal tender, entering into treaties or alliances, or (without the consent of Congress) levying import or export duties.

Article II vested the executive power in a president to serve for four years and to be eligible for unlimited reelection. Special presidential electors, equal to the total number of each state's representatives and senators and chosen in a manner decided by the state legislatures, were to meet on the same day in their home states and cast two ballots—one of which could not be for a resident of their state. The person receiving the highest number of votes would be elected president; the person with the second highest number would become vice president. If two or more people tied—each with electoral votes that totaled a majority of the electors appointed—the House of Representatives would by ballot choose the winner. If no person had a vote that was a majority of the number of the electors, the House of Representatives would choose the president by ballot from among those with the five highest numbers of electoral votes. The Senate, voting per capita, would elect the vice president.

The president—who had to be at least thirty-five years old, a natural-born citizen or a citizen at the time that the Constitution was adopted, and a resident of the United States for fourteen years—was to be commander in chief of the military and of the state militias whenever they were brought into federal service. He could grant pardons and reprieves—except in cases of impeachment—and, with the advice and consent of the Senate, make appointments (including diplomats and judges), enter into treaties (subject to the approval of a two-thirds vote of the Senate), and require in writing the opinions of the heads of the different executive departments. The president would receive a fixed salary that could not be raised or lowered during his term of office, and he would be required to take an oath to faithfully execute his duties and to defend the Constitution. From time to time the president was to make a "State of the Union" address to Congress containing "such Measures as he shall judge necessary and expedient." The president, vice president, and all other civil officers could be impeached by the House of Representatives for "Treason, Bribery, or other High Crimes and Misdemeanors." The Senate would try all impeachments, with conviction requiring a two thirds vote. The chief justice would preside over impeachment trials of the president. Punishment was limited to removal from office, but those convicted were also subject to regular criminal prosecution.

Article III provided for a federal judiciary to consist of one Supreme Court and such inferior courts as Congress deemed necessary. To be nominated by the president and confirmed by the Senate, federal judges were to serve during good behavior with salaries that could not be diminished. The judiciary's jurisdiction would extend to all cases of law and equity arising under the Constitution, federal laws, and treaties as well as to cases involving the United States, cases between citizens of different states, and cases involving foreigners. The original jurisdiction of the Supreme Court was delineated in the Constitution; in all other cases the Supreme Court would have appellate jurisdiction in law and fact, with such exceptions as provided by Congress. Unlike with the British House of Lords or in several state constitutions, no provision was made for legislative overview of Supreme Court decisions. By authority of the supremacy clause in Article VI, federal judges could declare state laws unconstitutional and thus null and void. As per the general principles of written constitutions, federal judges could also declare acts of Congress and of the president unconstitutional.

Jury trials were guaranteed in criminal cases within the state in which the crime had been committed. Treason was narrowly defined, and its punishment could not extend to the family of the traitor.

Article IV required that each state give "full Faith and Credit" to the public acts, records, and judicial proceedings of the other states. Citizens of each state would be entitled to the "Privileges and Immunities" of citizens in other states, while states would be required to extradite other states' fugitives from justice and runaway slaves. Congress could admit new states into the Union and could make rules and regulations for federal territories. The United States guaranteed each state a republican form of government, protection from foreign invasion, and assistance against domestic violence upon the application of the state legislature, or of the governor when the legislature was not in session.

Article V provided that amendments to the Constitution could be proposed either by a two-thirds vote in both houses of Congress or by a constitutional convention called on the application to Congress of two-thirds of the states. Proposed amendments could be ratified by three-quarters of the state legislatures or by state ratifying conventions, whichever method Congress directed.

Article VI provided that the new federal government assumed all the debts and engagements previously held by the Confederation government. It also specified that "This Constitution, and the Laws of the United States which shall be made in Pursuance thereof; and all Treaties made, or which shall be made, under the Authority of the United States, shall be the supreme Law of the Land; and the Judges in every State shall be bound thereby, any Thing in the Constitution or Laws of any State to the Contrary notwithstanding."

Article VII provided that the Constitution would be considered in each state by specially elected ratifying conventions and that whenever nine states ratified, the Constitution would go into effect among the ratifying states.

Essential Themes

The introduction and implementation of the Constitution had a profound impact on the nation. At a time when the principles of the American Revolution were being questioned, it provided a necessary and revolutionary change in how the United States would be governed. If the Constitution had not been either proposed or adopted, the United States might have stayed a loose confederation of states, evolved into a parliamentary system of government, become a monarchy, returned into the British Empire, become separate confederacies, or adopted a different form of government at a later time. All of the alternatives would have likely brought about dramatically different circumstances. As it is, the Constitution educated and continues to educate Americans about the nature of government and how best to preserve liberty, and it provided written historical assertions to help subsequent government officials, especially jurists such as John Marshall, interpret the Constitution. From the moment the Constitution was implemented, all sides endorsed it as an almost divinely inspired text. The debate then shifted from the topic of the quality of the Constitution to the question of how this veritably sacred text was to be interpreted.

Discussion over the nature of the new Constitution continued unabated from the time of its promulgation, through its ratification, and into and beyond the first decade of its implementation. During the first federal elections, Antifederalists continued their efforts to obtain amendments, while Federalists, many of whom had promised to support amendments after the Constitution had been ratified, opposed amendments and attacked those who campaigned for alterations. Ultimately, a set of additional rights was proposed by President Washington and Representative Madison. Sent to the states in October 1789, ten amendments were adopted in December 1791. Although unused throughout the nineteenth century, the Bill of Rights has become the most controversial part of the Constitution.

Throughout the 1790s a constitutional debate raged between Federalists and their opponents. The Federalists wanted an energetic federal government that would actively stimulate the economy and (in the late 1790s) suppress political opposition. The opponents of the Federalists (called Republicans, Democratic Republicans, or Jeffersonians) wanted a far more limited federal government with a laissez faire policy and with virtually no power to restrict the freedom of speech or the press. With the 1800 election of Thomas Jefferson as president and a Jeffersonian majority in both houses of Congress, a more laissez-faire interpretation of the Constitution took hold. Circumstances during the presidencies of Jefferson and Madison brought the constitutional interpretation of the Jeffersonians to a more centralist position, as Federalists became more extremist and isolated in New England. The presidency of James Monroe saw the demise of the Federalist Party and the emergence of what historians have called the Era of Good Feeling, during which a constitutional interpretation similar to what Federalists had advocated during the ratification debate of 1788 came to prominence—a view highlighted by several important constitutional decisions written by Chief Justice John Marshall.

Members of the old Federalist Party and many former Republicans now agreed on how to interpret the Constitution, but in the late 1820s a neo-Antifederalist party emerged that advocated states' rights with very limited powers for the federal government. A more democratic interpretation of the Constitution occurred under President Andrew Jackson and his successors. The role of the federal government with respect to slavery in federal territories created the greatest crisis in the interpretation of the Constitution—one that led nearly half of the states to secede from the Union in 1861 and adopt a written constitution providing for a far weaker central government. The catastrophic Civil War greatly strengthened the authority of the presidency. For the next three decades, the federal courts, citing the Constitution's commerce clause, broadly interpreted the Constitution in favor of private business interests. The progressive reformist movement beginning at the turn of the century, as bolstered by the enhanced roles of such dynamic leaders as Theodore Roosevelt, Woodrow Wilson, and Franklin D. Roosevelt—as well as by the crises of the two world wars and the Great Depression—called for an enlarged interpretation of the Constitution and a greatly expanded role for the federal government. Over the last half of the twentieth century, political leaders and social activists advocated various constitutional positions on civil rights for minorities and on the president's role as commander in chief.

Over the course of its history, the Constitution has provided each generation of Americans with a written form of government with enough elasticity to meet their needs. The assertions and laws presented in the Constitution continue to shape the policies of the federal and state governments and the lives of all Americans. This historic document will undoubtedly long remain the fulcrum of the most consequential national political debates.

——John P. Kaminski

Bibliography and Further Reading

Collier, Christopher, and James Lincoln Collier. *Decision in Philadelphia: The Constitutional Convention of 1787*. New York: Random House, Reader's Digest, 1986.

Conley, Patrick T., and John P. Kaminski, eds. *The Constitution and the States: The Role of the Original Thirteen in the Framing and Adoption of the Federal Constitution*. Madison, Wis. Madison House, 1988.

Elkins, Stanley, and Eric McKitrick. *The Age of Federalism*. New York: Oxford University Press, 1993.

Gillespie, Michael Allen, and Michael Lienesch, eds. *Ratifying the Constitution*. Lawrence: University Press of Kansas, 1989.

Levy, Leonard W. *Original Intent and the Framers' Constitution*. New York: Macmillan, 1988.

McGuire, Robert A. *To Form a More Perfect Union: A New Economic Interpretation of the United States Constitution*. Oxford, U.K. Oxford University Press, 2003.

Monk, Linda R. *The Words We Live By: Your Annotated Guide to the Constitution*. New York: Hyperion, 2003.

Web sites

"Constitution of the United States." National Archives "Charters of Freedom." http://www.archives.gov/national-archives-experience/charters/constitution.html [accessed October 5, 2007].

"The Federalist Papers." Founding Fathers. http://www.foundingfathers.info/federalistpapers/. [accessed January 25, 2008].

"United States Constitution." Library of Congress "Primary Documents in American History." http://www.loc.gov/rr/program/bib/ourdocs/Constitution.html. [accessed October 5, 2007].

Declaration of the Rights of Man and of the Citizen

Date: 1789
Author: Marie-Joseph du Motier, marquis de Lafayette
Genre: Statement of rights

Summary Overview

On August 26, 1789, the National Assembly of France approved the Declaration of the Rights of Man and of the Citizen, a document that ended the ancien régime in France. The term ancien régime refers to the old society before the outbreak of the French Revolution that year. As a society, it was characterized by an absolute monarch as ruler, a hierarchical social structure with each social class having a set of privileges, and a restrictive labor system controlled by the guilds (associations of tradesmen). In composing the Declaration of the Rights of Man and of the Citizen, the representatives of the French people organized as the National Assembly borrowed heavily on the writings of Marie-Joseph du Motier, marquis de Lafayette. In July 1789 Lafayette wrote a preamble to a future constitution of France, proclaiming that the principle of all sovereignty resided in the nation. This preamble provided a model for the version of the preamble written by the liberal Emmanuel Joseph Sieyès, also known as Abbé Sieyès. This later preamble, expanded in August 1789, was based on the motto of the French Revolution—"liberty, equality, and fraternity"—and was inspired by the U.S. Declaration of Independence (1776). Strongly influenced by Enlightenment ideas, the Declaration of the Rights of Man and of the Citizen was accepted by the French king Louis XVI on October 5, 1789, and was promulgated on November 3, 1789.

Defining Moment

At the beginning of the eighteenth century, France experienced a period of expansion, population growth, and increased urbanization, and the newer colonial empires of France began to pay off. By the end of the century, the population surge had begun to press against the food supply. Land hunger and food shortages went hand in hand with increasing social dissatisfactions in the country. France was experiencing growing pains. Although France was changing, the structure of French society, a system of privilege, was not. The social structure was more than one hundred years old. The population was divided into three "estates," each with its own set of privileges, although the privileges were not equal. The First Estate was the clergy, the Second Estate consisted of the nobility, and the Third Estate included everyone else. The economic crises of 1787, 1788, and 1789 showed the weakness of the social order. This situation stimulated suspicions between the lower and the upper classes and between all classes and the government; it gave rise to an indefinite fear of complacency. Moreover, there was a general lack of confidence in the established social and political order.

The response of King Louis XVI was to call an Assembly of Notables, a meeting of select members of the nobility. In 1788 he invited them to come to his palace at Versailles, in the hope that the nobility would agree to gifts to the crown and to a new taxation structure. Thus the nobility, by acting in concert with the crown, would relieve the fiscal crisis faced by Louis XVI and the government. The assembly failed to produce the desired results, however, and Louis was forced to call a meeting of the Estates-General of France in 1789. This medieval representative institution in France had not met for 175 years before Louis XVI reconvened it on May 5, 1789, to deal with the looming financial crisis. France was on the verge of bankruptcy.

The meeting of the Estates-General provided those elected to it with the opportunity to present their grievances. On June 20, 1789, the members of the newly formed National Assembly took the Tennis Court Oath, pledging to remain together until they had drafted and passed a new constitution. The National Assembly, also called the Constituent Assembly, is what the Third Estate's delegation to the Estates-General decided to call itself when, on June 16, 1789, it proclaimed itself the sole legitimate representative of the French nation. The name stuck when, after a failed attempt to undo this clear usurpation of royal authority, Louis XVI ordered the noble and clerical delegations to join the National Assembly on June 27, 1789. (The National Assembly differed greatly from the Estates-General. The latter organization, which dated to the fourteenth century, was primarily a consultative as-

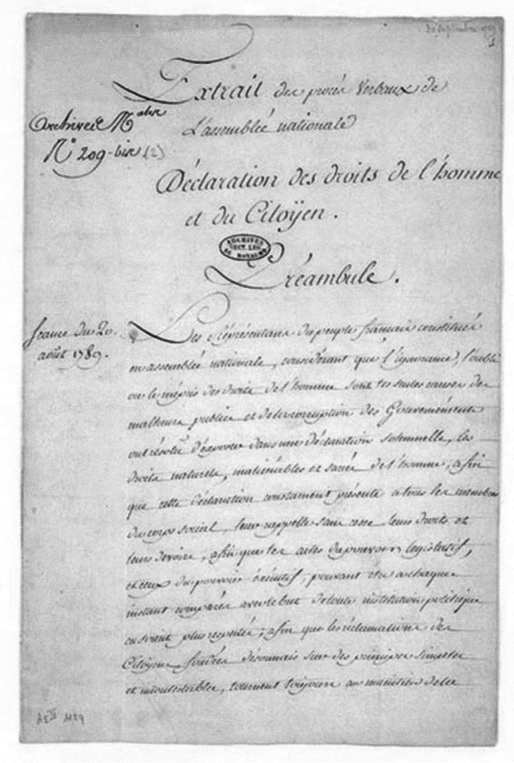

Declaration des droits de l'homme et du citoyen de 1789. Page 1 - Archives Nationales (commons.wikimedia.org) [Public Domain]

sembly, convoked at the pleasure of the king.) These events marked the birth of the Patriot Party, resulting in part from the success of a small pamphlet published by Emmanuel-Joseph Sieyès in January 1789 titled "What Is the Third Estate?" Sieyès's argument was based on the concepts of utility and nationalism. The Third Estate was the most useful class to the nation. The nobles constituted an *imperium in imperio*, or empire within an empire. The Third Estate's demands for equality were moderate. It was by itself the National Assembly and therefore should create a system that eliminated class privilege.

The traditional date marking the start of the French Revolution is July 14, 1789, when revolutionaries stormed and seized the royal prison, the Bastille, in Paris. The storming of the Bastille had few practical consequences, but symbolically it was of enormous significance. It represented the Revolution-inspired attack on the ancien régime. Today it is celebrated as Bastille Day, or French Independence Day. Shortly after the fall of the Bastille, in a series of disturbances in the countryside of France, rural peasants revolted against their feudal overlords during July and August 1789, a period known as the Great Fear. These revolts were occasioned by rumors of an aristocratic plot to hoard grain and drive up prices while sending gangs of bandits to ruin the peasants' crops in the countryside.

On August 4, 1789, Armand II, the duke of Aiguillon, a liberal nobleman, renounced feudal rights, prerogatives, and dues in order to satisfy the peasants and restore order to the countryside. Effectively, this action ended the feudal system in France. Fearful that the peasants would next begin to attack the property of the bourgeoisie, or middle class, the National Assembly in August issued a series of decrees that, in effect, destroyed the ancien régime.

On August 26, 1789, the National Assembly deputies faced the difficult task of composing a bill of rights that a majority of the deputies could accept. A lengthy debate ensued, with the following questions raised: Should the declaration be short and limited to general principles, or should it include a long explanation of the significance of each article? Should the declaration include a list of duties or only rights? What precisely were "the natural, inalienable, and sacred rights of man"? After several days of debate and voting, the deputies suspended their deliberations on the declaration, having agreed on seventeen articles

that laid out a new vision of government. The basis of authority was no longer the king but the will of the people. The duty of the government was to protect the natural rights of its citizens.

Author Biography

The Declaration of the Rights of Man and of the Citizen sought to define natural and civil rights for the citizens of France. Much of the document was taken from a draft done by General Lafayette, a liberal and a heroic participant in the American Revolution, at the request of the National Assembly during the summer of 1789.

Born to the Motier family in the Auvergne on September 6, 1757, Lafayette studied at the prestigious Collège du Plessis in Paris before joining the French army in 1771. Leaving France for America, he participated in the American War of Independence. He then fought in the French Revolutionary Wars, a series of conflicts (1792–1802) fought between the French Revolutionary government and several European states. Thus he became a hero on both sides of the Atlantic.

Politically liberal, Lafayette rose to leadership as early as 1788, favoring a parliamentary monarchy like England's but one based on a formal written constitution like that of the United States. Increasingly, Lafayette's efforts to hold the Revolution to a more moderate course grew difficult. Given the position of commander of the National Guard, Lafayette unwisely ordered the guard to fire on a crowd gathered in the Champs de Mars in 1791. The general refused to support Napoléon's Imperial France and returned to political life in France only after Napoléon's final abdication in 1815. Strongly opposing Louis XVIII and Charles X, Lafayette sat in the Chamber of Deputies as a member of the opposition party from 1818 to 1824. He died on May 20, 1834, in Paris.

The modifications of the Declaration of the Rights of Man and of the Citizen took place through a series of debates held from August 1 through August 4, 1789. The principal proponent of a declaration was Mathieu de Montmorency, duke of Montmorency-Laval. Montmorency was born in 1767 and, as an adolescent, had served along with his father in the American Revolution. He returned from that war imbued with democratic ideals. In 1789 he was elected deputy to the Estates-General, becoming closely allied with Lafayette and the reforming faction of nobles.

HISTORICAL DOCUMENT

The representatives of the French people, organized as a National Assembly, believing that the ignorance, neglect, or contempt of the rights of man are the sole cause of public calamities and of the corruption of governments, have determined to set forth in a solemn declaration the natural, unalienable, and sacred rights of man, in order that this declaration, being constantly before all the members of the Social body, shall remind them continually of their rights and duties; in order that the acts of the legislative power, as well as those of the executive power, may be compared at any moment with the objects and purposes of all political institutions and may thus be more respected, and, lastly, in order that the grievances of the citizens, based hereafter upon simple and incontestable principles, shall tend to the maintenance of the constitution and redound to the happiness of all. Therefore the National Assembly recognizes and proclaims, in the presence and under the auspices of the Supreme Being, the following rights of man and of the citizen:

Articles:

1. Men are born and remain free and equal in rights. Social distinctions may be founded only upon the general good.

2. The aim of all political association is the preservation of the natural and imprescriptible rights of man. These rights are liberty, property, security, and resistance to oppression.

3. The principle of all sovereignty resides essentially in the nation. No body nor individual may exercise any authority which does not proceed directly from the nation.

4. Liberty consists in the freedom to do everything which injures no one else; hence the exercise of the natural rights of each man has no limits except those which assure to the other members of the society the enjoyment of the same rights. These limits can only be determined by law.

5. Law can only prohibit such actions as are hurtful to society. Nothing may be prevented which is not forbidden by law, and no one may be forced to do anything not provided for by law.

6. Law is the expression of the general will. Every citizen has a right to participate personally, or through his representative, in its foundation. It must be the same for all, whether it protects or punishes. All citizens, being equal in the eyes of the law, are equally eligible to all dignities and to all public positions and occupations, according to their abilities, and without distinction except that of their virtues and talents.

7. No person shall be accused, arrested, or imprisoned except in the cases and according to the forms prescribed by law. Any one soliciting, transmitting, executing, or causing to be executed, any arbitrary order, shall be punished. But any citizen summoned or arrested in virtue of the law shall submit without delay, as resistance constitutes an offense.

8. The law shall provide for such punishments only as are strictly and obviously necessary, and no one shall suffer punishment except it be legally inflicted in virtue of a law passed and promulgated before the commission of the offense.

9. As all persons are held innocent until they shall have been declared guilty, if arrest shall be deemed indispensable, all harshness not essential to the securing of the prisoner's person shall be severely repressed by law.

10. No one shall be disquieted on account of his opinions, including his religious views, provided their manifestation does not disturb the public order established by law.

11. The free communication of ideas and opinions is one of the most precious of the rights of man. Every citizen may, accordingly, speak, write, and print with freedom, but shall be responsible for such abuses of this freedom as shall be defined by law.

12. The security of the rights of man and of the citizen requires public military forces. These forces are, therefore, established for the good of all and not for the personal advantage of those to whom they shall be intrusted.

13. A common contribution is essential for the maintenance of the public forces and for the cost of administration. This should be equitably distributed among all the citizens in proportion to their means.

14. All the citizens have a right to decide, either personally or by their representatives, as to the necessity of the public contribution; to grant this freely; to know to what uses it is put; and to fix the proportion, the mode of assessment and of collection and the duration of the taxes.

15. Society has the right to require of every public agent an account of his administration.

16. A society in which the observance of the law is not assured, nor the separation of powers defined, has no constitution at all.

17. Since property is an inviolable and sacred right, no one shall be deprived thereof except where public necessity, legally determined, shall clearly demand it, and then only on condition that the owner shall have been previously and equitably indemnified.

GLOSSARY

imprescriptible: not subject to loss or diminution for any reason

Document Analysis

The Declaration of the Rights of Man and of the Citizen expresses the liberal and universal goal of the philosophes, the general term for those academics and intellectuals who became the leading voices of the French Enlightenment during the eighteenth century. The most important of these men were Voltaire, Jean-Jacques Rousseau, Denis Diderot, and Charles-Louis de Secondat, baron of Montesquieu. The two fundamental ideas of the Enlightenment were rationalism and relativism. Rationalism was the belief that through the power of reason, humans could arrive at truth and improve human society. The philosophes were eager to demonstrate that human reason was the best guide for organizing society and government. Relativism, a philosophy that different ideas, cultures, and beliefs had equal worth, gripped the European mind as the impact of the Age of Exploration demonstrated that adherence to this philosophy had practical and intellectual value in any societal program for reform. Europeans were exposed to a variety of cultures and peoples worldwide.

The Declaration of the Rights of Man and of the Citizen also addressed the interests of the bourgeois, including their demands for government by the people and the idea that the aim of the government is to preserve the natural rights of the individual. The political ideas of John Locke and Montesquieu and Rousseau's work *The Social Contract*, along with Voltaire's thoughts on equality and an end to government censorship, spring from the pages of the document. In addition, the National Assembly helped businesses stop tariffs, ended the guild system, and decreed that French colonies trade only with France.

The document embodies the political ideas of Locke and Rousseau with regard to the idea of the social contract and the general will, as well as Montesquieu's work *The Spirit of the Laws*, which calls for a separation of powers. Montesquieu argues that the power of the government should be divided into separate branches, usually legislative, judicial, and executive, so that no one branch of government could gain too much authority. The ideas expressed in the Declaration of the Rights of Man and of the Citizen were influenced by the preamble to the U.S. Constitution. In his preamble to the French Constitution, Sieyès wrote in August 1789 that after having set forth the natural and civil rights of citizens, political rights would follow. He believed that all inhabitants of France were entitled to the right of protection of their person, their property, and their liberty; however, all did not have the right to take an active part in the formation of the public authorities—including women, children, foreigners, and those who contributed nothing to maintaining the public establishment. All could enjoy the benefits of society, but only those who contributed to the public establishment could declare themselves to be true active citizens, true members of the association.

Paragraph 1 states: "The representatives of the French people constituted as a National Assembly ... have resolved to set forth in a solemn declaration the natural, inalienable, and sacred rights of Man." Rather than ending debate about rights, the vote on the declaration opened it up in new ways. The people of France now possessed an official document based on universal principles; this document encouraged further discussion of human rights and, in fact, demanded clarification concerning who was included in the definition of "man and citizen." Should the definition include the poor, those without property, the religious minority, blacks, mulattoes (people of mixed race), or even women? Where should the lines defining citizenship be drawn? The question of citizenship helped drive the Revolution into increasingly radical directions after 1789. Each group excluded in 1789 began to assert its claims to the right to be citizens of France. French legislators approached the question of citizenship step by step over a period of five years after 1789. France was in flux, the Patriot Party walked a tightrope, and the Revolution was never on solid ground.

In proclaiming the Declaration of the Rights of Man and of the Citizen, the National Assembly defined liberty in broad terms in order to provide essential freedoms and liberties with few restrictions. This is evident in Article 1, which states that men are born and remain free and equal in rights. Article 2 provides a definition of the social contract theory's idea of natural rights: These rights are liberty, property, security, and resistance to oppression. Article 3 states the radical notions that the sovereignty of the nation resides in the nation; the nation is defined as the only source from which authority is delivered. This statement constituted an attack on the ancien régime concept of absolute monarchs ruling by divine right; the power of royalty was to be taken by the National Assembly, "the nation assembled." Article 4 offers an explanation of the limits of freedom and liberty and clearly puts all freedoms and protections under the written law.

Articles 5–9 deal with the establishment of new laws of the nation. These laws protect citizens from arbitrary arrest and imprisonment and grant equality to all citizens, especially in the eyes of the law. Article 5 is closely tied to the principles asserted in the previous article. Article 6 provides a direct statement of an important element in Jean-Jacques Rousseau's work *The Social Contract*. Here the idea that the general will expresses the law of the land provides for citizen political participation, whether directly or through elected representatives. Being equal before the law, every citizen is likewise entitled to all dignities and public positions—a strong statement that suggests the revolutionary principle that careers should be open only to those with talent. Articles 7–9

address the legal system. Under the ancien régime, each order had its own law courts, and certain provinces had their own courts. With enough influence one could have one's case transferred to the king's court. No member of the clergy could be tried in any court other than an ecclesiastical court. Taken together, these articles establish equality under the law and a more humane penal code. The importance of the written law as the foundation of these rights is evident.

Article 10 addresses the ancien régime's practice of censorship and the lack of "free speech." The written law is held up as the determinant of limits—citizens are free to communicate ideas and opinions, including speech related to religious beliefs, "provided their manifestation [speech] does not disturb the public order established by law." Article 11 makes clear that the right of free speech is "one of the most precious rights of man."

Article 12 addresses the need for public military forces—a national army, not the private army of the monarch—to be gathered by conscription, or the *levee en masse*. Article 13 redresses the ancien régime's secrecy in accounts—that is, how public funds are spent—and proposes an equitable distribution for the costs of administering the government, stating that citizens must be told exactly what their share of this cost would be. Article 14 takes the power of taxation out of the hands of the king and the Estates-General, reserving these decisions to either direct action by the individual or action through elected representatives. Included in this article is the right to determine not only the mode of assessment but the duration of the taxation.

Article 15 makes every civil servant, administrator, and public agent accountable for his administration. This article redresses the practice of venality under the ancien régime, where government offices were bought and accountability was owed only to the king. Article 16 demands that written law supersedes everything in creating a new society, for law legitimizes society. Clearly, this article makes the legislative separation of powers—the idea of the philosophe Montesquieu—and a written law governing all elements of this society the necessary foundation for a constitutional society. Finally, Article 17 establishes the right to own property, as described by John Locke. The article also sets forth the principle of eminent domain, or the right of the state to seize property in cases of necessity.

Essential Themes

The reforms of the National Assembly dismantled the ancien régime in France. The instrument by which this was done was the Declaration of the Rights of Man and of the Citizen. With the National Assembly's decrees of August 4, 1789, the equality demanded by the bourgeoisie was achieved. The declaration expressed the liberal and universal goal of Enlightenment philosophers and the middle class—government by the people—with the aim of ensuring that government would exist to preserve the natural rights of the individual.

Following August 26, 1789, the National Assembly proceeded to rebuild France from the ground up. The Great Reforms of 1789–1791, all rooted in the ideological foundations of the declaration and the writings of the philosophes, fall roughly into three categories. First, the Patriots wanted to limit the government by decentralizing the administration and the judiciary. On December 14, 1789, the National Assembly established a structure for municipal governments throughout France. For this purpose it created a distinction between active citizens (men who paid yearly taxes equal to three days' wages) who could vote and passive citizens who could not vote. On December 22, 1789, the assembly established a structure for new departmental administration. The number of departments throughout France was reduced. The departments were subdivided into districts and cantons. In the cantons only active citizens could vote and then only for electors who would choose deputies to the National Assembly and district officials who had to pay yearly taxes equal to ten days' wages. Deputies to the National Assembly had to pay yearly taxes equal to a silver mark. On August 16, 1790, cantons, districts, and departments were given courts staffed by elected judges.

Second, to deal further with the bankruptcy problem, the National Assembly on December 19, 1789, authorized the issuance of paper money (assignats) to be backed by church lands and to be redeemable when they were sold. The declaration struck at the Roman Catholic Church in France by ending tithes and taking church lands. On February 13, 1790, the National Assembly suppressed the monastic orders, thus creating a supply of salable land. Members of the National Assembly did not wish to destroy the church, which they considered to be a useful source of popular moral inspiration. On July 12, 1790, they issued the Civil Constitution of the Clergy, making departments and dioceses coterminous. Bishops and priests were to be elected in the same fashion as other departmental and district officials; they were paid by the state. Moreover, they were required to pledge allegiance to the constitution of the nation. Only a few members of the clergy did so; most clergy became refractory, or nonaccepting, clergy. Many left France or went into hiding. This issue divided the French people.

Finally, in more general financial and economic reforms, the National Assembly was strongly influenced by physiocratic doctrines (doctrines of utility or usefulness). In October 1790 it established a unified tariff for France. In November 1790 it set up two basic taxes—a contribution on land and a contribution on personal property. Also, on June 14, 1791, the National Assembly passed the Le Chapelier Law, which prohibited industrial and labor strikes. On May 21, 1791, the assembly established the metric system. The reorganization of France from the ground up was complete.

The 1791 constitution upheld the principles of the Declaration of the Rights of Man and of the Citizen by limiting the power of the king and guaranteeing equal taxation under the law. In June 1791 the royal family, fearing for their lives, attempted to flee France and were arrested at Varennes, France (the so-called "flight to Varennes"). Later, in October, the new Legislative Assembly met for the first time. By 1792 counterrevolutionary movements were forming, so in August of that year the king was imprisoned; that same month, the National Convention replaced the Legislative Assembly. The Revolution began to turn violent when prisoners, most of them aristocrats, were killed during the so-called September Massacres of 1792. In 1792 the monarchy was abolished, and the First French Republic was proclaimed. Louis XVI was executed on January 21, 1793, and in March the Revolutionary Tribunal was created, leading to the Reign of Terror under Maximilien de Robespierre and the radical Jacobins. Then, on October 16, 1793, Marie-Antoinette was executed. Further violence took place when Robespierre and other radicals were executed by moderates.

By 1794 the Reign of Terror had come to an end, as had the traditional phase of the French Revolution. Despite the revolution's excesses, the Declaration of the Rights of Man and of the Citizen has brought the French people to a stage in human history characterized by emancipation from superstition, prejudice, cruelty, and enthusiasm. Liberty had triumphed over tyranny.

———*Anne York*

Bibliography and Further Reading

Doyle, William. *The French Revolution: A Very Short Introduction*. Oxford, U.K. Oxford University Press, 2001.

Hunt, Lynn. *The French Revolution and Human Rights: A Brief Documentary History*. New York: Bedford Books, 1996.

Mason, Laura, and Tracey Rizzo. *The French Revolution: A Document Collection*. Boston: Houghton Mifflin, 1999.

Popkin, Jeremy. *A Short History of the French Revolution*, 5th ed. Englewood Cliffs, N.J. Prentice Hall, 2009.

Roberts, J. M. *The French Revolution*, 2nd ed. Oxford, U.K. Oxford University Press, 1997.

Web Sites

"Liberty, Equality, Fraternity: Exploring the French Revolution." George Mason University. http://chnm.gmu.edu/revolution [accessed February 25, 2017].

■ *Reflections on the Revolution in France*

Date: 1790
Author: Edmund Burke
Genre: Published book

Summary Overview

Edmund Burke's *Reflections on the Revolution in France* (1790) represents a controversial and impassioned plea in support of the hereditary principle of monarchical succession in England. Published against the advice of close friends, who feared it would open a Pandora's box to political reformers, its publication spawned a wave of pamphlet replies in the early 1790s, most notably by Thomas Paine, Mary Wollstonecraft, and James Mackintosh, who challenged his interpretation of the constitutional implications of the English Revolution of 1688. While Burke's rhetorical tour de force focused on events in France, they were also interpreted with an eye to their implications for the English political system.

In *Reflections on the Revolution in France*, Burke comprehensively rebutted the political doctrines advanced by the Revolution Society, a society founded to celebrate the centenary of the "Glorious Revolution." Against the assertions of its founding member Richard Price, outlined in his *Discourse on the Love of Our Country* (1789)—that the English people have the right to elect their own governors, to cashier (rebuke) them for misconduct, and to select the system by which they are governed—Burke drew the seductive picture of a stable and legally sanctioned hereditary monarchy.

Defining Moment

In 1789, at the point when the events of the French Revolution began to play out, Britain and its empire were at a low ebb in the history of their peoples. The empire had just lost thirteen of its colonies in British North America—not the most profitable colonies but the ones with the highest per capita income and therefore a useful captive market. An Australian penal colony had just been established at New South Wales, but its very need to exist hinted at the overbearing number of crimes committed by British subjects at home. The British East India Company's first governor general, Warren Hastings, was on trial in the House of Commons for corruption. Ireland threatened revolt, and in return got self-government, signaling an uncertain future. Thousands of impoverished Scottish peasants were forced onto ships to sail to the Americas in the Highland Clearances. The British economy was in transition to capitalism and industrialism, providing employment for new industrial workers but simultaneously replacing others with machines. The old feudal order where a wealthy aristocracy took care of the poor was in the mid-stages of collapse. In short, while British nationalists could rejoice at the turmoil taking place in England's traditional enemy state, there was understandable fear that the same turmoil might soon cross the English Channel.

There was also excitement over the same idea. Democrats, socialists, religious dissenters, radicals and others sympathized with both the American and French revolutionaries, cheered by the French people seizing control over their government. Most believed the French were following the English model from 1688. In that year, Parliament had united to oppose the continued reign of James II of the Stuart dynasty, because he was a converted Catholic and his wife had just produced a male heir who was born Catholic. Instead, members of Parliament asked the Protestant daughter of James, Mary, and her Protestant husband, Prince William of Orange, to assume the throne of their predominantly Protestant country. James fled England, and in the "Glorious Revolution," William and Mary signed a Bill of Rights protecting Englishmen's right to representation in government and freedom of expression. It was assumed that the French were on the same course.

Edmund Burke's faction in the House of Commons, led by Charles James Fox, was prominent in its rhetorical support of the revolutionaries, and Fox occasionally hinted that he would like to see the revolution spread to Britain. Burke himself called the revolution a "wonderful spectacle" when it began in 1789. The fall of the Bastille, however, filled Burke with disquiet—the French people were losing control of the institutions of their society, particularly the morality which, in Burke's opinion, supported the French state. By 1790 Burke saw the revolution as a threat to European stability and security.

Burke had a correspondence with a young French aristocrat named Charles-Jean-François Depont. In late summer 1789, Depont wrote a letter to Burke to ask his impressions of the Revolution; Burke's first response was friendly, courteous, short and derogatory of the revolutionaries, specifically the "swinish multitude" that had taken the Bastille. This was a surprise, and apparently Depont did not consider it Burke's last word on the subject. He sent Burke another letter, this time after reading a pamphlet by one Richard Price, a political radical with whom, Depont assumed, Burke had much in common.

The Unitarian minister Richard Price was a noted advocate of the French Revolution. He was also the founder of the Society for the Commemoration of the Glorious Revolution in Great Britain, known colloquially as the Revolution Society, which celebrated the 1688 Glorious Revolution that had deposed James II. In November 1789, Price gave a speech on William of Orange's birthday, comparing the French Revolution favorably with the events of 1688. In January 1790, Price published the speech as *A Discourse on the Love of Our Country*. In it, Price argued that the Glorious Revolution of 1688 occurred because the English people wanted to obtain their natural rights and liberties, and the French Revolution of a hundred years later now sought the same thing in France. Now that the French had reset the bar for personal liberty, perhaps the English might follow suit once again and hold another revolution.

Burke read Price and responded to Depont, this time with a book, *Reflections on the Revolution in France* (1790). At odds with both his political colleagues in the House of Commons and his own reputation, Burke was obliged to explain why he had supported so many radical causes before, but not this one. For one thing, Burke despised Price and his ideas. He was terrified that Price might be right and that a similar revolution might happen in Britain to mirror that in France. Thus the text is mostly a reinterpretation of the Glorious Revolution as a comparatively conservative event. Furthermore, as it turned out, Burke was actually not particularly radical at all: he believed in reform, not the overthrow of institutions, and in the case of every cause he espoused— American independence, Irish Catholic empowerment, the dismantling of the East India Company—the thing that had inspired a radical reaction had been a desire by the people in each society to be left alone to their own devices while other forces insisted upon change. To Burke, the French people were casting institutions aside without any regard for tradition, utility or moral-

ity, and the result would be anarchy and violence. He would soon be proved right.

Author Biography

Edmund Burke was born in Dublin, Ireland in 1729, a member of an Irish Anglican family surrounded by impoverished Irish Catholics. The exploitation of the poor bothered Burke all his life, and colored his attitudes toward politics and the British Empire. He earned a law degree, like his father, but the practice of law did not interest him so much as the philosophy behind laws and the societal institutions that underpinned the law. He became a published philosopher, producing *A Philosophical Enquiry into the Origin of our Ideas of the Sublime and Beautiful* (1757), and *A Vindication of Natural Society* (1756).

In 1765, the Marquis of Rockingham assumed government in Britain as prime minister, and made Burke his private secretary, embarking the young man on a career in politics. Burke was elected to office in his own right in the same year, and he remained in the House of Commons until 1794. He became the equivalent of an ideologue in Parliament, with his speeches and writings used to direct political organization and policymaking for the varying faction of Whig politicians he represented. He published many of his speeches, particularly on the rebellion of the thirteen colonies in British North America, for which he sympathized with the colonists and their desire to be left alone. In *Thoughts on the Cause of the Present Discontents* (1770), he described why a cabinet of all-the-talents was not an effective means of conducting government in comparison to a partisan cabinet—probably the first defense and advocacy of party in the history of republican politics. In the 1780s, he was the principle prosecutor of the governor general of the British East India Company Warren Hastings, accusing him of corruption and the abuse of his Indian subjects. He could also always be counted on to defend the rights of the impoverished Irish populace in the House of Commons.

For all his activities as a political pundit, however, Burke rarely held office in a cabinet. From Rockingham, he came to be associated with the radical wing of the Whig faction, led by Charles James Fox. In the Commons this affiliation associated him with the interests of the new moneyed classes in British society, industrial workers, managers and owners who benefited from the rise of capitalism. It also made Burke an outsider, since King George III loathed the Foxites and Burke agreed with the efforts to limit the king's power in the state. With a sparse record in power before 1790, Burke had a reputation as a supporter of radical causes—the American colonists, the Irish, the Indian people against the empire, parliamentary power against the king.

Therefore, Burke's opposition to the French Revolution came as a surprise to those who knew him. He was shunned by the Foxites, who supported the French in their experimentation with republicanism and democracy, and thus became something of a free agent in the Commons, a part of no political faction. As Britain went to war with France in 1792 and the Reign of Terror began in Paris in 1793, Burke's reputation improved and he came to be seen as an intelligent elder statesman. He died in 1794.

HISTORICAL DOCUMENT

Whatever may be the success of evasion in explaining away the gross error of *fact*, which supposes that his Majesty (though he holds it in concurrence with the wishes) owes his crown to the choice of his people, yet nothing can evade their full explicit declaration concerning the principle of a right in the people to choose; which right is directly maintained, and tenaciously adhered to. All the oblique insinuations concerning election bottom in this proposition, and are referable to it. Lest the foundation of the king's exclusive legal title should pass for a mere rant of adulatory freedom, the political divine proceeds dogmatically to assert, that, by the principles of the Revolution, the people of England have acquired three fundamental rights, all which, with him, compose one system, and lie together in one short sentence; namely, that we have acquired a right

"To choose our own governors."
"To cashier them for misconduct."
"To frame a government for ourselves."

This new, and hitherto unheard-of, bill of rights, though made in the name of the whole people, belongs to those gentlemen and their faction only. The body of the people of England have no share in it. They utterly disclaim it. They will resist the practical assertion of it with their lives and fortunes. They are bound to do so by the laws of their country, made at the time of that very Revolution which is appealed to in favour of the fictitious rights claimed by the Society which abuses its name.

These gentlemen of the Old Jewry, in all their reasonings on the Revolution of 1688, have a Revolution which happened in England about forty years before, and the late French Revolution, so much before their eyes, and in their hearts, that they are constantly confounding all the three together. It is necessary that we should separate what they confound. We must recall their erring fancies to the acts of the Revolution which we revere, for the discovery of its true principles. If the principles of the Revolution of 1688 are anywhere to be found, it is in the statute called the *Declaration of Right*. In that most wise, sober, and considerate declaration, drawn up by great lawyers and great statesmen, and not by warm and inexperienced enthusiasts, not one word is said, nor one suggestion made, of a general right "to choose our own governors; to cashier them for misconduct; and to form a government for ourselves."

This Declaration of Right (the act of the 1st of William and Mary, sess. 2, ch. 2) is the corner-stone of our constitution, as reinforced, explained, improved, and in its fundamental principles for ever settled. It is called "An Act for declaring the rights and liberties of the subject, and for settling the succession of the crown." You will observe, that these rights and this succession are declared in one body, and bound indissolubly together. ...

Unquestionably there was at the Revolution, in the person of King William, a small and a temporary deviation from the strict order of a regular hereditary succession; but it is against all genuine principles of jurisprudence to draw a principle from a law made in a special case, and regarding an individual person. *Privilegium non transit in exemplum*. If ever there was a time favourable for establishing the principle, that a king of popular choice was the only legal king, without all doubt it was at the Revolution. Its not being done at that time is a proof that the nation was of opinion it ought not to be done at any time. There is no person so completely ignorant of our history as not to know, that the majority in parliament of both parties were so little disposed to anything resembling that principle, that at first they were determined to place the vacant crown, not on the head of the Prince of Orange, but on that of his wife Mary, daughter of King James, the eldest born of the issue of that king, which they acknowledged as undoubtedly his. It would be to repeat a very trite story, to recall to your memory all those circumstances which demonstrated that their accepting King William was not properly a choice; but to all those who did not wish, in effect, to recall King James, or to deluge their country in blood, and again to bring their religion, laws, and liberties into the peril they had just escaped, it was an act of *necessity*, in the strictest moral sense in which necessity can be taken. ...

It is true, that, aided with the powers derived from force and opportunity, the nation was at that time, in some sense, free to take what course it pleased for filling the throne; but only free to do so upon the same grounds on which they might have wholly abolished their monarchy, and every other part of their constitution. However, they did not think such bold changes within their commission. It is indeed difficult, perhaps impossible, to give limits to the mere abstract competence of the supreme power, such as was exercised by parliament at that time; but the limits of a moral competence, subjecting, even in powers more indisputably sovereign, occasional will to permanent reason, and to the steady maxims of faith, justice, and fixed fundamental policy, are perfectly intelligible, and perfectly binding upon those who exercise any authority, under any name, or under any title, in the state. The House of Lords, for instance, is not morally competent to dissolve the House of Commons; no, nor even to dissolve itself, nor to abdicate, if it would, its portion in the legislature of the kingdom. Though a king may abdicate for his own person, he cannot abdicate for the monarchy. By as strong, or by a stronger reason, the House of Commons cannot renounce its share of authority. The engagement and pact of society, which generally goes by the name of the constitution, forbids such invasion and such surrender. The constituent parts of a state are obliged to hold their public faith with each other, and with all those who derive any serious interest under their engagements, as much as the whole state is bound to keep its faith with separate communities. Otherwise competence and power would soon be confounded, and no law be left but the will of a prevailing force. On this principle the succession of the crown has always been what it now is, an hereditary succession by law: in the old line it was a succession by the common law; in the new by the statute law, operating on the principles of the common law, not changing the substance, but regulating the mode, and describing the persons. Both these descriptions of law are of the same force, and are derived from an equal authority, emanating from the common agreement and original compact of the state, *communi sponsione reipublicae*, and as such are equally binding on king and people too, as long as the terms are observed, and they continue the same body politic. ...

A state without the means of some change is without the means of its conservation. Without such means it might even risk the loss of that part of the constitution which it wished the most religiously to preserve. The two principles of conservation and correction operated strongly at the two critical periods of the Restoration and Revolution, when England found itself without a king. ...At no time, perhaps, did the sovereign legislature manifest a more tender regard to that fundamental principle of British constitutional policy, than at the time of the Revolution, when it deviated from the direct line of hereditary succession. The crown was carried somewhat out of the line in which it had before moved; but the new line was derived from the same stock. It was still a line of hereditary descent; still an hereditary descent in the same blood, though an hereditary descent qualified with Protestantism. When the legislature altered the direction, but kept the principle, they showed that they held it inviolable. ...

A few years ago I should be ashamed to overload a matter, so capable of supporting itself, by the then unnecessary support of any argument; but this seditious, unconstitutional doctrine is now publicly taught, avowed, and printed. The dislike I feel to revolutions, the signals for which have so often been given from pulpits; the spirit of change that is gone abroad; the total contempt which prevails with you, and may come to prevail with us, of all ancient institutions, when set in opposition to a present sense of convenience, or to the bent of a present inclination: all these considerations make it not unadvisable, in my opinion, to call back our attention to the true principles of our own domestic laws; that, you, my French friend, should begin to know, and that we should continue to cherish them. We ought not, on either side of the water, to suffer ourselves to be imposed upon by the counterfeit wares which some persons, by a double fraud, export to you in illicit bottoms, as raw commodities of British growth, though wholly alien to our soil, in order afterwards to smuggle them back again into this country, manufactured after the newest Paris fashion of an improved liberty.

The people of England will not ape the fashions they have never tried, nor go back to those which they have found mischievous on trial. They look upon the legal hereditary succession of their crown as among their rights, not as among their wrongs; as a benefit, not as a grievance; as a security for their liberty, not as a badge of servitude. They look on the frame of their commonwealth, such as it stands, to be of inestimable value; and they conceive the undisturbed succession of the crown to be a pledge of the stability and perpetuity of all the other members of our constitution.

I shall beg leave, before I go any further, to take notice of some paltry artifices, which the abettors of election, as the only lawful title to the crown, are ready to employ, in order to render the support of the just principles of our constitution a task somewhat invidious. These sophisters substitute a fictitious cause, and feigned personages, in whose favour they suppose you engaged, whenever you defend the inheritable nature of the crown. It is common with them to dispute as if they were in a conflict with some of those exploded fanatics of slavery, who formerly maintained, what I believe no creature now maintains, "that the crown is held by divine hereditary and indefeasible right."—These old fanatics of single arbitrary power dogmatized as if hereditary royalty was the only lawful government in the world, just as our new fanatics of popular arbitrary power maintain that a popular election is the sole lawful source of authority. The old prerogative enthusiasts, it is true, did speculate foolishly, and perhaps impiously too, as if monarchy had more of a divine sanction that any other mode of government; and as if a right to govern by inheritance were in strictness indefeasible in every person, who should be found in the succession to a throne, and under every circumstance, which no civil or political right can be. But an absurd opinion concerning the king's hereditary right to the crown does not prejudice one that is rational, and bottomed upon solid principles of law and policy. If all the absurd theories of lawyers and divines were to vitiate the objects in which they are conversant, we should have no law and no religion left in the world. But an absurd theory on one side of a question forms no justification for alleging a false fact, or promulgating mischievous maxims, on the other.

The second claim of the Revolution Society is "a right of cashiering their governors for misconduct." Perhaps the apprehensions our ancestors entertained of forming such a precedent as that "of cashiering for misconduct," was the cause that the declaration of the act, which implied the abdication of King James, was, if it had any fault, rather too guarded, and too circumstantial. But all this guard, and all this accumulation of circumstances, serves to show the spirit of caution which predominated in the national councils in a situation in which men irritated by oppression, and elevated by a triumph over it, are art to abandon themselves to violent and extreme courses: it shows the anxiety of the great men who influenced the conduct of affairs at that great event to make the Revolution a parent of settlement, and not a nursery of future revolutions.

No government could stand a moment, if it could be blown down with anything so loose and indefinite as an opinion of "misconduct." They who led at the Revolution grounded the virtual abdication of King James upon no such light and uncertain principle. They charged him with nothing less than a design, confirmed by a multitude of illegal overt acts, to subvert the Protestant church and state, and their fundamental, unquestionable laws and liberties: they charged him with having broken the original contract between king and people. This was more than misconduct. A grave and overruling necessity obliged them to take the step they took, and took with infinite reluctance, as under that most rigorous of all laws. Their trust for the future preservation of the constitution was not in future revolutions. The grand policy of all their regulations was to render it almost impracticable for any future sovereign to compel the states of the kingdom to have again recourse to those violent remedies. They left the crown what, in the eye and estimation of law, it had never been, perfectly irresponsible. In order to lighten the crown still further, they aggravated responsibility on ministers of state. By the statute of the 1st of King William, sess. 2nd, called "the act for declaring the rights and liberties of the subject, and for settling the succession to the crown," they enacted, that the ministers should serve the crown on the terms of that declaration. They secured soon after the frequent meetings of parliament, by which the whole government would be under the constant inspection and active control of the popular representative and of the magnates of the kingdom. In the next great constitutional act, that of the 12th and 13th of King William, for the further limitation of the crown, and better securing the rights and liberties of the subject, they provided, "that no pardon under the great seal of England should be pleadable to an impeachment by the Commons in parliament." The rule laid down for government in the Declaration of Right, the constant inspection of parliament, the practical claim of impeachment, they thought infinitely a better security not only for their constitutional liberty, but against the vices of administration, than the reservation of a right so difficult in the practice, so uncertain in the issue, and often so mischievous in the consequences, as that of "cashiering their governors."

Dr. Price, in his sermon, condemns very properly the practice of gross, adulatory addresses to kings. Instead of this fulsome style, he proposes that his Majesty should be told, on occasions of congratulation, that "he is to consider himself as more properly the servant than the sovereign of his people." For a compliment, this new form of address does not seem to be very soothing. Those who are servants in name, as well as in effect, do not like to be told of their situation, their duty, and their obligations. The slave, in the old play, tells his master, *"Hæc commemoratio est quasi exprobatio."* It is not pleasant as compliment; it is not wholesome as instruction. After all, if the king were to bring himself to echo this new kind of address, to adopt it in terms, and even to take the appellation of Servant of the People as his royal style, how either he or we should be much mended by it, I cannot imagine. I have seen very assuming letters, signed, Your most obedient, humble servant. The proudest denomination that ever was endured on earth took a title of still greater humility than that which is now proposed for sovereigns by the Apostle of Liberty. Kings and nations were trampled upon by the foot of one calling himself "the Servant of Servants"; and mandates for deposing sovereigns were sealed with the signet of "the Fisherman."

I should have considered all this as no more than a sort of flippant, vain discourse, in which, as in an unsavoury fume, several persons suffer the spirit of liberty to evaporate, if it were not plainly in support of the idea, and a part of the scheme, of "cashiering kings for misconduct." In that light it is worth some observation.

Kings, in one sense, are undoubtedly the servants of the people, because their power has no other rational end than that of the general advantage; but it is not true that they are, in the ordinary sense, (by our constitution at least,) anything like servants; the essence of whose situation is to obey the commands of some other, and to be removable at pleasure. But the king of Great Britain obeys no other person; all other persons are individually, and collectively too, under him, and owe to him a legal obedience. The law, which knows neither to flatter nor to insult, calls this high magistrate, not our servant, as this humble divine calls him, but "our sovereign Lord the king;" and we, on our parts, have learned to speak only the primitive language of the law, and not the confused jargon of their Babylonian pulpits.

As he is not to obey us, but as we are to obey the law in him, our constitution has made no sort of provision towards rendering him, as a servant, in any degree responsible. Our constitution knows nothing of a magistrate like the Justicia of Arragon; nor of any court legally appointed, nor of any process legally settled, for submitting the king to the responsibility belonging to all servants. In this he is not distinguished from the Commons and the Lords; who, in their several public capacities, can never be called to an account for their conduct; although the Revolution Society chooses to assert,

in direct opposition to one of the wisest and most beautiful parts of our constitution, that "a king is no more than the first servant of the public, created by it, and responsible to it."

Ill would our ancestors at the Revolution have deserved their fame for wisdom, if they had found no security for their freedom, but in rendering their government feeble in its operations, and precarious in its tenure; if they had been able to contrive no better remedy against arbitrary power than civil confusion. Let these gentlemen state who that representative public is to whom they will affirm the king, as a servant, to be responsible. It will then be time enough for me to produce to them the positive statute law which affirms that he is not.

GLOSSARY

Old Jewry: the Old Jewry Meeting House, a Presbyterian chapel in central London; Burke uses this term to refer to Richard Price and his cronies in the Revolution Society

Declaration of Right[s]: the physical document that proclaimed that William and Mary were to replace James II as king of England, and which conveyed specific rights on all Englishmen that monarchs must obey

Privilegium non transit in exemplum: "A privilege does not become a precedent"

communi sponsione reipublicae: by the general agreement of all the people

sophisters: magicians of a deceitful nature

Hæc commemoratio est quasi exprobatio: From the Roman playwright Terence's play *Andria*—"For this reminder is, as it were, a rebuke"

'Kings and nations were trampled upon by the foot of one calling himself "the Servant of Servants"; and mandates for deposing sovereigns were sealed with the signet of "the Fisherman."': a reference to Jesus Christ

the Justicia of Arragon: the supreme legal authority in the Spanish kingdom of Aragon, superior in legal authority even to the king

Document Analysis

In the extract Burke outlines and staunchly defends the principle of hereditary succession to the English throne, emphasizing the role played by the English Revolution of 1688 in confirming this principle through lineal descent and statute law. This controversial interpretation challenged many political reformers, such as the Dissenting Minister Richard Price, who argued that

the monarch of England required popular consent to rule as a servant of the people—the very consent that William of Orange had gained through Parliament prior to his joint enthronement with Queen Mary.

By contrast, in *Reflections*, Burke argues that the accession of William of Orange to the throne, though it represented "a small and a temporary deviation" from the *direct* hereditary line, was nevertheless a succession "derived from the same stock"—"hereditary descent qualified with Protestantism." Nowhere in the process, Burke contended, had the English people exercised a determining will or been required to give their consent. The lead-up to the English Revolution was, he suggested, a moment of great emergency, a litmus test on the constitutional footing of the monarchy. The passive acceptance by the public of William of Orange as joint sovereign confirmed *in perpetuity* the binding nature of hereditary royal succession.

According to Burke, not only had the deeds of the English Revolution and the acquiescence of the people confirmed this principle, but it also had a legal basis, enshrined by statute in the form of the "Declaration of Right," which confirmed a Protestant line of succession. Layering his argument still further but moving into his own century, Burke also suggests that the public acceptance of the Hanoverian line commencing with George I, despite all the "dangers and inconveniences" of a foreign monarch, had straightened what had been a brief but necessary hereditary deviation, by reestablishing a *direct* descent to James I, albeit through the female line.

Hereditary succession was necessary according to Burke, because it was the only way to provide political and social stability, which in turn generated wealth and happiness. Throughout *Reflections* but particularly in this extract, Burke is careful to draw a distinction between the concept of the hereditary right of succession by statute law and the "divine heredity and indefeasible right" claimed by monarchs in the past, most notably Charles I. Burke therefore positioned himself as a moderate between two poles: the excesses of absolute monarchy associated with Louis XVI in France and the "new fanatics," English political radicals who claimed that "popular election is the sole lawful source of authority."

In addition to defending hereditary monarchy, Burke also addressed the issue raised by Price of whether the people had a right to "cashier" or rebuke their governors or rulers for misconduct, while attacking his assertion that the king should consider himself "more properly the servant than the sovereign of his people." In Burke's view, this analogy was as pernicious as it was false, for the king was in no way subservient to his people, could not be dismissed, and had the right to be obeyed. However, several pieces of legislation that had been passed under William and Mary already safeguarded the rights and liberties of subjects from arbitrary Crown rule, providing that "no pardon under the great seal of England should be pleadable to an impeachment by the Commons in parliament."

Burke's position in *Reflections on the Revolution in France* consists of a delicate and, some argue, contradictory balance between constitutional continuity and healthy correction. It hinges on the separation of the person of the monarch from the institution of the monarchy, for while a king could abdicate or forsake his crown in absentia as James II had done, the monarchy per se would continue in perpetuity. Burke's conservative defense of hereditary monarchy and his antagonism toward the French Revolution—"the newest Paris Fashion of an improved liberty," as he sarcastically writes—surprised his contemporaries, who remembered his progressive support for the American revolutionaries. However, his defection from the opposition to the government immediately prior to the writing of *Reflections* may well partly explain this political shift.

Essential Themes

While Burke wrote other works on the French Revolution before he died in 1794, it is his *Reflections* that have captured the attentions of later political thinkers, mostly because it is so polemical and so amazingly accurate in its plotting of the future of the revolution. This passage covers the history of the 1688 Glorious Revolution and the Revolution Settlement. Much of the rest of the book was a prediction of the depths of depravity to which the French people were soon to descend, having cast away all of their institutions of government. In late 1790, the violence of the Bastille and the royal family's forced march to the Tuileries Palace in Paris was a year in the past. The revolutionaries had written up laws and were working on a constitution, and any unrest in France had moved out to the countryside, where the enforcement of the Civil Constitution of the Clergy and the confiscation of Church lands met with resistance. The revolution seemed to be on its way to the establishment of a constitutional monarchy like that in Britain—hence Price's speech. Yet here was Burke, predicting that France would soon set off on a path of death and destruction; within two years he would be proven right.

That did not stop any number of other readers to Burke's work to condemn his diagnosis of the sickness of the revolution and praise its actions. The most articulate was Thomas Paine, former sympathizer with the American revolutionaries as the author of *Common Sense* (1776). In a point-by-point rebuttal of Burke called *The Rights of Man* (1791), Paine—a utopian agrarian socialist by the 1790s—argued that Britain simply did not have a true "constitution" since so little of it was on paper, that the monarchy's existence was always based on force and that therefore, a revolution in Britain would be welcome. In his time, Paine's rebuttal was more popular and more widely read than Burke's castigation of the revolution.

Yet it is telling that Burke's work is more widely read today and that legions of conservative ideologues consider him a modern philosophical hero; Paine is still read, but largely as a product of his time as opposed to a precursor of our own. Not that the conservatives are either right about Burke or that they follow in his allegedly conservative footsteps. Burke's advocacy of reform—"A state without the means of some change is without the means of its conservation"—tends to get lost in studies of him as a pre-modern conservative, and his anti-imperialism in regards to Ireland and India would be welcome in any liberal intellectual circle both then and now. Yet he was a "conservative" in the truest sense of the word. Burke would conserve the French regime the same way England had conserved its monarchy in 1688, by making whatever reforms were necessary, or radical, in order to maintain the order the institution represented. Whether that goal is fundamentally conservative or not depends on one's point of view. Regardless, Burke was a brilliant examiner of people and their motivations, and that has made him an influential political philosopher well past his own time.

———*Peter Robinson*

Bibliography and Further Reading

Bourke, Richard. *Empire and Revolution: The Political Life of Edmund Burke*. Princeton: Princeton University Press, 2015.

Dwan, David and Christopher Insole, editors. *The Cambridge Companion to Edmund Burke*. New York: Cambridge University Press, 2012.

Hodson, Jane. *Language and Revolution in Burke, Wollstonecraft, Paine, and Godwin*. Burlington, VT: Ashgate, 2007.

Web Sites

"Edmund Burke (1729 - 1797)." *BBC History* (2014) BBC.org http://www.bbc.co.uk/history/ historic_figures/burke_edmund.shtml [accessed March 1, 2017].

Harris, Ian. "Edmund Burke." *The Stanford Encyclopedia of Philosophy*, Edward N. Zalta, editor. (January 25, 2012) https://plato.stanford.edu/entries/burke/ [accessed March 1, 2017].

Smith, George H. *Edmund Burke, Intellectuals, and the French Revolution*. Libertarianism.org (March 14, 2014) https://www.libertarianism.org/columns/edmund-burke-intellectuals-french-revolution-part-1 [accessed March 1, 2017].

■ Constitution of Haiti

Date: 1801
Author: Haitian constitutional assembly; Toussaint-Louverture
Genre: Constitution

Summary Overview

The 1801 Constitution of Haiti, promulgated in the wake of the Haitian Revolution that had begun in 1791, was the first in a series of some twenty-three constitutions that have been adopted in that nation. Haiti, at the time called Saint Domingue, had been a French colony since the late seventeenth century; the name Haiti, from the indigenous name Ayiti ("mountainous land") was adopted at independence in 1804. Haiti produced the bulk of the world's sugar in a plantation economy built on the backs of slaves imported from Africa. The Haitian Revolution was essentially a slave revolt, the only successful slave revolt in modern history. As a result of the revolt, Haiti became the first independent nation in Latin America, the second in the Western Hemisphere (after the United States), and the first postcolonial nation led by blacks.

The Constitution of Haiti of 1801, sometimes called the Saint Domingue Constitution, was written by a ten-member committee, though the document the committee produced embodied the thinking of François-Dominique Toussaint-Louverture, a former slave who became a prominent leader of the revolution. In the 1790s he was able to expel Europeans from Haiti and establish Haiti as a self-governing polity with himself as governor. The 1801 constitution abolished slavery and named him governor for life, though his administration was brief, for in response to the constitution the French reasserted control over its colony. Nevertheless, Toussaint-Louverture and the 1801 Constitution of Haiti were of immense significance, for they launched the process of overthrowing European colonial rule in the Americas—rule that extended back some three centuries to the decades after Christopher Columbus's historic voyage to the New World.

Defining Moment

In 1697, the Treaty of Ryswick divided the island of Hispaniola between France, which controlled Saint Domingue (the western third of the island), and Spain, which controlled the Dominican Republic. Haiti became a leading supplier of sugar and France's most lucrative colony—in fact, the most lucrative European colony in the world. White landowners developed immense plantations for the raising of sugarcane, coffee, indigo, and other crops for export, all labor-intensive industries that depended on slave labor. Because they were vastly outnumbered, plantation owners lived in fear of slave rebellions. They passed repressive laws that had the effect of creating a caste system. At the top of the system, of course, were *blancs*, or the white planters, who in turn were divided into *grand blancs*, or wealthy, aristocratic planters, and *petit blancs*, a class consisting of shopkeepers, artisans, and free day laborers. Occupying a middle tier were free blacks and mixed-race people (often the offspring of white planters and slave mothers), frequently referred to as mulattoes or *gens de couleur*. Members of this tier were typically educated and either worked as overseers on the plantations or served in the army; most had formerly been slaves. The lowest caste were black slaves.

By the late 1700s, Haiti was riven by caste, racial, and national rivalries. The *petit blancs* resented the *grand blancs* because of their wealth and power. The *grand blancs* resented the French government's restrictions on their trade and supported the concept of an independent Haiti. The white colonists numbered about forty thousand, while the *gens de couleur* numbered about twenty-eight thousand. Meanwhile, the number of slaves was at least a half million, and the slaves resented not only the abuses of their masters but also the privileges of free blacks. Complicating matters was competition for control of the lucrative colony among the French, Spanish, and British. Throughout the colony could be found advocates for independence, French loyalists, those who were loyal to Spain, and those who saw the British as their allies and liberators. On top of that, there were strong regional rivalries, with the colony's southern and western regions vying for economic supremacy against the more fertile and profitable northern coast.

While this complex stew was brewing in the New World, the French Revolution began in 1789. Haitians of all classes and colors watched the revolution with interest. Free people of color were emboldened by the revolutionary government's Declaration of the Rights of Man and of the Citizen and consequently were often called Black Jacobins, a reference to political radicals in revolutionary France. The people of color agitated for civil rights, particularly the right to vote, sending emissaries to Paris to lobby for their cause. Whites supported the revolution, believing that it would lead to Haitian independence and that independence would give them a free hand in world trade. When the French government granted French citizenship and civil rights to free people of color in May 1791, white colonists refused to recognize the decision (which was later revoked). The result was a state of high tension between Haiti's former slaves and whites, particularly the *grand blancs*. Developments in France, where power after the revolution rapidly changed hands, added to the air of uncertainty.

The fuse was lit, and the explosion occurred on August 22, 1791, when the Haitian Revolution began at the instigation of Dutty Boukman, a Vodou priest and Maroon leader. Events over the next three years unfolded rapidly. In the early months, some hundred thousand slaves joined the revolt and embarked on a campaign of retaliation that killed two thousand whites and burned nearly two hundred plantations (out of a total of about eight thousand). Alarmed, the French dispatched six thousand troops to the island to quell the revolt. After the French declared war on England in 1793, white planters signed treaties with the British, intending for the British to gain sovereignty over the island. Meanwhile, the Spanish still occupied the Dominican Republic. Sensing an opportunity to expand their sphere of influence, the Spanish invaded Saint Domingue with the support of Saint Domingue's slaves.

By the time hostilities had been suspended in 1794, a hundred thousand blacks and twenty-four thousand whites had been killed. That year, the French National Convention abolished slavery and granted full civil and political rights to all blacks in Haiti. Napoléon Bonaparte issued the Proclamation on Saint Domingue in December 1799. In it, he asserted that he and the French government supported the colony's blacks: "The Consuls of the Republic, in announcing to you the new social pact, declare to you that the sacred principles of the freedom and equality of blacks will never suffer among you the least attack or modification."

Amid this chaos, Toussaint-Louverture emerged as the most dominant figure in Saint Domingue. A skilled, if untutored military commander, he initially fought on the side of the Spanish. In response to the arrival of British troops, he agreed to fight for France on the condition that slaves would be freed. Under his leadership, the Spanish were driven out of Saint Domingue. He subdued local rivals for preeminence, defeated a British contingent of forces in 1798, and in 1801 he even freed the slaves in Santo Domingo, the capital of the Dominican Republic. By this time he was the de facto ruler of an autonomous Haiti. He issued the constitution on May 9, 1801, and the constitution took effect on July 8 of that year.

Author Biography

Toussaint-Louverture called for a constitutional assembly to write a constitution for Saint Domingue, even though it was still technically a colony of France. The assembly, whose members' names are listed at the end of the document, was composed of three mulattoes and seven whites. Their deliberations were directed by Bernard Borgella, the mayor of Port-au-Prince and formerly a barrister in the French city of Bordeaux. Chief among the members was Julien Raimond, a free man of color who was born in 1744 on the island of Martinique. His mother was a mulatto, and his father, a French colonist, was a planter. Raimond achieved wealth as an indigo planter, and by the 1780s he owned about a hundred slaves. He gained fame in the history of Haiti, however, for his ultimate opposition to slavery. He moved to Paris, where he petitioned the colonial ministry for the end of slavery and full equality for blacks in France's colonies. Working with an abolitionist group called Société des Amis des Noirs, or Society of Friends of the Blacks, he presented his case so effectively that the French General Assembly took up the issue in 1790 and in 1792 granted political rights to mulattos and free blacks. He died in 1801, shortly after the constitution he helped write took effect.

The motive force behind the constitution, however, was Toussaint-Louverture. He was born into slavery on May 20, 1743, as Toussaint Bréda near Le Cap in northern Haiti. Legend holds that his father had been an African chieftain, but it is likely that his father was actually the man whom others have often called his godfather and whom Toussaint-Louverture claimed as his father: Pierre Baptiste Simon, an educated black slave. Toussaint-Louverture was somewhat fortunate in that the owners of the Bréda plantation treated their slaves with kindness, and Toussaint was able to acquire an informal education. He was granted his freedom in

1776 when he married, and in the ensuing years he would rent and work a farm.

Toussaint joined the military, serving initially as a doctor but rising to the rank of commander. Throughout the 1790s he demonstrated his skill as a military leader and as a diplomat. In 1793 he added "Louverture" to his name, meaning "the opener of the way." By the turn of the century he had consolidated his position as governor not just of Saint Domingue but, indeed, of the entire island of Hispaniola. In response to Toussaint-Louverture's constitution, Napoléon dispatched troops to the island under the command of his brother-in-law, General Victor Emmanuel Leclerc. Toussaint-Louverture put up resistance as long as he could, but the numbers were overwhelming, and he surrendered, signing a treaty with the French on May 7, 1802. He believed that he would be able to retire to his farm, but just a month later Leclerc had him arrested. He was taken to France, where he died in the Fort de Joux prison on April 7, 1803.

HISTORICAL DOCUMENT

First Title. On the Territory
Art 1—The entire extent of Saint-Domingue, and Samana, Tortuga, Gonave, the Cayemites, Ile-a-Vache, the Saone and other adjacent islands, form the territory of one colony, that is part of the French Empire, but is subject to particular laws.

Art 2—The territory of this colony is divided into departments, *arrondisements*, and parishes.

Title II. On Its Inhabitants
Art 3—There can be no slaves on this territory; servitude has been forever abolished. All men are born, live and die there free and French.

Art 4—All men can work at all forms of employment, whatever their color.

Art 5—No other distinctions exist than those of virtues and talents, nor any other superiority than that granted by the law in the exercise of a public charge. The law is the same for all, whether it punishes or protects.

Title III. On Religion
Art 6—The Catholic religion, Apostolic and Roman, is the only one publicly professed.

Art 7—Every parish provides for the maintenance of the religious cult and its ministers. Manufactured goods are especially destined for this expense and for presbyteries and the lodging of ministers.

Art 8—The governor of the colony assigns to each minister of the religion the scope of his spiritual administration, and these ministers can never, under any pretext, form a body within the colony.

Title IV. On Morals
Art 9—Since marriage, by its civil and religious institution, tends to the purity of morals, those spouses who practice the virtues demanded by their state, will always be distinguished and specially protected by the government.

Art 10—Divorce will not take place in the colony.

Art 11—The state of the rights of children born through marriage will be fixed by laws that will tend to spread and maintain social virtues, and to encourage and solidify family ties.

Title V. On Men in Society
Art 12—The Constitution guarantees individual freedom and safety. No one can be arrested except by virtue of a formally expressed order, issued by a functionary who the law gives the right to arrest and detain in a publicly designated place.

Art 13—Property is sacred and inviolable. Every person, either by himself or his representatives, has the free disposal and administration of that which is recognized as belonging to him. Whoever infringes upon this right renders himself criminal towards society and responsible as concerns the person troubled in his property.

Title VI. On Cultivation and Commerce
Art 14—The colony, being essentially agricultural, cannot allow the least interruption in its labor and cultivation.

Art 15—Every habitation is a manufactory that demands a gathering together of cultivators and workers; it's the tranquil asylum of an active and constant family, of which the owner of the land or his representative is necessarily the father.

Art 16—Every cultivator and worker is a member of the family and a shareholder in its revenues.

Any change in domicile on the part of cultivators brings with it the ruin of farming.

In order to do away with a vice so disastrous for the colony and contrary to public order, the governor makes all the police regulations that the circumstances render necessary in conformity with the bases of the police regulation of 20 Vendémiaire of the year 9, and the proclamation of General-in-Chief Toussaint-Louverture of the following 19 Pluviose.

Art 17—The introduction of the cultivators indispensable to the re-establishment and the growth of planting will take place in Saint-Domingue. The Constitution charges the governor to take the appropriate measures to encourage and favor this increase in arms, stipulate and balance the diverse interests, and assure and guarantee the carrying out of the respective engagements resulting from this introduction.

Art 18—The commerce of the colony consists only in the exchange of the goods and products of its territory; consequently the introduction of those of the same nature as its own is and remains prohibited.

Title VII. On Legislation and Legislative Authority

Art 19—The regime of the colony is determined by the laws proposed by the governor and rendered by an assembly of inhabitants who gather at fixed periods in the center of the colony under the title of Central Assembly of Saint-Domingue.

Art 20—No law relative to the internal administration of the colony can be promulgated unless it bears the following formula: the Central Assembly of Saint-Domingue, on the proposition of the Governor, renders the following law.

Art 21—Laws will only be obligatory for citizens from the day of their promulgation in the departmental capitals. The promulgation of a law occurs in the following fashion: in the name of the French colony of Saint-Domingue, the governor orders that the above law be sealed, promulgated, and executed in the whole colony.

Art 22—The Central Assembly of Saint-Domingue is composed of two deputies per department who, in order to be eligible, must be at least 30 years old and have resided in the colony five years.

Art 23—The Assembly is renewed every two years by half; no one can be a member six consecutive years. The election takes place thusly: the municipal administrations every two years name on 10 Ventose (March 1), each one with one deputy, who will meet ten days later in the capitals of their respective departments where they form as many departmental electoral assemblies, who will each name a deputy to the Central Assembly. The next election will take place the 10 Ventose of the eleventh year of the French republic (March 1, 1803). In case of death, resignation or otherwise of one or several members of the Assembly, the Governor will see to their replacement. He also designates the members of the current Central Assembly who, at the period of the first renewal, shall remain members of the Assembly for two more years.

Art 24—The Central Assembly votes on the adoption or rejection of laws proposed to it by the Governor. It expresses its wishes on the regulations made and on the application of laws already made, on the abuses to be corrected, on the improvements to be undertaken, on all parts of service of the colony.

Art 25—Its session begins every year the first of Germinal (March 22) and cannot exceed a duration of three months. The governor can convoke it extraordinarily. The sessions are not public.

Art 26—If need be, the Central Assembly determines the basis, the amount, the duration and the mode of collection of taxes based on the state of the receipts and expenses presented to it, and on their increase or decrease. These states will be summarily published.

Title VIII. On Government

Art 27—The administrative reins of the colony are confided to a Governor, who directly corresponds with the government of the metropole in all matters relating to the colony.

Art 28—The Constitution names as governor Citizen Toussaint-Louverture, General-in-Chief of the army of Saint-Domingue and, in consideration of the important services that the general has rendered to the colony in the most critical circumstances of the revolution, and per the wishes of the grateful inhabitants, the reins are confided to him for the rest of his glorious life.

Art 29—In the future each governor will be named for five years, and can be continued every five years for reason of good administration.

Art 30—In order to consolidate the tranquility that the colony owes to the firmness, the activity, the indefatigable zeal, and the rare virtues of General Toussaint-Louverture, and as a sign of the unlimited confidence of the inhabitants of Saint-Domingue, the Constitution attributes exclusively to this general the right to choose the citizen who, in the unhappy instance of his death, shall immediately replace him. This choice shall be secret. It will be consigned in a sealed packet that can only be opened by the Central Assembly in the presence of all the generals of the army of Saint-Domingue in active service and the commanders-in-chief of the departments.

General Toussaint-Louverture will take all the precautionary measures necessary to make known to the Central Assembly the place this important packet has been deposited.

Art 31—The citizen who will have been chosen by General Toussaint-Louverture to take the reins of government upon his death, will take a vow to the Central Assembly to execute the Constitution of Sant-Domingue and to remain attached to the French government, and will be immediately installed in his functions, all of this in the presence of the army generals in active service and the commanders-in-chief of the departments who will all, individually and without cease will pledge to the new governor the vow of obedience to his orders.

Art 32—No more than one month before the expiration of the five years set for the administration of each sitting governor, he will convoke the Central Assembly, the meeting of army generals in active service and the commanders- in- chief of the departments at the ordinary place of the meetings of the Central Assembly in order to name, along with the members of that Assembly, the new governor, or to maintain the sitting one in office.

Art 33—Any failure in convocation on the part of the sitting governor is a manifest infraction of the constitution. In this case the highest ranking general, or the one with the most seniority of the same rank, who is on active duty in the colony shall take, by right and provisionally, the reins of government. This general will immediately convoke the other active duty generals, the commanders-in-chief of the departments and the members of the Central Assembly, all of who must obey the convocation in order to proceed with the nomination of a new governor.

In case of death, resignation or otherwise of a governor before the expiration of his functions, the government in the same way passes into the hands of the highest ranking general or the one with the most seniority of the same rank, who will convoke to the same ends as above the members of the Central Assembly, the generals in active service and the commanders-in-chief of departments.

Art 34—The Governor seals and promulgates the laws; he names to all civil and military posts. He commands in chief the armed forces and is charged with its organization, the ships of State docked in the ports of the colony receive his orders. He determines the division of the territory in the manner most in conformity with internal relations. According to the law, he watches over and provides for the internal and external security of the colony, and given that the state of war is a state of abandonment, malaise and nullity for the colony, the governor is charged in that circumstance to take the measures necessary to assure the colony subsistence and provisioning of all kinds.

Art 35—He influences the general policies of the inhabitants and manufactories, and ensures that owners, farmers and their representatives observe their obligations towards the cultivators and workers, and the obligations of cultivators and workers towards the owners, farmers and their representatives.

Art 36—He proposes to the Central Assembly the propositions of law as well as those changes in the Constitution that experience can render necessary.

Art 37—He directs the collection, the payment and the use of the finances of the colony and, to this effect, gives all orders.

Art 38—Every two years he presents at the Central Assembly the state of the receipts and expenses of each department, year by year.

Art 39—He oversees and censors, via commissioners, every writing meant for publication on the island. He suppresses all those coming from foreign countries that will tend to corrupt the morals or again trouble the colony. He punishes the authors or sellers, according to the seriousness of the case.

Art 40—If the Governor is informed that there is in the works some conspiracy against the tranquility of the colony, he has immediately arrested the persons presumed to be its authors, executors or accomplices. After having had them submit to an extra-judiciary interrogation if it is called for he has them brought before a competent tribunal.

Art 41—The salary of the Governor is fixed at present at three hundred thousand francs. His guard of honor is paid for by the colony.

Title IX. On Tribunals

Art 42—The right of citizens to be amicably judged by arbitrators of their choice cannot be infringed.

Art 43—No authority can suspend or hinder the execution of decisions rendered by the tribunals.

Art 44—Justice is administered in the colony by *tribunaux de premiére instance* and appeal tribunals. The law determines the organization of the one and the other, their number, their competency, and the territory forming the field of each. These tribunals, according to their degree of jurisdiction, handle all civil and criminal affairs.

Art 45—The colony has a *tribunal de cassation*, which pronounces on all requests for appeals against the decisions rendered by appeals courts, and complaints against an entire tribunal. This tribunal has no knowledge of the essence of affairs, but it reverses decisions rendered on procedures in which form was violated, or that contain some kind of evident contravention of the law, and sends the essence of the trial to the tribunal that must deal with it.

Art 46—The judges of these diverse tribunals preserve their functions all their lives, unless condemned for heinous crimes. The government commissioners can be revoked.

Art 47—Crimes by those in the military are subject to special tribunals and particular forms of judgment. These tribunals also know all kinds of theft, the violation of asylum, assassinations, murders, arson, rape, conspiracy and revolt. Their organization belongs to the governor of the colony.

Title X. On Municipal Administration

Art 48—There is a municipal administration in every parish of the colony; in that in which is placed a *tribunal de premiére instance* the municipal administration is composed of a mayor and four administrators. The government commissioner attached to the tribunal fulfills the functions of commissioner attached to the municipal administration without pay. In the other parishes the municipal administrations are composed of a mayor and two administrators, and the functions of commissioner attached to them are filled without pay by substitute commissioners attached to the tribunal that are responsible for these parishes.

Art 49—The members of municipal administrations are named for two years, but they can be continued in office. Their nomination falls upon the government that, from a list of at least sixteen persons presented to it by each municipal administration, chooses those persons most apt to guide the affairs of each parish.

Art 50—The functions of the municipal administrations consist in the simple exercise of policing cities and towns, in the administration of funds, assuring the revenues of manufactured goods and the additional impositions of the parishes. In addition, they are especially charged with the keeping of registers of births, marriages and deaths.

Art 51—Mayors exercise particular functions determined by the law.

Title XI. On the Armed Force

Art 52—The armed force is essentially obedient; it can never deliberate. It is at the disposition of the Governor, who can only set it in motion for the maintenance of public order, the protection due to all citizens, and the defense of the colony.

Art 53—It is divided into paid colonial guard and unpaid colonial guard.

Art 54—The unpaid colonial guard does not leave the limits of its parish except in cases of imminent danger, and under orders from, and under the personal responsibility of, the military commander or his place. Outside the limits of its parish it becomes paid and is subject in this case to military discipline; in any other it is subject only to the law.

Art 55—The colonial gendarmerie is part of the armed force. It is divided into horseback and foot gendarmerie. The horseback gendarmerie is instituted for high police matters and the safety of the countryside. It is paid for from the colonial treasury. The foot gendarmerie is instituted for the police functions in cities and towns. It is paid for by the cities and towns where it accomplishes its service.

Art 56—The army recruits upon the proposal made by the Governor to the Central Assembly, and following the mode established by law.

Title XII. On Finances and Goods from Seized and Vacant Domains

Art 57—The finances of the colony are composed of:

Rights on imported goods, weights and measures

Rights on the rental value of houses in cities and towns, of those that produce manufactured goods other than those of cultivation, and salt

Revenue from ferries and post

Fines, confiscations, wrecks

Rights from the saving of shipwrecked ships

Revenue from colonial domains

Art 58—The product of the *fermage* of goods seized from absentee owners without representatives are provisionally part of the public revenue of the colony, and are applied to administrative expenses. Circumstances will determine the laws that can be made relative to the overdue public debt and the *fermage* of goods seized by the administration at a period prior to the promulgation of the current Constitution, and towards those that will have been collected in a later time; they can be demanded and reimbursed in the year following the lifting of the seizure of the good.

Art 59—The funds coming from the sale of movable goods and the price of vacant successions, open in the colony under the French government since 1789, will be deposited in a special cashbox and will only be available, along with the real estate combined in colonial domains, two years after the publication on the island of peace between France and the maritime powers. Of course, this time span is only relative to those successions whose delay of five years—fixed by the edict of 1781—will have expired; and as relates to those opened at eras closer

to peace, they can only be available and combined at the expiration of seven years.

Art 60—Foreigners inheriting in France from their foreign or French relatives will also inherit in Saint-Domingue. They can contract, acquire, and receive goods situated in the colony and can dispose of them just like Frenchmen by all the means authorized by the law.

Art 61—The mode of collection and administration of goods from seized and vacant domains will be determined by law.

Art 62—A temporary accounting commission regulates and verifies the accounting of receipts and expenses of the colony. This commission is composed of three members, chosen and named by the governor.

Title XIII. General Dispositions

Art 63—Every person's home is an inviolable asylum. During the night, no one has the right to enter there except in case of fire, flood or appeal from within. During the day it can be entered for a specially determined objective, or by a law or an order emanating from a public authority.

Art 64—In order for an act ordering the arrest of a person to be executed it is necessary that it:

Formally express the motive for the arrest and the law in execution of which it is ordered;

Emanate from a functionary who the law had formally given the power to do so;

The person arrested be given a copy of the order.

Art 65—All those who, not having been given by the law the power to arrest, will give, sign, execute, or have executed the arrest of a person will be guilty of the crime of arbitrary detention.

Art 66—All persons have the right to address individual petitions to any constituted authority, and especially to the governor.

Art 67—No corporation or association contrary to public order can be formed in the colony.

No assembly of citizens can qualify itself as popular society. Any seditious gathering shall be immediately broken up at first by verbal order and, if necessary, by the development of armed force.

Art 68—Every person has the right to form private establishments for the education and instruction of youth, with the authorization and under the surveillance of municipal administrations.

Art 69—The law particularly watches over those professions that deal with public morality, the safety, the health and the fortunes of citizens.

Art 70—The law provides for the recompense of inventors of rural machinery, or the maintenance of the exclusive property in their discoveries.

Art 71—In the entire colony there is a uniformity in weights and measures.

Art 72—The governor will distribute, in the name of the colony, recompense to warriors who have rendered striking service in fighting for the common defense.

Art 73—Absent owners, for whatever cause, preserve their rights over the goods belonging to them situated in the colony. In order to have the seizure lifted, it will suffice for them to present their titles of ownership or, lacking titles, supplicative acts whose formula the law determines. Nevertheless, those inscribed and maintained on the general list of émigrés from France are excepted from this disposition. In this case their goods will continue to be administered as colonial domains until they have been taken from the lists.

Art 74—As a guarantee of the public law, the colony proclaims that all the leases legally affirmed by the administration will have their full effect, if the adjudicators don't prefer to compromise with the owners or their representatives who will have obtained the lifting of the seizure.

Art 75—It proclaims that it is upon the respect of persons and property that the cultivation of land, all production, and all means of labor and all social order rests.

Art 76—It proclaims that every citizen owes his services to the land that nourishes him and that saw him born; to the maintenance of liberty equality and property every time the law calls him to defend them.

Art 77—The General-in-Chief Toussaint-Louverture is and remains charged with sending the present Constitution for the approval of the French government. Nevertheless, and given the absence of laws, the urgency of escaping from this state of peril, the necessity of promptly re-establishing culture and the well expressed unanimous wish of the inhabitants of Saint-Domingue, the General-in-Chief is and remains invited, in the name of public good, to put it into effect in the entire expanse of the territory of the colony.

"Done at Port-Républicain, 19 Floreal year 9 of the one and indivisible French Republic."

Signed:

Borgella (president)

Raimond, Collet, Gaston Nogérée Lacour, Roxas, Mugnos, Mancebo, E Viart (Secretary).

"After having learned of the Constitution I give it my approbation. The invitation of the Central Assembly is an order for me. Consequently, I will have it passed on to the French government for its aproval. As for as its execution in the colony, the wish expressed by the CentralAssembly will be equally fulfilled and executed."

Given at Cap-Francais, 14 Messidor, year 9 of the one and indivisible French Republic.

General-in Chief: Toussaint-Louverture

GLOSSARY

Samana: now a province of the Dominican Republic

Saone: Saona Island, close to the southeastern coast of the Hispaniola, in the Caribbean Sea and now part of the Dominican Republic

Tortuga, … , Ile-a-Vache: islands off the coast of Haiti

vacant successions: unclaimed inheritances, or those for which the heirs are unknown

Vendémiaire, … , Pluviose, … : months in the French Republican Calendar, which was in use in France and its possessions when the Haitian constitution was promulgated

Document Analysis

The language of the constitution of 1801 is simple and straightforward. It resembles other constitutions in that it establishes a system of laws and government for the colony in thirteen titles and seventy-seven articles. At the same time, it vests considerable authority in the hands of the colony's governor.

Title I, consisting of two articles, defines the extent of Saint Domingue, which included the mainland and several islands. This title also indicates that the colony was to be divided into departments, *arrondisements*, and parishes. These terms reflect the administrative organization of France. A department was analogous to a state, a parish was analogous to a county, and an *arrondisement* was analogous to a precinct or district in a city. All were administrative subdivisions. Particularly noteworthy is that the constitution does not proclaim complete independence. It defines Saint Domingue as a colony and part of the French Empire.

Article 3 is a core element of the constitution, declaring that there could be no slaves in the territory. The title goes on to grant freedom of employment and to eliminate distinctions based on skin color. All persons living in the colony were not only "free" but also "French." Again, the constitution does not declare independence from France.

Toussaint-Louverture was a lifelong Catholic, and since he identified himself as a Frenchman, it is not entirely surprising that he would impose Catholicism—specifically Roman Catholicism—on the colony. He was also opposed to Vodou. (In Haitian Vodou, various deities, called *loa*, are subordinate to Bondyè, a greater god who does not intervene in human affairs. Worship is therefore directed to the *loa*. Vodou also places great value on ancestor worship and avoidance of evil witchcraft.) The constitution calls for the maintenance of the Catholic Church in each parish and notes that resources would be directed to its support.

Title IV addresses marriage and children. It promotes marriage, which "tends to the purity of morals." Consistent with Catholicism, the constitution forbids divorce. It also provides for the passage of laws designed to protect the welfare of children and family ties. The constitution specifies children "born through marriage," suggesting that different laws could apply to children born as a result of sexual misconduct (for example, involving white planters and their black or mulatto employees).

Title V, along with Titles IX and XIII, is as close as the constitution comes to issuing a bill of rights. Two essential rights are recognized. Article 12 "guarantees individual freedom and safety" and states that a person could be arrested only "by virtue of a formally expressed order, issued by a functionary who the law gives the right to arrest and detain." Article 13 protects property rights, calling property "sacred and inviolable." This provision protected landowners from having their land seized illegally by the government, and it had the effect of protecting the rights of plantation owners to their property.

A chief reason why Toussaint-Louverture wanted to protect property rights was that he wanted to protect commerce. He recognized that Saint Dominguc depended on agricultural production and trade, and for that reason, he did not wish to permit "the least interruption in its labor and cultivation." The constitution goes on to note that "every habitation is a manufactory that demands a gathering together of cultivators and workers." It also asserts that changes in the habitation of cultivators would bring the ruin of farming, and it refers to the "introduction of cultivators indispensable to the re-establishment of planting." These are key provisions of the constitution, for essentially they tied black workers to the plantations where they worked. Toussaint-Louverture opposed slavery and mandated its abolition, but these provisions in the constitution limited the mobility of black workers in an attempt to ensure that Saint Domingue would remain a profitable French colony. Title VI shows other evidence of the constitution's authors' desire to assert their connection with France as well: It uses French revolutionary dating ("20 Vendémiaire" rather than October 11 and "19 Pluviôse" ["Pluviose" in the document]" rather than February 7).

Title VII turns to the specifics of government. It provides for an assembly and specifies rules for membership in the assembly, election procedures, meetings of the assembly, and similar practical matters. It is noteworthy that all bills passed by the assembly have to have been proposed by the governor. Further, the assembly functions largely in an advisory capacity: "It expresses its wishes on the regulations made and on the application of laws already made, on the abuses to be corrected, on the improvements to be undertaken."

The constitution places control of the colony firmly in the hands of Toussaint-Louverture and his successors. The governor "directly corresponds with the government of the metropole," a word used in France, England, and other European countries to refer to the mother country, independent of its colonies. The title goes on to praise Toussaint-Louverture for his services to the colony and to lay out provisions for him to name his successor. The constitution mandates that succeeding governors remain loyal to the French government. It puts the governorship in the hands of the highest-ranking general in the event that a governor died without naming a successor. Articles 34 through 40 specify the powers of the governor, giving him command of the military, oversight of the colony's finances, censorship authority, command of the colony's agricultural activities, and other authority as well. Historians have noted that the constitution was not a particularly democratic document, for it vested considerable control in the governor, particularly Toussaint-Louverture.

Title IX protects the right to a fair trial. It reflects the French judicial system by establishing *tribunaux de première instance*, meaning "courts of first instance," or trial courts, and also appeals courts. Additionally, it provides for a *tribunal de cassation*, otherwise known as a "court of error." This court—a court of final appeal—was analogous to the U.S. Supreme Court and to the *tribunal de cassation* established in France in 1790. Military tribunals were to be under the authority of the island's governor.

Title X turns to practical matters of administration in the cities, specifying that each was to have a mayor and administrators. The municipal administration was to be responsible for policing the area under its jurisdiction, administering funds, and similar basic functions.

The constitution places the armed forces under the command of the governor. It divides the armed forces into a paid regular army and an unpaid "national guard." The latter could operate only within its parish except in cases of emergency. The constitution specifies that the police (*gendarmerie*) were to be considered part of the armed forces.

After specifying the colony's sources of revenue, the constitution turns to one of the problems that arose from the Haitian Revolution: what to do about the properties of landowners who had lost their lives during the conflict and what to do about the contracts (*fermages*) between landowners and tenants. While the language of Title XII is in places obscure, essentially it grants the colonial administration power to seize goods and vacant lands but also obligates the administration to return those goods and lands with the restoration of peace between France and its adversaries.

As "General Dispositions" suggests, this title addresses a number of miscellaneous matters. It functions in part as a bill of rights by stating that "every per-

son's home is an inviolable asylum," that citizens were protected from arbitrary arrest, and that they could petition the government. Patent rights are protected, as is the right to form schools. A uniform system of weights and measures is mandated. Citizens had the obligation to come to the defense of the colony. The obligations of leases are protected. The general dispositions also provide for the payment of "warriors" and forbid "seditious gatherings."

The constitution concludes with a statement from Toussaint-Louverture, who approves it after—as he somewhat disingenuously claims—having learned of it. He also states, perhaps naively, that he has passed it on to the French government for its approval. Napoléon declined to approve the constitution and invaded the colony.

Essential Themes

The 1801 Constitution of Haiti was a short-lived document. In the estimation of Napoléon, Toussaint-Louverture had gone too far in writing a constitution for what was still a French colony. By 1801 Napoléon had signed peace treaties with many of his adversaries in the Napoleonic Wars, so he was able to turn his attention to internal problems—and to Haiti. Accordingly, he dispatched a fleet to the island, and by the end of February 1802 these forces had taken control of most of Haiti's cities and ports. Toussaint-Louverture and his generals, notably Jean-Jacques Dessalines, put up resistance, but the numbers were against them. Their only weapons were the large number of white hostages they held and Haiti's terrain, which forced the French to fight in jungles and to find their way around mountain gorges, where ambushes were a constant threat. The French, however, held a weapon of their own in the form of Toussaint-Louverture's two sons, whom they claimed as hostages. Running out of resources and with morale low among his troops, Toussant-Louverture surrendered and, on May 7, 1802, signed a peace agreement with the French. On May 20, 1802, Napoléon reestablished slavery in the French colonies.

Toussaint-Louverture retired to his farm, under house arrest. He continued to correspond with rebels and made plans for a new offensive against the French. At this point, an ally came to his aid: yellow fever. The illness devastated the French forces, reducing their numbers to fewer than ten thousand; General Leclerc died of the disease in November 1802. Meanwhile, news of Napoléon's reinstatement of slavery spread. Hostilities resumed and continued until November 18,

1803, when the rebels, led by General Dessalines, defeated the French at the Battle of Vertières. By the end of the year, all French troops had departed.

General Dessalines proclaimed Haitian independence on the first day of 1804. He, like Toussaint-Louverture, named himself governor-general for life, though on October 6 of that year he was crowned emperor as Jacques I. After massacring the French colonists who remained on the island, he instituted a system of serfdom to keep the sugar plantations running. Dessalines was assassinated on October 17, 1806, and at that point the country split. In the north, Henri Christophe, one of Toussaint-Louverture's generals, was elected president and, on March 26, 1811, was crowned King Henri I. The south proclaimed itself a republic under the presidency of Alexandre Pétion, another of Toussaint-Louverture's generals and Christophe's rival for power. Some observers alleged that Pétion may have been complicit in the assassination of Dessalines, but this charge was never proved. Still, power appears to have corrupted Pétion, who came to find his earlier democratic ideals restrictive and who suspended the legislature in 1816 until his death in 1818. Meanwhile, Haiti—or parts of it—had been governed by constitutions promulgated in 1804, 1805, 1806, 1807, 1811, and 1816. Numerous other constitutions followed throughout the nineteenth and twentieth centuries. Its latest was written in 1987.

Although Toussaint-Louverture's vision of Haiti did not last, at least not in its entirety, the rebellion he helped lead and the constitution he wrote had profound significance. Black slaves, a people repressed and denigrated as inhuman, rose up to shock the slave-owning populations of the Americas by establishing its second republic. The Haitian revolution and constitution were profound challenges to the prejudices that upheld slavery and colonialism.

——*Michael J. O'Neal, PhD*

Bibliography and Further Reading

Bell, Madison Smartt. *Toussaint-Louverture: A Biography*. New York: Pantheon, 2007.

Dubois, Laurent, and John D. Garrigus. *Slave Revolution in the Caribbean, 1789–1804: A Brief History with Documents*. Boston: Bedford/St. Martin's Press, 2006.

DuPuy, Alex. *Haiti in the World Economy: Class, Race, and Underdevelopment since 1700*. Boulder, Colo. Westview Press, 1989.

Hochschild, Adam. *Bury the Chains: Prophets and Rebels in the Fight to Free an Empire's Slaves*. Boston: Houghton Mifflin, 2005.

Ott, Thomas. *The Haitian Revolution: 1789–1804*. Knoxville: University of Tennessee Press, 1973.

Ros, Martin. *Night of Fire: The Black Napoleon and the Battle for Haiti*. Kent, U.K. Spellmount Publishers, 1994.

Toussaint L'Ouverture. *The Haitian Revolution*, ed. Nick Nesbitt. New York: Verso, 2008.

Web Sites

Beard, John Relly. *Toussaint L'Ouverture: A Biography and Autobiography*. Documenting the American South, University of North Carolina at Chapel Hill http://docsouth.unc.edu/neh/[accessed February 6, 2017].

The Louverture Project. http://thelouvertureproject.org/ [accessed February 6, 2017].

■ Cartagena Manifesto

Date: 1812
Author: Simón Bolívar
Genre: Statement of political philosophy

Summary Overview

The Cartagena Manifesto was a key document in the Spanish American wars of independence that took place in Mexico and South America from 1808 to 1829. Simón was one of the chief liberators of the nations of South America from Spanish rule. Bolívar was Venezuelan, but after the collapse of his nation's First Republic in 1812, he departed to live in exile in modern-day Colombia. In the city of Cartagena de Indias (Cartagena of the Indies), he wrote a manifesto outlining what he perceived to be the causes for the First Republic's collapse. In doing so, he implicitly outlined what he believed should be the shape of a future Venezuelan republic or of any South American republic. More explicitly, his goal in the Cartagena Manifesto was to seek support for an invasion of Venezuela to oust the Spanish.

Venezuela effectively achieved its independence in 1821, at least in part as a consequence of the Cartagena Manifesto and Bolívar's leadership. Bolívar also lent aid to revolutions in other countries, helping to liberate Peru, Chile, Bolivia, and Argentina and thus earning the sobriquet "Liberator of Five Nations." Because of his role and those of numerous other revolutionaries, Spanish rule in continental Central and South America came to an end after three centuries. After the early nineteenth century's wave of revolutionary activity, only Puerto Rico and Cuba remained under Spanish control, a state of affairs that lasted until the Spanish-American War of 1898.

Discussions of South American history during this period are complicated by the nomenclature used to refer to the states. In the modern world, the various nations of South America—Argentina, Bolivia, Colombia, Ecuador, Paraguay, Peru, Uruguay, Venezuela, and others—are established independent countries. In the eighteenth and early nineteenth centuries, however, these nations were in essence provinces of larger polities ruled by Spain. Borders were shifting, and Spain's territories were often carved up and recombined into new political entities. Venezuela, for example, began as a province of Spain's Viceroyalty of Peru. Later it was part of the Viceroyalty of New Granada and then what was called a captaincy general—all referring to administrative units of Spain's New World colonies. Accordingly, in historical context, modern country names such as "Venezuela" and "Peru" serve as shorthand devices for referring to the regions that would eventually become these nations.

The manifesto was Bolívar's first significant piece of political writing, and he used it to convince republicans of the errors they had made in forming the First Republic and confronting the challenges of uniting the provinces into a stable nation able to fend off its adversaries. Bolívar wrote the manifesto to ask the governing powers in New Granada for permission to lead a New Granada army into Venezuela. Bolívar believed that the defeat of the First Republic by royalist forces was in some measure his responsibility. Through the manifesto he wanted to rehabilitate his reputation among military leaders, for he was already planning his invasion of Venezuela, which would lead to the formation of the Second Republic.

Bolívar knew that like any infant country Venezuela would need aid from foreign nations, such as the United States and Great Britain; indeed, British and Irish troops would fight in Venezuela after the collapse of the First Republic. With his manifesto, Bolívar hoped to convince international leaders that the political leadership of a republican Venezuela—specifically he himself—would have the necessary political heft to forge and maintain a new nation, one worthy of assistance from other nations that support the goal of independence.

Defining Moment

As Spanish colonies in the New World expanded in the sixteenth century, they were divided into what were called viceroyalties, each under the command of a governor-general. The first two were the viceroyalties of New Spain and Peru. New Spain encompassed what is today California and the southwestern United States, Mexico, most of Central America, and the Caribbean islands. The Viceroyalty of Peru consisted essentially of all of Spain's South American holdings (with the notable exception of Brazil, which was a Portuguese colony). Later, in the eighteenth century, two additional viceroyalties were formed. In 1717 the Viceroyalty of New Granada was created out of what would become Panama, Columbia, Ecuador, and Venezuela. In 1776 the Viceroyalty of the Río de la Plata was formed out of what would become Argentina, Bolivia, Uruguay, and Paraguay. Thus, by the eighteenth century, a map of Spain's New World colonies would extend all the way from the southern tip of South America up through most of western South America, through Central America and the western regions of North America.

Spain's relationships with its Atlantic colonies were rarely smooth. Spanish colonists in the New World grew to resent the high taxes they paid to the Spanish Crown as well as interference in their affairs by Spain, and they began to agitate for political independence. Many Latin American colonists were influenced by ideas coming out of the European Enlightenment, which, during the eighteenth century, questioned the legitimacy of hereditary succession and the divine right of kings to rule. These democratic notions began to gather momentum after England's American colonies declared their independence in 1776 and achieved victory in the Revolutionary War in 1783. Then, in 1789, the French Revolution overthrew the monarchy in France. The spirit of revolt moved to Central America with the Haitian Revolution, which began in 1791 and led to Haitian independence from France in 1804. The time was ripe for revolutionary movements to spread to Spain's American colonies.

A key event that triggered revolutionary movements in Latin America was the 1808 invasion of Spain by Napoléon Bonaparte in what is called the Peninsular War (referring to the Iberian Peninsula, which comprises Spain and Portugal). This campaign was part of a larger series of wars called the Napoleonic Wars, waged when Napoléon, having declared himself emperor of France, fought to topple hereditary monarchies and impose unified rule over Europe. The French invasion led to the complete breakdown of Spanish administration, both in Spain and in its colonies. What followed was a long period of warfare—both guerrilla and conventional—instability, turmoil, and uncertainty in Spain. The chief outcome of Napoléon's invasion, at least from the standpoint of the Americas, was a breakdown in communication between the colonies and Spain, which now no longer had the might necessary to enforce its control across the Atlantic.

Almost immediately, the Spanish colonies began to take action. The first effort to achieve independence in Venezuela occurred in 1810, when the municipal council in Caracas, the capital of the Captaincy General of Venezuela, launched a movement to depose the governor-general and set up a governing congress. Several of Venezuela's provinces quickly joined the "Caracas Junta," though numerous others did not. On July 5, 1811, the Venezuelan congress declared the nation's independence from Spain and established the First Republic. Meanwhile, revolutionary fervor spread to other Spanish colonies. In 1799 rebels in Mexico had launched an unsuccessful revolt called the Conspiracy of the Machetes. The spirit of rebellion survived in Mexico, and in September 1810 Mexico launched its war for independence from Spain, which it would achieve through the Treaty of Córdoba, signed in 1821. Also in 1810 the United Provinces of South America was formed. This state would become the United Provinces of the Río de la Plata, which in turn would eventually become the nation of Argentina. The United Provinces deployed armies, including the Army of the North, to liberate northern Argentina and Upper Peru (modern-day Bolivia). On November 5, 1811, a rebellion called the Primer Grito de Independencia, or "First Shout of Independence," erupted in El Salvador. The Spanish Empire in the New World was crumbling.

In Venezuela, matters did not go well for the infant First Republic. Civil war erupted between republicans and those who wanted to remain loyal to the Spanish monarchy. Two major provinces, Maracaibo and Guiana, as well as the district of Coro, refused to recognize the rebellious junta in Caracas. The republicans launched a military operation to bring Coro and Guayana to heel, but the operation failed—though republican forces did succeed in suppressing a rebellion against the republicans in Valencia. Meanwhile Spain, now under Napoléon's brother Joseph Bonaparte, imposed a blockade. A further setback for the republican government was an earthquake on March 26, 1812, which hit republican areas particularly hard and killed some fifteen thousand to twenty thousand people. Amid all this turmoil, Francisco de Miranda, the First Republic's political leader, was able to assume dictatorial powers, but he was unable to stop the advance of royalist troops under the command of Domingo de Monteverde. On July 25, 1812, royalists dealt a decisive defeat to the republicans at the Battle of San Mateo. Miranda signed a cease-fire agreement with Monteverde, effectively ending the First Republic.

One of the key leaders of the republican movement was Simón Bolívar, a young aristocrat who supported complete independence from Spain. Bolívar regarded Miranda's surrender as an act of treason. He arrested Miranda and turned him over to Monteverde, who ignored the terms of the cease-fire and arrested and executed many of the rebels. To escape Monteverde's reprisals, Bolívar fled to Cartagena de Indias, where he wrote the Cartagena Manifesto and planned an invasion of Venezuela.

Author Biography

The author of the Cartagena Manifesto was Simón José Antonio de la Santísima Trinidad Bolívar y Palacios Ponte Blanco, known to history simply as Simón Bolívar. Bolívar was born in Caracas on July 24, 1783, to an aristocratic family that had made its immense fortune in sugar and mining, particularly of copper. He thus was a member of the caste called criollos, or people of pure Spanish descent born in the colonies. After completing his education in Spain and living for a time in France, he returned to Venezuela in 1807. After the Caracas Junta assumed control, he was dispatched to England as a diplomatic representative, but he returned to Venezuela in 1811. When republican forces surrendered to royalist forces in 1812, he fled to Cartagena, where he wrote the Cartagena Manifesto later that year.

Bolívar's life after 1812 was eventful. He was given a military command by the United Provinces of New Granada, and in 1813 he led an invasion of Venezuela known as the Admirable Campaign, liberating the provinces of Mérida, Barinas, Trujillo, and Caracas from Spanish rule. When he seized Caracas on August 6, 1813, he proclaimed the Second Republic and served as its president until it collapsed in 1814. After a series of successes and setbacks, including the need to flee to Jamaica and then to Haiti, Bolívar returned to fight for the political independence of New Granada. He led military campaigns that liberated Venezuela and Ecuador and then established the nation known as Gran Colombia (comprising Venezuela, Colombia, Panama, and Ecuador) on December 17, 1819, serving as the nation's first president. He was able to witness his dream of a sovereign Venezuela after republican forces won the Battle of Carabobo on June 24, 1821, ensuring his nation's independence. A later victory in the Battle of Lake Maracaibo on July 24, 1823, drove out the last vestiges of the Spanish.

On August 6, 1825, the Congress of Upper Peru created the nation of Bolivia—one of the few nations in the world named after a person. Bolívar had difficulty governing, however, and had to assume dictatorial powers to maintain some semblance of control of the fragile state. He resigned his presidency on April 27, 1830, and died of tuberculosis on December 17 that year in Santa Marta, Gran Colombia (now Colombia).

HISTORICAL DOCUMENT

To spare New Granada the fate of Venezuela and save it from its present suffering are the objects of this report. Consent, my countrymen, to accept it with indulgence, in light of its praiseworthy intentions.

I am, Granadans, a child of unhappy Caracas, who having miraculously escaped from the midst of her physical and political ruins, always faithful to the liberal and just system proclaimed by my country, have come here to follow the standards of independence, so gloriously waving in these states.

Motivated by a patriotic zeal, let me dare to address you, to outline for you the causes that led to Venezuela's destruction; flattering myself that the awful and exemplary lessons that extinguished Re-

public has given us persuade America to improve her conduct, correcting the errors of unity, strength, and energy that are manifested in her forms of government.

The gravest mistake Venezuela made, when they entered the political arena, was without a doubt the fatal adoption of a system of tolerance—a system that was rejected by the whole sensible world as weak and ineffective but that was held to tenaciously and with unexampled blindness until the end.

The first evidence that our government gave of its foolish weakness manifested with respect to the subject city of Coro, when it refused to recognize the city's legitimacy, pronounced it insurgent, and harassed it as an enemy.

Instead of subjugating that defenseless city, which was ready to surrender when our maritime forces arrived, the Supreme Council allowed it to fortify itself and to put on such a respectable façade that it later succeeded in subjugating the whole Confederation, almost as easily as we had previously done. The Council based its political policy on a mistaken understanding of humanity that does not allow any government to free by force stupid people who do not know the value of their rights.

The codes consulted by our magistrates were not those that could teach them the practical science of government but those that have formed certain visionaries who, imagining ethereal republics, have sought to attain political perfection, assuming the perfectibility of humankind. Thus we got philosophers for leaders; philanthropy for law, dialectics for tactics, and sophists for soldiers. With such a subversion of principles and things, the social order suffered enormously, and, of course, the state ran by leaps and bounds to a universal solution, which was soon realized.

Hence was born the impunity of crimes against the state committed brazenly by the discontented, and especially on the part of our born and implacable enemy, the Spanish Europeans, remained in our country with the malicious intent of causing constant unrest and promoting as many conspiracies as our forgiving judges allowed, even if their attacks were so enormous that the public well-being was threatened.

The doctrine supporting this behavior stemmed from the philanthropic maxims of certain writers who defend the notion that no one has to take the life of a man, even one who has committed a crime against the state. In the shelter of this pious doctrine, a pardon followed every conspiracy, and after every pardon came another conspiracy, which in turn was forgiven because liberal governments must be distinguished by leniency. But this clemency is criminal and contributed more than anything else to tearing down the machinery that had not yet quite been established!

From this source stemmed the determined opposition to the calling up of veteran troops, disciplined and able to appear in the battlefield, as instructed, to defend liberty with success and glory. Instead, countless undisciplined militia were established, which, in addition to exhausting the funds of the national treasury with huge salaries, destroyed agriculture, driving the peasants away from their homes and making hateful the government that had forced them to take up arms and abandon their families.

Our statesmen tell us, "Republics have no need of men paid to maintain their freedom. All citizens are soldiers when the enemy attacks us. Greece, Rome, Venice, Genoa, Switzerland, Holland, and recently North America defeated their opponents without the help of mercenary troops always ready to support despotism and subjugate their fellow citizens."

The simple-minded were fascinated by these impolitic and inaccurate arguments, but they failed to convince the wise, who knew well the vast difference between the peoples, times, and customs of those republics and ours. It is true that those republics paid no standing armies, but in ancient times it was for the reason that they did not have any and instead entrusted their salvation and the glory of the States to their political virtues, austere habits, and military character, qualities that we are very far from possessing. As for modern republics that have shaken off the yoke of tyrants, it is well known that they have maintained a considerable number of veterans to assure their security—except North America, which being at peace with everyone and bounded by the sea has not had the need in recent years to sustain a full complement of veteran troops to defend its borders and squares.

The result provided Venezuela with harsh evidence of the error of their calculation, because the militiamen who went to meet the enemy, ignorant of the use of weapons and not being accustomed to discipline and obedience, were overwhelmed at the start of the last campaign, despite the heroic and extraordinary efforts made by their leaders to lead them to victory. This produced a general feeling of discouragement among the soldiers and officers, because it is a military truth that only hardened armies are capable of overcoming the first fateful events of a campaign. The inexperienced soldier believes that everything is lost if he is once defeated, because experience has not proved that courage, skill, and perseverance make up for bad fortune.

The subdivision of the disputed province of Caracas, planned and sanctioned by the federal congress, awakened and fostered a bitter rivalry between the cities and outlying areas and the capital, which—so said the congressmen, ambitious to dominate their districts—was the tyranny of the cities and the leech of the State. In this way the flames of civil war were fanned in Valencia and were never put out, even with the defeat of that city. Secretly the torch was passed from adjacent towns to Coro and Maracaibo and grew in intensity, in this way facilitating the entry of the Spanish, who brought about the downfall of Venezuela.

The dissipation of public revenues on frivolous and harmful items—particularly in salaries for countless clerks, secretaries, judges, magistrates, provincial and federal legislators—dealt a fatal blow to the Republic because it was forced to resort to the dangerous expedient of establishing a paper currency, without other security than the strength and anticipated income of the Confederation. This new currency appeared in the eyes of most people to be a gross violation of property rights, because they saw themselves as being robbed of objects of intrinsic value in exchange for others whose price was uncertain and even imaginary. Paper money put the finishing touches on the discontent of the stolid people of the interior, who called upon the Commander of the Spanish troops to come and rescue them from a currency that they viewed with more horror than slavery.

But what weakened the government of Venezuela the most was the federal structure they adopted, following the most exaggerated notions of human rights. Authorizing each man to rule himself breaks the social compact and characterizes nations in anarchy. Such was the true state of the Confederation. Each province was governed independently and, following this example, each city sought to claim the same powers and adopt the theory that all men and all peoples have the prerogative to establish at will the government that suits them.

Although it is the most perfect and most capable of providing human happiness in society, the federal system is nonetheless the most contrary to the interests of our nascent states. Generally speaking, our citizens are not in a position to exert their rights fully, because they lack the political virtues that characterize the true republican—virtues that are not acquired in absolute governments, where the rights and duties of citizenship are not recognized.

On the other hand, what country in the world, no matter how temperate and Republican it is, will be able to rule itself, in the middle of internal strife and foreign warfare, by a system as complicated and weak as the federal government? No, it is not possible to maintain order in the turmoil of fighting and factions. The government needs to adjust itself, so to speak, to the nature of the circumstances, the times, and the men that surround it. If they are prosperous and serene, it should be temperate and protective, but if they are dire and turbulent, it has to be harsh and arm itself with strength equal to the dangers, with no regard for laws or constitutions until happiness and peace are restored.

Caracas had to suffer much in light of the defects of the Confederation, which, far from aiding her, exhausted her wealth and military supplies and, when danger came, abandoned her to her fate—without help, with the smallest contingent. Moreover, it augmented the problems by fostering competition between the federal and provincial powers, which allowed the enemy to get to the heart of the State, before it had resolved the question of which troops—federal or provincial—should be dispatched to drive them back, when they already had occupied a large portion of the province. This fatal disagreement produced a delay that was terrible for our forces. They were defeated in San Carlos before the reinforcements necessary for victory arrived.

I believe that as long as we do not centralize our American governments, our enemies will gain the most comprehensive advantages. We will be inevitably involved in the horrors of civil strife and abjectly defeated by the handful of bandits who infest our region.

Popular elections conducted by the rustics of the countryside and by those engaged in intrigue in the cities add a further obstacle to the practice of federation among us, because the former are so ignorant that they vote mechanically and the latter are so ambitious that they turn everything into factionalism. So in Venezuela a free and fair election has never been seen, which put government in the hands of men who are uncommitted to the cause, inept, and immoral. The party spirit decided all matters, thus creating more chaos than the circumstances dictated. Our own divisions and not the Spanish forces, has turned us to slavery.

The earthquake of March 26 certainly was as upsetting physically as psychically and can properly be called the immediate cause of the ruin of Venezuela. But this same event could have occurred without producing such deadly effect if Caracas had then been governed by a single authority that, acting with speed and force, could have repaired the damage unfettered by the hindrances and rivalries that retarded the effect of these measures until the destruction had become so devastating that it was beyond help.

If Caracas, instead of a languid and ineffectual Confederation, had set up a simple government—the kind it required for its political and military circumstances, you would exist today, O Venezuela, and you would enjoy freedom.

After the earthquake, the influence of the church played a large part in the uprising of the towns and cities and the introduction of the enemies into the country, sacrilegiously abusing the sanctity of its ministry in aid of the promoters of civil war. However, we must candidly confess that these traitorous priests were encouraged to commit the heinous crimes of which they are justly accused simply because impunity for their crimes was absolute, a condition that Congress shockingly aided. The situation came to such a pass that from the time of the insurrection of the city of Valencia—the pacification of which cost the lives of a thousand men—not a single rebel was given over to the vengeance of the law. All of them were left with their lives intact, and the majority also kept their property.

It follows from the foregoing that among the causes leading to the fall of Venezuela should be placed, first, the nature of its Constitution, which was, I repeat, as contrary to her own interests as it was favorable to those of her opponents. Second was the spirit of misanthropy that gripped our leaders. Third was the opposition to the establishment of a military force that could have saved the Republic and repelled the blows of the Spaniards. Fourth was the earthquake, accompanied by a fanaticism that succeeded in drawing from this phenomenon the most ominous interpretations. Finally, there were the internal factions that were, in fact, the deadly poison that had pushed the country into the grave.

These examples of mistakes and misfortunes are not entirely without value for the peoples of South America, who aspire to freedom and independence.

New Granada has seen the demise of Venezuela, so it should avoid the pitfalls that have destroyed her. To this end, I advocate the reconquest of Caracas as an essential measure for securing the safety of New Granada. At first glance, this project might seem irrelevant, costly, and perhaps impractical, but if we examine it more closely, attentively, and with foresight, it is impossible to ignore the necessity and not to implement it once its utility is established.

The first thing that speaks in support of this operation is the origin of the destruction of Caracas, which was none other than the contempt with which the city regarded the existence of an enemy that seemed inconsequential. It was not, considered in its true light.

Coro certainly could never have competed with Caracas, when compared with Caracas in terms of its intrinsic strength. But because, in the order of human events, it is not always the largest physical entity that tilts the political balance, but the one that has superior moral force, should not the government of Venezuela therefore have refrained from removing an enemy who, though seemingly weak, had the support of the province of Maracaibo, including all those bound to the Regency; the gold; and the cooperation of our eternal enemies, the Europeans who live among us; the clerical party, always addicted to its supporter and partner, despotism; and, above all, the confirmed regard of the ignorant and superstitious within the boundaries of our states. So, to dismantle the machinery of state, it required only one traitorous official to call in the enemy, after which the unprecedented and patriotic efforts of the advocates of Caracas could not prevent the collapse of a structure already toppling from the blow of a single man.

Applying the example of Venezuela to New Granada and expressing it mathematically as a ratio, we find that Coro is to Caracas as Caracas is to all America; consequently, the danger that threatens this country is due to the aforementioned formula, because Spain, possessing the territory of Venezuela, can easily obtain men and munitions of war such that, under the direction of leaders with experience against the masters of war, the French, they can penetrate from the provinces of Barinas and Maracaibo to the ends of America South.

Spain has many ambitious and courageous general officers, who, accustomed to dangers and privations, yearn to come here to find an empire to replace the one she just lost.

It is very likely that upon the decline of the Peninsula, there will be a prodigious emigration of all sorts of men, particularly cardinals, archbishops, bishops, canons, and revolutionary clerics capable not only of subverting our tender and languid States but also entangling the entire New World in a frightful anarchy. The religious influence, the rule of civil and military domination, and all the prestige they can use to seduce the human spirit are so many instruments available to subjugate these regions.

Nothing will prevent emigration from Spain. England is likely to assist the emigration of a group that weakens Bonaparte's forces in Spain and augments and strengthens their own power in America. Neither France nor America can stop it. Neither can we do so on our own; all of our countries lacking a respectable navy, our attempts will be in vain.

These defectors will indeed find a favorable reception in the ports of Venezuela, as they are reinforcing the oppressors of that country and supplying the means to undertake the conquest of independent states.

They will raise a force of fifteen or twenty thousand men who will promptly be brought to order by their leaders, officers, sergeants, corporals, and veteran soldiers. This army will be followed by another, even more fearsome—one consisting of ministers, ambassadors, counselors, judges, the entire church hierarchy, and the grandees of Spain, whose profession is deceit and intrigue and who will be decorated with flashy titles well suited to dazzle the crowd. They will engulf everything like a torrent, right down to the seeds and even the roots of the tree of freedom in Colombia. The troops will fight on the field, and the others will wage war from their ministries by means of seduction and fanaticism.

Thus, we have no other recourse to guard against these calamities than to pacify our rebellious provinces and then to take up our weapons against the enemy and in this way to form soldiers and officials worthy to be called the pillars of the country.

Everything conspires to make us adopt this measure; without mentioning the urgent need for us to close the doors to the enemy, there are other very strong reasons for us to take the offensive. It would be an inexcusable political and military failure to fail to do so. We have been invaded, and we are therefore forced to drive the enemy back beyond the border. Moreover, it is a principle of the art of war that any defensive war is injurious and ruinous to the country that conducts it, because it weakens without hope of compensation. Conversely, fighting in enemy territory is always advantageous, for the sake of the good that results from harming the enemy. For this reason we must not, under any circumstances, go on the defensive.

We should also consider the current state of the enemy, which is in a very vulnerable position, having been deserted by most of its Creole soldiers and having, at just this time, to defend the patriotic garrison cities of Caracas, Puerto Cabello, La Guaira, Barcelona, Cumaná and Margarita, where they have their supplies. They do not dare abandon these positions, fearing a general uprising when they leave. So it would be impossible for our troops to arrive at the gates of Caracas without engaging in a pitched battle.

It is certain that as soon as we arrive in Venezuela thousands of brave patriots who are longing for our arrival to help them shake off the yoke of their tyrants will join us, uniting their forces with ours to defend freedom.

The nature of this campaign gives us the advantage of approaching Maracaibo by way of Santa Marta and Barinas by way of Cucuta.

Let us therefore take hold of this propitious moment. Do not allow reinforcements that might arrive at any time from Spain to entirely alter this strategic balance. Do not lose, perhaps forever, the providential opportunity to ensure the fortune of these states.

The honor of New Granada absolutely requires us to chasten those audacious invaders, pursuing them to their last stronghold. Because her glory depends on our undertaking the enterprise of marching to Venezuela, to liberate the cradle of Colombian independence, its martyrs and the worthy people of Caracas, whose cries are directed only to their beloved compatriots of Granada, whom they eagerly await as their redeemers. Let us hasten to break the chains of those victims who groan in the dungeons, ever hopeful of rescue by us. Do not betray their confidence; do not be insensitive to the cries of your brothers. Fly to avenge the dead, to give life to the dying, ease to the oppressed, and freedom to all.

———*Cartagena de Indias, 15 December 1812*

GLOSSARY

Creole: in this context, a Spanish American, born in the Americas

Peninsula: the Iberian Peninsula

Regency: French-dominated junta that briefly attempted to govern Spain's colonial possessions in South America

traitorous official: Francisco de Miranda

Document Analysis

Bolívar addresses his manifesto specifically to the people of New Granada. His goal is to outline his experiences in Venezuela, particularly the collapse of the First Republic, with a view to helping the people of New Granada escape the state's errors. Essentially, he outlines five major problems with the First Republic: the ineffectiveness of the army, poor administration of public revenues, reliance on a weak federal system, the Caracas earthquake of 1812, and the opposition of the Catholic Church to republican views. He then outlines his reasons for wanting to launch an invasion of Venezuela.

The first section of the manifesto is sharply critical of the republican military. After brief introductory paragraphs, Bolívar launches into a discussion of the failure of the First Republic's military campaigns, particularly against the district of Coro. His tone is harsh. He refers to "the fatal adoption of a system of tolerance" that allowed Coro to resist republican rule. He then makes a startling statement regarding the governing council in Caracas: "The Council based its political policy on a mistaken understanding of humanity that does not allow any government to free by force stupid people who do not know the value of their rights." Bolívar was a liberator, but he was by instinct an aristocrat, and as such he was willing to impose his political vision even on those who did not share it. He then discusses what he regarded as misplaced idealism, referring to "ethereal republics" and "pious doctrine" where philosophers supplanted leaders and philanthropy supplanted law. Crimes against the new state were tolerated, thus allowing royalist supporters free rein in Venezuela. One consequence of this tolerance was that unchecked opposition prevented the First Republic from calling up veteran troops, leading to the creation of undisciplined militias that were not equal to the fight at hand. And because these militias were formed from the local laboring populations, the impact on agriculture was severe. He rejects the view that because earlier nations, from ancient Greece and Rome to the fledgling United States, did not need mercenary armies, Venezuela did not need them either. He counters this view by arguing that these states had "political virtues, austere habits, and military character" that the Venezuelans did not possess.

The collective impact of these failures was twofold. In paragraph 13, Bolívar argues that the First Republic's military was simply ineffective; enlistees lacked discipline, obedience, and even knowledge of the use of weapons. The forces were thus doomed to defeat. In paragraph 14, Bolívar notes that the republic's unwillingness to take harsh measures led to problems in the city of Valencia; although the republic subdued Valencia, there resulted a rivalry between city and country that allowed the Spanish to regain a foothold in Venezuela.

Paragraph 15 briefly discusses the First Republic's poor administration of public revenues—"the dissipation of public revenues on frivolous and harmful items." For example, he cites the bloated salaries given to legions of public bureaucrats. The consequence of this overspending was that the First Republic had to issue its own paper currency. The currency, though, lacked the backing of goods and productive capacity. It was essentially worthless, with no "intrinsic value." Under such conditions of fiscal irresponsibility, many Venezuelans concluded that life was better under the Spanish than it was under the First Republic.

The core of Bolívar's argument is contained in this sequence of paragraphs. His chief objection to the First Republic was its "federal structure," a term that in Bolívar's usage means decentralization. In his view, too much power and authority were given to Venezuela's districts and cities, and not enough was reserved for the central government. Interestingly, the fledgling United States had faced the same problem. Under the original Articles of Confederation, the nation's first constitution, power was decentralized. The nation was less a unified polity than a "confederation" of states. Centrifugal forces threatened to drive the independent states apart until the U.S. Constitution, in the form in which it survives today, strengthened the federal government—while also planting the seeds of the American Civil War, when regional factionalism would overcome allegiance to the nation. Venezuela experienced the same kind of factionalism during the First Republic and beyond, as local economic interests trumped allegiance to the national government.

Bolívar's position is clear: "Authorizing each man to rule himself breaks the social compact and characterizes nations in anarchy." He goes on to write that despite its being ideal in certain respects, "the federal system is nonetheless the most contrary to the interests of our nascent states," especially since "our citizens are not in a position to exert their rights fully, because they lack the political virtues that characterize the true republican." He defends this notion by appealing to the nature of the times. When a country is "prosperous and serene," it can afford to relinquish power to its citizens. But when a country is fighting both internal factionalism and a foreign enemy, the times require it to exhibit strength. One of the practical consequences of this diffusion of power in the First Republic was that the federal government and provincial authorities quarreled in Caracas about who was going to deploy troops while the Spanish poised to strike. The result was certain defeat. A second practical consequence was ineffectual elections. In Bolívar's view, the federal system encouraged divisiveness, for "popular elections conducted by the rustics of the countryside and by those engaged in intrigue in the cities" become obstacles because the rustics "are so ignorant that they vote mechanically" while those in the cities "are so ambitious that they turn everything into factionalism."

In paragraphs 22 and 23, Bolívar makes reference to the Caracas earthquake, which struck on March 26, 1812, killing some fifteen to twenty thousand people and causing widespread property damage. Because the earthquake was centered in republican-controlled areas of Venezuela, it represented a serious setback to the First Republic. While Bolívar acknowledges that the earthquake was the "immediate cause" of the collapse of the republic, he goes on to argue that its effects would not have been as devastating if there had been a strong central government to address the crisis. In essence, the earthquake helped to expose the weaknesses of the federal system of government of the First Republic.

Paragraph 24 briefly apportions some of the blame for the collapse of the First Republic on the Catholic Church. Bolívar argues that Catholic priests aided those who promoted civil war and allowed the Spanish sanctuary in the country. He is particularly shocked by the fact that none of these "traitorous priests" were punished for their "heinous crimes"—again, a failing that he attributes to the weak and overly tolerant federal congress.

In the manifesto's final sequence of paragraphs, after reiterating the key points of his argument, Bolívar turns to the future by outlining how New Granada can learn from the mistakes made in Venezuela. He first insists that New Granada forces should invade and subdue Caracas. He draws his readers' attention again to the factionalism in Caracas, where distinct groups pursued their selfish ends at the expense of the republic, as had occurred in Coro. Bolívar argues that only by retaining control over Caracas could New Granada spread the spirit of revolution through South America. He then notes that because of events in Spain, it was likely that large numbers of Spanish immigrants would arrive in South America. These immigrants, acting in concert with seasoned military officers and soldiers, would be in a position to subvert South American independence. Bolívar goes on to claim that nothing can stop this immigration, and he raises the specter of a new Spanish army bent on conquest.

The only solution to this looming problem was "to pacify our rebellious provinces and then to take up our weapons against the enemy." He makes clear that fighting a purely defensive war would be ruinous to the country; the only alternative was to take the fight to the enemy. He calls the moment "propitious," for the Spanish were confined to their garrisons, which they had to defend. New Granada had to strike before Spanish reinforcements arrived. The manifesto closes with an inspirational call to action. Bolívar points out the obligation of New Granada to "chasten those audacious invaders" and "liberate the cradle of Colombian independence."

Essential Themes

In the short term, the Cartagena Manifesto had a profound impact. Bolívar won the support of New Granada and launched his Admirable Campaign on February 16, 1813. During the campaign, Bolívar issued a document called the Decree of War to the Death, in which he announced that any Spaniard who failed to support independence would be put to death. On July 22 his forces met and defeated the royalists at the Battle of Horcones. In August his army occupied Valencia and La Victoria, and the royalist government surrendered, leading to the formation of the Second Republic—which itself ended up collapsing less than a year later. From 1817 to 1819, Bolívar was head of a rump government that created a legislative body called the Congress of Angostura, which wrote a constitution for Venezuela in 1819. Later, in the Battle of Lake Maracaibo on July 24, 1823, republicans drove out the last vestiges of the Spanish. Thus, Bolívar's dream of an independent Venezuelan Republic was realized. The official, formal name of the country became and remains the Bolivarian Republic of Venezuela.

In the longer term, Bolívar's goal of a free, unified, prosperous South America proved harder to realize. Although several nations gained their independence— largely through the efforts of Bolívar and numerous other republicans—factionalism, caste, and power plays undermined attempts at South American unity. Gran Colombia collapsed within a decade, and in the ensuing years the nations of South America fell under the control of caudillos, a term often translated as "strongmen" or "warlords." Thus, throughout the 1800s, South American nations—excepting Brazil, a stable nation under the Portuguese until 1889—were ruled by authoritarian dictators, and the century was one of revolts, coups, civil wars, and wars between states.

——*Michael J. O'Neal, PhD*

Bibliography and Further Reading

Chasteen, John Charles. *Americanos: Latin America's Struggle for Independence*. New York: Oxford University Press, 2008.

Graham, Richard. *Independence in Latin America: A Comparative Approach*, 2nd ed. New York: McGraw-Hill, 1994.

Humphreys, Robert A., and John Lynch, eds. *The Origins of the Latin American Revolutions, 1808–1826*. New York: Knopf, 1965.

Lynch, John. *Simón Bolívar: A Life*. New Haven, CT: Yale University Press, 2007.

Rodríguez, Jaime E. *The Independence of Spanish America*. Cambridge: Cambridge University Press, 1998.

Web Sites

John Lynch. "Simon Bolivar and the Spanish Revolutions." *History Today* 33 Issue 7 (July 1983) http://www.historytoday.com/john-lynch/simon-bolivar-and-spanish-revolutions [**accessed February 27, 2017**].

■ *Considerations on the Principal Events of the French Revolution*

Date: 1818
Author: Germaine de Staël
Genre: Historical study

Summary Overview

Napoleon Bonaparte is still one of the most controversial figures in European and world history. On one hand, he was an egotistical, narcissistic monster, killing millions of soldiers and civilians over the course of twenty years in pursuit of his ambition to surpass the conquests of Alexander the Great. On the other hand, he was a product of the French Revolution and he likewise advanced the political ambitions of millions of people in France and the rest of Europe toward their own freedom and equality, whether he intended to or not. Germaine de Staël was the daughter of Louis XVI's last minister of finance and a revolutionary and philosopher in her own right. Having been at the center of events during the French Revolution, she wrote a history of the revolution and the Napoleonic era at the end of her life, part memoir and part reflection. One of its most famous chapters concerns de Staël's early assessment of Napoleon when he was about thirty, on the verge of seizing power from the Directory that was running France in the 1790s. Despite Napoleon's persecution of her in opposition to his regime, de Staël is balanced and nuanced in her depiction of a man on the verge of remaking European history in his own image, for both better and worse.

Defining Moment

Like many of the earliest historians of the French revolutionary and Napoleonic periods, Germaine de Staël (1766–1817) lived through them. She supported the liberal ideas of the earlier phases of the revolution. She also had a high regard for the parliamentary political culture of Britain. Although she had admired the young Napoléon as a general under the French Republic, she turned against him shortly after his seizure of power in 1799. During the Napoleonic period, de Staël was one of the few French writers to explicitly oppose Napoléon. For her involvement with the political opposition, she was exiled from France in 1793, and her books were banned. She spent the next year at her Swiss country estate at Coppet (near Geneva, Switzerland), which became a center of anti-Napoleonic sentiment.

Considerations on the Principal Events of the French Revolution was originally conceived of as an examination of Jacques Necker's career, Germaine de Staël's father. Instead it grew into a history of revolutionary France from 1789 to 1815. De Staël was famed as the woman whom Napoleon hated the most. Her background—wealthy, educated, aristocratic yet comfortable in the revolutionary world—made her a model of the sort of person Napoleon Bonaparte hoped to impress with his credentials as a nationalist hero. Her opposition was likely all the more galling as a result.

Author Biography

Jacques Necker and his wife hosted famous intellectual get-togethers, "salons', in Paris in the 1770s and 1780s, at which their daughter Germaine met some of the most famous French political thinkers of the time. These same thinkers, people like Voltaire and Jean-Jacques Rousseau, became the inspiration for revolution in France in 1789, and Louis XVI's dismissal of Necker as his finance minister was part of inspiration for the storming of the Bastille prison, the defining moment of the revolution. After the Reign of Terror ended and the Directory assumed power in 1794, Germaine de Staël herself became the hostess of Paris' most esteemed salons, and thus came into contact with the most famous hero of the revolution at the time, the general Napoleon Bonaparte. He did not agree with her political ideology or ideas on constitutional government, and before long, de Staël's salons became centers of resistance to the dictatorship Napoleon imposed on France and its empire.

De Staël thus spent most of the Napoleonic Wars in exile at her father's old estate in Switzerland. She became the most famous critic of the regime all the way up to its collapse with the allied invasion of 1814. After Waterloo, she reestablished her famous salons, but constant harassment had taken a toll on her health, and she died in 1817. *Considerations on the Principal Events of the French Revolution* was published a year later by her children and friends. Besides her portraits

of figures like Napoleon, the book became renowned for its championing of liberal and constitutional values and the rule of law.

HISTORICAL DOCUMENT

Chapter XXVI

The Directory was disinclined to peace, not that it wished to extend the French dominions beyond the Rhine and the Alps, but because it thought the war useful for the propagation of the republican system. Its plan was to surround France with a belt of republics, like those of Holland, Switzerland, Piedmont, Lombardy, Genoa. Every where it established a directory, two councils, a constitution, in short, similar in every respect to that of France. It is one of the great failings of the French, and a consequence of their social habits, that they imitate one another, and wish to be imitated by every body. They take natural varieties in each man's, or even each nation's mode of thinking, for a spirit of hostility against themselves.

General Bonaparte was assuredly less serious and less sincere than the Directory in the love of republicanism; but he had much more sagacity in appreciating circumstances. He foresaw that peace would be popular in France, because the passions were subsiding into tranquillity, and the people were becoming weary of sacrifices; he therefore signed the treaty of Campo Formio with Austria. But this treaty contained the surrender of the Venetian Republic, and it is not easy to conceive, how he succeeded in prevailing upon the Directory, which yet was in some respects republican, to commit what, according to its own principles, was the greatest possible enormity. From the date of this proceeding, not less arbitrary than the partition of Poland, there no longer existed in the government of France the slightest respect for any political doctrine, and the reign of one man began, when the dominion of principle was at an end.

Bonaparte made himself remarkable by his character and capacity as much as by his victories, and the imagination of the French was beginning to attach itself warmly to him. His proclamations to the Cisalpine and Ligurian Republics were quoted. In

the one this phrase was remarked: *You were divided, and bent down by tyranny; you were not in a situation to conquer liberty.* In the other: *True conquests, the only conquests which cost no regret, are those which we make from ignorance.* In his style there reigned a spirit of moderation and dignity, which formed a contrast with the revolutionary bitterness of the civil leaders of France. The warrior then spoke like a magistrate, while magistrates expressed themselves with military violence.

Bonaparte in his army had not enforced the laws against emigrants. He was said to be much attached to his wife, whose character was full of gentleness; it was asserted that he was feelingly alive to the beauties of Ossian; people took delight in ascribing to him all the generous qualities which give a pleasing relief to extraordinary talents. Besides, the nation was so weary of oppressors who borrowed the name of liberty, and of oppressed persons who regretted the loss of arbitrary power, that admiration knew not what to attach itself to, and Bonaparte seemed to unite all that was fitted to take it captive.

It was with this sentiment, at least, that I saw him for the first time at Paris. I could not find words to reply to him, when he came to me to say, that he had sought my father at Coppet, and that he regretted having passed into Switzerland without seeing him. But, when I was a little recovered from the confusion of admiration, a strongly marked sentiment of fear succeeded. Bonaparte, at that time, had no power; he was even believed to be not a little threatened by the captious suspicions of the Directory; so that the fear which he inspired was caused only by the singular effect of his person upon nearly all who approached him. I had seen men highly worthy of esteem; I had likewise seen monsters of ferocity: there was nothing in the effect which Bonaparte produced on me, that could bring back to my recollection either the one or the other.

I soon perceived, in the different opportunities which I had of meeting him during his stay at Paris, that his character could not be defined by the words which we commonly use; he was neither good, nor violent, nor gentle, nor cruel, after the manner of individuals of whom we have any knowledge. Such a being had no fellow, and therefore could neither feel nor excite sympathy: he was more or less than man. His cast of character, his understanding, his language, were stamped with the impress of an unknown nature—an additional advantage, as we have elsewhere observed, for the subjugation of Frenchmen.

Far from recovering my confidence by seeing Bonaparte more frequently, he constantly intimidated me more and more. I had a confused feeling that no emotion of the heart could act upon him. He regards a human being as an action or a thing, not as a fellow creature. He does not hate more than he loves; for him nothing exists but himself; all other creatures are ciphers. The force of his will consists in the impossibility of disturbing the calculations of his egotism; he is an able chessplayer, and the human race is the opponent to whom he proposes to give check-mate. His successes depend as much on the qualities in which he is deficient as on the talents which he possesses. Neither pity, nor allurement, nor religion, nor attachment to any idea whatsoever, could turn him aside from his principal direction. He is for his self-interest what the just man should be for virtue; if the end were good, his perseverance would be noble.

Every time that I heard him speak, I was struck with his superiority; yet it had no similitude to that of men instructed and cultivated by study or society, such as those of whom France and England can furnish examples. But his discourse indicated a fine perception of circumstances, such as the sportsman has of the game which he pursues. Sometimes he related the political and military events of his life in a very interesting manner; he had even somewhat of Italian imagination in narratives which allowed of gayety. Yet nothing could triumph over my invincible aversion for what I perceived in him. I felt in his soul a cold sharp-edged sword, which froze the wound that it inflicted; I perceived in his understanding a profound irony, from which nothing great or beautiful, not even his own glory could escape; for he despised the nation whose suffrages he wished, and no spark of enthusiasm was mingled with his desire of astonishing the human race.

It was in the interval between the return of Bonaparte and his departure for Egypt, that is to say, about the end of 1797, that I saw him several times at Paris; and never could I dissipate the difficulty of breathing which I experienced in his presence. I was one day at table between him and the Abbé Sieyès; —a singular situation, if I had been able to foresee what afterwards happened. I examined the figure of Bonaparte with attention; but whenever he discovered that my looks were fixed upon him, he had the art of taking away all expression from his eyes, as if they had been turned into marble. His countenance was then immoveable, except a vague smile which his lips assumed at random, to mislead any one who might wish to observe the external signs of what was passing within.

The Abbé Sieyès conversed during dinner unaffectedly and fluently, as suited a mind of his degree of strength. He expressed himself concerning my father with a sincere esteem. *He is the only man*, said he, *who has ever united the most perfect precision in the calculations of a great financier to the imagination of a poet*. This eulogium pleased me, because it characterized him. Bonaparte, who heard it, also said some obliging things concerning my father and me, but like a man who takes no interest in individuals whom he cannot make use of in the accomplishment of his own ends.

His figure, at that time thin and pale, was rather agreeable; he has since grown fat, which does not become him; for we can scarcely tolerate a character which inflicts so many sufferings on others, if we do not believe it to be a torment to the person himself. As his stature is short, and his waist very long, he appeared to much more advantage on horseback than on foot. In every respect it is war, and only war, which suits him. His manners in society are constrained, without timidity; he has an air of vulgarity when he is at his ease, and of disdain when he is not; disdain suits him best, and accordingly he indulges in it without scruple.

By a natural vocation to the regal office, he already addressed trifling questions to all who were presented to him. Are you married? was his question to one of the guests. How many children have you? said he to another. How long is it since you arrived? When do you set out? and other interrogations of a similar kind, which establish the superiority of him who puts them over those who submit to be thus questioned. He already took delight in the art of embarrassing, by saying disagreeable things; an art which he has since reduced into a system, as he has every other mode of subjugating men by degrading them. At this epoch, however, he had a desire to please, for he confined to his own thoughts the project of overturning the Directory, and substituting himself in its stead; but in spite of this desire, one would have said that, unlike the prophet, he cursed involuntarily, though he intended to bless.

I saw him one day approach a French lady distinguished for her beauty, her wit, and the ardour of her opinions. He placed himself straight before her, like the stiffest of the German generals, and said to her, *Madam, I don't like women to meddle with politics. You are right, General,* replied she; *but in a country where they lose their heads, it is natural for them to desire to know the reason.* Bonaparte made no answer. He is a man who is calmed by an effective resistance; those who have borne his despotism deserve to be accused as much as he himself.

The Directory gave General Bonaparte a solemn reception, which in several respects should be considered as one of the most important epochs in the history of the Revolution. The court of the palace of the Luxembourg was chosen for this ceremony. No hall would have been large enough to contain the multitude which it attracted: all the windows, and all the roofs, were crowded with spectators. The five Directors, in Roman costume, were seated on a platform at the further end of the court, and near them the deputies of the two councils, the tribunals, and the institute. Had this spectacle occurred before the subjugation of the national representation to military power on the 18th Fructidor,

it would have exhibited an air of grandeur: patriotic tunes were played by an excellent band; banners served as a canopy to the Directors, and these banners brought back the recollection of great victories.

Bonaparte arrived, dressed very simply, followed by his aides-de-camp, all taller than himself, but nearly bent by the respect which they displayed to him. In the presence of whatever was most distinguished in France, the victorious General was covered with applauses: he was the hope of every one: republicans, royalists, all saw the present or the future in the support of his powerful hand. Alas! of the young men who then cried *Long live Bonaparte,* how many has his insatiable ambition left alive?

M. de Talleyrand, in presenting Bonaparte to the Directory, called him *the liberator of Italy, and the pacificator of the Continent.* He assured them, that *General Bonaparte detested luxury and splendour, the miserable ambition of vulgar souls, and that he loved the poems of Ossian, particularly because they detach us from the earth.* The earth would have required nothing better, I think, than to let him detach himself from its concerns. Bonaparte himself then spoke with a sort of affected negligence, as if he had wished to intimate, that he bore little love to the government under which he was called to serve.

He said that for twenty centuries royalty and feudality had governed the world, and that the peace which he had just concluded was the era of republican government. *When the happiness of the French,* said he, *shall be established upon better organical laws, all Europe will be free.* I know not whether by the organical laws of freedom he meant the establishment of his absolute power. However that might be, Barras, at that time his friend, and president of the Directory, made a reply which supposed him to be sincere in all that he had just said, and concluded by charging him specially with the conquest of England, a mission rather difficult. …

Alas! what is become of those days of glory and peace, with which France flattered herself twenty years ago! All these blessings were in the hand of a single man: what has he done with them?

Document Analysis

De Staël's presentation of the character of Napoléon portrays him not as the representative of a particular political position but as a man utterly focused on his own political ambition, to the point where other people did not really exist for him. Although she had admired Napoléon to some extent early in his career, she moved to opposition following his 1799 takeover in the coup of 18 Brumaire (November 9). She viewed Napoléon's seizure of power as the final assassination of liberty during the revolution and a betrayal of the revolution's promise. De Staël was also concerned to disabuse the French people of the idea that Napoléon was a patriotic Frenchman or a champion of French culture.

In the excerpted passages, de Staël depicts Napoléon at the time when he was a famous general but before he had seized power as dictator. She wanted to show that he had the same character before and after taking power and that the only real difference between the two phases of his career was that before taking power he had a greater need to be agreeable. She claims that the Treaty of Campo Formio, signed between France and Austria in 1797, at the end of Napoléon's campaigns in Italy, marked a turning point when the Republican tradition was betrayed both by Napoléon, then the French commander in Italy, and the Directory, which was at that time the government of France. The treaty gave Venice to Austria as compensation for the loss of her northern Italian possessions. Venice was a thousand-year-old republic, and French Republicans viewed Austria as a repressive monarchy. This shameful act revealed Napoléon's true ruthlessness and unscrupulousness as well as the weakness of the Directory.

De Staël draws on personal experience as well as historical analysis. As an intellectual woman, she represented a category Napoléon detested—a point she emphasizes. She discusses the history of her personal relations with Napoléon to bring out his inhumanity. However, she also tries to understand the roots of his appeal to the French. De Staël credits Napoléon with eloquence and good political instincts. She also points out that he was the right man at the right time, as the country was weary of its supposedly Republican rulers, the Directory, but was not sympathetic to the Royalists, who wished to restore the French monarchy. In this situation, Napoléon attracted the hopes of all.

Essential Themes

The note de Staël consistently sounds in her description of Napoléon is one of inhumanity. His emotional impact on her has no parallel either among good men or bad; "his character could not be defined in the words we commonly use." His manner is equally chilling, as he possessed an ability to remove "all expression from his eyes." No cause outside his struggle against the human race moved him. De Staël also uses her—and the reader's—knowledge of Napoléon's future to heighten the ironies of his ascent. She wonders how many of the young men cheering Napoléon on his presentation to the Directory survived his wars, and she recounts that the president of the Directory, Paul Nicolas, vicomte de Barras, charged Napoléon with the conquest of England. The anglophile de Staël remarks that that task was "rather difficult," and, of course, it was one that Napoléon was never to accomplish.

——*William Burns*

Bibliography and Further Reading

De Staël, Germaine. *Considerations on the Principal Events of the French Revolution*, vol. 1. Edited by Duke de Brogile and Baron de Staël. New York: James Eastburn, 1818.

Emsley, Clive. *Napoleon: Conquest, Reform, Reorganisation*. New York: Routledge, 2015.

Goodden, Angelica. *Madame de Staël: The Dangerous Exile*. New York: Oxford University Press, 2008.

"The French Revolution: Bliss Was It In That Dawn?" *The Economist* (December 24, 1988).

■ Treaty of Córdoba

Date: 1821
Authors: Agustín de Iturbide, Vicente Guerrero, Juan O'Donojú
Genre: International peace agreement

Summary Overview

On August 24, 1821, Agustín de Iturbide, general of the Mexican Army of the Three Guarantees, and Juan O'Donojú, captain general of New Spain and representative of the Spanish Crown, signed the Treaty of Córdoba, which granted independence to Mexico. (The accompanying document uses the anglicized spelling "Cordova" and the variant spelling "O'Donnoju.") The Treaty of Córdoba brought to a close the long and complex Mexican War of Independence (1810–1821).

The Mexican War of Independence occurred during what has been called the "Age of Revolution," a period from roughly 1760 to 1830, during which revolutionary movements flowered on both sides of the Atlantic. Countries broke free of absolutist monarchies and established republics. Enlightenment thought, particularly ideas about human equality and the relationship between government and the governed, encouraged both social and political revolution and caused people to challenge the established social hierarchy and the role of religion in politics. The Mexican War of Independence proved to be much more conservative than many other contemporaneous revolutions. It began with both social and political elements but ended largely as a political revolution, gaining Mexico independence but leaving its society largely unchanged. Additionally, like most of the Latin American wars of independence, the relationship between the Catholic Church and the state was largely unquestioned. The Catholic Church retained much of its authority, special rights, and powers after Mexican independence.

Nevertheless, with this treaty Mexico joined two other newly established American nations, the United States and Haiti, both of which had also fought for independence. On a global scale, by signing the Treaty of Córdoba, Mexico entered into world politics, becoming a sovereign nation.

Defining Moment

The Mexican War of Independence took place during a very turbulent time for the Spanish Empire. The colonies, increasingly unhappy with Spain, desired autonomy. At the same time, there was increasing social tension between the *criollos*, those of Spanish descent born in the New World, and the *peninsulares*, Spaniards from the mother country. The era saw the growth of *criollismo*, a movement promoting pride in American origin and empowering the *criollo* population. *Peninsulares* predominated in the highest offices of the government and Catholic Church in the colonies, including Mexico, even though *criollos* outnumbered them by a factor of ten or more. Compounding this social tension was the legal, organized discrimination against others under the *sistema de castas* (caste system), which differentiated between individuals by their *calidad*, or "quality." Under this system, mestizos (people of mixed European and Indian heritage) and Indians were denied many of the rights enjoyed by both *peninsulares* and *criollos*.

In 1808 France's Napoléon Bonaparte invaded Spain, deposed King Ferdinand VII, and installed his brother, Joseph Bonaparte, on the throne of Spain as Joseph I of Spain. This simultaneously diverted Spanish attention from the colonies and provided a rallying point for the fighters in the War of Mexican Independence and, indeed, for revolutionaries across the Americas. Many Spanish colonies broke away from the mother country when Napoleon deposed Ferdinand VII. The colonies cited Spanish law that declared that colonies belonged to the monarch, not to Spain. Therefore, the colonies would rule themselves while the "false king" was on the throne of Spain. By the time the Treaty of Valençay restored Ferdinand VII to the throne in December 1813, the colonies had grown accustomed to governing themselves. The independence movements, including Mexico's, grew from this. For the next decade, Spain fought wars all over Latin America, trying to keep its crumbling empire together. Mexico was the first of Spain's American colonies to successfully break away.

The Mexican War of Independence began on September 16, 1810, with the "Grito de Dolores" (Cry of Dolores), a speech delivered by the *criollo* priest Miguel Hidalgo y Costilla, who called upon his parishioners in the community of Dolores to revolt. Hidalgo had long worked to improve the welfare of his parishioners, trying to stimulate the local economy and provide employment through practices such as grape cultivation and beekeeping. Hidalgo's goals in the revolution included social and economic reform that would benefit both *criollos* and Indians. Soon after Hidalgo gave the "Grito de Dolores" speech, the Battle of Guanajuato, the first battle of the War of Independence, was fought.

Although Hidalgo's peasant army was largely successful (if undisciplined) for several months, within a year Hidalgo was captured, tried, and executed. After the death of Hidalgo, José María Morelos y Pavón arose as one of the leaders of the War of Independence. Like Hidalgo, Morelos was a priest who was dedicated to social reform. Under his leadership, the Congress of Chilpancingo was convened in 1813. In an initial document endorsed by Morelos, the Congress called for Mexican independence, the establishment of the Roman Catholic Church as the country's sole religion, division of government into executive, legislative, and judiciary branches, and the abolition of slavery and the ending of the *sistema de castas*. Morelos was captured and executed late in 1815.

From 1815 on, the war devolved into guerrilla activity led by Vicente Guerrero, Morelos's deputy, and Guadalupe Victoria, which continued until near the war's end in 1821. The guerrillas met with mixed success. In 1820 General Agustín de Iturbide was appointed to lead the royalist forces against the insurgents. The year 1820, however, also marked the outbreak of the Spanish Civil War, in which liberals sought to press constitutional reforms and limitations on the Spanish monarch. Faced with the loss of prestige, many conservative *criollos*, including Iturbide, chose to change allegiances and support the independence movement.

Iturbide's defection to the insurgents was codified in a document known as the Plan of Iguala, or the Plan of the Three Guarantees. Iturbide and Guerrero, the architects of the plan, agreed to unite their forces. The three guarantees that the plan laid out were Mexican independence, establishment of Roman Catholicism as the state religion, and legal codification of social equality through the abolition of the *sistema de castas*. Iturbide and Guerrero further agreed that Mexico would become a constitutional monarchy. The plan, signed on February 24, 1821, was the basis for the Treaty of Córdoba.

Iturbide, now head of the newly christened Army of the Three Guarantees, quickly cemented the in-

surgents' victory on the battlefield, which led to the resignation of Spain's highest-ranking political representative in New Spain, Juan O'Donojú. Iturbide and O'Donojú signed the Treaty of Córdoba on August 24, 1821, formalizing Mexican independence and establishing a constitutional monarchy.

In accordance with the treaty, Ferdinand VII was called upon to become king of Mexico. When he refused, the throne was offered to other members of his family, each of whom also declined, refusing to recognize Mexican independence. The Spanish legislature also declined to recognize Mexican independence, declaring it illegal on February 13, 1822. Ultimately, Iturbide himself assumed the throne. After a short reign (1822–1823), Iturbide was overthrown by General Antonio López de Santa Anna and Guadalupe Victoria, who called for the establishment of a republic. Spain tried to retake Mexico several times, most significantly through an invasion from Cuba in June 1829. Mexican forces defeated the invaders, and Spain was compelled to recognize Mexican independence in 1830.

Author Biographies

Agustín de Iturbide helped craft two of the documents that were foundational for the establishment of an independent Mexico: the Plan of Iguala and the Treaty of Córdoba. Iturbide was born into a high-status *criollo* family in Valladolid, New Spain (in the modern-day state of Michoacán, Mexico). He entered the army at an early age, and when the Mexican War of Independence broke out, he chose to fight for Spain, becoming one of the most important leaders of the royalist army. He fought against the insurgents with mixed success; ultimately, however, Iturbide was never able to defeat the insurgent leader Vicente Guerrero. This, coupled with the adoption in Spain of a liberal, republican constitution, led him to break with the royalist army and join with the insurgents.

Other authors of the treaty and its antecedent, the Plan of Iguala, include Vicente Guerrero and Juan O'Donojú. Guerrero was born in 1782 in Tixtla, a town in the Sierra Madre del Sur, a mountain range in southern Mexico. He joined the revolt against Spanish rule in 1810, rising through the ranks to become lieutenant colonel by 1812. Guerrero was one of the most effective commanders for the insurgents in the War of Mexican Independence and fought successfully against Iturbide before they joined forces to form the Army of the Three Guarantees.

O'Donojú was born of Irish descent in Seville, Spain, in 1762, joining the army at an early age. In 1814 he was appointed minister of war and then became aide de camp to Ferdinand VII. He served as the last viceroy of Mexico from July to September 1821. Upon his arrival in Mexico in July, he found tremendous support among the population for Iturbide and the Army of the Three Guarantees. O'Donojú, realizing that he had little hope of holding the colony for Spain, called for a meeting with Iturbide. The resulting treaty was modeled closely on the Plan of Iguala. The only real change between the treaty and the plan was the provision that if none of the members of the royal family of Spain would take the Mexican crown, the Mexican congress would choose the ruler. Some historians argue that this provision resulted from a collaboration between Iturbide and O'Donojú and that the two intended for Iturbide to assume the crown from the very beginning. After the signing of the treaty, O'Donojú supervised the removal of Spanish troops from the country. He died of pleurisy in October 1821.

HISTORICAL DOCUMENT

Agreement on the Independent Kingdom of Mexico
 24 Aug 1821
 Treaty concluded in the Town of Cordova on the 24th of August, 1821, between Don Juan O'Donnoju, Lieutenant-General of the Armies of Spain, and Don Augustín de Iturbide, First Chief of the Imperial Mexican Army of the "Three Guarantees."
 New Spain having declared herself independent of the mother country; possessing an army to support this declaration; her provinces having decided in its favour; the capital wherein the legitimate authority had been deposed being besieged; the cities of Vera Cruz and Acapulco alone remaining to the European government ungarrisoned, and without the means of resisting a well directed siege of any duration, Lieut.-Gen. Don Juan O'Donnoju arrived at the first, named port in the character and quality of Captain General and first political chief of this kingdom, appointed by his most Catholic Majesty, and being desirous of avoiding the evils that necessarily fall upon the people in changes of this description, and of reconciling the interests of Old and New Spain, he invited the First Chief of the imperial army, Don Augustín de Iturbide to an interview in order to discuss the great question of independence, disentangling without destroying the bonds which had connected the two Continents. This interview took place in the town of Cordova, on the 24th of August, 1821, and the former under the character with which he came invested, and the latter as representing the Mexican empire, having conferred at large upon the interests of each nation, looking to their actual condition and to recent occurrences, agreed to the following Articles, which they signed in duplicate, for their better preservation, each party keeping an original for greater security and validity.

1st. This kingdom of America shall be recognised as a sovereign and independent nation and shall, in future, be called the Mexican Empire.

2d. The government of the empire shall be monarchical, limited by a constitution.

3d. Ferdinand VII, Catholic king of Spain, shall, in the first place, be called to the throne of the Mexican Empire, (on taking the oath prescribed in the 10th Article of the plan) and on his refusal and denial, his brother, the most serene infante Don Carlos; on his refusal and denial, the most serene infante Don Francisco de Paula; on his refusal and denial, the most serene Don Carlos Luis, infante of Spain, formely heir of Tuscany, now of Lucca; and upon his renunciation and denial, the person whom the Cortes of the empire shall designate.

4th. The emperor shall fix his court in Mexico, which shall be the capital of the empire.

5th. Two commissioners shall be named by his excellency Señor O'Donnoju, and these shall proceed to the court of Spain, and place in the hands of his Majesty king Ferdinand VII a copy of this treaty, and a memorial which shall accompany it, for the purpose of affording information to his Majesty with respect to antecedent circumstances, whilst the Cortes of the empire offer him the crown with all the formalities and guarantees which a matter of so much importance requires; and they supplicate his Majesty, that on the occurrence of the case provided for in Article 3, he would be pleased to communicate it to the most serene infantes called to the crown in the same article, in the order in which they are so named; and that his Majesty would be pleased to interpose his influence and prevail on one of the members of his august family to proceed to this empire, inasmuch as the prosperity of both nations would be thereby promoted, and as the Mexicans would feel satisfaction in thus strengthening the bands of friendship, with which they may be, and wish to see themselves, united to the Spaniards.

6th. Conformably to the spirit of the "Plan of Iguala," an assembly shall be immediately named, composed of men the most eminent in the empire for their virtues, their station, rank, fortune, and influence; men marked out by the general opinion, whose number may be sufficiently considerable to insure by their collective knowledge the safety of the resolutions which they may take in pursuance of the powers and authority granted them by the following articles.

7th. The assembly mentioned in the preceding article shall be called the "Provisional Junta of Government."

8th. Lieutenant-General Don Juan O'Donnoju shall be a member of the Provisional Junta of Government, in consideration of its being expedient that a person of his rank should take an active and immediate part in the government, and of the indispensable necessity of excluding some of the individuals mentioned in the above Plan of Iguala, conformably to its own spirit.

9th. The Provisional Junta of Government shall have a president elected by itself from its own body, or from without it, to be determined by the absolute plurality of votes; and if on the first scrutiny the votes be found equal, a second scrutiny shall take place, which shall embrace those two who shall have received the greatest number of votes.

10th. The first act of the Provisional Junta shall be the drawing up of a manifesto of its installation, and the motives of its assemblage, together with whatever explanations it may deem convenient and proper for the information of the country, with respect to the public interests, and the mode to be adopted in the election of deputies for the Cortes, of which more shall be said hereafter.

11th. The Provisional Junta of Government after the election of its president, shall name a regency composed of three persons selected from its own body, or from without it, in whom shall be vested the executive power, and who shall govern in the name and on behalf of the monarch till the vacant throne be filled.

12th. The Provisional Junta, as soon as it is installed, shall govern ad interim according to the existing laws, so far as they may not be contrary to the "Plan of Iguala" and until the Cortes shall have framed the constitution of the state.

13th. The regency immediately on its nomination, shall proceed to the convocation of the Cortes in the manner which shall be prescribed by the Provisional Junta of Government, conformably to the spirit of Article No. 7 in the aforesaid "Plan."

14th. The executive power is vested in the regency, and the legislative in the Cortes; but as some time must elapse before the latter can assemble, and in order that the executive and legislative powers should not remain in the hands of one body, the junta shall be empowered to legislate; in the first place, where cases occur which are too pressing to wait till the assemblage of the Cortes, and then the junta shall proceed in concert with the regency; and, in the second place, to assist the regency in its determinations in the character of an auxiliary and consultative body.

15th. Every individual who is domiciled amongst any community, shall, on an alteration taking place in the system of government, or on the country passing under the dominion of another prince, be at full liberty to remove himself, together with his effects, to whatever country he chooses, without any person having the right to deprive him of such liberty, unless he have contracted some obligation with the community to which lie had belonged, by the commission of a crime, or by any other of those modes which publicists have laid down; this applies to the Europeans residing in New Spain, and to the Americans residing in the Peninsula. Consequently it will be at their option to remain, adopting either country, or to demand their passports (which cannot be denied them) for permission to leave the kingdom at such time as may be appointed beforehand, carrying with them their families and property; but paying on the latter the regular export duties now in force, or which may hereafter be established by the competent authority.

16th. The option granted in the foregoing article shall not extend to persons in public situations, whether civil or military, known to be disaffected to Mexican independence; such persons shall necessarily quit the empire within the time which shall be allotted by the regency, taking with them their effects after having paid the duties, as stated in the preceding article.

17th. The occupation of the capital by the Peninsular troops being an obstacle to the execution of this treaty, it is indispensable to have it removed. But as the Commander-in-Chief of the imperial army fully participating in the sentiments of the Mexican nation, does not wish to attain this object by force, for which, however, he has more than ample means at his command, notwithstanding the known valour and constancy of the Peninsular troops, who are not in a situation to maintain themselves against the system adopted by the nation at large, Don Juan O'Donnoju agrees to exercise his authority for the evacuation of the capital by the said troops without loss of blood, and upon the terms of an honourable capitulation.

Augustán de Iturbide, Juan O'Donnoju. (a true copy.) Jose Dominguez. Dated in the Town Of Cordova, 24th August, 1821

GLOSSARY

infante: a younger brother of a monarch, in this case Ferdinand VII

Peninsular troops: equivalent to the imperial army of Spain, from the Iberian Peninsula

regency: in this context, the temporary executive body described in the 11th article

Document Analysis

The two paragraphs and fourteen articles of the Treaty of Córdoba outline not only Mexico's new government but also the way in which Mexico should make the transition from war to peace with the establishment of a provisional government. The treaty sets up a constitutional monarchy and calls upon King Ferdinand VII of Spain to become the crowned head of Mexico. The treaty looks to the Plan of Iguala as a guideline, referencing the plan often. In particular, the treaty establishes the "three guarantees" of the Plan of Iguala: constitutional monarchy, establishment of Roman Catholicism as the nation's sole religion, and social equality under the law. These three guarantees were also known as "independence, religion, and union," and the three colors of the Mexican flag, designed by Iturbide, symbolize these guarantees: green for independence, white for religion, and red for union.

The Treaty of Córdoba begins with a statement of when and where it was signed and the names and titles of its signatories, establishing that it is a legal document. Paragraph 2 outlines the general provisions of the treaty and the condition of Mexico at the time of the treaty. It declares Mexico's independence from Spain, giving the reasons why Mexico has made the declaration and citing its power to do so. Mexico, it asserts, has effectively won the struggle for independence on the battlefield. Therefore, Juan O'Donojú, "desirous of … reconciling the interests of Old and New Spain," has agreed to meet with Iturbide. Both parties state that they are interested in continuing a relationship but say that the relationship must be altered. Mexico will be an independent country but one that still recognizes and celebrates its Spanish roots.

The remainder of the treaty lays out the way in which Mexico was to establish itself as an independent nation. First and most important, Mexico was to be an independent, sovereign nation referred to as the Mexican Empire. Second, Mexico would be a constitutional monarchy. That is, Mexico would have a monarch, but the monarch's powers would be limited by a constitution. By establishing itself as a constitutional monarchy, Mexico followed in the political steps of Spain and other European powers.

The third and fourth articles outline how the king of Mexico was to be chosen and where his court would be established. The throne of Mexico was to be located in Mexico City, and Mexico City was to be the capital of the empire. The throne was to be offered first to Ferdinand VII of Spain. Should he decline the throne, it was to be offered to Ferdinand's brothers, heirs to the Spanish throne. The desire of Iturbide and other *criollos* to maintain a relationship with Spain is evident here. The treaty provided for Mexico to be governed by the Spanish monarch himself but as a sovereign nation, not a colony; failing that, another member of the Bourbon royal family was to be offered the throne. However, the treaty recognized that Ferdinand and his brothers might refuse the throne: in that case, the Cortes, Mexico's new legislative body, was to choose the monarch. Some historians have suggested that Iturbide himself was behind the wording of this provision; they argue that Iturbide planned from the very beginning to assume the throne himself. Although this is a possibility, there is no direct evidence that it is so.

The fifth article outlines the manner in which Ferdinand VII of Spain was to be notified of Mexico's independence. It also details how the offer of the crown of Mexico should be delivered. The article asks Ferdinand, should he himself refuse the Mexican throne, to encourage one of his brothers to accept the throne for the economic good of both Spain and Mexico and to reaffirm the ties between the nations. Mexicans, it asserts, "wish to see themselves … united to the Spaniards."

The sixth through twelfth articles concern the interim government that would govern Mexico until such time as both the king and legislature were vested with power. The temporary government was to be known as the Provisional Junta. The Junta was to be made up of "eminent" men of the empire, including Juan O'Donojú. Here again we can see the Mexican desire to maintain an active relationship with Spain. The six articles charge the Junta with several responsibilities and duties, the first being to choose three people to govern as regent—that is, to be the executive power of the government until a monarch ascended the throne.

The Junta (and, by extension, the regents they chose) were to be charged with governing the Mexican Empire by the provisions outlined in the Plan of Iguala. Much of the Treaty of Córdoba concerns the first of the three

guarantees of the Plan: the establishment of a constitutional monarchy. Here, the second and third guarantees are referenced. The Junta was to ensure that Roman Catholicism became the state religion of Mexico and that the *sistema de castas* was abolished. As the Plan of Iguala states in article 11, in Mexico, "all the inhabitants of the country are citizens, and equal, and the door of advancement is open to virtue and merit" (Plan of Iguala).

The thirteenth and fourteenth articles outline how the regency and Junta was to be governed until the throne was filled and the Cortes convened. The regency was to govern as the executive body; the Junta was empowered to act as the legislative body. Moreover, the regency and the Junta were charged with determining how members of the Cortes would be chosen. Article 13 references the Plan of Iguala (article 7) again, saying specifically that the primary duty of the Junta, after its nomination, would be to "proceed to the convocation of the Cortes."

The last two articles concern the rights of individuals to remain in or to leave Mexico and Spain. The fifteenth article guarantees Europeans' right to leave Mexico if they so chose, provided, of course, that they paid their debts and were not serving a criminal sentence. Moreover, it asserts that Americans residing in Spain had the right to relocate to Mexico. The sixteenth article imposes limits on article 15: Any public figure, civil or military, who opposed Mexican independence would be exiled from Mexico.

Finally, O'Donojú agrees, in article 17, to evacuate the royalist army occupying Mexico City. The article makes two pointed statements: First, it acknowledges that the royal army had fought bravely. Second, it notes that although General Iturbide was not using military power to force the Spanish army to leave, he and his army were more than capable of doing so.

Essential Themes

When the new revolutionary government was unable to find a member of the Bourbon dynasty who was willing to take the crown of Mexico, Iturbide took the throne, becoming Emperor Agustín I. The nature of Iturbide's rise to power is hotly debated: some argue that he assumed the crown at the behest of his troops and the people of Mexico. Others contend that Iturbide's rise to power was nothing more than a coup and that public support for him was largely manufactured. Guerrero initially supported Iturbide, but Iturbide's support of the wealthy *criollos* turned Guerrero against him. Guerrero allied with Antonio López de Santa Anna to overthrow Iturbide, and Mexico became a republic. Sent into exile in 1823, Iturbide tried to return in 1824, only to be arrested and executed. Guerrero was elected Mexico's second president in 1829. Later that year he was deposed by his vice president, Anastasio Bustamante y Oseguera, who had him executed in 1831.

Although the Treaty of Córdoba established Mexican independence and allowed for a peaceful transition of power at the war's end, it did not ensure lasting changes in Mexico. Socioculturally, even though the *sistema de castas* had been abolished, the social hierarchy, in fact, remained. Race and color still determined one's place in society, with those of European descent at the top and those of Indian and African ancestry at the bottom. Politically, the constitutional monarchy that the treaty established did not last; Iturbide was overthrown within a year, and the Mexican Empire was no more. Economically, haciendas (plantations) were still the basis of much of the economy and remained in the hands of the elite.

Widespread change that brought greater equality came later during the mid-nineteenth century period known as La Reforma (the Reform), under the leadership of the Zapotec Indian Benito Pablo Juárez. Juarez sought to ensure that social equality and equality under the law would be enforced and would become part of the greater Mexican culture. After Juarez, the government of Mexico descended into dictatorship under Porfirio Diaz. The Mexican Revolution of 1910 eventually established the modern state of Mexico.

———*Tamara Shircliff-Spike*

Bibliography and Further Reading

Henderson, Timothy J. *The Mexican Wars for Independence*. New York: Hill and Wang, 2009.

Kinsbruner, Jay. *Independence in Spanish America: Civil Wars, Revolutions, and Underdevelopment*. Albuquerque: University of New Mexico Press, 1994.

Van Young, Eric. *The Other Rebellion: Popular Violence, Ideology, and the Mexican Struggle for Independence, 1810–1821*. Stanford, Calif. Stanford University Press, 2001.

Web Sites

"The Plan de Iguala." Historical Text Archive. http://historicaltextarchive.com/sections.php?op=viewarticle&artid=538 [accessed February 16, 2017].

■ Monroe Doctrine

Date: 1823
Authors: James Monroe, John Quincy Adams
Genre: Speech

Summary Overview

On December 2, 1823, in his seventh annual message to Congress, U.S. President James Monroe issued a bold statement on foreign policy that reaffirmed the nation's longstanding commitment to neutrality and offered an explicit warning to Europe that the entire Western Hemisphere was closed to further colonization. This pronouncement of American autonomy and hemispheric solidarity against European aggression, which came to be known as the Monroe Doctrine, is considered one of the most significant statements in American foreign policy and the greatest achievement of Monroe's two-term presidency. While Monroe discusses other issues in this presidential address, his statement on foreign policy is the most memorable.

The Monroe Doctrine, originally known as the American System, contains four major principles. First, the political systems of the Americas are different from those in Europe. Second, the United States will continue to remain neutral in foreign affairs, unless these matters directly affect American security or interests. Third, the Western Hemisphere is no longer available for new colonization. If a former colony becomes independent, European powers should respect its new status and not try to intervene. If a colony in the Western Hemisphere remains under European control, the United States will not interfere. Finally, the United States will interpret any new effort by Europe to colonize the Western Hemisphere as a direct threat to its security.

The Monroe Doctrine was primarily aimed at the European powers that had colonial designs on the Americas. Spain was the immediate target of such warnings because of its desire to reclaim its former territories, despite the independence movements sweeping through South America. Other intended audiences included Russia, which had tentative claims in the Pacific Northwest, and France, which had ambitions in South and Central America. Britain, which wished to stop the expansion efforts of the Spanish and French, was a sympathetic recipient. The American public, the press, and Congress all responded enthusiastically to this declaration of American neutrality and European nonintervention.

Defining Moment

While President Monroe and his secretary of state, John Quincy Adams, deserve most of the credit for establishing this doctrine, a confluence of events, some old and some new, created the environment permitting its issuance.

Beginning with George Washington's presidency in 1789, the nation's foreign policy stressed neutrality unless American interests were directly affected, and the Monroe Doctrine represented both a continuation and a reaffirmation of this approach. Diplomatic triumphs that occurred several years before the Monroe Doctrine was issued also laid the groundwork for this statement. The successful resolution of the War of 1812 through the Treaty of Ghent and the acquisition of Florida from Spain permitted the United States to gain greater control over trade and territory. These accomplishments also allowed American negotiators to approach European countries from a position of strength rather than weakness. European countries were also undergoing great change with the end of the Napoleonic Wars and the peace treaty known as the Congress of Vienna, and South American countries were successfully challenging Spanish colonial regimes and declaring their independence. As Europe restored its monarchies and South American countries resisted colonization, Americans were reminded of their own colonial heritage. They sympathize with an "American system" of independence and equality rather than with the "European system" of absolutism and tyranny from which they considered themselves liberated. The United States' identification with its southern neighbors also demonstrated its sense of vulnerability toward Europe, despite its recent diplomatic triumphs.

The final and most immediate impetus for the Monroe Doctrine came from the British foreign minister George Canning in August 1823. Concerned about the renewed alliance between France and Spain, Britain invited the United States to join it in issuing an Anglo-American statement opposing further Spanish and French colonization in the Americas. Spain's intention to send troops into South America to put down rebellions gave the British proposal a particular sense of urgency. While Monroe gave the British offer serious

Newspaper cartoon from 1912 about the Monroe Doctrine. (commons.wikimedia.org) [Public Domain]

consideration, including receiving favorable endorsements from both Thomas Jefferson and James Madison, he ultimately concluded that the United States should issue its own statement to demonstrate that America was truly independent and neutral and not merely an appendage of Britain.

The American System of the Monroe Doctrine should not be confused with Henry Clay's American System, an economic program consisting of tariffs, internal improvements and a national bank, originally proposed in 1824.

Author Biographies

The Monroe Doctrine has two principal authors, President James Monroe and Secretary of State John Quincy Adams. The best way to balance credit between these two men is a point of contention among historians. Most agree that Monroe was an advocate for the major principles of the doctrine—opposition to colonization, neutrality, and support for South American independence movements—but Adams's ideas and his diplomatic efforts created conditions that allowed Monroe's statement to be taken seriously by the European powers. The doctrine's original name, the American System, reflects its shared authorship as well as its debt to longstanding practices in American foreign policy, which involved the work of many individuals.

James Monroe was born in Virginia in 1758 into a slaveholding family of the landed gentry, a class slightly below that of the exalted planters. As a young man, Monroe participated in the American Revolution, fighting in the battles of Trenton and Monmouth under the command of General George Washington. Monroe had hoped this experience would lead to a career in the military, but he was unable to raise a regiment and sought a professional future in law and politics instead. For more than three decades, Monroe amassed a successful political career that included terms as Virginia's senator and governor as well as diplomatic experience as minister to France during Washington's presidency. He served as secretary of state during the War of 1812. A founding member of the Democratic-Republican Party, Monroe enjoyed a close political and personal association with his presidential predecessors, Virginia neighbors, and fellow partisans Thomas Jefferson and James Madison. After completing his second term as president, Monroe retired to New York City, where he died on July 4, 1831, at the age of seventy-three.

John Quincy Adams, the son of President John Adams, was born in Massachusetts in 1767. The younger Adams enjoyed a distinguished public career that began in foreign affairs and culminated with his election to the presidency in 1824. Before becoming secretary of state, Adams had served as the American ambassador in a string of European capitals, including Holland, Portugal, Prussia, Russia, and Britain. He also participated in the Treaty of Ghent negotiations that ended the War of 1812. Breaking with tradition, Adams abandoned his post-presidential retirement to become a member of Congress from Massachusetts, where he emerged as a major opponent of slavery. Adams died on February 23, 1848, at the age of eighty.

HISTORICAL DOCUMENT

... At the proposal of the Russian Imperial Government, made through the minister of the Emperor residing here, a full power and instructions have been transmitted to the minister of the United States at St. Petersburg to arrange by amicable negotiation the respective rights and interests of the two nations on the northwest coast of this continent. A similar proposal has been made by His Imperial Majesty to the Government of Great Britain, which has likewise been acceded to. The Government of the United States has been desirous by this friendly proceeding of manifesting the great value which they have invariably attached to the friendship of the Emperor and their solicitude to cultivate the best understanding with his Government. In the discussions to which this interest has given rise and in the arrangements by which they may terminate the occasion has been judged proper for asserting, as a principle in which the rights and interests of the United States are involved, that the American continents, by the free and independent condition which they have assumed and maintain, are henceforth not to be considered as subjects for future colonization by any European powers....

It was stated at the commencement of the last session that a great effort was then making in Spain and Portugal to improve the condition of the people of those countries, and that it appeared to be conducted with extraordinary moderation. It need scarcely be remarked that the results have been so far very different from what was then anticipated. Of events in that quarter of the globe, with which we have so much intercourse and from which we derive our origin, we have always been anxious and interested spectators. The citizens of the United States cherish sentiments the most friendly in favor of the liberty and happiness of their fellow-men on that side of the Atlantic. In the wars of the European powers in matters relating to themselves we have never taken any part, nor does it comport with our policy to do so. It is only when our rights are invaded or seriously menaced that we resent injuries or make preparation for our defense. With the movements in this hemisphere we are of necessity more immediately connected, and by causes which must be obvious to all enlightened and impartial observers. The political system of the allied powers is essentially different in this respect from that of America. This difference proceeds from that which exists in their respective Governments; and to the defense of our own, which has been achieved by the loss of so much blood and treasure, and matured by the wisdom of their most enlightened citizens, and under which we have enjoyed unexampled felicity, this whole nation is devoted. We owe it, therefore, to candor and to the amicable relations existing between the United States and those powers to declare that we should consider any attempt on their part to extend their system to any portion of this hemisphere as dangerous to our peace and safety. With the existing colonies or dependencies of any European power we have not interfered and shall not interfere. But with the Governments who have declared their independence and maintain it, and whose independence we have, on great consideration and on just principles, acknowledged, we could not view any interposition for the purpose of oppressing them, or controlling in any other manner their destiny, by any European power in any other light than as the manifestation of an unfriendly disposition toward the United States. In the war between those new Governments and Spain we declared our neutrality at the time of their recognition, and to this we have adhered, and shall continue to adhere, provided no change shall occur which, in the judgment of the competent authorities of this Government, shall make a corresponding change on the part of the United States indispensable to their security.

The late events in Spain and Portugal show that Europe is still unsettled. Of this important fact no stronger proof can be adduced than that the allied powers should have thought it proper, on any principle satisfactory to themselves, to have interposed by force in the internal concerns of Spain. To what extent such interposition may be carried, on the same principle, is a question in which all independent powers whose governments differ from theirs are interested, even those most remote, and surely none of them more so than the United States. Our policy in regard to Europe, which was adopted at an early stage of the wars which have so long agitated that quarter of the globe, nevertheless remains the same, which is, not to interfere in the internal concerns of any of its powers; to consider the government de facto as the legitimate government for us; to cultivate friendly relations with it, and to preserve those relations by a frank, firm, and manly policy, meeting in all instances the just claims of every power, submitting to injuries from none. But in regard to those continents circumstances are eminently and conspicuously different.

It is impossible that the allied powers should extend their political system to any portion of either continent without endangering our peace and happiness; nor can anyone believe that our southern brethren, if left to themselves, would adopt it of their own accord. It is equally impossible, therefore, that we should behold such interposition in any form with indifference. If we look to the comparative strength and resources of Spain and those new Governments, and their distance from each other, it must be obvious that she can never subdue them. It is still the true policy of the United States to leave the parties to themselves, in hope that other powers will pursue the same course.

Document Analysis

The Monroe Doctrine, issued by President James Monroe in his annual message to Congress in December 1823, offers a sweeping assertion of American autonomy in the southern and northern halves of the continent in the face of European colonization and aggression. This statement provides an elegant summation of the previous thirty years of American foreign policy, as it affirms the longstanding principles of neutrality and independence from European intervention.

The first principle of the Monroe Doctrine appears separately from the other three and offers the boldest and most memorable statement of the doctrine: the American continents are "not to be considered as subjects for future colonization by any European powers." Noting a common heritage that involved colonization and then liberation, this statement recognizes the "free and independent condition" of the American continents. By issuing this statement, the United States was asserting its autonomy as well as that of its southern brethren from all forms of European intervention and control, particularly colonization.

This end of European colonization in the Western Hemisphere is the part of the Monroe Doctrine most often associated with the ideas of John Quincy Adams, who previously had expressed similar anti-colonial sentiments in a Fourth of July address delivered in Washington in 1821. Adams had promoted this nonintervention position in July 1823 when he warned Russia that the United States would not tolerate its territorial claims in North America, particularly those in the Pacific Northwest.

The second principle of the Monroe Doctrine reaffirms the nation's longstanding policy of neutrality, stating, "In the wars of the European powers in matters relating to themselves we have never taken any part, nor does it comport with our policy to do so." At the time, the former colonial powers in Central and South America, Portugal and Spain, had just finished their own revolts, inspired by their colonists on the other side of the Atlantic. Both were put down savagely by their respective monarchies with the help of the French army; Italians in the state of Piedmont followed up themselves and were also crushed. The revolts had lasting impact, however; the term for the rebels fighting for their freedom in Spain, "liberales," is where the English term "liberal" derives from. Yet despite the United States' obvious ideological affinity to the advance of natural rights and the potential to secure Spanish colonial territories,

the Monroe administration stayed conspicuously neutral in the revolts. Later in this paragraph, the doctrine also stresses that the United States has not and will not interfere "with the existing colonies or dependencies of any European power" despite its opposition to further colonization in the Western Hemisphere. Both of these statements continue an American foreign policy that has stressed, since the government's establishment in 1789, the twin principles of neutrality and nonintervention in European affairs.

Despite its stated intention of remaining neutral, the United States struggled to attain this goal, particularly during the 1790s, as Britain and France each sought the allegiance of the young nation in its long-running animosities with the other. While the French Revolution and the resulting Reign of Terror permitted the United States to distance itself from France, Britain remained an overbearing ally, particularly in the area of transatlantic trade. The Jay Treaty, ratified in 1796, represented an unsuccessful effort to achieve a diplomatic solution. Later, the more assertive Embargo Act of 1807 sought to curtail British trading access as a way to produce concessions. Neither effort worked. Instead, the War of 1812 offered a military solution where diplomacy and economic pressure had failed. The two-year war was largely a stalemate, as each side enjoyed its share of military successes and failures, and the Treaty of Ghent mirrored these results by reaffirming the status quo of the prewar world. Nonetheless, the War of 1812 was a greater victory for the United States than the 1815 treaty indicated, because Britain finally recognized American autonomy by ceasing many of the aggressive trade policies that had led to the war. The world after the War of 1812 produced an environment in which the United States could issue a statement that reaffirmed its independence and increased its autonomy.

The third principle of the Monroe Doctrine concerns the historical and political similarities that exist among the sovereign nations of the American continents. Each country had once been a colony belonging to a European power and had fought to achieve its independence. The systems of government on each side of the Atlantic were also different—the United States had adopted a republican form of government that stressed popular sovereignty and representation, while European countries still embraced the monarchical government that the American Revolution had rejected. In fact, the aftermath of the Napoleonic Wars had witnessed the restoration of monarchy in France. As Monroe and Adams surveyed the post-1815 landscape, they realized that North and South America shared more than geographic proximity; the two continents also shared a common history that abhorred European intrusions. America's newfound strength after the War of 1812 permitted the formulation of a new foreign policy that affirmed the common ground among the American nations that rendered them historically and politically separate from Europe. The diplomatic recognition that President Monroe and Congress extended to the newly independent South American states of Argentina, Chile, Columbia, Mexico, and Peru in 1822 served as a significant step in an increasingly American-centered foreign policy. This recognition naturally paved the way for further expression of hemispheric solidarity in the Monroe Doctrine of 1823.

The fourth principle of the Monroe Doctrine deals with the consequences of Europe not respecting the statement's three principles: opposition to colonization, neutrality, and a shared tradition of independence and self-government. As the enforcement clause of the document, this fourth principle appears throughout the second section in various forms. Immediately following the declaration of the nation's long history of neutrality, the enforcement clause is then invoked to explain situations where the nation would get involved: "It is only when our rights are invaded or seriously menaced that we resent injuries or make preparation for our defense." A few sentences later, a similar warning appears, this time in relation to any efforts of new colonization or, a more pressing concern, re-colonization through military force: "We owe it, therefore, to candor and to the amicable relations existing between the United States and those powers to declare that we should consider any attempt on their part to extend their system to any portion of this hemisphere as dangerous to our peace and safety." Finally, in the last portion of the speech devoted to this doctrine, Monroe warns that both European political systems and military interference in the Western Hemisphere would be seen as "endangering our peace and happiness." Explicitly mentioning Spain for the first time, he says that Spanish attempts to retake their colonies would be impractical because of the expense and the distance. Instead, these new states should be allowed to prosper without interference. Nonetheless, Monroe ends with a final warning: Any interposition by Europe will not be met with indifference by the United States. While military action is never explicitly stated,

it is certainly implied throughout these sections, which are designed to enforce the three earlier provisions of the Monroe Doctrine.

Upon entering the presidency in 1817, Monroe encountered an international landscape that was substantially different from what had existed four years earlier when he had served as Madison's secretary of state. The 1815 Congress of Vienna had ended the Napoleonic Wars and had begun rebuilding Europe. In South America, independence movements were successfully overthrowing European colonial governments, particularly Spanish ones. As Europe regrouped and the Americas adopted an increasingly assertive approach to European incursions, the United States reoriented its foreign policy, which had been preoccupied with affairs in Europe and on the Atlantic, and looked to the West and the South. Building upon the successful outcome of the Treaty of Ghent as well as the acquisition of Florida from Spain through the Transcontinental Treaty of 1819, the United States was now in a position to assert a new approach to foreign policy that reflected strengthened American continents. The resulting pronouncement was the Monroe Doctrine, which boldly declares the Americas closed to colonization while also reiterating American neutrality. It also identifies a common political and historical heritage among the American continents that European countries did not and could not share. Finally, this doctrine warns that neutrality is not pacifism and that there would be consequences to any European attempt to interfere militarily or politically in the Western Hemisphere. Issued from a position of strength, the Monroe Doctrine serves as an enduring and effective statement of American autonomy and neutrality as well as hemispheric solidarity to warn against potential European incursions into the region's affairs.

Essential Themes

The Monroe Doctrine of 1823 emerged from a series of diplomatic triumphs that increased American independence and lessened European involvement in national affairs. The Monroe Doctrine affirmed the nation's new autonomy after the War of 1812 and the Transcontinental Treaty by reiterating its neutrality, while also expanding its influence by forging alliances with newly independent South American states and warning Europe that these states were off limits to further colonization. As the United States continued to grow economically and territorially during the nineteenth century, the Monroe Doctrine served as an important warning to Europe to mind its own affairs. Issued at a time of unusual peace, the doctrine anticipated that this harmony would not last and acted as a unilateral warning to thwart any potential European invasions or interferences before they began. Although the United States was by no means a military powerhouse after 1815, it had enjoyed enough military successes in the recent War of 1812 to competently challenge a foreign invasion. This experience, coupled with the difficulty of launching a war from Europe, made the doctrine's threat of retaliation a credible one. For these reasons, the Monroe Doctrine succeeded in keeping Europe out of American affairs and allowed the country to expand and prosper.

When Theodore Roosevelt issued his Corollaries to the Monroe Doctrine in 1904 and 1905, the United States' prerogative to defend South America from a European invasion took on a more sinister aspect. By the early twentieth century, the United States was becoming an economic and military power, and its interventions in South America had more to do with economic interests than regional solidarity. In many ways, the United States had become the colonizer the Monroe Doctrine was supposed to ban from the Western Hemisphere.

The Monroe Doctrine was a powerful and enduring statement of American independence, neutrality, and nonintervention that was issued at a time when the young nation was finally able to assert itself against European encroachments. This doctrine successfully insulated America from outside intrusions and enabled it to prosper, although, later, the doctrine's imperialistic possibilities became more pronounced as the United States grew in power. Even as late as 1962, the Monroe Doctrine retained its original intent: thwarting a European invasion of the Western Hemisphere. During the Cuban Missile Crisis, John F. Kennedy invoked the doctrine to impose a naval blockade on Cuba to challenge the presence of Soviet missiles.

——Sandy Moats

Bibliography and Further Reading

Borgens, Edward G. *Background of the Monroe Doctrine*. New York: Vantage Press, 2004.

May, Ernest R. *The Making of the Monroe Doctrine*. Cambridge, MA: Harvard University Press, 1975.

Nagel, Paul C. *John Quincy Adams: A Public Life, A Private Life*. New York: Alfred A. Knopf, 1997.

Sexton, Jay. *The Monroe Doctrine: Empire and Nation in Nineteenth-Century America*. New York: Hill and Wang, 2011.

Dangerfield, George. *The Era of Good Feelings*. Chicago: I.R. Dee, 1980.

Web Sites

"Monroe Doctrine (1823)." *100 Milestone Documents*. National Archive and Records Administration https://www.ourdocuments.gov/doc.php?flash=true&doc=23 [accessed March 6, 2017].

"Monroe Doctrine, 1823." *Milestones: 1801-1829*. Office of the Historian, Bureau of Public Affairs, United States Department of State https://history.state.gov/milestones/1801-1829/monroe [accessed March 6, 2017].

"Primary Documents in American History: Monroe Doctrine." Library of Congress, Virtual Services: Digital Reference Section https://www.loc.gov/rr/program/bib/ourdocs/Monroe.html [accessed March 6, 2017].

THE NINETEENTH CENTURY

The nineteenth century was the age of nationalism. After the American Revolution, the French Revolution, the Napoleonic wars and the wars of Latin American independence, concepts of nationalism and populism had spread all over the western world. Despite the best efforts of monarchs, who wanted people to take pride in and show loyalty to the states that the monarchs dominated, people had learned that one could take pride in and show loyalty to the idea of being French, or American, or British, German, Russian, Italian, Mexican, Venezuelan, Chilean or some other nationality. They had also discovered that they could run their own states without the mediating influence of an elite family of emperors, so long as they could get the right to vote, as the People's Charter asked.

Just because people believed that they did not need an emperor to run their nation's affairs, however, did not mean that they had abandoned the idea of empire. "Imperialism" was a nineteenth century concept itself, invented by the British Liberal politician William Gladstone as a pejorative term for other politicians who had "empire on the brain," as if it was a disease. Empires have existed almost since the beginning of civilization itself; indeed, it seems to be a stage of civilization, one people deciding that they had reached such a level of achievement that they should dominate another people, and in particular make them better for it. The difference in the nineteenth century was that westerners now expanded territories in the interest of nationalism, sometimes to the point not just of improving people but making them a part of the nation.

The Treaty of Guadalupe Hidalgo was an extreme example of "manifest destiny," the notion that the North American continent (at least) was a literally God-given territory to Americans. They therefore believed the United States had the right to take away a vast swathe of Mexico at the end of the Mexican-American War. It was no coincidence that at the point when Frederick Jackson Turner announced to Americans that the frontier was closed in his lecture, "The Significance of the Frontier in American History," the United States military began invading territories off the North American continent. American military forces invaded Cuba and the Philippines in the Spanish-American War, then other Central American and Caribbean states in the early twentieth century, ostensibly to "teach the S[panish] American republics to elect good men," in Woodrow Wilson's phrase. The Constitution Act of Canada was passed in 1867 in some part to keep the expansionist United States from casting its eyes northward too—in the same year, William Seward bought Alaska from the Russian Empire.

The two most expansionist powers of the nineteenth century in terms of occupied territory were the United States and the Russian Empire, presaging the major conflict to dominate the twentieth century. Yet the powers that expanded their control over the largest proportion of the world's population were Britain and France. The British Empire at its height controlled a quarter of the earth's surface and a quarter of its population, and having an empire contributed mightily to the British conception of national greatness. Colonies like India, Cape Colony (South Africa) and Egypt were economic, strategic and of great cultural importance—the tea at the center of the British 4 pm ritual wasn't grown in Britain, after all. To the French, their empire was proof of the benevolence of the revolutionary legacy. Algeria and Indochina were portions of France beyond the oceans, even sending members to the Chamber of Deputies to represent them in French government. The revolution was a responsibility to the French, its values a welcome burden to be brought to people around the world as a symbol of French greatness.

Of course, such sentiments worried other peoples around the world who had no interest in being "improved." Most of them found themselves prostrate before the Europeans and Americans who barged into their economies and asserted their own laws, religion and business practices as a sign of their alleged superiority. Japanese elites were alarmed enough with the coming of westerners that they made a conscious decision in the Meiji restoration to copy the westerners in everything they did (except Christianity) in order to avoid colonization and exploitation. The Meiji Constitution, unfinished until 1889, was partially meant to impress western powers with Japan's modernity and enlightenment-based values. In the long run, a few rather innocuous-sounding articles, in light of Japanese traditions, became the basis for the establishment of the most European institution the Japanese could copy: an empire, in East Asia, in the 1930s. Meanwhile, Theodor Herzl, an Austrian Jewish journalist, likewise hoped to copy European conceptions of nationalism: he wanted to literally invent a nation. Herzl hoped to provide a homeland for the Jewish population of Europe, to give people of a religious identity a new ethnic and cultural identity that would unite them across borders.

Nationalism and populism brought pride and progress to millions around the world at the turn of the twentieth century. In a matter of years, they would also bring two world wars to those same people and show how dangerous they could be as concepts.

■ National Petition from the People's Charter

Date: 1838
Authors: London Working Men's Association (William Lovett et al)
Genre: Petition

Summary Overview

The Chartist movement sought political and social reform in the United Kingdom in the middle of the nineteenth century through the fulfillment of the People's Charter of 1838. The main points of the original (1838) People's Charter included universal manhood suffrage, the ballot (secret), annual election of members of Parliament, no property qualifications for members of Parliament, and pay for members of Parliament. A sixth point was added to the petition submitted to Parliament in 1848: equal distribution of parliamentary constituencies.

Chartism was a product of the dissatisfaction within the working classes with the conditions in the United Kingdom during the early period of the Industrial Revolution. Chartism was one of several radical movements that sought a change in suffrage and representation in Great Britain. The Reform Act of 1832 lowered property qualifications, reformed the franchise, and gave the vote to male members of the middle class. Chartism sought to expand the franchise to include the working class.

Defining Moment

When Americans demanded "no taxation without representation" from the British parliament in the 1760s, the concept of that demand was considered ludicrous—92.5% of the British adult population could not vote at the time, and they were still expected to pay taxes. The House of Lords was populated with aristocrats who inherited their titles and seats in Parliament, and the House of Commons was elected by the small percentage of landowners who paid enough in land taxes to qualify, but did not have a noble title. The members of Parliament they voted for were expected to legislate in the best interests of the country at large, and only wealthier people were thought to have the education and values to determine who such people were. British elections, then, were not truly representative of the opinions of the whole of the British people.

In 1831 and 1832, popular pressure from the moneyed middle classes in Britain resulted in passage of the Reform Act of 1832, a law which extended the right to vote to people who paid far less in property taxes. Another 300,000 men now could exercise their franchise—which still left 82% of the adult male population without any choice as to who represented them in Parliament. Especially aggrieved were skilled industrial working men, many of whom made decent wages but did not own property; they paid heavily into the nation's taxes but had no say in how their money was spent. Even worse, the new Parliament elected in 1832 enacted a new Poor Law in 1834, placing the government-supported indigent population into workhouses and severely limiting their freedom of choice. The working classes in Britain were lacking in both representation and respect.

In 1836, a group of skilled workers came together with the radical agitator who had powered the popular movement in favor of the Reform Act, Francis Place. William Lovett made cabinets; Henry Hetherington was a publisher, and John Cleave and James Watson were printers. Together, they formed the London Working Men's Association, a sort of proto-union whose goal was to spread information and ideas amongst the working classes in Britain, to allow men to defend their own interests properly and seek equality for workers in British society and politics. At one of their meetings in 1838, the leaders of the LWMA drew up a petition to ask Parliament to consider a series of six demands oriented toward the political enfranchisement of the working classes; attached to the petition was a bill ready to be read into the parliamentary record and voted on, containing the six demands.

The entire petition became known as the People's Charter, and the people who advocated for it were referred to as "Chartists." The Charter was first presented to the public in Glasgow in May 1838, at a meeting attended by an estimated 150,000 people. Working people of all stripes signed the petition in an effort to attract Parliamentary attention. In May 1839, the MP Thomas Attwood present the Charter to Parliament, with more than a million signatures on it calling for reform. The petition sets out the six Chartist demands: universal suffrage, no property qualification, annual parliaments, equal representation, payment of members, and vote by ballot. Today all except one (annual parliaments, which is a de facto institution anyway) are enshrined in British law.

Author Biographies

At the meeting in 1838, a committee of six members of Parliament and six workingmen in the London Workingmen's Association accepted the responsibility to draw up a document presenting demands for universal men's suffrage to Parliament. The committee published it as the People's Charter in May 1838. The movement then presented it as a petition with signatures to the House of Commons in June 1839. By common consensus, the primary author of the petition and its attached sample bill was William Lovett, coupled with the help and advice of Francis Place.

William Lovett was born in 1800, and grew up poor in the port town of Penzance in southwest England. At 21 he moved to London and found work as a maker of cabinets. He got an education and became politicized by joining the available co-operative societies that then existed to provide a safety net to the working poor all over Britain—unions were illegal when he started to work, and he himself was an artisan, working out of his own shop. He met several important philosophical and political figures of the early nineteenth century and when unions were legalized, he joined the Grand National Consolidated Trades Union and the National Union of the Working Classes, where he met industrial workers who thought the same way about political issues as he did. In 1836, he became a founding member of the London Working Men's Association.

Lovett was a philosophical radical—his first draft of the People's Charter included a demand for women's suffrage, 70 years ahead of its time. Yet he was not a revolutionary; he disagreed with the wing of the Chartist movement that wanted revolution if the Charter was not adopted by Parliament. He was nevertheless arrested and tried numerous times over twenty years for plotting the overthrow of the British government, and was even thrown in jail in 1840 for twelve months. His pleas to avoid confrontation separated him from many of the other leaders of the Chartist movement, and he gradually withdrew from active political engagement as a result. By the 1850s he had become a science teacher at a grammar school. He died in 1877.

Francis Place was one of the most famous radical politicians of the early nineteenth century in Britain. He was born in 1771 and originally worked as a tailor in London, but he was always associated with working class causes. He made his name as a speaker at rallies in opposition to the Combination Acts, laws passed during the Napoleonic Wars that disallowed groups of more than ten men to meet in one place. As Place famously pointed out, the Combination Act—designed to keep radical groups from meeting to plot revolution—technically made Parliament illegal. By 1824, Place's agitation helped bring about the legalization of unions, though they had no right to strike. He was one of the leading voices in favor of the 1832 Reform Act, threatening Parliament with revolution if it was not passed. Chartism was his final major political cause; he died in 1854.

HISTORICAL DOCUMENT

National Petition

Unto the Honorable the Commons of the United Kingdom of Great Britain and Ireland in Parliament assembled, the Petition of the undersigned, their suffering countrymen,

Humbly Sheweth,

That we, your petitioners, dwell in a land whose merchants are noted for enterprise, whose manufacturers are very skilful, and whose workmen are proverbial for their industry.

The land itself is goodly, the soil rich, and the temperature wholesome; it is abundantly furnished with the materials of commerce and trade; it has numerous and convenient harbors; in facility of internal communication it exceeds all others.

For three-and-twenty years we have enjoyed a profound peace.

Yet, with all these elements of national prosperity, and with every disposition and capacity to take advantage of them, we find ourselves overwhelmed with public and private suffering.

We are bowed down under a load of taxes; which, notwithstanding, fall greatly short of the wants of our rulers; our traders are trembling on the verge of bankruptcy; our workmen are starving; capital brings no profit, and labor no remuneration; the home of the artificer is desolate, and the warehouse of the pawnbroker is full; the workhouse is crowded, and the manufactory is deserted.

We have looked on every side, we have searched diligently in order to find out the causes of a distress so sore and so long continued.

We can discover none in nature, or in Providence.

Heaven has dealt graciously by the people; but the foolishness of our rulers has made the goodness of God of none effect.

The energies of a mighty kingdom have been wasted in building up the power of selfish and ignorant men, and its resources squandered for their aggrandisement.

The good of a party has been advanced to the sacrifice of the good of the nation; the few have governed for the interest of the few, while the interest of the many has been neglected, or insolently and tyrannously trampled upon.

It was the fond expectation of the people that a remedy for the greater part, if not for the whole, of their grievances, would be found in the Reform Act of 1832.

They were taught to regard that Act as a wise means to a worthy end; as the machinery of an improved legislation, when the will of the masses would be at length potential.

They have been bitterly and basely deceived.

The fruit which looked so fair to the eye has turned to dust and ashes when gathered.

The Reform Act has effected a transfer of power from one domineering faction to another, and left the people as helpless as before.

Our slavery has been exchanged for an apprenticeship to liberty, which has aggravated the painful feeling of our social degradation, by adding to it the sickening of still deferred hope.

We come before your Honorable House to tell you, with all humility, that this state of things must not be permitted to continue; that it cannot long continue without very seriously endangering the stability of the throne and the peace of the kingdom; and that if by God's help and all lawful and constitutional appliances an end can be put to it, we are fully resolved that it shall speedily come to an end.

We tell your Honorable House that the capital of the master must no longer be deprived of its due reward; that the laws which make food dear, and those which by making money scarce, make labor cheap, must be abolished; that taxation must be made to fall on property, not on industry; that the good of the many, as it is the only legitimate end, so must it be the sole study of the Government.

As a preliminary essential to these and other requisite changes; as means by which alone the interests of the people can be effectually vindicated and secured, we demand that those interests be confided to the keeping of the people.

When the state calls for defenders, when it calls for money, no consideration of poverty or ignorance can be pleaded in refusal or delay of the call.

Required as we are, universally, to support and obey the laws, nature and reason entitle us to demand that in the making of the laws, the universal voice should be implicitly listened to.

We perform the duties of freemen; we must have the privileges of freemen.

WE DEMAND UNIVERSAL SUFFRAGE.

The suffrage, to be exempt from the corruption of the wealthy and the violence of the powerful, must be secret.

The assertion of our right necessarily involves the power of its uncontrolled exercise.

WE DEMAND THE BALLOT.

The connection between the representatives and the people, to be beneficial, must be intimate.

The legislative and constituent powers, for correction and for instruction, ought to be brought into frequent contact.

Errors which are comparatively light when susceptible of a speedy popular remedy, may produce the most disastrous effects when permitted to grow inveterate through years of compulsory endurance.

To public safety as well as public confidence, frequent elections are essential.

WE DEMAND ANNUAL PARLIAMENTS.

With power to choose, and freedom in choosing, the range of our choice must be unrestricted.

We are compelled, by the existing laws, to take for our representatives men who are incapable of appreciating our difficulties, or who have little sympathy with them; merchants who have retired from trade, and no longer feel its harassings; proprietors of and who are alike ignorant of its evils and their cure; lawyers, by whom the honors of the senate are sought after only as means of obtaining notice in the courts.

The labors of a representative who is sedulous in the discharge of his duty are numerous and burdensome.

It is neither just, nor reasonable, nor safe, that they should continue to be gratuitously rendered.

We demand that in the future election of members of your Honorable House the approbation of the constituency shall be the sole qualification; and that to every representative so chosen shall be assigned, out of the public taxes, a fair and adequate remuneration for the time which he is called upon to devote to the public service.

Finally, we would most earnestly impress on your Honorable House that this petition has not been dictated by any idle love of change; that it springs out of no inconsiderate attachment to fanciful theories; but that it is the result of much and long deliberation and of convictions, which the events of each succeeding year tend more and more to strengthen.

The management of this mighty kingdom has hitherto been a subject for contending factions to try their selfish experiments upon.

We have felt the consequences in our sorrowful experience—short glimmerings of uncertain enjoyment swallowed up by long and dark seasons of suffering.

If the self-government of the people should not remove their distresses, it will at least remove their repinings.

Universal suffrage will, and it alone can, bring true and lasting peace to the nation; we firmly believe that it will also bring prosperity.

May it, therefore, please your Honorable House to take this our petition into your most serious consideration; and to use your utmost endeavors, by all constitutional means, to have a law passed granting to every male of lawful age, sane mind, and unconvicted of crime the right of voting for members of Parliament; and directing all future elections of members of Parliament to be in the way of secret ballot; and ordaining that the duration of Parliaments so chosen shall in no case exceed one year; and abolishing all property qualifications in the members; and providing for their due remuneration while in attendance on their Parliamentary duties.

And your petitioners, &c.

GLOSSARY

Providence: the hand of God in everyday life

sedulous: diligent, dedicated

repinings: expressions of discontent

Document Analysis

The National Petition from the People's Charter of 1838 comprises two parts: a justification for the demanded changes and the changes themselves. The petition characterizes the nation as hardworking merchants, manufacturers, and workingmen; the land rich; the climate temperate; the resources generous; the harbors "numerous and convenient"; and the "internal communication" excellent. England was a nation at peace since 1815. Despite all the advantages, states the petition, "we find ourselves overwhelmed with public and private suffering." Heavy taxes, bankruptcy, starvation, no profit from capital, no remuneration for labor, empty homes, full pawnbrokers' warehouses, deserted factories and crowded workhouses oppressed the people. The answer could not be discovered in nature or in "Providence." The answer rested with the "foolishness of our rulers" who governed in the interest of the few at the expense of the many. The interest of the people "has been neglected, or insolently and tyrannously trampled upon." The Reform Act of 1832 had failed to fulfill the expectations of the people; it succeeded only in transferring power from "one domineering faction to another." "Our slavery has been exchanged for an apprenticeship to liberty, which has aggravated the painful feeling of our social degradation, by adding to it the sickening of still deferred hope." The situation could not continue without "endangering the stability of the throne and the peace of the kingdom."

The five demands of the petitioners are clear. First, "We Demand Universal Suffrage." The People's Charter refined the restrictions for the vote to those males over the age of twenty-one of sane mind and "unconvicted of crime." Second, "We Demand the Ballot." The suffrage must be secret "to be exempt from the corruption of the wealthy and the violence of the powerful." Third, "We Demand Annual Parliaments." Frequent elections are essential to the "public safety as well as public confidence." Fourth, "We demand that in the future election of members of your Honorable House the approbation of the constituency shall be the sole qualification." The petitioners sought to abolish property qualifications for office. Fifth, petitioners asked for payment for service: "Every representative so chosen shall be assigned, out of the public taxes, a fair and adequate remuneration for the time which he is called upon to devote to the public service."

The People's Charter concludes with the view that, though self-government might not relieve the distress of the people, "it will at least remove their repinings." Only through universal suffrage would the nation be granted "true and lasting peace" and prosperity. A brief restatement of the five demands ends the document.

Essential Themes

The House of Commons did nothing to acknowledge the presentation of the Charter; understandably, caving in to the Chartists' demands would open a Pandora's box of reform movements looking to intimidate Parliament in the same fashion. The lack of recognition divided the Chartists. Some thought the answer was to continue peaceful agitation and gather even more signatures demanding change; others thought there was no other way to bring about change short of revolutionary violence. At Newport in Wales in 1839, a peaceful Chartist march was fired upon by British soldiers, killing 22 people, and its leaders were transported to Australia after their arrests. The determination of the appropriate response divided the Chartists more than ever.

Fortunately, the advocates of peaceful pressure won out, at first. In 1842 the LWMA put together a second charter and petition. This time, they doubled the number of signatures they obtained to reach three million, meaning one in every five people in England and Wales signed the petition—or one in every three men, an amazing number. Again, the Commons rejected the petition, and agitation continued through the 1840s.

The year 1848 saw revolutions break out in all the major cities on the European continent; the advocates of Chartist revolution saw this period as their best opportunity. Hundreds of thousands of Chartists gathered on Kennington Common in April 1848, south of London, to present a third petition to Parliament, this one with two million signatures. The Chartist leaders exhorted the workers that if the Commons would not accept the petition this time, they would set up their own Parliament outside the doors of Westminster Abbey and see which one the British people considered more representative and responsive to their interests. Twenty thousand Chartists began to march to Westminster, but before they even made it off the common, they were met by 25,000 deputized Londoners who marched out to stop them.

It turned out that many of the two million signatures were false: Queen Victoria allegedly signed the petition 21 times, for example. So the Charter once again was rejected, and with it, the relevance of the Chartist movement. Yet by 1918, the British government had passed laws relating to five of the six Chartist demands, and without ever having to experience the revolution a branch of the Chartists had agitated for. Britain achieved democracy without violence, an anomaly in the western world.

——*Stephen Balzarini*

Bibliography and Further Reading

Brown, Richard. *Chartism*. Cambridge: Cambridge University Press, 1998.

Charlton, John. *The Chartists: The First National Workers' Movement*. Chicago: Pluto Press, 1997.

Chase, Malcolm. *Chartism: A New History*. New York: Manchester University Press, 2007.

Royle, Edward. *Chartism*. New York: Longman, 1996.

Saville, John. *1848: The British State and the Chartist Movement*. New York: Cambridge University Press, 1987.

Walton, John K. *Chartism*. New York: Routledge, 1999.

Web Sites

"A History of Chartism." *The Victorian Web* (April 29, 2014) http://www.victorianweb.org/history/ chartism/ index.html [accessed March 15, 2017].

"The People's Charter." *Learning: Dreamers and Dissenters*. British Library http://www.bl.uk/learning/ histcitizen/21cc/struggle/chartists1/historicalsources/ source4/peoplescharter.html [accessed March 15, 2017].

Chartist Ancestors. http://www.chartists.net/ [accessed March 15, 2017].

■ Treaty of Guadalupe Hidalgo

Date: 1848
Authors: Jose Bernardo Couto, Miguel Atristain, Luis G. Cuevas, Nicholas Trist
Genre: International peace agreement

Summary Overview

The Treaty of Guadalupe Hidalgo officially ended the Mexican-American War. The terms of peace set forth in the treaty were a catastrophe for Mexico and a triumph for the expanding United States. After a decisive military defeat, Mexico was forced to sell over half its national territory to the United States for the price of $15 million. The United States obtained clear legal title to more than 850,000 square miles of land, including territory that would eventually make up all or part of Arizona, California, Colorado, New Mexico, Nevada, Utah, and Wyoming.

The Treaty of Guadalupe Hidalgo had far-reaching consequences for both countries and set in motion a series of events that would lead to civil wars in both Mexico and the United States during the 1860s. In the United States the acquisition of the vast new territory exacerbated the conflict over slavery and led to the outbreak of the Civil War in 1861. In Mexico the sense of national humiliation inflicted by the treaty polarized Mexican politics and plunged the country into civil strife that endured throughout the 1850s and 1860s. The unequal terms of the treaty also called attention to the rising power of the United States. The territory the U.S. acquired in the treaty paved the way for rapid economic growth that would soon transform the United States into the dominant power in the Western Hemisphere. For Mexicans and other Latin Americans, the Treaty of Guadalupe Hidalgo would become an enduring symbol of U.S. territorial ambition and arrogance.

Defining Moment

When Mexico achieved independence from Spain in 1821, it inherited a long-standing border conflict with the United States. The conflict originated during the First Seminole War that began in December 1817, when U.S. forces under the command of Andrew Jackson occupied eastern Florida in defiance of Spain's claims to the area. Already fighting several wars and dealing with rebellion throughout its American colonies, Spain decided to bargain with the United States rather than fight. The result of these deliberations was the 1819 Adams-Onís Treaty, ratified by Spain in 1820 and the United States shortly thereafter and ratified again in 1831 after Mexican independence. In this agreement, Spain sold Florida to the United States and renounced its claims to the Pacific Northwest. In exchange, Spain received financial compensation and the promise that the United States would abandon its claim to Texas.

The Adams-Onís Treaty did not ultimately resolve the border dispute, however. Instead, it heightened tensions that would lead to war. The issue of who owned Texas continued to be a major source of contention. After independence, Mexicans pointed to the treaty as clear evidence of their right to Texas. Many Americans, however, continued to insist that Texas was rightfully part of the United States. In response to armed incursions into Texas by expansionist U.S. settlers, the Mexican government realized that the only way to substantiate its claim was to settle the area with people loyal to Mexico. Unable to entice Mexican citizens to migrate to a sparsely inhabited region, much of which was not well suited to agriculture, the Mexican government eventually handed out generous land grants to a group of U.S. settlers willing to relocate to the area and in effect colonize it. In return, Mexico required the settlers to respect Mexican sovereignty. Initially, men like Stephen F. Austin were willing to cooperate with the government in Mexico City, but during the 1820s and 1830s Texans found themselves increasingly at odds with Mexican policies. They revolted, prompting Mexico to send an army to restore order. After several skirmishes, the decisive battle took place on April 21, 1836, when soldiers under the command of Sam Houston defeated the Mexican army at the Battle of San Jacinto, thus forcing Mexican general Antonio López de Santa Anna to sign an agreement that put a temporary end to the fighting. Although Mexico never formally accepted this agreement, for all intents and purposes the victory made Texas an independent country.

Texas' independence put the United States and Mexico on a collision course toward war. In the 1830s and 1840s the idea of Manifest Destiny had become widespread in the United States. Originating in a belief in racial, religious, and political superiority, Manifest

Destiny was an ideology that insisted the United States was destined to extend its borders. In fact, many Texans wanted and expected that the United States would annex Texas after it became independent. The issue of annexation became a major political issue in the United States, however, as it quickly became the centerpiece in the battle between pro-slavery Southerners and anti-slavery Northerners. Slavery was important to the Texas economy, and Northerners worried that the admission of another slave state into the Union would upset the U.S. Congress's delicate political balance. At the same time, Mexico refused to recognize Texas independence, and Mexican leaders stated unequivocally that U.S. annexation would be considered an act of war. These tensions finally boiled over in 1845 and 1846. On March 1, 1845, just a few days before leaving office, President John Tyler signed a joint resolution that paved the way for Texas to be admitted to the United States. On December 29, 1845, President James Polk completed the process by signing the act that made Texas part of the United States. A determined expansionist, Polk sent U.S. troops into the disputed territory of the Texas-Mexico border in the spring of 1846, an act which provoked a skirmish between Mexican and U.S. forces on April 25, 1846. On May 13, 1846, the U.S. Congress declared Mexico and the United States to be at war.

From the start, the war did not go well for Mexico. As U.S. forces pushed south into central Mexico, an invasion force was deployed to the Gulf of Mexico port of Veracruz. In March 1847, Veracruz was subjected to heavy bombardment and seized by U.S. soldiers. On September 13, 1847, U.S. soldiers won a decisive victory at the Battle of Chapultepec and entered Mexico City the following day. In addition to military defeats, the war unleashed rebellions and revolts directed against the Mexican government that threatened its legitimacy.

In early 1847, President Polk sent Nicholas Trist to Mexico to negotiate a peace treaty. Trist was given specific instructions about the terms that would be acceptable to the United States. Following several failed efforts to work out a treaty in 1847, Polk sent a letter instructing Trist to abandon his mission and return to the United States. Trist prepared to leave Mexico, but at the last moment he decided that the time was right for negotiating and chose to ignore Polk's recall order. On January 2, 1848, Trist and three Mexican representatives began peace negotiations that culminated on February 2, 1848 with the signing of the Treaty of Guadalupe Hidalgo. The treaty was ratified by the U.S. Congress on March 10, 1848 and the Mexican Congress on May 30, 1848, and it was proclaimed on July 4, 1848.

Author Biographies

The Treaty of Guadalupe Hidalgo was negotiated entirely by four men. On the Mexican side were José Bernardo Couto, Miguel Atristain, and Luis G. Cuevas. Couto and Atristain were prominent lawyers who had been involved with earlier rounds of peace negotiations. Cuevas was also a well-known political figure and fluent in both English and Spanish. All three men were civilians and represented the political faction in Mexico that favored peace. The sole U.S. negotiator was Nicholas Trist. Then serving as an undersecretary of state, Trist had worked during the 1830s in the U.S. consul's office in Cuba, where he learned Spanish and became familiar with Latin America. A fervent supporter of slavery, Trist had been involved, while he was in Cuba, in various illegal schemes to sell Africans as slaves—schemes that alarmed many Northerners. In Latin America, however, he was generally seen as sympathetic and well intentioned.

The U.S. Congress also played a role in authoring the final version of the treaty. Most members of Congress did not support the comprehensive guarantees of Mexicans' rights that were included in Articles IX and X. These men believed that the U.S. judicial system would provide adequate legal protection for Mexicans living in the ceded territory, and their beliefs guided their decision to amend Article IX and to strike Article X altogether from the final version of the treaty.

HISTORICAL DOCUMENT

In the Name of Almighty God

The United States of America and the United Mexican States, animated by a sincere desire to put an end to the calamities of the war which unhappily exists between the two Republics and to establish Upon a solid basis relations of peace and friendship, which shall confer reciprocal benefits upon the citizens of both, and assure the concord, harmony, and mutual confidence wherein the two people should live, as good neighbors have for that purpose appointed their respective plenipotentiaries, that is to say: The President of the United States has appointed Nicholas P. Trist, a citizen of the United States, and the President of the Mexican Republic has appointed Don Luis Gonzaga Cuevas, Don Bernardo Couto, and Don Miguel Atristain, citizens of the said Republic; Who, after a reciprocal communication of their respective full powers, have, under the protection of Almighty God, the author of peace, arranged, agreed upon, and signed the following:

Treaty of Peace, Friendship, Limits, and Settlement between the United States of America and the Mexican Republic.

Article I

There shall be firm and universal peace between the United States of America and the Mexican Republic, and between their respective countries, territories, cities, towns, and people, without exception of places or persons.

Article II

Immediately upon the signature of this treaty, a convention shall be entered into between a commissioner or commissioners appointed by the General-in-Chief of the forces of the United States, and such as may be appointed by the Mexican Government, to the end that a provisional suspension of hostilities shall take place, and that, in the places occupied by the said forces, constitutional order may be reestablished, as regards the political, administrative, and judicial branches, so far as this shall be permitted by the circumstances of military occupation.

Article III

Immediately upon the ratification of the present treaty by the Government of the United States, orders shall be transmitted to the commanders of their land and naval forces, requiring the latter (provided this treaty shall then have been ratified by the Government of the Mexican Republic, and the ratifications exchanged) immediately to desist from blockading any Mexican ports and requiring the former (under the same condition) to commence, at the earliest moment practicable, withdrawing all troops of the United State then in the interior of the Mexican Republic, to points that shall be selected by common agreement, at a distance from the seaports not exceeding thirty leagues; and such evacuation of the interior of the Republic shall be completed with the least possible delay; the Mexican Government hereby binding itself to afford every facility in its power for rendering the same convenient to the troops, on their march and in their new positions, and for promoting a good understanding between them and the inhabitants. In like manner orders shall be dispatched to the persons in charge of the custom houses at all ports occupied by the forces of the United States, requiring them (under the same condition) immediately to deliver possession of the same to the persons authorized by the Mexican Government to receive it, together with all bonds and evidences of debt for duties on importations and on exportations, not yet fallen due. Moreover, a faithful and exact account shall be made out, showing the entire amount of all duties on imports and on exports, collected at such custom-houses, or elsewhere in Mexico, by authority of the United States, from and after the day of ratification of this treaty by the Government of the Mexican Republic; and also an account of the cost of collection; and such entire amount, deducting only the cost of collection, shall be delivered to the Mexican Government, at the city of Mexico, within three months after the exchange of ratifications.

The evacuation of the capital of the Mexican Republic by the troops of the United States, in virtue of the above stipulation, shall be completed in one month after the orders there stipulated for shall have been received by the commander of said troops, or sooner if possible.

Article IV

Immediately after the exchange of ratifications of the present treaty all castles, forts, territories, places, and possessions, which have been taken or occupied by the forces of the United States during the present war, within the limits of the Mexican Republic, as about to be established by the following article, shall be definitely restored to the said Republic, together with all the artillery, arms, apparatus of war, munitions, and other public property, which were in the said castles and forts when captured, and which shall remain there at the time when this treaty shall be duly ratified by the Government of the Mexican Republic. To this end, immediately upon the signature of this treaty, orders shall be dispatched to the American officers commanding such castles and forts, securing against the removal or destruction of any such artillery, arms, apparatus of war, munitions, or other public property. The city of Mexico, within the inner line of entrenchments surrounding the said city, is comprehended in the above stipulation, as regards the restoration of artillery, apparatus of war, &c.

The final evacuation of the territory of the Mexican Republic, by the forces of the United States, shall be completed in three months from the said exchange of ratifications, or sooner if possible; the Mexican Government hereby engaging, as in the foregoing article to use all means in its power for facilitating such evacuation, and rendering it convenient to the troops, and for promoting a good understanding between them and the inhabitants. ...

Article V

The boundary line between the two Republics shall commence in the Gulf of Mexico, three leagues from land, opposite the mouth of the Rio Grande, otherwise called Rio Bravo del Norte, or Opposite the mouth of its deepest branch, if it should have more than one branch emptying directly into the sea; from thence up the middle of that river, following the deepest channel, where it has more than one, to the point where it strikes the southern boundary of New Mexico; thence, westwardly, along the whole southern boundary of New Mexico (which runs north of the town called Paso) to its western termination; thence, northward, along the western line of New Mexico, until it intersects the first branch of the river Gila; (or if it should not intersect any branch of that river, then to the point on the said line nearest to such branch, and thence in a direct line to the same); thence down the middle of the said branch and of the said river, until it empties into the Rio Colorado; thence across the Rio Colorado, following the division line between Upper and Lower California, to the Pacific Ocean.

The southern and western limits of New Mexico, mentioned in the article, are those laid down in the map entitled "Map of the United Mexican States, as organized and defined by various acts of the Congress of said republic, and constructed according to the best authorities. Revised edition. Published at New York, in 1847, by J. Disturnell," of which map a copy is added to this treaty, bearing the signatures and seals of the undersigned Plenipotentiaries. And, in order to preclude all difficulty in tracing upon the ground the limit separating Upper from Lower California, it is agreed that the said limit shall consist of a straight line drawn from the middle of the Rio Gila, where it unites with the Colorado, to a point on the coast of the Pacific Ocean, distant one marine league due south of the southernmost point of the port of San Diego, according to the plan of said port made in the year 1782 by Don Juan Pantoja, second sailing-master of the Spanish fleet, and published at Madrid in the year 1802, in the atlas to the voyage of the schooners Sutil and Mexicana; of which plan a copy is hereunto added, signed and sealed by the respective Plenipotentiaries. ...

Article VI

The vessels and citizens of the United States shall, in all time, have a free and uninterrupted passage by the Gulf of California, and by the river Colorado below its confluence with the Gila, to and from their possessions situated north of the boundary line defined in the preceding article; it being understood that this passage is to be by navigating the Gulf of California and the river Colorado, and not by land, without the express consent of the Mexican Government.

If, by the examinations which may be made, it should be ascertained to be practicable and advantageous to construct a road, canal, or railway, which should in whole or in part run upon the river Gila, or upon its right or its left bank, within the space of one marine league from either margin of the river, the Governments of both republics will form an agreement regarding its construction, in order that it may serve equally for the use and advantage of both countries.

Article VII

The river Gila, and the part of the Rio Bravo del Norte lying below the southern boundary of New Mexico, being, agreeably to the fifth article, divided in the middle between the two republics, the navigation of the Gila and of the Bravo below said boundary shall be free and common to the vessels and citizens of both countries; and neither shall, without the consent of the other, construct any work that may impede or interrupt, in whole or in part, the exercise of this right; not even for the purpose of favoring new methods of navigation. Nor shall any tax or contribution, under any denomination or title, be levied upon vessels or persons navigating the same or upon merchandise or effects transported thereon, except in the case of landing upon one of their shores. If, for the purpose of making the said rivers navigable, or for maintaining them in such state, it should be necessary or advantageous to establish any tax or contribution, this shall not be done without the consent of both Governments.

The stipulations contained in the present article shall not impair the territorial rights of either republic within its established limits.

Article VIII

Mexicans now established in territories previously belonging to Mexico, and which remain for the future within the limits of the United States, as defined by the present treaty, shall be free to continue where they now reside, or to remove at any time to the Mexican Republic, retaining the property which they possess in the said territories, or disposing thereof, and removing the proceeds wherever they please, without their being subjected, on this account, to any contribution, tax, or charge whatever.

Those who shall prefer to remain in the said territories may either retain the title and rights of Mexican citizens, or acquire those of citizens of the United States. But they shall be under the obligation to make their election within one year from the date of the exchange of ratifications of this treaty; and those who shall remain in the said territories after the expiration of that year, without having declared their intention to retain the character of Mexicans, shall be considered to have elected to become citizens of the United States. ...

Article IX

The Mexicans who, in the territories aforesaid, shall not preserve the character of citizens of the Mexican Republic, conformably with what is stipulated in the preceding article, shall be incorporated into the Union of the United States. and be admitted at the proper time (to be judged of by the Congress of the United States) to the enjoyment of all the rights of citizens of the United States, according to the principles of the Constitution; and in the mean time, shall be maintained and protected in the free enjoyment of their liberty and property, and secured in the free exercise of their religion without restriction.

Article X
[Stricken out by the United States Amendments]

Article XI

Considering that a great part of the territories, which, by the present treaty, are to be comprehended for the future within the limits of the United States, is now occupied by savage tribes, who will hereafter be under the exclusive control of the Government of the United States, and whose incursions within the territory of Mexico would be prejudicial in the extreme, it is solemnly agreed that all such incursions shall be forcibly restrained by the Government of the United States whensoever this may be necessary; and that when they cannot be prevented, they shall be punished by the said Government, and satisfaction for the same shall be exacted all in the same way, and with equal diligence and energy, as if the same incursions were meditated or committed within its own territory, against its own citizens.

It shall not be lawful, under any pretext whatever, for any inhabitant of the United States to purchase or acquire any Mexican, or any foreigner residing in Mexico, who may have been captured by Indians inhabiting the territory of either of the two republics; nor to purchase or acquire horses, mules, cattle, or property of any kind, stolen within Mexican territory by such Indians.

And in the event of any person or persons, captured within Mexican territory by Indians, being carried into the territory of the United States, the Government of the latter engages and binds itself, in the most solemn manner, so soon as it shall know of such captives being within its territory, and shall be able so to do, through the faithful exercise of its influence and power, to rescue them and return them to their country or deliver them to the agent or representative of the Mexican Government. The Mexican authorities will, as far as practicable, give to the Government of the United States notice of such captures; and its agents shall pay the expenses incurred in the maintenance and transmission of the rescued captives; who, in the mean time, shall be treated with the utmost hospitality by the American authorities at the place where they may be. But if the Government of the United States, before receiving such notice from Mexico, should obtain intelligence, through any other channel, of the existence of Mexican captives within its territory, it will proceed forthwith to effect their release and delivery to the Mexican agent, as above stipulated. ...

Article XII

In consideration of the extension acquired by the boundaries of the United States, as defined in the fifth article of the present treaty, the Government of the United States engages to pay to that of the Mexican Republic the sum of fifteen millions of dollars. ...

Article XIII

The United States engage, moreover, to assume and pay to the claimants all the amounts now due them, and those hereafter to become due, by reason of the claims already liquidated and decided against the Mexican Republic, under the conventions between the two republics severally concluded on the elev-

enth day of April, eighteen hundred and thirty-nine, and on the thirtieth day of January, eighteen hundred and forty-three; so that the Mexican Republic shall be absolutely exempt, for the future, from all expense whatever on account of the said claims.

Article XIV

The United States do furthermore discharge the Mexican Republic from all claims of citizens of the United States, not heretofore decided against the Mexican Government, which may have arisen previously to the date of the signature of this treaty; which discharge shall be final and perpetual, whether the said claims be rejected or be allowed by the board of commissioners provided for in the following article, and whatever shall be the total amount of those allowed.

Article XV

The United States, exonerating Mexico from all demands on account of the claims of their citizens mentioned in the preceding article, and considering them entirely and forever canceled, whatever their amount may be, undertake to make satisfaction for the same, to an amount not exceeding three and one-quarter millions of dollars. To ascertain the validity and amount of those claims, a board of commissioners shall be established by the Government of the United States, whose awards shall be final and conclusive; provided that, in deciding upon the validity of each claim, the board shall be guided and governed by the principles and rules of decision prescribed by the first and fifth articles of the unratified convention, concluded at the city of Mexico on the twentieth day of November, one thousand eight hundred and forty-three; and in no case shall an award be made in favour of any claim not embraced by these principles and rules.

If, in the opinion of the said board of commissioners or of the claimants, any books, records, or documents, in the possession or power of the Government of the Mexican Republic, shall be deemed necessary to the just decision of any claim, the commissioners, or the claimants through them, shall, within such period as Congress may designate, make an application in writing for the same, addressed to the Mexican Minister of Foreign Affairs, to be transmitted by the Secretary of State of the United States; and the Mexican Government engages, at the earliest possible moment after the receipt of such demand, to cause any of the books, records, or documents so specified, which shall be in their possession or power (or authenticated copies or extracts of the same), to be transmitted to the said Secretary of State, who shall immediately deliver them over to the said board of commissioners; provided that no such application shall be made by or at the instance of any claimant, until the facts which it is expected to prove by such books, records, or documents, shall have been stated under oath or affirmation.

Article XVI

Each of the contracting parties reserves to itself the entire right to fortify whatever point within its territory it may judge proper so to fortify for its security.

Article XVII

The treaty of amity, commerce, and navigation, concluded at the city of Mexico, on the fifth day of April, A.D. 1831, between the United States of America and the United Mexican States, except the additional article, and except so far as the stipulations of the said treaty may be incompatible with any stipulation contained in the present treaty, is hereby revived for the period of eight years from the day of the exchange of ratifications of this treaty, with the same force and virtue as if incorporated therein; it being understood that each of the contracting parties reserves to itself the right, at any time after the said period of eight years shall have expired, to terminate the same by giving one year's notice of such intention to the other party.

Article XVIII

All supplies whatever for troops of the United States in Mexico, arriving at ports in the occupation of such troops previous to the final evacuation thereof, although subsequently to the restoration of the custom-houses at such ports, shall be entirely exempt from duties and charges of any kind; the Government of the United States hereby engaging and pledging its faith to establish and vigilantly to enforce, all possible guards for securing the revenue of Mexico, by preventing the importation, under cover of this stipulation, of any articles other than such, both in kind and in quantity, as shall really be wanted for the use and consumption of the forces of the United States during the time they may remain in Mexico. To this end it shall be the duty of all officers and agents of the United States to denounce to the Mexican authorities at the respective ports any attempts at a fraudulent abuse of this stipulation, which they may know of, or may have reason to suspect, and to give to such authorities all the aid in their power with regard thereto; and every such attempt, when duly proved and established by sentence of a competent tribunal, They shall be punished by the confiscation of the property so attempted to be fraudulently introduced.

Article XIX

With respect to all merchandise, effects, and property whatsoever, imported into ports of Mexico, whilst in the occupation of the forces of the United States, whether by citizens of either republic, or by citizens or subjects of any neutral nation, the following rules shall be observed:

(1) All such merchandise, effects, and property, if imported previously to the restoration of the custom-houses to the Mexican authorities, as stipulated for in the third article of this treaty, shall be exempt from confiscation, although the importation of the same be prohibited by the Mexican tariff.

(2) The same perfect exemption shall be enjoyed by all such merchandise, effects, and property, imported subsequently to the restoration of the custom-houses, and previously to the sixty days fixed in the following article for the coming into force of the Mexican tariff at such ports respectively; the said merchandise, effects, and property being, however, at the time of their importation, subject to the payment of duties, as provided for in the said following article.

(3) All merchandise, effects, and property described in the two rules foregoing shall, during their continuance at the place of importation, and upon their leaving such place for the interior, be exempt from all duty, tax, or imposts of every kind, under whatsoever title or denomination. Nor shall they be there subject to any charge whatsoever upon the sale thereof.

(4) All merchandise, effects, and property, described in the first and second rules, which shall have been removed to any place in the interior, whilst such place was in the occupation of the forces of the United States, shall, during their continuance therein, be exempt from all tax upon the sale or consumption thereof, and from every kind of impost or contribution, under whatsoever title or denomination.

(5) But if any merchandise, effects, or property, described in the first and second rules, shall be removed to any place not occupied at the time by the forces of the United States, they shall, upon their introduction into such place, or upon their sale or consumption there, be subject to the same duties which, under the Mexican laws, they would be required to pay in such cases if they had been imported in time of peace, through the maritime custom-houses, and had there paid the duties conformably with the Mexican tariff.

(6) The owners of all merchandise, effects, or property, described in the first and second rules, and existing in any port of Mexico, shall have the right to reship the same, exempt from all tax, impost, or contribution whatever.

With respect to the metals, or other property, exported from any Mexican port whilst in the occupation of the forces of the United States, and previously to the restoration of the custom-house at such port, no person shall be required by the Mexican authorities, whether general or state, to pay any tax, duty, or contribution upon any such exportation, or in any manner to account for the same to the said authorities.

Article XX

Through consideration for the interests of commerce generally, it is agreed, that if less than sixty days should elapse between the date of the signature of this treaty and the restoration of the custom houses, conformably with the stipulation in the third article, in such case all merchandise, effects and property whatsoever, arriving at the Mexican ports after the restoration of the said custom-houses, and previously to the expiration of sixty days after the day of signature of this treaty, shall be admitted to entry; and no other duties shall be levied thereon than the duties established by the tariff found in force at such custom-houses at the time of the restoration of the same. And to all such merchandise, effects, and property, the rules established by the preceding article shall apply.

Article XXI

If unhappily any disagreement should hereafter arise between the Governments of the two republics, whether with respect to the interpretation of any stipulation in this treaty, or with respect to any other particular concerning the political or commercial relations of the two nations, the said Governments, in the name of those nations, do promise to each other that they will endeavour, in the most sincere and earnest manner, to settle the differences so arising, and to preserve the state of peace and friendship in which the two countries are now placing themselves, using, for this end, mutual representations and pacific negotiations. And if, by these means, they should not be enabled to come to an agreement, a resort shall not, on this account, be had to reprisals, aggression, or hostility of any kind, by the one republic against the other, until the Government of that which deems itself aggrieved shall have maturely considered, in the spirit of peace and good neighbourship, whether it would not be better that such difference should be settled by the arbitration of commissioners appointed on each side, or by that of a friendly nation. And should such course be proposed by either party, it shall be acceded to by the other, unless deemed by it altogether incompatible with the nature of the difference, or the circumstances of the case.

Article XXII

If (which is not to be expected, and which God forbid) war should unhappily break out between the two republics, they do now, with a view to such calamity, solemnly pledge themselves to each other and to the world to observe the following rules; absolutely where the nature of the subject permits, and as closely as possible in all cases where such absolute observance shall be impossible:

(1) The merchants of either republic then residing in the other shall be allowed to remain twelve months (for those dwelling in the interior), and six months (for those dwelling at the seaports) to collect their debts and settle their affairs; during which periods they shall enjoy the same protection, and be on the same footing, in all respects, as the citizens or subjects of the most friendly nations; and, at the expiration thereof, or at any time before, they shall have full liberty to depart, carrying off all their effects without molestation or hindrance, conforming therein to the same laws which the citizens or subjects of the most friendly nations are required to conform to. …

(2) In order that the fate of prisoners of war may be alleviated all such practices as those of sending them into distant, inclement or unwholesome districts, or crowding them into close and noxious places, shall be studiously avoided. …

And it is declared that neither the pretense that war dissolves all treaties, nor any other whatever, shall be considered as annulling or suspending the solemn covenant contained in this article. On the contrary, the state of war is precisely that for which it is provided; and, during which, its stipulations are to be as sacredly observed as the most acknowledged obligations under the law of nature or nations.

Article XXIII

This treaty shall be ratified by the President of the United States of America, by and with the advice and consent of the Senate thereof; and by the President of the Mexican Republic, with the previous approbation of its general Congress; and the ratifications shall be exchanged in the City of Washington, or at the seat of Government of Mexico, in four months from the date of the signature hereof, or sooner if practicable.

In faith whereof we, the respective Plenipotentiaries, have signed this treaty of peace, friendship, limits, and settlement, and have hereunto affixed our seals respectively. Done in quintuplicate, at the city of Guadalupe Hidalgo, on the second day of February, in the year of our Lord one thousand eight hundred and forty-eight.

N. P. Trist
Luis P. Cuevas
Bernadro Cuoto
Migl. Atristain

GLOSSARY

30 leagues: 90 statute miles (1,449 kilometers)

cantonment: temporary quarters for military troops

plenipotentiaries: persons empowered by their respective governments to sign a treaty

sickly season: May through October, the period during which malaria was rampant in the treaty area

three millions of dollars: about $75 million in today's dollars

Document Analysis

The Treaty of Guadalupe Hidalgo put an official end to the Mexican-American War. Many of the treaty's twenty-three articles are still in effect today. The introductory paragraph lists the treaty's authors, states their credentials, and proclaims their authority to negotiate on behalf of their respective countries. Although the document states that each of the negotiators has "full powers" to act on behalf of their government, the truth was not so simple. In fact, the U.S. negotiator, Nicholas Trist, had been recalled by President Polk in a letter Trist received in November 1847. Trist ignored his instructions to return to the United States and negotiated the treaty in direct defiance of Polk's orders. The preamble also describes the treaty's scope by declaring it a treaty of "Peace, Friendship, Limits, and Settlement." Thus, the treaty was intended not only to end the war but also to resolve the long-standing question of Mexico's borders with the United States and to lay out a blueprint for a sustained and lasting peace between the two countries.

Article I declares an immediate end to the war and calls for a "firm and lasting peace" between the two countries. Despite many tensions, flare-ups, and even the occasional incursion of U.S. soldiers into Mexico since the signing of the treaty, Mexico and the United States have never again entered into a state of war with each other.

Articles II–IV lay out the details of the transition from war to peace. Article II calls for a cease-fire between the two countries and proclaims the reestablishment of "constitutional order" in Mexico. However, since the evacuation of U.S. troops from Mexico would take several months, the article asserts that the reestablishment of Mexican sovereignty would be limited by the "circumstances of military occupation." Article III requires the United States to end its blockade of Veracruz, which it had occupied since March 1847. It also restores control to Mexican authorities over the customhouse at the port and contains stipulations to return all taxes collected during the blockade and to remove all U.S. troops from Mexico City within one month. Article IV requires the return to Mexico of all military equipment and forts captured by U.S. forces during the war and the mutual exchange of all prisoners of war. It also states that the United States would remove its military personnel from Mexico within three months from the ratification of the treaty.

Article V defines the new boundaries of the United States and Mexico as a result of the treaty. The treaty cedes approximately 850,000 square miles of territory to the United States, including land that would eventually contain all or part of Arizona, California, Colorado, New Mexico, Nevada, Utah, and Wyoming. The beginning of the article settles the issue of the Texas-Mexico boundary that was the pretext for war by leaving no doubt that the southern border of Texas would be the Rio Grande, instead of the Rio Nueces, as Mexico had insisted. The California border with Mexico is also definitively settled. Despite Mexico's wish to retain the port of San Diego, the treaty states that the new border would be located one marine league south of the southernmost point of San Diego and run directly east in a straight line until meeting the point where the Colorado and Gila rivers intersect.

The southern border of the states that would become Arizona and New Mexico was more problematic. The treaty calls for a surveying team appointed by both countries to map the southern border within one year of the treaty's ratification. It states that the new border runs up the Rio Grande until it "strikes the southern boundary of New Mexico." The problem was that no one knew the exact boundaries of New Mexico. Trist wanted the Mesilla Valley to be included in the ceded territory, because he suspected it was the only feasible railroad route through the region. The authors of the treaty used a map made by John Disturnell, according to which the Mesilla Valley was north of the new boundary. However, when the surveyors mapped the area, they found that the Disturnell map was inaccurate, and they were subsequently unable to agree on the correct border. This dispute led to the Gadsden Purchase in 1854, in which the United States paid the Mexican government $10 million in exchange for territory that included the Mesilla Valley.

Articles VI and VII demonstrate the importance at the time of new transportation technologies, especially railroads and steam-powered ships. Article VI gives the United States the right of passage on the entire length of the Colorado River, which according to the terms of the new treaty begins in the United States but passes through Mexico before emptying into the Gulf of California. The article also paves the way for both countries to cooperate on the construction of a future transcontinental railroad. If the route needed to pass through Mexico, the article requires an agreement that the railroad would "serve equally for the use and advantage of both countries." Article VII grants both countries equal rights to the Rio Grande and Gila River for both navigation and commerce. It also states that neither country could collect taxes on the commerce of either river without the permission of the other.

Articles VIII and IX provide rules for determining citizenship and affirm the protection of the civil and property rights of people living in the annexed territories. These articles were extremely important to the Mexican negotiators. Article VIII first clarifies that all those living in the annexed territories would be "free to continue where they now reside" or to "remove at any time to the Mexican Republic." In other words, people in the annexed lands could choose to remain in the territory that had become part of the United States, or they could return to Mexico. The article states that their property rights would be respected if they chose to leave and that they would not be subject to any tax if they kept or sold their property. According to Article VIII, those who chose to remain in newly acquired U.S. territory would be free to decide if they wanted to retain their Mexican citizenship or renounce it and become citizens of the United States. However, the default position was the loss of Mexican citizenship; the treaty gave individuals one year from ratification to announce their decision to remain Mexican or else forfeit their rights to Mexican citizenship.

Article IX extends these guarantees to people who chose to become U.S. citizens but had not yet become so under U.S. law. This was especially important because the article is vague about when and how these people would gain U.S. citizenship. Rather than becoming citizens right away, the article explains that they would "be admitted at the proper time" to be decided by the U.S. Congress. In practice, this process was slow; many states, such as California, did not grant full citizenship under the terms of the treaty until the 1870s. The Mexican negotiators of the treaty tried to protect the rights of former Mexicans in this state of legal limbo by means of a long article that spelled out the precise protections they would be afforded. However, during the ratification process, the U.S. Congress voted to amend the article, replacing much of the text with subtler language promising that former Mexicans would be "protected in the free enjoyment of their liberty and property, and secured in the free exercise of their religion without restriction."

Article X asserts that all land claims made by the Mexican government in the annexed territories were valid. During the ratification process, it was stricken by the U.S. Congress and was not included in the final version of the treaty. Members of Congress believed that the article would revive old land claims, especially in Texas, and lead to conflict and confusion about property rights.

Article XI commits the United States to protecting Mexico from attacks and raids by Native Americans living in the annexed territory. Thousands of Native Americans inhabited the ceded area, many of whom had been in a prolonged state of conflict with U.S. and Mexican communities on both sides of the border. Mexican negotiators insisted that the United States bear the burden of forcibly controlling these groups. However, neither side during the negotiations appreciated the size of the Native American population and its determination to resist incursions into what they claimed as their territory. As a result, the article was a source of great tension in the years after the treaty's ratification, as Mexican leaders accused the United States of not fulfilling its obligations. The article was eventually canceled by the terms of the Gadsden Purchase in 1854.

Article XII determines the final price of $15 million that the United States was to pay Mexico in exchange for the ceded territory. This figure is equivalent to approximately $300 million in today's money. Trist had originally been authorized by President Polk to offer $20 million for similar territorial concessions, but he lowered the price to offset the cost in American lives and money spent by the United States during the war.

Articles XIII–XV lay out the terms by which the United States agrees to pay the financial claims of its own citizens against the Mexican government, up to the amount of $3.25 million. This resolved one of the outstanding disputes between the two countries. For decades, many U.S. citizens had sought money from the Mexican government for property damage, confiscation, or outstanding loans. The United States agreed to pay these claims itself to resolve the issue, essentially adding $3 million to the price the United States offered Mexico in exchange for the annexed territories.

Article XVI authorizes both countries to establish defensive fortifications anywhere within their respective territories. Article XVII makes it clear that the Adams-Onís Treaty, ratified in 1831, is still in effect. However, the article also states that all the terms of the Treaty of Guadalupe Hidalgo, once ratified, would overrule any from the previous treaty if at any point there should be a conflict between the two.

Articles XVIII–XX lay out the process by which taxes would be assessed during the time it took for all U.S. troops to leave Mexico. They also outline the procedure for the restoration of Mexican authority over its customhouses. The articles were written to ensure that the United States would not owe Mexico any taxes for equipment and materials brought into the country to supply its occupying army.

Articles XXI and XXII concern the resolution of any future conflicts that might arise between both countries. According to Article XXI, both Mexico and the United States pledged to arbitrate any disputes over the terms of the treaty or with respect to the "political or commercial relations of the two nations." In essence, this article attempts to prevent future wars by a mutual promise from both countries that they would use a third party to mediate disputes. Article XXII lays out two rules in the event of a future war. The first commits each country to respect the rights of civilians, and the second calls for fair and tolerable treatment of all prisoners of war. In the years since the treaty's ratification, there have been a number of disagreements submitted to arbitration. The decisions of arbitrators have not always been respected, but Mexico and the United States have remained at peace.

Article XXIII clarifies that the treaty must be ratified by the Congresses of both countries before it goes into effect. It also states that ratification should occur no more than four months from the signing of the treaty. The U.S. Congress ratified the treaty on March 10, 1848 and the Mexican Congress did so on May 30, 1848, three days shy of the required four months.

Essential Themes

Northern members of the Whig Party led by Daniel Webster opposed the treaty, because they feared the addition of so much new territory would encourage the spread of slavery. Some Southern legislators, on the other hand, such as Jefferson Davis and Sam Houston, opposed the treaty because it did not annex enough of Mexico. The terms negotiated by Trist were a compromise between these extreme positions that made ratification by the U.S. Congress possible.

Persuading Mexico's Congress to approve the treaty was more difficult. Mexican political factions were even more contentious than their counterparts in the United States regarding the end of the war. One faction, led by Manuel Crescencio Rejón, was convinced that the treaty would mean permanent economic subservience to the United States. Rejón and his supporters believed that Mexico could win a guerrilla war against the United States, and they recommended continuing the war. Another faction, under the leadership of Manuel de la Peña y Peña, who was serving as acting president of Mexico, viewed the treaty as the only way to prevent the loss of more territory or even the total annexation of Mexico by the United States. After a heated debate, the Mexican Congress agreed with Peña y Peña and ratified the treaty on May 30, 1848.

Mexico lost over half of its national territory to the United States in the treaty agreement. Although it was sparsely inhabited at the time, the ceded ter-ritory proved its economic importance immediately; the discovery of gold in California in 1848 set off a gold rush that transformed the region into an important economic center. Although much of the newly acquired land was arid, new technology and investment in irrigation allowed agriculture to flourish during the twentieth century. The acquisition of so much new territory made possible the rise of the United States as a world power.

The treaty also had important consequences for Native Americans and the approximately 100,000 Spanish-speaking inhabitants of the ceded territory. The westward expansion of the United States prompted a series of conflicts with Native American groups, including the Sioux, Apache, and Navajo nations. These groups were decimated by disease and defeated militarily. Despite the efforts of the Mexican government to encourage people to relocate, most of the former Mexicans who lived in the annexed territory chose to stay. Although the terms of the treaty legally protected their civil and property rights, in actuality many lost their land and struggled against racism and persecution. The importance of the treaty was resurrected in the 1960s and 1970s by Mexican Americans who participated in the Chicano movement. Chicanos invoked the treaty's legal protection of the rights of Mexicans and Mexican-Americans living in the United States in order to advance claims for social and economic justice.

——*Ben Fulwider*

Bibliography and Further Reading

Griswold del Castillo, Richard. *The Treaty of Guadalupe Hidalgo: A Legacy of Conflict*. Norman: University of Oklahoma Press, 1990.

Henderson, Timothy J. *A Glorious Defeat: Mexico and Its War with the United States*. New York: Hill and Wang, 2007.

Mahin, Dean B. *Olive Branch and Sword: The United States and Mexico, 1845–1848*. London: McFarland & Company, 1997.

Miller, David Hunter. "Treaty of Guadalupe Hidalgo." In *Treaties and Other International Acts of the United States of America*, vol. 5. Washington, D.C. Government Printing Office, 1937.

Pletcher, David M. *The Diplomacy of Annexation: Texas, Oregon, and the Mexican War*. Columbia: University of Missouri Press, 1973.

Web Sites

"The Treaty of Guadalupe Hidalgo." Hispanic Reading Room, Hispanic Division Area Studies, Library of Congress Web site. http://www.loc.gov/rr/hispanic/ghtreaty/.

"The U.S.-Mexican War: 1846–1848." Public Broadcasting Service Web site. http://www.pbs.org/kera/usmexicanwar/index_flash.html.

■ Constitution Act of Canada (British North America Act of 1867)

Date: 1867
Authors: John Alexander Macdonald, et al.
Genre: Constitution

Summary Overview

The Constitution Act of Canada of 1867, at the time called the British North America Act and still informally called the BNA Act, created the federal dominion of Canada. In conjunction with other documents, it continues to form the essence of Canada's constitution, defining its governmental structure, legislature, justice system, and system of taxation. Because the provinces of Canada were British colonies, the Constitution Act of Canada was, in effect, a petition to the British Parliament, which originally enacted the document as law; until 1982 any change in the Canadian constitution had to be made by the British Parliament. In 1982, however, the Constitution Act was "patriated," a term used in Canadian law, along with "patriation," to mean that it was made part of Canadian as opposed to British law. In effect, the Canadian constitution was "brought home." The Constitution Act of Canada represented the coalescence of Britain's North American colonies into a sovereign nation, although Canada remained part of the British Empire and England's monarch is the country's ceremonial head of state.

The legislation that was submitted to Parliament contains no ringing rhetoric declaring independence from Great Britain or denouncing Parliament. Rather, the Constitution Act is a sober, straightforward document outlining the structure and governmental functions of the proposed new federation. The document informed the citizens of the four original provinces of the provinces' intentions and the complexion of their new government. It was intended to be a unifying document that would enable the provinces, with their conflicting political views, nationalities, and ethnicities, to put aside differences for the common welfare. The constitution also provided for the admission of additional provinces and territories to the federation.

Defining Moment

The history of Canada came into focus with the passage of the Quebec Act of 1774, which established procedures for the governance of Britain's colony of Quebec. The Quebec Act expanded the province's territory to the west and south, encompassing portions of modern-day Ontario as well as territories that would become Ohio, Indiana, Illinois, Wisconsin, Michigan, and parts of Minnesota. From the standpoint of the disgruntled colonists in the thirteen coastal colonies to the south, the Quebec Act was one of the so-called Intolerable Acts, or Coercive Acts, passed to punish the American colonies for the Boston Tea Party; the act helped foment the American Revolution. Yet in Quebec, the act was generally well received and cemented the relationship between colonists and the Crown.

Another step in Canadian constitutional history was taken when the British Parliament passed the Constitutional Act of 1791, written to amend the Quebec Act. The purpose of the act was to alter the government of Quebec in a way that would accommodate the interests of "United Empire Loyalists" who had fled the American Revolution in the soon-to-be United States. The act divided Quebec into two parts: Upper Canada, which is now southern Ontario; and Lower Canada, which is now southern Quebec. (The words *upper* and *lower* refer to locations on the Saint Lawrence River, so Upper Canada was south of Lower Canada.) The act established English common law in Upper Canada and French civil law in Lower Canada. Most significant, the act provided for representative assemblies in both colonies; it also made Lower Canada, in effect, a Catholic colony, in contrast to the Protestant Upper Canada.

The result of the Constitutional Act was not what Parliament had hoped, however, for it increased rivalry and tension between the two Quebecs. *Canadiens* in the French-speaking Catholic Lower Canada came to believe that they were being dominated by English-speaking Protestants in Upper Canada; ironically, the latter believed that they were being dominated by French Catholics. The tension between the two eventually led to simultaneous revolts in Upper and Lower Canada in 1837. In Upper Canada, rebels engaged in armed skirmishes with the oligarchy of wealthy Anglican elites that essentially ran the colony. The revolt in Lower Canada was more sustained and was launched by both French-speaking and English-speaking colonists against the inept British colonial administration.

In the aftermath of hostilities, Britain investigated the causes of the unrest. The result of this investigation was the Act of Union of 1840. The act abolished Upper and Lower Canada and merged the two into the Province of Canada. The act allowed for the future emergence of "responsible government," a term used in British legislative history to refer to the practice of colonial administration bowing to the will of the electorate in a colony. This development was pivotal in Canadian constitutional history. The concept of responsible government was first realized in the Province of Canada and Nova Scotia in early 1848, followed by Prince Edward Island in 1851, New Brunswick in 1854, and Newfoundland in 1855. In the ensuing years the Province of Canada became more and more autonomous from Great Britain until it led the push for the Constitution Act of 1867. Canada joined with New Brunswick and Nova Scotia in petitioning the British Parliament to create the Dominion of Canada; Prince Edward Island was part of the original discussions, but it declined to join the confederation until 1873 after almost becoming part of the United States. Newfoundland, too, took part in early discussions but did not join the confederation until 1949. Under the terms of the act, the Province of Canada was again divided, with the western portion becoming Ontario and the eastern portion becoming Quebec. Thus, Canada, as the name is understood today, was formed of Ontario, Quebec, New Brunswick, and Nova Scotia by the Constitution Act of 1867.

Author Biography

Like any complex piece of legislation, the Constitution Act was the work of many hands. The chief author and the motive power behind Canadian federation, though, was Canada's first prime minister, John Alexander Macdonald. Macdonald was born in Glasgow, Scotland, on January 11, 1815. His family immigrated to Kingston, Upper Canada, in 1820. From 1830 to 1836 Macdonald studied and apprenticed at the law, and after he was admitted to the bar he earned a reputation as a capable lawyer in his defense of eight men charged with treason in the wake of the Rebellions of 1837. He entered politics in 1843, first as an alderman and then as a representative to the legislature. Over the next two decades he was an energetic member of the legislature and a party leader.

During these years, however, the legislature was frequently deadlocked as a result of party disputes. Liberals and conservatives warred with each other, and the French-speaking eastern portion of the Province of Canada proved to be a thorn in the government's side. It was in about 1864 that Macdonald began to formulate the idea of a Canadian confederation. He formed a coalition of liberals and conservatives, and over the next three years he conceived the legislation that would become the Constitution Act. He presented his ideas to the Maritime colonies (Nova Scotia, New Brunswick, and Prince Edward Island) and Newfoundland at a conference in Charlottetown, Prince Edward Island, in 1864. This conference was attended by thirty-six representatives who are often regarded as the "Fathers of the Confederation." Later that year, delegates who supported confederation met in Quebec City to draft the legislation. The agreement was completed at a conference in London in 1866 and passed by the British Parliament the following year.

Macdonald went on to become Canada's second-longest-serving prime minister, holding office from 1867 to 1873 and then from 1878 until his death on June 6, 1891. He remains an iconic figure in Canadian history despite a life that was marked by tragedy, including the twelve years of his first wife's illness ending with her death, the sudden death of his infant son, and the physical and mental disabilities of his daughter by a second marriage. Macdonald himself gambled heavily, was often in debt, and was sometimes given to using law practice funds to pay personal expenses. He had a vicious temper, once physically attacking a fellow legislator on the floor of the legislature. He was also a binge drinker, and at times he was so drunk that he became sick during debates, both in the legislature and on the campaign trail. Nevertheless, he can be said to be the founder of Canada, and he worked tirelessly to impose unity on a nation of diverse interests, nationalities, and ethnicities.

HISTORICAL DOCUMENT

An Act for the Union of Canada, Nova Scotia, and New Brunswick, and the Government thereof; and for Purposes connected therewith. ...

I. Preliminary

1. This Act may be cited as the *The British North America Act, 1867*.

2. The Provisions of this Act referring to Her Majesty the Queen extend also to the Heirs and Successors of Her Majesty, Kings and Queens of the United Kingdom of Great Britain and Ireland.

II. Union

3. It shall be lawful for the Queen, by and with the Advice of Her Majesty's Most Honourable Privy Council, to declare by Proclamation that, on and after a Day therein appointed, not being more than Six Months after the passing of this Act, the Provinces of Canada, Nova Scotia, and New Brunswick shall form and be One Dominion under the Name of Canada; and on and after that Day those Three Provinces shall form and be One Dominion under that Name accordingly.

4. The subsequent Provisions of this Act shall, unless it is otherwise expressed or implied, commence and have effect on and after the Union, that is to say, on and after the Day appointed for the Union taking effect in the Queen's Proclamation; and in the same Provisions, unless it is otherwise expressed or implied, the Name Canada shall be taken to mean Canada as constituted under this Act.

5. Canada shall be divided into Four Provinces, named Ontario, Quebec, Nova Scotia, and New Brunswick.

6. The Parts of the Province of Canada (as it exists at the passing of this Act) which formerly constituted respectively the Provinces of Upper Canada and Lower Canada shall be deemed to be severed, and shall form two separate Provinces. The Part which formerly constituted the Province of Upper Canada shall constitute the Province of Ontario; and the Part which formerly constituted the Province of Lower Canada shall constitute the Province of Quebec.

7. The Provinces of Nova Scotia and New Brunswick shall have the same Limits as at the passing of this Act.

8. In the general Census of the Population of Canada which is hereby required to be taken in the Year One thousand eight hundred and seventy-one, and in every Tenth Year thereafter, the respective Populations of the Four Provinces shall be distinguished.

III. Executive Power

9. The Executive Government and Authority of and over Canada is hereby declared to continue and be vested in the Queen.

10. The Provisions of this Act referring to the Governor General extend and apply to the Governor General for the Time being of Canada, or other the Chief Executive Officer or Administrator for the Time being carrying on the Government of Canada on behalf and in the Name of the Queen, by whatever Title he is designated.

11. There shall be a Council to aid and advise in the Government of Canada, to be styled the Queen's Privy Council for Canada; and the Persons who are to be Members of that Council shall be from Time to Time chosen and summoned by the Governor General and sworn in as Privy Councillors, and Members thereof may be from Time to Time removed by the Governor General.

12. All Powers, Authorities, and Functions which under any Act of the Parliament of Great Britain, or of the Parliament of the United Kingdom of Great Britain and Ireland, or of the Legislature of Upper Canada, Lower Canada, Canada, Nova Scotia, or New Brunswick, are at the Union vested in or exercisable by the respective Governors or Lieutenant Governors of those Provinces, with the Advice, or with the Advice and Consent, of the respective Executive Councils thereof, or in conjunction with those Councils, or with any Number of Members thereof, or by those Governors or Lieutenant Governors individually, shall, as far as the same continue in existence and capable of being exercised after the Union in relation to the Government of Canada, be vested in and exercisable by the Governor General,

with the Advice or with the Advice and Consent of or in conjunction with the Queen's Privy Council for Canada, or any Members thereof, or by the Governor General individually, as the Case requires, subject nevertheless (except with respect to such as exist under Acts of the Parliament of Great Britain or of the Parliament of the United Kingdom of Great Britain and Ireland) to be abolished or altered by the Parliament of Canada.

13. The Provisions of this Act referring to the Governor General in Council shall be construed as referring to the Governor General acting by and with the Advice of the Queen's Privy Council for Canada.

14. It shall be lawful for the Queen, if Her Majesty thinks fit, to authorize the Governor General from Time to Time to appoint any Person or any Persons jointly or severally to be his Deputy or Deputies within any Part or Parts of Canada, and in that Capacity to exercise during the Pleasure of the Governor General such of the Powers, Authorities, and Functions of the Governor General as the Governor General deems it necessary or expedient to assign to him or them, subject to any Limitations or Directions expressed or given by the Queen; but the Appointment of such a Deputy or Deputies shall not affect the Exercise by the Governor General himself of any Power, Authority, or Function.

15. The Command-in-Chief of the Land and Naval Militia, and of all Naval and Military Forces, of and in Canada, is hereby declared to continue and be vested in the Queen.

16. Until the Queen otherwise directs, the Seat of Government of Canada shall be Ottawa.

IV. Legislative Power

17. There shall be One Parliament for Canada, consisting of the Queen, an Upper House styled the Senate, and the House of Commons.

18. The Privileges, Immunities, and Powers to be held, enjoyed, and exercised by the Senate and by the House of Commons and by the Members thereof respectively shall be such as are from Time to Time defined by Act of the Parliament of Canada, but so that the same shall never exceed those at the passing of this Act held, enjoyed, and exercised by the Commons House of Parliament of the United

Kingdom of Great Britain and Ireland and by the Members thereof.

19. The Parliament of Canada shall be called together not later than Six Months after the Union.

20. There shall be a Session of the Parliament of Canada once at least in every Year, so that Twelve Months shall not intervene between the last Sitting of the Parliament in one Session and its first Sitting in the next Session.

Senate

21. The Senate shall, subject to the Provisions of this Act, consist of One Hundred and five Members, who shall be styled Senators.

22. In relation to the Constitution of the Senate, Canada shall be deemed to consist of Three Divisions: 1. Ontario; 2. Quebec; 3. The Maritime Provinces, Nova Scotia and New Brunswick; which Three Divisions shall (subject to the Provisions of this Act) be equally represented in the Senate as follows: Ontario by Twenty-four Senators; Quebec by Twenty-four Senators; and the Maritime Provinces by Twenty-four Senators, Twelve thereof representing Nova Scotia, and Twelve thereof representing New Brunswick.

In the Case of Quebec each of the Twenty-four Senators representing that Province shall be appointed for One of the Twenty-four Electoral Divisions of Lower Canada specified in Schedule A. to Chapter One of the Consolidated Statutes of Canada.

23. The Qualifications of a Senator shall be as follows:

(1) He shall be of the full age of Thirty Years:

(2) He shall be either a natural-born Subject of the Queen, or a Subject of the Queen naturalized by an Act of the Parliament of Great Britain, or of the Parliament of the United Kingdom of Great Britain and Ireland, or of the Legislature of One of the Provinces of Upper Canada, Lower Canada, Canada, Nova Scotia, or New Brunswick, before the Union, or of the Parliament of Canada after the Union:

(3) He shall be legally or equitably seised as of Freehold for his own Use and Benefit of Lands or Tenements held in Free and Common Socage, or seised or possessed for his own Use and Benefit of

Lands or Tenements held in Franc-alleu or in Roture, within the Province for which he is appointed, of the Value of Four thousand Dollars, over and above all Rents, Dues, Debts, Charges, Mortgages, and Incumbrances due or payable out of or charged on or affecting the same:

(4) His Real and Personal Property shall be together worth Four thousand Dollars over and above his Debts and Liabilities:

(5) He shall be resident in the Province for which he is appointed:

(6) In the Case of Quebec he shall have his Real Property Qualification in the Electoral Division for which he is appointed, or shall be resident in that Division.

24. The Governor General shall from Time to Time, in the Queen's Name, by Instrument under the Great Seal of Canada, summon qualified Persons to the Senate; and, subject to the Provisions of this Act, every Person so summoned shall become and be a Member of the Senate and a Senator.

25. Such Persons shall be first summoned to the Senate as the Queen by Warrant under Her Majesty's Royal Sign Manual thinks fit to approve, and their Names shall be inserted in the Queen's Proclamation of Union.

26. If at any Time on the Recommendation of the Governor General the Queen thinks fit to direct that Three or Six Members be added to the Senate, the Governor General may by Summons to Three or Six qualified Persons (as the Case may be), representing equally the Three Divisions of Canada, add to the Senate accordingly.

27. In case of such Addition being at any Time made the Governor General shall not summon any Person to the Senate except on a further like Direction by the Queen on the like Recommendation, until each of the Three Divisions of Canada is represented by Twenty-four Senators and no more.

28. The Number of Senators shall not at any Time exceed Seventy-eight.

29. A Senator shall, subject to the Provisions of this Act, hold his Place in the Senate for Life.

30. A Senator may by Writing under his Hand addressed to the Governor General resign his Place in the Senate, and thereupon the same shall be vacant. …

32. When a Vacancy happens in the Senate by Resignation, Death, or otherwise, the Governor General shall by Summons to a fit and qualified Person fill the Vacancy.

33. If any Question arises respecting the Qualification of a Senator or a Vacancy in the Senate the same shall be heard and determined by the Senate.

34. The Governor General may from Time to Time, by Instrument under the Great Seal of Canada, appoint a Senator to be Speaker of the Senate, and may remove him and appoint another in his Stead.

35. Until the Parliament of Canada otherwise provides, the Presence of at least Fifteen Senators, including the Speaker, shall be necessary to constitute a Meeting of the Senate for the Exercise of its Powers.

36. Questions arising in the Senate shall be decided by a Majority of Voices, and the Speaker shall in all Cases have a Vote, and when the Voices are equal the Decision shall be deemed to be in the Negative.

The House of Commons

37. The House of Commons shall, subject to the Provisions of this Act, consist of one hundred and eighty-one members, of whom Eighty-two shall be elected for Ontario, Sixty-five for Quebec, Nineteen for Nova Scotia, and Fifteen for New Brunswick.

38. The Governor General shall from Time to Time, in the Queen's Name, by Instrument under the Great Seal of Canada, summon and call together the House of Commons.

39. A Senator shall not be capable of being elected or of sitting or voting as a Member of the House of Commons.

40. Until the Parliament of Canada otherwise provides, Ontario, Quebec, Nova Scotia, and New Brunswick shall, for the Purposes of the Election of Members to serve in the House of Commons, be divided into Electoral Districts as follows:

(1) Ontario. Ontario shall be divided into the Counties, Ridings of Counties, Cities, Parts of Cities, and Towns enumerated in the First Schedule to this Act, each whereof shall be an Electoral District, each such District as numbered in that Schedule being entitled to return One Member.

(2) Quebec. Quebec shall be divided into Sixty-five Electoral Districts, composed of the Sixty-five Electoral Divisions into which Lower Canada is at the passing of this Act divided under Chapter Two of the Consolidated Statutes of Canada, Chapter Seventy-five of the Consolidated Statutes for Lower Canada, and the Act of the Province of Canada of the Twenty-third Year of the Queen, Chapter One, or any other Act amending the same in force at the Union, so that each such Electoral Division shall be for the Purposes of this Act an Electoral District entitled to return One Member.

(3) Nova Scotia. Each of the Eighteen Counties of Nova Scotia shall be an Electoral District. The County of Halifax shall be entitled to return Two Members, and each of the other Counties One Member.

(4) New Brunswick. Each of the Fourteen Counties into which New Brunswick is divided, including the City and County of St. John, shall be an Electoral District. The City of St. John shall also be a separate Electoral District. Each of those Fifteen Electoral Districts shall be entitled to return One Member.

41. Until the Parliament of Canada otherwise provides, all Laws in force in the several Provinces at the Union relative to the following Matters or any of them, namely,—the Qualifications and Disqualifications of Persons to be elected or to sit or vote as Members of the House of Assembly or Legislative Assembly in the several Provinces, the Voters at Elections of such Members, the Oaths to be taken by Voters, the Returning Officers, their Powers and Duties, the Proceedings at Elections, the Periods during which Elections may be continued, the Trial of controverted Elections, and Proceedings incident thereto, the vacating of Seats of Members, and the Execution of new Writs in case of Seats vacated otherwise than by Dissolution,—shall respectively apply to Elections of Members to serve in the House of Commons for the same several Provinces. …

43. In case a Vacancy in the Representation in the House of Commons of any Electoral District happens before the Meeting of the Parliament, or after the Meeting of the Parliament before Provision is made by the Parliament in this Behalf, the Provisions of the last foregoing Section of this Act shall extend and apply to the issuing and returning of a Writ in respect of such Vacant District.

44. The House of Commons on its first assembling after a General Election shall proceed with all practicable Speed to elect One of its Members to be Speaker.

45. In case of a Vacancy happening in the Office of Speaker by Death, Resignation, or otherwise, the House of Commons shall with all practicable Speed proceed to elect another of its Members to be Speaker.

46. The Speaker shall preside at all Meetings of the House of Commons.

47. Until the Parliament of Canada otherwise provides, in case of the Absence for any Reason of the Speaker from the Chair of the House of Commons for a Period of Forty-eight consecutive Hours, the House may elect another of its Members to act as Speaker, and the Member so elected shall during the Continuance of such Absence of the Speaker have and execute all the Powers, Privileges, and Duties of Speaker.

48. The Presence of at least Twenty Members of the House of Commons shall be necessary to constitute a Meeting of the House for the Exercise of its Powers, and for that Purpose the Speaker shall be reckoned as a Member.

49. Questions arising in the House of Commons shall be decided by a Majority of Voices other than that of the Speaker, and when the Voices are equal, but not otherwise, the Speaker shall have a Vote.

50. Every House of Commons shall continue for Five Years from the Day of the Return of the Writs for choosing the House (subject to be sooner dissolved by the Governor General), and no longer.

51. On the Completion of the Census in the Year One Thousand eight hundred and seventy-one, and of each subsequent decennial Census, the Representation of the Four Provinces shall be readjusted by such Authority, in such Manner, and from such Time, as the Parliament of Canada from Time to Time provides, subject and according to the following Rules:

(1) Quebec shall have the fixed Number of Sixty-five Members:

(2) There shall be assigned to each of the other Provinces such a Number of Members as will bear

the same Proportion to the Number of its Population (ascertained at such Census) as the Number Sixty-five bears to the Number of the Population of Quebec (so ascertained):

(3) In the Computation of the Number of Members for a Province a fractional Part not exceeding One Half of the whole Number requisite for entitling the Province to a Member shall be disregarded; but a fractional Part exceeding One Half of that Number shall be equivalent to the whole Number:

(4) On any such Re-adjustment the Number of Members for a Province shall not be reduced unless the Proportion which the Number of the Population of the Province bore to the Number of the aggregate Population of Canada at the then last preceding Re-adjustment of the Number of Members for the Province is ascertained at the then latest Census to be diminished by One Twentieth Part or upwards:

(5) Such Re-adjustment shall not take effect until the Termination of the then existing Parliament.

52. The Number of Members of the House of Commons may be from Time to Time increased by the Parliament of Canada, provided the proportionate Representation of the Provinces prescribed by this Act is not thereby disturbed....

VI. Distribution of Legislative Powers
Powers of the Parliament

91. It shall be lawful for the Queen, by and with the Advice and Consent of the Senate and House of Commons, to make Laws for the Peace, Order, and good Government of Canada, in relation to all Matters not coming within the Classes of Subjects by this Act assigned exclusively to the Legislatures of the Provinces; and for greater Certainty, but not so as to restrict the Generality of the foregoing Terms of this Section, it is hereby declared that (notwithstanding anything in this Act) the exclusive Legislative Authority of the Parliament of Canada extends to all Matters coming within the Classes of Subjects next hereinafter enumerated; that is to say,

1. The Public Debt and Property.
2. The Regulation of Trade and Commerce.
3. The raising of Money by any Mode or System of Taxation.
4. The borrowing of Money on the Public Credit.
5. Postal Service.
6. The Census and Statistics.
7. Militia, Military and Naval Service, and Defence.
8. The fixing of and providing for the Salaries and Allowances of Civil and other Officers of the Government of Canada.
9. Beacons, Buoys, Lighthouses, and Sable Island.
10. Navigation and Shipping.
11. Quarantine and the Establishment and Maintenance of Marine Hospitals.
12. Sea Coast and Inland Fisheries.
13. Ferries between a Province and any British or Foreign Country or between Two Provinces.
14. Currency and Coinage.
15. Issue of Paper Money.
16. Savings Banks.
17. Weights and Measures.
18. Bills of Exchange and Promissory Notes.
19. Interest.
20. Legal Tender.
21. Bankruptcy and Insolvency.
22. Patents of Invention and Discovery.
23. Copyrights.
24. Indians, and Lands reserved for the Indians.
25. Naturalization and Aliens.
26. Marriage and Divorce.
27. The Criminal Law, except the Constitution of Courts of Criminal Jurisdiction, but including the Procedure in Criminal Matters.
28. The Establishment, Maintenance, and Management of Penitentiaries.
29. Such Classes of Subjects as are expressly excepted in the Enumeration of the Classes of Subjects by this Act assigned exclusively to the Legislatures of the Provinces.

And any Matter coming within any of the Classes of Subjects enumerated in this Section shall not be deemed to come within the Class of Matters of a local or private Nature comprised in the Enumeration of the Classes of Subjects by this Act assigned exclusively to the Legislatures of the Provinces.

Exclusive Powers of Provincial Legislatures

92. In each Province the Legislature may exclusively make Laws in relation to Matters coming within the Classes of Subjects next hereinafter enumerated; that is to say,

1. The Amendment from Time to Time, notwithstanding anything in this Act, of the Constitution of the Province, except as regards the Office of Lieutenant Governor.

2. Direct Taxation within the Province in order to the raising of a Revenue for Provincial Purposes.

3. The borrowing of Money on the sole Credit of the Province

4. The Establishment and Tenure of Provincial Offices and the Appointment and Payment of Provincial Officers.

5. The Management and Sale of the Public Lands belonging to the Province and of the Timber and Wood thereon.

6. The Establishment, Maintenance, and Management of Public and Reformatory Prisons in and for the Province.

7. The Establishment, Maintenance, and Management of Hospitals, Asylums, Charities, and Eleemosynary Institutions in and for the Province, other than Marine Hospitals.

8. Municipal Institutions in the Province.

9. Shop, Saloon, Tavern, Auctioneer, and other Licences in order to the raising of a Revenue for Provincial, Local, or Municipal Purposes.

10. Local Works and Undertakings other than such as are of the following Classes:

a) Lines of Steam or other Ships, Railways, Canals, Telegraphs, and other Works and Undertakings connecting the Province with any other or others of the Provinces, or extending beyond the Limits of the Province:

(b) Lines of Steam Ships between the Province and any British or Foreign Country:

(c) Such Works as, although wholly situate within the Province, are before or after their Execution declared by the Parliament of Canada to be for the general Advantage of Canada or for the Advantage of Two or more of the Provinces.

11. The Incorporation of Companies with Provincial Objects.

12. The Solemnization of Marriage in the Province.

13. Property and Civil Rights in the Province.

14. The Administration of Justice in the Province, including the Constitution, Maintenance, and Organization of Provincial Courts, both of Civil and of Criminal Jurisdiction, and including Procedure in Civil Matters in those Courts.

15. The Imposition of Punishment by Fine, Penalty, or Imprisonment for enforcing any Law of the Province made in relation to any Matter coming within any of the Classes of Subjects enumerated in this Section.

16. Generally all Matters of a merely local or private Nature in the Province.

Education

93. In and for each Province the Legislature may exclusively make Laws in relation to Education, subject and according to the following Provisions:

(1) Nothing in any such Law shall prejudicially affect any Right or Privilege with respect to Denominational Schools which any Class of Persons have by Law in the Province at the Union:

(2) All the Powers, Privileges, and Duties at the Union by Law conferred and imposed in Upper Canada on the Separate Schools and School Trustees of the Queen's Roman Catholic Subjects shall be and the same are hereby extended to the Dissentient Schools of the Queen's Protestant and Roman Catholic Subjects in Quebec:

(3) Where in any Province a System of Separate or Dissentient Schools exists by Law at the Union or is thereafter established by the Legislature of the Province, an Appeal shall lie to the Governor General in Council from any Act or Decision of any Provincial Authority affecting any Right or Privilege of the Protestant or Roman Catholic Minority of the Queen's Subjects in relation to Education:

(4) In case any such Provincial Law as from Time to Time seems to the Governor General in Council requisite for the due Execution of the Provisions of this Section is not made, or in case any Decision of the Governor General in Council on any Appeal under this Section is not duly executed by the proper Provincial Authority in that Behalf, then and in every such Case, and as far only as the Circumstances of each Case require, the Parliament of Canada may make remedial Laws for the due Execution of the Provisions of this Section and of any Decision of the Governor General in Council under this Section....

IX. Miscellaneous Provisions
General

...

128. Every Member of the Senate or House of Commons of Canada shall before taking his Seat therein take and subscribe before the Governor General or some Person authorized by him, and every Member of a Legislative Council or Legislative Assembly of any Province shall before taking his Seat therein take and subscribe before the Lieutenant Governor of the Province or some Person authorized by him, the Oath of Allegiance contained in the Fifth Schedule to this Act; and every Member of the Senate of Canada and every Member of the Legislative Council of Quebec shall also, before taking his Seat therein, take and subscribe before the Governor General, or some Person authorized by him, the Declaration of Qualification contained in the same Schedule.

129. Except as otherwise provided by this Act, all Laws in force in Canada, Nova Scotia, or New Brunswick at the Union, and all Courts of Civil and Criminal Jurisdiction, and all legal Commissions, Powers, and Authorities, and all Officers, Judicial, Administrative, and Ministerial, existing therein at the Union, shall continue in Ontario, Quebec, Nova Scotia, and New Brunswick respectively, as if the Union had not been made; subject nevertheless (except with respect to such as are enacted by or exist under Acts of the Parliament of Great Britain or of the Parliament of the United Kingdom of Great Britain and Ireland), to be repealed, abolished, or altered by the Parliament of Canada, or by the Legislature of the respective Province, according to the Authority of the Parliament or of that Legislature under this Act.

130. Until the Parliament of Canada otherwise provides, all Officers of the several Provinces having Duties to discharge in relation to Matters other than those coming within the Classes of Subjects by this Act assigned exclusively to the Legislatures of the Provinces shall be Officers of Canada, and shall continue to discharge the Duties of their respective Offices under the same Liabilities, Responsibilities, and Penalties as if the Union had not been made.

131. Until the Parliament of Canada otherwise provides, the Governor General in Council may from Time to Time appoint such Officers as the Governor General in Council deems necessary or proper for the effectual Execution of this Act.

132. The Parliament and Government of Canada shall have all Powers necessary or proper for performing the Obligations of Canada or of any Province thereof, as Part of the British Empire, towards Foreign Countries, arising under Treaties between the Empire and such Foreign Countries.

133. Either the English or the French Language may be used by any Person in the Debates of the Houses of the Parliament of Canada and of the Houses of the Legislature of Quebec; and both those Languages shall be used in the respective Records and Journals of those Houses; and either of those Languages may be used by any Person or in any Pleading or Process in or issuing from any Court of Canada established under this Act, and in or from all or any of the Courts of Quebec.

The Acts of the Parliament of Canada and of the Legislature of Quebec shall be printed and published in both those Languages....

XI. Admission of Other Colonies

146. It shall be lawful for the Queen, by and with the Advice of Her Majesty's Most Honourable Privy Council, on Addresses from the Houses of the Parliament of Canada, and from the Houses of the respective Legislatures of the Colonies or Provinces of Newfoundland, Prince Edward Island, and British Columbia, to admit those Colonies or Provinces, or any of them, into the Union, and on Address from the Houses of the Parliament of Canada to admit Rupert's Land and the North-western Territory, or either of them, into the Union, on such Terms and Conditions in each Case as are in the Addresses expressed and as the Queen thinks fit to approve, subject to the Provisions of this Act; and the Provisions of any Order in Council in that Behalf shall have effect as if they had been enacted by the Parliament of the United Kingdom of Great Britain and Ireland.

147. In case of the Admission of Newfoundland and Prince Edward Island, or either of them, each shall be entitled to a Representation in the Senate

of Canada of Four Members, and (notwithstanding anything in this Act) in case of the Admission of Newfoundland the normal Number of Senators shall be Seventy-six and their maximum Number shall be Eighty-two; but Prince Edward Island when admitted shall be deemed to be comprised in the third of the Three Divisions into which Canada is, in relation to the Constitution of the Senate, divided by this Act, and accordingly, after the Admission of Prince Edward Island, whether Newfoundland is admitted or not, the Representation of Nova Scotia and New Brunswick in the Senate shall, as Vacancies occur, be reduced from Twelve to Ten Members respectively, and the Representation of each of those Provinces shall not be increased at any Time beyond Ten, except under the Provisions of this Act for the Appointment of Three or Six additional Senators under the Direction of the Queen.

GLOSSARY

Lords Spiritual and Temporal, and Commons: members of Parliament. At the time of the act, the lords spiritual were bishops and the lords temporal were members of the hereditary peerage; they comprised the House of Lords. "Commons," representatives of the towns and cities, sat in the House of Commons, as they do today.

Ridings: electoral districts in Canada

Royal Sign Manual: the queen's handwritten signature

Sable Island: a sparsely populated island off Nova Scotia; protected under the Canada Shipping Act

Document Analysis

The British North America Act of 1867 begins with a preamble in which the Province of Canada, New Brunswick, and Nova Scotia propose to form a united Dominion of Canada. Under the article titled "Union," the act specifies the provinces that shall make up the Dominion of Canada and notes that what formerly had been called Upper Canada and Lower Canada, joined by the Act of Union of 1840, were now severed into the provinces of Ontario and Quebec. The preamble also states that the dominion would have a constitution "similar in Principle to that of the United Kingdom." This was an important phrase, for in the ensuing decades it established a constitutional basis for Canadians to enjoy the same civil rights that citizens of the United Kingdom enjoyed. Throughout the Constitution Act, civil rights are implied, but they are not expressly stated in passages that would be analogous to the Bill of Rights of the U.S. Constitution. Canadians eventually made civil rights more explicit in the Canadian Charter of Rights and Freedoms, signed into law by England's Queen Elizabeth II in 1982.

The chief feature of Article III, "Executive Power," is that it vests executive authority over Canada in the monarch of England—at the time, Queen Victoria. Canada would have a governor general appointed by the queen, along with the queen's privy council, whose members would advise the governor general. A privy council is roughly equivalent to a cabinet, but the word *privy* implies that the deliberations and advice of this body of close advisers are secret or private. This section of the act vests the authority to appoint advisers with the queen. It also notes that the queen remains the commander in chief of the armed forces. In sum, the Constitution Act by no means represented a complete severance from Great Britain. Canada would occupy a middle ground between complete independence and membership in the British Commonwealth, with the monarch as its head of state.

Perhaps the core of the Constitution Act is that portion that deals with legislative authority. The act proposes a single parliament whose powers cannot exceed those of the British Parliament. The parliament would consist of a senate and a house of commons, and the act specifies the number of representatives each province would have as well as qualifications for becoming a senator. Interestingly, a number of these qualifications have to do with the prospective senator's finances. To be eligible, a prospective senator must be "seised as of Freehold," which means simply that he has to own property. "Socage" refers to agricultural lands. Alternatively, he could occupy lands in "Franc-alleu," a rare form of property ownership that is free of any kind of mortgage, tax, or any other obligation (the English equivalent is called allodial lands), or he could occupy lands in "Roture," which in French-Canadian law means essentially that a person can discharge duties to the owner of the land by payment of rent (as opposed to providing services, as would have been the case under feudalism in the Middle Ages). A prospective senator also had to have a net worth (assets minus debts) of at least $4,000, a significant sum of money in 1867. This provision was seen to lessen the likelihood that a senator would use his position for financial gain out of desperation or be subject to bribery from special interests. This article goes on to specify the details pertaining to increasing or decreasing the number of senators and to replacing senators in the case of a vacancy. It also provides for the formation of electoral districts. It should be noted that senators were to be appointed, not elected, and the tenure of a senator was for life; thus, the Canadian Senate was conceived as analogous to the British House of Lords, an upper chamber of men of means who would provide continuity in legislative government and who, presumably, could vote without regard to short-term political considerations.

The House of Commons was the lower chamber of representatives elected by males who were twenty-one years old or older. This portion of the act specifies in detail such matters as voting, the election of a speaker, and the like. It further specifies the number of elected representatives in the House of Commons and details procedures to be followed for increasing the number of representatives, presumably as the population of Canada grew. One interesting feature is that the representation of Quebec would be used as a fixed reference point. The number of representatives in that province is fixed at sixty-five; this number would not change. In each of the other provinces, the number of its representatives would bear the same proportion to its population as Quebec's sixty-five bore to its population. The House of Commons would sit for a five-year period. The requirement that a period of no more than a year pass between the closing of one session of the legislature and the opening of another was designed to help ensure the civil rights of Canadians. It eliminated the possibility that the monarch simply would not convene the legislature, as British monarchs had done in the past when they expected opposition from the people's representatives. Later, in section 128, the act specifies that members of the legislature must take an oath of allegiance.

Article VI, "Distribution of Legislative Powers," is quite particular in delineating the powers of the national, or federal, parliament and the parliaments of the individual provinces. Thus, for example, the national parliament was to have authority over the public debt, regulation of trade and commerce, borrowing, the postal system, the navigation system, coinage, and copyright law. The legislatures of the individual provinces were to have authority over direct taxation to raise revenue for provincial purposes. Later, section 102 specifies the division of revenues between the provinces and the federal government. In this sense, Canada was to operate in a manner similar to the United States at the time. Until the ratification of the Sixteenth Amendment to the U.S. Constitution in 1913, the federal government raised money from the states through indirect taxation; money was collected in the states and then paid by each state to the federal government. The Sixteenth Amendment imposed a system of direct income taxation whereby citizens pay tax directly to the federal government. The Constitution Act elsewhere specifies the amount of money each province was to pay to the federal government to fund its operations, but individual provinces could directly tax their citizens to raise revenues for provincial purposes. Additionally, the provincial governments were given authority over such matters as prisons, licenses, incorporation of businesses, marriage, and management of public lands and their timber in the provinces.

The section titled "Education" is a good example of the inclusion of civil rights by implication. The act turns education over to the provinces. However, it also asserts that "Nothing in any such Law shall prejudicially affect any Right or Privilege with respect to Denominational Schools." The act goes on to say that all the Powers, Privileges, and Duties at the Union by Law conferred and imposed in Upper Canada on the Separate Schools and School Trustees of the Queen's Roman Catholic Subjects shall be and the same are hereby extended to the Dissentient Schools of the Queen's Protestant and Roman Catholic Subjects in Quebec.

Thus, the Constitution Act recognized the religious tension that existed between the largely Catholic French-speaking people of Quebec and the largely Anglican English-speaking people of the other provinces.

The Constitution Act protects the civil rights of both populations. Later, section 133 notes that either English or French could be used in the legislature and records were to be kept in both languages. To this day, the principal—and official—language of Quebec is French, and Canada is officially a bilingual nation. Buyers of products made or traded in Canada will note that labels, owner's manuals, and the like are all printed in both French and English. This recognition of Quebec as in some sense unique, enjoying what its people call *statut particulier*, or "special status," in the Canadian body politic, has been a source of tension in that nation. As recently as 1995 the people of Quebec voted on whether to become a separate, sovereign nation. The bill was defeated by a margin of just 1 percent, but a majority of French speakers (about 79 percent of Quebec's population) voted in favor of the proposal.

Essential Themes

A number of factors influenced Canadians in their quest for greater unity and autonomy. One of the chief factors was political deadlock and a perceived need to reform the political structure of Canada. But various outside pressures played a role, too. One of these pressures was economic, the result of the United States' cancellation of its free-trade agreement with the Canadian provinces in 1865, partly because of Canadian unwillingness to back the Union in the Civil War; indeed, the Confederate "Gray Underground" freely conducted espionage operations in the North out of Canada during the war. The flight of many American slaves to Canada via the Underground Railroad also contributed to Canadians' sense that the provinces had to unite and firm up their borders. The U.S. doctrine of Manifest Destiny—the notion that expansion of the United States westward to the Pacific Ocean was inevitable— left many citizens in the provinces fearful of U.S. interference in their affairs. Additionally, the Fenian raids, conducted by the Irish Fenian Brotherhood, spilled over from the United States into Canada. These were raids conducted by Irish nationalists to pressure the British government into withdrawing from Ireland. These raids, in conjunction with Britain's expressed unwillingness to maintain troops in its colonies anymore, led to the growth of Canadian nationalism and the passage of the Constitution Act of 1867.

The Constitution Act was the final step in a century-long process of unifying Britain's remaining North American colonies into an autonomous, self-governing nation. Over the course of the next century, numerous acts titled British North America Act, each with a date appended, continued the process of settling Canada's relationship with Great Britain and of amending the original act.

While each gave the Canadian provinces more autonomy, Canada did not become entirely independent as a result of any of them. Great Britain retained authority over foreign policy, and the Judicial Committee of the Privy Council in England remained Canada's highest appeals court. Further, the act could be amended only by the action of the British Parliament. Nevertheless, over the ensuing decades Canada became more and more autonomous, and in 1931 the British Parliament passed the Statute of Westminster, which established full legislative equality between the British Parliament and the parliaments of the nations of the British Commonwealth, including Canada. (The others were Australia, New Zealand, Newfoundland, the Union of South Africa, and the Irish Free State.) The process was completed with the Canada Act of 1892, which patriated the Constitution Act of 1867 and subsequent acts, turning them over to Canada. The process of Canadian separation from Great Britain was complete, with the exception that the monarch of England remains Canada's ceremonial head of state.

In the years following passage of the Constitution Act, the Dominion of Canada grew, eventually extending across North America from the Atlantic to the Pacific Ocean. Manitoba and the Northwest Territories joined the confederation in 1870, British Columbia in 1871, Prince Edward Island in 1873, and the Yukon Territory in 1898. In the twentieth century, Saskatchewan and Alberta joined in 1905 and Newfoundland in 1949. The latest addition to the Canadian confederation was Nunavut, in 1999. With a land area of 3.85 million square miles, Canada is the world's second-largest country in area (following Russia) and is home to some 33 million people.

——Michael J. O'Neal, PhD

Bibliography and Further Reading

Conrad, Margaret, and Alvin Finkel. *Canada: A National History*. Toronto, Canada: Longman, 2003.

Francis, R. Douglas, and Donald B. Smith, eds. *Readings in Canadian History*, 2 vols., 5th ed. Toronto, Canada: Harcourt Brace Canada, 1998.

Hallowell, Gerald. *The Oxford Companion to Canadian History*. Don Mills, Ontario, Canada: Oxford University Press, 2004.

Morton, Desmond. *A Short History of Canada*, 5th ed. Toronto, Canada: McClelland and Stewart, 2001.

Taylor, M. Brook. *Canadian History: A Reader's Guide*. Vol. 1: *Beginnings to Confederation*. Toronto, Canada: University of Toronto Press, 1994.

Taylor, M. Brook, and Doug Owram. *Canadian History: A Reader's Guide*. Vol. 2: *Confederation to the Present*. Toronto, Canada: University of Toronto Press, 1994.

Web Sites

"Constitutional History." *Canada in the Making*. https://web.archive.org/web/ 20150317073736/http://www.canadiana.ca/citm/themes/constitution1_e.html [accessed February 6, 2017].

■ Meiji Constitution of Japan

Date: 1889
Author: Ito Hirobumi et al
Genre: Constitution

Summary Overview

Towns across Japan celebrated with fireworks and feasts when Emperor Meiji promulgated the Meiji Constitution of Japan, the country's first constitution, on February 11, 1889, while journalists around the globe recorded the popular joy. The exuberance was prompted as much by the constitution's symbolism as by its contents. The result of a decade of preparation, the Meiji Constitution of Japan represented an era of modernization, when Japan had moved quickly from pre-modern authoritarianism to monarchical constitutionalism, from the clip-clops of horse travel to the clickety-clack of rickshaws and the roar of trains. With the emperor's pronouncement, Japan became the first Asian nation to operate under a modern, democratic constitution.

Threatened by Western imperialism, the early Meiji leaders had set out to create a strong state—and to convince foreign powers that they had done so. On the one hand, they saw movement toward constitutionalism as essential to their efforts to revise unequal treaties that since the 1850s had deprived Japan of tariff autonomy and restricted its ability to try foreign residents in Japanese courts. Without a constitutional system, Japanese foreign diplomats maintained, treaty revision was unthinkable. On the other hand, Meiji leaders were convinced that without respect as a modern state Japan never would be taken seriously in imperialist circles. The constitution thus was proclaimed to the world as ultimate proof that Japan had become a modern state.

To intellectuals, the constitution was intended to demonstrate modernity and to prove the government's seriousness about instituting the rule of law and including a popular voice in governance. For the general populace, many of whom had been apathetic about the constitutional process, it was intended to stimulate loyalty to the state and expand engagement in public processes. While the campaign to engage the populace in promulgation festivities was quite successful, many observers found townspeople more interested in watching fireworks and consuming alcohol than in what the constitution said.

Among constitutions of the nineteenth century this document took a center-right approach, balancing imperial sovereignty with the elective powers of the people. The Meiji Constitution made the rule of law foundational; gave citizens limited freedom of speech, property, and religion; granted the legislature veto power over budgets; and set up an independent judiciary. At the same time, it created a powerful executive branch that was aloof from the legislature and placed final power for almost everything in the emperor. The Meiji Constitution would serve as the country's fundamental law until 1947, when the Showa Constitution replaced it following Japan's defeat in the Second World War.

Defining Moment

The Meiji Constitution was the culmination of two generations of national transformation in Japan. The changes had begun in earnest in 1854, when the ruling Tokugawa shogunate signed the Kanagawa Treaty with U.S. Commodore Matthew Perry, ending two centuries of Japanese isolation from most Western nations by opening two ports to American ships and providing for an American consulate in Japan. Four years later the 1858 Harris Treaty opened four more ports and initiated trade. Although the treaties were criticized by the Japanese as "unequal" because of the tariff and legal restrictions that they imposed on the country, they played an important role in bringing Japan into the global trade and diplomatic system.

Tokugawa officials put a great deal of energy into managing successful relations with the Western nations after Perry's incursion, but their rule was plagued by a spiraling set of problems: cumbersome administrative structures, serious financial crises, and rising opposition from a number of regional lords. Tradition-bound officials also found it difficult to conceive of the new approaches to governance that were demanded by the imperialist threat. As a result, when an ad hoc group of samurai staged an uprising—called the Meiji Restoration—in January 1868, the Tokugawa quickly fell. The coup leaders' youngest member was the twenty-seven-year-old Ito Hirobumi from the southwestern domain

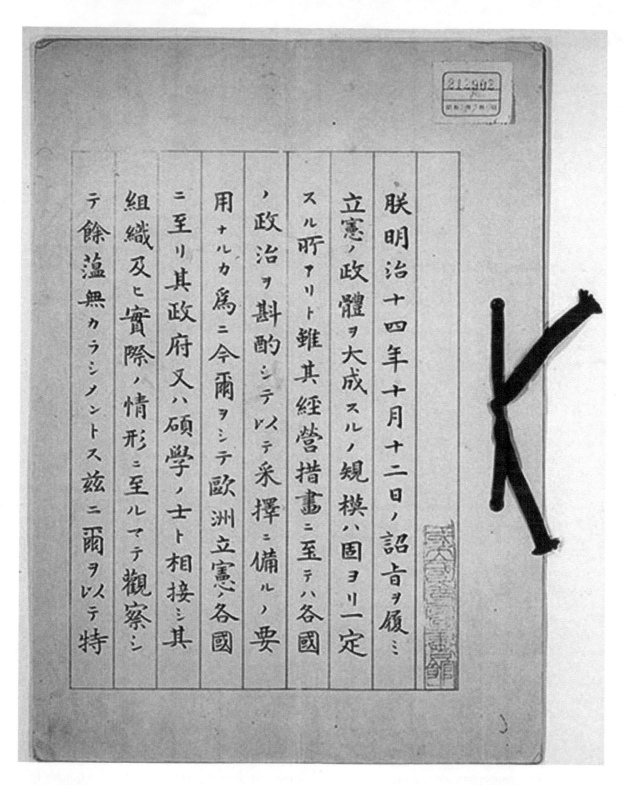

Imperial Order to Dispatch Mission Head Plenipotentiary Ito to Europe. (*commons.wikimedia.org*)
[*Public Domain*]

of Choshu. They quickly set out to move the nation in new directions. Acting in the name of the teenaged Emperor Meiji (whose birth name was Mutsuhito) but with little of his input, they moved the emperor from his ancient Kyoto palace to Edo (today's Tokyo), announced their determination to broaden the base of government, and set out to make Japan an international power.

Within a generation, change had forced its way into every mountain valley and urban alley of Japan. Modern prefectures replaced feudal daimyo domains. Japanese silks were being produced for Europe's trade centers. The world's first nationwide compulsory education system was adopted, along with a military draft and a standardized land-tax system. City streets displayed newspaper offices, brick buildings, beer halls, and a twelve-story tourist tower in Tokyo replete with an elevator and foreign gift shops. And officials worked endlessly on creating a government structure that would help them centralize power and make Japan strong. They also began talking, almost from the first, about the need for a constitutional system of government, partly to enable Japan to emulate Western political systems and partly to satisfy domestic critics.

Two events sped up the movement toward constitutionalism. In 1874 several men who had left the Meiji government in a dispute over policies submitted a petition to the throne, recommending the creation of a national legislature, on the ground that those who were taxed deserved a say in how the state used their tax money. The memorial sparked Japan's first newspaper editorial debates, with writers on all sides calling for the creation of a national assembly but arguing over the assembly's makeup and the kind of constitution needed to make an assembly government effective. Those debates inspired a "freedom and popular rights" movement that involved thousands of petitioners and speakers who demanded a voice in government. The second event was a corruption crisis in 1881, prompted by the secret sale of public properties to government insiders. When the press learned of the sale, uproar ensued, with critics complaining loudly that without a constitution or legislature they had no way to make officials accountable. To quiet the uproar, the emperor announced in October that a constitution would be drafted and a legislature would be convened by 1890.

Beginning in 1881, officials devoted themselves for seven years to laying the groundwork for constitutional governance. When Japan's first political parties emerged in response to the promise of a legislature, officials encouraged the formation of a pro-government counterpart. In 1882, Ito Hirobumi, who had been given responsibility for drafting the constitution, left on a trip to Europe, where he would spend more than a year studying governing systems, primarily in Germany and Austria. Upon his return, he worked with several advisers to develop a document that would make the emperor supreme yet provide a modicum of popular political input. In preparation for constitutional government, officials created a peerage (1884) that was designed as a pool for the upper house of a bicameral legislature, initiated a cabinet (1885) that would stand between the emperor and the legislature (with Ito as the first prime minister), and formed a civil service system (1887). They also enacted laws regulating speech and publication in a sometimes draconian effort to assure public tranquility under constitutional rule. Once the constitutional draft was completed in April 1888, forty-four secret discussion sessions of the Privy Council, a small body created in 1888 to advise the emperor, allowed cabinet members and a few other top officials to suggest changes. A draft then was approved, and the constitution was promulgated on February 11, 1889.

During the weeks before the big day, officials spread the word that the whole country should celebrate with festivals, sake drinking, and time off work. On the morning of the ceremony, Emperor Meiji dressed first in ancient court robes to secretly inform his departed ancestors of what was happening and then changed into Western military attire to issue the constitution in a new palace before an audience that included many Americans and Europeans. The empress wore a rose-colored gown and a diamond-studded crown in the European fashion. The aim of the ceremony—and of the document itself—was to convince both the Japanese public and the leaders of the imperial powers that Japan had become a powerful, "civilized" nation.

Author Biography

The Meiji Constitution was drafted by a team led by the politician and future prime minister Ito Hirobumi. Although he was only forty, Ito was already highly experienced in national affairs when the imperial edict was issued in 1881. Studies in England before the Meiji Restoration had convinced him that Japan must modernize along Western lines. They also had given him the expertise to earn appointment as the overseer of foreign affairs in the new Meiji government. By the end of the

1870s, after taking a series of top-level posts in a variety of governmental divisions, he generally was regarded as one of the country's two or three most powerful men, an intimate of the Meiji Emperor, equally at home with foreign affairs and domestic administration.

To draft the constitution, Ito chose a team of men even younger than he: his protégé Ito Miyoji, who was twenty-four when the edict was issued; Inoue Kowashi, age thirty-seven, who had studied European constitutions in the 1870s; and Kaneko Kentaro, age twenty-eight, who had studied law at Harvard University. Youth did not make these men liberal, however. All of them had a strong traditionalist bent, and all were determined to create a strong, emperor-centered state.

Assisting the constitutional team were several German scholars, foremost among them Hermann Roesler, a former professor at the University of Rostock. Brought to Japan as part of a broader government policy of hiring foreigners to give advice on modernizing the country, he had been giving legal advice to the foreign ministry since 1878. Roesler took part in all of the constitutional drafting discussions and played a key role in the decision to create a "social monarchy" that placed the emperor at the center but balanced his authority by ensuring the rights of citizens through elections and the rule of law. The Emperor Meiji attended all of the review sessions once the initial draft was completed, but as in other governmental matters, he had little impact on the content.

HISTORICAL DOCUMENT

Having, by virtue of the glories of Our Ancestors, ascended the throne of a lineal succession unbroken for ages eternal; desiring to promote the welfare of, and to give development to the moral and intellectual faculties of Our beloved subjects, the very same that have been favoured with the benevolent care and affectionate vigilance of Our Ancestors; and hoping to maintain the prosperity of the State, in concert with Our people and with their support, We hereby promulgate, in pursuance of Our Imperial Rescript of the 14th day of the 10th month of the 14th year of Meiji, a fundamental law of State, to exhibit the principles, by which We are to be guided in Our conduct, and to point out to what Our descendants and Our subjects and their descendants are forever to conform.

The rights of sovereignty of the State, We have inherited from Our Ancestors, and We shall bequeath them to Our descendants. Neither We nor they shall in future fail to wield them, in accordance with the provisions of the Constitution hereby granted.

We now declare to respect and protect the security of the rights and of the property of Our people, and to secure to them the complete enjoyment of the same, within the extent of the provision of the present Constitution and of the law.

The Imperial Diet shall first be convoked for the 23rd year of Meiji, and the time of its opening shall be the date, when the present Constitution comes into force.

When in the future it may become necessary to amend any of the provision of the present Constitution, We or Our successors shall assume the initiative right, and submit a project for the same to the Imperial Diet. The Imperial Diet shall pass its vote upon it, according to the condition imposed by the present Constitution, and in no otherwise shall Our descendants or Our subjects be permitted to attempt any alteration thereof.

Our Ministers of State, on Our behalf, shall be held responsible for the carrying out of the present Constitution, and Our present and future subjects shall forever assume the duty of allegiance to the present Constitution.

[His Imperial Majesty's Sign-Manual.]

[Privy Seal.]

The 11th day of the 2nd month of the 22nd year of Meiji. …

Chapter I: The Emperor
Article I

The Empire of Japan shall be reigned over (and governed) by a line of Emperors unbroken for ages eternal.

Article II

The Imperial Throne shall be succeeded to by Imperial male descendants, according to the provision of the Imperial House Law.

Article III

The Emperor is sacred and inviolable.

Article IV

The Emperor is the head of the Empire, combining in himself the rights of sovereignty, and exercises them, according to the provision of the present Constitution.

Article V

The Emperor exercises the legislative power with the consent of the Imperial Diet.

Article VI

The Emperor gives sanction to laws, and orders them to be promulgated and executed.

Article VII

The Emperor convokes the Imperial Diet, opens, closes, and prorogues it, and dissolves the House of Representatives.

Article VIII

The Emperor, in consequence of an urgent necessity to maintain public safety or to avert public calamities, issues, when the Imperial Diet is not sitting, Imperial Ordinances in the place of law.

Such Imperial Ordinances are to be laid before the Imperial Diet at its next session, and when the Diet does not approve the said Ordinance, the Government shall declare them to be invalid for the future.

Article IX

The Emperor issues, or causes to be issued, the Ordinances necessary for the carrying out of the laws, or for the maintenance of the public peace and order, and for the promotion of the welfare of the subjects. But no Ordinance shall in any way alter any of the existing laws.

Article X

The Emperor determines the organization of the different branches of the administration, and the salaries of all civil and military officers, and appoints and dismisses the same. Exceptions especially provided for in the present Constitution or in other laws, shall be in accordance with the respective provisions (bearing thereon).

Article XI

The Emperor has the supreme command of the Army and Navy.

Article XII

The Emperor determines the organization and peace standing of the Army and Navy.

Article XIII

The Emperor declares war, makes peace, and concludes treaties.

Article XIV

The Emperor proclaims the law of siege.

The conditions and effects of the law of siege shall be determined by law.

Article XV

The Emperor confers titles of nobility, rank, orders, and other marks of honor.

Article XVI

The Emperor orders amnesty, pardon, commutation of punishment, and rehabilitation.

Article XVII

A Regency shall be instituted in conformity with the provisions of the Imperial House Law.

The Regent shall exercise the powers appertaining to the Emperor in His name.

Chapter II: Rights and Duties of Subjects
Article XVIII

The condition necessary for being a Japanese subject shall be determined by law.

Article XIX

Japanese subjects may, according to qualifications determined in law or ordinances, be appointed to civil or military offices equally, and may fill any other public offices.

Article XX

Japanese subjects are amenable to service in the Army or Navy, according to the provisions of law.

Article XXI

Japanese subjects are amenable to the duty of paying taxes, according to the provision of law.

Article XXII

Japanese subjects shall have the liberty of abode and of changing the same within the limits of law.

Article XXIII

No Japanese subjects shall be arrested, detained, tried, or punished, unless according to law.

Article XXIV

No Japanese subject shall be deprived of his right of being tried by the judges determined by law.

Article XXV

Except in the cases provided for in the law, the house of no Japanese subject shall be entered or searched without his consent.

Article XXVI

Except in the cases mentioned in the law, the secrecy of the letters of every Japanese subject shall remain inviolate.

Article XXVII

The right of property of every Japanese subject shall remain inviolate.
  Measures necessary to be taken for the public benefit shall be provided for by law.

Article XXVIII

Japanese subjects shall, within limits not prejudicial to peace and order, and not antagonistic to their duties as subjects, enjoy freedom of religious belief.

Article XXIX

Japanese subjects shall, within the limits of law, enjoy the liberty of speech, writing, publication, public meetings, and associations.

Article XXX

Japanese subjects may present petitions, by observing the proper forms of respect, and by complying with the rules specially provided for the same.

Article XXXI

The provisions contained in the present Chapter shall not affect the exercise of the power appertaining to the Emperor, in times of war or in cases of a national emergency.

Article XXXII

Each and every one of the provisions contained in the preceding Articles of the present Chapter, that are not in conflict with the laws or the rules and discipline of the Army and Navy, shall apply to the officers and men of the Army and of the Navy.

Chapter III: The Imperial Diet
Article XXXIII

The Imperial Diet shall consist of two Houses, a House of Peers and a House of Representatives.

Article XXXIV

The House of Peers shall, in accordance with the Ordinance concerning the House of Peers, be composed of the members of the Imperial Family, of the orders of nobility, and of those persons who have been nominated thereto by the Emperor.

Article XXXV

The House of Representatives shall be composed of Members elected by the people, according to the provisions of the Law of Election.

Article XXXVI

No one can at one and the same time be a member of both Houses.

Article XXXVII

Every law requires the consent of the Imperial Diet.

Article XXXVIII

Both Houses shall vote upon projects of law submitted to it by the Government, and may respectively initiate projects of law.

Article XXXIX

A Bill, which has been rejected by either the one or the other of the two houses, shall not be again brought in during the same session.

Article XL

Both Houses can make representations to the Government, as to laws or upon any other subject. When, however, such representations are not accepted, they cannot be made a second time during the same session.

Article XLI

The Imperial Diet shall be convoked every year.

Article XLII

A session of the Imperial Diet shall last during three months. In case of necessity, the duration of a session may be prolonged by Imperial Order.

Article XLIII

When urgent necessity arises, an extraordinary session may be convoked, in addition to the ordinary one.

The duration of an extraordinary session shall be determined by Imperial Order.

Article XLIV

The opening, closing, prolongation of session, and prorogation of the Imperial Diet, shall be effected simultaneously for both houses.

In case the House of Representatives has been ordered to dissolve, the House of Peers shall at the same time be prorogued.

Article XLV

When the House of Representatives has been ordered to dissolve, Members shall be caused by Imperial Order to be newly elected, and the new House shall be convoked within five months from the day of dissolution.

Article XLVI

No debate can be opened and no vote can be taken in either House of the Imperial Diet, unless not less than one-third of the whole number of the members thereof is present.

Article XLVII

Votes shall be taken in both Houses by absolute majority. In the case of a tie vote, the President shall have the casting vote.

Article XLVIII

The deliberations of both Houses shall be held in public. The deliberations may, however, upon demand of the Government or by resolution of the Houses, be held in secret sitting.

Article XLIX

Both Houses of the Imperial Diet may respectively present addresses to the Emperor.

Article L

Both Houses may receive petitions presented by subjects.

Article LI

Both Houses may enact, besides what is provided for in the present Constitution and in the Law of the Houses, rules necessary for the management of their internal affairs.

Article LII

No member of either House shall be held responsible outside the respective Houses, for any opinion uttered or for any vote given in the House. When, however, a Member himself has given publicity to his opinions by public speech, by documents in printing or in writing, or by any other similar means he shall, in the matter, be amenable to the general law.

Article LIII

The members of both Houses shall, during the session, be free from arrest, unless with the consent of the House, except in cases of flagrant delicts, or of offences connected with a state of internal commotion or with a foreign trouble.

Article LIV

The Ministers of State and the Delegates of the Government may, at any time, take seats and speak in either House.

Chapter IV: The Ministers of State and the Privy Council

Article LV

The respective Ministers of State shall give their advice to the Emperor, and be responsible for it.

All Laws, Imperial Ordinances, and Imperial Rescripts of whatever kind that relate to the affairs of the State, require the countersignature of a Minister of State.

Article LVI

The Privy Council shall, in accordance with the provisions for the organization of the Privy Council, deliberate upon important matters of State, when they have been consulted by the Emperor.

Chapter V: The Judicature

Article LVII

The Judicature shall be exercised by the Courts of Law according to law, in the name of the Emperor.

The organization of the Courts of Law shall be determined by law.

Article LVIII

The judges shall be appointed from among those, who possess proper qualification according to law.

No judge shall be deprived of his position, unless by way of criminal sentence or disciplinary punishment.

Rules for disciplinary punishment shall be determined by law.

Article LIX

Trials and judgment of a Court shall be conducted publicly. When, however, there exists any fear that such publicity may be prejudicial to peace and order, or to the maintenance of public morality, the public trial may be suspended by provision of law or by the decision of the Court of Law.

Article LX

All matters, that fall within the competency of a special Court, shall be specially provided for by law.

Article LXI

No suit at law, which relates to rights alleged to have been infringed by the legal measures of the executive authorities, and which shall come within the competency of the Court of Administrative Litigation specially established by law, shall be taken cognizance of by a Court of Law.

Chapter VI: Finance
Article LXII

The imposition of a new tax or the modification of the rates (of an existing one) shall be determined by law.

However, all such administrative fees or other revenue having the nature of compensation shall not fall within the category of the above clause.

The raising of national loans and the contracting of other liabilities to the charge of the National Treasury, except those that are provided in the Budget, shall require the consent of the Imperial Diet.

Article LXIII

The taxes levied at present shall, in so far as are not remodelled by new law, be collected according to the old system.

Article LXIV

The expenditure and revenue of the State require the consent of the Imperial Diet by means of an annual Budget.

Any and all expenditures overpassing the appropriations set forth in the Titles and Paragraphs of the Budget, or that are not provided for in the Budget, shall subsequently require the approbation of the Imperial Diet.

Article LXV

The Budget shall be first laid before the House of Representatives.

Article LXVI

The expenditures of the Imperial House shall be defrayed every year out of the National Treasury, according to the present fixed amount for the same, and shall not require the consent thereto of the Imperial Diet, except in case an increase thereof is found necessary.

Article LXVII

Those already fixed expenditures based by the Constitution upon the powers appertaining to the Emperor, and such expenditures as may have arisen by the effect of law, or that appertain to the legal obligations of the Government, shall be neither rejected nor reduced by the Imperial Diet, without the concurrence of the Government.

Article LXVIII

In order to meet special requirements, the Government may ask the consent of the Imperial Diet to a certain amount as a Continuing Expenditure Fund, for a previously fixed number of years.

Article LXIX

In order to supply deficiencies, which are unavoidable, in the Budget, and to meet requirements unprovided for in the same, a Reserve Fund shall be provided in the Budget.

Article LXX

When the Imperial Diet cannot be convoked, owing to the external or internal condition of the country, in case of urgent need for the maintenance of public safety, the Government may take all necessary financial measures, by means of an Imperial Ordinance.

In the case mentioned in the preceding clause, the matter shall be submitted to the Imperial Diet at its next session, and its approbation shall be obtained thereto.

Article LXXI

When the Imperial Diet has not voted on the Budget, or when the Budget has not been brought into actual existence, the Government shall carry out the Budget of the preceding year.

Article LXXII

The final account of the expenditures and revenue of the State shall be verified and confirmed by the Board of Audit, and it shall be submitted by the Government to the Imperial Diet, together with the report of verification of the said Board.

The organization and competency of the Board of Audit shall be determined by law separately.

Chapter VII: Supplementary Rules

Article LXXIII

When it has become necessary in future to amend the provisions of the present Constitution, a proj-ect to that effect shall be submitted to the Imperial Diet by Imperial Order.

In the above case, neither House can open the debate, unless not less than two-thirds of the whole number of Members are present, and no amendment can be passed, unless a majority of not less than two-thirds of the Members present is obtained.

Article LXXIV

No modification of the Imperial House Law shall be required to be submitted to the deliberation of the Imperial Diet.

No provision of the present Constitution can be modified by the Imperial House Law.

Article LXXV

No modification can be introduced into the Constitution, or into the Imperial House Law, during the time of a Regency.

Article LXXVI

Existing legal enactments, such as laws, regulations, Ordinances, or by whatever names they may be called, shall, so far as they do not conflict with the present Constitution, continue in force.

All existing contracts or orders, that entail obligations upon the Government, and that are connected with expenditure shall come within the scope of Art. LXVII.

Document Analysis

Journalists and patriots universally praised the Meiji Constitution in 1889 as a sign of Japan's modernity. Scholars since then have been more nuanced, asking questions about the document's philosophy, balance, and impact. One reason for the debates about the document lay in the many opinions stimulated by the drafting process itself. When Ito and his colleagues began their work, they already had a host of written materials from which to draw, many of them quite contradictory in nature. In 1878, for example, the quasi-legislative, non-elective Genroin (Senate) had prepared a draft of a constitution that provided for power to be shared by the emperor and the people. Over the next few years, other constitutional opinions were written by the country's junior councilors (including Ito); most of those opinions favored a system with a strong emperor. Private groups and individuals, ranging from mountain villagers to newspaper editors, also drew up prospective drafts, most of which advocated a strong popular voice in the government. The result was a profusion of visions of what the constitution should mean and thus great differences in interpretations of what it meant in actual fact.

Another reason for these scholarly debates lies in the ambiguous nature of the constitution. In the constitution, classical symbols lend authority to its modern content. Even more important, it is a carefully balanced document, reflecting the drafters' often contradictory goals. All the members of Ito Hirobumi's commission agreed, for example, that the document must reflect Japan's kokutai (national essence) and that imperial rule was the central pillar of that kokutai. But at the same time, they were determined to establish the rule of law, to create a legislature, to make the judiciary independent, and to guarantee certain personal rights—all of which, at a fundamental level, ran contrary to absolute imperial sovereignty. From that contradiction has sprung much of the debate about the constitution's nature.

Chapter I: "The Emperor": The emperor's centrality permeates the constitution's preamble and serves as the focus of its first chapter. The language of the preamble is ancient, evoking a line "unbroken for ages eternal," a man who is sovereign and benevolent, who will make his "beloved subjects" prosperous, moral, and secure. (It bears noting that the original preamble mistakenly said that the imperial rescript promising a constitution was issued on October 14 of Meiji 14 (1881), two days after the actual date of the rescript. Most of the later versions changed the date to October 12.)

Chapter I states that the emperor is eternal (Article I), sacred (III), and sovereign (IV), with responsibility for supervising the country's administration (X) and making laws in times of "urgent necessity" when the Diet is not in session (VIII). The emperor is also placed in charge of the military (XI) and given sole responsibility for declaring war and peace (XIII). Of particular note is the fact that only males could reign (II), even though ancient emperors had included numerous women, among them, Suiko, who was on the throne when the famous Seventeen-Article Constitution was written in 604, and Jito, who oversaw the drafting of Japan's first comprehensive set of penal and administrative regulations in the late seventh century—a point that Ito ignored in his Commentaries on the constitution (Ito, p. 6).

The chapter about the emperor also has a populist side. Hermann Roesler had argued that an emperor's power should not be made absolute in a modern society, where it was important to guard the interests of all classes, including business people and farmers. It is in this spirit that the constitution's first chapter circumscribes the emperor's prerogatives in important ways, making him subject to the constitution itself (IV) and rendering his legislative powers dependent on the Diet's consent (V). The drafters ignored Roesler's advice that the emperor's role should be wholly secular, however, and instead declared him to be "sacred and inviolable" (III). Emperors thus would reign as both political sovereign and spiritual fountain, providing a connection to the mythical Sun Goddess, from whom Japan's imperial line was held to have descended. The divinity clause would help to inspire loyalty to the state; it also would make the imperial symbol easy to manipulate during the militarist 1930s in order to justify propagation of ancient mythologies and support for foreign aggression.

Chapter II: "Rights and Duties of Subjects": While the first chapter undergirds central governmental control, the second addresses popular initiatives. Although the people are referred to as "subjects" rather than citizens, the section's overriding theme is the rule of law, under provisions that make "law" the basis of citizenship (XVIII) and speak about rights more than duties. Some articles prohibit authorities from overextending their reach, whether from taxing without a legal basis (XXI) or from making extralegal searches (XXV) or arrests (XXIII). Others provide for laws that limit freedoms. But in every case (with the sole exception of wartime or periods of national emergency), citizens are required to follow the legal system; even the emperor is not exempt. In Meiji Japan the idea of rule by law was hardly new; the Tokugawa era had produced detailed, sophisticated sets of legal codes. It was new, however, to have a central set of laws approved by a publicly elected legislature and available for all to read.

This chapter has much to say about freedoms, though often in ambiguous language. The two duties that it demands are military service (XX) and the payment of taxes (XXI). Freedoms and rights, on the other hand, include property holding (XXVII), privacy (XXV, XXVI), freedom of religious belief (XXVIII), and freedom of speech (XXIX). These freedoms are not absolute, though. In most cases, the drafters included provisions for limiting freedoms through specific legislation. Such provisions, the 1920s and 1930s would show, carried with them the potential for thought police and the destruction of the very concept of free speech. That the Meiji drafters devoted so much space to subjects' rights, however, indicated how deeply they were committed to the welfare of the entire society.

Chapter III: "The Imperial Diet": The constitution's third chapter creates Japan's first national legislature, the Diet. Made up of twenty-two articles, this section gives flesh to the demands of freedom-and-rights campaigners that the public have a share in governmental decisions. Included in the chapter are articles creating a bicameral legislature (XXXIII), with an upper house selected from the imperial family and the national peerage (XXXIV) and a lower house "elected by the people" (XXXV). The Diet was to meet once a year for three months, unless the emperor prolonged the legislative session or called the Diet into an extraordinary session. Passage of bills would require an absolute majority (XLVII).

This chapter clearly addressed the drafters' worries about radical populism. It grants the Diet responsibility only for consenting to laws, leaving it little recourse when the government might refuse to accept its actions (XL). Nonetheless, the gains for citizens were immense. "Every law" has to be approved by the Diet (XXXVII); legislative discussions are to "be held in public" (XLVIII); and through the provisions of a later chapter, the Diet holds ultimate power over national budgets (LXIV). The people now had a formal role in the state; officials no longer could make laws without their input. Bureaucrats might have tried to mute the popular voice; they might have gotten the emperor to suspend a contentious Diet. But now that the populace had been given a legislative voice, the Japanese government never would be the same.

Chapter IV: "The Ministers of State and the Privy Council": The constitution's shortest chapter, which creates a cabinet of ministers (LV) and a privy council (LVI), is also one of its most important. While the Privy Council (intended to mediate cabinet-Diet disputes) seldom would play a crucial role in actual governance, the cabinet would operate at the heart of power. And the constitution's failure to create any connection between the cabinet and the Diet meant that the ministers of state could act on their own, without answering directly to the public. The omission was intentional. Fearful once more that popular passions might turn the Diet into a radical body, the constitutional drafters had decided to make the cabinet transcendent. Ironically, considering Roesler's opposition to declaring the emperor's divinity and power, these articles made the relationship between emperor, cabinet and the Diet almost

the same as that between emperor, cabinet and Reichstag in Germany. It reflects Hirobumi's strong impressions of the workings of the state in Germany when he visited there. While the constitution's sections on the Diet and subjects' rights would make this aloofness increasingly difficult as the decades progressed, Chapter IV assured that cabinets would retain considerable initiative in setting national policies until after the Meiji era ended in 1912.

Chapter V: "The Judicature": This short chapter, which establishes the judiciary, continues the balancing act between authority and "social" governance with the creation of an independent judiciary free even from imperial constraints. Judicial decisions are to be rendered "in the name of the Emperor" but without input or influence from him or any other branch of government (LVII). Decisions are to be made in open sessions (LIX). The article on public trials contains caveats that would allow occasional breaches in later years—as in 1911, for example, when a group of conspirators against the Emperor Meiji were tried and sentenced to death in complete secrecy. But the independence of the courts was hailed as one of the triumphs of the constitution, a victory that would be confirmed just two years later when judges defied heavy government pressure and refused to use laws intended for Japan's own imperial family in the trial of a police officer who had stabbed Russia's visiting crown prince.

Chapter VI: "Finance": The chapter on finance is particularly important to the Diet's powers. Not only does it give the Diet primary responsibility for a host of financial matters, including the creation of taxes (LXII) and the approval of the imperial household's spending increases (LXVI), but it also provides that the legislature establish the annual budget (LXIV), with budget proposals beginning in the lower house. The drafters added a provision that the previous year's budget would be used if the Diet failed to pass a budget. However, as the early 1890s would later prove, inflation and wartime costs could make a previous year's budget grossly inadequate. As a result, the Diet's budgetary power soon made the legislature almost as powerful as the oligarchs had feared that it might become.

Essential Themes

Contemporary press accounts praised the Meiji Constitution as a seminal document. They were right in many ways. Scholars have since agreed, for example, that the constitution paved the way for new treaties with the

Western powers that were signed five years later, which marked the beginning of the end of the unequal treaty system. The constitution also created a new governmental structure that was rooted in the rule of law and to some extent engaged average citizens in the nation's decision-making processes. The document also gained Japan worldwide recognition as a new leader of Asia. However, those who trace the constitution's impact over the long term usually write in more nuanced ways, often discussing one of two issues: the constitution's impact on the development of democracy or its role in nurturing the twentieth-century authoritarianism and militarism that ended in the Second World War.

Regarding the latter, there is no question that the constitution played into the hands of the militarists. Few, if any, doubt that the document's definition of the emperor as both sovereign and sacred undergirded the suppression of left-wing thought and the emergence of military cabinets in the years leading up to the Second World War. From the early 1900s onward, conservative officials worked hard at creating an emperor-system ideology, partly as an antidote to the corrupting impact of modern institutions and partly as a way to maintain a strong state. They revised textbooks repeatedly to emphasize the emperor's role as oracle and sovereign, they discouraged individualistic literature, and they supported the activities of patriotic societies—all in the name of loyalty to the emperor, whom the constitution described as "sacred and inviolable." Authoritarianism also was encouraged by the constitution's chapters on "subjects" (which made room for laws that circumscribed "dangerous" speech) and on the ministers of state (who were exempted from having to answer to the Diet). But even those chapters were grounded in the emperor's constitutional role, both in the provisions that gave him and his ministers such overriding authority and in the loyalist mindset that imperial sovereignty encouraged.

None of this made authoritarianism or militarism inevitable, however. Constitutions reflect the milieu in which they operate, and for two generations following the promulgation Japanese politics made it clear that democracy was highly feasible under the Meiji Constitution. Certainly, the constitution contains numerous provisions that encourage popular participation in an open, responsive system: the affirmation of rule by law, an independent judiciary, the creation of a popularly elected Diet, the assertion of fundamen-

tal rights, and the legislature's control over budgets, among other things. Even the emperor was subject to the constitution, and his legislative powers required the Diet's consent.

What is more, Japan experienced steady movement toward full-fledged democracy during the constitution's first four decades, with the document itself at the heart of democratic developments. By the early 1890s, Diet members were using their budgetary power to control cabinets. And they fought constantly for expansion of the electorate. While in 1890 the nation's electoral ordinance kept all but large landowners from voting, voting laws were continually changed in response to public demands, and by 1925 Japan had adopted universal male suffrage. In the late 1920s bills were being introduced in the Diet to give voting rights to women, as well. Moreover, political parties eventually took control of the cabinets, further expanding the country's democratic base. By 1918, even the most authoritarian oligarchs had to accept a system in which most cabinets would be headed by the leader of the dominant party in the Diet. At the theoretical level, scholars like Minobe Tatsukichi lent credence to these developments. Minobe dominated mainstream Japanese political theory in the 1920s with his "organ theory," which maintained that the nation's political body was composed of several political organs, the most important of which were the emperor and the Diet. The constitution, he maintained, called for them to rule jointly.

A mix of domestic and international forces undermined these democratic trends after the late 1920s. But the triumph of militarism and ultranationalism after the mid-1930s cannot hide the fact that democratic tendencies flourished for nearly forty years under the Meiji Constitution. The US-dominated occupation government, which ran Japan after the Second World War, demanded that Japan adopt a new fundamental law in 1947, the Showa Constitution, which made the people sovereign and the emperor a mere state "symbol." While there is no question that the new constitution cut the heart from Japan's military and expanded suffrage to women, the occupying forces who had thought they were giving democracy to Japan simply exposed their own historical ignorance. Democracy had come first under the Meiji Constitution.

———*James Huffman*

Bibliography and Further Reading

Banno, Junji. *The Establishment of the Japanese Constitutional System*, trans. J. A. A. Stockwin. New York: Routledge, 1992.

De Bary, William Theodore, et al., eds. *Sources of Japanese Tradition*. Vol. 2, part 2: *1868 to 2000*, 2nd ed. New York: Columbia University Press, 2006.

Irokawa, Daikichi. *The Culture of the Meiji Period*, trans. and ed. Marius B. Jansen. Princeton, N.J. Princeton University Press, 1985.

Jansen, Marius B. *The Making of Modern Japan*. Cambridge, MA: Belknap Press, 2000.

Takii, Kazuhiro. *The Meiji Constitution: The Japanese Experience of the West and the Shaping of the Modern State*, trans. David Noble. Tokyo: I-House of Japan Press, 2007.

Web Sites

"Birth of the Constitution of Japan." National Diet Library (2003) http://www.ndl.go.jp/constitution/e/ index.html [accessed March 5, 2017].

"The Meiji Restoration and Modernization." *Contemporary Japan: A Teaching Workbook*. Columbia University, East Asian Curriculum Project http://www. indiana.edu/~hisdcl/h207_2002/ meijiconstitution. htm [accessed March 5, 2017].

■ "The Significance of the Frontier in American History"

Date: 1893
Author: Frederick Jackson Turner
Genre: Speech/journal article

Summary Overview

In the 1893 *Report of the American Historical Association*, Frederick Jackson Turner published "The Significance of the Frontier in American History."Although some of Turner's assertions were perhaps a little overstated, the essay remains important because it essentially defined the frontier character of American life and how the frontier shaped American values and characteristics. It was an example of a new approach to historiography that historians and social scientists were beginning to take in the nineteenth century; rather than focusing on kings and popes, wars and treaties, historians were taking a closer look at economic and social factors and how those factors influenced historical events. Still in the twenty-first century, Americans tend to trace American individualism and enterprise to the "frontier thesis" Turner articulated just three years after the U.S. Census Bureau declared the American frontier closed.

Turner's essay picks up two themes that influenced historians throughout the nineteenth century. One was that, like the American frontier itself, democracy and civilization were progressively moving westward and that in time the New World would eclipse the Old World—Europe—as the center of progress and civilization. The other theme was the notion that at each step in the settlement of the frontier—not just in the Old West but along the eastern seaboard as America was first settled—the process of social evolution is recreated and renewed as "savagery" comes into conflict with "civilization." Progress inevitably followed the same arc: from hunting and trapping to agriculture and a settled way of life to the development of towns and eventually major urban, commercial, and industrial centers. Turner's frontier thesis provided Americans with assurance that their nation, still relatively new in the scheme of things, would follow this path into the future, ensuring a better life for all. Though few outside the history profession read Turner's article at the time, his ideas have been so influential that the article has been referred to as "the single most influential piece of writing in the history of American history."

Defining Moment

The 1893 World's Columbian Exposition at Chicago was, in some sense, the United States' coming-out party in world history and as a world power. The fair was held to mark the four hundredth anniversary of Columbus' voyage to the Americas. The massive "white city" that was built for the fair, the gigantic public turnout that made it the most heavily attended world's fair of its time, and the impressive fact that the fair was located in the United States' "second city," the gateway to the west, all signaled that the United States had achieved its "manifest destiny" and was now ready to meet the world and spread its principles beyond its borders.

At the same time, however, the fair was the end of an era. Historian Frederick Jackson Turner presented this paper to a special meeting of the American Historical Association held at the exposition, then published it in the proceedings of the meeting. In this speech, Turner discussed this concept in presenting his "frontier thesis." His assessment of the frontier's cultural significance was the first of its kind, and revolutionized American intellectual and historical thinking. It was also something of a portent; after all, now that the frontier was closed in the United States, what would replace it?

Author Biography

Frederick Jackson Turner was born in Portage, Wisconsin, in 1861. At the time, Wisconsin was at the very edge of American sovereignty in the Midwest, yet by 1893, it was the essence of middle America already, culturally as well as geographically. Turner received his PhD from Johns Hopkins University in 1890 and returned to the University of Wisconsin, where he taught history until 1910, when he moved on to Harvard. The ideas in this speech described not just a moment in American history but also Turner's entire life's work—the definition of the United States through the history of its ever-advancing frontiers.

To Turner, the frontier was essential to the United States' development of democracy, a concept the writers of the constitution feared. The frontier created a level of rugged individualism that led men to disdain just the sort of elitist leadership that the writers expected to provide the American people once the constitution was written—if they could make it on the edges of civilization, if men could *be* that civilization, they would be little inclined to show deference to others who might dictate how they were to live.

HISTORICAL DOCUMENT

In a recent bulletin of the Superintendent of the Census for 1890 appear these significant words: "Up to and including 1880 the country had a frontier of settlement, but at present the unsettled area has been so broken into by isolated bodies of settlement that there can hardly be said to be a frontier line. In the discussion of its extent, its westward movement, etc., it cannot, therefore, any longer have a place in the census reports." This brief official statement marks the closing of a great historic movement. Up to our own day American history has been in a large degree the history of the colonization of the Great West. The existence of an area of free land, its continuous recession, and the advance of American settlement westward, explain American development.

Behind institutions, behind constitutional forms and modifications, lie the vital forces that call these organs into life and shape them to meet changing conditions. The peculiarity of American institutions is the fact that they have been compelled to adapt themselves to the changes of an expanding people—to the changes involved in crossing a continent, in winning a wilderness, and in developing at each area of this progress out of the primitive economic and political conditions of the frontier into the complexity of city life. …Limiting our attention to the Atlantic coast, we have the familiar phenomenon of the evolution of institutions in a limited area, such as the rise of representative government; into complex organs; the progress from primitive industrial society, without division of labor, up to manufacturing civilization. But we have in addition to this a recurrence of the process of evolution in each western area reached in the process of expansion. Thus American development has exhibited not merely advance along a single line, but a return to primitive conditions on a continually advancing frontier line, and a new development for that area. American social development has been continually beginning over again on the frontier. This perennial rebirth, this fluidity of American life, this expansion westward with its new opportunities, its continuous touch with the simplicity of primitive society, furnish the forces dominating American character. The true point of view in the history of this nation is not the Atlantic coast, it is the Great West. Even the slavery struggle …occupies its important place in American history because of its relation to westward expansion.

In this advance, the frontier is the outer edge of the wave—the meeting point between savagery and civilization. Much has been written about the frontier from the point of view of border warfare and the chase, but as a field for the serious study of the economist and the historian it has been neglected.

The American frontier is sharply distinguished from the European frontier—a fortified boundary line running through dense populations. The most significant thing about the American frontier is that it lies at the hither edge of free land. …

The frontier is the line of most rapid and effective Americanization. The wilderness masters the colonist. It finds him a European in dress, industries, tools, modes of travel, and thought. It takes him from the railroad car and puts him in the birch canoe. It strips off the garments of civilization and arrays him in the hunting shirt and the moccasin. It puts him in the log cabin of the Cherokee and Iroquois and runs an Indian palisade around him. Before long he has gone to planting Indian corn and plowing with a sharp stick, he shouts the war cry and takes the scalp in orthodox Indian fashion. In short, at the frontier the environment is at first too strong for the man. He must accept the conditions which it furnishes, or perish, and so he fits himself into the Indian clearings and follows the Indian trails. Little by little he transforms the wilderness, but the outcome is not the old Europe, not simply the development of Germanic germs, any more than the first phenomenon was a case of reversion to the Germanic mark. The fact is, that here is a new product that is American. At first, the frontier was the Atlantic coast. It was the frontier of Europe in a very real sense. Moving westward, the frontier became more and more American. …Thus the advance of the frontier has meant a steady movement away from the influence of Europe, a steady growth of independence on American lines. And to study this advance, the men who grew up under these conditions, and the political, economic, and social results of it, is to study the really American part of our history. …

In [the advance of the American] frontier[] we find natural boundary lines which have served to mark and to affect the characteristics of the frontiers, namely: the "fall line;" the Allegheny Mountains; the Mississippi; the Missouri where its direction approximates north and south; the line of the arid lands, approximately the ninety-ninth meridian; and the Rocky Mountains. The fall line marked the frontier of the seventeenth century; the Alleghenies that of the eighteenth; the Mississippi that of the first quarter of the nineteenth; the Missouri that of the middle of this century (omitting the California movement); and the belt of the Rocky Mountains and the arid tract, the present frontier. Each was won by a series of Indian wars.

At the Atlantic frontier one can study the germs of processes repeated at each successive frontier. We have the complex European life sharply precipitated by the wilderness into the simplicity of primitive conditions. The first frontier had to meet its Indian question, its question of the disposition of the public domain, of the means of intercourse with older settlements, of the extension of political organization, of religious and educational activity. And the settlement of these and similar questions for one frontier served as a guide for the next. …Each tier of new States has found in the older ones material for its constitutions. Each frontier has made similar contributions to American character… .

But with all these similarities there are essential differences, due to the place element and the time element. It is evident that the farming frontier of the Mississippi Valley presents different conditions from the mining frontier of the Rocky Mountains.

The frontier reached by the Pacific Railroad, surveyed into rectangles, guarded by the United States Army, and recruited by the daily immigrant ship, moves forward at a swifter pace and in a different way than the frontier reached by the birch canoe or the pack horse. The geologist traces patiently the shores of ancient seas, maps their areas, and compares the older and the newer. It would be a work worth the historian's labors to mark these various frontiers and in detail compare one with another. Not only would there result a more adequate conception of American development and characteristics, but invaluable additions would be made to the history of society. …

The United States lies like a huge page in the history of society. Line by line as we read this continental page from West to East we find the record of social evolution. It begins with the Indian and the hunter; it goes on to tell of the disintegration of savagery by the entrance of the trader, the pathfinder of civilization; we read the annals of the pastoral stage in ranch life; the exploitation of the soil by the raising of unrotated crops of corn and wheat in sparsely settled farming communities; the intensive culture of the denser farm settlement; and finally the manufacturing organization with city and factory system. This page is familiar to the student of census statistics, but how little of it has been used by our historians. Particularly in eastern States this page is a palimpsest. What is now a manufacturing State was in an earlier decade an area of intensive farming. Earlier yet it had been a wheat area, and still earlier the "range" had attracted the cattleherder. Thus Wisconsin, now developing manufacture, is a State with varied agricultural interests. But earlier it was given over to almost exclusive grain-raising, like North Dakota at the present time. …

[T]he Indian trade pioneered the way for civilization. The buffalo trail became the Indian trail, and this became the trader's "trace;" the trails widened into roads, and the roads into turnpikes, and these in turn were transformed into railroads. The same origin can be shown for the railroads of the South, the Far West, and the Dominion of Canada. The trading posts reached by these trails were on the sites of Indian villages which had been placed in positions suggested by nature; and these trading posts, situated so as to command the water systems of the country, have grown into such cities as Albany, Pittsburgh, Detroit, Chicago, St. Louis, Council Bluffs, and Kansas City. Thus civilization in America has followed the arteries made by geology, pouring an ever richer tide through them, until at last the slender paths of aboriginal intercourse have been broadened and interwoven into the complex mazes of modern commercial lines; the wilderness has been interpenetrated by lines of civilization growing ever more numerous. It is like the steady growth of a complex nervous system for the originally simple, inert continent. If one would understand why we are to-day one nation, rather than a collection of isolated states, he must study this economic and social consolidation of the country. In this progress from savage conditions lie topics for the evolutionist.

The effect of the Indian frontier as a consolidating agent in our history is important. From the close of the seventeenth century various intercolonial congresses have been called to treat with Indians and establish common measures of defense. Particularism was strongest in colonies with no Indian frontier. This frontier stretched along the western border like a cord of union. The Indian was a common danger, demanding united action. …In this connection may be mentioned the importance of the frontier, from that day to this, as a military training school, keeping alive the power of resistance to aggression, and developing the stalwart and rugged qualities of the frontiersman. …

Omitting those of the pioneer farmers who move from the love of adventure, the advance of the more steady farmer is easy to understand. Obviously the immigrant was attracted by the cheap lands of the frontier, and even the native farmer felt their influence strongly. Year by year the farmers who lived on soil whose returns were diminished by unrotated crops were offered the virgin soil of the frontier at nominal prices. Their growing families demanded more lands, and these were dear. The competition of the unexhausted, cheap, and easily tilled prairie lands compelled the farmer either to go west and continue the exhaustion of the soil on a new frontier, or to adopt intensive culture. Thus the census of 1890 shows, in the Northwest, many counties in which there is an absolute or a relative decrease of population. These States have been sending farmers to advance the frontier on the plains, and have themselves begun to turn to intensive farming and to manufacture. A decade before this, Ohio had shown the same transition stage. Thus the demand for land and the love of wilderness freedom drew the frontier ever onward.

Having now roughly outlined the various kinds of frontiers, and their modes of advance, chiefly from the point of view of the frontier itself, we may next inquire [as to] what were the influences on the East and on the Old World. …

First, we note that the frontier promoted the formation of a composite nationality for the American people. The coast was preponderantly English, but the later tides of continental immigration flowed across to the free lands. This was the case from the early colonial days. The Scotch-Irish and the Palatine Germans, or "Pennsylvania Dutch," furnished the dominant element in the stock of the colonial frontier. …In the crucible of the frontier the immigrants were Americanized, liberated, and fused into a mixed race, English in neither nationality nor characteristics. The process has gone on from the early days to our own. [English] writers in the middle of the eighteenth century believed that Pennsylvania was "threatened with the danger of being wholly foreign in language, manners, and perhaps even inclinations." The German and Scotch-Irish elements in the frontier of the South were only less great. In the middle of the present century the German element in Wisconsin was already so considerable that leading publicists looked to the creation of a German state out of the commonwealth by concentrating their colonization. Such examples teach us to beware of misinterpreting the fact that there is a common English speech in America into a belief that the stock is also English. …

It was this nationalizing tendency of the West that transformed the democracy of Jefferson into the national republicanism of Monroe and the democracy of Andrew Jackson. The West of the War of 1812, the West of Clay, and Benton and Harrison, and Andrew Jackson, shut off by the Middle States and the mountains from the coast sections, had a solidarity of its own with national tendencies. On the tide of the Father of Waters, North and South met and mingled into a nation. Interstate migration went steadily on—a process of crossfertilization of ideas and institutions. The fierce struggle of the sections over slavery on the western frontier does not diminish the truth of this statement; it proves the truth of it. Slavery was a sectional trait that would not down, but in the West it could not remain sectional. It was the greatest of frontiersmen who declared: "I believe this Government can not endure permanently half slave and half free. It will become all of one thing or all of the other." Nothing works for nationalism like intercourse within the nation. Mobility of population is death to localism, and the western frontier worked irresistibly in unsettling population. The effect reached back from the frontier and affected profoundly the Atlantic coast and even the Old World.

The public domain has been a force of profound importance in the nationalization and development of the government. ... Administratively the frontier called out some of the highest and most vitalizing activities of the general government. The purchase of Louisiana was perhaps the constitutional turning point in the history of the Republic, inasmuch as it afforded both a new area for national legislation and the occasion of the downfall of the policy of strict construction. But the purchase of Louisiana was called out by frontier needs and demands. As frontier States accrued to the Union, the national power grew. ...

[I]t was not merely in legislative action that the frontier worked against the sectionalism of the coast. The economic and social characteristics of the frontier worked against sectionalism. ...The Middle region was less English than the other sections. It had a wide mixture of nationalities, a varied society, the mixed town and county system of local government, a varied economic life, many religious sects. In short, it was a region mediating between New England and the South, and the East and the West. It represented that composite nationality which the contemporary United States exhibits, that juxtaposition of non-English groups, occupying a valley or a little settlement, and presenting reflections of the map of Europe in their variety. It was democratic and nonsectional, if not national; "easy, tolerant, and contented;" rooted strongly in material prosperity. It was typical of the modern United States. It was least sectional, not only because it lay between North and South, but also because with no barriers to shut out its frontiers from its settled region, and with a system of connecting waterways, the Middle region mediated between East and West as well as between North and South. Thus it became the typically American region. ...

But the most important effect of the frontier has been in the promotion of democracy here and in Europe. As has been indicated, the frontier is productive of individualism. Complex society is precipitated by the wilderness into a kind of primitive organization based on the family. The tendency is anti-social. It produces antipathy to control, and particularly to any direct control. The tax-gatherer is viewed as a representative of oppression. ...The frontier individualism has from the beginning promoted democracy. The frontier States that came into the Union in the first quarter of a century of its existence came in with democratic suffrage provisions, and had reactive effects of the highest importance upon the older States whose peoples were being attracted there. An extension of the franchise became essential. ...

So long as free land exists, the opportunity for a competency exists, and economic power secures political power. But the democracy born of free land, strong in selfishness and individualism, intolerant of administrative experience and education, and pressing individual liberty beyond its proper bounds, has its dangers as well as its benefits. Individualism in America has allowed a laxity in regard to governmental affairs which has rendered possible the spoils system and all the manifest evils that follow from the lack of a highly developed civic spirit. ...

The East has always feared the result of an unregulated advance of the frontier, and has tried to check and guide it. The English authorities would have checked settlement at the headwaters of the Atlantic tributaries and allowed the "savages to enjoy their deserts in quiet lest the peltry trade should decrease." ...But the attempts to limit the boundaries, to restrict land sales and settlement, and to deprive the West of its share of political power were all in vain. Steadily the frontier of settlement advanced and carried with it individualism, democracy, and nationalism, and powerfully affected the East and the Old World.

From the conditions of frontier life came intellectual traits of profound importance. The works of travelers along each frontier from colonial days onward describe certain common traits, and these traits have, while softening down, still persisted as survivals in the place of their origin, even when a higher social organization succeeded. The result is that to the frontier the American intellect owes its striking characteristics. That coarseness and strength combined with acuteness and inquisitiveness; that practical, inventive turn of mind, quick to find expedients; that masterful grasp of material things, lacking in the artistic but powerful to effect great ends; that restless, nervous energy; that dominant individualism, working for good and for evil, and withal that buoyancy and exuberance which comes with freedom—these are traits of the frontier, or traits called out elsewhere because of the existence of the frontier.

Since the days when the fleet of Columbus sailed into the waters of the New World, America has been another name for opportunity, and the people of the United States have taken their tone from the incessant expansion which has not only been open but has even been forced upon them. He would be a rash prophet who should assert that the expansive character of American life has now entirely ceased.

Movement has been its dominant fact, and, unless this training has no effect upon a people, the American energy will continually demand a wider field for its exercise. But never again will such gifts of free land offer themselves. For a moment, at the frontier, the bonds of custom are broken and unrestraint is triumphant. There is not tabula rasa. The stubborn American environment is there with its imperious summons to accept its conditions; the inherited ways of doing things are also there; and yet, in spite of environment, and in spite of custom, each frontier did indeed furnish a new field of opportunity, a gate of escape from the bondage of the past; and freshness, and confidence, and scorn of older society, impatience of its restraints and its ideas, and indifference to its lessons, have accompanied the frontier. What the Mediterranean Sea was to the Greeks, breaking the bond of custom, offering new experiences, calling out new institutions and activities, that, and more, the ever retreating frontier has been to the United States directly, and to the nations of Europe more remotely. And now, four centuries from the discovery of America, at the end of a hundred years of life under the Constitution, the frontier has gone, and with its going has closed the first period of American history.

Document Analysis

It is possible to extract from Turner's dense essay a number of critical points. The first is that the American frontier has shaped the American character: "American social development has been continually beginning over again on the frontier. This perennial rebirth, this fluidity of American life, this expansion westward with its new opportunities, its continuous touch with the simplicity of primitive society, furnish the forces dominating American character." Turner traces the westward movement of the frontier, noting that the Atlantic seaboard was in effect the western frontier of Europe. Over time, frontier settlers progressively moved westward. At each step along the way—the Allegheny Mountains, the Mississippi River, the Rocky Mountains—settlers confronted a virgin wilderness and, over time, tamed it. Civilization and "savagery" clashed as settlers encountered the Indian tribes and, at first, adopted their modes of life until ranches, settled farms, and industries emerged.

Turner places considerable emphasis on the prospect of free land for settlers: "Year by year the farmers who lived on soil whose returns were diminished by unrotated crops were offered the virgin soil of the frontier at nominal prices." This induced a kind of "pick up and move on" mind-set that fueled westward expansion. This thirst for land created a number of characteristics that define American culture and values. First, he says, "the frontier promoted the formation of a composite nationality for the American people." This nationalizing trend had an enormous influence on legislation and the administration of the country throughout the nineteenth century. "Mobility of population," Turner writes, "is death to localism, and the western frontier worked irresistibly in unsettling population. The effect reached back from the frontier and affected profoundly the Atlantic coast and even the Old World."

Turner then articulates his boldest thesis: "But the most important effect of the frontier has been in the promotion of democracy here and in Europe. ...The frontier individualism has from the beginning promoted democracy." Some historians disagree, yet Turner's emphasis on the presumed individualistic character of Americans has persisted for over a century. Likewise, Turner's thesis continues to influence views of American "intellectual traits": "That coarseness and strength combined with acuteness and inquisitiveness; that practical, inventive turn of mind, quick to find expedients; that masterful grasp of material things, lacking in the artistic but powerful to effect great ends; that restless, nervous energy; that dominant individualism, working for good and for evil, and withal that buoyancy and exuberance which comes with freedom—these are traits of the frontier."

Essential Themes

Frederick Jackson Turner was perhaps the first articulate and original theorist of a type of American nationalism—finding cultural values in the demographic expansion across North America. The historical profession has since moved well beyond Turner's thesis. His dismissal of the native American population as little more than a vanguard providing the skills necessary to establish civilization in non-Europeanized parts of North America is seen as in tune with the racism of its times. Today, historians see other factors in American history like race and slavery, capitalism, religious tolerance and intolerance and immigration as keys to understanding the nature of what it means to be an American. Others have noted that the frontier really presented a conflict to European Americans between freedom and equality—the individual on the move in an unknown country could only expect to survive with help from people like him that settled nearby, establishing an equality and interdependence that would drive the next generation to leave in search of an oxymoronic freedom and opportunity with like-minded individuals.

On a more prosaic level, some commentators have noted that the American "frontier" has simply changed. At about the same time Turner presented his ideas, the United States annexed Hawaii; five years later, war with Spain brought Cuba, Puerto Rico and the Philippines into the American orbit. The beginnings of the twentieth century brought with them the Roosevelt Corollary to the Monroe Doctrine, arguing that the United States had a duty to teach Latin American states the principles of democracy and capitalism, often at the price of military occupation in Central America and the Caribbean. And of course, the First World War was an adventure in world-building as defined by President Woodrow Wilson's Fourteen Points. In effect, it has become possible to argue that American nationalism has taken the frontier and redefined it as the extension of American values throughout the world. Where in Turner's time, American exceptionalism was focused inward and people outside the US had to come here to indulge in the nation's bounties of freedom and economic opportunity, with the closing of the frontier Americans began to focus their sense of exceptionalism outward, to "make the world safe for democracy," as Wilson called it. For better or worse, this trend has only extended itself well into the twentieth century.

———Michael J. O'Neal, PhD

Bibliography and Further Reading

Aron, Stephen. *The American West: A Very Short Introduction.* New York: Oxford University Press, 2015.

Bogue, Allan G. *Frederick Jackson Turner: Strange Roads Going Down.* Norman, OK: University of Oklahoma Press, 1998.

Brown, David S. *Beyond the Frontier: The Midwestern Voice in American Historical Writing.* Chicago: The University of Chicago Press, 2009.

Hodgson, Godfrey. *The Myth of American Exceptionalism.* New Haven CT: Yale University Press, 2009.

King, Desmond. *The Liberty of Strangers: Making the American Nation.* New York: Oxford University Press, 2005.

Monahan, Peter, editor. *America in Literature, Volume 2: The West.* Max Bogart, general editor. New York: Scribner, 1979.

Web Sites

"Frederick Jackson Turner (1861-1932)." New Perspectives on the West. *PBS.org (2001)* http://www.pbs.org/weta/thewest/people/s_z/turner.htm [accessed February 26, 2017].

Blackhawk, Ned. "The Development of the West." The Gilder Lehrman Institute of American History https://www.gilderlehrman.org/history-by-era/development-west/essays/development-**west** [**accessed February 26, 2017**].

■ "A Solution to the Jewish Question"

Date: 1896
Author: Theodor Herzl
Genre: Newspaper essay

Summary Overview

Theodor Herzl's essay "A Solution to the Jewish Question" appeared in a London weekly newspaper, the *Jewish Chronicle*, in 1896. In it, Herzl argued that the world's Jews needed a homeland and that the homeland should be Palestine—an ancient region on the eastern Mediterranean that encompasses the modern-day nation of Israel. At the time that Herzl wrote "A Solution to the Jewish Question," Israel did not exist. Indeed, the Jewish population in what is today Israel numbered less than one hundred thousand people, who lived among their Muslim and Christian Arab neighbors as part of the Ottoman Empire. This state of affairs would abruptly change in the twentieth century, primarily because of the activities of European Jewish intellectuals and activists, including Herzl. While Herzl was not the only actor in creating a Jewish homeland in Palestine, he contributed significantly to the effort through a number of publications, including "A Solution to the Jewish Question."

Defining Moment

Historically, Jews had been a minority population in Palestine after the Romans destroyed the Temple of Solomon in Jerusalem in 70 CE. This event led to the expulsion and dispersal of much of the Jewish population from the region, with the majority fleeing to other parts of the Middle East or Europe. Afterward, the remaining Jews were ruled as a minority by various Muslim powers. The last of these rulers were the Ottomans, after the Ottoman Turks conquered Syria and Palestine during the Ottoman-Mamluk War (1485–1491) and established the Ottoman Empire in 1516.

Jewish migration to Palestine began soon after the Ottoman conquest. A Jewish population came from Spain as part of the exodus resulting from the Reconquista, or the Christian reconquest of the Iberian Peninsula from Muslims. Thus began a pattern; with every new persecution of the Jews in the different states of Europe, a small group of Jews would migrate back to the land that the Pentateuch had defined for them as a homeland, for safety. In Herzl's time, thousands of Jews fled from the Russian Empire after the pogroms of 1881–1884 and 1903–1906; in Russia the government used the Jews as scapegoats for many of the nation's ills.

They sought religious toleration, and they found it in Muslim lands, where they were considered *dhimmis*, or "people of the Book"—those who, like Muslims, had received a revelation from God but, unlike Muslims, had not accepted the teachings of Muhammad. Thus, they had rights and were protected as citizens of the Ottoman Empire.

The Ottoman Empire was not the only state to deal with large numbers of Jewish immigrants. More Jews came from eastern to western Europe—like Herzl himself. The sudden influx of immigrants thus prompted the "Jewish question," which was a series of questions that boiled down to one: How do the Jews fit into a Western secular society? Underlying this question were old prejudices in a secular, yet very Christian society that viewed Jews as outsiders who refused to assimilate into Western society. Indeed, with the influx of eastern European Jews, the differences between the Jews and Western society became more apparent. Although many western European Jews had become more assimilated, while retaining their religion as part of their identity, eastern European Jews were different. They had lived apart from their Christians neighbors in what were termed "ghettos," or Jewish quarters in cities. Although at times they could be poor, many ghettos were often affluent areas. This separation, once required by medieval law, helped keep alive prejudices dating back centuries.

The true turning point, however, came with the advent of Zionism, or what might be termed Jewish nationalism. This movement came as a reaction to the pogroms and persecution of the Jewish Diaspora throughout Europe. Although Jews received much better treatment in western Europe, many Jewish intellectuals and religious leaders became concerned that the secular environment of the industrialized West could lead to their absorption and loss of identity. Integration was not unacceptable, but the concern was that latent prejudice among Europeans would prevent Jews from ever fully becoming part of Western society. A Jewish minority would always be outsiders no matter how long their families had lived in a particular country.

Author Biography

Theodor Herzl was one of the founders of the Zionist movement and convened the first World Zionist Congress in 1897. The ideas of Zionism existed well before he came into prominence, but his influence became seminal. Herzl was born in 1860 in Budapest, in the Austro-Hungarian Empire, but he was raised and educated in a secular German world. While Judaism played a role in his background, for much of his life he possessed only a cursory understanding of it. In 1878 Herzl's family moved to the capital of the Austro-Hungarian Empire, Vienna. There, Herzl attended the University of Vienna and obtained a doctorate in law in 1884.

After graduation, Herzl earned a living as a civil servant and a writer of plays, short stories, and articles. Eventually he secured a job as a journalist for the prestigious Viennese newspaper *Neue Freie Presse* ("New Free Press"), which stationed him in Paris as their correspondent. This was the transforming event of Herzl's life, as he would experience anti-Semitism firsthand when he covered the treason trial of Alfred Dreyfus, a Jewish officer in the French army, for his newspaper. Earlier, in 1894, he had published a drama titled *The Ghetto* that he hoped would serve as a vehicle for discussion and a step toward harmony between Christians and Jews. Prior to the Dreyfus affair, Herzl was fully committed to assimilation into the culture of secular Europe, but the widespread anti-Semitism he witnessed during the Dreyfus affair convinced him that the only solution was a Jewish state. Toward that end, in 1896 he published a pamphlet titled *Der Judenstaat* ("The Jewish State"), which was ridiculed by many Jewish leaders who could not conceive it as reality. "The Solution to the Jewish Question" (also published in 1896) is a modified version of *Der Judenstaat* intended for a British audience.

Herzl's ideas found rapid acceptance among the general Jewish public, but the leaders of the Jewish Diaspora were skeptical as to whether it was feasible. Herzl eventually found sufficient support to call for a meeting of Jewish leaders in Basel, Switzerland, in 1897. This was a significant step, for it was the first international meeting of major Jewish leaders. There the World Zionist Congress was formed with Herzl as its president..

As president, Herzl attempted to find a solution to the "Jewish question," and he even traveled to the Ottoman Empire in 1898 to pursue his dream. Ultimately, his visit was a failure. He did not meet the Ottoman sultan, Abdul Hamid II, at that time, though he did eventually meet with him in 1901. Still, Ottoman officials informed him that the Ottomans were opposed to autonomous regions or self-rule. He also timed his 1898 visit so that he could meet with the German emperor, Kaiser Wilhelm II, who was visiting the Middle East. He finally met with Kaiser Wilhelm, hoping to recruit him as an ally in the Zionist effort, but the kaiser was dismissive of the idea. A trip to Britain resulted in a modest proposal of Uganda as a potential autonomous homeland. The fact that Herzl considered this as a temporary solution undermined his support in the World Zionist Congress. His death in 1904 ensured that the Uganda plan was forgotten.

HISTORICAL DOCUMENT

The Jewish Question still exists. It would be foolish to deny it. It exists wherever Jews live in perceptible numbers. Where it does not yet exist, it will be brought by Jews in the course of their migrations. We naturally move to those places where we are not persecuted, and there our presence soon produces persecution. This is true in every country, and will remain true even in those most highly civilised—France itself is no exception—till the Jewish Question finds a solution on a political basis. I believe that I understand antisemitism, which is in reality a highly complex movement. I consider it from a Jewish standpoint, yet without fear or hatred. I believe that I can see what elements there are in it of vulgar sport, of common trade, of jealousy, of inherited prejudice, of religious intolerance, and also of ligitimate self-defence....

We are one people—One People. We have honestly striven everywhere to merge ourselves in the social life of surrounding communities, and to preserve only the faith of our fathers. It has not been permitted to us. In vain are we loyal patriots, in some places our loyalty running to extremes; in vain do we make the same sacrifices of life and property as our fellow-citizens; in vain do we strive to increase the fame of our native land in science and art, or her Wealth by trade and commerce. In countries where we have lived for centuries we are still cried down as strangers; and often by those whose ancestors were not yet domiciled in the land where Jews had already made experience of suffering. Yet, in spite of all, we are loyal subjects, loyal as the Huguenots, who were forced to emigrate. If we could only be left in peace....

We are one people—our enemies have made us one in our despite, as repeatedly happens in history. Distress binds us together, and thus united, we suddenly discover our strength. Yes, we are strong enough to form a state, and a model state. We possess all human and material resources necessary for the purpose.... The whole matter is in its essence perfectly simple, as it must necessarily be, if it is to come within the comprehension of all.

Let the sovereignty be granted us over a portion of the globe large enough to satisfy the requirements of the nation—the rest we shall manage for ourselves. Of course, I fully expect that each word of this sentence, and each letter of each word, will be torn to tatters by scoffers and doubters. I advise them to do the thing cautiously, if they are themselves sensitive to ridicule. The creation of a new state has in it nothing ridiculous or impossible. We have, in our day, witnessed the process in connection with nations which were not in the bulk of the middle class, but poor, less educated, and therefore weaker than ourselves. The governments of all countries, scourged by antisemitism, will serve their own interests, in assisting us to obtain the sovereignty we want. These governments will be all the more willing to meet us half-way, seeing that the movement I suggest is not likely to bring about any economic crisis. Such crisis, as must

follow everywhere as a natural consequence of Jew-baiting, will rather be prevented by the carrying out of my plan. For I propose an inner migration of Christians into the parts slowly and systematically evacuated by Jews. If we are not merely suffered to do what I ask, but are actually helped, we shall be able to affect a transfer of property from Jews to Christians in a manner so peaceable and on so extensive a scale as has never been known in the annals of history....

Shall we choose [the] Argentine [Republic] or Palestine? We will take what is given us and what is selected by Jewish public opinion. Argentina is one of the most fertile countries in the world, extends over a vast area, and has a sparse population. The Argentine Republic would derive considerable profit from the cession of a portion of its territory to us. The present infiltration of Jews has certainly produced some friction, and it would be necessary to enlighten the Republic on the intrinsic difference of our new movement.

Palestine is our ever-memorable historic home. The very name of Palestine would attract our people with a force of extraordinary potency. Supposing His Majesty the Sultan were to give us Palestine, we could in return pledge ourselves to regulate the whole finances of Turkey. There we should also form a portion of the rampart of Europe against Asia, an outpost of civilisation as opposed to barbarism. We should remain a neutral state in intimate connection with the whole of Europe, which would guarantee our continued existence. The sanctuaries of Christendom would be safeguarded by assigning to them an extra-territorial status, such as is well known to the law of nations. We should form a guard of honour about these sanctuaries, answering for the fulfillment of this duty with our existence. This guard of honour would be the great symbol of the solution of the Jewish Question after nearly nineteen centuries of Jewish suffering.

Document Analysis

Herzl's essay "A Solution to the Jewish Question" was a radical proposal that sought to ameliorate the oppression and persecution of Jews throughout Europe. In it, Herzl is appealing not only to his fellow Jews but also to the governments of Europe. His work was crucial for laying the foundations of the modern state of Israel but also detrimental, in that it led to the oppression of another group, the Palestinians—an unintended consequence that Herzl did not imagine and probably could not have conceived.

What exactly was the Jewish question? The readers of the *Jewish Chronicle* knew what Herzl meant: How did Jews fit into any country's society and culture? What was their role? It is not a single question but a series of questions that all countries and cultures ask themselves when they receive or possess a large minority who are considered outsiders by virtue of race, culture, or custom. Herzl speaks both about the abominable pogroms against Jews in the Russian Empire and other parts of eastern Europe and about the prejudice against Jews in western Europe. While the intellectual movement of the Enlightenment—the cultural shift coinciding with the eighteenth century in Europe, when reason replaced tradition as the source of authority—had alleviated most outright religious hostility, Jews remained a minority in a largely Christian, albeit secular, western Europe. Jews remained separate because they lived in communities apart from non-Jews, and this contributed to a fear of the unknown.

A contributing factor to Herzl's publication of "A Solution to the Jewish Question" is also revealed when he makes a specific reference to France: "France itself is no exception." Herzl is referring to one of the major headlines of his day, the so-called Dreyfus affair. This incident concerned the trial of a Jewish French army officer, Alfred Dreyfus, who was convicted of treason by a military tribunal in 1894 on charges of spying for the Germans. Ultimately, the court reversed the conviction, and Dreyfus was proved innocent of all charges.

Nonetheless, the Dreyfus affair awakened anti-Semitism in French society—a society that since the French Revolution in 1789 had generally been regarded as a secular and tolerant country. At all levels of society, debates raged about the trial as well as the place of Jews in France: Could they be trusted? Did they owe their allegiance to France or to their religion? The trial immediately became a key event in the formation of Zionism, for Herzl covered it as a reporter. There he witnessed crowds chanting "Death to the Jews," and the now open anti-Semitism did not dissipate after Dreyfus was proclaimed to be innocent.

In Herzl's eyes, Jews had to view themselves as a single group—not Russian Jews or French Jews but a single nation of Jews. He also laments here that no matter how loyal Jews are to the countries they live in, they are still outsiders. Even though they have died in battle or sacrificed for their respective countries, they remain unaccepted. Again he turns to France, using the Huguenots to illustrate his point that ultimately people's differences outweigh their loyalty. The Huguenots were French Protestants who followed the teachings of John Calvin during the Protestant Reformation of the sixteenth and seventeenth centuries. They suffered greatly in the religious wars that occurred throughout the Reformation, but eventually they achieved a degree of official tolerance by the French government with the Edict of Nantes in 1598. This toleration was fleeting, however, for King Louis XIV ignored the edict and then declared Protestantism illegal, despite Protestants' loyalty to France in time of war. Hundreds of thousands of Huguenots fled to other European countries and the New World. "Yet," Herzl concludes, "in spite of all, we are loyal subjects, loyal as the Huguenots, who were forced to emigrate." In other words, the situation of France's Jews is analogous to that of the French Huguenots.

Herzl then calls for the Jewish Diaspora—the term used to refer to Jews dispersed throughout the world—to unite together in the common goal of forming a state. In the fourth paragraph he asks for a nation to grant them territory and says that the Jewish community will manage the rest. Herzl may have been appealing to Great Britain. "The Solution to the Jewish Question" appeared in a British newspaper so it could gain the attention of the government, which did have some Jewish members. Furthermore, as the world's most powerful nation, the British were in a position to exert their influence overseas on behalf of a Jewish homeland.

This section also reveals that Herzl was not simply an idealist, although naive idealism is not absent. He understands that many Jews and non-Jews would not comprehend what he is proposing. He illustrates his point by noting that new states had appeared in Europe, and these states had been created largely from the wreckage of older empires. Nevertheless, the new nations were populated by people who were linguistically and culturally unified; examples include Italy in 1870 and Germany in 1871. Jews, however, were united only in religion. Hebrew was a dead language, spoken only by rabbis during religious services. Russian Jews had little in common with those in Great Britain and France. In many of these western European countries, the bulk of the population was poorly educated with fewer economic resources, whereas the Jewish population tended to be largely middle class and well educated. Herzl also argues that granting sovereignty to a Jewish homeland would be beneficial to the state through the transfer of property. At the same time, land within other countries, such as Great Britain, would be freed up by the exodus of the Jews.

Herzl ponders where the Jews should make their new homeland—Argentina or Palestine. He points out that Argentina is a rich and vast land with a sparse population, so there would be room. Herzl notes that some anti-Semitism already exists there—probably as a result of immigration from Europe in the second half of the nineteenth century. Many Europeans, including Jews, moved to Argentina to take advantage of Argentina's economic boom in the 1880s. Herzl's statement that Jews need to demonstrate "the intrinsic difference of our new movement" simply indicates that they hope to establish an independent state and not to be outsiders within an existing state. One might wonder how the Argentine government reacted to an offer by someone to take a portion of "unused" territory and create a new state.

In the final paragraph Herzl turns to Palestine—the biblical Promised Land of the Jews. He notes that the ideal of a homeland there has tremendous appeal to the Jewish Diaspora. He also offers a proposal to the Ottoman sultan, Abdul Hamid II: In return for land, the Jews would manage the finances of the Turks. It is curious how at one point Herzl decries anti-Semitism based on stereotypes and yet, when it suits him, he plays it to his advantage. To be fair, the Ottomans in the late nineteenth century suffered from acute fiscal shortfalls, and thus Herzl assumed that the sultan would be eager to take whatever assistance was offered. Indeed, by making the offer that the World Zionist Congress would pay off the considerable Ottoman debt, Herzl demonstrates that he commanded extensive financial resources. Still, it is doubtful that Abdul Hamid would have been pleased with Herzl's remark that the Jewish presence would then serve as a rampart of civilization against the barbarism of Asia. Thus, while Herzl denigrates European anti-Semitism, he himself is not above adopting European airs of superiority over the non-Europeans. It is thus not surprising that not long after Herzl's publications and visit, the Ottomans forbade the sale of land to foreign Jews and decreed that Jewish immigrants could settle in Syria and Iraq but not Palestine.

Herzl also proposes that the Jewish state would be neutral, thus suggesting that in return for managing the fiscal affairs of the Ottoman Empire, he expected full independence for his new state. To allay the fears of the Europeans, he grants extraterritorial status to the sanctuaries of Christendom—in other words, they would be protected and not officially incorporated into the state. He obviously recognized that in order to procure the support of European powers for this project, any settlement in Palestine must include protection for Christian holy sites.

What is most interesting about this paragraph is that Herzl never mentions what would happen to the people already dwelling in Palestine or the portion of Argentina that he hoped to claim. One supposes that in Argentina, he envisioned the Pampas, the great plains of Argentina that were largely empty except for vast cattle ranches and a Native American presence. Meanwhile, already living in Palestine were tens of thousands of Arab Christians and Muslims. Indeed, it is not clear what Herzl thought—whether there was plenty of room or that only Jews should live there. Like many Europeans, he may have held a simplistic view that the area was devoid of people. Herzl must have later realized, though, that a large population did live in the area, as he visited the region two years after he wrote his "Solution." Nonetheless, in the appeal for Palestine, this fact was often conveniently overlooked under the slogan that Zionists later adopted: "A land without a people for a people without a land."

Essential Themes

Herzl's article had an enormous impact. It planted the seed of the idea for a Jewish homeland among like-minded Zionists and other Jews and in the minds of others as well. If nothing else, he outlined a plan and its necessity. For Herzl, the article helped propel him to the forefront of the Zionist movement. He transformed from a bystander to one of the leaders of Zionism. His influence and charisma became most evident with his success in organizing the First World Zionist Congress and his subsequent election as president of the organization.

The First World Zionist Congress met in Basel, Switzerland, in 1897, with approximately two hundred delegates from fifteen countries. While enthusiasm for a Jewish state grew, widespread disagreement arose about where the state should be. Initially, Herzl had no strong preference. One suggestion, prompted by the British government, was Uganda, while others proposed that the Jews should follow the model of the Mormons and settle in the western United States, Canada, or Australia, where they could form a state within an existing country. In view of the already significant Jewish presence in the United States, it was a serious consideration. Yet Herzl turned to an ancient biblical covenant made between God and the first Jews—the Hebrews.

Although Herzl did not live long enough to see the creation of an independent Jewish state, he laid the foundation for the future establishment of a homeland in Palestine. Such a homeland was impossible during his lifetime simply because of the existence of the Ottoman Empire. His British friends could exert only so much pressure and influence on the Ottomans, who were concerned with not only waves of immigrants but also the increasing European influence within the empire—influence that undermined Ottoman authority within their own territories. Not until the First World War did the opportunity manifest itself: Herzl's seed, first planted in the "The Solution to the Jewish Question," ultimately matured into a possibility through the 1917 Balfour Declaration, in which Britain offered supported for a Jewish state in Palestine.

——*Timothy May*

Bibliography and Further Reading

Gelvin, James L. *The Israel-Palestine Conflict: One Hundred Years of War.* Cambridge: Cambridge University Press, 2005.

Marcus, Amy Dockser. *Jerusalem 1913: The Origins of the Arab-Israeli Conflict.* New York: Viking, 2007.

Milton-Edwards, Beverley. *The Israeli-Palestinian Conflict: A People's War.* New York: Routledge, 2009.

Web Sites

"Herzl's 'The Jewish State.'" MidEastWeb. http://www.mideastweb.org/thejewishstate.htm [accessed February 12, 2017].

"Theodor Herzl." Jewish Virtual Library. http://www.jewishvirtuallibrary.org/jsource/ biography/Herzl.html [accessed February 12, 2017].

■ "The White Man's Burden"

Date: 1899
Author: Rudyard Kipling
Genre: Poem

Summary Overview

"The White Man's Burden" was written by the British author Rudyard Kipling (1865–1936) in 1899 and published in *McClure's Magazine* with the subtitle "The United States and the Philippine Islands." Kipling wrote the poem in the aftermath of the Spanish-American War as a means to advocate for U.S. expansion into the Philippines, Guam, Cuba, and Puerto Rico.

While the piece was meant to influence U.S. policy, it clearly reflects Kipling's own perspective on British imperialism, particularly in British India, where Kipling spent much of his childhood. He presents a classic rationale for empire as a necessary and noble intervention by the more "civilized" European white nations in other parts of the world. While much analysis has been done on the motivations for empire, Kipling's poem remains a particularly bald expression of the white supremacist ideology behind colonialism. Some have speculated that the poem could have been written as a satire, but the pro-imperial perspective it presents is consistent with Kipling's defense of imperialism throughout his life. In addition, the poem was not received as satire by popular audiences, and Kipling himself never gave an indication that it was intended in any way contrary to this popular reception.

The legacy of the poem has been significant. In response to the poem, several writers penned anti-imperial rebuttals, such as Henry Labouchère's poem "The Brown Man's Burden" (1899) and E. D. Morel's "The Black Man's Burden" (1903). In the years following the poem, the phrase "White Man's Burden" has been used as a metaphor for cultural chauvinism and neo-colonialism, and it has been regularly used to critique policies of intervention by Western governments in Global South nations.

Defining Moment

The expansion of empire is hardly a nineteenth century phenomenon. Since men have adopted agriculture and city life, they have wanted to dominate other men as a sign of their own advancement. However, "imperialism"—that is, the idea that empire is a *necessary* stage of civilization, that men's empires are a sign of their level of civilization—is very much a nineteenth century phenomenon. The combination of nationalism, industrialization, morality and economy became the necessary witches' brew to produce an empire; status as a great power could only be achieved by taking colonies, the way nuclear weapons became the litmus test of power a hundred years later. Add the concept of Darwinism into the mix—that there was something biological in the notion of the occupation of empires, that the nation that was not evolving into an imperial power was instead degenerating—and the brew became intoxicating, and deadly.

No power had a bigger empire in the nineteenth century, in terms of total land mass and population, than the British Empire. Not surprisingly, no power was as fully developed in terms of nationalism and industrialization either, and morality and economy in the form of free market capitalism had been invented in Britain. Darwin himself was English. By Rudyard Kipling's time, the British controlled India's manufacturing and mining, managed diamond and gold mines in Cape Colony, controlled the Suez Canal and the Egyptian "condominium" that surrounded it, held naval bases in Malaysia and trade factories in Hong Kong, and had five settler colonies that ran their own governments, or dominions, in Canada, Newfoundland, Australia, New Zealand and South Africa. The British Empire was such a model of world power to other Europeans by the turn of the twentieth century that they copied it, occupying colonies all over the world in order to play catch-up and hope to get in on some of the riches and prestige that the British state received from its empire. The focus of expansion was Africa, which was almost entirely colonized in a mere 35 years, from 1875 to 1910, and to a lesser extent China's ports, most of which were forced to accept domination by European merchants and the militaries behind them in the 1890s.

Amazingly, this was all true despite the fact that the empire was not exactly popular in Britain except for that short period of time at the end of the nineteenth and early twentieth century when Kipling wrote his works. For all the wealth the British economy got out of its empire, the

THE WHITE (?) MAN'S BURDEN.

The cartoonist William H. Walker ridicules the colonial hypocrisy inherent to "the white man's burden". (Life magazine)

burdens of administering to so many other lands cost the British taxpayer well more than they believed they got out of the colonies. The empire tended to make newspapers when something was wrong—an 1865 rebellion in Jamaica, the viceroy being assassinated in India in 1874, an army slaughtered by Zulus in 1877, General Charles George Gordon losing his head to Sudanese nationalists in 1885, the South African or Boer War from 1899 to 1902. To most Britons, empire was a headache, even though it seemed indefinably important to actually have one.

Ultimately, if they had to define it, most educated British subjects would likely argue that the empire was indeed a sign of their civilization, and a necessary one. The British nations (minus Ireland, which was really still a colony) were made up of peoples who defined themselves largely as Protestant, maritime, commercial and free. These values demanded that the British expand their power around the world, for their own good and everyone else's. Furthermore, despite the fact that millions died trying to keep British occupiers out of their lands and exploitation was the very purpose of imperialism, an educated Briton asked to define the purpose of empire would almost surely say it was for the betterment of the colonized peoples too. Empire was, as the French called it, "a civilizing mission," and despite the hatred they elicited and the hypocrisies that they had to trample over, the British were out to make a better world, whether the world liked it or not.

It was in this context in 1898 that world newspapers carried stories of the Spanish-American War and the United States' foray into empire-building. The American army and navy occupied Cuba, Puerto Rico, Guam and the Philippines. There was little controversy engendered in the first three islands but the Philippines had a well-established independence movement already in place when the US Navy arrived in Manila in 1898, and despite the cooperation of the rebels in driving out the Spanish, American forces simply replaced them as colonizers, leading to a long and violent insurgency that would last until 1902 and cost 9000 American casualties, and the lives of 25 times as many Filipinos. It was this insurgency that inspired Kipling, already the poet laureate of the British Empire, to warn the United States—the original colonial rebel power—as to exactly what sort of a business they had gotten themselves into.

Author Biography

Joseph Rudyard Kipling was the most well-known British poet of his time, and for a while the most popular.

He was born in 1865 in India, a colony to which he would always be sympathetic, and educated back home in England, an experience he hated. He spent time at a public school for the children of army officers and colonial officials, and there he began to write poems of such facility that his parents actually published many of them as a book when he was sixteen. At seventeen he returned to India to become a journalist, where his true literary career began to take shape.

As a journalist, Kipling made many friends and traveled all over south Asia, writing poems and occasionally publishing them. Gradually his talent was recognized, and his editors allowed him to produce short stories, travelogue and poems for his newspapers as opposed to actual news articles. His travelogues would eventually be collected in his book *From Sea to Sea* (1900). His short stories, most about British officers in India, were collected in *Plain Tales from the Hills* (1888), his first commercial success. After published further short stories in newspapers, Kipling left India for England in 1889.

In England, the young Kipling became acquainted with other writers about imperial subjects like H. Rider Haggard, and writers about English social life like Thomas Hardy. But he was mostly a loner, and if he was interested in companionship, he preferred army officers and other people he perceived as adventurous. Not surprisingly, he saw the empire itself as an adventure of sorts, acquired by heroes and maintained by moral pillars. He was also sympathetic to the peoples of the empire, too, however, and he had a vivid imagination, best displayed perhaps in *The Jungle Book* (1894) or *Kim* (1901), both becoming popular children's books too. Yet he was best known as the poet of empire, particularly of British India. Kipling was motivated by the fact that so few of the British people actually knew anything whatsoever about the empire, and he determined to entertain them into a level of understanding. Particularly striking in his work was his sense of fate as a determining factor in people's lives and works, the personification of animals as archetypal human personalities, and the occasional touch of the supernatural and weird, perhaps a nod to his rudimentary understanding of India's many religions.

In 1892, Kipling married an American woman and moved to Vermont, where his work thrived and he contrived to meet Americans he admired, like Theodore Roosevelt, for whom he wrote "The White Man's Burden." Perhaps not coincidentally, Roosevelt was the United States' most convincing version of an imperialist, a hero of the Spanish-American War later on. He bounced back and forth between England and America for a time before taking ill and moving to South Africa for the warm climate. There, he had a first-hand view of the Boer War (1899-1902) and made the acquaintance of the men who ran Cape Colony and the war effort, including Alfred Milner and Cecil Rhodes. The British army was woefully unprepared to fight the South African Afrikaaner population, and the shock of their early failures in the field led Kipling to push for military preparedness and sacrifice in the name of the empire for the rest of his life. His works were never as popular as in this period, but he also became more strident politically and began to alienate readers.

Kipling returned to England permanently in 1908. A year earlier, he won the Nobel Prize for literature, which cemented his status as the embodiment of empire. His causes tended to be reactionary; he supported Protestant rebellion in Ireland and was positively excited with the coming of the Great War. Then his only son, John, went missing at the battle of Loos in 1915, an experience that devastated him—John's body was never found in Rudyard Kipling's lifetime. He became embittered due to his inability to find his son, contracting an ulcer that gave him regular gastrointestinal difficulties. He also published dark poems reflecting his sense of loss. In 1917, he was contracted by the Imperial War Graves Commission to write inscriptions for its memorials and epitaphs for soldiers. His production tailed off in the last twenty years of his life, and he died in 1936.

HISTORICAL DOCUMENT

Take up the White Man's burden—
Send forth the best ye breed—
Go bind your sons to exile
To serve your captives' need;
To wait in heavy harness,
On fluttered folk and wild—
Your new-caught, sullen peoples,
Half-devil and half-child.
Take up the White Man's burden—
In patience to abide,
To veil the threat of terror
And check the show of pride;
By open speech and simple,
An hundred times made plain
To seek another's profit,
And work another's gain.
Take up the White Man's burden—
The savage wars of peace—
Fill full the mouth of Famine
And bid the sickness cease;
And when your goal is nearest
The end for others sought,
Watch Sloth and heathen Folly
Bring all your hopes to nought.
Take up the White Man's burden—
No tawdry rule of kings,
But toil of serf and sweeper—
The tale of common things.

The ports ye shall not enter,
The roads ye shall not tread,
Go mark them with your living,
And mark them with your dead.
Take up the White Man's burden—
And reap his old reward:
The blame of those ye better,
The hate of those ye guard—
The cry of hosts ye humour
(Ah, slowly!) toward the light:—
"Why brought he us from bondage,
Our loved Egyptian night?"
Take up the White Man's burden—
Ye dare not stoop to less—
Nor call too loud on Freedom
To cloke your weariness;
By all ye cry or whisper,
By all ye leave or do,
The silent, sullen peoples
Shall weigh your gods and you.
Take up the White Man's burden—
Have done with childish days—
The lightly proferred laurel,
The easy, ungrudged praise.
Comes now, to search your manhood
Through all the thankless years
Cold, edged with dear-bought wisdom,
The judgment of your peers!

Document Analysis

"The White Man's Burden" is significant in its depiction of both the colonized and the colonizer. The poem is addressed to a colonizing nation. In the first stanza, Kipling calls on his audience to "Take up the White Man's burden— / Send forth the best ye breed— / Go bind your sons to exile." He thus frames the colonizing nation as one making a great sacrifice and the colonial troops as being the best of the nation, being sent "to serve your captives' need." He depicts the colonizer as a servant to the colonized people, which he describes as ungrateful "sullen peoples, / Half-devil and half-child."

Indeed, the image of a half-devil and half-child creates a dual personality for those who are colonized, and it serves to justify different aspects of imperialism. The half-child portrayal establishes a need for a more knowledgeable colonizer to teach the innocent and ignorant colonized about life and civilization. This patronizing view of the colonized consigns all indigenous knowledge to the less advanced and less developed. At the same time, the half-devil depiction reflects a fundamental mistrust of the colonized and relegates all resistance to their inherent savagery and moral inferiority—justifying military tactics and often brutal systems of control and separation between the colonizer and colonized.

The themes of colonialism as a burden and of a self-sacrificing colonial official continue throughout the poem. The tone becomes increasingly bitter, as when Kipling complains in the third stanza that after all the colonizers' hard work to "Fill full the mouth of Famine / And bid the sickness cease," they must "Watch sloth and heathen Folly / Bring all your hopes to nought." The resentment Kipling holds toward the ungrateful colonized people is best seen in the fifth stanza of the poem. Here Kipling describes the "reward" as "The blame of those ye better / The hate of those ye guard." Native resistance to colonialism is deemed ignorant and devoid of political understanding.

In response to any resistance, Kipling points out that the colonizer is obligated to maintain his honor and composure. The sixth stanza of the poem characterizes the duty of the colonizer to be a constant representative of the West. Despite weariness, Kipling forewarns the young colonizer, "By all ye cry or whisper / By all ye leave or do / The silent, sullen peoples / Shall weigh your gods and you." Thus, Kipling adds another level of burden on the colonizer, who is constantly representing civilization to the natives.

In the final stanza of the poem, Kipling makes a case for imperialism as part of growing into manhood. The individual in this case serves to represent national maturation as well, and in the final line Kipling presents the true reward, in his eyes, of imperialism: "The judgment of your peers." In this way, Kipling argues that even if the colonized people do not appreciate the sacrifices of the colonizer, the rest of the "civilized" world will.

In the final analysis, "White Man's Burden" treats colonialism as a purely humanitarian effort on the part of the colonizer. Kipling's imperialism is devoid of any taint of economic or political gain for the imperial powers. There is also no mention of suffering of the colonized people under the abuses of colonialism—only the suffering that colonialism seeks to alleviate.

Essential Themes

The point at which Kipling published "The White Man's Burden" was actually the high watermark for imperialism in both Britain and the United States. The insurgency in the Philippines did little to stem enthusiasm for American efforts at nation-building; from Central America and the Caribbean all the way to the wars in Iraq and Afghanistan, the United States has taken on the "burden" of bettering peoples around the world at the end of a gun, never an optimal way to create democracy or flourishing capitalist economies. The idea of actually colonizing those places, however, disappeared after the Spanish-American war, much as it did for Britain after the Boer War at the same time. Colonization seemed to fall out of fashion as fears ratcheted up about a general European war coming in the early twentieth century.

The war would cost Britain's poet of imperialism his son; it also cost Britain the similar assuredness with which its empire was conducted. Though the British Empire picked up valuable oil fields in southwest Asia with the conclusion of the war, its global hegemony was mortally damaged; Britain could not win the war without the help of its empire, and the slaughter entailed wounded the goodwill that Britain had accumulated and that Kipling's "white man's burden" claimed the British looked to foster overseas. The Philippines would become independent in 1946, after the Second World War; most of Britain's colonies would follow soon after.

———*Samantha Christiansen*

Bibliography and Further Reading

Brendon, Piers. *The Decline and Fall of the British Empire, 1781-1997*. New York: Vintage Books, 2010.

Gilmour, David. *The Long Recessional: The Imperial Life of Rudyard Kipling*. New York: Farrar, Straus and Giroux, 2002.

Judd, Denis. *Diamonds are Forever? Kipling's Imperialism*. New York : Longman, 1998.

Karnow, Stanley. *In Our Image: America's Empire in the Philippines*. New York: Ballantine Books, 1989.

Kinzer, Stephen. *The True Flag: Theodore Roosevelt, Mark Twain, and the Birth of American Empire*. New York: Henry Holt, 2016.

Morris, Jan. *Pax Britannica: The Climax of an Empire*. New York: Harcourt, Brace & World, 1968.

Musicant, Ivan. *Empire by Default: The Spanish-American War and the Dawn of the American Century*. New York: Henry Holt, 1998.

THE FIRST WORLD WAR

One of the inevitable results of the rise of nationalism and populism was progress—competition led to the desire to be better than the people one competed against, and thus Europe and the United States were the most advanced areas of the world in the early twentieth century. The other inevitable result of the rise of nationalism and populism was war: the ultimate competition. It was one thing to prove a nation's greatness by dominating less materially-developed peoples on other continents. It was another thing entirely to take on the neighbors, powers of comparative equality in industry and military might, to win the social Darwinist struggle for existence and hold the future of civilization in your hands. Or so the western powers believed.

The Great War began soon after the Austro-Hungarian ultimatum to Serbia was issued. It is often referred to as the First World War—not a wrong title, but no one knew at the time there would be a second one. Also, in some respects the Seven Years' War of the eighteenth century was a "world war" in that it took place over a larger span of territory. Yet every other war paled in significance to the Great War—the real First World War—because of nationalism and populism. The war involved all people in civilization in one way or another in its conduct, either as a soldier or a supplier or a victim or an exploiter; it was a function of nationalism, of the division of peoples into competing ethnicities, cultures, religions, economies and languages as well as states. Nations fought against empires, not only on the other side but the empires they were a part of, such as the Irish rebels in the Easter Rebellion. Other nations found their roots in the war, such as the Israeli people in the Balfour Declaration.

The First World War especially put the concept of the nation-state quite literally on the map. Old empires like the Russians, the Ottomans and the Austro-Hungarians were sept aside in favor of "national self-determination," the notion that peoples should form states for themselves based on their national distinctions. There were many hypocrisies in the application of this idea when the war ended; Woodrow Wilson, who came up with the idea, was specifically talking about the ethnic peoples of eastern Europe and had little interest in people in the rest of the world. Yet imperialism had spread the concept of nationalism to these peoples, and the war had shown that the Europeans had no business asserting the superior level of their civilization over anyone. Anti-slavery and anti-war activist Edmund Dene Morel explained the deleterious impact of imperialism on Africans in *The Black Man's Burden*, for example.

Even more, though, the war asserted that the world should be split up into nations, free, distinct from and equal to one another, and empires seemed clearly to be the state organization of the past. The League of Nations existed to create such a situation; why couldn't every people on earth participate in it? Koreans declared their independence from the Japanese empire, abortively. Sun Yixian called on the Chinese people to implement nationalism, socialism and democracy in a Chinese manner, to bring the emperor's old territories together as one people and one power. Some people even defined themselves as a nation when nothing else whatsoever brought them together. "Syria," as that section of the carved-up Ottoman Empire came to be called, was an ethnic and religious hodgepodge; its peoples have had almost nothing in common with one another since their borders were drawn. Yet they were drawn together when the war ended by the desire to avoid becoming a French mandate of the League: a temporary colony. As has been proven since, Syrians have little in common, but one thing that united all of them was the desire not to colonized by the French.

If the nineteenth century had been the age of nationalism, the twentieth century became the age of the nation-state. The idea of empire was not finished, as the Second World War proved in horrible fashion. But the idea of people's uniqueness requiring unique state organization became the organizing principle of the century. It would not last very long.

■ Austro-Hungarian Ultimatum to Serbia and the Serbian Reply

Date: 1914
Authors: Foreign Ministries of the Austro-Hungarian Empire and Kingdom of Serbia
Genre: Diplomatic communiqués

Summary Overview

On June 28, 1914, Archduke Franz Ferdinand of Austria, heir apparent to the Austro-Hungarian throne, and his wife, Sophie, were assassinated in Sarajevo, the capital of Bosnia-Herzegovina, by a Bosnian Serb, Gavrilo Princip. One month later, on July 23, 1914, the Austrian government presented the Serbian government with an ultimatum demanding that certain conditions be met in order to stabilize bilateral relations. Serbia was given two days to respond to the ultimatum. On July 25, the Serbian government answered the ultimatum in a manner unacceptable to Austria-Hungary, which three days later declared war on Serbia. Thus began World War I.

Defining Moment

The Austro-Hungarian ultimatum to Serbia and the Serbian reply (1914) came at the end of a long chain of events leading up to world war. The nineteenth century was an extremely turbulent period in the history of the Balkans. "The sick man of Europe," as the Ottoman Empire was called colloquially, lost a considerable part of its territories, out of which new independent states such as Serbia, Romania, and Bulgaria were formed. Three empires tried to exert direct pressure and influence on these lands: Austria-Hungary, Russia, and Ottoman Turkey. Following the Russian invasion of Turkey in 1877, a congress held in Berlin in 1878 put Bosnia-Herzegovina under Austrian jurisdiction. In 1908 the province was annexed to Austria and became a province of the Austrian part of the Austro-Hungarian Empire—a fact that Serbia was made to accept in a formal declaration a year later in March 1909. This province was inhabited by Serbs, Croats, and Muslim Bosnians, and Serbia was not satisfied with the solution.

At that time Europe was divided between two military blocks. The first, the Triple Alliance, had been constituted in 1882 and was made up of Germany, Austria-Hungary, and Italy. The second, the Triple Entente, brought together Great Britain, France, and Russia in 1907. The diplomatic and political situation in Europe was tense, and any spark could result in a global conflict. Both sides were arming themselves, making military plans, and looking for any occasion to weaken the enemy. The assassination of Franz Ferdinand proved to be that occasion, when the following declarations proved unacceptable to either power involved. A week after this ultimatum was promulgated, the Austro-Hungarian Empire's government declared war on Serbia. The tsarist regime in the Russian Empire pledged itself to defend Serbia; the German government had given a 'blank check' to Austria-Hungary promising their unconditional support whatever the outcome of the ultimatum. The result was a general European war that would eventually engulf not only the continent's major powers but many other states around the world besides, and cost the lives of an estimated ten million people.

Author Biographies

The original Austrian communiqué was issued by the empire's foreign minister, Count Leopold von Berchtold (1863-1942). Berchtold was not an imaginative diplomat but he was stately and well-connected. He was respected enough to have served ambassadorships in Britain, France and Russia over the course of his career, yet when the moment of European war arrived, Berchtold was not prescient enough to realize that any one of the European powers that he had lived in might declare war on Austria-Hungary—let alone all of them—should his state declare war on Serbia. He saw the assassination of the heir to the Austro-Hungarian throne as an opportunity to lay Serbia low diplomatically and militarily. His ultimatum was designed to be rejected; while delivering it, the Austrian ambassador to Serbia carried his suitcases with him, expecting to be thrown out of the country. Despite the Serb government's acceptance of most of the terms, Berchtold and everyone else in the Austro-Hungarian government saw the reply as a rejection, and declared war on July 28.

Serbia's prime minister, Nikola Pasic (1845-1926) wrote the Serbian reply and delivered it personally to the Austrian embassy in Belgrade. Pasic was a natural intriguer as a politician, having been arrested for plotting against his own crown and government multiple times since his political career began in 1878. He had served as prime minister since 1903. In that office, Pasic often had to curb the ambitions of his own generals as they spoiled for a war in southern Europe that would increase the size of Serbia. At the same time, he certainly knew about and supplied most of the activities of the Black Hand (Narodna Odbrana), the group that assassinated the archduke. It is likely that he did not approve of the assassination plot, and may have issued orders to arrest the conspirators before they left for Bosnia. Yet when it came time to respond to Austria-Hungary's challenge, Pasic brilliantly parried Berchtold's ultimatum by accepting all of its demands except one, thus placing the blame for aggressive action for war on Austria-Hungary.

HISTORICAL DOCUMENT

Austria-Hungary's Ultimatum to Serbia

On the 31st of March, 1909, the Serbian Minister in Vienna, on the instructions of the Serbian Government, made the following declaration to the Imperial and Royal Government:

"Serbia recognizes that the fait accompli regarding Bosnia has not affected her rights and consequently she will conform to the decisions that the Powers may take in conformity with Article 25 of the Treaty of Berlin. In deference to the advice of the Great Powers, Serbia undertakes to renounce from now onwards the attitude of protest and opposition which she has adopted with regard to the annexation since last autumn.

She undertakes, moreover, to modify the direction of her policy with regard to Austria-Hungary and to live in future on good neighborly terms with the latter."

The history of recent years, and in particular the painful events of the 28th June last, have shown the existence of a subversive [Serbian] movement with the object of detaching a part of the territories of Austria-Hungary from the monarchy. The movement, which had its birth under the eye of the Serbian Government, has gone so far as to make itself manifest on both sides of the Serbian frontier in the shape of acts of terrorism and a series of outrages and murders.

Far from carrying out the formal undertakings contained in the declaration of the 31st March, 1909, the Royal Serbian Government has done nothing to repress these movements. It has permitted the criminal machinations of various societies and associations directed against the monarchy and [it] has tolerated unrestrained language on the part of the press, the glorification of the perpetrators of outrages, and the participation of officers and functionaries in subversive agitation. It has permitted an unwholesome propaganda in public instruction. In short, it has permitted all manifestations of a nature to incite the Serbian population to hatred of the monarchy and contempt of its institutions.

This culpable tolerance of the Royal Serbian Government had not ceased at the moment when the events of the 28th June last proved its fatal consequences to the whole world.

It results from the depositions and confessions of the criminal perpetrators of the outrage of the 28th June that the Sarajevo assassinations were planned in Belgrade, that the arms and explosives with which the murderers were provided had been given to them by Serbian officers and functionaries belonging to the Narodna Odbrana, and, finally, that the passage into Bosnia of the criminals and their arms was organized and effected by the chiefs of the Serbian frontier service.

The above-mentioned results of the magisterial investigation do not permit the Austro-Hungarian Government to pursue any longer the attitude of expectant forbearance which it has maintained for years in face of the machinations hatched in Belgrade, and thence propagated in the territories of the monarchy. The results, on the contrary, impose on it the duty of putting an end to the intrigues which form a perpetual menace to the tranquility of the monarchy.

To achieve this end the Imperial and Royal Government sees itself compelled to demand from the Royal Serbian Government a formal assurance that it condemns this dangerous propaganda against the monarchy; in other words, the whole series of tendencies, the ultimate aim of which is to detach from the monarchy territories belonging to it, and that it undertakes to suppress by every means this criminal and terrorist propaganda.

In order to give a formal character to this undertaking the Royal Serbian Government shall publish on the front page of its Official Journal of the 26th July the following declaration:

"The Royal Government of Serbia condemns the propaganda directed against Austria-Hungary—i.e., the general tendency of which the final aim is to detach from the Austro-Hungarian monarchy territories belonging to it, and it sincerely deplores the fatal consequences of these criminal proceedings.

"The Royal Government regrets that Serbian officers and functionaries participated in the above-mentioned propaganda and thus compromised the good neighborly relations to which the Royal Government was solemnly pledged by its declaration of the 31st March, 1909.

"The Royal Government, which disapproves and repudiates all idea of interfering or attempting to interfere with the destinies of the inhabitants of any part whatsoever of Austria-Hungary, considers it its duty formally to warn officers and functionaries, and the whole population of the kingdom, that henceforward it will proceed with the utmost rigor against persons who may be guilty of such machinations, which it will use all its efforts to anticipate and suppress."

This declaration shall simultaneously be communicated to the royal army as an order of the day by his Majesty the King and shall be published in the Official Bulletin of the army.

The Royal Serbian Government further undertakes:

1. To suppress any publication which incites to hatred and contempt of the Austro-Hungarian Monarchy and the general tendency of which is directed against its territorial integrity;
2. To dissolve immediately the society styled Narodna Odbrana, to confiscate all its means of propaganda, and to proceed in the same manner against other societies and their branches in Serbia which engage in propaganda against the Austro-Hungarian Monarchy. The Royal Government shall take the necessary measures to prevent the societies dissolved from continuing their activity under another name and form;
3. To eliminate without delay from public instruction in Serbia, both as regards the teaching body and also as regards the methods of instruction, everything that serves, or might serve, to foment the propaganda against Austria-Hungary;
4. To remove from the military service, and from the administration in general, all officers and functionaries guilty of propaganda against the Austro-Hungarian Monarchy whose names and deeds the Austro-Hungarian Government reserves to itself the right of communicating to the Royal Government;
5. To accept the collaboration in Serbia of representatives of the Austro-Hungarian Government in the suppression of the subversive movement directed against the territorial integrity of the monarchy;
6. To take judicial proceedings against accessories to the plot of the 28th June who are on Serbian territory. Delegates of the Austro-Hungarian Government will take part in the investigation relating thereto;
7. To proceed without delay to the arrest of Major Voija Tankositch and of the individual named Milan Ciganovitch, a Serbian State employee, who have been compromised by the results of the magisterial inquiry at Sarajevo;
8. To prevent by effective measures the co-operation of the Serbian authorities in the illicit traffic in arms and explosives across the frontier, to dismiss and punish severely the officials of the frontier service at Schabatz and Loznica guilty of having assisted the perpetrators of the Sarajevo crime by facilitating their passage across the frontier;
9. To furnish the Imperial and Royal Government with explanations regarding the unjustifiable utterances of high Serbian officials, both in Serbia and abroad, who, notwithstanding their official position, did not hesitate after the crime of the 28th June to express themselves in interviews in terms of hostility to the Austro-Hungarian Government; and, finally,
10. To notify the Imperial and Royal Government without delay of the execution of the measures comprised under the preceding heads.

The Austro-Hungarian Government expects the reply of the Royal Government at the latest by 6 o'clock on Saturday evening, the 25th July.

A memorandum dealing with the results of the magisterial inquiry at Sarajevo with regard to the officials mentioned under heads (7) and (8) is attached to this note.

Serbia's Reply to Austria-Hungary's Ultimatum (1914)

The Royal Serbian Government have received the communication of the Imperial and Royal Government of the 10th instant, and are convinced that their reply will remove any misunderstanding which may threaten to impair the good neighborly relations between the Austro-Hungarian Monarchy and the Kingdom of Serbia.

Conscious of the fact that the protests which were made both from the tribune of the national Skupshtina [the Serbian parliament] and in the declarations and actions of the responsible representatives of the State—protests which were cut short by the declaration made by the Serbian Government on the 18th (31st) March, 1909—have not been renewed on any occasion as regards the great neighboring Monarchy, and that no attempt has been made since that time, either by the successive Royal Governments or by their organs, to change the political and legal state of affairs created in Bosnia and Herzegovina, the Royal Government draw attention to the fact that in this connection the Imperial and Royal Government have made no representation except one concerning a schoolbook, and that on that occasion the Imperial and Royal Government received an entirely satisfactory explanation. Serbia has several times given proofs of her pacific and moderate policy during the Balkan crisis, and it is thanks to Serbia and to the sacrifice that she has made in the exclusive interest of European peace that that peace has been preserved. The Royal Government cannot be held responsible for manifestations of a private character, such as articles in the press and the peaceable work of societies—manifestations which take place in nearly all countries in the ordinary course of events, and which as a general rule escape official control. The Royal Government are all the less responsible in view of the fact that at the time of the solution of a series of questions which arose between Serbia and Austria-Hungary they gave proof of a great readiness to oblige, and thus succeeded in settling the majority of these questions to the advantage of the two neighboring countries.

For these reasons the Royal Government have been pained and surprised at the statements according to which members of the Kingdom of Serbia are supposed to have participated in the preparations for the crime committed at Sarajevo; the Royal Government expected to be invited to collaborate in an investigation of all that concerns this crime, and they were ready, in order to prove the entire correctness of their attitude, to take measures against any persons concerning whom representations were made to them. Falling in, therefore, with the desire of the Imperial and Royal Government, they are prepared to hand over for trial any Serbian subject, without regard to his situation or rank, of whose complicity in the crime of Sarajevo proofs are forthcoming, and more especially they undertake to cause to be published on the first page of the *Journal Officiel*, on the date of the 13th (26th) July, the following declaration:

"The Royal Government of Serbia condemn all propaganda which may be directed against Austria-Hungary, that is to say, all such tendencies as aim at ultimately detaching from the Austro-Hungarian Monarchy territories which form part thereof, and they sincerely deplore the baneful consequences of these criminal movements. The Royal Government regret that, according to the communication from the Imperial and Royal Government, certain Serbian officers and officials should have taken part in the above-mentioned propaganda, and thus compromise the good neighborly relations to which the Royal Serbian Government was solemnly engaged by the declaration of the 18th (31st) March, 1909, which declaration disapproves and repudiates all idea or attempt at interference with the destiny of the inhabitants of any part whatsoever of Austria-Hungary, and they consider it their duty formally to warn the officers, officials, and entire population of the kingdom that henceforth they will take the most rigorous steps against all such persons as are guilty of such acts, to prevent and to repress which they will use their utmost endeavor."

This declaration will be brought to the knowledge of the Royal Army in an order of the day, in the name of his Majesty the King, by his Royal Highness the Crown Prince Alexander, and will be published in the next official army bulletin.

The Royal Government further undertake:

1. To introduce at the first regular convocation of the Skupshtina a provision into the press law providing for the most severe punishment of incitement to hatred or contempt of the Austro-Hungarian Monarchy, and for taking action against any publication the general tendency of which is directed against the territorial integrity of Austria-Hungary. The Government engage at the approaching revision of the Constitution to cause an amendment to be introduced into Article 22 of the Constitution of such a nature that such publication may be confiscated, a proceeding at present impossible under the categorical terms of Article 22 of the Constitution.

2. The Government possess no proof, nor does the note of the Imperial and Royal Government furnish them with any, that the "Narodna Odbrana" and other similar societies have committed up to the present any criminal act of this nature through the proceedings of any of their members. Nevertheless, the Royal Government will accept the demand of the Imperial and Royal Government and will dissolve the "Narodna Odbrana" Society and every other society which may be directing its efforts against Austria-Hungary.

3. The Royal Serbian Government undertake to remove without delay from their public educational establishments in Serbia all that serves or could serve to foment propaganda against Austria-Hungary, whenever the Imperial and Royal Government furnish them with facts and proofs of this propaganda.

4. The Royal Government also agree to remove from military service all such persons as the judicial inquiry may have proved to be guilty of acts directed against the integrity of the territory of the Austro-Hungarian Monarchy, and they expect the Imperial and Royal Government to communicate to them at a later date the names and the acts of these officers and officials for the purposes of the proceedings which are to be taken against them.

5. The Royal Government must confess that they do not clearly grasp the meaning or the scope of the demand made by the Imperial and Royal Government that Serbia shall undertake to accept the collaboration of the organs of the Imperial and Royal Government upon their territory, but they declare that they will admit such collaboration as agrees with the principle of international law, with criminal procedure, and with good neighborly relations.

6. It goes without saying that the Royal Government consider it their duty to open an inquiry against all such persons as are, or eventually may be, implicated in the plot of the 15th (28th) June, and who happen to be within the territory of the kingdom. As regards the participation in this inquiry of Austro-Hungarian agents or authorities appointed for this purpose by the Imperial and Royal Government, the Royal Government cannot accept such an arrangement, as it would be a violation of the Constitution and of the law of criminal procedure; nevertheless, in concrete cases communications as to the results of the investigation in question might be given to the Austro-Hungarian agents.

7. The Royal Government proceeded, on the very evening of the delivery of the note, to arrest Commandant Voislav Tankositch. As regards Milan Ciganovitch, who is a subject of the Austro-Hungarian Monarchy and who up to the 15th (28th) June was employed (on probation) by the directorate of railways, it has not yet been possible to arrest him.

8. The Austro-Hungarian Government are requested to be so good as to supply as soon as possible, in the customary form, the presumptive evidence of guilt, as well as the eventual proofs of guilt which have been collected up to the present time, at the inquiry at Sarajevo, for the purposes of the latter inquiry.

9. The Serbian Government will reinforce and extend the measures which have been taken for preventing the illicit traffic of arms and explosives across the frontier. It goes without saying that they will immediately order an inquiry and will severely punish the frontier officials on the Schabatz-Loznica line who have failed in their duty and allowed the authors of the crime of Sarajevo to pass.

10. The Royal Government will gladly give explanations of the remarks made by their officials, whether in Serbia or abroad, in interviews after the crime, and which, according to the statement of the Imperial and Royal Government, were hostile towards the Monarchy, as soon as the Imperial and Royal Government have communicated to them the passages in question in these remarks, and as soon as they have shown that the remarks were actually made by the said officials, although the Royal Government will itself take steps to collect evidence and proofs.

11. The Royal Government will inform the Imperial and Royal Government of the execution of the measures comprised under the above heads, in so far as this has not already been done by the present note, as soon as each measure has been ordered and carried out.

If the Imperial and Royal Government are not satisfied with this reply, the Serbian Government, considering that it is not to the common interest to precipitate the solution of this question, are ready, as always, to accept a pacific understanding, either by referring this question to the decision of the International Tribunal of The Hague, or to the Great Powers which took part in the drawing up of the declaration made by the Serbian Government on the 18th (31st) March, 1909.

Document Analysis

The Austro-Hungarian Ultimatum to Serbia opens with a reference to the Serbian statement from the time of Bosnia-Herzegovina's annexation and Serbia's assurance that it would abide by the undertaken action ("the fait accompli"). The next three paragraphs lay out accusations that Serbia was tolerating and, in fact, aiding acts of terror and attacks on the Austro-Hungarian administration in the annexed territory. These actions had led to the murder of Archduke Franz Ferdinand and his wife.

The Austro-Hungarian authorities put forward several demands to be met by Serbia. First, Serbia was to condemn all actions directed against Austria-Hungary, particularly those aimed at detachment of provinces from the empire. A statement to this effect was to be published by the Serbian government in an official state journal on July 26. Next follow ten precise conditions that the Serbs had to resolve in order to satisfy the Austro-Hungarian authorities and secure peace. These include imposition of censorship, dissolution of the nationalist group Narodna Odbrana (accused of taking part in the assassination), stopping of all anti-Austrian propaganda, acceptance of Austro-Hungarian collaboration in the inquiry into "subversive movements" against the empire in Serbia, arrest and trial of those involved in the assassination, cessation of cross-border supply of arms, and explanation of hostile statements by Serbian officials after the murder. The execution of these points was to take place immediately, and Austria-Hungary was to be informed about the undertaken measures.

The second document is the Serbian Reply to the Austro-Hungarian Ultimatum. This document shows double dating, because Serbia was still using the old Julian calendar. In 1914 the difference between Julian and Gregorian dating was thirteen days. The reply opens with a paragraph in which the Serbian government points to the fact that since 1909 it has not undertaken any actions against Austria-Hungary, particularly concerning the status of Bosnia-Herzegovina. In the second paragraph the Serbian government displays surprise that it was not asked to take part in the investigations after the murder with respect issues relating to Serbian participants.

There follows a detailed answer to the Austro-Hungarian requests. The Serbian government agrees to publish the demanded declaration practically unchanged, as an army order and in the official army publication. Serbia next addresses each of the ten points of the ultimatum. The Serbian Royal Government agrees to implement laws to block incendiary statements in the press and to suppress Narodna Odbrana, although the reply stresses the lack of any evidence against this and similar organizations. Serbia further promises to put an end to any anti-Austro-Hungarian propaganda in public life and in the army. Showing a good-faith effort to meet the demands of its powerful neighbor, Serbia also consents to open an inquiry into the plot to kill the archduke and informs Austria-Hungary that one arrest has been made. The Serbian government requests documented evidence with which to proceed. In the end, if Austria-Hungary were to remain dissatisfied, Serbia agrees to put the matter before either the Hague Tribunal (referring to the Permanent Court of Arbitration in the Hague) or the "Great Powers" who had been involved in the 1909 declaration concerning ceding of Serbian territory.

The only Austrian request rejected by the Serbian government is found in the fifth point, where Austria asks Serbia to allow Austro-Hungarian officials (in reality, police) to conduct their investigations on Serbian territory. The document clearly stipulates that Serbia is willing to collaborate in the investigations and agrees to fulfill all regulations demanded by international law but refuses to allow foreign interference into their domestic affairs. It was this very point that effectively made the Serbian answer unacceptable to Vienna and caused Austria-Hungary to declare war on its neighbor.

Essential Themes

The diplomatic exchange between Austria-Hungary and Serbia achieved its objectives on both sides. The Austro-Hungarians got the war that they wanted to punish Serbia; the Serbian government deflected enough blame from events to secure help from the Russian Empire. Yet the war they conducted was worse than any of the diplomats and politicians involved in the exchange could have imagined. By 1916 Serbia had lost one out of six of its people, civilian and military, and the country was wiped from the European map, not to

reemerge until the 1990s. By 1918 the Russian Empire had fallen into Bolshevism and civil war. By 1919, the Austro-Hungarian Empire was starving and divvied up into its constituent ethnic parts, creating a new Europe of small and poor nation-states.

The kind of political calculations involved in the Austro-Hungarian ultimatum and the Serbian reply have certainly lasted, however, largely because nationalism is still a motivating factor in world power politics. The essence of these two carefully-crafted letters was not about their effort to craft a diplomatic solution to an international crisis, despite their language. They were really about stoking the nationalist fires of their populations—in Austria-Hungary, in defense of the monarchy, and in Serbia, in defense of its borders and in offense to take Bosnia-Herzegovina. The As many politicians and diplomats since have discovered, like Berchtold, Pasic and everyone involved in these letters, it is important to be careful of what a nation-state's people wish for, because they might get it.

———*Jakub Basista*

Bibliography and Further Reading

Clark, Christopher. *The Sleepwalkers: How Europe Went to War in 1914*. Boston: Harper Perennial, 2014.

MacMillan, Margaret. *The War that Ended Peace: The Road to 1914*. New York: Random House, 2014.

McMeekin, Sean. *July 1914: Countdown to War*. New York: Basic Books, 2013.

Tuchman, Barbara. *The Guns of August*. New York: Ballantine Books, 1962.

■ 1916 Proclamation of the Provisional Government of the Irish Republic

Date: April 24, 1916
Authors: Patrick Pearse et al.
Genre: Declarative speech

Summary Review

On the Monday after Easter, April 24, 1916, a ragtag body of civilian soldiers, led by members of the Catholic paramilitary Irish Volunteers, seized the General Post Office in Dublin as the headquarters of what was supposed to be a rebellion against the British Empire. The leaders of what came to be called the 1916 Rising were romantics—poets, politicians and professors, as opposed to professionally-trained soldiers. When they took the Post Office in the morning, one of their leaders, Patrick Pearse, strode out the front door of the building at noon to proclaim Ireland's independence from the British Empire.

The Republic of Ireland today dates its beginnings to this moment, similar to the way the United States dates its independence to its own declaration in 1776. The similarities do not end there. Just as in the colonies in 1776, there was a viable alternative of home rule available under the British crown. There was also a very similar division of sentiment amongst the people whose independence was being declared. There was a similar sense that the signatories to each declaration of independence were taking their own lives in their hands. In Ireland, however, the writers and signatories to the 1916 Easter Proclamation expected to fail, to give themselves as a "blood sacrifice" to the cause of their nation's independence. In that respect, they were very different from the Americans in 1776. Moreover, despite their correct assumption that they would all fail and die—or perhaps because of it—they launched Ireland on the path of rebellion against the British Empire that would finally end in the island's freedom.

Defining Moment

The rebels of Easter 1916 were the product of the long-term enmity between Britain and Ireland. The British never seemed able to appropriately define what Ireland was in their empire and what it meant to them. The Irish always knew—both Catholics and Protestants—that they were considered inferiors by the British, and thus they never accommodated themselves to British rule.

In the early twentieth century, several historical events came together to establish a real breaking point for this contentious relationship. In a climate of European nationalism, the Irish people rediscovered their Gaelic cultural roots, and intellectuals wanted to define themselves as separate from their English overlords. For a century, Ireland had been one of the four nations in the United Kingdom, but the combination of English arrogance and neglect meant that there was a strong political demand for what was called Home Rule, the establishment of a subordinate national government separate from the British Parliament but still under the English crown. For even longer, the predominantly Catholic Irish people had developed a strong and educated Protestant minority in their midst that clung to its connection to Protestant England, and were therefore determined that Home Rule would never happen, on pain of civil war. Only the beginning of the Great War in 1914 had kept Irishmen from killing one another, and most of the paramilitary soldiers who had sworn to fight each other over Ireland's state status had instead marched off to fight in France. All of these events were central to understanding the authors and the intentions of the 1916 Proclamation.

Most Irish seemed content with the concept of Home Rule in the prewar era; those who were not wanted to stay connected to the British Empire and its protection one way or another. So when war broke out, both groups were willing to fight for the British Empire under the assumption that their differences would be hammered out once the war was over. Not everyone wanted to wait, however. Amongst them were a small number of members of the Irish Volunteers, the Catholic paramilitary in Dublin, most of who had only just learned to carry a gun and fight. They included Eoin Mac Neill, founder of the Gaelic League, an organization promoting traditional Irish culture; Patrick Pearse, promoter of the Gaelic language at his school, St. Enda's, in Dublin;

Thomas MacDonagh, another poet and teacher at St. Enda's and founder of the Irish Theater; and Joseph Mary Plunkett, also a poet and playwright, and editor of the *Irish Review*, an important literary magazine that connected the Irish nationalist community.

They formed a Central Executive in Dublin, and combined forces with a socialist paramilitary group, the Irish Citizens Army, led by one James Connolly and the future playwright Sean O'Casey. Through contacts in America, they contacted the German government to get a boatload of weapons shipped to the Irish coast. Idealists all, the rebels hoped that an organized uprising with German support would excite the wider Irish populace into general revolt. Ireland would force its independence in the middle of the war, and the new republic would even secure for itself a place at the peace conference when the war ended.

All of this proved illusory, as was usual in Irish history. The German government agreed to ship the guns, but lost interest in fomenting rebellion, since it seemed clear the Irish population was uninterested, if not hostile. The ship carrying the guns never met its contact on the Irish shore and was scuttled before the British navy captured it. Yet the romantics in Dublin were determined to go forward with the rising anyway, because only "blood sacrifice" could rid Ireland of its servitude to the British crown and dependence on English culture. The Easter rebels determined that the blood sacrifice would be their own, for their nation's good.

Author Biography

While Thomas MacDonagh is thought to have contributed to the wording, Patrick Pearse was the acknowledged author of the 1916 Proclamation and perhaps the most romantic of any of the rebels. Born in Dublin in 1879, he was an early exponent of Irish cultural nationalism. He was considered an extremist by many of his colleagues; the nominal leader of the Gaelic League and the Irish Volunteers, Eoin Mac Neill, even pulled his children out of St. Enda's because he feared the violent rhetoric of revolt to which Pearse exposed them. Fifteen of Pearse's teenaged pupils actually joined the Easter Rising, inspired by their teacher.

Pearse had few illusions about the success of the Rising. Yet his poetic nature and that of his colleagues allowed them to believe that a rebellion would have an almost mystical effect on the Irish people. "Bloodshed is a cleansing and sanctifying thing, and the nation which regards it as the final horror has lost its manhood," wrote Pearse. His death and that of the other people occupying the General Post Office would be a victory because it would galvanize the Irish people into fighting for their freedom. It was certainly no mistake, then, that the 1916 Rising and its proclamation of a new Irish Republic was to take place over the Easter week—Pearse and the other rebels thought of themselves as almost Christ-like in their willingness to sacrifice themselves in service to the greater good of the Irish people.

HISTORICAL DOCUMENT

The Provisional Government of the Irish Republic to the People of Ireland

Irishmen and Irishwomen: In the name of God and of the dead generations from whom she receives her old traditions of nationhood, Ireland, through us, summons her children to her flag and strikes for her freedom.

Having organized and trained her manhood through her secret revolutionary organization the Irish Republican Brotherhood, and through her open military organizations, the Irish Volunteers and the Irish Citizen Army, having patiently perfected her discipline, having resolutely waited for the right moment to reveal itself, she now seizes that moment, and, supported by her exiled children in America and her gallant allies in Europe, but relying in the first on her own strength, she strikes in full confidence of victory.

We declare the right of the people of Ireland to the ownership of Ireland, and to the unfettered control of Irish destinies, to be sovereign and indefeasible. The long usurpation of that right by a foreign people and government has not extinguished the right, nor can it ever be extinguished except by the destruction of the Irish people. In every generation the Irish people have asserted their right to national freedom and sovereignty: six times during the past three hundred years they have asserted it in arms. Standing on that fundamental right and again asserting it in arms in the face of the world, we hereby proclaim the Irish Republic as a Sovereign Independent State, and we pledge our lives and the lives of our comrades-in-arms to the cause of its freedom, of its welfare, and of its exaltation among the nations.

The Irish Republic is entitled to, and hereby claims, the allegiance of every Irishman and Irishwoman. The Republic guarantees religious and civil liberty, equal rights and equal opportunities to all its citizens, and declares its resolve to pursue the happiness and prosperity of the whole nation and of all its parts, cherishing all the children of the nation equally, and oblivious of the differences carefully fostered by an alien government, which have divided a minority from the majority in the past.

Until our arms have brought the opportune moment for the establishment of a permanent National Government, representative of the whole people of Ireland and elected by the suffrages of all her men and women, the Provisional Government, hereby constituted, will administer the civil and military affairs of the Republic in trust for the people.

We place the cause of the Irish Republic under the protection of the Most High God, Whose blessing we invoke upon our arms, and we pray that no one who serves that cause will dishonor it by cowardice, inhumanity or rapine. In this supreme hour the Irish nation must, by its valor and discipline and by the readiness of its children to sacrifice themselves for the common good, prove itself worthy of the august destiny to which it is called.

Signed on Behalf of the Provisional Government.
Thomas J. Clarke,
Seán Mac Diarmada,
Thomas MacDonagh,
P. H. Pearse,
Éamonn Ceannt,
James Connolly, and
Joseph Plunkett.

Document Analysis

Upon seizing the Post Office, a flag with the brand-new Irish tricolor was raised over the building, and Pearse walked outside to read his proclamation to a confused group of passersby. It was titled "Poblacht na hEireann," or Republic of Ireland; most Irishmen did not know Gaelic, and thus had no idea what the title meant. Pearse opened by calling on the Irish public, its "children," to take up arms in the name of the "dead generations" that had established Ireland as a nation. He then named all of the revolt's supporters and actors—the IRB, the Irish Volunteers, the Irish Citizens' Army, American supporters and "gallant allies in Europe," the Germans, who by that time had already failed the rising.

Pearse then asserted the right of Irishmen to "ownership" of their island and their destinies, declaring that the Irish people would sooner disappear than submit that right to the British occupiers. He hearkened back to previous rebellions as proof, and declared Ireland's independence, to which he pledged the lives of all the rebels. Considering his expectation that the rebellion would fail, this was brave indeed. Still, he called on all Irishmen and Irishwomen—showing a striking equality and lack of chauvinism for the time—to join the rebellion, and promised that everyone would be treated equally, meaning Protestants. Pearse chalked up the hatreds between Protestants and Catholics to the deliberate policies of the British government, which was an exceptionally biased reading of the history of the same six rebellions he had appealed to in Ireland's past—in all of them, Protestants had been slaughtered by Catholics.

Pearse reaffirmed the provisional nature of the republic as constituted in the officers of the Rising, and then called upon God to protect the cause and keep it from devolving into the usual horrors of war, "cowardice, inhumanity, or rapine." He noted that the Irish nation had to be "worthy of the august destiny to which it is called," and read off the names of the signatories. Then he turned and walked back into the building, and the Rising began.

Essential Themes

Despite being outnumbered three to one, the rebels held out for nearly a week. From the beginning the Irish populace rejected them, considering the insurgents to be traitors in leading a rebellion against the British Empire in the midst of the deadliest war in history. When they surrendered, they were spat upon and jeered at by surrounding crowds as British soldiers escorted them to jail. British forces under Sir John Maxwell arrested 3400 people and held them without trial, some for more than a year. Under the rules of martial law, Maxwell convened military courts martial as if they took place on the battlefield in France. This meant there would be no jury and no defense witnesses. Almost two hundred civilians were tried and ninety of them received death sentences. The leaders of the Rising, as expected, received the opportunity to give their "blood sacrifice," all of them being executed by firing squad over ten days in May. The methods and reasons behind the executions circulated widely soon after they took place. Patrick Pearse's little brother Willie was executed for no more reason than for worshipping his brother. Joseph Mary Plunkett was ill after having had an operation on the glands in his neck; just before his execution, he married the sister of Thomas MacDonagh's wife and thus both sisters were left widows. James Connolly was so gravely wounded that the firing squad had to prop him up in a chair to shoot him. They received no funerals; their bodies were covered in quicklime as if they were corpses left to rot after a battle.

During his court martial, Pearse spoke, saying "You cannot conquer Ireland. You cannot extinguish the Irish passion for freedom. If our deed has not been sufficient to win freedom, then our children will win it by a better deed." He was right. If the insurgents had been considered fools and traitors during the 1916 Rising, they became martyrs immediately after they had died. It was one thing for the British government and army to put down a rebellion run by a group of addled patriots in the middle of a war; it was a worse thing entirely for them to simply throw away Britain's own legal rules and execute the lot in an act of vengeance. Wasn't Ireland supposed to be on the verge of governing itself after the war? Couldn't these rebels have been held until then to allow the Irish people to show the loyalty of a Home Rule government to the English crown by putting them on trial themselves? The summary nature of the executions made it clear that the British did not trust the Irish to manage themselves, and that the British still believed the Irish needed to be punished to understand the gravity of their own actions. The conduct of the executions turned Irish public opinion decidedly in favor of the Rising. Masses were said in the names of the rebels, and numerous public demonstrations followed throughout the war. In early 1918, the British government tried to introduce conscription in Ireland; this was the last straw for many, who had not gone to war earlier to die for their colonial overlords and certainly would not now after the Rising. In the end, nationwide resistance to the draft meant it was never implemented, and furthermore, Catholic southern Ireland was virtually united for independence—just as Pearse and the other rebels had hoped.

In December 1918, the British government held a general election. After it ended, seventy-three of the 108 winning candidates representing Ireland refused to accept their seats in London. All of them were members of Sinn Fein, a political party bent on the independence of Ireland. Instead, they stayed home in Dublin to form their own Dáil Eireann, an Irish parliament. The Irish War of Independence began in January 1919, the Irish Volunteers having renamed themselves the Irish Republican Army. Two years later, a truce was signed and the Irish nation was divided in peace negotiations between north and south. By the end of 1922, most of the promises of the 1916 Proclamation were achieved. It would take another year of civil war to force acceptance of the geographic and religiously-based split on the Irish population; the 1916 rebels' prediction of "blood sacrifice" came true with a vengeance.

———*David Simonelli*

Bibliography

O'Brien, Conor Cruise. "The Embers of Easter." *Massachusetts Review* 7, no. 4 (Autumn 1966): 621-637.

Gerson, Gal. "Cultural Subversion and the Background of the Irish 'Easter Poets'." *Journal of Contemporary History* 30, no. 2 (April 1995): 333-347.

Wills, Clair. *Dublin 1916: The Siege of the GPO.* London: Profile Books, 2009.

Coogan, Tim Pat. *Ireland in the 20ᵗʰ Century.* New York: Palgrave Macmillan, 2006.

Duffy, Sean. *The Illustrated History of Ireland.* Chicago: Contemporary Books, 2002.

Fry, Peter and Fiona Somerset Fry. *A History of Ireland.* New York: Barnes & Noble Books, 1988.

Judd, Denis. *Empire: The British Imperial Experience from 1765 to the Present.* London: HarperCollins, 1996.

O Broin, Leon. *Dublin Castle and the 1916 Rising.* New York: New York University Press, 1971.

Web Sites

"The 1916 Rising." Department of the Taoiseach, Government of Ireland. http://www.taoiseach.gov.ie/eng/Taoiseach_and_Government/History_of_Government/1916_Commemorations/The_1916_Rising. html.

Kissane, Dr. Noel, Researcher and Author. "1916: The 1916 Rising—Personalities and Perspectives." The

National Library of Ireland. http://www.nli.ie/1916/credits.html.

"Wars & Conflict: 1916 Easter Rising." BBC History. http://www.bbc.co.uk/history/british/easterrising/. "The White Man's Burden" (1899). Notes by Mary Hamer. The Kipling Society (October 18 2009) http://www.kiplingsociety.co.uk/rg_burden1.htm [accessed March 20, 2017].

◼ Balfour Declaration

Date: 1917
Authors: Arthur Balfour [David Lloyd George, Alfred Milner, Leopold Amery]
Genre: Letter

Summary Overview

The Balfour Declaration was conveyed in a letter addressed by Arthur James Balfour, the British secretary of state for foreign affairs, to Lord Walter Rothschild, a prominent member of the British Jewish community. In the letter, Balfour proclaimed that Britain would support Zionist aspirations by facilitating in Palestine the establishment of "a national home for the Jewish people." By declaring Britain to be Zionism's patron, Balfour's signature completed a process begun twenty years earlier at the First Zionist Congress, held in 1897 in Basel, Switzerland. It was then that a small group of Jewish leaders acted on their conviction that anti-Semitism in Europe was too deeply embedded to ever be eliminated and started canvassing political leaders—in Britain and Germany especially, but also in the Ottoman Empire itself—for a "charter" granting Jews the right to develop Palestine as a state of their own.

The Balfour Declaration was one of a number of contradictory pledges made by Britain during the course of World War I regarding the future disposition of Ottoman territories. Vague and ambiguous, it nonetheless stood as official policy until World War II. Throughout the interwar period, Britain provided Zionism with the necessary protective umbrella without which Jewish immigration, settlement, and state building in Palestine could not have succeeded. At the time of World War I, the Jewish contingent in Palestine was only 10 percent of the population, the other 90 percent consisting of an Arab community whose rights and aspirations Balfour had effectively ignored. Britain assumed that the problematic balancing act was one that could be upheld, but this was a gross misjudgment that would come back to haunt the empire.

Defining Moment

The outbreak of World War I in 1914 forced profound changes in Britain's Middle East policies. During the next three years the nation signed a number of controversial treaties and agreements with different partners. Prior to the war, Britain's long-standing concern in this strategic region was to protect the sea routes to its colony in India. Britain had been able to satisfy its own interests in the late nineteenth century by securing control over Egypt and the Suez Canal. Beyond that, the main aim of British diplomacy was to preserve the territorial integrity of the Ottoman Empire as a way to guard against Russian expansionism. However, with the Ottoman entry into the war as an ally of Germany, new policies had to be adopted. Often hesitant and ambiguous, British wartime policies resulted in a confusing array of declarations. Despite the best efforts of British diplomats in the postwar years to square the contradictions, the promises concerning that part of the Ottoman Empire known as Palestine—the future disposition of which Britain pledged to no fewer than three different allies—have remained the source of much controversy.

Prior to being presented in November 1917 to Zionist leaders, the fate of Palestine was the subject of two separate British agreements concluded with Arab and French negotiators. Britain was greatly concerned over the potential impact of war with the Ottoman sultan-caliph and so quickly directed its attention to establishing an alliance with Sharif Husayn ibn 'Ali, the Arab emir of the Muslim holy city of Mecca and head of the Hashemite family. In return for the launching of an Arab rebellion against the Ottomans by Husayn's son, Faisal, the British high commissioner in Egypt, Sir Henry McMahon, promised Husayn money, munitions, and the right to establish an independent Arab state. The negotiation was worked out in an exchange of letters between July 1915 and March 1916, in what later became known as the McMahon-Husayn correspondence. The ambiguity of territorial boundaries set out in this correspondence resulted in great confusion over whether Palestine was in fact promised to the Arabs, as part of Husayn's Arab state, or was deliberately excluded by Britain in order to accommodate the interests of France.

Even while negotiating with Husayn, the British were secretly carving up the Middle East into spoils of war to be shared with European allies. Through the secret 1916 Sykes-Picot Agreement, the Ottoman provinces of the Hashemite's hoped-for Arab kingdom were divided into a number of successor states, each of them

Foreign Office,
November 2nd, 1917.

Dear Lord Rothschild,

I have much pleasure in conveying to you, on behalf of His Majesty's Government, the following declaration of sympathy with Jewish Zionist aspirations which has been submitted to, and approved by, the Cabinet

'His Majesty's Government view with favour the establishment in Palestine of a national home for the Jewish people, and will use their best endeavours to facilitate the achievement of this object, it being clearly understood that nothing shall be done which may prejudice the civil and religious rights of existing non-Jewish communities in Palestine, or the rights and political status enjoyed by Jews in any other country"

I should be grateful if you would bring this declaration to the knowledge of the Zionist Federation.

Balfour declaration by Alfred Balfour. (commons.wikimedia.org) [Public Domain]

under some degree of control by Britain or France. The repercussions of this calculated yet arbitrary drawing of new state boundaries resonate to this day. As for Palestine specifically, Britain resisted the attempts of French negotiators to secure for themselves control over the whole of Syria down to the Egyptian border, and in the end the agreement placed Palestine under the control of an international administration.

By the end of the following year, however, Britain had recalculated its own strategic interests in Palestine. The region had become the site of important military operations, and government officials concluded that Palestine's value as a buffer to Egypt was too high to make tolerable any sort of foreign presence there after the war. These new calculations were emerging just as British forces were amassing on the Sinai Peninsula to push back the Ottoman forces and break through to Palestine. Most significantly, the new calculations were developed in tandem with efforts of the British Jewish community to persuade the country's leaders that Zionist interests in developing Palestine for themselves complemented British interests. In November 1917, Britain issued the Balfour Declaration, thus concluding in less than three years a third round of negotiations over the promised land. The following month, British imperial forces occupied Jerusalem, ending over four hundred years of Ottoman rule and initiating over thirty years of British rule.

Author Biography

The Balfour Declaration underwent successive drafts between July and October 1917. The main responsibility for the phrasing and rephrasing of the declaration was shared by Arthur Balfour, Prime Minister David Lloyd George, Lord Alfred Milner, and Leopold Amery. Balfour, a former prime minister (1902–1905), had graduated from Cambridge University in 1869 and became a Conservative member of Parliament in 1874. In what is sometimes referred to as "the first Balfour declaration," he had, as prime minister in 1903, supported a proposal to build a Jewish national presence in Uganda.

David Lloyd George, a Liberal member of Parliament since 1890, was appointed secretary of state for war in mid-1916 and became prime minister by the end of the year. For Lloyd George, support for Zionism was deeply rooted in his Christian faith, and he would refer to Palestine by its ancient name of Canaan. Like Balfour, Lloyd George viewed Jews as a separate race whose global influence could so benefit Britain that, as he wrote later, Britain had no real choice other than to "make a contract with Jewry" (Segev, p. 38).

Such racial perceptions of identity were also readily apparent in the thought of Lord Milner, who was brought into the war cabinet as a minister without portfolio in December 1916, largely because of his administrative capabilities. Milner had graduated from Oxford University in 1877 imbued with notions of imperial service and had been appointed governor of the Cape Colony and high commissioner of southern Africa in 1897. He believed firmly in the primordial nature of racial bonds. Significantly, his protégé from the colonial administration of South Africa, Leopold Amery—a lifelong imperialist and Zionist, appointed in 1917 as assistant secretary to the war cabinet secretariat—proposed in one draft of the declaration that the term "the Jewish people" be replaced with "the Jewish race."

HISTORICAL DOCUMENT

Foreign Office
November 2nd, 1917
Dear Lord Rothschild,

I have much pleasure in conveying to you, on behalf of His Majesty's Government, the following declaration of sympathy with Jewish Zionist aspirations which has been submitted to, and approved by, the Cabinet:

"His Majesty's Government view with favour the establishment in Palestine of a national home for the Jewish people, and will use their best endeavours to facilitate the achievement of this object, it being clearly understood that nothing shall be done which may prejudice the civil and religious rights of existing non-Jewish communities in Palestine, or the rights and political status enjoyed by Jews in any other country."

I should be grateful if you would bring this declaration to the knowledge of the Zionist Federation.

Yours sincerely,
Arthur James' Balfour

Document Analysis

The Balfour Declaration begins with the muted promise on the part of Britain to "favour" and "use their best endeavours to facilitate" Jewish aspirations. There was never an agreed consensus on how exactly Britain would facilitate Zionism, and rather than promise "a Jewish state," the declaration refers to "a national home." That phrase was an invention of the Zionist leadership in London who worried about demanding too much too soon. Zionist leaders certainly envisioned a state as the ultimate objective, but they sought to disguise their true intentions in order to lessen opposition. The use of the indefinite article "a," as is often the case in diplomatic negotiations that actually aim for ambiguous interpretations that accommodate the widest number of supporters, is also noteworthy. An early draft submitted by Jewish leaders entailed Britain's recognizing Palestine "as the National Home for the Jewish people" (qtd. in Fieldhouse, p. 149). The unease expressed by some cabinet officials resulted in the definite article later being replaced by the indefinite—"the National Home" being replaced by "a national home"—implying a much more open-ended commitment on the part of the British.

Vague as this declaration was—to somehow foster somewhere in Palestine something called a home—further questions were raised by the need to reconcile the ambiguous promise with the considerable provisos added to it. The first proviso clearly states that "nothing shall be done which may prejudice the civil and religious rights of existing non-Jewish communities in Palestine." Dismissive as this phrasing was to the national and political rights of the overwhelming Arab majority, which the document fails to cite by name, it constituted an attempt to meet the concerns of those British officials, particularly soldiers in the field, who were genuinely concerned about running the risk of antagonizing the Arab populations. The second proviso adds that nothing shall be done to prejudice "the rights and political status enjoyed by Jews in any other country." This met the objections from leading figures in the British Jewish community, most prominent among them being the only Jew in the cabinet, Edwin Montagu, secretary of state for India. In mid-1917, Montagu brought negotiations to a standstill when he made clear that he saw Zionism as a threat to his own position as a citizen of British society. In their non-Zionism, British Jewish leaders such as Montagu may in fact have been speaking for the majority when they rejected any implication that Palestine, and not Britain, was their proper nation. Montagu worried that the Balfour Declaration's emphasis on Jewish national distinctiveness would, in fact, exacerbate European anti-Semitism.

Essential Themes

For Zionist leaders the Balfour Declaration clearly represented, at long last, a triumph for their hard work. However, celebrations aside, the letter otherwise made very little impact in the short term. In Russia, the significance of the declaration was completely outweighed by the Bolshevik seizure of power. By the end of 1917, the new Bolshevik regime had not only withdrawn Russia from the war but had also proceeded to embarrass the Allies with the publication of secret wartime negotiations such as the Sykes-Picot Agreement. In the United States, there was no discernible change in official policy; in fact, the Zionist movement continued well into the interwar period to attract only a small minority of American Jews. As for the wartime fears that Germany might have preempted the entente with a declaration of its own, it was found that Germany had not been close to making such a decision.

In Palestine, British authorities did everything they could to tone down the effect of the pro-Zionist policy. Much to the chagrin of the Zionist leadership, no practical initiatives were allowed by the military administration, which was trying to restore order and stability to a destroyed landscape. But the rhetoric that had spread across Europe and North America made its way also to Palestine, and an increasingly wary Palestinian Arab population became as convinced as the Zionist leadership of the challenge Zionism posed to Arab patrimony of the country. On the first anniversary of the Balfour Declaration, which coincided with the end of the war and an opening up of political activity, Arab dignitaries and representatives petitioned the British denouncing the Balfour Day parade that was held in Jerusalem. From then on, Zionism became the chief oppositional factor in the articulation of a Palestinian Arab nationalist identity.

The hostility directed toward Zionism in Palestine did not deter the British government, which maintained its regard for Zionism into the immediate postwar period. This was especially important when the Allied Supreme Council awarded Britain the Mandate for Palestine at the 1920 San Remo conference. In many ways, the mandate system originated as a way for Britain and France to disguise old-fashioned imperial acquisition as enlightened tutelage. In one important aspect, however, the mandate was more than just a fig leaf. Once the Balfour Declaration was written into the terms of the League of Nations mandate sanctioning British rule in Palestine, one of several competing wartime promises was turned into a binding contract mediated by the League of Nations. Restrained in this way, British officials found it very difficult to even consider rescinding the promise of support for a Jewish national home, whatever the pressure being felt by British officials in Palestine caught in the simmering conflict between the nationalist demands of the Jewish and Arab communities. These pressures, which in the end Britain proved unable to contain, exploded in the bloody Arab revolt of 1936–1939.

———*Martin Bunton*

Bibliography and Further Reading

Articles

Vereté, Mayir. "The Balfour Declaration and Its Makers." *Middle Eastern Studies* 6, no. 1 (January 1970): 48–76.

Books

Fieldhouse, D. K. *Western Imperialism in the Middle East, 1914–1958.* Oxford, U.K. Oxford University Press, 2006.

Fromkin, David. *A Peace to End All Peace: Creating the Modern Middle East, 1914–1922.* New York: Henry Holt, 1989.

Renton, James. *The Zionist Masquerade: The Birth of the Anglo-Zionist Alliance, 1914–1918.* New York: Palgrave Macmillan, 2007.

Segev, Tom. *One Palestine, Complete: Jews and Arabs under the Mandate.* New York: Metropolitan Books, 2000.

Shlaim, Avi. "The Balfour Declaration and Its Consequences." In *Yet More Adventures with Britannia: Personalities, Politics, and Culture in Britain,* ed. William Roger Louis. London: I. B. Tauris, 2005.

Tomes, Jason. *Balfour and Foreign Policy: The International Thought of a Conservative Statesman.* New York: Cambridge University Press, 1997.

Yapp, M. E. *The Making of the Modern Near East, 1792–1923.* London: Longman, 1987.

■ Covenant of the League of Nations

Date: 1919
Authors: Woodrow Wilson (Jan Smuts) et al.
Genre: International organizational charter

Summary Overview

The Covenant of the League of Nations was an integral part of the Treaty of Versailles concluding the First World War. The Covenant of the League of Nations is the first section of the treaty and differs markedly from the main treaty itself, which is distinguished by its unmitigated vengeance toward the defeated Germany. The Covenant's preamble and twenty-six articles define the scope, objectives, organization, and operations of a world body that would prevent future wars. The League of Nations, as described, would have representatives from all nations, though it at first excluded those nations that had lost the recent war. The League was to be a permanent organization that would bring into practice the principles of negotiation, arbitration, respect for treaties, and international law. U.S. President Woodrow Wilson was the leader of the Treaty of Versailles discussions, and the League of Nations was the physical manifestation of the last of his Fourteen Points, a speech defining United States war aims, that had called for an international peacekeeping organization.

The audience for the Covenant of the League of Nations was the entire world, which had just gone through four years of total war. The defeated nations that had allied themselves with Germany were reminded that they had disregarded international law when they began the conflict in 1914. The retribution against Germany contained in the rest of the Treaty of Versailles drove home the point. The new nations of central and eastern Europe that had come into being as a result of the collapse of the Russian, German, and Austro-Hungarian empires were given a body of doctrine to govern their relations with the rest of the continent. Their rights in their conflicts against one another and potential threats from larger nations were to be guaranteed by the League as described in the Covenant.

In the end, however, the League was hamstrung from the beginning by the U.S. Senate and the people of the United States. Wilson sought to convince them of the League's value, which was clear in the antiwar provisions of the League's activities. The Covenant also guaranteed the validity of the Monroe Doctrine, which Americans felt to be essential to their security. The Senate had to ratify the treaty for it to go into effect. It did not, and neither the Covenant nor the Treaty of Versailles was adopted. The Senate's opposition was based largely on the strengthening mood of isolationism in the United States. The United States' people and businesses were more than willing to play a dominant role in international trade, but they did not want to be drawn into political arrangements that involve them in another war. Further, despite assurances that the Monroe Doctrine would be unaffected, membership in an international organization was seen as a sure means of limiting American sovereignty and independence of action. The United States would eventually conclude a separate peace with Germany and would not participate in the League of Nations, and the League's effectiveness was therefore reduced as a result.

Defining Moment

The First World War changed the world in many ways. Between 1914 and 1918 millions of people were killed or wounded in battle, and millions more died in a Spanish influenza outbreak that was exacerbated by the large transfers of soldiers and civilians. The winners, having suffered temporary but traumatic losses of territory and damage that can still be seen, were in a mood to exact revenge on the losing powers. The losing powers themselves were in the midst of revolutions, famine and ethnic clashes; over everything loomed the specter of the Bolsheviks in the old Russian Empire and worldwide communist revolution. Many of the old assumptions about the progress of humankind toward a better state through education, technical development, and a sense of culture and refinement had been destroyed. Empires that had existed for hundreds of years and that a short time before had seemed to be immortal had disintegrated. The dissolution and the accompanying turmoil indicated that the old world order was dead.

However, as the Paris Peace Conference took place in the first half of 1919, the sense of bitterness and disillusion that would characterize the 1920s in Europe had not yet set in. While many senior statesmen did not hold great expectations for an international diplomatic organization dedicated to peace and doubted how effective it might be, the concept held enough merit in the eyes of many at least to warrant an attempt. The idea sprang directly from the Fourteen Points that U.S. President Woodrow Wilson had articulated in a speech delivered before a joint session of the U.S. Congress in 1918, outlining Wilson's idea of what would need to be accomplished as a result of victory over Germany and its allies. Wilson's view was quite idealistic, and parts of the speech were in direct opposition to what he and many Americans had come to believe were the evils that had created the war. His Fourteen Points included freedom of the seas (a point with which his British allies did not agree), the end to secret treaties, and independence for such populations as the Poles and the nationalities that had been part of the Austro-Hungarian and Ottoman empires. The final point was a call to establish an international organization that would promote peace in the world.

The Fourteen Points were seen as an idealistic program that would benefit many of the peoples that had been part of prewar empires and bring about a just peace. It did have an effect in Germany and, coupled with the fact that American soldiers were arriving in great numbers in Europe, influenced Germany's decision to surrender. It was the final point that Wilson considered to be the most important. At his insistence, discussions that would define the covenant of a new organization, the League of Nations, were conducted as the first discussions of the entire Treaty of Versailles, which ended the war with Germany. With the signing of the Treaty of Versailles on June 28, 1919, both the treaty and the Covenant of the League went into effect. The first session of the League's Council and, later, the Assembly occurred early the following year.

Author Biography

Although the Covenant was a compromise document, it basically had a single author, U.S. President Woodrow Wilson, who was the leader of all discussions on its creation. Formerly a president of Princeton University and a governor of New Jersey, Wilson was elected president of the United States in 1912. Reelected in 1916 on the basis of his ability to keep the United States out of the conflict, Wilson asked Congress to declare war against Germany within two months of his second inauguration. As the war progressed, Wilson sounded an idealistic note as he made statements concerning the just treatment of nations in the world after the war, and he called for an international organization to maintain peace. He went to Paris in 1919 to help create the League of Nations and shape the peace. Largely on the basis of his efforts to form the League, he was awarded the Nobel Peace Prize that year. He died in 1924.

Wilson's final draft leaned heavily on a book entitled *The League of Nations: A Practical Suggestion*, by General Jan Smuts of South Africa. During the First World War, Smuts had led his forces against the Germans in Africa. In the last two years of the war he served Prime Minister David Lloyd George as one of five members of the British government's Imperial War Cabinet. In the Second World War, he acted as a field marshal in the British army and joined Prime Minister Winston Churchill's War Cabinet. He was the only person to sign the peace treaties ending both world wars. Smuts was elected prime minister of South Africa twice; he served from 1919 until 1924 and then again from 1939 to 1948. In May 1945 he represented South Africa in San Francisco at the drafting of the UN Charter. Smuts was an author of the preamble to the charter of the United Nations and was the only person to sign both the League Covenant and the UN Charter. He died in Pretoria, South Africa, in 1950.

HISTORICAL DOCUMENT

The High Contracting Parties,

In order to promote international co-operation and to achieve international peace and security

by the acceptance of obligations not to resort to war,

by the prescription of open, just and honorable relations between nations,

by the firm establishment of the understandings of international law as the actual rule of conduct among Governments, and

by the maintenance of justice and a scrupulous respect for all treaty obligations in the dealings of organized peoples with one another Agree to this Covenant of the League of Nations.

Article 1.

The original Members of the League of Nations shall be those of the Signatories which are named in the Annex to this Covenant and also such of those other States named in the Annex as shall accede without reservation to this Covenant. Such accession shall be effected by a Declaration deposited with the Secretariat within two months of the coming into force of the Covenant. Notice thereof shall be sent to all other Members of the League.

Any fully self-governing State, Dominion or Colony not named in the Annex may become a Member of the League if its admission is agreed to by two-thirds of the Assembly, provided that it shall give effective guarantees of its sincere intention to observe its international obligations, and shall accept such regulations as may be prescribed by the League in regard to its military, naval and air forces and armaments.

Any Member of the League may, after two years' notice of its intention so to do, withdraw from the League, provided that all its international obligations and all its obligations under this Covenant shall have been fulfilled at the time of its withdrawal.

Article 2.

The action of the League under this Covenant shall be effected through the instrumentality of an Assembly and of a Council, with a permanent Secretariat.

Article 3.

The Assembly shall consist of Representatives of the Members of the League.

The Assembly shall meet at stated intervals and from time to time, as occasion may require, at the Seat of the League or at such other place as may be decided upon.

The Assembly may deal at its meetings with any matter within the sphere of action of the League or affecting the peace of the world.

At meetings of the Assembly each Member of the League shall have one vote, and may have not more than three Representatives.

Article 4.

The Council shall consist of Representatives of the Principal Allied and Associated Powers (United States of America, the British Empire, France, Italy, and Japan), together with Representatives of four other Members of the League. These four Members of the League shall be selected by the Assembly from time to time in its discretion. Until the appointment of the Representatives of the four Members of the League first selected by the Assembly, Representatives of Belgium, Brazil, Greece and Spain shall be members of the Council.

With the approval of the majority of the Assembly, the Council may name additional Members of the League whose Representatives shall always be members of the Council; the Council, with like approval may increase the number of Members of the League to be selected by the Assembly for representation on the Council.

The Council shall meet from time to time as occasion may require, and at least once a year, at the Seat of the League, or at such other place as may be decided upon.

The Council may deal at its meetings with any matter within the sphere of action of the League or affecting the peace of the world.

Any Member of the League not represented on the Council shall be invited to send a Representative to sit as a member at any meeting of the Council during the consideration of matters specially affecting the interests of that Member of the League.

At meetings of the Council, each Member of the League represented on the Council shall have one vote, and may have not more than one Representative.

Article 5.

Except where otherwise expressly provided in this Covenant, or by the terms of the present Treaty, decisions at any meeting of the Assembly or of the Council shall require the agreement of all the Members of the League represented at the meeting.

All matters of procedure at meetings of the Assembly or of the Council, including the appointment of Committees to investigate particular matters, shall be regulated by the Assembly or by the Council and may be decided by a majority of the Members of the League represented at the meeting.

The first meeting of the Assembly and the first meeting of the Council shall be summoned by the President of the United States of America.

Article 6.

The permanent Secretariat shall be established at the Seat of the League. The Secretariat shall comprise a Secretary-General and such secretaries and staff as may be required.

The first Secretary-General shall be the person named in the Annex; thereafter the Secretary-General shall be appointed by the Council with the approval of the majority of the Assembly.

The secretaries and staff of the Secretariat shall be appointed by the Secretary-General with the approval of the Council.

The Secretary-General shall act in that capacity at all meetings of the Assembly and of the Council.

The expenses of the Secretariat shall be borne by the Members of the League in accordance with the apportionment of the expenses of the International Bureau of the Universal Postal Union.

Article 7.

The Seat of the League is established at Geneva. The Council may at any time decide that the Seat of the League shall be established elsewhere.

All positions under or in connection with the League, including the Secretariat, shall be open equally to men and women.

Representatives of the Members of the League and officials of the League when engaged on the business of the League shall enjoy diplomatic privileges and immunities.

The buildings and other property occupied by the League or its officials or by Representatives attending its meetings shall be inviolable.

Article 8.

The Members of the League recognize that the maintenance of peace requires the reduction of national armaments to the lowest point consistent with national safety and the enforcement by common action of international obligations.

The Council, taking account of the geographical situation and circumstances of each State, shall formulate plans for such reduction for the consideration and action of the several Governments.

Such plans shall be subject to reconsideration and revision at least every ten years.

After these plans shall have been adopted by the several Governments, the limits of armaments therein fixed shall not be exceeded without the concurrence of the Council.

The Members of the League agree that the manufacture by private enterprise of munitions and implements of war is open to grave objections. The Council shall advise how the evil effects attendant upon such manufacture can be prevented, due regard being had to the necessities of those Members of the League which are not able to manufacture the munitions and implements of war necessary for their safety.

The Members of the League undertake to interchange full and frank information as to the scale of their armaments, their military, naval and air programs and the condition of such of their industries as are adaptable to warlike purposes.

Article 9.

A permanent Commission shall be constituted to advise the Council on the execution of the provisions of Articles 1 and 8 and on military, naval and air questions generally.

Article 10.

The Members of the League undertake to respect and preserve as against external aggression the territorial integrity and existing political independence of all Members of the League. In case of any such aggression or in case of any threat or danger of such aggression the Council shall advise upon the means by which this obligation shall be fulfilled.

Article 11.

Any war or threat of war, whether immediately affecting any of the Members of the League or not, is hereby declared a matter of concern to the whole League, and the League shall take any action that may be deemed wise and effectual to safeguard the peace of nations. In case any such emergency should arise the Secretary-General shall on the request of any Member of the League forthwith summon a meeting of the Council.

It is also declared to be the friendly right of each Member of the League to bring to the attention of the Assembly or of the Council any circumstance whatever affecting international relations which threatens to disturb international peace or the good understanding between nations upon which peace depends.

Article 12.
The Members of the League agree that if there should arise between them any dispute likely to lead to a rupture, they will submit the matter either to arbitration or to inquiry by the Council, and they agree in no case to resort to war until three months after the award by the arbitrators or the report by the Council.

In any case under this Article the award of the arbitrators shall be made within a reasonable time, and the report of the Council shall be made within six months after the submission of the dispute.

Article 13.
The Members of the League agree that whenever any dispute shall arise between them which they recognize to be suitable for submission to arbitration or judicial settlement and which cannot be satisfactorily settled by diplomacy, they will submit the whole subject matter to arbitration or judicial settlement.

Disputes as to the interpretation of a treaty, as to any question of international law, as to the existence of any fact which if established would constitute a breach of any international obligation, or as to the extent and nature of the reparation to be made for any such breach, are declared to be among those which are generally suitable for submission to arbitration or judicial settlement.

For the consideration of any such dispute the court of arbitration to which the case is referred shall be the Court agreed on by the parties to the dispute or stipulated in any convention existing between them.

The Members of the League agree that they will carry out in full good faith any award or decision that may be rendered, and that they will not resort to war against a Member of the League which complies therewith. In the event of any failure to carry out such an award or decision, the Council shall propose what steps should be taken to give effect thereto.

Article 14.
The Council shall formulate and submit to the Members of the League for adoption plans for the establishment of a Permanent Court of International Justice. The Court shall be competent to hear and determine any dispute of an international character which the parties thereto submit to it. The Court may also give an advisory opinion upon any dispute or question referred to it by the Council or by the Assembly.

Article 15.
If there should arise between Members of the League any dispute likely to lead to a rupture, which is not submitted to arbitration in accordance with Article 13, the Members of the League agree that they will submit the matter to the Council. Any party to the dispute may effect such submission by giving notice of the existence of the dispute to the Secretary-General, who will make all necessary arrangements for a full investigation and consideration thereof.

For this purpose the parties to the dispute will communicate to the Secretary-General, as promptly as possible, statements of their case with all the relevant facts and papers, and the Council may forthwith direct the publication thereof.

The Council shall endeavor to effect a settlement of the dispute, and if such efforts are successful, a statement shall be made public giving such facts and explanations regarding the dispute and the terms of settlement thereof as the Council may deem appropriate.

If the dispute is not thus settled, the Council, either unanimously or by a majority vote, shall make and publish a report containing a statement of the facts of the dispute and the recommendations which are deemed just and proper in regard thereto.

Any Member of the League represented on the Council may make public a statement of the facts of the dispute and of its conclusions regarding the same.

If a report by the Council is unanimously agreed to by the members thereof other than the Representatives of one or more of the parties to the dispute, the Members of the League agree that they will not go to war with any party to the dispute which complies with the recommendations of the report.

If the Council fails to reach a report which is unanimously agreed to by the members thereof, other than the Representatives of one or more of the parties to the dispute, the Members of the League reserve to themselves the right to take such action as they shall consider necessary for the maintenance of right and justice.

If the dispute between the parties is claimed by one of them, and is found by the Council, to arise out of a matter which by international law is solely within the domestic jurisdiction of that party, the Council shall so report, and shall make no recommendation as to its settlement.

The Council may in any case under this Article refer the dispute to the Assembly. The dispute shall be so referred at the request of either party to the dispute, provided that such request be made within fourteen days after the submission of the dispute to the Council.

In any case referred to the Assembly, all the provisions of this Article and of Article 12 relating to the action and powers of the Council shall apply to the action and powers of the Assembly, provided that a report made by the Assembly, if concurred in by the Representatives of those Members of the League represented on the Council and of a majority of the other Members of the League, exclusive in each case of the Representatives of the parties to the dispute, shall have the same force as a report by the Council concurred in by all the members thereof other than the Representatives of one or more of the parties to the dispute.

Article 16.

Should any Member of the League resort to war in disregard of its covenants under Articles 12, 13, or 15, it shall *ipso facto* be deemed to have committed an act of war against all other Members of the League, which hereby undertake immediately to subject it to the severance of all trade or financial relations, the prohibition of all intercourse between their nationals and the nationals of the covenant-breaking State, and the prevention of all financial, commercial or personal intercourse between the nationals of the covenant-breaking State and the nationals of any other State, whether a Member of the League or not.

It shall be the duty of the Council in such case to recommend to the several Governments concerned what effective military, naval or air force the Members of the League shall severally contribute to the armed forces to be used to protect the covenants of the League.

The Members of the League agree, further, that they will mutually support one another in the financial and economic measures which are taken under this Article, in order to minimize the loss and inconvenience resulting from the above measures, and that they will mutually support one another in resisting any special measures aimed at one of their number by the covenant-breaking State, and that they will take the necessary steps to afford passage through their territory to the forces of any of the Members of the League which are co-operating to protect the covenants of the League.

Any Member of the League which has violated any covenant of the League may be declared to be no longer a Member of the League by a vote of the Council concurred in by the Representatives of all the other Members of the League represented thereon.

Article 17.

In the event of a dispute between a Member of the League and a State which is not a Member of the League, or between States not Members of the League, the State or States not Members of the League shall be invited to accept the obligations of membership in the League for the purposes of such dispute, upon such conditions as the Council may deem just. If such invitation is accepted, the provisions of Articles 12 to 16, inclusive, shall be applied with such modifications as may be deemed necessary by the Council.

Upon such invitation being given the Council shall immediately institute an inquiry into the circumstances of the dispute and recommend such action as may seem best and most effectual in the circumstances.

If a State so invited shall refuse to accept the obligations of membership in the League for the purposes of such dispute, and shall resort to war against a Member of the League, the provisions of Article 16 shall be applicable as against the State taking such action.

If both parties to the dispute, when so invited, refuse to accept the obligations of membership in the League for the purposes of such dispute, the Council may take such measures and make such recommendations as will prevent hostilities and will result in the settlement of the dispute.

Article 18.

Every treaty or international engagement entered into hereafter by any Member of the League shall be forthwith registered with the Secretariat and shall as soon as possible be published by it. No such treaty or international engagement shall be binding until so registered.

Article 19.

The Assembly may from time to time advise the reconsideration by Members of the League of treaties which have become inapplicable and the consideration of international conditions whose continuance might endanger the peace of the world.

Article 20.

The Members of the League severally agree that this Covenant is accepted as abrogating all obligations or understandings *inter se* which are inconsistent with the terms thereof, and solemnly undertake that they will not hereafter enter into any engagements inconsistent with the terms thereof.

In case any Member of the League shall, before becoming a Member of the League, have undertaken any obligations inconsistent with the terms of this Covenant, it shall be the duty of such Member to take immediate steps to procure its release from such obligations.

Article 21.

Nothing in this Covenant shall be deemed to affect the validity of international engagements, such as treaties of arbitration or regional understandings like the Monroe Doctrine, for securing the maintenance of peace.

Article 22.

To those colonies and territories which as a consequence of the late war have ceased to be under the sovereignty of the States which formerly governed them and which are inhabited by peoples not yet able to stand by themselves under the strenuous conditions of the modern world, there should be applied the principle that the well-being and development of such peoples form a sacred trust of civilization and that securities for the performance of this trust should be embodied in this Covenant.

The best method of giving practical effect to this principle is that the tutelage of such peoples should be entrusted to advanced nations who by reason of their resources, their experience or their geographical position can best undertake this responsibility, and who are willing to accept it, and that this tutelage should be exercised by them as Mandatories on behalf of the League.

The character of the mandate must differ according to the stage of the development of the people, the geographical situation of the territory, its economic conditions and other similar circumstances.

Certain communities formerly belonging to the Turkish Empire have reached a stage of development where their existence as independent nations can be provisionally recognized subject to the rendering of administrative advice and assistance by a Mandatory until such time as they are able to stand alone. The wishes of these communities must be a principal consideration in the selection of the Mandatory.

Other peoples, especially those of Central Africa, are at such a stage that the Mandatory must be responsible for the administration of the territory under conditions which will guarantee freedom of conscience and religion, subject only to the maintenance of public order and morals, the prohibition of abuses such as the slave trade, the arms traffic and the liquor traffic, and the prevention of the establishment of fortifications or military and naval bases and of military training of the natives for other than police purposes and the defense of territory, and will also secure equal opportunities for the trade and commerce of other Members of the League.

There are territories, such as South-West Africa and certain of the South Pacific Islands, which, owing to the sparseness of their population, or their small size, or their remoteness from the centers of civilization, or their geographical contiguity to the territory of the Mandatory, and other circumstances, can be best administered under the laws of the Mandatory as integral portions of its territory, subject to the safeguards above mentioned in the interests of the indigenous population.

In every case of mandate, the Mandatory shall render to the Council an annual report in reference to the territory committed to its charge.

The degree of authority, control, or administration to be exercised by the Mandatory shall, if not previously agreed upon by the Members of the League, be explicitly defined in each case by the Council.

A permanent Commission shall be constituted to receive and examine the annual reports of the Mandatories and to advise the Council on all matters relating to the observance of the mandates.

Article 23.

Subject to and in accordance with the provisions of international conventions existing or hereafter to be agreed upon, the Members of the League:

(a) Will endeavor to secure and maintain fair and humane conditions of labor for men, women, and children, both in their own countries and in all countries to which their commercial and industrial relations extend, and for that purpose will establish and maintain the necessary international organizations;

(b) Undertake to secure just treatment of the native inhabitants of territories under their control;

(c) Will entrust the League with the general supervision over the execution of agreements with regard to the traffic in women and children, and the traffic in opium and other dangerous drugs;

(d) Will entrust the League with the general supervision of the trade in arms and ammunition with the countries in which the control of this traffic is necessary in the common interest;

(e) Will make provision to secure and maintain freedom of communications and of transit and equitable treatment for the commerce of all Members of the League. In this connection, the special necessities of the regions devastated during the war of 1914–1918 shall be borne in mind;

(f) Will endeavor to take steps in matters of international concern for the prevention and control of disease.

Article 24.

There shall be placed under the direction of the League all international bureaus already established by general treaties if the parties to such treaties consent. All such international bureaus and all commissions for the regulation of matters of international interest hereafter constituted shall be placed under the direction of the League.

In all matters of international interest which are regulated by general conventions but which are not placed under the control of international bureaus or commissions, the Secretariat of the League shall, subject to the consent of the Council and if desired by the parties, collect and distribute all relevant information and shall render any other assistance which may be necessary or desirable.

The Council may include as part of the expenses of the Secretariat the expenses of any bureau or commission which is placed under the direction of the League.

Article 25.

The Members of the League agree to encourage and promote the establishment and co-operation of duly authorized voluntary national Red Cross organizations having as purposes the improvement of health, the prevention of disease and the mitigation of suffering throughout the world.

Article 26.

Amendments to this Covenant will take effect when ratified by the Members of the League whose Representatives compose the Council and by a majority of the Members of the League whose Representatives compose the Assembly.

No such amendments shall bind any Member of the League which signifies its dissent therefrom, but in that case it shall cease to be a Member of the League.

Document Analysis

The Covenant of the League of Nations brought that organization into being as an integral part of the Treaty of Versailles, signed in 1919 and ending the First World War. It was the first part of the treaty to appear in the completed document and was also the first part to be written, before the specific clauses determining the conditions of the peace were drafted. The charter was purposely broad in many aspects. While laying down basic rules for conduct, membership, scope, and operations, it left many decisions about procedure to be determined by the League's Assembly and Council once they finally met in 1920. Despite the vagueness concerning procedures, there is a fair degree of specificity in the Covenant about the types of issues it would treat, which evidenced a strong desire to avoid what were considered to be the actions that had begun the war just ended.

Another significant element is that in both practical and symbolic ways, there were concessions to the United States in several areas. It was believed that the League would not function successfully without U.S. participation. Thus, statements about sovereignty, immigration law, and regional influence were shaped with the idea of making it easier for Woodrow Wilson to persuade the U.S. Senate to approve the treaty and join the League. These concessions ultimately failed to persuade the American public in general or the Senate in particular.

The preamble to the Covenant identifies the League's objectives as an organization dedicated to maintaining peace and security in the world. The League would promote international law and the avoidance of war. It would ensure that all treaty obligations were honored. This last item was considered quite important. Before the start of the First World War, Belgium's status as a neutral nation had been guaranteed by a treaty signed by several nations, including Germany. When, in August 1914, Germany invaded Belgium, German Chancellor Theobald von Bethmann-Hollweg roared at the British ambassador to Berlin that the treaty safeguarding the smaller country had been only "a scrap of paper." The preamble specifically included this mention of the inviolability of treaties as a direct response to Germany's actions.

Two proposals were raised but not accepted. France proposed that the preamble contain a specific condemnation of Germany as an aggressor in the last war, but this stipulation was rejected. The Japanese delegation attempted to add the phrase "by the endorsement of the principles of equality of nations and the just treatment of nationals," to follow the phrase "relations between nations." The proposal was voted down ostensibly because it would dictate domestic policy. The real reason was an objection from the United States based on its immigration policy. The proposal as written would have run counter to U.S. immigration quotas, which were being applied to significantly limit the numbers of Chinese and Japanese entering the country.

The first seven articles of the Covenant describe the organization, where it would meet, the functions of the Council and the Assembly, and the general rules about how the League would conduct business and function. Article 1 defines the qualifications for membership for both original and subsequent League members. Because the League was originally comprised of the victorious Allies and neutral nations, some provision for later membership had to be made for the defeated nations (Germany, Austria, and Hungary) as well as others that did not belong to the original body. The manner in which a member nation could withdraw was also defined, an action that would be taken in the 1920s principally by smaller nations, followed by the significant departures of Germany, Japan, Italy, and the Soviet Union in the 1930s. The second article states that the League would operate as an assembly of nations with a smaller council of members who would act as an executive body and a secretariat that would bear responsibility for daily operations.

Article 3 declares that each member nation was to have only one vote, thereby negating the influence that the larger nations would have gained on the basis of population, size, or wealth. Further, while a nation could have as large a staff as it wished, it would be restricted to only three official delegates. The League would meet regularly (though, like many provisions in the Covenant, the details were left to be worked out later), and the League's scope included anything that it considered relevant to maintaining the peace of the world.

The fourth article defined the composition and activities of the League Council, a subset of the total membership that would provide leadership and direction. It would contain five permanent members, consisting of the war's major winning powers (the United States, Great Britain, France, Italy, and Japan). The United States never took its seat, but in the 1920s, when Germany was granted membership, that country became the fifth permanent member. The smaller powers were to be represented on the Council as well, with rotating memberships lasting three years. The number of temporary members was an issue from the beginning, and eventually their number would increase from four to eleven. The Council's scope of activities was purposely wide-ranging; the membership addressed any matter concerned with world peace or the operations of the League.

Article 5 declares that decisions adopted by the Council or the Assembly required unanimous approval. There were exceptions. Matters of procedure could be adopted by a simple majority, and amendments to the Covenant would be adopted by a majority vote. The first meeting of the Assembly would be called by the president of the United States, an honor recognizing Wilson's role in creating the League.

Article 6 concerns operations of the League and describes the role and responsibilities of the permanent secretary-general in conducting regular operations. As was the case in other portions of this document, detailed procedures were left to be settled by a future annex to the Covenant. The expenses of the secretariat were to be paid by the members in "accordance with the apportionment of the expenses of the Bureau of the Universal Postal Union." This bureau is an international organization that coordinates postal policies among member nations and thus the worldwide postal system. What is significant here is the adoption of standards already in use by an internationally recognized organization and the application of those rules to the League.

Article 7 stipulates that the League headquarters were to be in Geneva, Switzerland, and that all positions would be open to both men or women. All League representatives and League buildings would have diplomatic privileges and immunity.

Articles 8 through 12 describe in general terms the League's scope of activities in its major mission, which was to prevent war. This set of articles, while they are not as detailed as those that follow in Articles 13 through 17, address responsibilities incumbent on members to avoid war among themselves, in addition to other League peace initiatives.

The arms race between nations to build up military and naval forces, particularly navies, in the years before the First World War was seen by many as a major precipitating cause of the war. Article 8 addresses the issue of arms control, such that each nation would have enough military strength to protect itself but not enough

to wage aggressive war. The Council would form plans for disarmament, which would be reviewed and revised at least once every ten years. Based on a French proposal, the article states that the review would take into consideration the circumstances specific to each region and country, which essentially meant that because France feared another invasion by Germany, German forces would be restricted while the French government would be allowed to arm itself as it saw necessary.

In addition to government armament programs, there was before the war a very strong private arms industry, which made a wide range of weapons available to the highest bidder. These commercial concerns were seen as another danger to peace. In response, the Council would study and advise the best course of action to counter the effects of the private armaments manufacturers and merchants. Wilson had proposed abolishing all private arms companies, an idea opposed by smaller nations, such as Portugal and Romania, which did not have their own national arms manufacturers. Member nations would freely exchange information on their own military and naval and air and munitions industries. One effect of this last provision was an annually published listing, issued throughout the 1920s and 1930s, of detailed descriptions of the armies of the members.

Because military matters required the advice of experts, Article 9 established a permanent commission to advise the Council on how to perform the activities covered by articles 1 and 8 as well as on any questions concerning naval, air, and military matters. This commission would not act independently but rather solely on the Council's instructions. France attempted to amend this article so that the League could use military force—that is, form an international army to intervene in crisis situations—but that idea was rejected.

As part of the general revulsion toward war that informed so many postwar projects and plans, the issue of aggression, such as Germany's at the beginning of the war, was considered key. Article 10 states that the League would protect the territorial integrity of all members against external aggression. If such a case occurred, the Council would advise on what had to be done. The article is of great interest, because the eventual failure of the League was strongly signaled in 1935, when one member, Italy, invaded another member, Ethiopia. While sanctions were implemented, they were ineffectively planned and indifferently enforced. Second, the use of the word *external* reflects the article's aim to exclude civil wars. That restriction was considered necessary to prevent a government from seeking League assistance in the event of a civil war (such as would occur in Spain from 1936 to 1939).

Article 11 declares that the League's scope of interest was anything that threatened world peace, specifically war or the threat of war. The League would take any action considered appropriate. Upon the request of any member nation, the secretary-general could summon a meeting of the Council. Further, any nation could bring to the attention of the Council or the Assembly anything that had the potential of disturbing international peace.

Article 12 stipulates that in the event of any disagreements between members, they would submit the issue for arbitration or inquiry by the Council. Further, they would not engage in any military activity for three months after the award by arbitration or report from the inquiry if they disagreed with the result. Decisions would be made in a reasonable time, and a report would be issued within six months. This particular insistence on time limits before a declaration of war could be made was proposed by France, based on the extraordinarily short time from the assassination of the Austrian archduke Franz Ferdinand on June 28, 1914, to the escalation to national mobilizations through July, followed almost immediately by ultimatums and invasions.

While the previous five articles described general obligations, especially among members of the League, the following five articles provided detailed procedures for handling disputes that could not be resolved satisfactorily by the involved parties. According to Article 13, members having disputes that could not be resolved diplomatically would submit them for arbitration. These disputes could include, but were not restricted to, issues of international law or possible breaches of international obligations. The body to adjudicate these disputes would be a court mutually agreed upon by the parties involved in a dispute or whatever tribunal might be stipulated by a convention that existed between the parties. Article 14 established the authority and the responsibility of the League Council to bring to the Assembly plans to create and implement a Permanent Court of International Justice. The court would hear and adjudicate international disputes and would also provide legal opinions on any question raised by either the Council or the Assembly.

Article 15 expanded the possible number of parties that could be involved in bringing about peaceful solutions. If two members of the League engaged in a dispute that could lead to a breaking off of relations and they did not submit the dispute to arbitration as described in Article 13, the matter could be submitted to the Council by any concerned party. The secretary-general would publish the details and make arrangements for the case to be brought to the Council, which would provide a settlement. The Council would report on its findings and recommendations. If members of the Council unanimously agreed, excluding any nations involved in the dispute, League members would not go to war with any party complying with the recommendations. The article also stipulates that in any dispute stemming from domestic policies and not international law for both parties, the Council would not become involved. The Council could refer the dispute to the Assembly.

Article 16 states that any League member declaring war on another member would be declaring war on all members. The League would impose sanctions against offending members. The Council would recommend whatever military or naval activity it deemed necessary. League members would mutually support one another to mitigate economic hardships resulting from the conflict. Finally, the offending member would be expelled from the League. Article 17 made the process for conflict resolution an option open to any nation. The article specifically states that nations engaged in disputes and not belonging to the League would be invited to join. After accepting, they would abide by the League's rules, starting with conflict resolution, and articles 12 though 16 of the Covenant would apply.

Treaties and alliances, whether open or secret, were seen, along with the arms race, to have been a major cause of the war. While building alliances might have been a means of guaranteeing security, the obligations imposed on members to join their allies automatically in mobilizing and deploying their armies had led to a rapid and uncontrollable escalation that had brought about the recently ended war. Among Woodrow Wilson's Fourteen Points, one of which had specifically called for the formation of a League of Nations, was a point calling for treaties and covenants to be arrived at in a public fashion. The regulation and publicity of treaties and where previous treaties might or might not bind participants were addressed in these five articles.

Article 18 provided for a means of ensuring that treaties were made public. It states that no treaties entered into by any League member would be valid and binding until registered with the League's secretariat and formally published by the League. This stipulation affected only new treaties and did not apply to treaties formed before the existence of the League. In Article 19 the League declares its role to caution and advise members when they contemplate treaties that could present a danger to world peace. The League would request that members reconsider if a treaty seemed to pose that danger. The issue of the degree of power of the League over the rights and sovereignty of nations came up as a subject of debate. It was finally decided that the issue of sovereignty would not be a serious problem, as condemnation of a treaty by the League would require a unanimous vote. Further, it was declared that this article did not mean that the League had the right to refuse to register any treaties under the rules of Article 18.

While Article 19 discusses future treaties, Article 20 is concerned with past treaties in addition to future treaties that might create problems in maintaining world peace. By this article, the members of the League would cancel any past treaty obligations that would run counter to the Covenant and they would refrain from making any such agreements in the future. A nation wishing to join the League would have to repudiate any such treaties to which it had earlier agreed. While the League sought to provide advice and influence in the matter of treaties in the future, Article 21 states that nothing in the Covenant would negate any regional understandings that were not inconsistent with the Covenant. This article was inserted at the insistence of the United States, which had concerns that the Monroe Doctrine (the policy that opposed European interference in the Western Hemisphere) not be undermined in any fashion.

A direct effect of losing the war was that Germany and Turkey were to forfeit their colonies and other imperial possessions. The victorious nations were determined that these territories not be given back, but there had to be a mechanism to administer these territories until they were ready for independence. The winning powers (principally Britain, France, and Japan) would administer these territories as League mandates, report annually to the Council, and prepare the territories for eventual freedom. One of these mandates, the former Ottoman provinces combined to form Iraq, was administered by the British until 1932, when it became a fully independent nation. Most of the others, including Syria, Palestine (later to become Israel), and nations in

Africa such as Tanganyika did not reach independence until after the Second World War.

The League of Nations is commonly associated with grand failures, such as its ineffective methods to stop Italian aggression in Africa or to halt Japanese and German territorial advances. It is not so well understood, however, that the League was actually quite successful in implementing several initiatives beyond the prevention of war. Some of these initiatives made progress toward improving the lives of people in many countries, especially on health issues. These articles specify the League's interests in "social activities" as well as in supporting already existing organizations.

Article 23 defines the League's actions to resolve international problems that did not result from individual governmental actions but that adversely affected the well-being of all people. Specifically, the League would work on such issues as safe working conditions, fair treatment of native populations, international trafficking of women and children, and drug trafficking. These efforts attracted a great deal of support; even the United States, which never joined the League, participated in such endeavors as the antidrug-trafficking programs. Further, the League would monitor arms traffic and work to prevent and control disease.

Article 24 stipulates that the League would pay for the activities described in Article 23. If members agreed, it would take over existing international organizations and assume their expenses. The League would share any relevant information it had with organizations not affiliated with it. Under Article 25, League members would encourage and promote organizations to improve world health, prevent disease, or mitigate any form of suffering. The League pledged to support existing humanitarian organizations, such as the Red Cross.

The final article lays out the rules concerning amendments to the Covenant. Members would not have to abide by amendments, but if they chose not to do so, they forfeited their membership. Discussions centered on whether a simple majority or a three-fourths majority would be required. Those who favored a simple majority argued that a three-fourths majority might not be attainable and would give the impression that no changes could ever be made. The requirement of a simple majority carried the day.

Essential Themes

During negotiations for the Treaty of Versailles and the League Covenant, the French premier George Clemenceau was famously skeptical of its eventual success. Asked about its implementation, he stated "God gave us Ten Commandments, and we broke them all. Wilson gave us Fourteen Points; we shall see." He was unfortunately prescient, especially in the application of the League's rules in situations that warranted the application of international pressure to keep the peace.

With the signing of the Treaty of Versailles on June 28, 1919, both the treaty and the Covenant of the League of Nations went into effect. The first session of the League's Council (an executive body comprising four permanent and four rotating members) was held in 1920. The Assembly, made up of representatives from all member nations, met the same year. The League of Nations then began what was effectively its nineteen-year existence, ending for all purposes in 1939, though it would officially exist until 1946, when it was replaced by the United Nations. Its failure largely resulted from the lack of will to impose the rules and ideals of the Covenant. The Covenant of the League of Nations was the product of conflicting national objectives, even among the victors of the First World War, a situation that ultimately made it more difficult to enforce the League's role.

The League of Nations described in the Covenant did, still, come into existence, and for twenty years sought to contain the pressures leading to conflict between nations. The effects of the Covenant were immediate. In 1920 the first session of the League was held, and by the end of the 1920s it had begun to engage in several successful projects, such as halting Greece's invasion of Bulgaria in 1925, ending the Chaco War between Bolivia and Paraguay in the 1930s, and initiating the World Court. League programs to abolish drug trafficking were active and even benefited from the activities of the United States, a nonmember. The League did indeed function, despite the misgivings of many. Part of the League's failure must be attributed to the lack of strength given the organization as well as the absence of some sort of military option. There was no provision for an armed force or any equivalent to the peacekeeping activities that would later be performed by the United Nations.

While the Covenant and the League can be seen as failures in their inability to exercise control over the activities of aggressive nations or to prevent the outbreak of war, both did exert a positive outcome even after their demise. During the Second World War, the Allies, especially the United States, saw the need for an international organization. Weaknesses in both structure and organization served as a model for how things could go wrong. The League, as defined by its Covenant, was an innovation. Nothing like it had been tried before. Despite its failure, the League that men emerging from an old world that had been thoroughly destroyed were capable of going beyond their desire for vengeance to at least try to create a system to preserve peace in a new world. That they made the effort and achieved some successes were significant achievements.

————*Robert N. Stacy, MA*

Bibliography and Further Reading

MacMillan, Margaret. *Paris 1919: Six Months That Changed the World*. New York: Random House, 2002.

Miller, David Hunter. *The Drafting of the Covenant*. Buffalo, N.Y. W. S. Hein, 2002.

Reisser, Wesley J. *The Black Book: Woodrow Wilson's Secret Plan for Peace*. Lanham, MD: Lexington Books, 2012.

Walters, F. P. *A History of the League of Nations*. Westport, Conn. Greenwood Press, 1986.

Web Sites

Duffy, Michael, editor. "Primary Documents: Treaty of Versailles, 28 June 1919." First World War.com http://www.firstworldwar.com/source/versailles.htm [accessed February 24, 2017].

"The Treaty of Versailles June 28, 1919." The Avalon Project at Yale Law School. http://avalon.law.yale.edu/subject_menus/versailles_menu.asp [accessed February 24, 2017].

"The Paris Peace Conference and the Treaty of Versailles." US Department of State Web Site, Bureau of Public Affairs: Office of the Historian. https://history.state.gov/milestones/1914-1920/paris-peace [accessed February 24, 2017].

■ Korean Declaration of Independence

Date: 1919
Authors: Son Byonghui, O Sechang, Choe Namson, Han Yongun
Genre: Declarative statement/speech

Summary Overview

On March 1, 1919, at Pagoda Park in Seoul, Korea, a student nationalist read aloud to the crowd the Korean Declaration of Independence, giving rise to the nationwide March First Movement. In response to the unjust colonization of Korea by Japan in 1910, the Korean Declaration of Independence proclaimed to the world that Korea had the right to exist as a free and independent nation. Among the thirty-three signers were sixteen Protestant Christians, fifteen leaders of Chondogyo (also called Cheondoism, the "religion of the Heavenly Way"), and two Buddhists. The Chondogyo leaders Son Byonghui, O Sechang, Kwon Dongjin, and Choe Rin were most influential in producing the Declaration. They quietly arranged for Choe Namseon, a pioneering poet and publisher-scholar, to draft it, and they reached a consensus on its moderate tone and content, espousing the ideals of peace, humanity, and freedom. They then clandestinely printed the Korean Declaration of Independence and disseminated it among the Korean people.

Since the early 1900s exiled nationalists such as Ahn Changho, the preeminent leader of the independence movement, had created myriad overseas organizations and transnational networks agitating for Korean independence. Foremost was the Korean National Association, which was founded in 1908 and served as the proto-provisional government, with more than a hundred branches in the United States, Manchuria, China, Russia, and Mexico, among other countries. The movement for independence finally came home in 1919. Sparked by the Korean Declaration of Independence, the March First Movement proved unprecedented in magnitude and scope, galvanizing Korean men and women of all ages and backgrounds, with more than two million participants joining over several months. The movement surprised the Japanese police, who reacted with violence against unarmed and peaceful Korean demonstrators, accounting for some 47,000 arrests, 7,500 deaths, and 16,000 injuries. The uprising against the Japanese inspired overseas revolutionaries to form the Provisional Government of the Republic of Korea in April 1919 in Shanghai, China.

Defining Moment

Following the First Sino-Japanese War (1894–1895) and the Russo-Japanese War (1904–1905), both of which were fought in part over control of Korean territory, Japan's takeover of Korea began in earnest with the forced signing of a protectorate treaty in 1905. The Korean royal military was disbanded in 1907, but a Korean "righteous army"—irregular militias—bitterly fought the Japanese throughout the country. Finally, in 1910, the nation was formally colonized by Japan, effectively ending the Choson Dynasty (1392–1910). According to Japanese statistics, over 2,800 clashes between Koreans and the Japanese army occurred during the period 1907–1910. By 1910 at least 17,600 Korean soldiers had died, though the numbers may have been higher.

When the First World War ended, America emerged as a global leader, setting the agenda for international peace. President Woodrow Wilson expressed his vision for the postwar settlement in his Fourteen Points speech to the U.S. Congress on January 8, 1918. The Fourteen Points would later guide Wilson's approach to the Paris Peace Conference and the Treaty of Versailles, signed in 1919 to bring the war to an official close. The Fourteen Points advocated, among other ideals, international cooperation and respect for the right of self-determination of people. Koreans were not entirely persuaded that Wilson's statement would soon lead to Korean independence, but the nationalist leadership, both domestic and abroad, was quick to seize upon the statement as an opportunity to appeal for independence from Japan.

On January 21, 1919, King Kojong, the last king of the Choson Dynasty, died, possibly having been poisoned by the Japanese. Following Kojong's death, Korean nationalist activities accelerated. As anti-colonial efforts intensified among exiled revolutionaries in China, Manchuria, Russia, the United States, and Japan, nationalists within Korea began to ponder the course of the independence movement. As most of the nationalist Korean leaders were either exiled or imprisoned, the domestic leadership was centered on religious communities such as Chondogyo and Protestant Christianity, which often served as shelters for covert nationalist activities. Chondogyo is an indigenous religion that teaches values of equality, justice, and brotherhood and incorporates Christian and egalitarian values found within the Korean and Eastern traditions. Confucians did not participate in nationalist activities, because they had incurred severe losses during the fight against Japan before the annexation; the mainstream Buddhist establishment, in turn, declined to participate. With overwhelming numbers of Koreans expected to attend the funeral of Kojong, the nationalist leaders secretly planned demonstrations across the country for March 1. They also agreed to petition foreign representatives in Tokyo and send a message to President Wilson.

Meanwhile, Korean students in Tokyo were laying the foundations for the Korean Declaration of Independence. Choe Nam-seon based the Declaration on an earlier version, the Tokyo declaration of Korean independence, which was drafted by Korean students and read before an assembled crowd in Tokyo in February 1919. In asserting Korean independence, the Tokyo declaration noted that Korea had a 4,300-year history of sovereignty and had been guaranteed independence in the aftermath of the Sino-Japanese War, but the Japanese had forcibly reduced Korea to a protectorate following the Russo-Japanese War. The Korean people had unsuccessfully resisted the Japanese protectorate, which was opposed to the wishes of the Korean people. Japan, this declaration asserted, had seen fit to exploit Korea, but the Japanese need for domination over Korea had passed, as Chinese and Russian influences no longer existed in Korea and were therefore no longer threats to Japanese security.

The Tokyo declaration pointed to the series of Japanese lies and deceits that had led to the annexation of Korea, dating back to the Treaty of Ganghwa, also called the Japanese-Korea Treaty of Amity—an unequal treaty signed by the two nations in 1876 that opened Korean ports and commerce to Japanese domination. The Tokyo declaration presented a long litany of political betrayals and deceptions committed by Japan against Korea and detailed the moral outrage and frustrations of Koreans. Whereas the Korean Declaration of Independence would prove tactful and emotionally detached, the Tokyo declaration displayed the raw emotions of a morally and physically wounded Korea. These emotions would erupt in conflagration in the March First Movement, as sparked by the initial reading of the Korean Declaration of Independence.

Author Biographies

Among the most influential leaders behind the Korean Declaration of Independence was Son Byonghui (1861–1922), the supreme leader of Chondogyo, who signed first on the document. A formidable character and charismatic leader, Son possessed the best-organized and best-financed network of followers within Korea. He had lived in exile in Japan in the early 1900s to avoid persecution—a fate that befell several Chondogyo leaders who opposed what they regarded as an oppressive government. Uprisings in 1894 had led King Kojong to invite Chinese forces into the nation to quell the unrest. Claiming that korea was in their sphere of influence, the Japanese claimed that the Chinese court should have informed them of their intent to place troops in Korea, which incidentally provided the Japanese with a pretext to invade Korea themselves. These events initiated the First Sino-Japanese War, which in turn paved the way for the Japanese colonization of Korea. This sequence of events created the conditions that allowed Son to become the leader of the Chondogyo and, while still in exile, to spearhead an anti-Japanese movement in Korea.

O Sechang (1864–1953), also a Chondogyo leader, had served as a government interpreter and official and became a journalist after studying in Japan. Having been in charge of the printing and distribution of the Declaration, O Sechang was imprisoned for three years for his involvement in the March First Movement, as was Son Byonghui. Following his prison term, he prepared a series of biographical dictionaries about Korean art and calligraphy, based on the collected art in his family possession. In his later years, he came to be known as the foremost Korean calligrapher, a connoisseur-scholar of Korean paintings and calligraphy, and a seal engraver.

The Korean Declaration of Independence was drafted by Choe Nam-seon (1890–1957), a leading Korean intellectual of his time who was knowledgeable about both traditional Chinese scholarship and new modern learning. He was persuaded to complete the draft by the Chondogyo leader Choe Rin. A poet whose work *From Sea to a Youth* introduced new Korean vernacular idioms, Choe Nam-seon was a writer, journalist, and scholar. Although he did not sign the Declaration, he was jailed for two and a half years after the March First Movement for his overall involvement. Following his imprisonment, he wrote an encyclopedic multivolume history of ancient and premodern Korea. His works covered a wide range of topics, including Korean origins, folklore, language, culture, history, and ethnography.

The "Three Open Pledges" at the close of the Korean Declaration of Independence were added by Han

Yong'un (1879–1944). Prior to Han's becoming an avid patriot, his father and brother were involved in anti-colonial activities. A leading Buddhist reformer, he wrote a book of poetry, *Silence of Love*, which is one of the most representative and beloved works in Korean literature. At the heart of his poetic concep-

tion was the yet-to-be liberated Korea. Han Yong'un and Choe Nam-seon disagreed over the Declaration's tone and content, as Han wanted it to be more ardent. In the end, a more moderate tone was adopted. Han was jailed for three years for his role in the March First Movement.

HISTORICAL DOCUMENT

We hereby declare that Korea is an independent state and that Koreans are a self-governing people. We proclaim it to the nations of the world in affirmation of the principle of the equality of all nations, and we proclaim it to our posterity, preserving in perpetuity the right of national survival. We make this declaration on the strength of five thousand years of history as an expression of the devotion and loyalty of twenty million people. We claim independence in the interest of the eternal and free development of our people and in accordance with the great movement for world reform based upon the awakening conscience of mankind. This is the clear command of heaven, the course of our times, and a legitimate manifestation of the right of all nations to coexist and live in harmony. Nothing in the world can suppress or block it.

For the first time in several thousand years, we have suffered the agony of alien suppression for a decade, becoming a victim of the policies of aggression and coercion, which are relics from a bygone era. How long have we been deprived of our right to exist? How long has our spiritual development been hampered? How long have the opportunities to contribute our creative vitality to the development of world culture been denied us?

Alas! In order to rectify past grievances, free ourselves from present hardships, eliminate future threats, stimulate and enhance the weakened conscience of our people, eradicate the shame that befell our nation, ensure proper development of human dignity, avoid leaving humiliating legacies to our children, and usher in lasting and complete happiness for our posterity, the most urgent task is to firmly establish national independence. Today when human nature and conscience are placing the forces of justice and humanity on our side, if every one of our twenty million people arms himself for

battle, whom could we not defeat and what could we not accomplish?

We do not intend to accuse Japan of infidelity for its violation of various solemn treaty obligations since the Treaty of Amity of 1876. Japan's scholars and officials, indulging in a conqueror's exuberance, have denigrated the accomplishments of our ancestors and treated our civilized people like barbarians. Despite their disregard for the ancient origins of our society and the brilliant spirit of our people, we shall not blame Japan; we must first blame ourselves before finding fault with others. Because of the urgent need for remedies for the problems of today, we cannot afford the time for recriminations over past wrongs.

Our task today is to build up our own strength, not to destroy others. We must chart a new course for ourselves in accord with the solemn dictates of conscience, not malign and reject others for reasons of past enmity or momentary passions. In order to restore natural and just conditions, we must remedy the unnatural and unjust conditions brought about by the leaders of Japan, who are chained to old ideas and old forces and victimized by their obsession with glory.

From the outset the union of the two countries did not emanate from the wishes of the people, and its outcome has been oppressive coercion, discriminatory injustice, and fabrication of statistical data, thereby deepening the eternally irreconcilable chasm of ill will between the two nations. To correct past mistakes and open a new phase of friendship based upon genuine understanding and sympathy—is this not the easiest way to avoid disaster and invite blessing? The enslavement of twenty million resentful people by force does not contribute to lasting peace in the East. It deepens the fear and suspicion of Japan by the four hundred million Chinese who constitute the main axis for stability in the East, and it will lead to the tragic downfall of all nations in our region. Independence for Korea today shall not only enable Koreans to lead a normal, prosperous life, as is their due; it will also guide Japan to leave its evil path and perform its great task of supporting the cause of the East, liberating China from a gnawing uneasiness and fear and helping the cause of world peace and happiness for mankind, which depends greatly on peace in the East. How can this be considered a trivial issue of mere sentiment?

Behold! A new world is before our eyes. The days of force are gone, and the days of morality are here. The spirit of humanity, nurtured throughout the past century, has begun casting its rays of new civilization upon human history. A new spring has arrived prompting the myriad forms of life to come to life again. The past was a time of freezing ice and snow, stifling the breath of life; the present is a time of mild breezes and warm sunshine, reinvigorating the spirit. Facing the return of the universal cycle, we set forth on the changing tide of the world. Nothing can make us hesitate or fear.

We shall safeguard our inherent right to freedom and enjoy a life of prosperity; we shall also make use of our creativity, enabling our national essence to blossom in the vernal warmth. We have arisen now. Conscience is on our side, and truth guides our way. All of us, men and women, young and old, have firmly left behind the old nest of darkness and gloom and head for joyful resurrection together with the myriad living things. The spirits of thousands of generations of our ancestors protect us; the rising tide of world consciousness shall assist us. Once started, we shall surely succeed. With this hope we march forward.

Three Open Pledges

1. Our action today represents the demand of our people for justice, humanity, survival, and dignity. It manifests our spirit of freedom and should not engender anti-foreign feelings.
2. To the last one of us and to the last moment possible, we shall unhesitatingly publicize the views of our people, as is our right.
3. All our actions should scrupulously uphold public order, and our demands and our attitudes must be honorable and upright.

Document Analysis

Simply titled "Declaration" (Seon-eon-seo), the Korean Declaration of Independence is written in poetic language. Although it is fresh and modern for 1919, the Sino-Korean literary form used for the Declaration manifests established Confucian educational traditions. It also reveals the authors' classical scholarship, intellectual resources and frame of reference, and literary aesthetics, as well as their moral outrage and political intuition. With majestic words that echo the emerging new world order of the postwar era, the Declaration reads like a poem of self-determination, championing national freedom, equality, and justice. With idealism and optimism, it rests its case upon universal claims of humanitarian ethics and humanistic values in search of Korean freedom, independence, and self-determination.

In proclaiming independence and the right of national survival, Choe and the leaders of the March First Movement who drafted the Declaration were clearly deeply aware and proud of the long history, culture, and civilization of Korea—"the strength of five thousand years of history." The basis of the moral right to independence and democratic sovereignty of Koreans is thus understood to be the principle of equality of nations and the historical authority of Korea's five thousand years of existence. The most spiritual phrase in the Declaration appears early: "This is the clear command of heaven, the course of our times, and a legitimate manifestation of the right of all nations to coexist and live in harmony." Certainly, the Chondogyo and Christian figures who comprised the March First leadership and led the drafting of the Declaration purposefully invoked the command of "heaven" or God in the inspirational beginning of the document. The Sino-Korean character *chon* can actually be translated as "heaven," "God," or "sky"; the Neoconfucian or Chondogyo notion of heaven is akin to the Christian notion of an omniscient and omnipresent moral God. Therefore, the phrase "command of Heaven" also implies the will of God.

The main point of the second paragraph can be found in the first sentence: "For the first time in several thousand years, we have suffered the agony of alien suppression for a decade, becoming a victim of the policies of aggression and coercion, which are relics from a bygone era." Being a small nation surrounded by larger neighbors—China, Russia, and Japan—Korea had been repeatedly invaded in its long history. Yet this was indeed the first time in "several thousand years" that it had been annexed or colonized by another country. For Koreans, it was infuriating and particularly humiliating to be colonized by Japan, which had long been considered a culturally inferior nation. Throughout history, the peninsular Korea had been a vital source of cultural and intellectual transmission to the islands of Japan, such as with Buddhism, a writing system, printing technology, and pottery-making methods, among other ideas and advances.

The original Korean language of the Declaration has both denotative and connotative aspects. For example, the Korean text uses the word *chimnyak*, which can be translated as "invasion" or "aggression," with a connotation of "territorial expansionism." The word *kanggeon* can be translated as "coercion" or "force," with connotations of "military force" or "brute might." The word *jui* means "principle" or also "ideology." The drafters wanted to express the awful reality of imperialism or colonialism for the colonized and highlight the associated aggressive, repressive, and coercive positionings as immoral and illegal strategies of a bygone era. That bygone era can be understood to be the sixteenth century, when Japan's invasion of Korea was repelled by Admiral Yi Sunshin's navy during the early Choson Dynasty.

The third paragraph describes the tragic plight and suffering of the colonized, with which all Koreans could empathize. Myriad reasons for Koreans to struggle for independence are listed in a long, oratorical sentence. Directly addressing the Korean people, the second sentence builds up to the ultimate message: "The most urgent task is to firmly establish national independence." The highlight of the paragraph comes at the end in the reminder to Koreans that the collective conscience of humanity is now on their side. Adopting martial language, the Declaration affirms that Koreans are assisted by "the forces of justice and humanity" and that independence can be achieved if "every one of our twenty million people arms himself for battle."

An intriguing part of the Korean Declaration of Independence, this paragraph is an artful rhetorical exercise. From the outset, the authors choose not to criticize or attack Japan directly for the annexation of

Korea or the exploitation of Koreans; instead, they attempt to take the moral high ground by stating, "We do not intend to accuse Japan of infidelity for its violation of various solemn treaty obligations since the Treaty of Amity of 1876." They also include an admission of collective self-blame for the colonial predicament: "We shall not blame Japan; we must first blame ourselves before finding fault with others." However, the paragraph stresses that "Japan's scholars and officials, indulging in a conqueror's exuberance, have denigrated the accomplishments of our ancestors and treated our civilized people like barbarians." The concepts of civilization versus barbarism are juxtaposed to emphasize the barbarically debased and humiliated state of subjugated Koreans and to remind Koreans of the history and beauty of their civilization. Here, the Korean intelligentsia's acute awareness of the underlying political significance of scholarship and discourse on history and civilization is revealed. The writers of the Declaration observe that the sins of distorting history and truth by Japanese scholars and historians have consequences that are just as grave as the sins committed by Japanese officials, whether politicians or military officers.

Shifting the focus to the Korean people as an audience, the authors state that the task at hand is "to build up our own strength, not to destroy others." A new beginning to shape a new destiny for the future of Korea is championed: "We must chart a new course for ourselves in accord with the solemn dictates of conscience, not malign and reject others for reasons of past enmity or momentary passion." Rather astutely, the Japanese leaders are described as actually being victims, as they are "chained to old ideas and old forces and victimized by their obsession with glory." A number of dichotomies appear in this paragraph: build versus destroy, conscience versus glory, natural versus unnatural, just versus unjust, and old versus new. Drawing on postwar optimism about a coming new world order and on perceptions of opportunity for change, the Declaration implies that the constructive and future-oriented task for Koreans is not necessarily anti-colonial but rather is pro-democratic. The foremost task of Koreans is to build a new order, new society, new culture, new civilization, and new democracy.

From the outset, this paragraph intends to clarify the situation of the annexation of Korea by Japan, which clearly "did not emanate from the wishes of the people." As such, the outcome was "oppressive coercion, discriminatory injustice, and fabrication of statistical data," which in turn has deepened "the eternally irrec-oncilable chasm of ill will between the two nations." While the opening of the Declaration is addressed to all nations of the world, the text has thus far been directed to Koreans and Japanese. Here, the targeted audience is expanded to include the greater Far East, especially China, with whom Koreans have long shared histori-cal ties. Japan's militarist ambitions extended not just to the Korean Peninsula but also to continental China and Southeast Asia, so the Declaration broadly calls for "peace in the East." The entwined historical destiny and political fate of Korea and China as well as their brotherhood and shared victimhood at the hands of Ja-pan are narrated: "The enslavement of twenty million resentful people by force does not contribute to lasting peace in the East. It deepens the fear and suspicion of Japan by the four hundred million Chinese who consti-tute the main axis for stability in the East."

Essentially, the core message of the paragraph is an urging of Japan to "correct past mistakes and open a new phase of friendship based upon genuine under-standing and sympathy," as a way to "avoid disaster and invite blessing." Perhaps the most forthright statement of moral and intellectual logic in the Declaration is found in the statement that independence will enable Koreans to lead normal lives and also will help Japan "leave its evil path" and bring stability to the East by freeing China from fear.

In the most poetic and metaphorical of the para-graphs, the Declaration speaks of the arrival of the "new world" and a "new spring" in which the "days of force" are being replaced by the "days of morality." With March 1 being the date of the collective uprising, the double meaning of "spring" dominates the paragraph, lending heightened connotations to such phrases as "rays of new civilization," "myriad forms of life to come to life again," "breath of life," "mild breezes," "warm sunshine," and "reinvigorating the spirit." The rhythm of the poetic language reinforces the image of a "uni-versal cycle" characterized by the "changing tide of the world" between good and evil and between right and wrong. The notion of the "universal cycle," in this sense, connotes not only the seasonal cycle but also historical cycles of morality and justice.

The final paragraph of the Declaration reiterates the Korean will for independence: "We shall safeguard our inherent right to freedom and enjoy a life of prosperity; we shall also make use of our creativity, enabling our national essence to blossom in the vernal warmth." The

reference to an inherent right to a "life of prosperity" is reminiscent of the U.S. Declaration of Independence, with Thomas Jefferson's assertion of the rights to "life, liberty, and the pursuit of happiness." Through the metaphor of growth, on the other hand, what is evoked is the national culture rather than the more politicized concepts of democracy or national self-determination. This focus originates from the drafters' worldview and pride in Korea's long history and civilization as well as their conception of a new national culture as a new political order. Empowering the Korean people with words of moral strength, the Declaration pronounces, "Conscience is on our side, and truth guides our way." Then it calls for all people, of all ages, to "head for joy-ful resurrection together with the myriad living things." Incorporating the imagery of nature in springtime, "resurrection" is, of course, an allusion to Christ's mi-raculous rise after his sacrificial death on the cross. An-nouncing that "the spirits of thousands of generations of our ancestors protect us," the Declaration ends with assurances of success.

Appended to the Declaration are three pledges for the future. The first notes that the Declaration is a de-mand for freedom and dignity, not a document to create anti-foreign feeling. In the second pledge the drafters assert their right to communicate the Declaration to the people of Korea. Finally, the drafters reject violence and urge their followers to maintain public order.

Essential Themes

As sparked by the Declaration, the March First Move-ment demonstrated Koreans' desire for independence and democracy. The demonstrators marched into the streets not only in Seoul but, indeed, in virtually ev-ery town, village, and county. People who had come to Seoul for the funeral of King Kojong joined the move-ment with shouts of "Long live Korea!" and "Long live Korean independence!" while waving forbidden Korean flags. The demonstrations were peaceful, for no armed revolt or violence had been planned by the organizers; in spearheading the movement, the Chondogyo lead-ers espoused three principles: popularization, unifica-tion, and nonviolence. The thirty-three signatories of the Declaration made no attempt to hide and allowed themselves to be arrested. The subsequent nationwide demonstrations lasted for months. Even by conserva-tive estimates, the nation witnessed some fifteen hun-dred demonstrations in the first three months, with the participation of over two million people. Among those arrested, about ten thousand, including 186 women, were tried and convicted.

On March 17, 1919, the Korean National Council was created in Vladivostok, Russia, to represent more than half a million Koreans in Manchuria and Siberia. Although a provisional government could not be openly established within Korea, an underground meeting named a roster of leaders and adopted a constitution in Seoul in April. Korean nationalists also emerged one by one in Shanghai, and many committed revolutionaries from Korea, China, and Japan gathered there. During this time, collective efforts to unify the nationalists in China, Manchuria, Siberia, and America began. The nationalists in Shanghai declared the formation of the Provisional Government of the Republic of Korea on April 9, 1919. The next day, the Provisional Assembly was created by representatives from eight provinces in Korea and from Russia, China, and America. At the meeting of the Provisional Assembly on April 11, the formal name of the sovereign nation was proclaimed as Taehan Minguk (Republic of Korea), and the initial outline of the constitution was drafted. The constitution's preface included the Korean Declaration of Independence.

The March First Movement did not lead to Korean independence from Japanese colonialism, yet it was significant in that it exposed to the world the abuses of Japanese colonial rule. Rising publicity and criticism worldwide led to Japan's "cultural policy" of appeasement in the 1920s under a new governor-general. However, from the late 1930s through the Second World War, Japan essentially tried to exterminate Korean culture. Japanese colonials forced the people to adopt Japanese religious practices and Japanese names, forbidding the use of the Korean language in publications, and destroying or stealing Korean artifacts. One of the horrors of the war was Japan's conscription of some two hundred thousand Korean women to serve as "comfort women," or sex slaves, for Japanese troops. Korea remained under Japanese control until the end of the war and Japan's unconditional surrender to Allied forces on August 15, 1945. In the war's immediate aftermath, the country was divided into North Korea and South Korea, with the south under U.S. control and the north under the control of the Soviet Union. The arrangement was intended to be temporary, but cold war tensions between the Communists and the West led to the outbreak of war between North Korea and South Korea in 1950, with the south backed by the United States and the north eventually receiving support from China. The war ended in a stalemate in 1953 with the establishment of the two-mile-wide Korean Demilitarized Zone at latitude thirty-eight degrees north. The peninsula continues to be divided between the Democratic People's Republic of Korea (Communist "North Korea") and the Republic of Korea ("South Korea") in the twenty-first century.

———*Jacqueline Pak*

Bibliography and Further Reading

Buswell, Robert E., Jr., and Timothy S. Lee, eds. *Christianity in Korea*. Honolulu: University of Hawaii Press, 2006.

Lee, Ki-baik. *A New History of Korea*, trans. Edward W. Wagner. Cambridge, MA: Harvard University Press, 1984.

Lee, Peter H., and Theodore de Bary, eds. *Sources of Korean Tradition*. 2 vols. New York: Columbia University Press, 1997.

Myers, Ramon H., and Mark R. Peattie. *The Japanese Colonial Empire, 1895–1945*. Princeton, N.J. Princeton University Press, 1984.

Nahm, Andrew, ed. *Korea under Japanese Colonial Rule: Studies of the Policy and Techniques of Japanese Colonialism*. Kalamazoo: Center for Korean Studies, Western Michigan University, 1973.

Web Sites

Masayuki, Nishi. "March 1 and May 4, 1919 in Korea, China and Japan: Toward an International History of East Asian Independence Movements." Asia-Pacific Journal: Japan Focus. http://apjjf.org/-Nishi-Masayuki/2560/article.html [accessed March 2, 2017].

Resolution of the General Syrian Congress

Date: 1919
Author: General Syrian Congress
Genre: Declarative statement/statement of principles

Summary Overview

The Resolution of the General Syrian Congress, composed at the behest of Emir Faisal, the head of the provisional Arab government in Damascus, reflected nationalist sentiments that were widely held in the aftermath of The First World War. At the time, the disposition of territory formerly governed by the Ottoman Empire became an issue of concern, both to the inhabitants of that territory and to the victorious Entente powers meeting in Paris. At the suggestion of President Woodrow Wilson, who was the leader of the American delegation, the Big Four powers—Britain, France, the United States, and Italy—authorized a commission of inquiry to be sent to the former Asiatic Arab provinces of the empire to ascertain the wishes of their inhabitants with regard to their future political status. Soon thereafter Faisal called for a General Syrian Congress to draft a document that would represent to the commission the political aspirations of a majority of those living in "Greater Syria"—the territory that now includes Syria, Lebanon, Israel-Palestine, and Jordan.

The resulting document, the Resolution of the General Syrian Congress, called on the Entente powers to honor their commitment to national self-determination, demanding complete and immediate independence for a united Syria. If Syria had to become a temporary ward (mandate) of any foreign power, that foreign power should be the United States or, if necessary, Britain. Finally, the resolution denounced French and Zionist ambitions in the region.

The General Syrian Congress directed the resolution at the commission of inquiry (the King-Crane Commission) that was visiting Greater Syria at the time of its drafting and, more broadly, at the Paris Peace Conference. By agreeing to the charter of the League of Nations, the representatives to that conference committed themselves to the proposition that the wishes of former subjects of empires defeated in the war would be paramount in determining the political future of those populations. The General Syrian Congress sought to hold the representatives to that proposition.

Defining Moment

During the First World War the Ottoman Empire fought in alliance with Germany and the Austro-Hungarian Empire, among others, against the Entente powers, an alliance that included Britain, France, Russia, and, eventually, the United States. During the war Britain, France, and Russia signed secret agreements that arranged for the division of the territory of the Ottoman Empire among themselves after the war. Each of the powers viewed these agreements as a means to safeguard its interests and enhance its strategic position in the Middle East. France, for example, claimed "historic rights" in "Syria"—an ambiguously defined geographic unit. The French based their claims on their historical relationship with Catholic and near-Catholic minorities (such as the Maronite Christians of Lebanon) who lived there and on French economic interests in the region, such as investments in railroads and silk production.

The British also made wartime pledges to a number of local warlords and nationalist groups, promising to support their goals if they allied themselves with the Entente. Two of these pledges were particularly important. In 1915 the British made contact with Sharif Husayn ibn 'Ali, an Arabian warlord based in Mecca. Husayn promised to delegate his son Faisal to launch a revolt against the Ottoman Empire to harass the empire from within—the famous Arab Revolt, guided by the British colonel T. E. Lawrence. In exchange, the British promised Husayn gold, guns, and, once the war ended, the right to establish an Arab "state or states" with ill-defined borders in the predominantly Arab territories of the empire. The second relevant pledge made by the British during the war was to the Zionist (Jewish nationalist) movement. In July 1917 the British foreign secretary Alfred Balfour placed a notice in the *Times* of London, stating that "His Majesty's Government view with favour the establishment in Palestine of a national home for the Jewish people." The Balfour Declaration provided the first real diplomatic victory for the Zionist movement.

The postwar settlement was complicated by three factors. First, the various agreements and pledges made during the war were mutually contradictory. Second,

Faisal's army had lodged itself in the territory of inland Syria (now labeled Occupied Enemy Territory–East, or OET-E), and with British cooperation Faisal established a rudimentary administration based in Damascus. Finally, in an address to the US Congress, President Wilson announced his famous Fourteen Points—a summary of American (and later Entente) war aims. Among them, Wilson called for the application of the right of peoples to national self-determination, and promised the non-Turkish portion of the Ottoman Empire the chance to achieve their independence and the autonomous development of nation-states.

To unravel their competing claims and arrange a final peace settlement, Entente leaders met in Paris. There they agreed to establish a League of Nations and initialed its charter. Article 22 of the charter deals directly with the Asiatic Arab provinces of the Ottoman Empire. Because the inhabitants of the region were not yet ready "to stand by themselves under the strenuous conditions of the modern world," the document states, they require assistance by a "mandatory" power until they are. Article 22 further stipulates that the wishes of the community were to be the principal concern in the choice of the mandatory power.

To determine those wishes, President Wilson proposed that a commission of inquiry be sent to the former Asiatic Arab provinces. Although both Britain and France acquiesced, neither country participated. Even the American government soon lost interest. Nevertheless, the announcement of the commission (named the King-Crane Commission after its two leaders) stirred great interest in Greater Syria. Faisal, who had been in Paris representing the interests of "Asiatic Arabs," returned home and called for an assembly to formulate a program expressing the wishes of a majority of the inhabitants. On July 2, 1919, the congress adopted the Damascus Program, also known as the Resolution of the General Syrian Congress. The announcement and site visits of the commission also stirred unprecedented and widespread nationalist agitation throughout inland Syria as the administration of Faisal attempted to win over the congress and the populace to his more conciliatory position, while various nationalist groups maneuvered to have their voices heard. In the end, the mobilization and the agitation of those nationalist groups outside the congress most influenced the resolution.

Author Biography

The General Syrian Congress was made up of delegates from the Arab-, British-, and French-administered areas of Greater Syria. Eighty-five representatives from the Arab-administered areas were elected in two stages: Voters first elected representatives to local assemblies; then those representatives chose the delegates. Faisal selected an additional thirty-five tribal and religious leaders as delegates. No elections took place in the British- and French-administered areas. Instead, local nationalist committees decided on the delegates. Seats were set aside for minority (Christian and Jewish) representation.

Two social groups were particularly well represented in the congress. One group consisted of urban notables, a stratum of society that had dominated local and provincial politics throughout the late Ottoman period. The other group included delegates who tended to be younger, more radical, and less socially prominent than the notables. Both groups contributed to the drafting of the resolution.

HISTORICAL DOCUMENT

We the undersigned members of the General Syrian Congress, meeting in Damascus on Wednesday, July 2nd, 1919, made up of representatives from the three Zones, viz., the Southern, Eastern, and Western, provided with credentials and authorizations by the inhabitants of our various districts, Muslims, Christians, and Jews have agreed upon the following statement of the desires of the people of the country who have elected us to present them to the American Section of the International Commission: the fifth article was passed by a very large majority; all the other articles were accepted unanimously.

1. We ask absolutely complete political independence for Syria within these boundaries. The Taurus System on the North; Rafah and a line running from Al Jauf to the south of the Syrian and the Hejazian line to Akaba on the south; the Euphrates and Khabur Rivers and a line extending east of Abu Kamal to the east of Al Jauf on the east; and the Mediterranean on the west.

2. We ask that the Government of this Syrian country should be a democratic civil constitutional Monarchy on broad decentralization principles, safeguarding the rights of minorities, and that the King be the Emir Feisal [Faisal], who carried on a glorious struggle in the cause of our liberation and merited our full confidence and entire reliance.

3. Considering the fact that the Arabs inhabiting the Syrian area are not naturally less gifted than other more advanced races and that they are by no means less developed than the Bulgarians, Serbians, Greeks, and Romanians at the beginning of their independence, we protest against Article 22 of the Covenant of the League of Nations, placing us among the nations in their middle stage of development which stand in need of a mandatory power.

4. In the event of the rejection by the Peace Conference of this just protest for certain considerations that we may not understand, we, relying on the declarations of President Wilson that his object in waging war was to put an end to the ambition of conquest and colonization, can only regard the mandate mentioned in the Covenant of the League of Nations as equivalent to the rendering of economical and technical assistance that does not prejudice our complete independence. And desiring that our country should not fall a prey to colonization and believing that the American Nation is farthest from any thought of colonization and has no political ambition in our country, we will seek the technical and economical assistance from the United States of America, provided that such assistance does not exceed 20 years.

5. In the event of America not finding herself in a position to accept our desire for assistance, we will seek this assistance from Britain, also provided that such assistance does not infringe the complete independence and unity of our country and that the duration of such assistance does not exceed that mentioned in the previous article.

6. We do not acknowledge any right claimed by the French Government in any part whatever of our Syrian country and refuse that she should assist us or have a hand in our country under any circumstances and in any place.

7. We oppose the pretentions of the Zionists to create a Jewish commonwealth in the southern part of Syria, known as Palestine, and oppose Zionist migration to any part of our country; for we do not acknowledge their title but consider them a grave peril to our people from the national, economical, and political points of view. Our Jewish compatriots shall enjoy our common rights and assume the common responsibilities.

8. We ask that there should be no separation of the southern part of Syria, known as Palestine, nor of the littoral western zone, which includes Lebanon, from the Syrian country. We desire that the unity of the country should be guaranteed against partition under whatever circumstances.

9. We ask complete independence for emancipated Mesopotamia and that there should be no economical barriers between the two countries.

10. The fundamental principles laid down by President Wilson in condemnation of secret treaties impel us to protest most emphatically against any treaty that stipulates the partition of our Syria country and against any private engagement aiming at the establishment of Zionism in the southern part of Syria; therefore we ask the complete annulment of these conventions and agreements.

The noble principles enunciated by President Wilson strengthen our confidence that our desires emanating from the depths of our hearts, shall be the decisive factor in determining our future; and that President Wilson and the free American people will be our supporters for the realization of our hopes, thereby proving their sincerity and noble sympathy with the aspiration of the weaker nations in general and our Arab people in particular.

We also have the fullest confidence that the Peace Conference will realize that we would not have risen against the Turks, with whom we had participated in all civil, political, and representative privileges, but for their violation of our national rights, and so will grant us our desires in full in order that our political rights may not be less after the war than they were before, since we have shed so much blood in the cause of our liberty and independence.

We request to the allowed to send a delegation to represent us at the Peace Conference to defend our rights and secure the realization of our aspirations.

> ## GLOSSARY
>
> **decentralization principles:** conventions supporting the removal of power from a single national authority in favor of regional and local authorities
>
> **littoral:** near a shore (here, the coast of the Mediterranean Sea)
>
> **mandatory power:** power assumed by a country that had received a commission from the League of Nations to set up a government in a conquered territory

Document Analysis

The General Syrian Congress was more of a bellwether than an architect of public opinion. While the deliberations that resulted in the drafting of the resolution remain unknown, it is evident that the resolution emerged as a compromise between the two main ideological blocs that dominated the politics of the Arab-administered area of Greater Syria.

The first bloc (which might be called the Arabist bloc) included the supporters of Faisal and his policies. Like most who had fought in the Arab Revolt, Faisal came from outside the territory of Greater Syria. As a result, he and his followers, many of whom also came from other areas, championed the eventual establishment of the *Arab* state that the British had promised his father. This state would include the Hejaz (the western region of Arabia from which Faisal came) and perhaps Iraq. Like Faisal, members of this bloc were also willing to bow to reality and accept a mandate, but only if France was not the mandatory power. Finally, while Zionist immigration into Palestine was not a central issue for this bloc, Faisal reached an accord with the Zionists that would have permitted continued Jewish immigration into Palestine.

The second bloc (which might be called the Syrianist bloc) included those who had belonged to or embraced ideas originally espoused by the Syrian Union, an organization formed by Syrian exiles in Egypt during the war. By the time the congress convened, this bloc had already begun to dominate the nationalist camp in the Syrian interior. Its members demanded complete independence for a unified Syria within clearly delineated borders, no connection to the Hejaz, separation from Iraq, no mandate, and an end to Zionist immigration—in their view, Palestine was southern Syria. Because members distrusted Husayn and his son, they sought decentralization and limitations on the power

of any government headed by Faisal. Because they also distrusted the British, who had sponsored Faisal's Arab Revolt and supported Zionist aspirations, they believed a British mandate to be no better than a French one.

The resolution begins with a prologue establishing the credentials of the General Syrian Congress and its right to represent to the commission of inquiry the wishes of the entire Syrian nation. That right rested on three grounds. First, the congress represented all regions of Greater Syria— Occupied Enemy Territory -E, Occupied Enemy Territory -W, and Occupied Enemy Territory–South, or Occupied Enemy Territory -S (Palestine)—despite the fact that the French discouraged elections in the coastal zone and Palestine lacked the infrastructure for holding them. Second, delegates to the congress were authorized by the populations of their districts to act on their behalf. Finally, the congress included delegates who represented the three major religious communities living in Syria. Ensuring the representation of religious minorities was essential for both domestic and foreign reasons. The minority population of Greater Syria was not negligible, and its support was necessary for any government that wished to rule effectively. In addition, many from minority communities looked with suspicion on an emir who claimed descent from the prophet Muhammad and on an administration associated so closely with the Hejaz, the region of Arabia in which the two holy cities of Islam, Mecca and Medina, are located. By putting the issue of minority rights up front, the congress hoped to minimize foreign (particularly French) interference in the domestic affairs of Syria as well as to demonstrate to the Entente powers that the "religious fanaticism" about which those powers had frequently complained during the nineteenth century was a thing of the past. In other words, ensuring minority representation in the congress assured foreign observers that Syria had reached a "level of civilization" commensurate with independence.

Ten articles follow the prologue. The first article calls for the complete independence of Syria within a fixed set of boundaries. The wording is complex and allows for multiple interpretations. Nevertheless, it can be assumed that the boundaries of a future Syrian state stipulated by the resolution corresponded to the so-called "natural boundaries" of Syria found in other documents written at the same time. The northern boundary was demarcated by the Taurus Mountains in the southern part of contemporary Turkey. The eastern boundary followed the Euphrates and Khabur rivers in the north and then stretched from the town of Abu Kamal (on the borders of present-day Syria and Iraq), continued through the town of al-Jawf, and terminated around the town of Mada'in Salih. (Both al-Jawf and Mada'in Salih are located in the northwest of present-day Saudi Arabia.) The southern boundary followed a line stretching southeast from Rafah (on the present-day Gaza-Egypt border) through Aqaba (a port city in the south of present-day Jordan) until it met the eastern boundary in the proximity of Mada'in Salih.

Several aspects of Article 1 are significant. In its opening sentence, the article calls for "absolutely complete independence for Syria." Thus, in this article the General Syrian Congress rejected mandatory control. Moreover, by calling for "absolutely complete independence for Syria," this article rebuffed those, including Husayn and Faisal, who would have preferred an Arab state over a Syrian state. Indeed, the boundaries were deliberately drawn to sever the Syrian state from the Hejaz and from Iraq. In spite of the artificiality of Syria's "natural" boundaries, the victory of the Syrianist bloc over the Arabist bloc in the congress indicated that most delegates found a Syrian identity more compelling than an Arab one. While there were immediate political reasons for delegates to favor severing national bonds with the Hejaz and Iraq (including resentment over the preeminent role played by Hejazis and Iraqis in the Damascus administration), a number of factors—migratory patterns, marriage alliances, economic exchange, and infrastructure development—had combined to make a Syrian identity plausible, while Syrian nationalists had acted to make it accepted.

Article 2 lays out the structure of the future Syrian state. It calls for the establishment of a decentralized constitutional monarchy that would safeguard the rights of minorities. It also nominated Faisal to serve as the first king of Syria, arguing that he merited the position because of his wartime service.

While the first article reflected a clear victory for the Syrianists over the Arabists, Article 2 represented a compromise between the two camps. On the one hand, it strongly limited the power of the monarch by compelling him to abide by constitutional strictures and by insisting upon local checks to decision making. These stipulations were undoubtedly the work of the Syrianist bloc, which distrusted the intentions of Faisal and his father. On the other hand, the Arabist bloc achieved its own success with the selection of Faisal as first king of Syria. Placing Syrian independence in the context of the Arab Revolt represented another victory for the Arabist bloc, integrating the Arab Revolt into the Syrian national narrative and proclaiming Faisal the liberator of Syria.

Article 3 protests the inclusion of Syria in the category of "Class A" mandates—that is, nations that were, according to the Covenant of the League of Nations, "inhabited by peoples not yet able to stand by themselves under the strenuous conditions of the modern world," whose independence could be "provisionally recognized" but whose complete independence had to be delayed to allow one or another "advanced nation" time to render them advice and assistance (Hurewitz, p. 179). Class A mandates occupied an intermediate space between nations worthy of independence and such territories as most of Africa and Micronesia, whose independence was indefinitely postponed. The article lists people of other nationalities—Bulgarians, Serbians, Greeks, and Romanians—who, like the Syrians, had once been subject peoples of the Ottoman Empire but who had been no more advanced at the time of their independence than Syrians were in 1919.

Backtracking somewhat from the demand for complete and immediate independence for Syria articulated in Article 1, Articles 4–6 corresponded more closely to the more pragmatic views of the Arabist bloc than to those of the Syrianist bloc. Acknowledging that the League of Nations might not acquiesce to the demand for immediate independence, these articles sought to define the conditions under which mandate status would be acceptable and to identify a suitable mandatory power. Citing the position of President Wilson that the United States joined the war effort to end "conquest and colonization," Article 4 limited the role of any mandatory power to providing economic and technical assistance, which in no way would affect Syrian independence adversely.

That the General Syrian Congress would attempt to provide its own definition of the role of the mandatory power and the status of the mandate underscored the novelty of the mandates system. That system emerged as a compromise between the British and the French positions on the one hand and the American position on the other. The British and the French wanted the peace conference to put its imprimatur on imperial rule over less-developed areas; the Americans demanded an open door to those areas and the abolition of imperial trade preferences, a position that was inconsistent with British and French imperial policies. While the mandatory power would have enhanced access to and influence upon its mandates, the special access and influence were to be temporary, and all nations were to have equal rights in the mandates' markets.

Articles 4–6 also identify the United States and, if the United States refused, Britain as possible mandatory powers for Syria, rejecting the idea of a French mandate. While Article 4 cites the American reputation for anticolonialism, historians have attributed the appeal of an American mandate to a number of other causes as well, including President Wilson's renown in the region, the disinterest of the United States and its disinclination to project its power into a region that had been of little concern to it, and a misreading of the American colonial experience in the Philippines, which Syrians believed to have been more benign than it actually was. Even so, Article 4 limited an American mandate to twenty years. Britain was popular with the Arabist bloc because of its wartime support for the Arab Revolt (from whose ranks the Arab administration drew much of its personnel) and for a postwar Arab state or states. As opposed to the United States, Britain had a long history in the region and had periodically offered support to national movements seeking independence from the Ottoman Empire. France also had a long history in the region but had too close a relationship to Syria's Christians (particularly Maronite Christians) to satisfy many non-Christians in Syria, and France was sympathetic to the establishment of a separate Christian enclave on the Syrian coast. In addition, French missionary activity in the region had given France a reputation for being anti-Muslim. Finally, many Syrians feared that once it was established in Syria, France would never relinquish control because of its economic interests there.

Articles 7, 8, and 10 address threats to Syrian unity posed by Zionism (Articles 7 and 10) and by the pos-sible detachment of the Syrian littoral (Lebanon) and southern Syria (Palestine) from Greater Syria (Articles 8 and 10). These articles once again enunciate a fundamental plank of the platform of the Syrianist bloc. Article 7 protests Zionist plans to establish a separate Jewish commonwealth in Palestine and Zionist immigration to any part of Syria, citing the national, economic, and political threat posed to Syria by Zionism. The article differentiates between Zionists, who were devoted to the partition of Syria, and Syrian Jews, who would enjoy the rights and obligations of citizenship in common with other Syrians after independence. By making this distinction, the article affirms that the opposition of the congress to Zionism rested on political, not religious, grounds.

Article 10 makes the argument against Zionism and partition from a different angle, citing President Wilson's oft-repeated condemnation of secret treaties secretly arrived at. While the British pledge to the Zionists had, in fact, been made publicly, the 1916 Sykes-Picot Agreement had been secret. This agreement would have divided Syria and much of the Middle East into zones of direct and indirect British and French control and would have established an international zone of Jerusalem. When the Bolsheviks took power in Russia in 1917, they published the secret treaties and agreements to which the czarist government had been party. Article 10 demands the annulment of those treaties and agreements.

Clearly the work of the Syrianist bloc, Article 9 requests that Mesopotamia also receive "complete independence" and that no economic barriers be established obstructing trade between Syria and Mesopotamia. During the war the British had occupied Mesopotamia, whose name originally referred to the territory between the Tigris and Euphrates rivers but subsequently referred to the larger territory roughly coincident with present-day Iraq. The Syrianist position of separating the two countries was supported by economic realities. During the nineteenth century the interregional caravan trade between Syria and Mesopotamia collapsed, though international trade increased as a result of the invention of steamships and the opening of the Suez Canal. Thereafter the international trade of Syria oriented west toward the Mediterranean, while that of Mesopotamia oriented south toward the Persian Gulf. Ironically, then, by the time this article was written, trade between the two regions had virtually disappeared. It is ironic as well that after the French established their mandate over Syria and Faisal was forced to flee Damascus, the British found a throne for him as the first king of Iraq.

The resolution concludes with three paragraphs. The first addresses what had become an American commission of inquiry and affirms the congress's confidence that its demands, rooted in Wilsonian principles, would be met and that President Wilson and the American people would demonstrate their compassion for weaker nations and the Arab world by assisting in their achievement. In the second paragraph, the congress reminded the representatives to the peace conference that Syrians had not rebelled against the Ottoman Empire because they had been denied civil, political, or representational rights in the empire; rather, they had rebelled because they were denied rights as a nation. The paragraph argues that after Syrians had shed so much blood for their independence, it was incumbent on the representatives to the peace conference not to leave them with fewer political rights than they had enjoyed before the war. The resolution concludes by requesting permission to send a delegation to the peace conference to ensure that Syrians rights would not be denied and to secure Syrian independence.

Essential Themes

The resolution of the General Syrian Congress had no impact on the deliberations in Paris. Britain and France divided the territory of Greater Syria between them as mandates and worked out an understanding of their own. Having already ceded the coastal plain and the contiguous hinterland to the French (an area designated as Occupied Enemy Territory–West, or OET-W), the British withdrew their forces to Palestine from the interior. This decision, in effect, created three separate administrative units in Greater Syria and challenged the demand of the congress and most nationalist groups in the Arab administrative zone for a unified, independent Syria. In March 1920 the congress proclaimed Syria independent, with Faisal as its monarch. A little over a month later, the San Remo Conference awarded France the mandate for a truncated Syria.

In Syria, nationalist groups successfully rallied the population that was politically engaged around the Syrianist position. Within several months, the slogan "We demand complete independence for Syria within its natural boundaries, no protection, no tutelage, no mandate" became virtually ubiquitous in nationalist rhetoric, while support for the promised "Arab state or states" evaporated. The Arab administration of Faisal brought the population of Damascus and other cities into the streets to display to the commission of inquiry the popular will in action. Soon after, nationalist groups representing the Syrianist view also took to the streets and began organizing mass-based political associations and popular militias. The mobilizing activities of these associations and militias led directly to the proclamation of Syrian independence in March 1920.

Tensions rose between the French on the coast and nationalist guerrillas who were launching raids into French territory, and nationalist agitation spread throughout inland Syria. As a result, the French delivered an ultimatum to the newly proclaimed Arab government, invaded inland Syria, and assumed mandatory control over what would become Lebanon and Syria in July 1920.

———*James L. Gelvin*

Bibliography and Further Reading

Fromkin, David. *A Peace to End All Peace: The Fall of the Ottoman Empire and the Creation of the Modern Middle East*. New York: Holt, 2009.

Hurewitz, J. C. *The Middle East and North Africa in World Politics: A Documentary Record*. Vol. 2: *British-French Supremacy, 1914–1945*. New Haven: Yale University Press, 1979.

Web Sites

"The King-Crane Commission Report, August 28, 1919." Hellenic Resources Network. http://www.hri.org/docs/king-crane/ [accessed March 9, 2017].

Collelo, Thomas, editor. *Syria: A Country Study*. Washington: Government Printing Office for the Library of Congress, 1987 http://countrystudies.us/syria/ [accessed March 9, 2017].

■ *The Black Man's Burden*

Date: 1920
Author: Edmund Dene Morel
Genre: Book

Summary Review

E. D. Morel was a British crusader against slavery and the slave trade in the early twentieth century. He wrote several books over the course of his lifetime, but his most famous work was a summation of the focus of most of his political life, *The Black Man's Burden: The White Man in Africa from the Fifteenth Century to World War I*. The title was a play on the title of a famous poem written by the imperialist writer Rudyard Kipling, entitled "The White Man's Burden" (1899). Kipling's poem referred to "the white man's burden" as the improvement of the peoples of the non-western world, despite their hatreds of the benefits of western civilization. Morel's work was therefore meant to strike a note of irony; by describing Europeans' exploitation of Africans, Morel made the point that there were excellent reasons for non-westerners to reject western "civilization," and that the burden of enslavement was worse than any imagined and hypocritical difficulties encountered in the colonization of the world's free peoples.

Defining Moment

In 1895, Edmund Dene Morel worked for a Liverpool shipping company, as the head clerk of a department in charge of imports and exports headed to the Belgian Congo. He began to notice that, for all the ivory and rubber shipping out of the Congo and making its way through Liverpool, there seemed to be little else in the way of compensation and maintenance going back to the Congo for the native workers, short of rifles. Morel came to the correct conclusion—that the Congolese people were enslaved to King Leopold's International African Association—and resigned his post on moral grounds in

1901. Thereafter, Morel's life focus was on the eradication of slavery, in all its forms: as the actual chained labor of impoverished Africans, or in the barely-livable wage compensation of European industrial workers. By 1920, the First World War and socialist politics had risen to occupy Morel's attentions, but the publication of *The Black Man's Burden*—in essence, a history of European exploitation of Africans over centuries—reminded his admiring public of what made him a major public figure in the first place. *The Black Man's Burden* was published after the war ended, as the victorious British, Belgian and French empires divvied up Germany's African colonies between them. Morel's work, then, was also meant as an indictment of the Peace of Paris and its dismissal of the freedom of national self-determination for the world's non-western peoples.

Author Biography

Edmund Dene Morel was primarily a journalist, and one of the best-known anti-slavery crusaders of his time in Britain. Over the course of his career, he ran a newspaper, the *African Mail*, which publicized abuses in the Belgian Congo, and he founded the Congo Reform Association in 1904. He was a committed socialist and pacifist, opposing the First World War and even serving time in prison for his pacifist activities in 1917. Eventually he stood as a candidate for Parliament as a member of the Labour Party in 1922, and won office. He was considered for the post of Foreign Secretary in the Labour government of 1924, and his fellow Labour members put him up for the Nobel Peace Prize at the same time. However, he died of a heart attack later in the year.

HISTORICAL DOCUMENT

Chapter I: The White Man's Burden

The bard of a modern Imperialism has sung of the White Man's burden.

The notes strike the granite surface of racial pride and fling back echoes which reverberate through the corridors of history, exultant, stirring the blood with memories of heroic adventure, deeds of desperate daring, ploughing of unknown seas, vistas of mysterious continents, perils affronted and overcome, obstacles triumphantly surmounted.

But mingled with these anthems to national elation another sound is borne to us, the white peoples of the earth, along the trackless byways of the past, in melancholy cadence. We should prefer to close our ears to its haunting refrain, stifle its appeal in the clashing melodies of rapturous self-esteem. We cannot. And, as to-day, we tear and rend ourselves, we who have torn and rent the weaker folk in our Imperial stride, it gathers volume and insistence.

What of that other burden, not our own self-imposed one which national and racial vanity may well over-stress; but the burden we have laid on others in the process of assuming ours, the burden which others are bearing now because of us? Where are they whose shoulders have bent beneath its weight in the dim valleys of the centuries? Vanished into nothingness, pressed and stamped into that earth on which we set our conquering seal. How is it with those who but yesterday lived free lives beneath the sun and stars, and to-day totter to oblivion? How shall it be to-morrow with these who must slide even more swiftly to their doom, if our consciences be not smitten, our perception be not responsive to the long-drawn sigh which comes to us from the shadows of the bygone?

These contemplations are not a fit theme for lyrical outpourings. These questions are unbidden guests at the banquet of national self-laudation. They excite no public plaudits, arouse no patriotic enthusiasms, pander to no racial conceits. They typify the skeleton at the imperial feast.

But this is a time of searching inquiry for the white races; of probing scrutiny into both past and present; of introspection in every branch of human endeavour.

And these questions must be asked. They must be confronted in the fullness of their import, in the utmost significance of their implications—and they must be answered.

I respectfully ask the reader to face them in these pages.

My canvas is not crowded with figures. One figure only fills it, the figure which has incarnated for us through many generations the symbol of helplessness in man - the manacled slave stretching forth supplicating hands.

The figure on my canvas is the African, the man of sorrows in the human family.

And the reason he alone is represented there is that the question of "native races" and their treatment by the white races, centres henceforth upon the Black man, as the African is called, although few Africans are wholly black. The statement needs amplifying perhaps.

Wherever, in Asia, in Australasia and in America, the invading white man has disputed with the aboriginal coloured man the actual occupation and exploitation of the soil, the latter has either virtually disappeared, as in Northern America, the West Indies, and Western Australia; or is rapidly dying out; or is being assimilated and absorbed; the two processes operating in combination in Southern America, while in New Zealand assimilation is the chief factor.

On the other hand where, in Asia, the white man is political over-lord, as in Hindustan, Indo-China, and the East Indies, the problem of contact is not one in which the decay and disappearance of the Asiatic is even remotely problematical. Taking into account the incalculable forces which events are quickening throughout the East, the problem is whether the days of white political control south of the Great Wall are not already numbered. Europe's delirious orgy of self-destruction following the unsuccessful effort of her principal Governments to apportion China among themselves, "the most stupendous project yet imagined," has set vibrating chords of racial impulse, whose diapason may yet shake the Western world as with the tremors of approaching earthquake. For, conceding every credit to force of character, innate in the white imperial peoples, which has enabled, and enables, a handful of white men to control extensive communities of non-white peoples by moral suasion, is it not mere hypocrisy to conceal from ourselves that we have extended our subjugating march from hemisphere to hemisphere because of our superior armament? With these secrets of our power we have new parted. We have sold them to Asia, to an older civilisation than our own. We thrust them, at first under duress and with humiliation, upon brains more profound, more subtle, more imitative, more daring perhaps than our own. Then, for lust of gain, we admitted into partnership those we earlier sought to subdue. Nay more. We have invited our apt pupils to join with us in slaughtering our rivals for-the-time-being; bidden them attend the shambles, inspect the implements, study at their ease the methods of the business.

And so, to-day, after long years of furious struggle with some of its peoples, long years of rough insolence towards others, White imperialism finds itself confronted with a racial force in Asia, which it can neither intimidate nor trample underfoot. Equipped with the knowledge our statesmen and capitalists have themselves imparted to it, this racial force faces us with its superior millions, its more real spiritual faith, its greater homogeneousness, its contempt of death. As the mists of fratricidal passion lessen, our gaze travels eastwards and vainly strives to read the purpose which lurks beneath the mask of imperturbable impassivity which meets us. Do we detect behind it no more than an insurance against white exploitation, or do we fancy that we perceive the features of an imperialism as ruthless as our own has been, which shall mould to its will the plastic myriads our own actions have wrenched from agelong trodden paths of peace? Do we hope that the "colour line," we ourselves have drawn so rigidly and almost universally, may operate between brown and yellow; that the ranges of the Himalayas and the forests of Burma may prove a national barrier to a more intimate fusion of design than the white races have yet shown themselves capable of evolving?

The answer to these riddles lies hidden in the womb of the future. But to this at least we may testify. In Asia the question is no longer, "How have we, the White imperial peoples, treated the Asiatic peoples in the past?"; nor is it, even, "How do we propose to treat them in the future?" It is, "How will they deal with us in their continent, perchance beyond its frontiers, in the days to come?"

Chapter II: The Black Man's Burden

It is with the peoples of Africa, then, that our inquiry is concerned. It is they who carry the "Black man's" burden. They have not withered away before the white man's *occupation*. Indeed, if the scope of this volume permitted, there would be no difficulty in showing that Africa has ultimately absorbed within itself every Caucasian and, for that matter, every Semitic invader too. In hewing out for himself a fixed abode in Africa, the white man has massacred

the African in heaps. The African has survived, and it is well for the white settlers that he has.

In the process of imposing his political dominion over the African, the white man has carved broad and bloody avenues from one end of Africa to the other. The African has resisted, and persisted.

For three centuries the white man seized and enslaved millions of Africans and transported them, with every circumstance of ferocious cruelty, across the seas. Still the African survived and, in his land of exile, multiplied exceedingly.

But what the partial occupation of his soil by the white man has failed to do; what the mapping out of European political "spheres of influence" has failed to do; what the maxim and the rifle, the slave gang, labour in the bowels of the earth and the lash, have failed to do; what imported measles, smallpox and syphilis have failed to do; what even the oversea slave trade failed to do, the power of modern capitalistic exploitation, assisted by modern engines of destruction, may yet succeed in accomplishing.

For from the evils of the latter, scientifically applied and enforced, there is no escape for the African. Its, destructive effects are not spasmodic: they are permanent. In its permanence resides its fatal consequences. It kills not the body merely, but the soul. It breaks the spirit. It attacks the African at every turn, from every point of vantage. It wrecks his polity, uproots him from the land, invades his family life, destroys his natural pursuits and occupations, claims his whole time, enslaves him in his own home.

Economic bondage and wage slavery, the grinding pressure of a life of toil, the incessant demands of industrial capitalism—these things a landless European proletariat physically endures, though hardly. . . . The recuperative forces of a temperate climate are there to arrest the ravages, which alleviating influences in the shape of prophylactic and curative remedies will still further circumscribe. But in Africa, especially in tropical Africa, which a capitalistic imperialism threatens and has, in part, already devastated, man is incapable of reacting against unnatural conditions. In those regions man is engaged in a perpetual struggle against disease and an exhausting climate, which tells heavily upon child-bearing; and there is no scientific machinery for salving the weaker members of the community. The African of the tropics is capable of tremendous physical labours. But he cannot accommodate himself to the European system of monotonous, uninterrupted labour, with its long and regular hours, involving, moreover, as it frequently does, severance from natural surroundings and nostalgia, the condition of melancholy resulting from separation from home, a malady to which the African is specially prone. Climatic conditions forbid it. When the system is forced upon him, the tropical African droops and dies.

Nor is violent physical opposition to abuse and injustice henceforth possible for the African in any part of Africa. His chances of effective resistance have been steadily dwindling with the increasing perfectibility in the killing power of modern armament. Gunpowder broke the effectiveness of his resistance to the slave trade, although he continued to struggle. He has forced and, on rare occasions and in exceptional circumstances beaten, in turn the old-fashioned musket, the elephant gun, the seven-pounder, and even the repeating rifle and the gatling gun. He has been known to charge right down repeatedly, foot and horse, upon the square, swept on all sides with the pitiless and continuous hail of maxims. But against the latest inventions, physical bravery, though associated with a perfect knowledge of the country, can do nothing. The African cannot face the high-explosive shell and the bomb-dropping aeroplane. He has inflicted sanguinary reverses upon picked European troops, hampered by the climate and by commissariat difficulties. He cannot successfully oppose members of his own race free from these impediments, employed by his white adversaries, and trained in all the diabolical devices of scientific massacre. And although the conscripting of African armies for use in Europe or in Africa as agencies for the liquidation of the white man's quarrels must bring in its train evils from which the white man will be the first to suffer, both in Africa and in Europe; the African himself must eventually disappear in the process. Winter in Europe, or even in Northern Africa, is fatal to the tropical or sub-tropical African, while in the very nature of the case anything approaching real European control in Africa, of hordes of African soldiery armed with weapons of precision is not a feasible proposition. The

Black man converted by the European into a scientifically-equipped machine for the slaughter of his kind, is certainly not more merciful than the white man similarly equipped for like purposes in dealing with unarmed communities. And the experiences of the civilian population of Belgium, East Prussia, Galicia and Poland is indicative of the sort of visitation involved for peaceable and powerless African communities if the white man determines to add to his appalling catalogue of past misdeeds towards the African, the crowning wickedness of once again, as in the day of the slave trade, supplying him with the means of encompassing his own destruction.

Thus the African is really helpless against the material gods of the white man, as embodied in the trinity of imperialism, capitalistic-exploitation, and militarism. If the white man retains these gods and if he insists upon making the African worship them as assiduously as he has done himself, the African will go the way of the Red Indian, the Amerindian, the Carib, the Guanche, the aboriginal Australian, and many more. And this would be at once a crime of enormous magnitude, and a world disaster.

An endeavour will now be made to describe the nature, and the changing form, which the burden inflicted by the white man in modern times upon the black has assumed. It can only be sketched here in the broadest outline, but in such a way as will, it is hoped, explain the differing causes and motives which have inspired white activities in Africa and illustrate, by specific and notable examples, their resultant effects upon African peoples. It is important that these differing causes and motives should be understood, and that we should distinguish between them in order that we may hew our way later on through the jungle of error which impedes the pathway to reform. Diffused generalities and sweeping judgments generate confusion of thought and hamper the evolution of a constructive policy based upon clear apprehension of the problem to be solved.

The history of contact between the white and black peoples in modern times is divisible into two distinct and separate periods: the period of the slave trade and the period of invasion, political control, capitalistic exploitation, and, the latest development, militarism.

Document Analysis

Morel opens by setting the stage of European colonization from the romantic perspective of the Europeans themselves. He describes Europeans as having "racial pride" in "memories of heroic adventure, deeds of desperate daring, ploughing of unknown seas, vistas of mysterious continents, perils affronted and overcome, obstacles triumphantly surmounted." But he asks the reader not to ignore or discount "the burden which others are bearing now because of us"—meaning the legacy of slavery and exploitation in Africa, "the skeleton at the imperial feast."

Morel sees a negative legacy in "the white man's burden." Outside of Africa, in North America, South America, the Caribbean, New Zealand and Australia, white men exterminated or assimilated non-white populations. By comparison, European colonization and economic exploitation of India (Hindustan), Southeast Asia (Indo-China), and China - "the most stupendous project yet imagined," in the phrase of a famous multiple edition history of England—had resulted in independence movements by 1920. The destruction wrought by the First World War, or Great War (1914-1918) as Morel would have known it, threatened to undo the positive nature of European imperialism. Though he "conced[es] every credit to force of character, innate in the white imperial peoples," he identifies guns as the main reason they have managed to colonize Asia. The Great War taught Asians how to use those selfsame guns, potentially to achieve their independence—and Morel warns, with "its superior millions, its more real spiritual faith, its greater homogeneousness, its contempt of death," Asian states might end up conquering and colonizing the Europeans in the long run.

In his second chapter, Morel turns to the peoples of Africa. Morel outlines the numerous political and demographic disasters wrought by European exploitation: artificial political divisions into colonies, war, murder and slavery, diseases brought from Europe and the Americas. He asserts that "the power of modern capitalistic exploitation, assisted by modern engines of destruction," might yet destroy Africa and the Africans, because it threatens not just to kill the man, but to kill his soul and spirit.

While Morel was certainly out of step with his times in condemning the abuses of Europeans in Africa, the modern reader should not have much doubt that he was a racialist in the social Darwinian sense. He harbored no doubts that contact with white people should be an improving force for the colonized peoples of the world. Morel believed that there were biological distinctions between the alleged "races" of the world, based mostly on their adaptations to climate. For example, he compares the "[e]conomic bondage and wage slavery" of European workers to that of Africans, but notes that Europe's "temperate climate … arrest[s] the ravages" of capitalism, while "tropical Africa[ns]" are "engaged in a perpetual struggle against disease and an exhausting climate, … and there is no scientific machinery for salving the weaker members of the community. … When the system is forced upon him, the tropical African droops and dies." Such are not the sentiments of a man who considers Africans his racial equals.

Nevertheless, Morel blames European guns for the subjugation of Africans, from the time of the slave trade to the present. He notes the extraordinary bravery, and occasional successes, of Africans in resisting European armaments in the face of certain death, but in the era of the Gatling gun, the howitzer and the airplane, their resistance has become only more hopeless. Morel believes that Africans face virtual extinction in the face of "the material gods of the white man, as embodied in the trinity of imperialism, capitalis[m], and militarism." The black man's burden is a legacy of the slave trade and colonial exploitation.

Essential Themes

Though the book was written two decades after Morel's greatest fame as an anti-slavery crusader, the fact that there was enough interest in the subject for him to write *The Black Man's Burden* in 1920 said a lot about the continued interest in slavery in Africa. Morel was one of the major founders of the Congo Reform Association, along with a member of the Guinness brewing family and Sir Roger Casement. Their agitation in the international press forced the king of Belgium to give up control of the colony to his government in 1908, which was widely perceived as a triumph for Morel and his colleagues. Slavery was ended in the Congo, and the Association was finished by 1912; it was for this work that Morel was nominated for his Nobel Prize. While there is still a slave trade operating out of West and Central Africa today, it is far more circumscribed and definitely better monitored by the United Nations than it had been in Morel's time. His campaign was a prime example of the power of publicity and the average person in the face of injustice, a general theme of twentieth century history.

———*David Simonelli*

Bibliography and Further Reading

Cline, Catherine Ann. *E.D. Morel, 1873-1924: The Strategies of Protest*. Belfast: Blackstaff, 1980.

Hochschild, Adam. *King Leopold's Ghost: A Story of Greed, Terror, and Heroism in Colonial Africa*. London: Pan, 2002.

Mitchell, Angus. "New Light on the 'Heart of Darkness.'" *History Today* 49, no. 12 (December 1999): 20-27.

Mitchell, Donald. *Politics of Dissent: A Biography of E.D. Morel*. Bristol, UK: Silverwood Books, 2014.

Websites

Ceadel, Martin. "Morel, Edmund Dene (1873–1924)." *Oxford Dictionary of National Biography*. Oxford University Press (2008) http://www.oxforddnb.com/view/article/37782 [accessed December 26, 2016].

Snider, Christy Jo. "Morel, Edmund Dene." *1914-1918 Online: International Encyclopedia of the First World War* (June 14, 2016) http://encyclopedia.1914-1918-online.net/article/ morel_edmund_dene [accessed December 26, 2016].

■ "The Three Principles of the People"

Date: 1921
Author: Sun Yixian
Genre: Speech

Summary Overview

Sun Yixian's speech "The Three Principles of the People" ("*Sanmin zhuyi*") was delivered on March 6, 1921, at a meeting of the Executive Committee of the National People's Party in the southern Chinese city of Guangzhou (Canton). In this speech, Sun, the founder of the Republic of China, elaborated on the three primary tenets of his political doctrine: the ethnic nation (*minzu*), the people's rights (*minquan*), and the well-being of the people (*minsheng*). In English, these principles have often been translated as nationalism, democracy, and socialism. In Chinese, each of these principles contains the character *min*, which means "people." Sun likened his principles to U.S. president Abraham Lincoln's ideals of government (expressed in the Gettysburg Address) "of the people" (nationalism), "by the people" (democracy), and "for the people" (Socialism).

As early as 1905, Sun had drafted the first version of "The Three Principles of the People" in collaboration with some of his followers. Initially, the principles constituted a guideline for his revolutionary plan to overthrow the Qing (Manchu) Dynasty, which had ruled China since 1644. However, Sun repeatedly refined his political program as reflected in "The Three Principles of the People" and amended his thought on democratic and constitutional ideals in further writings. Sun envisioned China as a republic in which all Chinese people could exert their political rights and secure their material well-being. Today, Sun is revered as the founder of modern China not only by the Chinese Communist Party in the People's Republic of China on the mainland but also in the Republic of China on the island of Taiwan, where "The Three Principles of the People" have become part of the constitution.

Defining Moment

Since the mid-seventeenth century, China had been ruled by the Qing, or Manchu, Dynasty, which was considered culturally and racially foreign by the majority of the Han Chinese. During the first 150 years of their rule, the Qing gradually expanded their influence over vast parts of today's China. In the nineteenth century, however, their rule was continually challenged by local and regional insurrections as well as the court's inability to deal with Western nations. After China's defeat by the British in the First Opium War (1840–1842), the country was forcefully opened to the West by treaties that were considered unequal by the Chinese, as they were not the result of negotiation but rather were imposed on China by the Western powers through threat of force. Although the treaties' direct impact was hardly felt beyond the capital (Beijing), Hong Kong, and the port cities in the southeast (Shanghai, Xiamen, Fuzhou, Ningbo, and Guangzhou), Qing rule was enormously weakened when religious sects and ethnic groups started rebellions throughout the country. In 1853 the Taiping, a Christian religious sect, even declared its own independent country in the former capital of Nanjing. The Qing Dynasty eventually managed to crush the Taiping Rebellion (1850–1864) and other insurrections; however, it never fully recovered from these challenges to its authority.

China's hegemony in East Asia faded at the same moment. The Qing armies were defeated by France in the Sino-French War of 1883–1885, fought over economic and political dominance in Vietnam. A decade later, China lost to Japan in the first Sino-Japanese War of 1894–1895, fought over political supremacy in Korea. At last, the Qing court appeared ready to embrace reform. Emperor Guangxu encouraged the Hundred Days' Reform of 1898, which was led by Chinese scholars who had been educated in Japan and aimed at making comprehensive social and institutional changes within China. But the reform movement was soon suppressed at the behest of the Empress Dowager Cixi, who staged a coup and took over power in September. Foreign intervention to end the Boxer Rebellion, a violent anti-imperialist uprising of 1900–1901, further weakened Qing rule.

As early as 1894, Sun had submitted reform proposals to Li Hongzhang, the governor-general of the province of Zhili who was known as a reformer at court. When Sun was rebuffed, he called for the abolition of the monarchy. The Qing court's reintroduction of re-

form policies from 1902 onward failed to placate opposition groups such as Sun's Revive China Society, which
he had founded in 1894 in Honolulu. Most members
were Chinese living overseas (including Sun), and the
goal was primarily to overthrow the Qing and set up a
central, unified Han Chinese government. In 1905 the
Revive China Society and other revolutionary groups
met in Tokyo (where Sun was living in exile) to form
the Revolutionary Alliance, known in Chinese as Tongmenghui, under Sun's leadership. The alliance stated
its political goals as the expulsion of the Qing, revival of
China, establishment of a republic, and equal land distribution. In his first version of "The Three Principles
of the People," published in the Tongmenghui's *People's
Paper* (*Min bao*) as early as 1905, Sun called for the
Han Chinese ethnic majority to realize the principle of
nationalism by overthrowing the Qing Dynasty and assuming political control of China.

The Qing Dynasty was finally overthrown in 1911,
after which Sun returned to China and was elected provisional president of the first Chinese Republic in 1912.
Sun transformed his Revolutionary Alliance into the
National People's Party (also known as the Nationalist
Party, or Guomindang in Chinese), and tried to build a
democratic republic. Yet the weakness of the new government was exploited by regional army leaders, who
gained control of vast territories and challenged Sun's
efforts at unity. Despite his political prominence and
his party's win of a majority of seats in the new National
Assembly, Sun was compelled to resign as provisional
president of the republic by the powerful General Yuan
Shikai, who in 1915 established himself briefly as qua-
si-emperor. Sun fled once more into exile. From Yuan's
death in 1916 to Jiang Jieshi's establishment of a central government in Nanjing in 1928, China remained
divided and ruled by regional warlords. Political divisions were compounded in 1921 with the founding of
the Chinese Communist Party in Shanghai, while Sun
was in the process of reviving the Guomindang in its
regional stronghold of Guangzhou.

From 1916, when he returned to China, until his
death in 1925, Sun undertook several attempts to extend his influence from Guangzhou to other parts of
the country. His reiteration and reinterpretation of the
"The Three Principles of the People" in 1921 must be
seen against the background of continuing domestic
power struggles. In view of popular calls for extending
political rights and achieving national independence,

Sun's combination of Socialist, democratic, and nationalist ideas appeared particularly promising. Although
Sun was well known and respected abroad, he failed to
gain international support for his campaign to establish
central authority in China under his leadership. His last
effort at national unity—the alliance of the reorganized
Guomindang with the newly founded Chinese Communist Party in 1923—ended prematurely when he fell
sick in late 1924 while on his way to Beijing to attend a
conference on national reconstruction. He died weeks
later, in March 1925.

Author Biography

Sun Yixian was born in 1866 in southeastern China near
Guangzhou in today's Guangdong Province. In 1879
he left China to study medicine in Hawaii and then
moved to Hong Kong. In 1895, after China's defeat in
the First Sino-Japanese War, he led his first insurrection against the Qing Dynasty. When it failed, Sun was
banned from Hong Kong and went into exile in Japan.
He also traveled widely and lived in other Asian and
Western countries, where he sought support for his revolutionary cause. While he was in London in 1896, he
was kidnapped by Chinese agents and detained by the
Chinese legation. The event was well publicized and
immediately elevated Sun to the ranks of a celebrity. In
1905 he brought several anti-Qing forces together and
founded the Revolutionary Alliance (Tongmenghui) in
Tokyo. Several of Sun's attempts to overthrow the Qing
Dynasty and establish a Chinese republic failed before
the successful Chinese Revolution of 1911.

Outside his native base in southern China, Sun
lacked the support and means to unify the country. In
1912 he had to allow general Yuan Shikai to become
president. After Yuan undermined the power of the
Chinese National Assembly in 1913, Sun was forced
into exile again. Upon his return to China in 1916, Sun
attempted to reestablish his political power base in
Guangzhou, where in 1919 he reorganized the Guomindang. He recruited new and more powerful internal allies, such as Jiang Jieshi, then an army officer. He also
gained the support of the newly founded Communist
Party. Yet in the end, he failed to expand his Guangzhou
base of operations into a national government. In 1924
he accepted an invitation by northern militarists to a
conference about national reconstruction. On his way
there, Sun fell ill; he died in Beijing of liver cancer on
March 12, 1925.

HISTORICAL DOCUMENT

Comrades, ...

To-day, at the opening of our Executive session, the question involuntarily arises before me: what does our organisation represent? This in brief is its history, and the principles which guide it.

Our Party was formed after the overthrow of the Qing (Manchu) dynasty and the establishment of a republican form of Government. It has to play a tremendous part in the future of our country. From the time this Party was dissolved, China has been constantly in a state of disorder. It is, of course, natural that the reason for the disturbances and sufferings of the Chinese people was the dissolution of our Party. For many years we have fought, and are still fighting, against the traitors to the people who live to this day in the northern provinces of China, where the influence of our Party is very small: nevertheless, sooner or later the northerners will join us. In the south of China, in the sphere of influence of the Party, there is only the single province of Kwantung.

Our Party is revolutionary. In the second year after the establishment of the republican order, many of its members went abroad, where they worked energetically for the development of the revolutionary movement in China. Hence the name of the Party. While it was working in Tokyo, the Party was known as the "National League": the difference of names, of course, does not alter the character and essence of the aims it pursues. Our Republic is already ten years old, but we still cannot look upon it as a fully perfected type, or consider that our aim has been achieved. Our work is not yet completed: we must continue the struggle.

Our Party is radically different from all the other parties of China. Thus, there was a Party which strove for the overthrow of the Qing dynasty and the establishment of another dynasty, Ming. Of course, the principles of this party were opposed to ours. When in the last years of the Qing dynasty, we were forced to establish ourselves in Tokyo, we determined the following as the fundamental principles of our Party: nationalism, democracy and Socialism.

At that time, power in China was still in the hands of the Manchus, and the Revolution had only arrived at its first stage, nationalism, passing over the other two principles. "The Fivefold Constitution" has great importance for our country in the sense of establishing a firm and just form of government; but, before the overthrow of the Qing dynasty, many thought that the overthrow of that dynasty was the ultimate aim of our Party, and that thereafter China would proceed along the road of universal development and success. But has that proved to be the case? It is now clear that the reason for all that has happened is that our comrades despised—in the name of nationalism—the other two principles of democracy and Socialism. This once again proves that our work did not conclude with the overthrow of the Qing dynasty. We must firmly know and remember that, so long as all three principles have not been carried into real life (even if one of them had been completely realised), there can be no stable conditions of existence.

Furthermore, in fact, our nationalism has not yet been completely realised. The principles of President Lincoln completely coincide with mine. He said: "A government of the people, elected by the people and for the people." These principles have served as the maximum of achievement for Europeans as well as Americans. Words which have the same sense can be found in China: I have translated them: "nationalism, democracy and Socialism." Of course, there can be other interpretations. The wealth and power of the United States are a striking example of the results of great men's teachings in that country. I am glad to observe that my principles, too, are shared by the greatest political minds abroad and are not in contradiction to all the world's democratic schools of thought.

I now wish to speak of nationalism.

(1) Nationalism

What meaning do we impart to the word "nationalism"? With the establishment of the Manchu dynasty in China, the people remained under an incredible yoke for over two hundred years. Now that dynasty has been overthrown, and the people, it would seem, ought to enjoy complete freedom. But do the Chinese people enjoy all the blessings of liberty? No. Then what is the reason? Why, that our Party has as yet far from fulfilled its appointed tasks, and has carried out only the negative part of its work, without doing anything of its positive work.

Since the end of the great European War, the world position has sharply changed: the eyes of the whole world are now turned to the Far East, particularly to China. Strictly speaking, amongst all the nations of the Far East only Siam and Japan are completely independent. China, vast territorially and exceeding dozens of times in population the independent countries, is yet in effect only semi-independent. What is the reason?

After the overthrow of the monarchy and the establishment of the republican system in the territory populated by the five nationalities (Chinese, Manchus, Mongols, Tartars and Tibetans), a vast number of reactionary and religious elements appeared. And here lies the root of the evil. Numerically, these nationalities stand as follows: there are several million Tibetans, less than a million Mongols, about ten million Tartars, and the most insignificant number of Manchus, Politically their distribution is as follows: Manchuria is in the sphere of Japanese influence, Mongolia, according to recent reports, is under the influence of Russia, and Tibet is the booty of Great Britain. These races have not sufficient strength for self-defence but they might unite with the Chinese to form single State.

There are 400 million Chinese: if they cannot organise a single nation, a united State, this is their disgrace, and moreover a proof that we have not given complete effect even to the first principle, and that we must fight for a long while yet to carry out our tasks to the full. We shall establish a united Chinese Republic in order that all the peoples—Manchus, Mongols, Tibetans, Tartars and Chinese—should constitute a single powerful nation. As an example of what I have described, I can refer to the people of the United States of America, constituting one great and terrible whole, but in reality consisting of many separate nationalities: Germans, Dutch, English, French, etc. The United States are an example of a united nation. Such a nationalism is possible, and we must pursue it.

The name "Republic of Five Nationalities" exists only because there exists a certain racial distinction which distorts the meaning of a single Republic. We must facilitate the dying out of all names of individual people inhabiting China, i.e. Manchus, Tibetans, etc. In this respect we must follow the example of the United States of America, i.e. satisfy the demands and requirements of all races and unite them in a single cultural and political whole, to constitute a single nation with such a name, for example, as "Chunhua" (China—in the widest application of the name). Organise the nation, the State.

Or take another case of a nation of mingled races—Switzerland. It is situated in the heart of Europe: on one side it borders on France, on another on Germany, on a third, Italy. Not all the parts of this State have a common tongue, yet they constitute one nation. And only the wise cultural and political life of Switzerland makes its people of many races united and strong. All this is the consequence of the citizens of this Republic enjoying equal and direct electoral rights. Regarding this country from the aspect of international policy, we see that it was the first to establish equal and direct electoral rights for all the population. This is an example of "nationalism."

But let us imagine that the work of uniting all the tribes who inhabit China has been completed, and one nation, "Chunhua," has been formed. Still the object has not been achieved. There are still many peoples suffering from unjust treatment: the Chinese people must assume the mission of setting free these people from their yoke, in the sense of direct aid for them or uniting them under the banner of a single Chinese nation. This would give them the opportunity to enjoy the feeling of equality of man and man, and of a just international attitude, i.e. that which was expressed in the declaration of the American President Wilson by the words "self-determination of nations." Up to the moment of reaching this political stage, our work cannot be considered as finished. Everyone who wishes to join China must be considered Chinese. This is the meaning of nationalism—but "positive" nationalism, and to this we must give special attention.

(2) Democracy

I have already said that in Switzerland democracy has reached its highest point of development: but at the same time the system of representation prevailing there does not constitute real democracy, and only the direct right of the citizen fully answers to the requirements of democracy. Although revolutions took place at various times in France, America and England, and resulted in the establishment of the existing representative system, nevertheless that system does not mean direct and equal rights for all citizens, such as we are fighting for to-day. The most essential of such rights are: the franchise for all citizens: the right of recall (the officials elected by the people can be dismissed by them at will): the right of referendum (if the legislative body passes a law contrary to the wishes of the citizens, the latter may reject the law): the right of initiative (the citizens may propose draft laws, to be carried and adopted by the legislative body).

These four fundamental clauses constitute the basis of what I call "direct electoral right."

(3) Socialism

The theory of Socialism has become known in China comparatively recently. Its chief advocates usually limit their knowledge of this tendency to a few empty words, without having any definite programme. By long study I have formed a concrete view of this question. The essence of Socialism amounts to solving the problem of land and capital.

Above I have set forth the general main idea of the "three principles." The efforts of the whole world, including the Chinese people, are directed to this aim, and I say that our Party must immediately set about carrying these principles into effect.

Summing up the above, I want also to make a few additional observations.

(1) *Nationalism.*—Since the overthrow of the Qing dynasty, we have carried out only one part of our obligations: we have fulfilled only our passive duty, but have done nothing in the realm of positive work. We must raise the prestige of the Chinese people, and unite all the races inhabiting China to form one Chinese people in eastern Asia, a Chinese National State.

(2) *Democracy.*—To bring about this ideal we must first of all adopt all the four points of direct electoral rights: universal suffrage, the referendum, the initiative and the right of recall.

(3). *Socialism.*—Here I have my plan.

The first task of my plan is to bring about the proportional distribution of the land. During my stay at Nanjing (as Provisional President), I tried to carry out this proposal, but my desire was not fulfilled, as I was not understood. Social questions arise from the inequality between rich and poor. What do we understand by inequality? In ancient times, although there was a distinction between rich and poor, it was not so sharp as to-day. Today the rich own all the land, while the poor have not even a little plot. The reason for this inequality is the difference in productive power. For example, in ancient times timber-cutters used axes, knives, etc., for their work, whereas to-day industry is greatly developed, machines have replaced human labour, and the result is that a much greater quantity of products is secured at the expense of much less human energy.

Take another example, from the sphere of agriculture. In ancient times only human labour was employed in this sphere; but with the introduction of plowing with horses and oxen, the process of tilling became more speedy and greatly reduced human effort. In Europe and America electrical energy is now used to till the soil, which affords the opportunity of plowing in the best possible way more than a thousand acres a day, thus eliminating the use of horses and oxen. This has created a truly amazing difference, expressed by the ratio of a thousand to one. If we take the means of communication, however, we see that the introduction of steamships and railways has made communications more than a thousand times more rapid in comparison with human energy.

Those who discuss the question of the brotherhood of peoples in America and Europe have in view only two problems—labours and capital; but European conditions are very different from our own. The thing is that in Europe and America all their misfortunes arise from an extremely unfair distribution of products, whereas in China there is general poverty, since there are no large capitalists. But this, of course, should not serve as a reason for not advocating Socialism: this would be a great mistake. If we see mistakes in Europe and America, we are bound to correct them: disproportion in the distribution of products, both in America and in Europe, are a bad example for us. Therefore I agitate for Socialism—the socialisation of land and capital.

First we shall speak of the socialisation of land. The land systems of Europe and America are very different. In England up to this day the feudal system of land-holding has survived, whereas in the United States all the land is private property. But my social theory advocates the proportionalisation of the land, as a means of providing against future evils. We can see the latter beginning even at the present day. Take what is going on under our very eyes since the reorganisation of the Canton municipality: communications have improved, and in consequence the price of land along the embankment and in other most thickly populated districts has begun to increase daily, some estates selling for tens of thousands of dollars per mu. And all this belongs to private persons, living by the labour of others.

The old Chinese land system partially conforms to the principle of proportionalisaton of land. In the event of this principle being applied, the two following conditions must be observed: taxation according to the value of the land, and compensation according to declared value. In China up to this day the so-called three-grade system of collection of land taxes has been preserved, but, owing to the weak development of transport and industry, land values were not so high in the past as they are to-day. Well developed means of communication and developing industry have led, owing to the maintenance of the old system, to an extremely unequal rise in the value of the land. There are, for example, lands worth 2,000 dollars per mu, while there are also lands worth 20,000 dollars per mu, while between these two extremes of values there are a large number of the most varying values. But if taxes continue to be collected on the old system, both the tax collectors and taxpayers will be put in such a position that dishonest collectors and landowners can make easy profits thereby.

Therefore if we want to abolish this evil and introduce the graduation of taxes, we must adopt the following method: to collect one per cent of the value of the land. For example, if a given piece of land is worth 2,000 dollars its owner pays 20 dollars. The collection of further taxes will depend on an increase in the value of the land. The process of State purchase of the land must begin with the establishment of its definite value. In England, at one time, special offices for collection of land tax and purchase of land were set up, which fixed definite

assessments: these methods are not suitable for introduction in China. In my opinion, it is much more profitable and certain to leave it to the landowner himself to determine and fix the value and the tax, and to inform accordingly the Government department in charge of these matters.

The question arises: will not the landowner communicate a smaller value for his land, and thus pay a smaller tax? But if we adopt the system of compensation for lands according to their value, all illegal activities must disappear of themselves. For example, there is a piece of land of one mu, worth 1,000 dollars, for which the owner must pay 10 dollars yearly in to the tax office. He may declare that the value of his land is only 100 dollars, and thus pay only one dollar; but the application of the principle whereby the Government can compulsorily purchase his land at its declared value obliges the owner to declare its real value, as otherwise he runs the risk of being left without his land. If these two methods are applied, the proportionalisation of land will achieve itself; we can leave other processes on one side for the time being.

Thus I have discussed the land question. There still remains the issue of how to settle the problem of capital.

Last year I published a book entitled: *The International Development of China*. In this book I discussed the question of utilising foreign capital for the purpose of developing Chinese industry and commerce. Look at the Beijing-Wuhan and Beijing-Shenyang railways, and also at the Tianjin-Pukow line, built by foreign capital and yielding enormous profits. At the present time the total length of the Chinese railways is 5000–6000 miles, and their profits amount to 70–80 millions—more even than the land tax. But if the total length is increased to 50 or 60 thousand miles, the profits will also increase considerably. My opinion about the application of foreign capital to our industry is the following: all branches of our industry, for example mining, which represent, with any management worth its salt, profitable undertakings, are awaiting foreign capital.

When I speak of a loan in this connection, I mean the procuring of various machines and other necessary appliances for our industry. For example, after the construction of the Beijing-Wuhan railway, the profits of which were enormous, the foreigners would have given us the chance to acquire it, with its future profit-making possibilities. These were so great that we could have completed the Beijing-Xuanhua line, which now reaches Sunyang. In brief, we can easily incur debt to foreign capital, but the question is—how shall we utilise it, productively or otherwise?

There are also other questions of which I must speak. The British and American diplomats are undoubtedly a skilful race, but still the spectre of social revolution is extremely menacing in these countries. Why? Because the principles of Socialism have not been fully realised there.

We must admit that the degree of sacrifice required for the social revolution will be higher than for the political. The Revolution of 1911 and the overthrow of the Manchus only partially realised the principle of nationalism, while neither the theory of democracy nor the theory of Socialism left any impression. But we must strive our utmost not only to secure the triumph of our first Party principle, but, in accordance with modern world ideas, to develop if possible the principles of democracy, which are also old principles of our Party. Although both England and America are politically developed, political authority there still remains in the hands, not of the people as a whole, but of a political party.

I remember that, on my return to Kwantung, a well-known Hong Kong paper stated the meaning of our return to be that Guangdong was governed, not by the people of the province, but by a "Party." There was a certain point in this declaration. At all events, I was pleased to hear a confirmation that it was governed by a "Party," as the same was true of England and America. If we succeed in achieving our Party ends, this will undoubtedly be a great achievement for the people of Kwantung. We must energetically set about organising, explaining our principles, spreading them far and wide. If we want to awaken others, we must first of all wake up ourselves.

Now there is a committee of the Guomindang at Canton, where propaganda will be concentrated. In this respect there will be no limitations. We shall soon find that the province of Guangdong will not only be the soil on which our principles will grow into reality, but will be the birthplace of the idea of democracy and its practical realisation. From here these principles and their realisation will spread all over China. The people of the Yangtse and Yellow River valleys will follow our example. The haste of our action is explained by the fact that the people which has been actually living in the Republic set up by itself over ten years ago is quite ignorant of what the word means: the explanation of the significance of the Republic must be our task.

During the great European War, President Wilson put forward the watchword: "self-determination of peoples." This corresponds to our Party principle of "nationalism." After the Peace Conference at Versailles, a number of small but independent republics were formed, living without any common tie. This must clearly show you the principal tendency in the modern life of nations. Now the time is approaching to carry into effect our great principles of nationalism, democracy and Socialism. Only by the transformation of all three principles into reality can our people live and develop freely. But the explanation and application of these principles depends very largely on the display of your forces and the degree of energy shown in your propaganda.

We now have a favourable occasion for the propaganda of our ideas: the whole Guangdong Province, with its population of 30 millions, is in our hands. We must immediately tackle the work of explaining in detail to all citizens the essential principles of our Party programme.

GLOSSARY

Canton: the old name of the city of Guangzhou

great European War: The First World War (1914-1918)

Manchu: the ethnic origins of the Qing dynasty emperors—traditional Chinese considered them foreign interlopers and therefore an embarrassment to Chinese history

mu: a Chinese land measurement—one mu = 666.66 square meters, or 0.1647 acres

Our Party: the Guomindang, or Nationalist Party

Siam: the old name of Thailand

Document Analysis

In March 1921 prominent members of the Guomindang assembled in Guangzhou for a meeting of the party's Executive Committee. In a speech given on March 6, Sun addressed the committee with the intent of strengthening the ideological unity of the Guomindang. His central message was the necessity of awakening the Chinese people to the significance of "The Three Principles of the People." According to Sun, it was the party members' task to work toward the realization of these principles in order to unify China under his leadership.

Paragraphs 1–6: The 1921 version of "The Three Principles" begins with a brief historical overview of the early days of the Guomindang. Sun then devotes most of his speech to elaborating on his principles, here translated as "nationalism," "democracy," and "Socialism." Against the rising influence of Marxist forces after the Russian Revolution, Sun calls his comrades to take seriously not only the principle of nationalism—which he viewed as partially realized after the overthrow of the Qing Dynasty (often called "the Manchus" in the text)—but also those of democracy and Socialism. Notwithstanding the nationalist and anti-imperialist political trends of the times, Sun emphasizes his openness to foreign ideas and makes numerous references to political and social conditions abroad from which the Chinese could learn.

In his opening paragraphs, Sun addresses the role of the Guomindang in the establishment of the Chinese republic and briefly introduces the main points of his speech. By likening the dissolution of the party to the political disorder in China, Sun implies that the country can be saved only if the party and its members work as a cohesive unit. Moving on to the "fundamental principles of our Party," Sun emphasizes that the party's mission had not been fulfilled simply with the overthrow of Qing rule and the implementation of the principle of nationalism. Rather, the principles of democracy and Socialism needed to be realized, too, in order to achieve national stability.

Sun then presents the United States as a model for China and compares his three principles to Abraham Lincoln's principles of government of, by, and for the people. Sun counters claims of cultural essentialists—and older versions of his own principles—that demanded an approach to modernization based on ancient Chinese virtues. Instead, Sun stresses the international trend of times, within which his Western-inspired teachings were strongly rooted.

Sun argues that the party has failed to bring "complete freedom" and "the blessings of liberty" to the people since the Chinese Revolution. Consequently, China must be characterized as "only semi-independent." Sun offers both internal and external reasons for this failure. Out of the five primary nationalities that he names (Han Chinese, Manchurians, Mongols, Tartars, and Tibetans), Sun observes that three were still under foreign control: Manchuria was controlled by the Japanese, Mongolia by Russia, and Tibet by Britain. Sun also attacks the failure of the Han Chinese majority to form a "single nation, a united State." As models of national unity, Sun lifts up the United States and Switzerland. Just as members of different ethnic groups consider themselves citizens of the United States or Switzerland, all ethnic groups in China should unite as one nation and stop identifying themselves primarily by ethnic background. They ought to commit themselves to the cause of *zhonghua* (called "Chunhua" in the document)—referring essentially to the Chinese nationality as a whole.

At the end of this section, Sun refers to the principle of "self-determination of nations," as expressed by U.S. president Woodrow Wilson in 1918 in his Fourteen Points. Sun employs this phrase to define his "positive," or voluntary, conception of nationalism, which assumes that an individual is free to become a citizen of the country of his or her choice. At the same time, however, Sun's statements reveal vestiges of Han centrism, which asserted the cultural superiority of the Han over all other ethnicities in China. This assumption has remained the cornerstone of China's policy toward minorities to this day. According to this reasoning, the Han's mission is one of "setting free" China's other ethnic groups and uniting them "under the banner of a single Chinese nation"—if necessary, against their will.

The shortest section of Sun's speech is dedicated to the principle of the rights of the people, or democracy. Sun again mentions Switzerland and deems it the country in which democracy has reached "its highest point of development." However, he criticizes the Swiss form of representative government for having not fully provided for the rights of all citizens. He contends that this was also true in France, the United States, and the United Kingdom. Herein lies Sun's revolutionary approach to democracy. Instead of a representative democratic system, Sun advocates the implementation of direct and equal rights for all citizens. As the four cornerstones of this direct form of democracy, Sun names universal suffrage ("the franchise for all citizens"), the right to recall elected officials, the right to reject laws by referendum, and "the right of initiative," in which citizens may propose legislation to be "carried and adopted" by the legislative body.

This section does not represent a comprehensive summary of Sun's concept of a democratic political order. Rather, Sun here briefly explains his views on the rights of the people within the general framework of constitutional democracy. However, the Fivefold Constitution, to which Sun alludes in his introductory remarks, did not actually grant such broad rights to the people. The Fivefold Constitution provided for a highly structured Chinese government consisting of executive, legislative, judicial, examining, and supervisory branches. Moreover, Sun's three stages of the revolution—military dictatorship, political tutelage, and constitutional government, none of which are mentioned in this speech—placed considerable limitations on the rights to be enjoyed by the people.

The longest section of the speech is dedicated to the principle of the well-being or livelihood of the people, usually translated as "Socialism." After a brief recapitulation of all three of his principles, Sun moves on to his explanation of "solving the problem of land and capital," which he identifies as underlying the inequality between rich and poor.

Sun first notes the disproportional distribution of land in China. As a solution to this problem, he proposes the socialization of land. By this, however, Sun does not mean the immediate and coercive nationalization of all land. Rather, he proposes a proportional distribution of land, that is, the equalization of land ownership by implementing a new taxation system. According to Sun's proposal, the state or a local authority such as a municipality would have the right to purchase land at a price fixed by the owner. In return, according to the system of graduated taxes, the landowner would pay taxes based on the self-declared value of the land. Thus, the state would have the right to buy any privately owned land at a price fixed by the owner. The state normally would not do so, so the land would remain privately owned and subject to taxation. This way, Sun thought, the state could make a fair deal with the land owner without losing money to the potentially corrupt tax collectors. However, the land would be taxed according to the price fixed by the land owner. If the landowner sought to betray the state (by naming too low a price in order to save annual taxes), he would have to fear that the state might actually buy the land at this low price. This system, according to Sun, would naturally eliminate dishonesty among tax collectors and landowners.

The last paragraphs of this section deal with "the problem of capital." Sun refers to his book *The International Development of China*, first published in 1920, and affirms that the party should be open to utilizing foreign capital for the development of China's key industries and infrastructure, such as mining and railways. Sun's openness to anything foreign—whether foreign ideas or foreign capital—is again well reflected in this section. His phrasing, however, remains more careful, as many Chinese feared that depending too much on foreign aid would obstruct China's struggle for independence and autarky, both economically and politically. This fear was particularly widespread with regard to financial aid from Japan, which, however, was Sun's favored source of help owing to his long-cultivated contacts there. On the other hand, Sun had little choice but to accept loans from any side, as his southern regime needed to raise huge sums not only to develop industry and infrastructure there but also to compete with the government in the north of China over the claim for central authority.

In his ending remarks, Sun addresses the role of the party in implementing his three fundamental principles. In Sun's view, the political revolution had been achieved in 1911, but the social revolution was yet to come. He calls on the party to work toward a social revolution in which his principles "will grow into reality." On one hand, Sun expresses his satisfaction with the strong position the party has regained in the province of Guangdong. On the other, though, he warns his fellow party members not to stop at this stage. Rather, starting from Guangzhou, the party should strive to implement Sun's principles all over the country and thus realize the true meaning of the word "republic," or *minguo*, which literally translates as "country of the people." Sun closes with an appeal to his comrades to use the Guomindang's return to power in Guangzhou as a springboard for propagating the party program, namely, the "great principles of nationalism, democracy, and Socialism."

Essential Themes

The most immediate impact of Sun's speech was the affirmation of his role as the theoretical and practical leader of the Guomindang and, potentially, the Chinese nation. This claim was affirmed one month later on April 7, 1921, when Sun was elected extraordinary president of the Republic of China. More significantly, the speech revealed that Sun had already largely formulated a blueprint for what would become his final version of "The Three Principles," which was set forth in his final series of lectures, given in Guangzhou between January and August 1924. This last version was transcribed from the lectures and became canonical after Sun's death in 1925. It is unlikely, however, that most of Sun's followers read the entire 250-page text of the final version.

"The Three Principles of the People" became Sun's central political and ideological legacy, and his potential successors fought harshly over the interpretation of his fundamental tenets. Eventually, the traditionalist interpretation of the principles prevailed. This interpretation was put forth by so-called rightists within the Guomindang; two of the most prominent were Sun's disciple and translator, Dai Jitao (1890–1949), and Sun's son-in-law and eventual successor, Jiang Jieshi (1887–1975). Chinese Communists, with whom the Guomindang were allied in the 1920s and during the war against Japan,

and Soviet advisers to both parties attempted to place more emphasis on the Socialist, revolutionary, and anti-imperialistic character of the principles.

The issues Sun addressed in "The Three Principles" remained of central concern for China in the decades following his death. In accordance with Sun's principle of Socialism, the Communists emphasized fair treatment of common people, as opposed to the Guomindang's protection of the bourgeoisie and capitalists. Jiang Jieshi gave priority to the cause of national unification and justified his authoritarian rule in the name of Sun's principle of nationalism. During the Japanese invasion of China, a third position emerged under Jiang's rival, Wang Jingwei, who had been a close follower of Sun since his earliest days. Wang argued for close cooperation with the Japanese in order to bring peace to China and allow for national reconstruction as a precondition to the fulfillment of Sun's ideology. Sun's legacy remained central to the political history of China until the civil war between Mao Zedong's Communists and Jiang Jieshi's Nationalists, which divided China. While Sun's legacy on the mainland today is overshadowed by that of Mao Zedong, on Taiwan he is still referred to by his honorary title, "father of the country" (*guofu*), and the national anthem is named after "The Three Principles."

——*Torsten Weber*

Bibliography and Further Reading
Books

Bergère, Marie-Claire. *Sun Yixian*, trans. Janet Lloyd. Stanford, Calif. Stanford University Press, 1998.

Eto, Shinkichi, and Harold Z. Schiffrin, eds. *China's Republican Revolution*. Tokyo: University of Tokyo Press, 1994.

Schiffrin, Harold Z. *Sun Yixian, Reluctant Revolutionary*. Boston: Little, Brown, 1980.

Sun Yixian. *Kidnapped in London*. London: China Society, 1969.

———. *Prescriptions for Saving China: Selected Writings of Sun Yixian*, trans. and ed. Julie Lee Wei et al. Stanford, Calif. Hoover Institution Press, 1994.

■ Treaty of Lausanne

Date: 1923
Authors: George Curzon, Horace Rumbold, Eleutherios Venizelos, Ismet Pasa
Genre: International peace agreement

Summary Overview

The Treaty of Lausanne is a peace treaty signed in 1923 at Lausanne, Switzerland, between Turkey and the British Empire, France, Italy, Japan, Greece, Romania, and the Serb-Croat-Slovene State. It was the final treaty that brought World War I (1914–1918) to a close. The Treaty of Lausanne was based on respect for the independence and sovereignty of the states on both sides and reestablished friendly relations among them.

The treaty was signed after the Turkish War of Independence came to a successful end. The Treaty of Sèvres of 1920 (between the Ottoman Empire and the Allies in World War I) became an invalid document, and a new agreement was negotiated between the Allies and Turkey. The negotiations started on November 20, 1922, and lasted about eight months. They broke up due to Turkish protest on February 4, 1923, and restarted on April 23, continuing until the final agreement was reached on July 24, 1923. The Turkish delegation was headed by the foreign minister Ismet Pasa (later named Ismet Inönü). The chief negotiator for the Allies was the British foreign secretary Lord George Curzon, while the statesman Eleuthérios Venizélos represented Greece. The Treaty of Lausanne brought the six hundred year old Ottoman Empire to an end, and recognized the Grand National Assembly of Turkey, based in Ankara, as representative of a new Turkish state that the treaty created. It also drew the boundaries of the new Turkish state, with Turkey making no claims to the former Ottoman territories. The terms of the Treaty of Lausanne thus prepared the ground for the declaration of a new state in place of the Ottoman Empire—the Republic of Turkey, established on October 29, 1923.

Defining Moment

In the twentieth century, the Ottoman Empire collapsed and disintegrated into a number of nation-states on the Balkan Peninsula and in the Middle East. The Turks sided with the Central Powers and Germany during the First World War, in part to try to regain control of their lost provinces; instead, they were on the losing side and faced the total disintegration of the empire. At the end of the war, the empire was forced to sign first the Armistice of Moudros on October 30, 1918, and then the Treaty of Sèvres on August 10, 1920. The terms of the armistice and treaty were so burdensome that the two together ensured the demise of the Ottoman Empire.

The First World War ended in political turmoil and created a power vacuum in the former territories of the Ottoman Empire, which now passed to the British and their allies, who intended to recreate them as colonies and friendly nation-states. Under the terms of the armistice, the Allies occupied the Bosporus and Dardanelles straits. The Ottoman army was demobilized, and ports, railways, and strategic points were to be used by the Allies. Soon after signing the armistice, a joint army of British, French, Greeks, and Italians occupied Constantinople and divided Anatolia among themselves in accordance with the terms of the Armistice of Moudros. The key port of Izmir was occupied by the Greeks.

During the two years between the Armistice of Moudros and Treaty of Sèvres, a Turkish nationalist movement formed a new government in Ankara on April 23, 1920, headed by the military hero of the war, Mustafa Kemal. The occupation by the Greeks posed the most serious threat to the Ankara government, and the Greek army expanded its control of western Anatolia in a series of attacks that led to war between Greece and the new Turkish state. Kemal persuaded the assembly to give him full power as commander in chief, and he drove out the invading Greek army in a series of renewed attacks. The Greeks fled, and the Turkish troops entered Izmir on September 9, 1922. Anatolia was cleared of the Greeks, but there were still Greeks in Thrace, across the straits. A small number of British troops were guarding the straits, backed by naval units. Kemal's forces advanced up to the straits zone and stopped. Here, both sides agreed to negotiate.

The Armistice of Mudanya was signed on October 11, 1922, with the Allied powers agreeing to restore Turkish control in Constantinople, Thrace, and the Bosporus and Dardanelles straits and to convene a peace conference. Thus, the Turks were victorious in the Turkish War of Independence, and the Treaty of

Sèvres became an invalid document, with a new treaty yet to be made. The Allies sent formal invitations to the Turkish governments in Ankara and in Constantinople for a peace conference to be held in Lausanne, Switzerland. The representation of the Turkish government by two delegations would injure Turkish prospects at the forthcoming negotiations. Therefore, after a long discussion, Ankara's Grand National Assembly abolished Constantinople's sultanate on November 1, 1922, and chose Abdülmecid II as the new caliph of the Ottoman line. The thirty-sixth and last sultan of the Ottoman Empire, Mehmed VI (Vahideddin), left Constantinople on November 17 on a British warship, to live in exile in San Remo, Italy, until his death. Thus, the Ankara government alone represented Turkey at the Lausanne conference, which began on November 20.

Lord Curzon, the British foreign secretary and head of the British delegation, was the chief negotiator on behalf of both his own nation and the Allies. Greece was represented by a separate negotiator. It was Lord Curzon who prepared and proposed the first draft of the agreement on behalf of Britain and the Allies. The Turkish delegation did not present its own draft agreement but instead prepared a document consisting of their points for consideration. Initial discussions were carried out based on Curzon's draft agreement, most of which was rejected by the Turkish delegation. Curzon refused to compromise on the draft agreement and insisted that it was the Turks who had to bend and accept the terms offered to them, while the Turkish delegation insisted that they should be treated on a basis of equality. Curzon's demands and Ismet Pasa's reactions and counter-demands remained contradictory throughout the negotiation process. In fact, almost all issues discussed at the conference were met by opposition on both sides.

Curzon presented a draft treaty on January 31, 1923, incorporating all the agreements reached in the three main committees and including the provisions that he wanted but that the Turkish delegation refused to accept. He demanded that Ismet Pasa accept the proposal as it was written, but Pasa communicated with Ankara and was instructed to refuse to sign the agreement. The French and Italian delegations attempted to arrange a compromise, and new meetings were held between February 1 and 5. However, the Turkish delegation was not ready to accept Curzon's demands, while the British refused to make any changes to Curzon's draft treaty. Therefore, the conference adjourned before any agreement was reached or a common document was produced.

Ismet Pasa and the Turkish delegation returned to Turkey on February 16, 1923, and met with Mustafa Kemal to discuss the proceedings of the conference. Debate over the conference by the Grand National Assembly in a secret session started on February 21 and lasted two weeks. Meeting on March 7, the Ankara government revised Curzon's text, formulated its own treaty in about a hundred pages, and sent it to the Allied governments. On March 11, the British government called the Allies to London to discuss the Turkish proposal. The Allies at first suggested many changes to the Turkish proposal but then responded more favorably in the interest of resuming talks. With the conference resuming in Lausanne on April 23, 1923, Britain was represented by two new delegates, Horace Rumbold and Andrew Ryan. The British delegation sought to meet Ismet Pasa's objections, and most of the problems were handled through compromise. The final treaty was signed by all the states involved.

Author Biography

The Treaty of Lausanne was authored by the delegates to the conference. Several delegates played major roles in composing the final treaty, including Lord Curzon, Horace Rumbold, Eleuthérios Venizélos, and Ismet Pasa. George Curzon was an educated British statesman from an aristocratic background. He became undersecretary of state for India in 1891 and undersecretary of state for foreign affairs in 1895. In 1899 he was appointed viceroy of India, where he introduced a series of reforms and became familiar with the affairs of the East. During World War I, he joined the war cabinet of Prime Minister David Lloyd George and became involved in Middle Eastern affairs. He opposed the Greek occupation of Anatolia and wanted to offer peace to Turkey. Because of his involvement and expertise in Eastern affairs, he became foreign secretary and represented Britain at the Lausanne conference. He was a tough negotiator, playing a major role in arbitrating population exchanges between Greece and Turkey, and uncompromising in his views. He served as foreign secretary from 1919 until his retirement in 1924.

Horace Rumbold was also an aristocratic British diplomat. He was fluent in Eastern languages, and between 1900 and 1913 he was appointed as an attaché in Cairo, Egypt; Tehran, Iran; Munich, Germany; and Vienna, Austria. Because of his knowledge and understanding of the Middle East, he was appointed ambassador to Constantinople, serving from 1920 to 1924. Joining the second phase of conference negotiations, he compromised on the terms of the final agreement and signed the treaty on Britain's behalf. He then served as an ambassador in Madrid and Berlin before retiring in 1933.

Born as an Ottoman citizen in Crete in 1864, Eleuthérios Venizélos became a Greek statesman. He was the architect of the Megali Idea, the concept of expanding the Greek state to include all ethnic Greeks, and worked for the annexation of Anatolia to Greece. In 1910 he became prime minister of the military administration of Greece, which allied with Serbia, Bulgaria, and Montenegro against the Ottoman Empire during the Balkan Wars. He managed to keep his nation neutral during World War I but went to war with Turkey afterward, with the Turkish War of Independence being waged against the Greek occupation of Anatolia. Venizélos signed the Treaty of Sèvres, and he joined the Lausanne conference negotiations as head of the Greek

delegation. He maintained peace with Turkey after 1928 but ultimately proved unsuccessful in his policies and resigned from the government in 1935. Venizélos died as a Greek citizen in Paris in 1936.

Ismet Pasa would adopt the name Ismet İnönü and serve as prime minister of Turkey and as the country's second president, from 1938 to 1950. He graduated from the Turkish Military Academy in 1903 and from the Artillery War Academy in 1906 and joined the army the same year. He fought in the Balkan Wars, World War I, and the Turkish War of Independence. After the establishment of the Republic of Turkey, he became prime minister under Mustafa Kemal. Because of his success during the war for liberation, he was selected to defend the nation's interests at the Lausanne conference negotiations. After the death of Atatürk in 1938, Ismet İnönü became president. During his administration, Turkey shifted to a multiparty system. He was a close follower of Atatürk's ideas on modernization of the Turkish Republic, development of parliamentary democracy, and foreign policy.

HISTORICAL DOCUMENT

The Convention Respecting the Regime of the Straits and Other Instruments Signed at Lausanne

The British Empire, France, Italy, Japan, Greece, Roumania and the Serb-Croat-Slovene State, of the one part, and Turkey, of the other part; Being united in the desire to bring to a final close the state of war which has existed in the East since 1914,

Being anxious to re-establish the relations of friendship and commerce which are essential to the mutual well-being of their respective peoples,

And considering that these relations must be based on respect for the independence and sovereignty of States,

Have decided to conclude a Treaty for this purpose, and have appointed as their Plenipotentiaries:

His Majesty the King of the United Kingdom of Great Britain and Ireland and of the British Dominions Beyond the Seas, Emperor of India: The Right Honourable Sir Horace George Montagu Rumbold, Baronet, G.C.M.G., High Commissioner at Constantinople;

The President of the French Republic: General Maurice Pelle, Ambassador of France, High Commissioner of the Republic in the East, Grand Officer of the National Order of the Legion of Honour;

His Majesty the King of Italy: The Honourable Marquis Camillo Garroni, Senator of the Kingdom, Ambassador of Italy, High Commissioner at Constantinople, Grand Cross of the Orders of Saints Maurice and Lazarus, and of the Crown of Italy;

M. Giulio Cesare Montagna, Envoy Extraordinary and Minister Plenipotentiary at Athens, Commander of the Orders of Saints Maurice and Lazarus, Grand Officer of the Crown of Italy;

His Majesty the Emperor of Japan: Mr. Kentaro Otchiai, Jusammi, First Class of the Order of the Rising Sun, Ambassador Extraordinary and Plenipotentiary at Rome;

His Majesty the King of the Hellenes: M. Eleftherios K. Veniselos, formerly President of the Council of Ministers, Grand Cross of the Order of the Saviour;

M. Demetrios Caclamanos, Minister Plenipotentiary at London, Commander of the Order of the Saviour;

His Majesty the King of Roumania: M. Constantine I. Diamandy, Minister Plenipotentiary;

M. Constantine Contzesco, Minister Plenipotentiary;

His Majesty the King of the Serbs, the Croats and the Slovenes: Dr. Miloutine Yovanovitch, Envoy Extraordinary and Minister Plenipotentiary at Berne;

The Government of the Grand National Assembly of Turkey: Ismet Pasha, Minister for Foreign Affairs, Deputy for Adrianople; Dr. Riza Nour Bey, Minister for Health and for Public Assistance, Deputy for Sinope; Hassan Bey, formerly Minister, Deputy for Trebizond;

Who, having produced their full powers, found in good and due form, have agreed as follows:

Part I. Political Clauses

Article 1.

From the coming into force of the present Treaty, the state of peace will be definitely re-established between the British Empire, France, Italy, Japan, Greece, Roumania and the Serb-Croat-Slovene State of the one part, and Turkey of the other part, as well as between their respective nationals. Official relations will be resumed on both sides and, in the respective territories, diplomatic and consular representatives will receive, without prejudice to such agreements as may be concluded in the future, treatment in accordance with the general principles of international law.

Section I
1. TERRITORIAL CLAUSES

Article 2.

From the Black Sea to the Aegean the frontier of Turkey is laid down as follows:

(1) With Bulgaria: From the mouth of the River Rezvaya, to the River Maritza, the point of junction of the three frontiers of Turkey, Bulgaria and Greece: the southern frontier of Bulgaria as at present demarcated;

(2) With Greece: Thence to the confluence of the Arda and the Maritza: the course of the Maritza;

then upstream along the Arda, up to a point on that river to be determined on the spot in the immediate neighbourhood of the village of Tchorek-Keuy: the course of the Arda; thence in a south-easterly direction up to a point on the Maritza, 1 kilom. below Bosna-Keuy: a roughly straight line leaving in Turkish territory the village of Bosna-Keuy. The village of Tchorek-Keuy shall be assigned to Greece or to Turkey according as the majority of the population shall be found to be Greek or Turkish by the Commission for which provision is made in Article 5, the population which has migrated into this village after the 11th October, 1922, not being taken into account; thence to the Aegean Sea: the course of the Maritza.

Article 3.

From the Mediterranean to the frontier of Persia, the frontier of Turkey is laid down as follows:

(1) With Syria: The frontier described in Article 8 of the Franco-Turkish Agreement of the 20th October, 1921

(2) With Iraq: The frontier between Turkey and Iraq shall be laid down in friendly arrangement to be concluded between Turkey and Great Britain within nine months.

In the event of no agreement being reached between the two Governments within the time mentioned, the dispute shall be referred to the Council of the League of Nations.

The Turkish and British Governments reciprocally undertake that, pending the decision to be reached on the subject of the frontier, no military or other movement shall take place which might modify in any way the present state of the territories of which the final fate will depend upon that decision. ...

Article 12.

The decision taken on the 13th February, 1914, by the Conference of London, in virtue of Articles 5 of the Treaty of London of the 17th–30th May, 1913, and 15 of the Treaty of Athens of the 1st–14th November, 1913, which decision was communicated to the Greek Government on the 13th February, 1914, regarding the sovereignty of Greece over the islands of the Eastern Mediterranean, other than the islands of Imbros, Tenedos and Rabbit Islands, particularly the islands of Lemnos, Samothrace, Mytilene, Chios, Samos and Nikaria, is confirmed, subject to the provisions of the present Treaty respecting the islands placed under the sovereignty of Italy which form the subject of Article 15.

Except where a provision to the contrary is contained in the present Treaty, the islands situated at less than three miles from the Asiatic coast remain under Turkish sovereignty.

Article 13.

With a view to ensuring the maintenance of peace, the Greek Government undertakes to observe the following restrictions in the islands of Mytilene, Chios, Samos and Nikaria:

(1) No naval base and no fortification will be established in the said islands.

(2) Greek military aircraft will be forbidden to fly over the territory of the Anatolian coast. Reciprocally, the Turkish Government will forbid their military aircraft to fly over the said islands.

(3) The Greek military forces in the said islands will be limited to the normal contingent called up for military service, which can be trained on the spot, as well as to a force of gendarmerie and police in proportion to the force of gendarmerie and police existing in the whole of the Greek territory.

Article 14.

The islands of Imbros and Tenedos, remaining under Turkish sovereignty, shall enjoy a special administrative organisation composed of local elements and furnishing every guarantee for the native non-Moslem population in so far as concerns local administration and the protection of persons and property. The maintenance of order will be assured therein by a police force recruited from amongst the local population by the local administration above provided for and placed under its orders.

The agreements which have been, or may be, concluded between Greece and Turkey relating to the exchange of the Greek and Turkish populations will not be applied to the inhabitants of the islands of Imbros and Tenedos.

Article 15.

Turkey renounces in favour of Italy all rights and title over the following islands: Stampalia (Astrapalia), Rhodes (Rhodos), Calki (Kharki), Scarpanto, Casos (Casso), Piscopis (Tilos), Misiros (Nisyros), Calimnos (Kalymnos), Leros, Patmos, Lipsos (Lipso), Simi (Symi), and Cos (Kos), which are now occupied by Italy, and the islets dependent thereon, and also over the island of Castellorizzo. ...

2. SPECIAL PROVISIONS

Article 23.

The High Contracting Parties are agreed to recognise and declare the principle of freedom of transit and of navigation, by sea and by air, in time of peace as in time of war, in the strait of the Dardanelles, the Sea of Marmora and the Bosphorus, as prescribed in the separate Convention signed this day, regarding the regime of the Straits. This Convention will have the same force and effect in so far as the present High Contracting Parties are concerned as if it formed part of the present Treaty. ...

Article 27.

No power or jurisdiction in political, legislative or administrative matters shall be exercised outside Turkish territory by the Turkish Government or authorities, for any reason whatsoever, over the nationals of a territory placed under the sovereignty or protectorate of the other Powers signatory of the present Treaty, or over the nationals of a territory detached from Turkey.

It is understood that the spiritual attributions of the Moslem religious authorities are in no way infringed.

Article 28.

Each of the High Contracting Parties hereby accepts, in so far as it is concerned, the complete abolition of the Capitulations in Turkey in every respect. ...

Section II
NATIONALITY

Article 30.

Turkish subjects habitually resident in territory which in accordance with the provisions of the present Treaty is detached from Turkey will become ipso facto, in the conditions laid down by the local law, nationals of the State to which such territory is transferred. ...

Section III
PROTECTION OF MINORITIES

Article 37.

Turkey undertakes that the stipulations contained in Articles 38 to 44 shall be recognised as fundamental laws, and that no law, no regulation, nor official action shall conflict or interfere with these stipulations, nor shall any law, regulation, nor official action prevail over them.

Article 38.

The Turkish Government undertakes to assure full and complete protection of life and liberty to all inhabitants of Turkey without distinction of birth, nationality, language, race or religion.

All inhabitants of Turkey shall be entitled to free exercise, whether in public or private, of any creed, religion or belief, the observance of which shall not be incompatible with public order and good morals.

Non-Moslem minorities will enjoy full freedom of movement and of emigration, subject to the measures applied, on the whole or on part of the territory, to all Turkish nationals, and which may be taken by the Turkish Government for national defence, or for the maintenance of public order.

Article 39.

Turkish nationals belonging to non-Moslem minorities will enjoy the same civil and political rights as Moslems.

All the inhabitants of Turkey, without distinction of religion, shall be equal before the law. ...

Article 40.

Turkish nationals belonging to non-Moslem minorities shall enjoy the same treatment and security in law and in fact as other Turkish nationals. In particular, they shall have an equal right to establish, manage and control at their own expense, any charitable, religious and social institutions, any schools and other establishments for instruction and education, with the right to use their own language and to exercise their own religion freely therein. ...

Article 44.

Turkey agrees that, in so far as the preceding Articles of this Section affect non-Moslem nationals of Turkey, these provisions constitute obligations of international concern and shall be placed under the guarantee of the League of Nations. They shall not be modified without the assent of the majority of the Council of the League of Nations. The British Empire, France, Italy and Japan hereby agree not to withhold their assent to any modification in these Articles which is in due form assented to by a majority of the Council of the League of Nations. ...

Article 45.

The rights conferred by the provisions of the present Section on the non-Moslem minorities of Turkey will be similarly conferred by Greece on the Moslem minority in her territory.

Part II. Financial Clauses
Section I
OTTOMAN PUBLIC DEBT

Article 46.

The Ottoman Public Debt, as defined in the Table annexed to the present Section, shall be distributed under the conditions laid down in the present Section between Turkey, the States in favour of which territory has been detached from the Ottoman Empire after the Balkan wars of 1912–13, the States to which the islands referred to in Articles 12 and 15 of the present Treaty and the territory referred to in the last paragraph of the present Article have been attributed, and the States newly created in territories in Asia which are detached from the Ottoman Empire under the present Treaty. All the above States shall also participate, under the conditions laid down in the present Section, in the annual charges for the service of the Ottoman Public Debt from the dates referred to in Article 53.

From the dates laid down in Article 53, Turkey shall not be held in any way whatsoever responsible for the shares of the Debt for which other States are liable.

For the purpose of the distribution of the Ottoman Public Debt, that portion of the territory of Thrace which was under Turkish sovereignty on the 1st August, 1914, and lies outside the boundaries of Turkey as laid down by Article 2 of the present Treaty, shall be deemed to be detached from the Ottoman Empire under the said Treaty.

Article 47.

The Council of the Ottoman Public Debt shall, within three months from the coming into force of the present Treaty, determine, on the basis laid down by Articles 50 and 51, the amounts of the annuities for the loans referred to in Part A of the Table annexed to the present Section which are payable by each of the States concerned, and shall notify to them this amount.

These States shall be granted an opportunity to send to Constantinople delegates to check the calculations made for this purpose by the Council of the Ottoman Public Debt.

The Council of the Debt shall exercise the functions referred to in Article 134 of the Treaty of Peace with Bulgaria of the 27th November, 1919.

Any disputes which may arise between the parties concerned as to the application of the principles laid down in the present Article shall be referred, not more than one month after the notification referred to in the first paragraph, to an arbitrator whom the Council of the League of Nations will be asked to appoint; this arbitrator shall give his decision within a period of not more than three months. The remuneration of the arbitrator shall be determined by the Council of the League of Nations, and shall, together with the other expenses of the arbitration, be borne by the parties concerned. The decisions

of the arbitrator shall be final. The payment of the annuities shall not be suspended by the reference of any disputes to the above-mentioned arbitrator.

Article 48.

The States, other than Turkey, among which the Ottoman Public Debt, as defined in Part A of the Table annexed to this Section is attributed, shall, within three months from the date on which they are notified, in accordance with Article 47, of their respective shares in the annual charges referred to in that Article, assign to the Council of the Debt adequate security for the payment of their share. If such security is not assigned within the above-mentioned period, or in the case of any disagreement as to the adequacy of the security assigned, any of the Governments signatory to the present Treaty shall be entitled to appeal to the Council of the League of Nations.

The Council of the League of Nations shall be empowered to entrust the collection of the revenues assigned as security to international financial organisations existing in the countries (other than Turkey) among which the Debt is distributed. The decisions of the Council of the League of Nations shall be final. ...

Article 50.

The distribution of the annual charges referred to in Article 47 and of the nominal capital of the Ottoman Public Debt mentioned in Article 49 shall be effected in the following manner:

(1) The loans prior to the 17th October, 1912, and the annuities of such loans shall be distributed between the Ottoman Empire as it existed after the Balkan wars of 1912–13, the Balkan States in favour of which territory was detached from the Ottoman Empire after those wars, and the States to which the islands referred to in Articles 12 and 15 of the present Treaty have been attributed; account shall be taken of the territorial changes which have taken place after the coming into force of the treaties which ended those wars or subsequent treaties.

(2) The residue of the loans for which the Ottoman Empire remained liable after this first distribution and the residue of the annuities of such loans, together with the loans contracted by that Empire between the 17th

October, 1912, and the 1st November, 1914, and the annuities of such loans shall be distributed between Turkey, the newly created States in Asia in favour of which a territory has been detached from the Ottoman Empire under the present Treaty, and the State to which the territory referred to in the last paragraph of Article 46 of the said Treaty has been attributed.

The distribution of the capital shall in the case of each loan be based on the capital amount outstanding at the date of the coming into force of the present Treaty. ...

Section II
MISCELLANEOUS CLAUSES

Article 58.

Turkey, on the one hand, and the other Contracting Powers (except Greece) on the other hand, reciprocally renounce all pecuniary claims for the loss and damage suffered respectively by Turkey and the said Powers and by their nationals (including juridical persons) between the 1st August, 1914, and the coming into force of the present Treaty, as the result of acts of war or measures of requisition, sequestration, disposal or confiscation.

Nevertheless, the above provisions are without prejudice to the provisions of Part III (Economic Clauses) of the present Treaty.

Turkey renounces in favour of the other Contracting Parties (except Greece) any right in the sums in gold transferred by Germany and Austria under Article 259 (I) of the Treaty of Peace of the 28th June, 1919, with Germany, and under Article 210 (I) of the Treaty of Peace of the 10th September, 1919, with Austria. ...

Article 59.

Greece recognises her obligation to make reparation for the damage caused in Anatolia by the acts of the Greek army or administration which were contrary to the laws of war.

On the other hand, Turkey, in consideration of the financial situation of Greece resulting from the prolongation of the war and from its consequences, finally renounces all claims for reparation against the Greek Government.

Article 60.

The States in favour of which territory was or is detached from the Ottoman Empire after the Balkan wars or by the present Treaty shall acquire, without payment, all the property and possessions of the Ottoman Empire situated therein.

It is understood that the property and possessions of which the transfer from the Civil List to the State was laid down by the Irades of the 26th August, 1324 (8th September, 1908) and the 20th April, 1325 (2nd May, 1909), and also those which, on the 30th October, 1918, were administered by the Civil List for the benefit of a public service, are included among the property and possessions referred to in the preceding paragraph, the aforesaid States being subrogated to the Ottoman Empire in regard to the property and possessions in question. The Wakfs created on such property shall be maintained. ...

Part III. Economic Clauses

Article 64.

In this part, the expression "Allied Powers" means the Contracting Powers other than Turkey. The term "Allied nationals" includes physical persons, companies and associations of the Contracting Powers other than Turkey, or of a State or territory under the protection of one of the said Powers.

The provisions of this Part relating to "Allied nationals" shall benefit persons who without having the nationality of one of the Allied Powers, have, in consequence of the protection which they in fact enjoyed at the hands of these Powers, received from the Ottoman authorities the same treatment as Allied nationals and have, on this account, been prejudiced.

Section I
PROPERTY, RIGHTS AND INTERESTS

Article 65.

Property, rights and interests which still exist and can be identified in territories remaining Turkish at the date of the coming into force of the present Treaty, and which belong to persons who on the 29th

October, 1914, were Allied nationals, shall be immediately restored to the owners in their existing state.

Reciprocally, property, rights and interests which still exist and can be identified in territories subject to the sovereignty or protectorate of the Allied Powers on the 29th October, 1914, or in territories detached from the Ottoman Empire after the Balkan wars and subject to-day to the sovereignty of any such Power, and which belong to Turkish nationals, shall be immediately restored to the owners in their existing state. The same provision shall apply to property, rights and interests which belong to Turkish nationals in territories detached from the Ottoman Empire under the present Treaty, and which may have been subjected to liquidation or any other exceptional measure whatever on the part of the authorities of the Allied Powers.

All property, rights and interests situated in territory detached from the Ottoman Empire under the present Treaty, which, after having been subjected by the Ottoman Government to an exceptional war measure, are now in the hands of the Contracting Power exercising authority over the said territory, and which can be identified, shall be restored to their legitimate owners, in their existing state. The same provision shall apply to immovable property which may have been liquidated by the Contracting Power exercising authority over the said territory. All other claims between individuals shall be submitted to the competent local courts.

All disputes relating to the identity or the restitution of property to which a claim is made shall be submitted to the Mixed Arbitral Tribunal provided for in Section V of this Part. ...

Article 67.

Greece, Roumania and the Serb-Croat-Slovene State on the one hand, and Turkey on the other hand undertake mutually to facilitate, both by appropriate administrative measures and by the delivery of all documents relating thereto, the search on their territory for, and the restitution of, movable property of every kind taken away, seized or sequestrated by their armies or administrations in the territory of Turkey, or in the territory of Greece, Roumania or the Serb-Croat-Slovene State respectively, which are actually within the territories in question.

Such search and restitution will take place also as regards property of the nature referred to above seized or sequestrated by German, Austro-Hungarian or Bulgarian armies or administrations in the territory of Greece, Roumania or the Serb-Croat-Slovene State, which has been assigned to Turkey or to her nationals, as well as to property seized or sequestrated by the Greek, Roumanian or Serbian armies in Turkish territory, which has been assigned to Greece, Roumania or the Serb-Croat-Slovene State or to their nationals.

Applications relating to such search and restitution must be made within six months from the coming into force of the present Treaty.

Article 68.

Debts arising out of contracts concluded, in districts in Turkey occupied by the Greek army, between the Greek authorities and administrations on the one hand and Turkish nationals on the other, shall be paid by the Greek Government in accordance with the provisions of the said contracts. ...

Article 72.

In the territories which remain Turkish by virtue of the present Treaty, property, rights and interests belonging to Germany, Austria, Hungary and Bulgaria or to their nationals, which before the coming into force of the present Treaty have been seized or occupied by the Allied Governments, shall remain in the possession of these Governments until the conclusion of arrangements between them and the German, Austrian, Hungarian and Bulgarian Governments or their nationals who are concerned. If the above-mentioned property, rights and interests have been liquidated, such liquidation is confirmed.

In the territories detached from Turkey under the present Treaty, the Governments exercising authority there shall have power, within one year from the coming into force of the present Treaty, to liquidate the property, rights and interests belonging to Germany, Austria, Hungary and Bulgaria or to their nationals.

The proceeds of liquidations, whether they have already been carried out or not, shall be paid to the Reparation Commission established by the Treaty of Peace concluded with the States concerned, if the property liquidated belongs to the German, Austrian, Hungarian or Bulgarian State. In the case of liquidation of private property, the proceeds of liquidation shall be paid to the owners direct.

The provisions of this Article do not apply to Ottoman limited Companies.

The Turkish Government shall be in no way responsible for the measures referred to in the present Article. ...

Article 143.

The present Treaty shall be ratified as soon as possible.

The ratifications shall be deposited at Paris.

The Japanese Government will be entitled merely to inform the Government of the French Republic through their diplomatic representative at Paris when their ratification has been given; in that case, they must transmit the instrument of ratification as soon as possible.

Each of the Signatory Powers will ratify by one single instrument the present Treaty and the other instruments signed by it and mentioned in the Final Act of the Conference of Lausanne, in so far as these require ratification. ...

In faith whereof the above-named Plenipotentiaries have signed the present Treaty.

Done at Lausanne, the 24th July, 1923, in a single copy, which will be deposited in the archives of the Government of the French Republlc, which will transmit a certified copy to each of the Contracting Powers.

GLOSSARY

Balkan wars of 1912–13: wars over the possession of European territories of the Ottoman Empire

Capitulations in Turkey: agreements whereby Ottoman sultans granted rights and privileges to foreign nationals living or doing business in Ottoman territories

gendarmerie and police: authorities responsible for security in the countryside and in the city, respectively

Hedjaz: region bordering on the Red Sea that includes the sacred Muslim sites Mecca and Medina

spiritual attributions: rights accruing to Muslim authorities

Wakfs: property grants for religious or charitable purposes

Document Analysis

The Treaty of Lausanne was signed at Lausanne, Switzerland, on July 24, 1923, and deposited in the archives of the government of the French Republic. It was signed by Horace Rumbold, Maurice Pelle, Camillo Garroni, Giulio Cesare Montagna, Kentaro Otchiai, Eleuthérios K. Venizélos, Demetrios Caclamanos, Constantine Diamandy, Constantine Contzesco, Ismet Pasa, Riza Nour Bey, and Hassan Bey. The treaty consists of 143 articles divided into five parts, with each part divided into a number of sections. A number of conventions, agreements, and protocols are annexed to the treaty, including separate peace treaties with Greece, England, Italy, Japan, Romania, and France. The treaty opens with an expression of the desire to bring to a final close the state of war which has existed in the East since 1914. It continues with an expression of anxiety to reestablish relations of friendship and commerce and considers that these relations must be based on respect for the independence and sovereignty of the states involved. The expressions of the desire for peace, friendship, and respect for independence were very important for Turkey, as they show that Turkey has been treated as equal and that the terms of the treaty were negotiated among equals, not imposed.

Part I of the treaty includes three sections, on territorial clauses, nationality, and the protection of minorities. Section I, concerning territorial issues, draws the boundaries of Turkey with the surrounding countries. The boundaries were essentially those demanded by the Turks, except that around Mosul. Turkey insisted that this region was included in the National Pact (a resolution, dated 1920, stating the goals of independence of Turkey and forming the basis of the negotiating position of Turkey) and was overwhelmingly inhabited by Turks; therefore, it should belong to Turkey. However, Britain was not ready to relinquish the oil-rich area. The problem of Mosul was not resolved during the conference negotiations and was left to further negotiations between Britain and Turkey, to be held within nine months of the signing of the treaty. Mosul eventually remained under British jurisdiction as a part of their mandate in Iraq.

The border with Greece was resolved by acceptance of the Turkish proposal to draw the boundary at the deepest point in the middle of the Maritsa (or Maritza) River. In return, Turkey agreed that the island of Castellorizzo (Kastellórizon) would go to Italy. Western Thrace remained in Greece on the condition of respect for the rights and freedoms of the Turkish minority living there.

The border with Syria remained as described in the Franco-Turkish Agreement of October 20, 1921. Antakya (formerly Antioch) and Iskenderun (formerly Alexandretta), which were acquired by Turkey in 1938 after the withdrawal of France from Syria, would remain in Syria. The islands of Imbros (now Gökçeada) and Tenedos (now Bozcaada) and the Rabbit Islands would belong to Turkey, while the islands of Lemnos, Samothrace, Mytilene, Chios, Sámos, and Ikaria (or Nikaria) would belong to Greece. Turkey's complete control of the straits was recognized, but it had to demilitarize the zone around the straits and establish an international commission to supervise the transmission of ships. Thus, Soviet control of the straits was avoided. Meantime, other islands in the Aegean were given over to Italy, as provisions of the Treaty of London of April 1915, by which Italy joined the war with the Allies. Most of the rest of the articles in Part I, Section I dismantled the Ottoman Empire and renounced Turkish claims to its territory.

As to population issues, to minimize minority problems in a nation state, the Turks and Greeks agreed to exchange the Greeks living in Anatolia with the Turks living in Greece. Only Greeks of Constantinople and the Turks of Western Thrace were excepted from the population exchange.

As to the protection of minorities, Turkish nationals belonging to non-Muslim minorities were not granted any privileges; they were to enjoy the same treatment and security as other Turkish nationals. They would have equal right to establish charitable, religious, and social institutions and schools for education. They would have the right to use their own languages and to exercise their own religions freely. The Allies did not ask for any war reparations. Greece did not pay any compensation but instead gave Karaagaç to Turkey.

Part II of the treaty is concerned with financial issues and is divided into two sections, the first covering the Ottoman public debt and the second containing miscellaneous clauses. The Ottoman public debt was the main financial problem of the treaty negotiations. The Allies agreed that Turkey would have to pay only its portion of the debt; the former Ottoman territories would pay their shares as well. The Turks won the right to have their debt set in francs, regardless of its value in gold. Among the miscellaneous clauses, capitulations, which were the trade concessions given to European countries during the Ottoman Empire, were abolished completely. Another clause is concerned with the foreign concessions within Turkey awarded by the Ottoman Empire. The Allies insisted that these concessions had to be recognized by Turkey, too. It was finally agreed that some payment would be made for the loss of the concessions and that Turkey would award future concessions to whomever it wanted.

Part III concerns economic issues, with Section I covering property, rights, and interests and Section II taking up contracts, prescriptions, and judgments. According to the treaty, all property, rights, and interests that still existed which could be identified, in territories detached from the Ottoman Empire after the Balkan Wars, as belonging to Turkish nationals, were to be immediately restored to the owners.

Essential Themes

The treaty was first introduced in the newly elected Grand National Assembly of Turkey and was ratified on August 23, 1923. Mustafa Kemal made a speech in support of the terms, and members of the assembly voted to accept it.

Most of the Turkish people of the era considered the treaty a major Turkish victory. It overturned the vindictive provisions of the Treaty of Sèvres, which was perceived as a means for the Allies to destroy the national identity of the Turkish people. However, some people, from the time of the signing of the treaty until the present, have considered the treaty a defeat, behind the notion that if Ismet Pasa and the Ankara government had held out longer and even refused to sign the treaty, they could have gotten much more of the territories included in the National Pact, such as Western Thrace, Mosul, and the port of Batumi. These places had substantial Turkish populations that could well have justified their inclusion in Turkey. Also, Turkey might have received considerable war reparations from all the Allies, particularly from Greece, for the monumental damage caused during their occupation. Detractors of the treaty also claim that negotiators should not have allowed the Greek Orthodox Ecumenical Patriarchate to remain in Constantinople and that Turkey should never have agreed to allow the international community to maintain a role in establishing regulations for passage through the straits. Kemal responded to these conservative critiques by asserting that after twelve years of war, the Turkish people had reached the limit of their endurance, and the Turkish army had gone as far as it could. Further efforts might have jeopardized all the achievements of the national movement.

The conclusion of the treaty led to the recognition of the Republic of Turkey by the international community as the successor state of the Ottoman Empire. Peace gave Mustafa Kemal and the nationalist government sufficient prestige to take further steps. The Allied forces began to move out of Constantinople on August 23, 1923, and left the city on October 2; the Turkish army entered Constantinople on October 6. Ankara was named the capital of Turkey officially on October 13, while the Turkish Republic was proclaimed by the assembly on October 29. On the same day, Atatürk was elected president, and the next day İnönü became prime minister. A series of reforms were then undertaken to modernize the newly established republic.

A meeting was held between Turkey and Britain to negotiate the Mosul problem on May 19, 1924. However, no result was obtained, and the problem was transferred to the League of Nations. Turkey accepted the League of Nations' decision to give Mosul to Iraq on June 5, 1926. By the terms of the 1926 treaty, Turkey surrendered its right to a permanent share in the exploitation of Mosul oil in return for a single payment of £500,000 together with twenty-five years of annual payments of a 10 percent share in the oil revenues.

Antakya and Iskenderun, which were left to Syria under French mandate, were acquired by Turkey in 1938 after the withdrawal of France from Syria. According to the population exchange agreement signed between Turkey and Greece on January 30, 1923 (prior to the signing of the Treaty of Lausanne), around two million Greeks living in Turkey and five hundred thousand Turks living in Greece were exchanged. This entailed a large-scale transfer of peoples out of their homelands, which caused a proportional degree of human misery.

The agreement concerning the Bosporus and Dardanelles straits lasted only thirteen years, as a new agreement was signed in 1936 giving more control to Turkey. This became important in the 1990s when the international community demanded that Turkey continue to allow unrestricted passage by huge oil tankers, whose contents constituted a danger to the lives of the local people and the ecology of the region.

———*Fatma Acun*

Bibliography and Further Reading

Davison, Roderic. *Turkey*. Englewood Cliffs, N.J. Prentice-Hall, 1968.

Demirci, Sevtap. *Strategies and Struggles: British Rhetoric and Turkish Response—The Lausanne Conference (1922–1923)*. Istanbul: Isis Press, 2005.

Knudsen, Erik Lance. *Great Britain, Constantinople, and the Turkish Peace Treaty, 1919- 1922*. New York: Garland Publishing, 1987.

Shaw, Stanford. *From Empire to Republic: The Turkish War of National Liberation, 1918–1923, A Documentary Study*. Ankara: Turkish Historical Association, 2000.

Web Sites

"The Demographic Consequences of Lausanne Treaty in Turkey." Forced Migration Online. http://repository.forcedmigration.org/show_metadata.jsp?pid=fmo:1824 [accessed February 20, 2017].

"The Treaty of Lausanne: Turkey's International Recognition." Turkish Coalition of America http://tcamerica.org/issues-information/turkish-history/the-treaty-of-lausanne-116.htm [accessed February 20, 2017].